The Romantic South

Books by HARNETT T. KANE

AMERICAN VISTA SERIES

The

Edited, with introduction and commentary by

Romantic South

Harnett T. Kane

COWARD-McCANN, INC.   NEW YORK

THE MEN OF THE ALAMO: From *Readings in Texas History* edited by Eugene C. Barker. published by the Southwest Press of Dallas, copyright 1929. Reprinted by permission of the publisher.

THE INCREASED SUMMER: From *Collected Essays* of John P. Bishop, essay originally entitled *The South Revisited*, published by Charles Scribner's Sons, copyright 1948. Reprinted by permission of the publishers.

JOHN RANDOLPH ALWAYS HAD A WORD FOR IT: From *John Randolph of Roanoke* by William Cabell Bruce, copyright 1939. Reprinted by permission of G. P. Putnam's Sons, publishers.

MAKING A YANKEE OUT OF HIM and THE SOUTH IN THE SOUTH PACIFIC: From *The Sword Over the Mantel* by J. Bryan, III, published by the McGraw-Hill Book Company. Copyright © 1960 by J. Bryan, III. Reprinted by permission of the McGraw-Hill Book Company.

THE NEGRO IN THE WELL: A short story by Erskine Caldwell, published by Little, Brown & Co. Reprinted by permission of the publishers and Mr. Caldwell's agent.

HOW ISAAC REMEMBERED THE MASTER: From *Memoirs of a Monticello Slave* as dictated to Charles Campbell, published by the University of Virginia Press, Charlottesville, copyright 1951. Reprinted by permission of the director of the press.

AN ECCENTRIC, CHILDLIKE UNIVERSE: From *Local Color* by Truman Capote, published by Random House. Copyright 1950. Reprinted by permission of the publishers.

"THE LOSERS ALWAYS REMEMBER LONGER . . .": From *The Angry Scar* by Hodding Carter, published by Doubleday & Co., Inc. Copyright © 1959 by Hodding Carter. Reprinted by permission of Doubleday & Company, Inc.

A SOUTHERNER PROBES THE SOUTH'S MIND: From *The Mind of the South* by W. J. Cash, published by Alfred A. Knopf Incorporated. Copyright 1941 by Alfred A. Knopf Incorporated. Reprinted by permission of the publisher.

EPITAPH TO A DEAD SLAVE: From *Liberalism in the South* by Virginius Dabney, published by the University of North Carolina Press, copyright 1932. Reprinted by permission of the publisher.

RED NECK, BURR HEAD: From *A Southerner Discovers the South* by Jonathan Daniels, published by The Macmillan Company. Copyright 1938 by Jonathan Daniels. Reprinted by permission of the author.

TWO INNOCENTS, AND THE MINSTRELS OF ST. LOUIS: From *Mark Twain in Eruption* edited by Bernard DeVoto, published by Harper & Brothers. Copyright 1922 by Harper & Brothers; copyright 1940 by The Mark Twain Company. Reprinted by permission of the publishers.

A ROSE FOR EMILY: A short story by William Faulkner, published by Random House. Copyright 1931, reprinted by permission of the publishers.

TILL YOU GET IT IN THE NECK: From *I Remember Another Texas* by Charles J. Finger, an essay published by the Southwest Review, copyright 1927. Reprinted by permission of the Estate of Charles J. Finger and The Southwest Review.

INTO THE WEST-LYING VALLEY: From *A New Look at the Old Dominion* by Marshall Fishwick, published by Harper & Brothers, copyright © 1957. Reprinted by permission of the publishers.

A MEETING AT APPOMATTOX: From Volume 4 of *R. E. Lee, A Biography* by Douglas Southall Freeman, published by Charles Scribner's Sons, copyright 1047. Reprinted by permission of the publishers.

"OIL IS LIKE THAT": From *Houston: Land of the Big Rich* by George Fuermann, published by Doubleday & Company, Inc. Copyright 1951 by George Fuermann. Reprinted by permission of Doubleday & Company, Inc.

TWO GIRLS VISIT A GENTLEMAN: From *Memories of a Southern Woman of Letters* by Grace King, published by The Macmillan Company, copyright 1932. Reprinted by permission of the publishers.

A SAD CAFE AND ITS BALLAD:. From *The Ballad of the Sad Café* by Carson McCullers, published by the Houghton Miflin Company. Copyright 1951. Reprinted by permission of the publishers.

GLORY THAT WAS, GRANDEUR THAT WASN'T: From *The Way of the South* by Howard W. Odum, published by The Macmillan Company, copyright 1945. Reprinted by permission of the publishers.

CHANGED, YET ETERNALLY THE SAME: From *Lanterns of the Levee* by William Alexander Percy, published by Alfred A. Knopf, copyright 1941. Reprinted by permission of the publishers.

TALE OF TWO CITIES: From *Cities of America* by George Sessions Perry, published by McGraw-Hill Book Company. Copyright 1947 by George Sessions Perry. Reprinted by permission of the author's estate.

"IS IT TRUE WHAT THEY SAY ABOUT DIXIE?": From *Southern Accent: From Uncle Remus to Oak Ridge* by William T. Polk, copyright 1953 by William T. Polk, reprinted by permission of William Morrow and Company, Inc.

THE GRAVE: A short story by Katherine Anne Porter, published by Harcourt, Brace and Company. Reprinted by permission of the publishers.

WHAT FOLKS WERE LIKE AT CROSS CREEK: From *Cross Creek* by Marjorie K. Rawlings, published by Charles Scribner's Sons, copyright 1942. Reprinted by permission of the publishers.

A TOAST OF TWO WORLDS and MISS PATSY JEFFERSON OF PARIS AND AMERICA: From *Old Time Belles and Cavaliers* by Edith Tunis Sale, published by J. B. Lippincott Company, copyright 1912. Reprinted by permission of the publishers.

REVOLT OF A DAMNYANKEE: From *The Rebel Yell* by H. Allen Smith, published by Doubleday and Company. Copyright 1954 by H. Allen Smith. Reprinted by permission of the Harold Matson Company.

"IF WE SUCCEED . . .": From *Jefferson Davis: American Patriot 1808–1861* by Hudson Strode, published by Harcourt, Brace & World, Inc., copyright 1955. Reprinted by permission of the pubishers.

INTIMATE SECRETS FROM A STRANGER ON A BUS: From *The Romantic New Orleanians* by Robert Tallant, published by E. P. Dutton & Company, Inc. Copyright 1950 by Robert Tallant. Reprinted by permission of the publishers.

THE ODE OF A LATTER-DAY POET: From "Ode to the Confederate Dead" in *Poems, 1922–1947* by Allan Tate, published by Charles Scribner's Sons, New York, copyright 1948. Reprinted by permission of the publishers.

BEGUN IN DEFEAT, ENDED IN RESURRECTION: From *Thirteen Days to Glory* by Lon Tinkle, published by McGraw-Hill Company of New York, copyright © 1959. Reprinted by permission of the publishers.

A CHRISTIAN EDUCATION: From *Circus in the Attic and Other Stories* by Robert Penn Warren, published by Harcourt, Brace and Company. Reprinted by permission of the publishers.

SOME NOTES ON RIVER COUNTRY: From *Notes on River Country* by Eudora Welty, published by Harper's Bazaar, February, 1944. Reprinted by permission of Harper's Bazaar and Eudora Welty.

HADN'T HUGGED FOR SO LONG, HE WAS OUT OF PRACTICE: From "The Gentler Sentiments," Chapter XIV of *The Life of Johnny Reb* by Bell Irvin Wiley, copyright 1943 by The Bobbs-Merrill Company, Inc., used by special permission of the publishers.

A TIME OF FAMILY TROUBLE AFTER SHILOH: From *So Red The Rose* by Stark Young, published 1942 by Charles Scribner's Sons. Reprinted by permission of the publishers.

THOMAS WOLFE RE-CREATES CATAWBA'S DISCOVERY: From *The Face of a Nation 1934*, edited by John Hall Wheelock, 1939. Published by Charles Scribner's Sons. Reprinted by permission of the publishers.

Library of Congress Catalog Card Number: 61-5424

MANUFACTURED IN THE UNITED STATES OF AMERICA

To James Kane,

My great-grandfather, of County Cork, Ireland, and New Orleans, Louisiana, a Confederate who died as a result of war privations; who belonged to a small, select group—one of the few privates who ever served in the Southern armies

Contents

The Romantic South

"For the Romance of Thing"

*. . . A certain heritage abounding in the concepts and experiences
of good living, strong loyalties . . . strong individuality.*

—HOWARD W. ODUM

A little more than a century ago, shortly before the South and the North directed guns at each other, an Ohio schoolteacher went to one of the Gulf states and met a handsome fellow tutor with "the bloom of the Northern rose in her cheek." He inquired: Why had she come here? Her answer was prompt: "For the romance of the thing."

For many decades men and women ventured into the American South by stagecoach, horseback, boat, even laboriously on foot, with the expectation of finding a scene and a people overtly or subtly different from other places and other folk. In the words of one of my friends, not meant unkindly, such individuals arrived with a nostalgia for something that they had never known.

Some callers left with a slow shake of the head, repelled or at least not pleased with what they encountered. Certain Southerners themselves have agreed with objectors who felt that this most regional of America's regions was far removed from the rank of Eden-on-earth that its advocates claimed for it. Among the area's earliest critics were eminent Virginians, Marylanders and North Carolinians who labored against internal trends which, they believed, would eventually destroy it.

Many nevertheless beheld there a warming beauty, a fragrant panorama and a mood ranging from the gently amiable to the beguiling. "We smelt so sweet, and so strong a smell, as if we had been in the midst of some delicate garden abounding with all kinds of odoriferous flowers." So wrote one of the Old Dominion's earliest English guests, and those who followed echoed the admiring words with variations during several hundred years. They recalled long, serene days under a kindly (now and then a bit too kindly) sun, vistas of shining valleys, lakes like silver shields below the low-hanging skies, fields reaching without a break to the hushed forests at their edges; the deep, moist green of the canebrake, and the shadowed swamps, their buttressed cypresses draped in moss, with trumpet vine and the distant white of the iris along their bases.

The Shadows, one of the best-maintained of surviving great houses in the Deep South, was left by
its owner, Weeks Hall of New Iberia, to the
National Trust for Historic Preservation.

The natives and their friends also remembered a plantation people who were partly relaxed, partly volatile, who spoke casually, slowly, but also moved with swift decision when they wished; who grew hotly emotional, then lapsed into a composed calm for the rest of the heat-drowsy afternoon. Their setting, many felt, was the most magnificent in this New World—opulent, semitropical in places, spotted with residences of a rare grace, the tempered Georgian in the oldest colonies, the soaring lines of the Greek Revival or West Indian in the later, lower South, or combinations of the several elements in ironwork and sweeping roofs.

Like the other Souths of the world, of Italy and France and Spain, this land had a scented loveliness with which men identified themselves through the generations. Here was *their* home, their family's acres, its landing at the river edge, first built by a long-dead ancestor. Early and late, the Southern plantation locale had the appeal of *dolce far niente*, of contented hours in garden houses, of quiet conversation during the long spring and unending summer of the region.

Like people in other hot lands of the world, such Southerners acquired a "manner" of their own, not the smallest part of which was an art of manners; a rule of good behavior, of courtesy between man and man, between man and woman; casual grace in the drawing room, the ballroom, or the carriage that jostled its passengers over the muddy roads and dangerous water crossings of an earlier America.

To be sure, there were frequent violations of the standard, intermittent crudities—linen that was not quite fresh, examples of slothful acts. Whatever their prescriptions of polite behavior, certain planters staggered foolishly after too-alcoholic indulgences; mistreated helpless slaves, at times to the death, and quarreled with neighbors in half-savage outbursts under a code of "honor" which frequently gave its rewards to the man of dishonor.

Nevertheless, for many thousands, it was a golden land, a golden age—several such ages, in fact: the colonial era in the earliest colonies; the post-Revolutionary times when the South spread in a still more southerly and also westerly direction; and then the flush decades when wealth piled highest of all and cotton became monarch of lands reaching to the Mississippi and beyond it.

Increasingly as the years went by, the rest of America viewed it as a place (for better or for worse, and debators did not agree which it was) sharply different from the rest of the growing country. Yet there was never a single South, or a completely unified one, but a series of somewhat overlapping Souths: the tidewater lowlands about the spreading Chesapeake Bay of Virginia and Maryland, with long tongues of water about the tobacco-growing country; the ripely endowed South Carolina of Charleston and the rice-enriched lowlands; the earliest Georgia of the Atlantic edge; the Piedmont beyond the "fall line" of coastal waters, the hilly expanses to which men went for fresh lands; the old West of Kentucky and Tennessee; then the teeming, steamy flatlands of Louisiana and Mississippi and Alabama, accepting the march of cotton toward the Mississippi River, with its own unique life along its banks up to St. Louis, and stretches of the Missouri banks that shared a Southern style and outlook. Beyond the great river of the South waited a still newer region with pungent differences, Arkansas and East Texas of the cotton fields. In the background there existed from an early date a sub-civilization, the Southern mountaineer folk of the Smokies, the Cumberlands, the Alleghenies, and later of the Ozarks, cut off from the world of their fellows.

Those who joined the life of the South were not quite the homogeneous

English group that has sometimes been pictured. They included Scotch-Irish of Western Virginia and the Carolinas, "Dutch" or Germans who took the less opulent land behind the tidewater; Moravians and other Protestant groups; the French and Spanish who created a large spur of Latin Europe along the lower Mississippi; the Spaniards of Florida and also of Texas; the sizable German element in the Lone Star state; the French Huguenots of Charleston and West Indian settlers who joined them there; clusters of the French in Mobile and elsewhere on the Gulf. For a time, as representatives of the three cultures met in repeated clashes, it appeared that France or Spain, rather than Britain, might win the South.

The Southerners of the plantations made up far from a majority of the region's people. They were, in fact, a meager fraction, living usually a short distance from hard-working yeomen farmers without slaves or only a few; from occasional artisans and other workers in Williamsburg, New Orleans, Charleston; in Louisville, Richmond, Pensacola, Natchez and the other enlarging towns and cities. Yet—and here is the essential fact—the large growers of tobacco, of cotton and rice came to dominate their areas and their people, taking leadership in office, setting the rules, presiding over economic and social affairs. Occasionally the Piedmont or the back settlements tried revolt; in most cases the older elements won.

They were the aristocracy of their land, but a self-made element. Few among the European nobility went to the South or to the North; "dukes don't emigrate," nor do many of their sons. The first Southerners appeared as a mixed group, country farmers, city craftsmen, individuals without known occupation and some who wrote the word "gent." after their names—and died soonest of all under the privations at Jamestown and in Maryland and the Carolinas. A limited number had stamina, courage, a will to succeed. Taking advantage of the astonishing fertility of the soil, they made a place and a name for themselves. About their early tobacco fields they achieved what colonial America would know as its first gentry.

Yet between these Atlantic coastal Southerners and the men of, say, New England, there seemed little difference in origin; there was small basis for later claims that the Southern groups were "cavaliers" and the more northerly pioneers men of less elevated stock. All were settlers who labored in ways determined by the soil and the climate they found. And until 1860 and the Confederacy, Southerners beheld a changing frontier that beckoned from a distance, with new rivers, new plains, new hills to provide a fresh start. Opportunity, a safety valve for men who yearned for a chance . . . The frontier answered several needs, and its influence gave the South a continuing vigor, a rambunctious quality of speech and act. For the tidewater family or the resident of Charleston's Battery often had cousins in the rural stretches near Memphis or over in Texas.

The original workers in Southern fields were whites, indentured servants who agreed to labor for a few years in return for their passage from home and their maintenance in the new land. But at an early date, 1619, the Virginians saw an original shipment of Negroes, and another pattern was set, that of slaves attached to the fields and their owners. Thus the future of the South was determined.

The single-crop economy proved wasteful, devouring the soil, and in time slavery's early end was indicated. By the late 1700s the South, like the rest of the new United States, appeared on its way toward a solution of the problem.

With the generation of Thomas Jefferson, the region provided the emerging nation with its greatest galaxy of leaders—George Washington, Patrick Henry, James Madison, and others. For a time it seemed that these Southerners might bring an end to slavery, or a restriction of it, with other reforms in the direction of a greater democracy. But the forces of economy were against them. With the perfection of the cotton gin, a vast new crop came to the forefront, blanketing the South as never before.

For several generations Southerners, feeling guilt over the existence of bondage, had apologized for it. Now the region turned against Jefferson's beliefs, insisted that slavery was a "positive good," one that was even sanctioned by the Bible, and made fervent, furious attacks or counterattacks on its opponents. The South carried on as the last part of the civilized world with such bondage, and proposed to extend it to new territories of the West. In time came the conflict in which it was almost inevitably doomed to defeat.

In the years since 1865 "New Souths" have been frequently proclaimed, and basic change has occurred in section after section. Yet meanwhile a still-romantic area has continued to exist, little diminished in its essentials. Here is a part of America in which tradition and the past remain close at hand, in which the role of forebears, of the family and its older ways, is a matter of unaltered importance. "Are you related to the Allens, by any chance?" a newcomer is asked. "I heard your mother was a Dabney, and we have some Dabney kin up in Kentucky." Eventually the new resident will discover a connection, perhaps five generations back and four states away. Without such a relationship, he may well be accepted; but any such vague tie will make the process much the easier.

This South is, as ever, a place of great talk, of artful conversationalists happy to speak on without letup—sometimes, it appears, determined to do so. A pause in an exchange may bring embarrassment; in the words of a Tennessee woman whom I have known for years: "At such a time, silence is plain impoliteness, don't you think?" And we talked happily on.

In a clear fashion, the South came to think of itself in terms of romance. It approached its peak during the great Romantic movement which swept Europe from about 1760 to 1860—a movement which emphasized feeling, imagination. As they turned from formal methods, from formal reasoning, the Romanticists embraced the past, the richly colored elements, the days and the ways of Greece and Rome and the medieval era.

In the South, as in England and on the Continent, the Romanticists praised nature and its glories, the classicism of Southern Europe; and also, not least, the delights of the rural, the pastoral, life. More and more, the Southerners regarded themselves as a people apart from other Americans, occupying a land vividly different from other areas.

In time they spoke out buoyantly, excitedly, in behalf of a new Southern nation, powerful, expanding into Mexico at one extreme and to Cuba and the other Caribbean islands at the other. Slavery provided a feudal touch; great crops gave a secure status to the classes. The Southern leaders were "the Chivalry"; in the words of some, an aristocratic (or "aristocratical," as others put it) group which had little in common with the folk of the North.

And writers such as Sir Walter Scott, with his scenes of pageantry and tournaments, spurred Southerners to consider themselves as allied with such Old World elements. Sir Walter became the South's favorite of all writers, and booksellers told how they sent his novels in enormous shipments to fulfill the demand from Virginia to Louisiana, Florida to Missouri. Ultimately Mark Twain would blame the whole Confederate war on Sir Walter. While others have not gone so far, they have recognized the influence of the Scottish revivalist of the glories of chivalric times. . . . Like their visitors, the Southerners themselves came to savor "the romance of the thing."

At the side of the white man or woman of the South the Negro stands, and his daily life touches or crosses that of the whites at a hundred unseen points, in relationships interconnected in a fashion seldom clearly perceived by the stranger or even the native himself. In his recent perceptive study of South Carolina, William Francis Guess offers the poignant remark of a nursemaid to a complaining child who was her charge: "Honey, you has to learn to want and not git." A naked truth, says this authority, which "no one ever put plainer or better." Related in clear fashion is his story of the not altogether unfriendly words of one Ella Mae to her employer: "Lord, Miss Maggie, you don't have to tell me what a fool I is. I wouldn't of been working for you seventeen years if I wasn't."

HARNETT T. KANE

New Orleans, La.

I

Finders and Founders

THEY came to the South from one European power after the other—adventurous men whose rulers distrusted one another, who remained at "peace" but ready in a moment to order throats slit in sporadic contests for a new world. For centuries this part of America was probed by mixed bands with a yearning for territory, for gleaming metals and jewels, and (sometimes as an afterthought) for heathen souls to be enlisted under God's banners.

Long before they took their places on the soil of the upper Atlantic or along the Hudson, Europeans were drawn to the future South. Their imaginations catching fire, they put down words of wonder: teeming shores, an astonishing prodigality of massive plants and trees, great birds and animals, rippling lakes and gray-green distant mountains. . . .

Slowly, following one failure after another, the newcomers discovered ways to subdue the far-stretched plains, and to realize something of the wealth at their finger tips. The British of the silver bays and inlets of Virginia and the Carolinas; the Spaniards in swampy Florida, the French along the moist edges of Louisiana . . . which element would prevail? Ultimately the English, with their genius for steady settlement, were to give their impress to most of the area, but the Gallic and Hispanic areas maintained much of their separate identities.

From early days, climate and the shape of the earth determined the kind of life that would develop. The South had little of the rocky hills known to Maine or Massachusetts, or of the icy winds that roared down upon the upper East Coast or the Great Lakes, and none of the parching sands that would support only cactus and lizards for hundreds of miles of the Far West.

This land, almost bursting with fertility, did not welcome small trades or industries, but major crops that would spread over many acres reaching to the horizon. It would be a civilization to be enjoyed in the open—a place with the shade of many trees against the sun, and wind-swept porches and galleries. The pattern emerged: big agriculture, large labor forces and black men to work the fields. White laborers, used in the first days, were supplanted by slaves, and slowly the stage was set for clashes with other sections over the issue of bondage, and eventual catastrophe for the South.

With the late 1600's the South had begun to set up a replica of countryside England as its people remembered it. As time passed, cities were to crystallize at Richmond, New Orleans, Charleston, Mobile, Atlanta, but for generations the region existed as a rural area, and successful planters tried to model their ways after those of the squires on the other side of the Atlantic.

Thus a large-handed tradition arose: a new version of the old country, dominated by families fond of balls and dances, "fish feasts," hunts, long visits among friends. Visitors reported a certain high gloss of living, a good-humored hospitality that was evident from the earliest times.

With all this went a growing pride; the people of the plantations seldom undervalued themselves. The habit of command, acquired in contacts with their servants, extended to other matters. "Arrogant," a number of outsiders called them. Yet others found only a warmth of disposition, a will to please, and a quick capacity for enjoyment. At the same time they acquired a sense of responsibility, of public duty, and in time they were to contribute some of America's greatest figures.

The doors of the colonial and post-colonial drawing rooms were not tightly closed ones. Men could manage by energy and good luck—and also, let it be noted, sometimes, through the marriage bed of a rich widow—to enter the ranks of the ruling element. And throughout the South, as in England itself during the seventeenth and eighteenth and nineteenth centuries, members of various classes rose and fell and now and then rose again.

Many of these Virginians and Carolinians had a high temper, or at least high spirit, a measure of gallantry and, with it, a liking for their own way in most things. Some sent sons and daughters to Europe for education and a seasoning in worldly manners. (It must be admitted, however, that when certain youths returned with all *too* worldly a style, the fathers and mothers sighed and yearned for simpler days and simpler ways.) While outsiders thought the majority of the planters indolent or "plain lazy," records exist to show that a typical large tobacco grower had to function as might a business executive, looking after a dozen enterprises at the same time.

Meanwhile the plantation masters worked to hold their place in the sun against plainer families who started farms to the westward, and against occasional Indian raiders—and, not least, occasionally against the King's Governors and other agents disinclined to recognize the full rights of the colonials. Good Englishmen the colonists considered themselves, but gradually they were becoming something else: Americans whose attitudes were determined by their new interests, their new experiments.

With the mid-1700's the Southerners, like the colonials of New England, reacted furiously to overauthoritative English rulers and, step by step, the men of Virginia, South and North Carolina and Georgia asserted themselves in the front rank of the Revolutionists. Washington, Jefferson, Patrick Henry . . . they and others like them gave inspiration to the emerging nation; Jefferson spoke eloquently in behalf of the highest hopes, the more enlightened principles of their day.

In particular, Thomas Jefferson envisioned a new day of opportunity among men, as he urged a "natural aristocracy" of character and virtue, not an "artificial" one of birth and family position. About him and his associates there was an aura of high good will, of imagination and something that approached vision. They declared, for the world to applaud and later generations around the world to quote, that all men were created equal and entitled to a chance to show their capacities.

At the same time, of course, Jefferson and his followers passed over the contradiction between such a principle and existence of human bondage in their midst. Yet many such Southerners freed their slaves; others worked for plans of freedom, transportation of former bondsmen to other places. For all of its existence, the pre-Confederate South was to know distinguished individuals who dared stand out for general freedom, and insisted upon speaking their minds on the subject.

And meanwhile many Southerners turned their faces to the West, and moved along the mountain gaps to outlying Virginia and the remote parts of the Carolinas, while others marched or rode slowly to Kentucky and Tennessee and other open lands in the direction of the Mississippi. In the well-rutted lines of steady travel, in the ever-growing fields of green, and no less in the thoughts of men, the South was shaping itself.

"They Hugged Him with Great Affection"

GIOVANNI DA VERRAZZANO

THE precise identity of the first European to put foot on the shores of the South will never be established. For many years adventurers had advanced westward, stopping at islands, touching at beaches of what would eventually be Latin America. In dim accounts, half lost in prehistory, such explorers gave descriptions puzzling in their vagueness, but filled with hope of future achievement. In 1524 Giovanni da Verrazzano, Florentine navigator in the pay of France's king, sailed along the North Carolina coast in the Outer Banks area, probably above Cape Fear. Without notable modesty Giovanni named the land "Verrazzano Isthmus," and speculated about the "oriental sea" which doubtless extended about "the extremity of India, China and Cathay." Many after him also concluded that a narrow ledge of North Carolina was all that existed between the Atlantic and Pacific oceans. The earliest Indians, be it noted, were friendly and affectionate. It would take them time to learn better about such newcomers to their South. This account is from Richard Hakluyt's classic Divers Voyages Touching the Discovery of America and the Islands Adjacent.*

ON the 17th of January we set sail from a desolate rock near the Island of Madeira, belonging to his Most Serene Majesty, the King of Portugal, with fifty men, having provisions sufficient for eight months. . . . On the 24th of February we encountered as violent a hurricane as any ship ever weathered, from which we escaped unhurt by the divine assistance and goodness. . . . Pursuing our voyage towards the West, a little northwardly, in twenty-four days more we reached a new country, which had never before been seen by anyone, either in ancient or modern times. . . . On approaching it to within a quarter of a league from the shore, we perceived, by the great fires near the coast, that it was inhabited.

Many people who were seen coming to the sea-side fled at our approach, but occasionally stopping, they looked back upon us with astonishment, and some were at length induced, by various friendly signs, to come to us. These showed the greatest delight on beholding us, wondering at our dress, countenances and complexions. They then showed us by signs where we could more conveniently secure our boat, and offered us some of their provisions. . . .

They go entirely naked, except that about the loins they wear skins of small animals like martens fastened by a girdle of plaited grass, to which they tie, all round the body, the tails of other animals hanging down to the knees. Some wear garlands similar to birds' feathers. . . . Their hair is black and thick, and not very long; it is worn tied back upon the head in the form of a little tail. In person they are of good proportions, of middle stature, a little above our own, broad across the breast, strong in the arms, and well-formed in the legs and other parts of the body; the only exception to their good looks is that they have broad faces, but not all, however, as we saw many that had sharp ones, with large black eyes and a fixed expression.

We found not far from this people another whose mode of life we judged to be similar. The whole shore is covered with fine sand, about fifteen feet thick, rising in the form of little hills. . . . An outstretched country appears at a little distance rising somewhat above the sandy shore in beautiful fields and broad plains, covered with immense forests of trees, more or less dense, too various in colors, and too delightful and charming in appearance to be described. . . .

We set sail from this place, continuing to coast along the shore. . . . Many of the natives came to the beach, indicating by various friendly signs that we might trust ourselves on shore. . . . A young sailor was attempting to swim ashore through the surf to carry them some knick-knacks, as little bells, looking glasses, and other like trifles; when he came near three or four of them he tossed the things to them and turned about to get back to the boat, but he was thrown over by the waves, and so dashed by them that he lay as it were dead. . . . They ran and took him up by the head, legs and arms. . . . The young man, finding himself borne off, uttered very loud shrieks in fear and dismay, while they answered in their language, showing him that he had no cause for fear.

Afterwards they laid him down at the foot of a little hill, when they took off his shirt and trowsers, and examined him, expressing the greatest astonishment at the whiteness of his skin. Our sailors, seeing a great fire made up, imagined that the natives were about to roast him for food. But as soon as he had recovered his strength, showing by signs that he wished to return aboard, they hugged him with great affection, and accompanied him to the shore. . . .

Departing hence, we came in the space of fifty leagues to another land, which appeared very beautiful. We found that the people had fled and hid themselves. By searching around, we discovered in the grass a very old woman and a young girl of about eighteen or twenty; the old woman carried two infants on her shoulders and behind her neck a little boy eight years of age; when we came up to them they began to shriek. We gave them a part of our provisions, which they accepted with delight, but the girl threw down in great anger. We took the little boy from the old woman to carry with us to France, and would have taken the girl also, who was very beautiful and very tall, but it was impossible because of the loud shrieks she uttered. . . . We found also wild roses, violets, lilies and many sorts of plants and fragrant flowers different from our own. . . . After having remained here three days, riding at anchor on the coast, as we could find no harbour, we determined to depart.

The Lady Gave Her Life for Her Pearls

A bizarre Southern-Spanish saga of rapacity and determination is the tale of Hernando de Soto, whose band marched for three years across most of the Lower South, murdering and burning as they went. In 1539 the conquistadores sailed upon Florida, with a party of some 625 knights and soldiers, hundreds of hogs and horses. From the Tampa Bay vicinity they advanced across Florida, the Georgia of today, Alabama, Louisiana, Arkansas; they went short distances into North Carolina and Tennessee and discovered the great Mississippi. In time the expedition fell apart; De Soto's body was dropped into the stream he had located, and remnants of the party finally reached Mexico. These passages, from B. F. French's Historical Collections of Louisiana and Florida, *New York, 1875, picture some of the more brutal moments of the story. For a century and a half afterward, the Europeans stayed away from the Mississippi.*

AS soon as March was come, Governor de Soto determined to depart from Chicaça, and demanded of the *cacique* two hundred men for carriages. The *cacique* sent him answer that he would speak with his principal men. Upon Tuesday, the eighth of March, 1541, the Governor went to the town where he was, to ask him for the men; the *cacique* told him he would send them the next day. As soon as the Governor was come to Chicaça he told Luys de Moscoso, the camp-master, that he misliked the Indians, and that he should keep a strong watch that night, which the camp-master remembered but a little.

The Indians came at the second watch in four squadrons, every one by itself, and as soon as they were descried, they sounded a drum, and gave the assault with a great cry, and with so great celerity, that presently they entered with the scouts, that were somewhat distant from the camp. And when they were perceived of them which were in the town, half the houses were on fire, which they had kindled.

That night three horsemen chanced to be scouts; two of them were of base calling, and the worst men in all the camp, and the other, which was a nephew of the Governor, which until then was held for a tall man, showed himself there as great a coward as any of them: for all of them ran away.

And the Indians without any resistance came and set the town on fire; and tarried without behind the doors for the Christians, which ran out of the houses, not having any leisure to arm themselves; and as they ran hither and thither amazed with the noise, and blinded with the smoke and flame of the fire, they knew not which way they went, neither could they light upon their weapons, nor saddle their horses, neither saw they the Indians that shot at them.

Many of the horses were burned in the stables, and those which could break their halters got loose. The disorder and flight was such that every man fled which way he could, without leaving any to resist the Indians. But God (which chastiseth according to his pleasure, and in the greatest necessities and dangers sustaineth them with his hand) so blinded the Indians, that they saw not what they had done, and thought that the horses

which ran loose, were men on horseback, that gathered themselves to set upon them. The Governor only rode on horseback, and with him a soldier called Tapia, and set upon the Indians, and striking the first he met with his lance, the saddle fell with him, which with haste was evil girded, and so he fell from his horse.

And all the people that were on foot were fled to a wood out of the town, and there assembled themselves together. And because it was night, and that the Indians thought the horses were men on horseback which came to set upon them, as I said before, they fled; and one only remained dead, and that was he whom the Governor slew with his lance.

The town lay all burnt to ashes. There was a woman burned, who, after she and her husband were both gone out of their house, went in again for certain pearls which they had forgotten, and when she would have come out, the fire was so great at the door that she could not, neither could her husband succor her. Three other Christians came out of their lodgings so cruelly burned, that one of them died within three days, and the other two were carried many days each of them, upon a couch between staves, which the Indians carried on their shoulders, for otherwise they could not travel.

There died in this hurlyburly eleven Christians, and fifty horses; and there remained a hundred hogs, and four hundred were burned. If any perchance had saved any clothes from the (earlier) fire of Mavilla, here they were burned, and many were clad in skins, for they had no leisure to take their coats. They endured much cold in this place, and the chiefest remedy were great fires. They spent all night in turnings without sleep; for if they warmed one side, they froze on the other. Some invented the weaving of certain mats of dry ivy, and did wear one beneath, and another above: many laughed at this device, whom afterward necessity enforced to do the like.

Incredible Abundance "Even in the Midst of Summer..."

ARTHUR BARLOWE

Arriving at a comparatively late date, a pioneer set Englishmen sailed nearly a half century after De Soto to the Atlantic coast of the South. Two ships, sent out by the ambitious Walter Raleigh, halted off North Carolina, and one of the Captains wrote his version of the exciting incident. As a result Raleigh became a knight, and the name of Virginia, for the Virgin Queen Elizabeth, was fixed upon a wide, vague region extending far into the interior. There followed attempted British settlement along the North Carolina shores, sadly aborted by ill luck, but the way was pointed for a future colony in the South—specifically, the beginnings of Anglo-Saxon America. The following is Captain Arthur Barlowe's 1584 report to his superior, Raleigh.

THE 27 day of April, in the year of our redemption, 1584, we departed the West of England, with two barks well furnished with men and victuals. . . . The tenth of May we arrived at the Canaries, and the tenth of June . . . we were fallen with the Islands of the West Indies. . . . The second of July, we found shoal water, where we smelt so sweet, and so strong a smell, as if we had been in the midst of some delicate garden abounding with all kind of odoriferous flowers. . . . The fourth of the same month we arrived upon the coast, which we supposed to be a continent and firm land. . . .

The first river that appeared to us, we entered, though not without some difficulty, and cast anchor about three harquebus-shot within the haven's mouth; after thanks given to God for our safe arrival thither, we manned our boats, and went to view the land next adjoining, and to take possession of the same, in the right of the Queen's most excellent Majesty, as rightful Queen and princess of the same, and after delivered the same over to your use, according to her Majesty's grant and letters patent. . . .

We viewed the land about us, being, whereas we first landed, very sandy and low toward the water's side, but so full of grapes, as the very beating and surge of the sea overflowed them, of which we found such plenty, as well there as in all places else, both on the sand and on the green soil on the hills, as in the plains, as well on every little shrub, as also climbing towards the tops of high cedars, that I think in all the world the like abundance is not to be found. . . .

We passed from the sea side towards the tops of those hills next adjoining, being but of mean height, and from thence we beheld the sea on both sides to the north, and to the south, finding no end any of both ways. . . . Having discharged our harquebus-shot, such a flock of cranes (the most part white) arose under us, with such a cry redoubled by many echoes, as if an army of men had shouted all together. This island had many goodly woods full of deer, conies, hares and fowl, even in the midst of summer in incredible abundance. . . . We remained by the side of this island two whole days before we saw any people of the country. The third day we spied one small boat rowing toward us having in it three persons.

This boat came to the island side, four harquebus-shot from our ships, and there two of the people remaining, the third came along the shoreside and we being then all within board, he walked up and down upon the point of land. Then myself and others rowed to the land, whose coming this fellow attended, never making any show of fear or doubt. And after he had spoken of many things not understood by us, we brought him with his own good liking aboard the ships, and gave him a shirt, a hat and some other things, and made him taste of our wine and our meat, which he liked very well; and after having viewed both barks he departed. . . .

As soon as he was two bow shot into the water, he fell to fishing, and in less than half an hour, he had laden his boat as deep as it could swim, with which he came again to the point and divided his fish into two parts, pointing one part to the ship and the other to the pinnace. . . .

The next day there came unto us divers boats and in one of them the King's brother, accompanied with forty or fifty men, very handsome and goodly people, and in their behavior as mannerly and civil as any of Europe. . . . His servants spread a long mat upon the ground, on which he sat down and at the other end of the mat four others of his company did the like. The rest of his men stood round about him, somewhat a far off. When we came to the shore to him with our weapons, he never moved from his place, nor any of the other four, nor never mistrusted any harm to be offered from us, but sitting still he beckoned us to come and sit by him, which we performed; and being set he made all signs of joy and welcome, striking on his head and his breast and afterwards on ours, to show we were all one, smiling and making show the best he could of all love and familiarity. . . .

After we had presented this his brother with such things as we thought he liked, we likewise gave somewhat to the other that sat with him on the mat. But presently he arose and took all from them and put it into his own basket, making signs and tokens that all things ought to be delivered to him, and the rest were but his servants and followers. . . . A day or so after this, of all things that he saw, a bright tin dish most pleased him, which he presently took up and clapped it before his breast, and after made a hole in the brim thereof and hung it about his neck, making signs that it would defend him against his enemies' arrows.

"Many Rare and Wonderful Experiments"

THOMAS HARRIOT

Without the Indian crop of tobacco there might have been no Virginia or no South as they developed from the original settlements. Gaping as they watched the red men "suck" or "drink" the peculiar smoke, the Englishmen tried it, liked it, and history was made. Virginia had its first great crop, the basis of its colonial existence, and Europeans had a new habit. Thomas Harriot, brilliant young scientist from Oxford, gave armchair travelers some significant accounts—dependable, carefully balanced—of the life of Virginia. Not least important was this section of his Brief and True Report of the New Found Land of Virginia, *1588, in which he describes "Uppowoc, or Tabacco."*

THERE is an herbe which is sowed apart by it selfe, and is called by the inhabitants Uppowoc: in the West Indies it hath divers names, according to the severall places and countreys where it groweth and is used: the Spanyards generally call it Tabacco. The leaves thereof being dried and brought into pouder, they use to take the fume or smoake thereof, by sucking it thorow pipes made of clay, into their stomacke and head; from whence it purgeth superfluous fleame and other grosse humours, and openeth all the pores and passages of the body: by which meanes the use thereof not onely preserveth the body from obstructions, but also (if any be, so that they have not bene of too long continuance) in short time breaketh them: whereby their bodies are notably preserved in health, and know not many grievous diseases, wherewithall we in England are often times afflicted.

This Uppowoc is of so precious estimation amongst them, that they thinke their gods are marvellously delighted therewith: whereupon sometime they make hallowed fires, and cast some of the pouder therin for a sacrifice: being in a storme upon the waters, to pacifie their gods, they cast some up into the aire and into the water: so a weare for fish being newly set up, they cast some therein and into the aire: also after an escape of danger, they cast some into the aire likewise: but all done with strange gestures, stamping, sometime dancing, clapping of hands, holding up of hands, and staring up into the heavens, uttering therewithall, and chattering strange words and noises.

We our selves, during the time we were there, used to sucke it after their manner, as also since our returne, and have found many rare and woonderfull experiments of the vertues thereof: of which the relation would require a volume by it selfe: the use of it by so many of late men and women of great calling, as els, and some learned Physicians also, is sufficient witnesse.

"Kindly Intreating Us, Daunsing and Feasting Us with Strawberries"

JOHN SMITH

Had there been no John Smith, the story of the South might have taken a somewhat different turn at a number of early points. The energetic, hot-tempered little redhead of a man fumed and fought with the others with whom he went to Virginia in 1607. At least once he faced execution at the hands of his fellows. But the self-made leader from Lincolnshire had zest and a hard will, and he did much to make Jamestown succeed in its most hazardous days. He had the tastes of an explorer, and he worked hard to establish relations with the Indians (not excluding the females of the tribe). In his True Relation of Virginia *of 1608 John gives his version of the scene and what happened there.*

KINDE Sir, commendations remembred, &c. You shall understand that after many crosses in the downes by tempests, wee arrived safely uppon the Southwest part of the great Canaries: within foure or five daies after we set saile for Dominica, the 26. of April: the first land we made, wee fell with Cape Henry, the verie mouth of the Bay of Chissiapiacke, which at that present we little expected, having by a cruell storme bene put to the Northward. Anchoring in this Bay twentie or thirtie went a shore with the Captain, and in coming aboard, they were assalted with certaine Indians which charged them within Pistoll shot: in which conflict, Captaine Archer and Mathew Morton were shot: whereupon Captaine Newport seconding them, made a shot at them, which the Indians little respected, but having spent their arrowes retyred without harme.

And in that place was the Box opened, wherin the Counsell for Virginia was nominated: and arriving at the place where wee are now seated, the Counsel was sworn, and the

President elected, which for that yeare was Maister Edm. Maria Wingfield, where was made choice for our scituation, a verie fit place for the erecting of a great cittie, about which some contention passed betwixt Captaine Wingfield and Captain Gosnold: notwithstanding, all our provision was brought a shore, and with as much speede as might bee wee went about our fortification.

The two and twenty day of Aprill, Captain Newport and my selfe with divers others, to the number of twenty two persons, set forward to discover the River, some fiftie or sixtie miles, finding it in some places broader, and in some narrower, the Countrie (for the moste part) on each side plaine high ground, with many fresh Springes, the people in all places kindely intreating us, daunsing and feasting us with strawberries, Mulberies, Bread, Fish, and other their Countrie provisions wherof we had plenty: for which Captaine Newport kindely requited their least favours with Bels, Pinnes, Needles, beades, or Glasses, which so contented them that his liberallitie made them follow us from place to place, and ever kindely to respect us.

In the midway staying to refresh our selves in a little Ile foure or five savages came unto us which described unto us the course of the River, and after in our journey, they often met us, trading with us for such provisions as wee had, and arriving at Arsatecke, hee whom we supposed to bee the chiefe King of all the rest, moste kindely entertained us, giving us in a guide to go with us up the River to Powhatan, of which place their great Emperor taketh his name, where he that they honored for King used us kindely.

But to finish this discoverie, we passed on further, where within an ile we were intercepted with great craggy stones in the midst of the river, where the water falleth so rudely, and with such a violence, as not any boat can possibly passe, and so broad disperseth the streame, as there is not past five or six Foote at a low water, and to the shore scarce passage with a barge, the water floweth foure foote, and the freshes by reason of the Rockes have left markes of the inundations 8. or 9. foote: The South side is plaine low ground, and the north side is high mountaines the reckes being of a gravelly nature, interlaced with many vains of glistring spangles.

That night we returned to Powhatan: the next day (being Whitsunday after dinner) we returned to the fals, leaving a mariner in pawn with the Indians for a guide of theirs; hee that they honoured for King followed us by the river. That afternoone we trifled in looking upon the Rockes and river (further he would not goe) so there we erected a crosse, and that night taking our man at Powhatan, Captaine Newport congratulated his kindenes with a Gown and a Hatchet: returning to Arseteche, and stayed there the next day to observe the height therof, and so with many signes of love we departed. The next day the Queene of Agamatack kindely intreated us, her people being no lesse contented then the rest, and from thence we went to another place (the name whereof I do not remember) where the people shewed us the manner of their diving for Mussels, in which they finde Pearles.

That night passing by Weanock some twentie miles from our Fort, they according to their former churlish condition, seemed little to affect us, but as wee departed and lodged at the point of Weanocke, the people the next morning seemed kindely to content us, yet we might perceive many signes of a more Jealousie in them then before, and also the Hinde that the King of Arseteck had given us, altered his resolution in going to our Fort, and with many kinde circumstances left us there.

This gave us some occasion to doubt some mischiefe at the Fort, yet Capt. Newport intended to have visited Paspahegh and Tappahanocke, but the instant change of the winde being faire for our return we repaired to the fort with all speed where the first we heard was that 400. Indians the day before had assalted the fort, and supprised it, had not God (beyond al their expectations) by meanes of the shippes, at whom they shot with their Ordinances and Muskets, caused them to retire, they had entred the fort with our own men, which were then busied in setting Corne, their Armes beeing then in driefats and few ready but certain Gentlemen of their own, in which conflict, most of the Counsel was hurt, a boy slain in the Pinnas, and thirteene or fourteene more hurt. With all speed we pallisadoed our Fort: (each other day) for sixe or seaven daies we had alarums by ambuscadoes, and four or five cruelly wounded by being abroad: the Indians losse wee know not, but as they report three were slain and divers hurt.

Captaine Newport having set things in order, set saile for England the 22d of June, leaving provision for 13. or 14. weeks. The day before the Ships departure, the King of Pamaunke sent the Indian that had met us before in our discoverie, to assure us peace; our fort being then palisadoed round, and all our men in good health and comfort, albeit, that throgh some discontented humors, it did not so long continue, for the President and Captaine Gosnold, with the rest of the Counsell, being for the moste part discontented with one another, in so much, that things were neither carried with that discretion nor any busines effected in such good sort as wisdome would, nor our owne good and safetie required, whereby, and through the hard dealing of our President, the rest of the counsell beeing diverslie affected through his audacious commaund; and for Captaine Martin, albeit verie honest, and wishing the best good, yet so sicke and weake; and my selfe so disgrac'd through others mallice: through which disorder God (being angrie with us) plagued us with such famin and sicknes, that the living were scarce able to bury the dead: our want of sufficient and good victualls, with continuall watching, foure or five each night at three Bulwarkes, being the chiefe cause: onely of Sturgion wee had great store, whereon our men would so greedily surfet, as it cost manye their lives: the Sack, Aquavitie, and other preservatives for our health, being kept onely in the Presidents hands, for his owne diet, and his few associates.

Thomas Wolfe Re-creates Catawba's Discovery

THOMAS WOLFE

In this vivid and evocative passage the remarkable Thomas Wolfe speculated over the early explorations of his native North Carolina. Nearly always skillful in his descriptive writings, Wolfe drew freely upon his imagination to achieve a vivid effect in re-creating the past. Adroitly he set a mood and brought to life a forgotten hour, in this section from The Face of a Nation, *collection of Wolfe's writings about the American scene, edited by John Hall Wheelock, Scribner's, New York, 1939.*

CATAWBA got discovered in this way: a one-eyed Spaniard, one of the early voyagers, was beating up the American coasts out of the tropics, perhaps on his way back home, perhaps only to see what could be seen. He does not tell us in the record he has left of the voyage how he happened to be there, but it seems likely that he was on his way home and had been driven off his course. Subsequent events show that he was in a very dilapidated condition, and in need of overhauling: the sails were rent, the ship was leaking, the food and water stores were almost exhausted. During the night in a storm off one of the cruelest and most evilly celebrated of the Atlantic capes, the one-eyed Spaniard was driven in and almost wrecked. By some miracle of good fortune he got through one of the inlets in the dark, and when light broke he found himself becalmed in an enormous inlet of pearl-gray water.

As the light grew he made out seawards a long almost unbroken line of sandy shoals and islands that formed a desolate barrier between the sea and the mainland, and made this bay or sound in which he found himself. Away to the west he descried now the line of the shore: it was also low, sandy, and desolate-looking. The cool gray water of morning slapped gently at the sides of his ship: he had come from the howling immensity of the sea into the desert monotony of this coast. It was as bleak and barren a coast as the one-eyed Spaniard had ever seen.

And indeed, for a man who had come up so many times under the headlands of Europe, and had seen the worn escarpments of chalk, the lush greenery of the hills, and the minute striped cultivation of the earth that greet the sailor returning from a long and dangerous voyage—and awaken in him the unspeakable emotion of earth which has been tilled and used for so many centuries, with its almost personal bond for the men who have lived there on it, and whose dust is buried in it—there must have been something particularly desolate about this coast which stretched away with the immense indifference of nature into silence and wilderness. The Spaniard felt this, and the barren and desert quality of the place is duly recorded in his log. . . .

But here a strange kind of exhilaration seizes the Spaniard; it gets into his writing, it begins to color and pulse through the gray stuff of his record. The light of the young rising sun reddened delicately upon the waters; immense and golden it came up from the sea behind the line of the sea-dunes, and suddenly he heard the fast drumming of the wild ducks as they crossed his ship high up, flying swift and straight as projectiles. Great heavy gulls of a size and kind he had never seen before, swung over his ship in vast circles, making their eerie creaking noises. The powerful birds soared on their strong even wings, with their feet tucked neatly in below their bodies; or they dove and tumbled through the air, settling to the water with great flutterings and their haunted creaking clamor; they seemed to orchestrate this desolation, they gave a tongue to loneliness and they filled the hearts of the men who had come there with a strange exultancy. For, as if some subtle and radical changes had been effected in the chemistry of their flesh and blood by the air they breathed, a kind of

wild glee now possessed the one-eyed Spaniard's men. They began to laugh and sing, and to be, as he says, "marvellous merry."

During the morning the wind freshened a little; the Spaniard set his sails and stood in toward the land. By noon he was going up the coast quite near the shore, and by night he had put into the mouth of one of the coastal rivers. He took in his sails and anchored there. There was nearby on shore a settlement of "the race that inhabits these regions," and it was evident that his arrival had caused a great commotion among the inhabitants, for some who had fled away into the woods were now returning, and others were running up and down the shore, pointing and gesticulating and making a great deal of noise. But the one-eyed Spaniard had seen Indians before; that was an old story to him now, and he was not disturbed. As for his men, the strange exuberance that had seized them in the morning does not seem to have worn off; they shouted ribald jokes at the Indians, and "did laugh and caper as if they had been madde."

Nevertheless, they did not go ashore that day. The one-eyed Spaniard was worn out, and the crew was exhausted: they ate such food as they had, some raisins, cheese, and wine, and after posting a watch they went to sleep, unmindful of the fires that flickered in the Indian village, of sounds and chants and rumors, or of the forms that padded softly up and down the shore.

Then the marvellous moon moved up into the skies, and blank and full, blazed down upon the quiet waters of the sound, and upon the Indian village. It blazed upon the one-eyed Spaniard and his lonely little ship and crew, on their rich dull lamps, and on their swarthy sleeping faces; it blazed upon all the dirty richness of their ragged costumes, and on their greedy little minds, obsessed then as now by the European's greedy myth about America, to which he remains forever faithful with an unwearied and idiot pertinacity: "Where is the gold in the streets? Lead us to the emerald plantations, the diamond bushes, the platinum mountains, and the cliffs of pearl. Brother, let us gather in the shade of the ham and mutton trees, by the shores of ambrosial rivers: we will bathe in the fountains of milk, and pluck hot buttered rolls from the bread vines."

Early the next morning the Spaniard went ashore with several of his men. "When we reached land," he writes, "our first act was to fall down on our knees and render thanks to God and the Blessed Virgin without Whose intervention we had all been dead men." Their next act was to "take possession" of this land in the name of the King of Spain, and to ground the flag. As we read today of this solemn ceremony, its pathos and puny arrogance touch us with pity. For what else can we feel for this handful of greedy adventurers "taking possession" of the immortal wilderness in the name of another puny fellow four thousand miles away, who had never seen or heard of the place and could never have understood it any better than these men? For the earth is never "taken possession of": it possesses.

A *Te Deum* in Gratitude for Entrance into the Mississippi's Mouth

Even later than the English, the French arrived eventually from Europe and Canada for a historic exploration along the Gulf Coast. After their difficult entry through the hazardous mouths of the Mississippi River they set up primitive homes along the sandy or muddy shores, culminating about 1718 in the founding of the Latin-spirited New Orleans. A member of the expedition commanded by Pierre Le Moyne d'Iberville marveled at the alluvial edges of the uncertain land, the spreading green marshes, the almost impenetrable canebrake and the slothful alligator-residents of the locale. From these tentative beginnings arose the great city of the South, polyglot, languid, worldly New Orleans. The report is from B. F. French's Historical Collections of Louisiana and Florida, *New York, 1875.*

ON Monday, March 2, 1699, we sighted the mainland and coasted along the whole distance in our long-boats. A few of our company were in bark canoes. The seas ran so high that we were obliged to fix up tarred canvas on the gunwales about a foot in height to prevent the water from breaking into the boats. We drew nearer the land for fear of missing the river. . . .

After beating about in the seas for two hours, and fearing the waves would fill the bark canoes, M. d'Iberville, our commander, made us run before the wind. At this moment we perceived a pass between two banks, which appeared like islands. We saw that the color of the water had changed. We tasted it and found it fresh, a circumstance that gave us great consolation in that moment of consternation.

Soon after we beheld the thick, muddy water. As we advanced, we saw the passes of the river, three in number. The current was such that we could not ascend it without difficulty, although the wind was fair and favorable. . . . The coast consists of nothing more than two narrow strips of land, about a musket shot in width having the sea on both sides of the river, which flows between these two strips of land, and frequently overflows them. At four o'clock, after having ascended the river one league and a half, we landed in a thick cane-brake, which grows so tall and thick on both banks of the river, that it is difficult to see across, and is impossible to pass through without cutting it down. Beyond the canes are impenetrable marshes. The banks are also bordered by trees of prodigious heights, which the current of the river draws down to the sea, with their roots and branches. . . .

On Tuesday 3d, mass was performed, and a *Te Deum* sung in gratitude for our discovery of the entrance of the Mississippi River. . . . At the quarter of a league from our encampment we found a large arm of water, which broke over everywhere. At nine oclock, we were dismasted in a squall. We landed as soon as possible to adjust our masts, and found an abundance of blackberries, nearly ripe. . . . There are bushes on each side [of the river bank], but as you ascend, the banks appear more and more submerged, the land being scarcely visible. We saw a great quantity of wild game, such as ducks, geese, snipe, teal, bustards and other birds. . . . Some of our men found a variety of animals, such as stags, deer and buffaloes. . . .

On the 4th, which was Ash Wednesday, religious ceremonies were attended by everyone. Mass was said and a cross was planted. . . . We saw some small canoes, each made from three bundles of cane, bound with thin wooden straps. The Indians make use of these in the chase and in crossing from one side of the river to the other. . . . One of our bark canoes, which had remained behind with three hunters, reported they saw three crocodiles on the bank. . . .

The forest trees began to assume larger dimensions, but not very close together, for we could see across the country, which was very marshy. . . . On Thursday, the 5th, three of our men went hunting at daylight; they saw many tracks and heard the howlings of wild beasts. . . . Saw a large crocodile on the river banks, sunning himself. Some of our men fired at him, when he immediately threw himself into the river. At eleven o'clock we saw smoke arising from the burning grass, to which the Indians had set fire, either to drive out the game or obtain easier access to fire upon us. . . . At three o'clock, in going up the river, saw a canoe which had been hollowed out by burning from the trunk of a large tree. . . .

On Friday, the 6th . . . two of our men told us they had seen three crocodiles, one of which was a monster. At seven o'clock a buffalo was killed. . . . On Saturday, the 7th, after having marked some trees, we embarked. We saw three buffaloes lying down on the bank. We landed five men to go in pursuit of them, which they could not do, as they soon got lost in the thick forest and cane-brakes. A short time after, in turning a point, we saw a canoe manned by two Indians, who took to land the moment they saw us and concealed themselves in the woods. A little farther on we saw five more who executed the same manoeuvre, with the exception of one, who waited for us at the brink of the river. We made signs to him. M. d'Iberville gave him a knife, some beads and other trinkets. In exchange he gave us some dried bear's meat. M. d'Iberville commanded all of our men to go on board the long-boats for fear of intimidating him, and made signs to him to recall his comrades. They came singing their song of peace, extending their hands towards the sun and rubbing their stomachs, as a sign of admiration and joy. After joining us they placed their hands upon their breasts and extended their arms over our heads as a mark of friendship. M. d'Iberville asked them, by signs, if their village was far off. They told him it was five days' journey hence.

What troubled us most was that our provisions were falling short. M. d'Iberville gave them some beads, knives and looking-glasses; in return they gave us dried bear's meat, which they had in their canoes. Our men also trafficked with them for some trifling objects. One good old man extended his meat upon the ground, after the same manner our butchers do in our markets of Europe, and sat down beside it. Two of our men went to him, and each one gave him a knife and took the whole of the meat, consisting of at least one hundred pounds. All seemed satisfied with their bargain. M. d'Iberville asked them if they would show him their village. They gave him to understand they were going on a hunt, and could not accompany him. But having offered a hatchet to one of them, who seemed very desirous to possess it, he agreed to go. We asked them if they had heard the sound of the swivel; they said they had heard it twice. We fired it again before them, at which they were greatly astonished, for it was the first time they had ever heard it so near them.

They Became "Joyful Mothers"

JOHN LAWSON

There are few more poignant stories than that of John Lawson, onetime surveyor-general of North Carolina. He was a man of good will, with marked sympathy toward the Indians, a warm humor and comprehension unusual among people of his day. The red men, he said, were "really better to us than we to them." He gave valuable accounts of the natives' everyday life in his A New Voyage to Carolina, *London, 1709, and he sought fairer treatment for the tribes he met. But a few years later he was trapped in the moiled warfare of the day; a European associate apparently made little or no effort to save Lawson when the Indians seized him. And the man who here describes the Indians' harsh treatment of their captives seems to have been burned to death in much the manner that he himself pictured to the world.*

THE inhabitants of Carolina, through the richness of the soil, lead an easy and pleasant life. . . . With a small trouble of fencing, almost every man may enjoy, to himself, an entire plantation, or rather park. These, with the other benefits of plenty of fish, wild-fowl, venison, and the other conveniences which this summer-country naturally furnishes, have induced a great many families to leave the more northerly plantations and sit down under one of the mildest governments in the world; in a country that, with moderate industry, will afford all the necessaries of life. . . .

Some of the men are very laborious, and make great improvements in their way; but I dare hardly give them that character in general. The easy way of living in that plentiful country makes a great many planters very negligent. . . . The women are the most industrious sex in that place, and, by their good housewifery, make a great deal of cloath of their own cotton, wool and flax; some of them keeping their families, (though large) very decently appareled. . . . The Christian natives are a straight, clean-limbed people; the children being seldom or ever troubled with rickets, or those other distempers that the Europeans are visited withal. 'Tis next to a miracle to see one of them deformed in body.

The vicinity of the sun makes impression on the men who labour out of doors, or use the water. As for those women that do not expose themselves to the weather, they are often very fair, and generally as well featured as you shall see any where, and have very brisk, charming eyes which sets them off to advantage. They marry very young; some at thirteen or fourteen; and she that stays till twenty is reckoned a stale maid, which is a very indifferent character in that warm country.

The women are very fruitful, most houses being full of little ones. It has been observed that women long married and without children in other places, have removed to Carolina and become joyful mothers. They have very easy travail in their childbearing, in which they are so happy as seldom to miscarry. . . . Many of the women are very handy in canoes and will manage them with great dexterity and skill. . . . They are ready to help their husbands in any servile work, as planting, when the season of the weather requires expedition; pride seldom banishing good housewifery.

The girls are not bred up to the wheel and sewing only, but the dairy, and affairs of the house they are very well acquainted withal; so that you shall see them, whilst very young, manage their business with a great deal of conduct and alacrity. The children of both sexes are very docile. . . . The young men are commonly of a bashful, sober behavior; few proving prodigals to consume what the industry of their parents has left them, but commonly improve it. The marrying so young, carries a double advantage with it, and that is that the parents see their children provided for in marriage, and the young married people are taught by their parents how to get their living.

.   .   .

When an aged [Indian] man is speaking, none ever interrupts him, (the contrary practice the English and other Europeans too much use,) the company yielding a great deal of attention to his tale with a continued silence and an exact demeanor, during the oration. Indeed, the Indians are a people that never interrupt one another in their discourse; no man so much as offering to open his mouth till the speaker has uttered his intent: When an Englishman comes among them, perhaps every one is acquainted with him, yet, first the King bids him welcome, after him the War Captain, so on gradually from high to low; not one of all these speaking to the white guest, till his superior has ended his salutation.

Amongst women, it seems impossible to find a scold; if they are provoked or affronted, by their husbands, or some other, they resent the indignity offered them in silent tears, or by refusing their meat. Would some of our European daughters of thunder set these Indians for a pattern, there might be more quiet families found amongst them, occasioned by that unruly member, the tongue.

.   .   .

Next morning we set out early, breaking the ice we met withal in the stony runs. . . . We passed by several cottages, and about 8 of the clock came to a pretty big town, where we took up our quarters in one of their statehouses, the men being all out hunting in the woods. . . . Our fellow traveler, having a great mind for an Indian lass for his bed-fellow that night, spoke to our guide, who soon got a couple, reserving one for himself.

That which fell to our companion's share was a pretty young girl. Though they could not understand one word of what each other spoke, yet the female Indian, being no novice at her game, but understanding what she came thither for, acted her part dexterously enough

with her cully, to make him sensible of what she wanted, which was to pay the hire before he rode the hackney. He showed her all the treasures he was possessed of, as beads, red cadis, &c., which she liked very well, and permitted him to put them into his pocket again, endearing him with all the charms which one of a better education than Dame Nature had bestowed upon her, could have made use of to render her consort a surer captive.

After they had used this sort of courtship a small time, the match was confirmed by both parties, with the approbation of as many Indian women as came to the house to celebrate our Winchester-Wedding. Every one of the bride-maids were as great whores as Mrs. Bride, though not quite so handsome. Our happy couple went to bed together before us all, and with as little blushing as if they had been man and wife for seven years. The rest of the company, being weary with traveling, had more mind to take their rest, than add more weddings to that hopeful one already consummated; so that, though the other virgins offered their service to us, we gave them their answer and went to sleep.

About an hour before day, I awaked and saw somebody moving up and down the room, in a seemingly deep melancholy. . . . It proved to be Mr. Bridegroom, who, in less than twelve hours, was batchelor, husband and widower, his dear spouse having picked his pocket of the beads, cadis and what else should have gratified the Indians for the victuals we received of them; however, that did not serve her turn, but she also got his shoes away. . . . After the Indians had laughed their sides sore at the figure Mr. Bridegroom made, with much ado, we mustered up another pair of shoes or moggisons, and set forward, the company lifting up their prayers for the new married couple, whose wedding had made away with that which should have purchased our food.

.   .   .

The Indians will endure a great many misfortunes, losses and disappointments without showing themselves, in the least, vexed or uneasy. When they go by water, if there proves a headwind, they never vex or fret as the Europeans do, and let what misfortune comes to them as will or can happen, they never relent. Besides there is one vice very common everywhere, which I never found among them, which is, envying other men's happiness, because their station is not equal to, or above their neighbors. . . .

If they are taken captives and expect a miserable exit, they sing; if death approach them in sickness, they are not afraid of it; nor are ever heard to say, Grant me some time. They know by instinct, and daily example, that they must die; wherefore they have that great and noble gift to submit to everything that happens, and value nothing that attacks them.

Their cruelty to their prisoners of war is what they are seemingly guilty of an error in, (I mean as to a natural failing) because they strive to invent the most inhuman butcheries for them that the devils themselves could invent or hammer out of hell; they esteeming death no punishment, but rather an advantage to him, that is exported out of this into another world.

Therefore, they inflict on them torments, wherein they prolong life in that miserable state as long as they can, and never miss skulping of them as they call it, which is, to cut off the skin from the temples and taking the whole head of hair along with it, as if it was a nightcap. Sometimes they take the top of the skull along with it; all which they preserve and carefully keep by them, for a trophy of their conquest over their enemies. Others keep their enemies teeth which are taken in war, whilst others split the pitch-pine into splinters, and stick them into the prisoner's body yet alive. Thus they light them which burn like so many torches; and in this manner they make him dance round a great fire, every one buffeting and deriding him, till he expires, when every one strives to get a bone or some relick of this unfortunate captive.

Into The West-Lying Valley

MARSHALL FISHWICK

An epochal hour for the South arrived when, in 1716, Governor Alexander Spotswood of Virginia led a party of his followers in exploring a future green passageway to the early "West" of the Shenandoah Valley—a thoroughfare that was to be traveled by hundreds of thousands on their way toward the frontier. In his Virginia, A New Look at the Old Dominion *(Harper's, 1959) Marshall Fishwick makes clear that the expedition had spirit and also spirits, and several kinds of glow, human and otherwise. The exploit also opened the way to a long series of clashes with Indians who resented the steady encroachment upon their domain.*

"And stepping Westward seemed to be a kind of heavenly destiny."—William Wordsworth

WHAT a shame that the spectators consisted largely of reptiles and black bears. There the Governor stood, a-tiptoe on the crest of the Blue Ridge, his peacock plume poking a hole in the sky, his green velvet cape flapping in the fall breeze, his Russian leather boots and eyes sparkling.

September 7, 1716. Governor Alexander Spotswood, knowing full well this was a memorable day, fondled it tenderly as it passed. By claiming this magnificent valley which the Indians called Shenandoah, the English would sever communications between French outposts to the north and those along the Mississippi. Just west of the mountains ahead lay the Great Lakes and destiny.

As sparkling as lake water was, this occasion conjured up stronger stuff. "Gentlemen," said the Governor, "let us drink a toast to King George!" On this "for men only" outing, toasts were easily come by. Though the Williamsburg gentry involved complained of stiffness in their bones, "because they had not good beds to lie on," and had a close call with a bear, they could take consolation in the knowledge that they would not suffer from thirst. Lieutenant John Fontaine, a young Huguenot who had joined the British army and attached himself to Spotswood, listed the following provisions: "several sorts of liquor, viz: Virginia red wine and white wine, Irish usquebaugh, brandy, shrub, two sorts of rum, champagne, canary, cherry punch, cider, etc., etc." The gentlemen explorers were seemingly prepared to float the Shenandoah Valley into the British Empire.

The grand manner came naturally to Spotswood. In an age of dazzling individuals, he had won early distinction as a British officer. He had been "dangerously wounded" at Blenheim. What attracted attention was not his wound, but the fact that instead of having it treated, he rushed off to retrieve the offending cannon ball as a souvenir. For this, and other plucky feats, he was at the age of twenty-eight made a quartermaster general by Marlborough. Politically ambitious, Spotswood came to Virginia in 1710 as royal Governor. As his Council soon discovered, he could and did "swear like our army in Flanders," set up iron works, import artisans, and plot to move the Union Jack Westward. He was proficient with the pen, the sword, and the flask. September 6, 1716, was definitely a day for the flask.

Champagne corks popped merrily atop the Great Blue Ridge. Fitting ceremonies were held on the peaks, one of which was named Mt. George, and another Mt. Spotswood, and there was a feast of wild deer, turkey, currants, cucumbers, and grapes. The last-named item apparently set off a chain reaction which extended back to the vineyards of the Old World. After the meal, Lieutenant Fontaine tells us in his diary, "we drank the King's health in champagne, and fired a volley; the Princess' in Burgundy, and fired a volley; all the rest in claret, and fired a volley. We drank the Governor's health, and fired yet another volley." By this time the valley was dancing.

On the hazy horizon a river meandered through the tall grass. To the well-plied Governor it seemed so grand a stream that he promptly named it the Euphrates. (At a later and soberer moment, the name was changed to Shenandoah.) Utilizing one of the innumerable empty bottles, Spotswood buried a paper on which was written the claim that this place was now in the possession of King George I of England. After centuries of service as an international hunting ground for Delaware, Catawba, and Shawnee Indians, the valley was to become an outpost for white Europeans.

Back in Williamsburg, Alexander Spotswood had miniature gold horseshoes made for his jolly companions. . . . The Knights of the Golden Horseshoe had cast a golden glow over the Valley which it would never lose.

Spotswood was not the first white man to see the Shenandoah. . . . As early as 1654 Colonel Abraham Wood crossed the mountains further South, as did Captain Henry Batts in 1671. They tell that the adventurous German John Lederer made three such expeditions in 1669. "A modest ingenuous person and a pretty scholar," in Sir William Talbott's words, Lederer prepared a map and account of his adventures in Latin. . . .

Fine plumes and velvets were not standard equipment for the German and Scotch-Irish pioneers who followed in the eighteenth century. Long rifles and scalping knives were more functional. These small farmers, owning no slaves, hated the highhanded Tidewater slaveholders. They were . . . essentially Westerners, with the traditional frontier hostility to the East. The reason they would play such a small part in the Virginia tradition was that the planters who perpetuated traditions, passed laws and wrote histories would accord them no larger one.

Indians, incensed by the invasion of their best hunting ground, fought the oncoming settlers with a peculiar ferocity, as men like George Painter found out. They raided his house near Woodstock. When he tried to escape, he was shot and his bloody body dragged back into the house, which was then set on fire. The rest of the family, and several neighbors who had sought refuge in the cellar, came out and surrendered. Four babies were hanged on trees, riddled with rifle shots, and left dangling in the wind. A stable full of sheep and cows was burned, and all the animals roasted.

The remaining whites were forced to march to an Indian village beyond the Allegheny Mountains. One of the prisoners was Jacob Fisher, a plump German lad of twelve. The Indians forced him to collect a pile of faggots. These were ignited, and the boy was goaded with sharp sticks until he ran through the flames again and again. After the braves had tired of the goading, the squaws took over. Hours later, while his family watched helplessly, the screams stopped. Bleeding from a hundred wounds, Jacob Fisher found relief in death. No wonder, when the white men were able to revenge such atrocities, they answered in kind and fed their dogs on Indian flesh.

Those who mastered the Valley were strong and resourceful. Men like Jost Hite, allegedly a baron from Alsace, who sailed his own schooner over from Germany. At first he lived in a log cabin, but he soon set to work to build the first stone home in the Valley, five miles southwest of the site of Winchester. Although Governor Gooch confirmed his 100,000-acre grant, the court ruled against it. Jost Hite didn't budge. Then Lord Fairfax, who owned most of the Northern Neck, told him to give way. Jost Hite didn't budge. Instead he planted more fields, planted more corn, and said more prayers. He slept on a feather bed, ate sauerkraut, and kept his stock indoors all winter. When he had lived his life out, he died on his own Virginia soil and was buried in it.

Men like John Lewis, who came to Virginia from Ireland with a price on his head, having killed his landlord, Lord Clonmithgairn, in an argument over rents. He came over the Blue Ridge with thirty faithful tenants and founded Staunton in 1732. They set their rude cabins in thick grass that unrolled like gaudy carpeting. It was the best grass they had ever seen. Snowdrop, the white cow, waddled in every evening, her legs stained crimson by wild strawberries. Even the Indians, who came by full-painted, looked like fragments of rainbows or mountebanks at the Irish fairs. There were many bad moments, but even more good ones, in John Lewis's life. Then there was the epitaph, which summed the whole thing up:

HERE LIES THE REMAINS OF JOHN LEWIS
WHO SLEW THE IRISH LORD
SETTLED IN AUGUSTA COUNTY
LOCATED THE TOWN OF STAUNTON
AND FURNISHED FIVE SONS TO FIGHT THE BATTLES
OF THE AMERICAN REVOLUTION.

Women like Isabel Stockton, Hannah Dennis, Mary Moore, or "Mad Ann" Baily, who could "hew with an ax as good as airy man." Born Ann Hennis in Liverpool, England, Mad Ann came to Virginia in 1750 as an indentured servant. Her husband, James Trotter, was still a boy when the Indians scalped him at the battle of Point Pleasant. After the news came, Ann left her only child, William, with a neighbor, dressed in buckskins, carried a tomahawk, and hunted Indians. She found them, and began her scalp collection. When John Baily turned up, she took time off to marry him. All the dowry she could supply was a horse, bridle and saddle, and covers enough to keep a bed warm. Soon she went back to scalping Indians.

Mad Ann's finest moment came when the Redskins laid siege to Fort Lee, a stockade outpost near present-day Charleston, West Virginia. She slipped out during the night, rode to Fort Union (near Lewisburg), and returned with enough powder to turn the contest. Not many men could have done it; none who were there even dared it. What men did do was erect a monument to her memory, on top of Hot Springs Mountain. It still stands.

Through the Night They Dreamed of Scalpings

WILLIAM BYRD

William Byrd, grandson of an English goldsmith, inherited wealth from his Virginia father and increased it heavily by shrewd management. A man of parts, Byrd went to London for his education, became a friend of some of the great of his day and roistered about inns and other establishments with gentlemen and ladies high and low. Back in Virginia, he reconstructed Westover, one of the great mansions of the South, lived a full life and talked and wrote (though hardly ever for publication) wittily, lustily and well. In two major works he showed a sharp eye, ironic humor and an overweening contempt for his North Carolina neighbors. Toward men of Byrd's cast, the North Carolinians returned the contempt with compound interest. These accounts are based on The History of the Dividing Line and Other Tracts, from the Papers of William Byrd . . . *Richmond, 1866. He died in 1744 at seventy.*

SEPTEMBER 11th [1733]. Having recommended my family to the protection of the Almighty, I crossed the river with two servants and four horses, and rode to Col. Mumford's. . . . I proceeded to Major Mumford's [and] was the more obliged to him, because he made me the compliment to leave the arms of a pretty wife, to lie on the cold ground for my sake. She seemed to chide me with her eyes, for coming to take her bedfellow from her, now the cold weather came on.

12th. Then we fortified ourselves with a beef-steak, kissed our landlady for good luck, and mounted about ten. . . . Tom Short had promised to attend me, but had married a wife and could not come. . . . The major was ill of a purging and vomiting, attended by a fever which had brought him low; but I prescribed him a gallon or two of chicken broth, which washed him as clean as a gun. . . . We sent for an old Indian called Shacco-Will. . . . To comfort his heart, I gave him a bottle of rum, with which he made himself very happy, and all the family very miserable by the horrible noise he made all night.

16th. My landlady could not forbear discovering some broad signs of the fury, by breaking out into insolent and passionate expressions against the poor negroes. And if my presence could not awe her, I concluded she could be very outrageous when I was a hun-dred miles off. This inference I came afterwards to understand was but too true, for, between the husband and the wife, the negroes had a hard time of it.

18th. There are so many appearances of copper in these parts, that the inhabitants seem to be all mine-mad, and neglect making of corn for their present necessities, in hopes of growing very rich hereafter.

19th. The heavens lowered a little upon us in the morning, but, like a damsel ruffled by too bold an address, it soon cleared up again. . . . We laid the foundation of two large cities. One at Shacco's, to be called Richmond, and the other at the point of Appomattox river, to be named Petersburg. . . . The truth of it is, that these two places being the uppermost landing of James and Appomattox rivers, are naturally intended for marts, where the traffic of the outer inhabitants must center. Thus we did not build castles only, but cities in the air.

20th. In our way we killed two very large rattlesnakes, one of fifteen and the other of twelve rattles. They were both fat, but nobody would be persuaded to carry them to our quarters, although they would have added much to the luxury of our supper. . . . Our Indians killed three deer, but were so lazy they brought them not to camp, pretending for their excuse that they were too lean.

21st. It was strange we met with no wild

turkeys, this being the season in which great numbers of them used to be seen towards the mountains. . . . So that we could not commit that abomination, in the sight of all Indians, of mixing the flesh of deer and turkeys in our broth.

23d. Our Indians having no notion of the sabbath, went out to hunt for something for dinner, and brought a young doe back along with them. They laughed at the English for losing one day in seven; though the joke may be turned upon them for losing the whole seven, if idleness and doing nothing to the purpose may be called loss of time.

25th. We had no sooner pitched the tents, but one of our woodsmen alarmed us with the news that he had followed the track of a great body of Indians to the place where they had lately encamped. . . . These tidings I could perceive were a little shocking to some, and particularly the little major, whose tongue had never lain still, was taken speechless for sixteen hours. . . . It took the edge off most of our appetites for everything but the rum bottle.

26th. My servant had fed so intemperately upon bear, that it gave him a scouring, and that was followed by the piles, which made riding worse to him than purgatory. But anointing with the fat of the same bear, he soon grew easy again.

27th. In the night our sentinel alarmed us with an idle suspicion that he heard the Indian whistle (which amongst them is a signal for attacking their enemies). This made every one stand manfully to his arms in a moment . . . but after we had put ourselves in battle array, we discovered this whistle to be nothing but the nocturnal note of a little harmless bird. We were glad to find the mistake. . . . However, some of the company dreamed of nothing but scalping all the rest of the night.

29th. In our way to this place we treed a bear, of so mighty a bulk that when we fetched her down she almost made an earthquake. But neither the shot nor the fall disabled her so much, but she had like to have hugged one of our dogs to death in the violence of her embrace. We exercised the discipline of the woods, by tossing a very careless servant in a blanket for losing one of our axes.

30th. Of other work (than fighting and hunting) the men do none, thinking it below the dignity of their sex, but make the poor women do all the drudgery. They have a blind tradition amongst them, that work was first laid upon mankind by the fault of the female, and therefore it is but just that sex should do the greatest part of it. This they plead in their excuse; but the true reason is, that the weakest must always go to the wall, and superiority has from the beginning ungenerously imposed slavery on those who are not able to resist it.

[Oct.] 2d. One of our men, Joseph Colson by name, a timorous, lazy fellow, had squandered away his bread, and grew very uneasy when his own ravening had reduced him to short allowance. He was one of those drones who love to do little and eat much, and are never in humor unless their bellies are full. . . . He began to break the rules by complaining and threatening to desert. This had like to have brought him to the blanket, but his submission reprieved him.

3d. One of the Indians shot a wild goose, that was very lousy, which nevertheless was good meat. 4th. Peter Jones had a smart fit of ague which shook him severely, though he bore it like a man; but the small major had a small fever, and bore it like a child. He groaned as if he had been in labor, and thought verily it would be his fate to die like a mutinous Israelite in the wilderness, and be buried under a heap of stones.

5th. Our invalids found themselves in traveling condition this morning, and began to conceive hopes of returning home and dying in their own beds. . . . We had the fortune to knock down a young buffalo, two years old. 6th. We made our supper on the tongue and udder of the buffalo, which were so good, that a cardinal legate might have made a comfortable meal upon them during the carnival. Nor was this all, but we had still a rarer morsel, the bunch rising up between the shoulders of this animal, which is very tender and very fat.

8th. We knocked down an ancient she bear that had no flesh upon her bones, so we left it to the free-booters of the forest. In coming back to the camp we discovered a solitary bull buffalo, which boldly stood his ground, contrary to the custom of that shy animal. We spared his life, from a principle of never slaughtering an innocent creature to no purpose. However, we made ourselves some diversion, by trying if he would face our dogs. He was so far from retreating at their approach, that he ran at them with great fierceness, cocking up his ridiculous little tail, and grunting like a hog. The dogs in the meantime only played about him, not venturing within reach of his horns, and by their nimbleness came off with a whole skin.

11th. My landlady received us with a grim sort of a welcome, which I did not expect, since I brought her husband back in good health, though perhaps that might be the reason. It is sure something or other did tease her. . . . We now returned to that evil custom of lying in a house, and an evil one it is, when ten or a dozen people are forced to pig together in a room . . . troubled with the squalling of peevish dirty children into the bargain.

12th. I put my friend (one of the party) in mind of many things he had done amiss, which he promised faithfully to reform. I was so much an infidel to his fair speeches (having been many times deceived by them), that I was forced to threaten him with my highest displeasure. . . . I also let him know that he was not only to correct his own errors, but likewise those of his wife, since the power certainly belonged to him, in virtue of his conjugal authority. He scratched his head at this last admonition, from whence I inferred that the gray mare was the better horse.

Mr. John Butcher received us kindly, and we had a true Roanoke entertainment of pork upon pork, and pork again upon that. He told us he had been one of the first seated in that remote part of the country, and in the beginning had been forced, like the great Nebuchadnezzar, to live a considerable time upon grass. . . . The people are all mine mad, and neglecting to make corn, starve their families in hopes to live in great plenty hereafter. . . . As you ride, you see all the large stones knocked to pieces, nor can a poor marcasite rest quietly in its bed for these curious inquirers.

13th. After breaking our fast with a sea of milk and potatoes, we took our leave, and I crossed my landlady's hand with a piece of money. She refused the offer at first, but, like a true woman, accepted of it when it was put home to her. She told me the utmost she was able to do for me was a trifle in comparison of some favor I had formerly done her; but what that favor was, neither I could recollect, nor did she think proper to explain. . . . Then I came to the plantation of Joshua Nicholson, where Daniel Taylor lives for halves. There was a poor dirty house, with hardly anything in it but children, that wallowed about like so many pigs. It is a common case in this part of the country, that people live worse upon good land; and the more they are befriended by the soil and the climate, the less they will do for themselves.

14th. We got to church in decent time, and Mr. Betty entertained us with a good honest sermon, but whether he bought it or borrowed it, would have been uncivil in us to inquire. . . . He is a decent man, with a double chin that sits gracefully over his band, and his parish, especially the female part of it, like him well. . . . What women happened to be there, were very gim [sic] and tidy in the work of their own hands, which made them look tempting in the eyes of us foresters. The distance (to the next house) was reputed fifteen miles, but appeared less by the company of a nymph of those woods, whom innocence, and wholesome flesh and blood made very alluring.

15th. Mr. Banister's good humored little wife was glad to see her runaway spouse returned in safety. . . . In the gayety of our hearts we drank our bottle a little too freely, which had an unusual effect on persons so long accustomed to simple element. We were both of us raised out of our beds in the same manner, and near the same time, which was a fair proof that people who breathe the same air, and are engaged in the same way of living, will be very apt to fall into the same indispositions. And this may explain why distempers sometimes go round a family, without any reason to believe they are infectious, according to the superstition of the vulgar.

16th. As much in haste as I was to return to my family, I spent an hour or two at that place, but could by no means be persuaded to stay for dinner, nor could even Madame de Graffenriedt's smiles on one side of her face shake my resolution. . . . I had not passed the courthouse before it began to pour down like a spout upon me. Nevertheless I pushed forward and got dripping wet before I could reach Merchant's Hope Point. . . . The good fortune that attended me, and my whole company, will I hope stick fast in my memory, and make me everlastingly thankful.

History of the Dividing Line

[March 10, 1728] We observed very few cornfields in our walks. . . . Both cattle and hogs ramble into the neighboring marshes and swamps, where they maintain themselves the whole winter long, and are not fetched home till the spring. Thus these indolent wretches, during one half of the year, lose the advantage of the milk of their cattle, as well as their dung, and many of the poor creatures perish in the mire, into the bargain, by this ill management. Some, who pique themselves more upon industry than their neighbors, will, now and then in compliment to their cattle, cut down a tree whose limbs are loaden with the moss. The trouble would be too great to climb the tree in order to gather this provender, but the shortest way (which in this country is always counted the best) is to fell it, just like the lazy Indians, who do the same by such trees as bear fruit, and so make one harvest for all. By this bad husbandry milk is so scarce, in the winter season, that were a big-bellied woman to long for it, she would lose her longing. And, in truth, I believe this is often the case, and at the same time a very good reason why so many people in this province are marked with a custard complexion.

The only business here is raising of hogs, which is managed with the least trouble, and affords the diet they are most fond of. The truth of it is, that the inhabitants of North Carolina devour so much swine's flesh, that it fills them full of gross humors. For want too of a constant supply of salt, they are commonly obliged to eat it fresh, and that begets the highest taint of scurvy. Thus, whenever a severe cold happens to constitutions thus vitiated, tis apt to improve into the yaws, called there very justly the country-distemper. This has all the symptoms of the pox [syphilis], with this aggravation, that no preparation of mercury will touch it. First it seizes the throat, next the palate, and lastly shows its spite to the poor nose, of which tis apt in a small time treacherously to undermine the foundation.

This calamity is so common and familiar here, that it ceases to be a scandal. . . . Tis said that once, after three good pork years, a motion had like to have been made in the house of burgesses, that a man with a nose should be incapable of holding any place of profit in the province; which extraordinary motion could never have been intended without some hopes of a majority.

11th. . . . We came upon a family of mulattoes that called themselves free, though by the shyness of the master, who took care to keep least in sight, their freedom seemed a little doubtful. It is certain many slaves shelter themselves in this obscure part of the world, nor will any of their righteous neighbors discover them. On the contrary, they find their account in settling such fugitives on some out-of-the-way corner of their land, to raise stocks for a mean and inconsiderable share, well knowing their condition makes it necessary for them to submit to any terms.

Nor were these worthy borders content to shelter runaway slaves, but debtors and criminals have often met with the like indulgence. But if the government of North Carolina has encouraged this unneighborly policy in order to increase their people, it is no more than what ancient Rome did. . . . And considering how fortune delights in bringing great things out of small, who knows but Carolina may, one time or other, come to be the seat of some great empire?

. . . Surely there is no place in the world where the inhabitants live with less labor than in North Carolina. It approaches nearer to the description of Lubberland than any other, by the great felicity of the climate; the easiness of raising provisions, and the slothfulness of the people. . . . The men, for their parts just like the Indians, impose all the work upon the poor women. They make their wives rise out of their beds early in the morning, at the same time that they lie and snore, till the sun has risen one third of his course, and dispersed all the unwholesome damps. Then, after stretching and yawning for half an hour, they light their pipes, and, under the protection of a cloud of smoke, venture into the open air; though, if it happens to be never so little cold, they quickly return shivering into the chimney corner. . . . To speak the truth, tis a thorough aversion to labor that makes people file off to North Carolina, where plenty and a warm sun confirm them in their disposition to laziness for their whole lives.

A Toast of Two Worlds

EDITH TUNIS SALE

In contrast with that of her glittering father, Evelyn Byrd's life eventually became a shadowed one. William Byrd's wealth and rank opened nearly all doors to her, but he closed the one which she wished above everything else to enter. Whether or not the girl's death came of a broken heart, or whether anyone really dies of a fractured romance, Virginians have told this romantic story through many generations. The following account comes from Old Time Belles and Cavaliers, *by Edith Tunis Sale, J. B. Lippincott Company, New York, 1912.*

IN the early part of the eighteenth century, about the year 1725, a gentleman of great wealth returned from England, bringing with him, in his own sailing vessel, his young daughter whose presentation had shortly before taken place at the Court of St. James, and about whose beauty and charm the fashionable tongues of two countries were wagging.

The gentleman was . . . the Honorable William Byrd, while the high-bred maiden who sat so passively beside him in his gilded coach as it rolled to his vast plantation, was the beautiful Evelyn, fresh from her triumphs abroad to try her fortune at the gay little Colonial Capital of Williamsburg.

Evelyn, the daughter of Colonel William and Lucy Parke Byrd, was born in 1708, upon her father's fair estate of Westover in Virginia, and though other children came to him, it was always this beautiful daughter who held first place in his heart. As a child, the little Evelyn had her own corps of black attendants; when she rowed upon the river, it was in a galley manned by stalwart negro oarsmen; when she dined, an ebony page stood stolidly behind her chair, while her women servants were many, from the old black mammy to the errand girl of contemporary age. Never was a life more joyous and care free than that led by this little Virginia maid.

When she was about eight years old, her father had her brought to London where he then was staying, and in a time-worn letter to his great friend, the Honorable John Custis, dated 1714, he speaks of his plans for her. "My daughter Evelyn has arrived safe, thank God, and I hope I shall manage her in such a manner that she may be no discredit to her country."

That the haughty Virginian realized this fond wish, all social history of the early eighteenth century proves, for when, after as good a schooling as could be gained in Europe, Evelyn Byrd, at sixteen, made her initial bow before George II, the Hanoverian monarch exclaimed in amazement: "Are there many other as beautiful *birds* in the forests of America?" Perhaps it was this play upon words that suggested to Sir Godfrey Kneller the pretty thought of painting in the background of his superb portrait of Mistress Evelyn a cardinal bird.

This exquisite likeness of America's greatest Colonial belle represents her in a gown of silvery blue fashioned without adornment save at the low neck, where a ruffle of the satin falls; the tight sleeves reach only to the elbow where they are finished with a frill. The poise of the figure is queenly almost to haughtiness; the dark brown hair, so plainly dressed, is carried back severely from the forehead to end in a loose curl over the right shoulder. . . .

The slender hands with such tapering fingers show very plainly that they could never have accomplished a harder task than that in which the fair young girl is engaged —wreathing a chain of wild flowers about the crown of her leghorn hat. The neck is flawless, the shoulders a bit sloping; the throat full, yet slender. But even all this beauty may, perhaps, be overlooked when one's glance reaches the lovely face; oval in shape, lit by sad brown eyes set obliquely, the high-bred nose and sweetly drooping mouth recall to the mind of the observer the cause of the piteous, resigned expression.

There is more than one story of the love affair that brought so soon to a close the life of Evelyn Byrd. Some old writers would have us believe that she pined for her cousin, Daniel Parke Custis, whom her father was eager to have her marry, and who later became the husband of Martha Dandridge.* Others say that it was for the old Earl of Peterborough, a roué of sixty years, though this is given little credence; the girl was too fair, too innocent for that.

The most probable version of all seems that in which Charles Mordaunt, grandson and heir of the old Lord Peterborough, figures. That these two met to love each other, can well be believed; Mordaunt was noble, manly, as handsome as a Greek god; Evelyn Byrd was aristocratic, wealthy, beautiful, and had drawn the eyes of the world towards her, and in the match the smart world, with one exception, seems to have seen perfection: that exception —the haughty father of the would-be bride.

Though William Byrd and Lord Peter-

* After her first husband's death, Martha became Mrs. George Washington.

borough had been staunch friends, something came to pass which changed them into the bitterest of enemies; some say it was cards, others religion, and again a darker reason is hinted. Be that as it may, Colonel Byrd refused to sanction the love affair, and regardless of the triumphs she was leaving, brought his daughter back to Westover. . . .

Accustomed in every way to obey her father, the sad girl made no remonstrance, but accepted the fate which robbed her of her life. Her beauty, if changed at all, was made greater by the suffering heart it hid; for admirers she never lacked; for belledom she was created; but as her father never withdrew his tyranny, though he saw her life slipping away day by day, neither did Evelyn ever falter in her devotion to Charles Mordaunt, and after a few pitiful years the light of Westover went out all too soon, and Evelyn Byrd was but a memory. . . .

Of this lovely maid of Colonial days, whose innocence and naïveté never suffered from contact with the gayest of courts, one of William Byrd's biographers says: "Her hand was kissed by my Lords Oxford and Chesterfield; of whom sneering Harvey deigned to approve; who supped with Pope at his Twickenham villa, while yet the town was ringing with the success of his Odyssey; who was noticed by Beau Nash, the autocrat of Bath; who saw Cibber and Mrs. Oldfield play; who read Gulliver's Travels as they were first presented to the public by his reverence the dean of St. Patrick's, then resident in Dublin; who from the presence-chamber of unroyal royalty, through a society reeking with wine and musk and snuff and scandal, passed back to her plantation home in the new country as unblemished as she came."

At beautiful old Brandon, where Sir Godfrey Kneller's famous portrait hangs, there is entered in an aged family record just opposite the name of Evelyn Byrd: "Refusing all offers from other gentlemen, she died of a broken heart."

A sigh is the outcome of the thoughts upon the sad life of the wistful girl whose years should have been so many and so fair. Through the quiet corners of old Westover, up and down its broad stairway, softly glides sometimes an ethereal figure said to be Evelyn Byrd. Those who sleep in the room that was hers when a little Colonial maid and to which she returned from the brilliant English Court, admit visits from the long dead beauty who comes as gently as she did in life.

There are some who say that they have felt the light touch of her exquisite fingers, others who have seen the white wraith hover near one of her favorite haunts; but there are none who fear the ghostly presence of the tender, lovely Evelyn, who asked of life the one thing it denied her.

Under the oaks of Westover this beauty found a grave in which to rest forever. Darkened by time and roughened by storms, a massive stone is placed over the spot where, "in the sleep of deep peace," reposes the fairest flower of old Virginia, whose life has never been reproduced in all the time that has passed since the thirteenth day of November, in 1737. The lengthy inscription upon her heavy tomb is guarded jealously by mosses and lichens which screen as best they can the piteous words from idle gaze. This tiny bit of God's earth, sacred to the memory of one of His most beautiful human creatures, is thickly carpeted with the periwinkle vine, evergreen through dreary winter months in remembrance of her who sleeps beneath, and bright with smiling blue blossoms at the first bird song of early spring.

The days that Mistress Evelyn knew belonged to that unique and beautiful era when high-heeled dames coquetted with gold-laced cavaliers; to that delightful and remarkable period which produced minds and masters, belles and beauties in whom vanity was blended with bravery with such wonderful results that the American people are what they are today. Hers was a time of filial obedience, which made it an age of tyranny and selfish parents. More than all, it was a day of pretty love stories, sometimes of pathetic disappointments and broken hearts, yet never has there been such a picturesque age, never will there be again such famous belles, and never will life be so unique and well worth living as when Evelyn Byrd was the toast of two worlds.

Epitaphs, Buckskin Breeches and Sweet Marrage Vows

"Annals of Old Virginia" might be the subtitle to the following newspaper items, reflecting the daily life of the colonials. They mirror the formality and also the casual doings of the Virginians. They are taken from Historical Collections of Virginia, *edited by Henry Howe, Charleston, 1845.*

WILLIAMSBURG, Nov. 12, 1736.—On this day sen'night, being the 5th of November, the president, masters, and scholars, of *William* and *Mary* college went, according to their annual custom, in a body, to the governor's, to present his honor with two copies of Latin verses, in obedience to their charter, as a grateful acknowledgment for two valuable tracts of land given the said college by their late *K. William* and *Q. Mary.* Mr. President delivered the verses to his honor; and two of the young gentlemen spoke them. It is further observed there were upwards of 60 scholars present; a much greater number than has been any year before since the foundation of the college.

.   .   .

Williamsburg, Sept. 21, 1739.—An epitaph on Miss M. Thacker (daughter of Col. Edwin

Thacker, of Middlesex,) who died at Williamsburg on Wednesday last:

"Pensively pay the tribute of a tear,
    For one that claims our common grief
    lies here.
Good-natured, prudent, affable, and mild,
In sense a woman, in deceit a child.
Angels, like us, her virtues shall admire,
And chant her welcome thro' the Heav-
    enly choir."

.   .   .

September 21, 1739—EDWARD MORRIS, *Breeches-Maker* and *Glover*, from London, is set up in his business, near the college, in Williamsburg, where he makes and sells the best *buckskin breeches*, either of the common tanned color, black, or any other cloth colors, after the English manner. Also buckskin gloves with high tops. Any persons that have occasion to make use of him, in any of the above particulars, may depend upon kind usage, and at very reasonable rates.

.   .   .

Williamsburg, April 13, 1768.—A hog was brought to town this week, from Sussex, as a show, raised by Mr. Henry Tyler there, who, though only four years old, is near three feet and a half high, about nine and a half long, and, it is supposed, weighs near twelve hundred pounds. He much exceeds any animal of the kind ever raised on this continent, and, indeed, we do not remember to have heard of any so large in England.

.   .   .

EDMUND RANDOLPH, Esq., Attorney-General of Virginia, to Miss BETSEY NICHOLAS, a young lady whose amiable sweetness of disposition, joined with the finest intellectual accomplishments, cannot fail of rendering the worthy man of her choice completely happy.

Fain would the aspiring muse attempt to sing
    The virtues of this amiable pair;
But how shall I attune the trembling string,
    Or sound a note which can such worth
    declare?
Exalted theme! too high for common lays!
    Could my weak verse with beauty be
    inspired,
In numbers smooth I'd chant my BETSEY'S
    praise,
        And tell how much her RANDOLPH
        is admired,
To light the hymeneal torch since they've
    resolved,
    Kind Heaven I trust will make them
    truly blest;
And when the *Gordian knot* shall be dis-
    solved,
        Translate them to eternal peace and rest.

Their Flaps were Just Too Narrow

MINGO EMMITTA

This piquant complaint was spoken in 1772 by the Indian Mingo Emmitta to the Superintendent in Mobile, part of the British province of West Florida, which changed ownership several times among the European powers of Southern colonial days. He appeared to have a just grievance, though perhaps not a world-shaking one. His words appear in "Peter Chester, Third Governor of West Florida Under British Dominion . . ." in Publications of the Mississippi Historical Society, Centenary Series, *Volume 2, by Mrs. Dunbar Rowland.*

WHEN I return to my Nation It will be asked what have you seen? I will answer That I saw my Father and the Chief of the Red men the Great Governor and Chief of the white men in this Country and the Chief Leader and General of the Great Kings Warriors who received me kindly and as a proof I will Show them what I shall receive from my Father, what can we ask or Expect from our white Brethren but to Supply our wants.

Our Father is like a Turkey perched upon the Top of a High Tree we are his Brood of Chickens eagerly looking up at but cannot reach him at our return to our Houses our Young our Old our Fathers our Wives our Children will all rejoyce and be happy in having their wants Supplied.

What can our White Brethren think of us by giving us such narrow Flaps, they don't cover our Secret parts, and are in danger of being deprived of our Manhood, by every Hungry dog that approaches us, these Flaps are too narrow I hope this will be altered.

Joy, Festivity, Happiness at Charleston, and Also Misery

J. HECTOR ST. JOHN CRÈVECOEUR

The remarkable J. Hector St. John Crèvecoeur was born in France and lived in England, Canada and ultimately the United States. A great traveler, an individual of strong convictions on such matters as liberty and man's rights, Crèvecoeur had a warm love of nature, considerable literary skill and a strong idealism which make him almost unique among interpreters of the America of his day. A friend of Washington and Franklin, he had gifts which sometimes touched the poetic. Under some circumstances, Crèvecoeur offered an almost too enthusiastic picture of America; on the other hand, some have questioned his description of the grim treatment of an offending slave ,which is part of this selection from his Letters from an American Farmer, 1782, London.

CHARLES-TOWN is, in the north, what Lima is in the South; both are Capitals of the richest provinces of their respective hemispheres: you may therefore conjecture, that both cities must exhibit the appearances necessarily resulting from riches. Peru abounding in gold, Lima is filled with inhabitants who enjoy all those gradations of pleasure, refinement and luxury, which proceed from wealth. Carolina produces commodities, more valuable perhaps than gold, because they are gained by greater industry; it exhibits also on our northern stage, a display of riches and luxury, inferior indeed to the former, but far superior to what are to be seen in our northern towns.

Its situation is admirable, being built at the confluence of two large rivers, which receive in their course a great number of inferior streams; all navigable in the spring, for flat boats. Here the produce of this extensive territory concentrates; here therefore is the seat of the most valuable exportation; their wharves, their docks, their magazines, are extremely convenient to facilitate this great commercial business.

The inhabitants are the gayest in America; it is called the centre of our beau monde, and it is always filled with the richest planters of the province, who resort hither in quest of health and pleasure. Here are always to be seen a great number of valetudinarians from the West-Indies, seeking for the renovation of health, exhausted by the debilitating nature of their sun, air, and modes of living. Many of these West-Indians have I seen, at thirty, loaded with the infirmities of old age; for nothing is more common in those countries of wealth, than for persons to lose the abilities of enjoying the comforts of life, at a time when we northern men just begin to taste the fruits of our labour and prudence.

The round of pleasure, and the expenses of those citizens' tables, are much superior to what you would imagine: indeed the growth of his town and province has been astonishingly rapid. It is pity that the narrowness of the neck on which it stands prevents it from increasing; and which is the reason why houses are so dear. The heat of the climate, which is sometimes very great in the interior parts of the country, is always temperate in Charles-Town; though sometimes when they have no sea breezes the sun is too powerful. The climate renders excesses of all kinds very dangerous, particularly those of the table; and yet, insensible or fearless of danger, they live on, and enjoy a short and a merry life: the rays of their sun seem to urge them irresistably to dissipation and pleasure: on the contrary, the women, from being abstemious, reach to a longer period of life, and seldom die without having had several husbands. An European at his first arrival must be greatly surprised when he sees the elegance of their houses, their sumptuous furniture, as well as the magnificence of their tables; can he imagine himself in a country, the establishment of which is so recent?

The three principal classes of inhabitants are, lawyers, planters and merchants; this is the province which has afforded to the first the richest spoils, for nothing can exceed their wealth, their power and their influence. They have reached the *ne plus ultra* of worldly felicity; no plantation is secured, no title is good, no will is valid, but what they dictate, regulate and approve. The whole mass of provincial property is become tributary to this society; which, far above priests and bishops, disdain to be satisfied with the poor Mosaical portion of the tenth. I appeal to the many inhabitants, who, while contending perhaps for their right to a few hundred acres, have lost by the mazes of the law their whole patrimony.

These men are more properly law givers than interpreters of the law; and have united here, as well as in most other provinces, the skill and dexterity of the scribe with the power and ambition of the prince: who can tell where this may lead in a future day? The nature of our laws, and the spirit of freedom, which often tends to make us litigious, must necessarily throw the greatest part of the property of the colonies into the hands of these gentlemen. In another century, the law will possess in the north, what now the church possesses in Peru and Mexico.

While all is joy, festivity, and happiness in Charles-Town, would you imagine that scenes of misery overspread in the country? Their ears by habit are become deaf, their hearts are hardened; they neither see, hear nor feel for the woes of their poor slaves, from whose painful labours all their wealth proceeds. Here the horrors of slavery, the hardship of incessant toils, are unseen; and no one thinks with compassion of those showers of sweat and of tears which from the bodies of Africans, daily drop, and moisten the ground they till. The cracks of the whip urging these miserable beings to excessive labour, are far too distant from the gay Capital to be heard.

The chosen race eat, drink and live happy, while the unfortunate one grubs up the ground, raises indigo, or husks the rice; exposed to a sun full as scorching as their native one; without the support of good food, without the cordials of any chearing liquor.

This great contrast has often afforded me subjects of the most afflicting meditation. On the one side, behold a people enjoying all that life affords most bewitching and pleasurable, without labour, without fatigue, hardly subjected to the trouble of wishing. With gold . . . they order vessels to the coasts of Guinea; wars, murders and devastations are committed where dwelt innocent people. The daughter torn from her weeping mother, the child from the wretched parents, the wife from the loving husband. . . . There, arranged like horses at a fair, they are branded like cattle, and then driven to toil, to starve and to languish for a few years on the different plantations of these citizens.

And for whom must they work? For persons they know not, and who have no other power over them than that of violence; no other right than what this accursed metal has given them! Strange order of things! Oh,

Nature, where are thou?—Are not these blacks thy children as well as we?

Their paternal fondness is embittered by considering, that if their children live, they must live to become slaves like themselves; no time is allowed them to exercise their pious office; the mothers must fasten them on their backs, and, with this double load, follow their husbands in the fields, where they too often hear no other sound than that of the voice or whip of the task-master. . . .

A clergyman settled a few years ago at George-Town, and feeling as I do now, warmly recommended to the planters, from the pulpit, a relaxation of severity; he introduced the benignity of Christianity, and pathetically made use of the admirable precepts of that system to melt the hearts of his congregation into a greater degree of compassion. . . . "Sir" (said one of his hearers) "we pay you a genteel salary to read to us the prayers of the liturgy, and to explain to us such parts of the Gospel as the rule of the church directs; but we do not want you to teach us what we are to do with our blacks." The clergyman found it prudent to with-hold any farther admonition.

.   .   .

I was not long since invited to dine with a planter who lived three miles from ————, where he then resided. In order to avoid the heat of the sun, I resolved to go on foot, sheltered in a small path, leading through a pleasant wood. I was leisurely travelling along, attentively examining some peculiar plants which I had collected, when all at once I felt the air strongly agitated; though the day was perfectly calm and sultry. I immediately cast my eyes toward the cleared ground, from which I was but at a small distance, in order to see whether it was not occasioned by a sudden shower; when at that instant a sound resembling a deep rough voice, uttered, as I thought, a few inarticulate monosyllables.

Alarmed and surprized, I precipitately looked all around, when I perceived at about six rods distance something resembling a cage, suspended to the limbs of a tree; all the branches of which appeared covered with large birds of prey, fluttering about, and anxiously endeavouring to perch on the cage.

Actuated by an involuntary motion of my hands, more than by any design of my mind, I fired at them; they all flew to a short distance, with a most hideous noise; when, horrid to think and painful to repeat, I perceived a negro, suspended in the cage, and left there to expire! I shudder when I recollect that the birds had already picked out his eyes, his cheek bones were bare; his arms had been attacked in several places, and his body seemed covered with a multitude of wounds. From the edges of the hollow sockets and from the lacerations with which he was disfigured, the blood slowly dropped, and tinged the ground beneath. No sooner were the birds flown, than swarms of insects covered the whole body of this unfortunate wretch, eager to feed on his mangled flesh and to drink his blood.

I found myself suddenly arrested by the power of affright and terror; my nerves were convulsed; I trembled, I stood motionless, involuntarily contemplating the fate of this negro, in all its dismal latitude. The living spectre, though deprived of his eyes, could still distinctly hear, and his uncouth dialect begged me to give him some water. . . .

Humanity itself would have recoiled back with horror; she would have balanced whether to lessen such reliefless distress, or mercifully with one blow to end this dreadful scene of agonizing torture! Had I had a ball in my gun, I certainly would have despatched him; but finding myself unable to perform so kind an office, I sought, though trembling, to relieve him as well as I could. A shell ready fixed to a pole, which had been used by some negroes, presented itself to me; I filled it with water, and with trembling hands I guided it to the quivering lips of the wretched sufferer.

Urged by the irresistible power of thirst, he endeavoured to meet it, as he instinctively guessed its approach by the noise it made in passing through the bars of the cage. "Tankè, you whitè man, tankè you, putè some poyson and givè me." How long have you been hanging there? I asked him. "Two days, and me no die; the birds, the birds; aah me!" Oppressed with the reflections which this shocking spectacle afforded me, I mustered strength enough to walk away, and soon reached the house at which I intended to dine. There I heard that the reason for this slave being thus punished, was on account of his having killed the overseer of the plantation. They told me that the laws of self-preservation rendered such executions necessary; and supported the doctrine of slavery with the arguments generally made use of to justify the practice; with the repetition of which I shall not trouble you at present.

Planters "Don't Much Admire Labour . . . Except Horse-Racing"

HUGH JONES

An individual of marked balance and perception, a teacher and minister, Hugh Jones looked judiciously at his Virginia fellows when he wrote his The Present State of Virginia *in 1721. While he liked those around him, he set down all of their qualities that he noted, the not-so-good ones as well as the not-so-bad, including their lack of inclination to "dive into books." As a faculty member at the College of William and Mary, he gave one of the best available descriptions of Williamsburg.*

THE first metropolis, James Town, was built in the most convenient place for trade and security against the Indians, but often received much damage, being twice burnt down; after which it never recovered its perfection, consisting at present of nothing but abundance of brick rubbish, and three or four good inhabited houses. . . . When the state house and prison were burnt down, Governor Nicholson removed the residence of the governor, with the meeting of General Courts and General Assemblies to Middle Plantation, seven miles from James Town, in a healthier and more convenient place, and freer from the annoyance of muskettoes.

Here he laid out the city of Williamsburgh (in the form of a cypher, made of W. and M.) on a ridge at the head springs of two great creeks, one running into the James, and the other into York River . . . so that this town is most conveniently located, in the middle of the lower part of Virginia . . . and is much more commodious and healthful than if built upon a river.

Publick buildings here of note are the College, the Capitol, the Governor's House and the church. The college front which looks due east is double and is 136 foot long. It is a lofty pile of brick building adorned with a cupola. At the north end runs back a large wing, which is a handsome hall, answerable to which the chapel is to be built; and there is a spacious piazza on the west side, from one wing to the other. It is approached by a good walk, and a grand entrance by steps, with good courts and gardens about it . . . and a large pasture enclosed like a park with about 150 acres of land adjoining. . . .

The building is beautiful and commodious, being first modelled by Sir Christopher Wren, adapted to the nature of the country by the gentlemen there; and since it was burnt down, it has been rebuilt, and nicely contrived, altered and adorned by the ingenious direction of Governor Spotswood. . . . This royal foundation was granted and established by charter, by King William and Queen Mary, and endowed by them, with some thousand acres of land, with duties upon furs and skins, and a penny a pound for all tobacco transported. . . .

For some causes that I can't account for,

the revenue is not improved as much as might be wished; neither is the College brought to that method of education and advantage, as it might be. . . . The nature of the country scarce yet admits of a possibility of reducing the collegians to the nice methods of life and study observed in Oxford and Cambridge; though by degrees they may copy from thence many useful customs and constitutions. . . .

Fronting the College at near its whole breadth, is extended a noble street mathematically streight . . . just three quarters of a mile in length: at the other end of which stands the Capitol, a noble, beautiful and commodious pile as any of its kind . . . the best that I have seen or heard of. Here the Governor and twelve counsellors sit as judges. . . . Here are also held courts martial, by judges appointed on purpose, for the trial of pyrates. . . . The whole is surrounded with a neat area, encompassed with a good wall, and near it is a strong sweet prison for criminals. . . . Because the State House, James Town and the College have been burnt down, therefore is prohibited in the Capitol the use of fire, candles and tobacco. . . .

Near the middle stands the Church, which is a large strong piece of brickwork in the form of a cross, nicely regular and convenient, and adorned as the best churches in London. This from the parish is called Bruton Church. . . . From the Church runs a street northward called Palace Street; at the other end of which stands the Palace or Governor's House, a magnificent structure, built at the publick expence, finished and beautified with gates, fine gardens, offices, walks, a fine canal, orchards, etc, with a great number of the best arms nicely posited. . . . This likewise has the ornamental addition of a good cupola or lanthorn, illuminated with most of the town, upon birthnights, and other nights of occasional rejoicings. At the Capitol, at publick times, may be seen a great number of handsom, well-dressed, compleat gentlemen.

And at the Governor's House upon birthnights, and at balls and assemblies, I have seen as fine an appearance, as good diversion, and as splendid entertainments in Governor Spottswood's time as I have seen any where else. These buildings here described are justly re-

puted the best in all of English America, and are exceeded by few of their kind in England. . . . Here dwell several very good families, and more reside here in their own houses at publick times. They live in the same neat manner, dress after the same modes and behave themselves exactly as the gentry in London; most families of any note having a coach, chariot, berlin or chaise. . . .

London . . . they esteem their home; and for the most part have contemptible notions of England, and wrong sentiments of Bristol and the other out-ports, which they entertain from seeing and hearing the common dealers, sailors and servants that come from those towns, and the country places in England and Scotland, whose language and manners are strange to them; for the planters, and even the native negroes generally talk good English without idiom or tone, and can discourse handsomely upon most common subjects; and conversing with persons belonging to trade and navigation from London, for the most part they are much civilized, and wear the best of cloaths according to their station; nay, sometimes too good for their circumstances, being for the generality comely handsom persons, of good features and fine complexions (if they take care), of good manners and address. . . .

Thus they have good natural notions, and will soon learn arts and sciences; but are generally diverted by business or inclination from profound study, and prying into the depth of things; being ripe for management of their affairs, before they have laid so good a foundation of learning, and had such instructions, and acquired such accomplishments, as might be instilled into such good natural capacities. . . .

They are more inclinable to read men by business and conversation, than to dive into books, and are for the most part only desirous of learning what is absolutely necessary, in the shortest and best method. . . . They are not very easily persuaded to the improvement of useful inventions . . . neither are they great encouragers of manufactures, because of the trouble and certain expence in attempts of this kind, with uncertain prospect of gain; whereas by their staple commodity, tobacco, they are certain to get a plentiful provision; nay, often very great estates. . . .

As for education, several are sent to England for it; though the Virginians being naturally of good parts . . . neither require nor admire as much learning, as we do in Britain. . . . When they come to England they are generally put to learn to persons that know little of their temper, who keep them drudging on in what is of least use to them, in pedantic methods, too tedious for their volatile genius. . . .

Most other plantations . . . are inferior to Virginia. . . . Virginia is esteemed one of the most valuable gems in the crown of Great Britain. . . . If New England be called a receptacle of dissenters and an Amsterdam of religion, Pennsylvania the nursery of Quakers, Maryland the retirement of Roman Catholicks, North Carolina the refuge of run-aways and South Carolina the delight of buccaneers and pyrates, Virginia may be justly esteemed the happy retreat of true Britons and true churchmen for the most part; neither soaring too high nor drooping too low. . . .

The common planters leading easy lives don't much admire labour, or any manly exercise, except horse-racing, nor diversion, except cock-fighting, in which some greatly delight. This easy way of living, and the heat of the summer makes some very lazy, who are then said to be climate-struck. . . . They are such lovers of riding, that almost every ordinary person keeps a horse; and I have known some to spend the morning in ranging several miles in the woods to find and catch their horses only to ride two or three miles to church, to the court house or to a horse-race, where they generally appoint to meet upon business; and are more certain of finding those that they want to speak or deal with, than at their home.

No people can entertain their friends with better cheer and welcome; and strangers and travellers are here treated in the most free, plentiful and hospitable manner; so that a few inns or ordinaries on the road are sufficient. . . .

The ships . . . bring over frequently white servants, which are of three kinds. 1. such as come upon certain wages by agreement for a certain time. 2. such as come bound by indenture, commonly call'd kids, who are usually to serve four or five years; and 3. those convicts or felons that are transported, whose room they had much rather have than their company; for abundance of them do great mischiefs, commit robbery and murder, and spoil servants, that were before very good. But they frequently there meet with the end they deserved at home, though indeed some of them prove indifferent good.

Their being sent thither to work as slaves for punishment is but a mere notion, for few of them ever lived so well and so easy before, especially if they were good for any thing. These are to serve seven, and sometimes fourteen years, and they and servants by indentures have an allowance of corn and cloaths, when they are out of their time, that they may be therewith supported, till they can be provided with services or otherwise settled. . . . They that have a mind to it, may serve their time with ease and satisfaction to themselves and their masters, especially if they fall into good hands.

The plenty of the country, and the good wages given to workfolks occasion very few poor, who are supported by the parish, being such as are lame, sick or decrepit through age, distempers, accidents or some infirmities. For where there is a numerous family of poor children the vestry takes care to bind them out apprentices, till they are able to maintain themselves by their own labour; by which means they are never tormented with vagrant and vagabond beggers, there being a reward for taking up run-aways that are a small distance from their home, if they are not known, or are without a pass from their master, and can give no good account of themselves, especially negroes. . . .

With Thomas Jefferson and other Southerners in active leadership, the world rang with the words of the Declaration of Independence: ". . . all men are created equal."

"Cry Peace, Peace...But There Is No Peace"

PATRICK HENRY

A great document of Southern and American history is Patrick Henry's celebrated speech of 1775, ending with his echoing cry: "Give me liberty, or give me death!" As a powerful, trenchant speaker, Henry became the orator of the Revolution. Later he took a place as Governor of Virginia and in other offices. In time, as one blunt commentator has said, Patrick Henry grew richer and shifted his views. Nevertheless his fiery words will long ring through the story of the South and of the country. The speech is taken from William Wirt's Sketches of the Life and Character of Patrick Henry, *1817.*

MR. President, it is natural to man to indulge in the illusions of hope. We are apt to shut our eyes against a painful truth — and listen to the song of that siren, till she transforms us into beasts. Is this the part of wise men, engaged in a great and arduous struggle for liberty? Are we disposed to be of the number of those who, having eyes, see not, and having ears, hear not, the things which so nearly concern their temporal salvation? For my part, whatever anguish of spirit it may cost, I am willing to know the whole truth; to know the worst, and to provide for it.

I have but one lamp by which my feet are guided, and that is the lamp of experience. I know of no way of judging the future but by the past. And judging by the past, I wish to know what there has been in the conduct of the British ministry for the last ten years to justify those hopes with which gentlemen have been pleased to solace themselves and the house? Is it that insidious smile with which our

"Make the most of it!" In this idealized scene the hawk-faced, redheaded Patrick Henry stirred the Virginia burgesses. "If this be treason . . ."

John Randolph, who was related to two of the most conspicuous families of colonial Virginia and was a descendant of the Indian Princess Pocahontas, had great influence on the thought and social life of his time.

petition has been lately received? Trust it not, sir; it will prove a snare to your feet. Suffer not yourself to be betrayed with a kiss. Ask yourself how this gracious reception of our petition comports with those warlike preparations which cover our waters and darken our land.

Are fleets and armies necessary to a work of love and reconciliation? Have we shown ourselves so unwilling to be reconciled that force must be called in to win back our love? Let us not deceive ourselves, sir. These are the implements of war and subjugation — the last arguments to which kings resort. I ask gentlemen, sir, what means this martial array if its purpose be not to force us to submission? Can gentlemen assign any other possible motive to it? Has Great Britain any enemy in this quarter of the world, to call for this accumulation of navies and armies? No, sir, she has none. They are meant for us: they can be meant for no other. They are sent over to bind and rivet upon us those chains which the British ministry have been so long forging.

And what have we to oppose to them? Shall we try arguments? Sir, we have been trying that for the last ten years. Have we anything new to offer upon the subject? Nothing. We have the subject up in every light of which it is capable; but it has been all in vain. Shall we resort to entreaty and humble supplication? What terms shall we find which have not been already exhausted? Let us not, I beseech you, sir, deceive ourselves longer. Sir, we have done everything that could be done to avert the storm which is now coming on. We have petitioned — we have remonstrated — we have supplicated — we have prostrated ourselves before the throne, and we have implored its interposition to arrest the tyrannical hands of the ministry and Parliament.

Our petitions have been slighted; our remonstrances have produced additional violence and insult; our supplications have been disregarded; and we have been spurned with contempt from the foot of the throne. In vain, after these things, may we indulge the fond hope of peace and reconciliation. *There is no longer any room for hope.* If we wish to be free — if we mean to preserve inviolate those inestimable privileges for which we have been so long contending — if we mean not basely to abandon the noble struggle in which we have been so long engaged, and which we have pledged ourselves never to abandon until the glorious object of our contest shall be obtained — we must fight! — I repeat it, sir, we must fight; an appeal to arms and to the God of Hosts is all that is left us!

They tell us, sir, that we are weak — unable to cope with so formidable an adversary. But when shall we be stronger? Will it be the next week or the next year? Will it be when we are totally disarmed, and when a British guard shall be stationed in every house? Shall we gather strength by irresolution and inaction? Shall we acquire the means of effectual resistance by lying supinely on our backs and hugging the delusive phantom of hope, until our enemy shall have bound us hand and foot?

Sir, we are not weak, if we make a proper use of those forces which the God of nature hath placed in our power. Three millions of people armed in the holy cause of liberty, and in such a country as that which we possess, are invincible by any force which our enemy can send against us. Besides, sir, we shall not fight our battles alone. There is a just God who presides over the destinies of nations, and who will raise up friends to fight our battles for us. The battle, sir, is not to the strong alone; it is to the vigilant, the active, the brave. Besides, sir, we have no election. If we were base enough to desire it, it is now too late to retire from the contest. There is no retreat but in submission and slavery! Our chains are forged. Their clanking may be heard on the plains of Boston! The war is inevitable — and let it come! I repeat it, sir, let it come!

It is vain, sir, to extenuate the matter. Gentlemen may cry, Peace, peace—but there is no peace. The war is actually begun! The next gale that sweeps from the north will bring to our ears the clash of resounding arms! Our brethren are already in the field! Why stand we here idle? What is it that gentlemen wish? What would they have? Is life so dear, or peace so sweet, as to be purchased at the price of chains and liberty? Forbid it, Almighty God! I know not what course others may take; but as for me, give me liberty, or give me death!

A Surprise Meeting

JOHN BERNARD

John Bernard, English comedian who became a successful American theatrical manager, told simply and engagingly of a happy incident in his life, when he accidentally met up with a famous Virginian. Perhaps a bit overimpressed by his contact with Southern planters, Bernard wrote gracefully and with a certain common sense about American life as he had studied it. The account is from his Retrospections of America, 1797–1811, *published in 1887.*

THE capital of Maryland — Annapolis — might well be termed the Bath of America. In this little spot all the best of Philadelphia and Virginia society was concentrated, and here, I am convinced, the most stubborn anti-republican could not but have perceived the absurdity of the common notion that all must be on a level socially because they are so politically. America really contained a true nobility, men of talent, probity and benevolence, who had been raised by the public voice to a station which the public feeling bowed down to — a station not hereditary, or due to one man's caprice or another's intrigue, but unassailably based on merit. . . .

Perhaps Mr. Carroll, one of the subscribers to the Declaration of Independence, as much as any man, was an illustration of my remarks. From the refinement of his manners, a stranger would have surmised that he had passed all his days in the *salons* of Paris. He had all that suavity and softness, in combination with dignity, which bespeak the perfection of good taste. . . . But Mr. Carroll possessed higher qualities than mere external polish. He had a heart that colored all his thoughts and deeds with the truest hues of humanity. . . .

A few weeks after my location at Annapolis I met with a most pleasing adventure. . . . I had been to pay a visit on the banks of the Potomac, a few miles below Alexandria, and was returning on horseback, in the rear of an old-fashioned chaise, the driver of which was strenuously urging his steed to an accelerated pace . . . until a lash, directed with more skill than humanity, took the skin from an old wound. The sudden pang threw the poor animal on his hind legs, and the wheel swerving upon the bank, over went the chaise, flinging out upon the road a young woman who had been its occupant.

The minute before I had perceived a horseman approaching at a gentle trot, who now broke into a gallop, and we reached the scene of the disaster together. The female was our first care. She was insensible, but had sustained no material injury. My companion supported her, while I brought some water in the crown of my hat, from a spring some way off. The driver of the chaise had landed on his legs, and, having ascertained that his spouse was not dead, seemed very well satisfied with the care she was in, and set about extricating his horse.

A gush of tears announced the lady's return to sensibility, and then, as her eyes opened, her tongue gradually resumed its office, and assured us that she retained at least one faculty in perfection, as she poured forth a volley of invectives on her mate. The horse was now on his legs, but the vehicle still prostrate, heavy in its frame, and laden with at least half a ton of luggage. My fellow-helper set me an example of activity in relieving it of the external weight; and, when all was clear, we grasped the wheel between us and, to the peril of our spinal columns, righted the conveyance. The horse was then put in, and we lent a hand to help up the luggage.

All this helping, hauling, and lifting occupied at least half an hour, under a meridian sun in the middle of July, which fairly boiled the perspiration out of our foreheads. Our unfortunate friend somewhat relieved the task with his narrative. He was a New Englander who had emigrated to the South when young, there picked up a wife and some money, and was now on his way home, having, he told us, been "made very comfortable" by the death of his father; and when all was right, and we had assisted the lady to resume her seat, he begged us to proceed with him to Alexandria, and take a drop of "something sociable."

Finding, however, that we were unsociable, he extended his hand (no distant likeness of a seal's fin), gripped ours as he had done the heavy boxes, and, when we had sufficiently *felt* that he was grateful, drove on. My companion, after an exclamation at the heat, offered very courteously to dust my coat, a favor the return of which enabled me to take a deliberate survey of his person. He was a tall, erect, well-made man, evidently advanced in years, but who appeared to have retained all the vigor and elasticity resulting from a life of temperance and exercise. His dress was a blue coat buttoned to the chin, and buckskin breeches.

Though, the instant he took off his hat, I could not avoid the recognition of familiar lineaments — which, indeed, I was in the habit of seeing on every sign post and over every fireplace — still I failed to identify him, and, to my surprise, I found that I was an object of equal speculation in his eyes. A smile at length lighted them up, and he exclaimed, "Mr. Bernard, I believe?" I bowed. "I had the pleasure of seeing you perform last winter in Philadelphia." I bowed again, and he added, "I have heard of you since from several of my friends at Annapolis. You are acquainted with Mr. Carroll?"

I replied that that gentleman's society had made amends for much that I had lost in quitting England. He then learned the cause of my presence in the neighborhood, and remarked, "You must be fatigued. If you will ride up to my house, which is not a mile distant, you can prevent any ill effects from this exertion, by a couple of hours' rest." I looked round for his dwelling, and he pointed to a building which, the day before, I had spent an hour in contemplating. "Mount Vernon!" I exclaimed; and then, drawing back, with a stare of wonder, "Have I the honor of addressing General Washington?"

With a smile, whose expression of benevolence I have rarely seen equaled, he offered his hand, and replied, "An odd sort of introduction, Mr. Bernard; but I am pleased to find you can play so active a part in private, and without a prompter," and then pointed to our horses (which had stood like statues all this time, as though in sympathy with their fallen brother), and shrugged his shoulders at the inn. I needed no further stimulus to accept his friendly invitation. As we rode up to his house we entered freely into conversation, first in reference to his friends at Annapolis, then respecting my own success in America and the impressions I had received of the country.

Flattering as such inquiries were from such a source, I must confess my own reflections on what had just passed were more absorbing. Considering that nine ordinary country gentlemen out of ten, who had seen a chaise upset near their estate, would have

As commander of the American troops, George Washington met a time of trial at Monmouth. In this engraving after a well-known painting by Chappel, the Virginian awaited a climax in his fortunes and his country's.

The South's and America's man of vision, greatest of its democrats, was the well-born Thomas Jefferson, who fought firmly against special rights and inherited privileges.

thought it savored neither of pride nor ill-nature to ride home and send their servants to its assistance, I could not but think that I had witnessed one of the strongest evidences of a great man's claim to his reputation — the prompt, impulsive working of a heart which, having made the good of mankind — not conventional forms — its religion, was never so happy as in practically displaying it. On reaching the house (which, in its compact simplicity and commanding elevation, was no bad emblem of its owner's mind), we found that Mrs. Washington was indisposed; but the General ordered refreshments in a parlor whose windows took a noble range of the Potomac, and, after a few minutes' absence, rejoined me. . . .

Whether you surveyed General Washington's face, open yet well-defined, dignified

but not arrogant, thoughtful but benign; his frame, towering and muscular, but alert from its good proportion — every feature suggested a resemblance to the spirit it encased, and showed simplicity in alliance with the sublime. The impression, therefore, was that of a most perfect whole; and though the effect of proportion is said to be to reduce the idea of magnitude, you could not but think you looked upon a wonder . . . a man fashioned by the hand of Heaven, with every requisite to achieve a great work. . . .

In conversation his face had not much variety of expression: a look of thoughtfulness was given by the compression of the mouth and the indentation of the brow (suggesting an habitual conflict with and mastery over passion), which did not seem so much to dis-

Center of a busy life—home duties, calls by friends and others who simply dropped in—was George Washington's Mount Vernon on the Potomac River.

dain a sympathy with trivialities as to be incapable of denoting them. Nor had his voice, so far as I could discover in our quiet talk, much change, or richness of intonation, but he always spoke with earnestness and his eyes . . . burned with a steady fire which no one could mistake for mere affability; they were one grand expression of the well-known line: "I am a man, and interested in all that concerns mankind."

In our hour and a half's conversation he touched on every topic that I brought before him with an even current of good sense, if he

embellished it with little wit or verbal elegance. He spoke like a man who had felt as much as he had reflected, and reflected more than he had spoken; like one who had looked upon society rather in the mass than in detail; and who regarded the happiness of America but as the first link in a series of universal victories; for his full faith in the power of these results of civil liberty which he saw all around him led him to foresee that it would, ere long, prevail in other countries. . . .

When I remarked that his observations were flattering to my country, he replied, with great good humor: . . . "Liberty in England is a sort of idol; people are bred up in the belief and love of it, but see little of its doings. They walk about freely, but then it is between high walls; and the error of its government was in supposing that after a portion of their subjects had crossed the sea to live upon a common, they would permit their friends at home to build up those walls about them."

A black coming in at this moment . . . I could not repress a smile. . . . "This may seem a contradiction," the General continued, "but I think you must perceive that it is neither a crime nor an absurdity. When we profess, as our fundamental principle, that liberty is the inalienable right of every man, we do not include madmen or idiots; liberty in their hands would become a scourge. Till the mind of the slave has been educated to perceive what are the obligations of a state of freedom, and not confound a man's with a brute's, the gift would insure its abuse. We might as well be asked to pull down our old warehouses before trade had increased to demand enlarged new ones. Both houses and slaves were bequeathed to us by Europeans, and time alone can change them; an event, sir, which, you may believe me, no man desires more heartily than I do. Not only do I pray for it, on the score of human dignity, but I can clearly foresee that nothing but the rooting out of slavery can perpetuate the existence of our union, by consolidating it in a common bond of principle." . . .

I have never heard of but one jest of Washington's, which was related to me by his aide-de-camp, my good friend, Colonel Humphreys. The General, rather priding himself on his riding, the Colonel was induced, one day when they were out hunting together, to offer him a bet that he would not follow him over one particular hedge. The challenge was accepted, and Humphreys led the way and took the leap boldly, but, to his consternation, discovered that he had mistaken the spot, and was deposited, up to his horse's girths, in a quagmire. The General either knew the ground better, or had suspected something, for, following at an easy pace, he reined up at the hedge, and, looking over at his engulfed aide, exclaimed, "No, no, Colonel, you are too *deep* for me!"

The Blind Preacher

WILLIAM WIRT

Although composed in fictional form, William Wirt's The Letters of a British Spy, 1832, *dealt in various sections with factual situations. German and Swiss in descent, Wirt was a native Marylander, son of an innkeeper. Of high legal rank, he kept his writings in a place secondary to his law practice. The* Letters *appeared without his name in a Richmond paper, drew wide attention and then came out in book form. The blind minister was James Waddell.*

IT was one Sunday, as I travelled through the county of Orange, that my eye was caught by a cluster of horses tied near a ruinous, old wooden house in the forest, not far from the roadside. Having frequently seen such objects before, in travelling through those states, I had no difficulty in understanding that this was a place of religious worship.

Devotion alone should have stopped me, to join in the duties of the congregation; but I must confess that curiosity to hear the preacher of such a wilderness, was not the least of my motives. On entering, I was struck with his preternatural appearance. He was a tall and very spare old man; his head, which was covered with a white linen cap, his shrivelled hands, and his voice, were all shaking under the influence of a palsy; and a few moments ascertained to me that he was perfectly blind.

The first emotions that touched my breast were those of mingled pity and veneration. But how soon were all my feelings changed! The lips of Plato were never more worthy of a prognostic swarm of bees, than were the lips of this holy man. . . . It was a day of the administration of the sacrament; and his subject was, of course, the passion of our Saviour. I have heard the subject handled a thousand times; I had thought it exhausted long ago. Little did I suppose that in the wild woods of America, I was to meet with a man whose eloquence would give to this topic a new and more sublime pathos than I had ever before witnessed.

As he descended from the pulpit to distribute the mystic symbols, there was a peculiar, a more than human solemnity in his air and manner, which made my blood run cold, and my whole frame shiver. He then drew a picture of the sufferings of our Saviour; his trial before Pilate; his ascent up Calvary; his crucifixion and his death. . . . Never until then had I heard the circumstances so selected, so arranged, so colored . . . and I seemed to have heard it for the first time in my life. His enunciation was so deliberate that his voice trembled on every syllable; and every heart in the assembly trembled in union. His peculiar phrases had the force of description, that the original scene appeared to be at that moment acting before our eyes . . . and my hands were involuntarily and convulsively clinched.

But when he came to touch on the patience, the forgiving mildness of our Saviour; when he drew, to the life, his blessed eyes streaming in tears to heaven; his voice breathing to God a soft and gentle prayer of pardon on his enemies, "Father, forgive them, for they know not what they do"—the voice of the preacher, which had all along faltered, grew fainter and fainter, until, his utterance being entirely obstructed by the force of his feelings, he raised his handkerchief to his eyes, and burst into a loud and irrepressible flood of grief. . . . The whole house resounded with the mingled groans, and sobs and shrieks of the congregation.

It was some time before the tumult had subsided, so far as to permit him to proceed. Indeed, judging by the usual, but fallacious standard of my own weakness, I began to be very uneasy for the situation of the preacher. For I could not conceive how he would be able to let his audience down from the height to which he had wound them, without impairing the solemnity and dignity of his subject, or perhaps shocking them by the abruptness of the fall. But—no: the descent was as beautiful and sublime as the elevation had been rapid and enthusiastic. . . .

Never before did I completely understand what Demosthenes meant by laying such stress on delivery. You are to bring before you the venerable figure of the preacher; his blindness, constantly recalling to your recollection old Homer, Ossian, and Milton, and associating with his performance the melancholy grandeur of their geniuses; imagine that you hear his slow, solemn, well-accented enunciation, and his voice of affecting, trembling melody; remember the pitch of passion and enthusiasm to which the congregation was raised; and then the few moments of portentous, deathlike silence which reigned throughout the house; the preacher removing his white handkerchief from his aged face and slowly stretching forth the palsied hand which holds it, begins the sentence, "Socrates died like a philosopher,"—then, pausing, raising his other hand, pressing them both, clasped together, with warmth and energy, to his breast, lifting his "sightless balls" to heaven, and pouring out his whole soul into his tremulous voice—"but Jesus Christ—like a God!" If it had indeed and in truth been an angel of light, the effect could scarcely have been more divine.

Bring No Dogs to Church

CHARLES WOODMASON

A series of well-pointed directions to country folk for attending church services, celebrating weddings and similar events is provided in Charles Wood-mason's The Carolina Backcountry on the Eve of the Revolution, *published for the Institution of Early American History and Culture, Williamsburg, University of North Carolina Press, Chapel Hill, 1953.*

ALWAYS contrive to come before service begins—which you may do, as we begin so late. 'Tis but putting and getting things in order over night—whereas many will hardly set about it till Sunday morning. Contrive too, to go as early as possible to rest on Saturday night so that you may rise early and refresh'd on the Lord's day and not be hurry'd in dressing, and ordering matters.

The coming late to sermon discourages people, for lack of company—and coming in after service is begun is very troublesome—disturb both me and ev'ry one and should be avoided as much as possible—But if it is unavoidable, pray enter leisurely—tread softly—nor disturb any who are on their knees or are intent on their devotions. Bring no dogs with you—they are very troublesome—and I shall inform the magistrate of those who do it, for it is an affront to the divine presence which we invoke, to be in the midst of us, and to hear our prayers, to mix unclean things with our services.

When you are seated—do not whisper, talk, gaze about—shew light airs, or behavior—for this argues a wandering mind and irreverence towards God; is unbecoming religion, and may give scandal and offence to weak Christians:—Neither sneeze or cough, if you can avoid it—and do not practice that unseemly, rude, indecent custom of chewing or of spitting, which is very ridiculous and absurd in public, especially in women and in Gods house.

If you are thirsty—Pray drink before you enter or before service begins, not to go out in midst of prayer, nor be running to and fro . . . except your necessary occasions should oblige you—Do you see anything like it in Charles Town or among well bred people. Keep your children as quiet as possible. If they will be fractious, carry them out at once for I will not have divine worship *now* consider'd by you, as if I were officiating in a private house. . . .

When banns are published—Don't make it a matter of sport; but let it stir you up to put up a petition to heav'n for a blessing of God upon the parties.

A Grandmother Saw Her Boy Again

ANDREW BURNABY

Two striking episodes illustrative of a phase of Southern life were set down in telling style by Andrew Burnaby, whose Incidents of Travel *was published in 1798. Each is a meaningful one. However, like others who were not always completely accurate in their observations, the author declared Virginia planters largely "indolent" and "unenterprising." Records show that many such growers applied themselves as steadily as any businessmen-administrators, handling a wide variety of operations in agriculture and related activities.*

WE ascended up the Rappahannock to Spotswood's iron-mines, and in our way had a fine view of the Appalachian mountains, or Blue Ridge, at a distance of seventy miles. At this place I was much affected by the following incident.

A gentleman in our company had a small negro boy with him, about fourteen years of age, that had lived with him in a remote part of the country some time as a servant. An old woman who was working in the mines, and who proved to be the boy's grandmother, accidentally cast her eyes on him; she viewed him with great attention for some time; then screamed out, saying that it was her child, and flung herself down upon the ground.

She lay there some seconds; rose up, looked on him again in an ecstasy of joy, and fell upon his neck and kissed him. After this, she retired a few paces, examined him afresh with fixed attention, and immediately seemed to lose herself in thoughtful and profound melancholy. The boy all this while stood silent and motionless, reclining his head on one side, pale and affected beyond description. It would not have been in the power of painting to exhibit a finer picture of distress.

. . .

An occurrence happened . . . which I should not have thought of sufficient moment to be recorded had not the intellectual powers of the African negroes been frequently of late made the subject of conversation. . . . I was rowed by an old gray-headed negro who seemed quite exhausted and worn down by age and infirmity. I inquired into his situation, and received for answer that he had been a slave from his youth, and had continued to work for his master till age had rendered him unfit for service; that his master had then kindly given him a small piece of ground, and the profits of the ferry, which were indeed very inconsiderable . . . and that with these means of subsistence he awaited the hour when it might please God to call him to another life.

I observed that he must naturally wish for that hour, as it would release him from his present sufferings. His answer was, no; for he was afraid to die. On my questioning him, why he was afraid to die: whether he had any thing upon his conscience that gave him uneasiness; or whether he had not been honest and faithful to his master?

He answered, yes; I have always done my duty to the best of my power; but yet I am afraid to die; and was not our Saviour himself afraid to die? The answer was so unexpected, and so far beyond what I supposed to be the intellectual capacity of the poor negro, that it sunk deep into my mind, and I was lost for a moment in silence.

. . .

A little below a plantation on a high hill on the Pamunky river stands the Pamunky Indian town, where at present are the few remaining of that large tribe. They live in little wigwams or cabins upon the river; and have a very fine tract of land of about 2000 acres. . . . Their employment is chiefly hunting or fishing for the neighboring gentry. They commonly dress like the Virginians, and I have sometimes mistaken them for the lower sort of that people.

The night I spent here they went out into an adjoining marsh to catch soruses; and one, as I was informed, caught near a hundred dozen. The manner of taking these birds is remarkable. The sorus is not known to be in Virginia, except for about six weeks from the latter end of September: at that time they are found in the marshes in prodigious numbers, feeding upon the wild oats. At first they are exceeding lean, but in a short time grow so fat, as to be unable to fly: in this state they lie upon the reeds, and the Indians go out in canoes and knock them on the head with their paddles.

Natural Aristocracy, Artificial Aristocracy

THOMAS JEFFERSON

In a letter to John Adams, October 28, 1813, the South's spokesman for democracy gave a telling summary of his views on the merits of men. Although his family had a place in the Virginia gentry, Jefferson had lived near the frontier as a boy and there acquired his innate feeling for the average man and his instinct for war upon privilege and special rights. In public affairs his voice became one of the most ringing of his day; he succeeded in ending Virginia laws which favored the first-born of the family; he labored for separation of church and state and for wider public education. And he saw the South's slavery as an injustice.

. . . I agree with you that there is a natural aristocracy among men. The groups of this are virtue and talents. Formerly, bodily powers gave place among the aristoi. But since the invention of gunpowder has armed the weak as well as the strong with missile death, bodily strength, like beauty, good humor, politeness and other accomplishments, has be-

With a backdrop of mountain peaks stood Thomas Jefferson's "academic village," the University of Virginia at Charlottesville. He wanted even women to go to school.

come but an auxiliary ground of distinction. There is also an artificial aristocracy, founded on wealth and birth, without either virtue or talents; for with these it would belong to the first class.

The natural aristocracy I consider as the most precious gift of nature, for the instruction, the trusts, and government of society. And indeed, it would have been inconsistent in creation to have formed man for the social state, and not to have provided virtue and wisdom enough to manage the concerns of the society. May we not even say, that that form of government is the best, which provides the most effectually for a pure selection of these natural aristoi into the offices of government?

The artificial aristocracy is a mischievous ingredient in government, and provision should be made to prevent its ascendency. . . . Nor do I believe [it] necessary to protect the wealthy; because enough of these will find their way into every branch of the legislation, to protect themselves. From fifteen to twenty [Virginia] legislatures of our own, in action for thirty years past, have proved that no fears of an equalization of property are to be apprehended from them. I think the best remedy is exactly that provided by all our constitutions, to leave to the citizens the free election and separation of the aristoi from the pseudo-aristoi, of the wheat from the chaff. In general they will elect the really good and wise. In some instances, wealth may corrupt, and birth may blind them; but not in sufficient degree to endanger the society. . . .

At the first session of our legislature after the Declaration of Independence, we passed a law abolishing entails. And this was followed by one abolishing the privilege of primogeniture, and dividing the lands of intestates equally among all their children, or other representatives. These laws, drawn by myself, laid the axe to the foot of pseudo-aristocracy. And had another one which I prepared been adopted by the legislature, our work would have been complete. It was a bill for the more general diffusion of learning. This proposed to divide every county into wards of five or six miles square; to establish in each ward a free school for reading, writing and common arithmetic; to provide for the annual selection of the best subjects from these schools, who might receive, at the public expense, a higher degree of education at a district school; and from these district schools to select a certain number of the most promising subjects, to be completed at a university, where all the useful sciences should be taught. Worth and genius would thus have been sought out from every condition of life, and completely prepared by education for defeating the competition of wealth and birth for public trusts.

Miss Patsy Jefferson of America and Paris
EDITH TUNIS SALE

Jefferson's favorite daughter Patsy is seen in an admirable light, and her father in that of the anxious parent, in this portrait of the girl who knew the New World and the Old. In the selection from Edith Tunis Sale's Old Time Belles and Cavaliers *(J. B. Lippincott Co., Philadelphia and London, 1912) the father amusingly seeks so much training and education for poor Patsy that she seemingly had no time for anything else.*

In the classic style which he did much to encourage in the South, Thomas Jefferson constructed his stately, impressive Monticello.

IT has frequently been said that the sons of great men must always suffer the handicap of comparison, which, too often, falls pitifully short of what might naturally be expected. Consequently, the sonless man of brains and ability is to be congratulated, for, no matter how many daughters he may have, neither they nor he need have cause for dissatisfaction. Yet, curiously enough, and history proves the right for the assertion, more than one daughter of a distinguished father has added lustre to his name, and this has been amply proven in the life of Martha Jefferson.

The eldest child of Thomas and Martha Wayles Jefferson, Martha Jefferson, was born September 25th, 1772, and was very young when her beautiful mother died. Perhaps it was this fact that served so materially to develop her so well, for the little girl was naturally thrown much in the company of her father, and at an early age became his constant companion when he was near. That Jefferson took an intense interest in the early education of his daughter, and that he expected rather difficult things of her as a mere child, is shown in old family letters which read laughably to us, but must have caused tremors of fear in the heart of the small scholar, who seems to have been left no hours for play time.

Added to all this, he states that he expects a letter from her by every post, and that she must also correspond dutifully with her aunts. Poor little Martha! It was a hard schooling, but the wisdom of her illustrious father was proven in her after life.

When Martha reached her fifteenth year, Jefferson then being American Minister to France, she joined him in Paris, where the finishing touches were put upon what was already a superior education, at the Convent at Parthemont; the correspondence which took place between her and her renowned father at that period is more than ordinarily interesting.

The first glimpse that Martha Jefferson had of the great world of society was in Paris, where she remained a while after leaving school, being under the chaperonage of Mrs. John Adams. Here she came in contact with the most notable French and American women of the time, and Mrs. William Bingham, that authorized leader of fashion in both countries, shows the American girl's success in a letter written to Jefferson from New York. "Be so kind as to remember me with affection to Miss Jefferson," she writes. "Tell her she is the envy of all the young ladies in America, and that I should wish nothing so much as to place my nice little girl under her inspection, should she not leave Paris before I revisit it."

It is gratifying to know that this young American head was in no wise turned by the adulation of the wealth and fashion of Europe, for it remained for Thomas Mann Randolph, her second cousin, who visited Paris in 1788, to win her from titles and old world dignitaries. On the 23d of February, 1790, Martha Jefferson became Mrs. Randolph, the wedding uniting two of our country's most distinguished families . . . who would live their lives together at "Edge Hill," in Albermarle County, Virginia.

Though Jefferson approved highly of his daughter's choice, some biographers would lead us to believe that he and Thomas Mann Randolph were never upon very friendly terms, yet history tells us that the President described his son-in-law as "a man of science, sense, virtue and competence." In any event, young Randolph was a true Virginian, of splendid bearing, good looks and broad intellect, possessing the chivalry and bravery of his race. . . .

When Thomas Jefferson became President, it was to Martha Randolph that the arduous duties of Lady of the White House fell, for all of which her noble qualities of head and heart well fitted her. Prior to her first visit to the Presidential mansion, Mrs. Randolph wrote her friend, Dolly Madison, to send her a wig of the latest design, adding that it would serve the double purpose of making her appear in the latest fashion and take away the trouble of arranging her own coiffure. So it would seem that no age, nor the most intellectual among women, is above the craze for puffs and curls that may be pinned on rather than grown.

In 1803, Thomas Mann Randolph was elected to Congress, his honor bringing a great pride to his wife, but in 1805 she was deeply saddened by the loss of her sister, Maria Eppes, and in order to help her father bear this great grief, spent the entire winter of 1805–06 at the White House, where her second son was born, he being the first child of the White House.

When her husband became Governor of Virginia in 1819, Martha Jefferson's cup of happiness was filled to the brim. Being forced into public life through both father and husband, notwithstanding the cares of a young family, she filled her various positions with ability. . . . It was Mrs. Randolph who was the victim (?) when Mrs. Merry, wife of the British Minister, undertook to be revenged for the fancied indignities she chose to think the President had heaped upon her, and but for the quick wit of the former, serious international complications might have arisen.

As it was, when Mrs. Merry wrote Mrs. Randolph begging to know if she were a guest at the White House as the daughter of the President or the wife of a Virginia gentleman, stating that if the first were true, she would call upon her, but in the latter case, would expect to be called upon, Mrs. Randolph, with ready tact, sent an instant reply. She announced that she was there as the wife of a Virginia gentleman, and, according to Jeffersonian etiquette, as visitors to the Capital should be called upon by residents, they would naturally expect the first call.

Martha Jefferson lived to be the mother of twelve children, the eldest, Thomas Jefferson Randolph, proving the greatest solace to the old age of his grandfather. The Sully portrait shows her in a bewitching mob cap, and was evidently done about the time she married, while Gilbert Stuart's painting portrays her as the young matron of the world with features resembling somewhat those of Thomas Jefferson, and character in every line of her face.

Mrs. Randolph's daughter relates the following incident: "I accompanied her to Mr. Sully's studio, and, as she took her seat before him, she said playfully: 'Mr. Sully, I shall never forgive you if you paint me with wrinkles.'

"I quickly interrupted, 'Paint her just as she is, Mr. Sully, the picture is for me.'

"He said, 'I shall paint you, Mrs. Randolph, as I remember you twenty years ago.'

"The picture does represent her younger —but failed to restore the expression of health and cheerful, ever-joyous vivacity which her countenance then habitually wore. My mother's face owed its greatest charm to its expressiveness, beaming, as it ever was, with kindness, good humor, gayety and wit. She was tall and very graceful; her complexion naturally fair, her hair of a dark chestnut color, very long and very abundant. Her manners were uncommonly attractive from their vivacity, amiability and high breeding. . . ."

Polly Jefferson, Mrs. Eppes, may have been the beauty of the family, but Martha, known to her father as "Patsy," was blessed with more lasting qualities. She was the friend of the rich, the comfort of the poor; the associate of the most gifted men in Europe and America, yet she was most charming of all in her beautiful domesticity, and though John Randolph of Roanoke had quarreled with both her husband and father, he rightly summed up her life and character when he toasted her as "the noblest woman in Virginia."

Thomas Jefferson to His Daughter

Annapolis, Nov. 28, 1783

MY DEAR PATSY—After four days' journey, I arrived here without any accident, and in as good health as when I left Philadelphia. The conviction that you would be more improved in the situation I have placed you than if still with me, has solaced me on my parting with you, which my love for you has rendered a difficult thing. The acquirements which I hope you will make under the tutors

I have provided for you will render you more worthy of my love; and if they cannot increase it, they will prevent its diminution. Consider the good lady who has taken you under her roof, who has undertaken to see that you perform all your exercises, and to admonish you in all those wanderings from what is right or what is clever, to which your inexperience would expose you: consider her, I say, as your mother, as the only person to whom, since the loss with which Heaven has pleased to afflict you, you can now look up; and that her displeasure or disapprobation, on any occasion, will be an immense misfortune, which should you be so unhappy as to incur by any unguarded act, think no concession too much to regain her good-will. With respect to the distribution of your time, the following is what I should approve:

From 8 to 10, practice music. From 10 to 1, dance one day and draw another. From 1 to 2, draw on the day you dance, and write a letter next day. From 3 to 4, read French. From 4 to 5, exercise yourself in music. From 5 till bedtime, read English, write, etc.

Communicate this plan to Mrs. Hopkinson, and if she approves of it, pursue it. As long as Mrs. Trist remains in Philadelphia, cultivate her affection. She has been a valuable friend to you, and her good sense and good heart make her valued by all who know her, and by nobody on earth more than me. I expect you will write me by every post. Inform me what books you read, what times you learn, and inclose me your best copy of every lesson in drawing. Write also one letter a week either to your Aunt Eppes, your Aunt Skipwith, your Aunt Carr, or the little lady from whom I now inclose a letter, and always put the letter you so write under cover to me. Take care that you never spell a word wrong. Always before you write a word consider how it is spelt, and, if you do not remember it, consult a dictionary. It produces great praise to a lady to spell well. I have placed my happiness on seeing you good and accomplished; and no distress which this world can now bring on me would equal that of your disappointing my hopes. If you love me, then strive to be good under every situation and to all living creatures, and to acquire those accomplishments which I have put in your power, and which will go far towards insuring you the warmest love of your affectionate father,

Th. Jefferson.

P.S.—Keep my letters and read them, at times, that you may always have present in your mind those things which will endear you to me.

. . .

Annapolis, Dec. 11th, 1783

I hope you will have good sense enough to disregard those foolish predictions that the world is to be at an end soon. The Almighty has never made known to anybody at what time he created it; nor will he tell anybody when he will put an end to it, if he ever means to do it. As to preparations for that event, the best way is for you always to be prepared for it. The only way to be so is, never to say or do a bad thing. . . .

. . .

Annapolis, Dec, 22d, 1783

I omitted . . . to advise you on the subject of dress, which I know you are a little apt to neglect. I do not wish you to be gayly clothed at this time of life, but that your wear should be fine of its kind. But above all things and at all times let your clothes be neat, whole and properly put on. Do not fancy you must wear them till the dirt is visible to the eye. You will be the last one who is sensible of this. Some ladies think they may, under the privileges of the deshabille, be loose and negligent of their dress in the morning. But be you, from the moment you rise till you go to bed, as cleanly and properly dressed as at the hours of dinner or tea. A lady who has been seen as a sloven or a slut in the morning, will never efface the impression she has made, with all the dress and pageantry she can afterwards involve herself in. Nothing is so disgusting to our sex as a want of cleanliness and delicacy in yours. I hope, therefore, the moment you rise from bed, your first work will be to dress yourself in such style, as that you may be seen by any gentleman without his being able to discover a pin amiss, or any other circumstance of neatness wanting.

Mr. Jefferson at His Ease

FRANCIS HALL

A British Lieutenant, Francis Hall went to the United States shortly after the War of 1812 and, despite lingering bitterness on both sides, saw the new nation in a generous and friendly light. In his Travels in Canada and the United States in 1816 and 1817 *(published in 1818) he gave a striking portrait of perhaps the greatest of Southerners and one of the greatest of Americans, Thomas Jefferson. Although no liker of slavery, Lieutenant Hall admired Americans for their energy, determination, intelligence and their "taciturnity, which is the offspring of thought."*

I ASCENDED his little mountain on a fine morning. . . . The whole of the sides and base are covered with forest, through which roads have been cut circularly, so that the winding may be shortened or prolonged at pleasure. The summit is an open lawn, near to the south side of which the house is built, with its garden just descending the brow; the saloon, or central hall, is ornamented with several pieces of antique sculpture, Indian arms, mammoth bones, and other curiosities collected from various parts of the Union.

I found Mr. Jefferson tall in person, but stooping and lean with old age; thus exhibiting that fortunate mode of bodily decay, which strips the frame of its most cumbersome parts, leaving it still strength of muscle and activity of limb. His deportment was exactly such as the Marquis de Chastellux describes it, above thirty years ago: "At first serious, nay even cold," but in a very short time relaxing into a most agreeable amenity; with an unabated flow of conversation on the most interesting topics, discussed in the most gentlemanly and philosophical manner.

I walked with him round his grounds, to visit his pet trees, and improvements of various kinds; during the walk, he pointed out to my observation a conical mountain, rising singly at the edge of the southern horizon of the landscape: its distance, he said, was forty miles, and its dimensions those of the greater Egyptian pyramid; so that it accurately represents the appearance of the pyramid at the same distance; there is a small cleft visible on its summit, through which the true meridian of Monticello exactly passes; its most singular property, however, is that on different occasions it *looms* or alters its appearance, sometimes becoming cylindrical, sometimes square, and sometimes assuming the form of an inverted cone.

Mr. Jefferson had not been able to connect this phenomenon with any particular season, or state of the atmosphere, except that it most commonly occurred in the forenoon; he observed that it was not only unaccounted for by the laws of vision but that it had not yet engaged the attention of philosophers so far as to acquire a name; that of *looming* being in fact a term applied by sailors to appearances of a similar kind at sea. The Blue Mountains are also observed to loom, though not in so remarkable a degree.

It must be interesting to recall and preserve the political sentiments of a man who has held so distinguished a station in public life as Mr. Jefferson. He seemed to consider much of the freedom and happiness of America to rise from local circumstances: "Our population," he observed, "has an elasticity, by which it would fly off from oppressive taxation." He instanced the beneficial effect of a free government in the case of New Orleans, where many proprietors who were in a state of indigence under the dominion of Spain have risen to sudden wealth solely by the rise in the value of the land, which followed a change of government.

Their ingenuity in mechanical inventions,

agricultural improvements, and that mass of general information to be found among Americans of all ranks and conditions he ascribed to that ease of circumstances which afforded them leisure to cultivate their minds, after the cultivation of their lands was completed.—In fact, I have frequently been surprised to find mathematical and other useful works in houses which seemed to have little pretension to the luxury of learning.

Another cause, Mr. Jefferson observed, might be discovered in the many court and county meetings, which brought men frequently together on public business, and thus gave them habits, both of thinking and of expressing their thoughts on subjects, which in other countries are confined to the consideration of the privileged few. . . .

Mr. Jefferson related an anecdote of the Abbé Reynal, which serves to show how history, even when it calls itself philosophical, is written. The Abbé was in company with Dr. Franklin and several Americans at Paris, when mention chanced to be made of his anecdote of Polly Baker, related in his sixth volume, upon which one of the company observed that no such law as that alluded to . . . existed in New England. The Abbé stoutly maintained the authenticity of his tale, when Dr. Franklin, who had hitherto remained silent, said, "I can account for all this; you took the anecdote from a newspaper of which I was at that time editor, and, happening to be very short of news, I composed and inserted the whole story." "Ah! Doctor," said the Abbé, making a true French retreat, "I had rather have your stories than other men's truths."

How Isaac Remembered the Master

CHARLES CAMPBELL

In 1840, long after Jefferson's death, one of his ancient Negro servants gave a straightforward and impressive series of recollections of the Virginian. Memoirs of a Monticello Slave, as Dictated to Charles Campbell, *University of Virginia Press, Charlottesville, 1951, offers an aspect of Thomas Jefferson which is rather different from the ones that his associates presented to the world.*

MR. Jefferson was a tall straight-bodied man as ever you see, right square-shouldered; nary man in this town walked so straight as my Old Master; neat a built man as ever was seen in Vaginny, I reckon, or any place—a straight-up man: long face, high nose. . . .

Old Master wore Vaginny cloth and a red waist-coat (all the gentlemen wore red waistcoats in dem days) and small clothes; arter dat he used to wear red breeches too.

Old Master was never seen to come out before breakfast—about 8 o'clock. If it was warm weather he wouldn't ride out till evening: studied upstairs till bell ring for dinner. When writing he had a copyin machine; while he was a-writin he wouldn't suffer nobody to come in his room: had a dumb-waiter: when he wanted anything he had nothin to do but turn a crank and the dumb-waiter would bring him water or fruit on a plate or anything he wanted. Old Master had abundance of books: sometimes would have twenty of 'em down on the floor at once: read fust one, then tother. Isaac has often wondered how Old Master came to have such a mighty head: read so many of them books: and when they go to ax him anything, he go right straight to the book and tell you all about it.

He talked French and Italian. Madzay [Mazzei, an Italian writer] talked with him. . . . Madzay lived at Monticello with Old Master some time . . . [and] brought to Monticello

Antoine, Jovanini, Francis, Modena and Belligrini, all gardiners. My Old Master's garden was monstrous large: two rows of palings, all round ten feet high.

Mr. Jefferson had a clock in his kitchen at Monticello; never went into the kitchen except to wind up the clock. He never would have less than eight covers at dinner—if nobody at dinner but himself; had from eight to thirty two covers for dinner; plenty of wine, best old Antigua rum and cider: very fond of wine and water. Isaac never heard of his being disguised in drink. He kept three fiddles: played in the afternoons and sometimes arter supper. This was in his early time. When he begin to git so old, he didn't play: kept a spinnet made mostly in shape of a harpsichord; his daughter played on it. Mr.

Fauble, a Frenchman that lived at Mr. Walker's, a music-man, used to come to Monticello and tune it. There was a forte piano and a guitar there: never seed anybody play on them, but the French people. Isaac never git acquainted with them: could hardly larn their names. Mr. Jefferson always singing when ridin or walkin: hardly see him anywhar out doors but what he was a-singin; had a fine clear voice, sung minnits [minuets] and sich: fiddled in the parlor. Old Master very kind to servants. . . .

The likeness of Mr. Jefferson [in Linn's Life of him] . . . is not much like him. Old Master never dat handsome in dis world; dat likeness right between Old Master and Ginral Washington; Old Master was squar-shouldered.

A Celebrated Virginian Affirms the Power of the Supreme Court

JOHN MARSHALL

A unique role in the development of his native South and of America has been played by John Marshall, Virginia-born, Virginia-reared political figure who became Chief Justice of the United States Supreme Court, changed its role and held his place for thirty-five years. Until then that court had no great authority; Marshall asserted its power and set his impress forever on the court's role in America. A hard-willed conservative, a zealous defender of property, Marshall ruled consistently that the highest judicial body had wide authority in the nation's life. In recent years, ironically, his belief has been steadily maintained in behalf of liberal movements rather than those favored by Marshall. In the following words, from Allen B. Magruder's John Marshall, 1885, *the justice states his opinions with emphasis.*

IT [the Supreme Court] is authorized to decide all cases of every description arising under the constitution or laws of the United States. From this general grant of jurisdiction no exception is made of those cases in which a State may be a party.

When we consider the situation of the government of the Union and of a State in relation to each other, the nature of our Constitution, the subordination of the state governments to that Constitution, the great purpose for which jurisdiction over all cases arising under the Constitution and laws of the United States is confided to the judicial department, are we at liberty to insert in this general grant an exception of those cases in which a State may be a party? Will the spirit of the Constitution justify this attempt to control its words?

We think it will not. We think a case arising under the Constitution or laws of the United States is cognizable in the courts of the Union, whoever may be the parties to that case. The laws must be executed by individuals acting within the several States. If these individuals may be exposed to penalties, and if the courts of the Union cannot correct the judgments by which these penalties may be enforced, the course of the government may be at any time arrested by the will of one of its members. Each member will possess a *veto* on the will of the whole.

That the United States form, for many and for most important purposes, a single nation has not yet been denied. These States are constituent parts of the United States. They are members of one great empire, for some purposes sovereign, for some purposes subordinate. In a government so constituted, is it unreasonable that the judicial power should be competent to give efficacy to the constitutional laws of the legislature?

That department can decide on the validity of the Constitution or law of the United States. Is it unreasonable that it should also be empowered to decide on the judgment of a state tribunal enforcing such unconstitutional law? Is it so very unreasonable as to furnish a justification for controlling the words of the Constitution? We think not. . . .

The exercise of the appellate power over those judgments of the state tribunals which may contravene the Constitution or laws of the United States is, we believe, essential to the attainment of those objects.

Colonel Boone Looked Back Over The Past

DANIEL BOONE

In his lifetime Daniel Boone became a near-legendary character, central figure in hundreds of tales. He was a true pioneer in the slow, relentless advance of Southerners to the early "West" of Kentucky and nearby areas. He led exploratory bands into the Indians' "dark and bloody ground," put up a fort at Boonesborough, coped with Indians, occasional white enemies and other hazards. He suffered many reverses, when he lost land that he had settled, and was robbed of thousands of dollars in his possession. "Civilized" men sometimes seemed harder to deal with than had the savages, and in his later years Boone moved on again, beyond the Mississippi, to end his days as a hunter reliving his past. In his Autobiography *he recalled some of his exploits.*

IT was on the first day of May, in the year 1769, that I resigned my domestic happiness for a time, and left my family and peaceful habitation on the Yadkin River, in North Carolina, to wander through the wilderness of America, in quest of the country of Kentucky, in company with John Finley, John Stewart, Joseph Holden, James Monay, and William Cool. We proceeded successfully, and after a long and fatiguing journey through a mountainous wilderness, in a westward direction. On the 7th of June following we found ourselves on Red River, where John Finley had formerly been trading with the Indians, and, from the top of an eminence, saw with pleasure the beautiful level of Kentucky.

Here let me observe that for some time we had experienced the most uncomfortable weather, as a prelibation of our future sufferings. At this point we encamped, and made a shelter to defend us from the inclement season, and began to hunt and reconnoiter the country. We found everywhere abundance of wild beasts of all sorts, through this vast forest. The buffalo were more frequent than I have seen cattle in the settlements, browsing on the leaves of the cane, or cropping the herbage on those extensive plains, fearless, because ignorant of the violence of man. Sometimes we saw hundreds in a drove, and the numbers about the salt springs were amazing. In this forest, the habitation of beasts of every kind natural to America, we practiced hunting with great success until the 22d day of December. . . .

This day John Stewart and I had a pleasing ramble, but fortune changed the scene in the close of it. We had passed through a great forest, on which stood myriads of trees, some gay with blossoms, and others rich with fruits. Nature was here a series of wonders, and a fund of delight. Here she displayed her ingenuity and industry in a variety of flowers and fruits, beautifully colored, elegantly shaped, and charmingly flavored; and we were diverted with innumerable animals presenting themselves perpetually to our view.

In the decline of the day, near Kentucky River, as we ascended the brow of a small hill, a number of Indians rushed out of a thick canebrake upon us, and made us prisoners. The time of our sorrow was now arrived, and the scene fully opened. The Indians plundered us of what we had, and kept us in confinement seven days, treating us with common savage usage. During this time we discovered no uneasiness or desire to escape, which made them less suspicious of us; but in the dead of night, as we lay in a thick canebrake by a large fire, when sleep had locked up their senses, my situation not disposing me for rest, I touched my companion and gently awoke him.

We improved this favorable opportunity and departed . . . speedily directed our course toward our old camp, but found it plundered, and the company dispersed and gone home. About this time my brother, Squire Boone, with another adventurer, who came to explore the country shortly after us, was wandering through the forest, determined to find me if possible, and accidentally found our camp. Notwithstanding the unfortunate circum-

stances of our company, and our dangerous situation, as surrounded with hostile savages, our meeting so fortunately in the wilderness made us reciprocally sensible of the utmost satisfaction. So much does friendship triumph over misfortune. . . .

Soon after this, my companion in captivity, John Stewart, was killed by the savages, and the man that came with my brother returned home by himself. We were then in a dangerous, helpless situation, exposed daily to perils and death among savages and wild beasts —not a white man but ourselves.

Thus situated, many hundred miles from our families in the howling wilderness, I believe few would have equally enjoyed the happiness we experienced. I often observed to my brother, "You see now how little nature requires to be satisfied. Felicity, the companion of content, is rather found in our own breasts than in the enjoyment of external things . . . a resigned soul finds pleasure in a path strewed with briers and thorns."

We remained there undisturbed during the winter, and on the first day of May, 1770, my brother returned home to the settlement by himself, for a new recruit of horses and ammunition, leaving me by myself, without bread, salt, or sugar, without company of my fellow-creatures, or even a horse or dog. I confess I never before was under greater necessity of exercising philosophy and fortitude. . . . The idea of a beloved wife and family, and their anxiety upon the account of my absence and exposed situation, made sensible impressions on my heart. . . .

One day I undertook a tour through the country, and the diversity and beauties of nature expelled every gloomy thought. Just at the close of day the gentle gales retired, and left the place to the disposal of a profound calm. I had gained the summit of a commanding ridge, and, looking round with astonishing delight, beheld the ample plains, the beauteous tracts below. On the other hand, I surveyed the famous river Ohio, that rolled in silent dignity, marking the western boundary of Kentucky with inconceivable grandeur. . . . I laid me down to sleep, and I awoke not until the sun had chased away the night. . . .

Thus, through an uninterrupted scene of

sylvan pleasures, I spent the time until the 27th day of July following, when my brother met me at our old camp. Soon after I returned home to my family, with a determination to bring them as soon as possible to live in Kentucky, which I esteemed a second paradise, at the risk of my life and fortune. I sold my farm on the Yadkin, and what goods we could not carry with us and proceeded on our journey in company with five families more, and forty men that joined us in Powell's valley, one hundred and fifty miles from the now-settled parts of Kentucky.

This promising beginning was soon overcast; for, upon the 10th day of October, the rear of our company was attacked by a number of Indians, who killed six and wounded one man. Of these, my eldest son was one that fell in the action. Though we defended ourselves and repulsed the enemy, yet this unhappy affair scattered our cattle, brought us into extreme difficulty, and so discouraged the whole company, that we retreated forty miles to the settlement on Clinch River. The mountains are in the wilderness as we pass from Virginia to Kentucky; their aspect is so wild that it is impossible to behold them without terror. The spectator is apt to imagine that nature has formerly suffered some violent convulsion, and that these are the dismembered remains. . . .

I remained with my family on Clinch until the 6th of June, 1774, when I and one Michael Stoner were solicited by Governor Dunmore of Virginia to go to the falls of the Ohio to conduct into the settlements a number of surveyors that had been sent hither by him; this country having about this time drawn the attention of many adventurers. We completed a tour of eight hundred miles, through many many difficulties, in sixty-two days. . . .

To conclude, I can now say that I have verified the saying of an old Indian who signed Colonel Henderson's deed. Taking me by the hand, at the delivery thereof—"Brother," said he, "we have given you a fine land, but I believe you will have much trouble in settling it." My footsteps have often been marked with blood, and therefore I can truly subscribe to its original name. Two darling sons and a brother have I lost by savage hands, which have also taken from me forty valuable horses, and abundance of cattle. Many dark and sleepless nights have I been a companion for owls, separated from the cheerful society of men, scorched by the summer's sun, and pinched by the winter's cold—an instrument ordained to settle the wilderness. But now the scene is changed: peace crowns the sylvan shade.

The Ladies *Will* Make Themselves Fine

JOHANN DAVID SCHOEPF

The Teutonic Johann David Schoepf in 1783-84, in his Travels in the Confederation, *turned a shrewd eye on the tastes and manners of the newly liberated Americans. Like many after him, Schoepf noted the way the women enjoyed dressing to the teeth, while the men often arrayed themselves in far plainer fashion. As a frugal European farmer, he was repelled by the waste in the slave system and the way the Southerners gave little care to their soil. And he saw the Virginia Legislature as rather less decorous than some have pictured it.*

THE fair sex in America cannot resist the propensity to make themselves fine, even when, remotely situated, they must forego the pleasure of being admired except by the casual traveller. We had gone many miles through the woods, had seen only a few wretched cabins, and arrived finally at a house that had been indicated to us, which appeared not greatly different from the rest, not a whole pane in the windows, neither rum, nor whiskey, nor bread to be had, a draughty, empty place. But in return we had the altogether unexpected pleasure of making our devoirs to several ladies dressed tastefully in silk and decked with plumes.

But it must be observed that in the love of display the fair of the southern provinces go far beyond those of the northern, and that similar phenomena in similar circumstances are not to be looked-for in Pennsylvania; as also, that the carelessness of the men in their dress is quite as striking as the vanity of the women. . . .

We spent a night at a plantation where, according to the custom here, travellers are lodged for a price, under the style of "Private Entertainment," but no tavern is kept. In the item of public houses Virginia and other southern provinces are worse off than the northern. The distinction between Private and Public Entertainment is to the advantage of the people who keep the so-called Private houses, they avoiding in this way the tax for permission to dispense rum and other drinks and not being plagued with noisy drinking-parties. . . .

Here one eats with the family both thick and thin hominy, drinks water at pleasure, is not free to demand and has no right to expect what he wants, but pays quite as much as elsewhere, in houses where he lives as he pleases, is better served and not obliged on coming and going to be very grateful for the reception. On the other hand, it must be said for these "private houses" that in them one has to submit to a general interrogation but once, on the part of the family, whereas in the taverns every person coming in must be thoroughly answered. . . .

[Later a plantation owner told of his desire to find leaseholders.]

He would prefer Germans for tenants, but so long as land is to be bought in the interior of America these will be wise enough not to spend their sweat on any land that is not their own, even if they must be content with very little. For other reasons as well, the German and Irish servants brought over in such numbers have been unwilling to apprentice themselves in Virginia or Carolina, nor have they cared to settle there if not possessed of considerable property and able to buy slaves themselves. . . .

For the Virginians as such are an indolent, haughty people whose thoughts and designs are directed solely towards playing the lord, owning great tracts of land and numerous troops of slaves. Any man whatever, if he can afford so much as 2–3 negroes, becomes ashamed of work and goes about in idleness, supported by his slaves. Thus the introduction of the negroes has been injurious to the moral principles of the inhabitants of these provinces, has made them sluggish and arrogant; and at times cruel, because of the despotic power they have over their slaves. Besides, the cultivation of the land merely by negroes is not the most profitable, which the people themselves see plainly enough and would like to get rid of them, but what is to be done with them and where are other working hands to be found? . . .

The rich Virginians who, from their luxury and love of display, have for many years been of evil repute among their more frugal neighbors to the north, prefer generally to live in the country rather than in towns, and according to their circumstances and opportunities spare nothing in rendering their houses agreeable both outside and in. . . .

Hannovertown was the first and only market-town on the record from Fredericksburg to Richmond. . . . Here and at other places along the navigable creeks and rivers, the English factor is to be seen again, who supplies the planter, in exchange for his tobacco and timber, with manufactured articles and other wares; but rich planters also, here and there, have set up their own warehouses, whence their neighbors may get what they need. Here too new land is always taken in for tobacco as soon as the old is impoverished, albeit the people know and admit that old well-dunged land would be quite as profitable; but the trouble of laying down grass, and gathering feed for winter so as to keep the cattle in stalls or folds to make dung, all this they regard as more irksome than cutting down trees and rooting up stumps; preferring to let the cattle wander about in the woods and swamps to seek a meagre winter support. . . .

The James River, up from its mouth in the Bay, is one of the greatest and most beautiful of American streams, and on account of the profitable tobacco-trade which it facilitates and furthers, one of the richest. It is navigable for large merchantmen as far up as three miles below Richmond, that is, below the falls. . . . Before the founding of Williamsburg, Jamestown, now in ruins, was the capital of the province. But after the settlement of the interior progressed more and more, it was found convenient to desert Williamsburg also and to establish the seat of government at Richmond, sixty miles to the west.

The Assembly had just now come together. . . . It is said of the Assembly: It sits; but this is not a just expression, for these members show themselves in every possible position rather than that of sitting still, with dignity and attention. An assembly of men whose object is the serious and important one of making laws, should at least observe a certain *decorum*, but independence prevails even here. During the visits I made I saw this estimable assembly quiet not five minutes together; some are leaving, others coming in, most of them talking of insignificant or irrelevant matters, and to judge from the indifference and heedlessness of most of the faces it must be a trifling business to make laws. At the open door of the hall stands a door-keeper, who is almost incessantly and with a loud voice calling out for one member after another.

In the ante-room there is a tumult quite as constant; here they amuse themselves zealously with talk of horse-races, runaway negroes, yesterday's play, politics, or it may be, with trafficking. . . . In the same clothes in which one goes hunting or tends his tobacco-fields, it is permissible to appear in the Senate or the Assembly. There are displayed boots, trowsers, stockings, and Indian leggings; greatcoats, ordinary coats, and short jackets, according to each man's caprice or comfort, and all equally honorable. . . .

Among the orators here is a certain Mr. Henry who appears to have the greatest influence over the House. He has a high-flown and bold delivery, deals more in words than in reasons, and not so long ago was a country schoolmaster. Men of this stamp, either naturally eloquent or become so through their occupation, as e.g. lawyers, invariably take the most active . . . part in these assemblies. . . .

In general this province is poor in literary productions. I could hear only of a Mr. Jefferson, at this time a member of the Congress, as the author of several excellent political brochures, with the contents of which nobody seemed familiar. . . . However, if little is written in Virginia, there is all the more of speaking, for the Virginians are very conversable. They boast that among all the American colonies the English language is with them preserved purest and most complete, and one cannot altogether deny them. But here and there a few negroisms have crept in, and the salmagundy of the English language has here been enriched even by the words of African origin . . . e.g., the negro expression "toat," to carry something on the shoulder, for which there is no word in the English.

The coming together of so many gentlemen from all parts of the province brought hither a great number of very fine horses. One could almost fancy it was an Arabian village; there were to be seen the whole day long saddled horses at every turn, and a swarming of riders in the few and muddy streets, for a horse must be mounted, if only to fetch a prise of snuff from across the way; but of coaches there were none, which in the larger towns elsewhere jolt through all the streets. Horses are a prime object with the Virginians; but they give their attention chiefly to racers and hunters, of which indubitably they have the finest in America, their custom formerly being to keep up and improve the strain by imported English stallions and mares.

But the province has no good draught and work-horses, and their teams, in the low country at least, are in general extremely sorry. One sees everywhere little, thin animals, hitched to wagons made of wood throughout. . . . The reason lies merely in the great negligence with which the Virginians, and all Americans, treat their horses as well as their other useful animals, making it impossible for them to show a better condition. . . . [They] are let run about in the fields for pasture . . . and in winter many of these poor beasts are actually forced to get what little nourishment they can from under ice and snow.

Jefferson's First Inaugural Address

CALLED upon to undertake the duties of the first Executive office of our country, I avail myself of the presence of that portion of my fellow citizens which is here assembled to express my grateful thanks for the favor with which they have been pleased to look towards me, to declare a sincere consciousness that the task is above my talents, and that I approach it with those anxious and awful presentiments which the greatness of the charge and the weakness of my powers so justly inspire. A rising nation, spread over a wide and fruitful land, traversing all the seas with the rich productions of their industry, engaged in commerce with nations who feel power and forget right, advancing rapidly to destinies beyond the reach of mortal eye, when I contemplate these transcendent objects, and see the honour, the happiness, and the hopes of this beloved country committed to the issue and the auspices of this day, I shrink from the contemplation, and humble myself before the magnitude of the undertaking.

Utterly indeed should I despair, did not the presence of many, whom I here see, remind me, that in the other high authorities provided by our constitution, I shall find resources of wisdom, of virtue, and of zeal, on which to rely under all difficulties. To you, then, gentlemen, who are charged with the sovereign functions of legislation, and to those associated with you, I look with encouragement for that guidance and support which may enable us to steer with safety the vessel in which we are all embarked amidst the conflicting elements of a troubled world.

During the contest of opinion through which we have past, the animation of discussions and of exertions has sometimes worn an aspect which might impose on strangers unused to think freely and to speak and to write what they think. But this being now decided by the voice of the nation enounced according to the rules of the constitution, all will of course arrange themselves under the will of the law, and unite in common efforts for the common good. All too will bear in mind this sacred principle, that though the will of the majority is in all cases to prevail, that will, to be rightful, must be reasonable; that the minority possess their equal rights, which equal laws must protect, and to violate [which] would be oppression.

Let us then, fellow citizens, unite with one heart and one mind, let us restore to social intercourse that harmony and affection without which liberty, and even life itself, are but dreary things. And let us reflect that having banished from our land that religious intolerance under which mankind so long bled and suffered, we have yet gained little if we countenance a political intolerance as despotic, as wicked, and capable of as bitter and bloody persecutions. During the throes and convulsions of the antient world, during the agonizing spasms of infuriated man, seeking through blood and slaughter his long-lost liberty, it was not wonderful that the agitation of the billows should reach even this distant and peaceful shore; that this should be more felt and feared by some and less by others; and should divide opinions as to measures of safety.

But every difference of opinion is not a difference of principle. We have called by different names brethren of the same principle. We are all republicans: we are all federalists. If there be any of us who would wish to dissolve this Union or to change its republican form, let them stand undisturbed as monuments of the safety with which error of opinion may be tolerated, where reason is left free to combat it. I know indeed that some honest men fear that a republican government cannot be strong, that this government is not strong enough. But would the honest patriot in the full tide of successful experiment abandon a government which has so far kept us free and firm, on the theoretic and visionary fear, that this government, the world's best hope, may, by possibility, want energy to preserve itself? I trust not.

I believe this, on the contrary, the strongest government on earth. I believe it is the only one, where every man, at the call of the law, would fly to the standard of the law, and would meet invasions of the public order as his own personal concern. Sometimes it is said that man cannot be trusted with the government of himself. Can he then be trusted with the government of others? Or have we found angels, in the form of kings, to govern him? Let history answer this question.

Let us then, with courage and confidence, pursue our own federal and republican principles; our attachment to our union and representative government. Kindly separated by nature and a wide ocean from the exterminating havoc of one quarter of the globe; too high-minded to endure the degradations of the others; possessing a chosen country, with room enough for our descendants to the thousandth and thousandth generation; enjoying the most favourable temperateness of climate; entertaining a due sense of our equal right to the use of our own faculties, to the acquisitions of our industry, to honour and confidence from our fellow citizens, resulting not from birth but from our actions and their sense of them; enlightened by a benign religion, professed indeed and practiced in various forms, yet all of them inculcating honesty, truth, temperance, gratitude, and the love of man, acknowledging and adoring an overruling providence, which by all its dispensations proves that it delights in the happiness of man here, and his greater happiness hereafter; with all these blessings, what more is necessary to make us a happy and prosperous people?

Still one thing more, fellow citizens, a wise and frugal government which shall restrain men from injuring one another, shall leave them otherwise free to regulate their own pursuits of industry and improvement, and shall not take from the mouth of labor the bread it has earned. This is the sum of good government, and this is necessary to close the circle of our felicities.

About to enter, fellow citizens, on the exercise of duties which comprehend everything dear and valuable to you, it is proper that you should understand what I deem the essential principles of our government, and consequently those which ought to shape its administration. I will compress them within the narrowest compass they will bear, stating the general principle, but not all its limitations. Equal and exact justice to all men, of whatever state of persuasion, religious or political; peace, commerce, and honest friendship with all nations, entangling alliances with none; the support of the state governments in all their rights, as the most competent administrations for our domestic concerns and the surest bulwarks against anti-republican tendencies; the preservation of the general government in its whole constitutional vigour as the sheet anchor of our peace at home and safety abroad; a jealous care of the right of election by the people, a mild and safe corrective of abuses which are lopped by the sword of the revolution where peaceable remedies are unprovided; absolute acquiescence in the decisions of the majority, the vital principle of republics, from which there is no appeal but to force, the vital principle and immediate parent of despotism; a well-disciplined militia—our best reliance in peace and for the first moments of war, till regulars may relieve them; the supremacy of the civil over the military authority; economy in the public expense, that labor may be lightly burthened; the honest payment of our debts and sacred preservation of the public faith; encouragement of agriculture, and of commerce as its handmaid; the diffusion of information and arraignment of all abuses at the bar of public reason; freedom of religion; freedom of the press; and freedom of person, under the protection of the habeas corpus; and trial by juries, impartially selected.

These principles form the bright constellation which has gone before us and guided our steps through an age of revolution and reformation. The wisdom of our sages and blood of our heroes have been devoted to their attainment. They should be the creed of our political faith; the text of civil instruction, the touchstone by which to try the services of those we trust; and should we wander from them in moments of error or of alarm, let us hasten to retrace our steps and to regain the road which alone leads to peace, liberty, and safety.

I repair, then, fellow citizens, to the post you have assigned me. With experience enough in subordinate offices to have seen the difficulties of this, the greatest of all, I have learnt to expect that it will rarely fall to the lot of imperfect man to retire from this station with the reputation and the favor which bring him into it. Without pretensions to that high confidence you reposed in our first and greatest revolutionary character, whose pre-eminent services had entitled him to the first place in his country's love, and destined for him the fairest page in the volume of faithful history, I ask so much confidence only as may give firmness and effect to the legal administration of your affairs. I shall often go wrong through defect of judgment. When right, I shall often be thought wrong by those whose positions will not command a view of the whole ground. I ask your indulgence for my own errors, which will never be intentional; and your support against the errors of others who may condemn what they would not, if seen in all its parts. The approbation implied by your suffrage is a great consolation to me for the past; and my future solicitude will be to retain the good opinion of those who have bestowed it in advance, to conciliate that of others by doing them all the good in my power, and to be instrumental to the happiness and freedom of all.

An Indian Combo

CHRISTIAN SCHULTZ, JR.

Mr. Schultz, a youthful, clear-sighted observer of the American scene, captured a bright flash of local color when he chanced upon a dusty, raffish band of somewhat corrupted Indians in Natchez along the Mississippi River about 1808. The selection is from his Travels on an Inland Voyage Through the States . . . , *published in New York, 1810.*

THERE is a gang of idle Choctaw, Natchez and Muskogee Indians, who stroll about the city, or rather are settled down on the Levee, which being the landing-place of the cargoes of whiskey and provisions that continually arrive, has attracted them to that spot. They are about forty in number, of both sexes, and of every age. They are provided with a full band of music, with which they serenade the different boats as they arrive morning and evening, or as often as they want a little money, whiskey, or provisions. You would no doubt have been surprised, if you had inspected the band, with their instruments, before the beginning of the performance; but you would have been satisfied, after hearing the music, that a given quantity of discord may produce harmony. I must certainly do them the justice to say, that I was never more agreeably disappointed in my life, and the harmony produced by such an unpromising collection of instruments and performers, exceeded all my expectations.

As I was very particular in examining the instruments used on this occasion, I must not omit giving you a description of them. The first and largest was a joint of thick cane, open at both ends, which, when applied to the mouth, and sung or blown through with a strong voice, served as a bass for the whole. The next was also a joint of cane with both ends closed, containing a few small pebbles: this was used by shaking it to the time and motion of the piece. The third was two separate joints of cane, each of which were cracked in several places, and used by suspending the one between the fingers of the left hand, and striking the other upon it with the right; producing a kind of rattling jarring sound.

The fourth was likewise a joint of cane open at one end, having a small slip of cane inserted directly across the aperture. This was held in a perpendicular direction, when by contracting the lips, and blowing or singing through the aperture upon the slip, it produced a hollow hissing sound. The fifth was another joint of cane closed at both ends, with a narrow strip out from end to end, over which was extended a strong deer sinew; which being set in vibration by the thumb, produced a dull monotonous sound, something like the lowest string of the African jumbo. The sixth and last instrument was a two gallon tin kettle, with a drest buckskin extended over the mouth, not unlike a drum, which it was intended to represent. This was held under one arm, and beat with a stick held in the hand, producing a dull sound like a drum.

The first five instruments were of various sizes, according to the ages of the persons using them, those of the children being the smallest. Their manner of performance was as follows: Having first formed their company under a tree a small distance from the boats, they advance singing short stanzas of "ho ha." When near the boats, the captain or leader advances before with a white or striped silk banner, taking long and solemn strides, and then halting a moment for the rest to come up. After reaching the boat, he stands still as a post, not moving his eyes, or any of his limbs. The men approach next, and form a circle round him: then follow the boys; after them the squaws with the girls in the rear.

The music now becomes slow and solemn for about five minutes, when it gradually increases to a brisker motion, during which you will first perceive the captain move his eyes, next his lips, then his head and hands, and at last a very curious and pleasing pantomimical dance strikes up, which continues for about a quarter of an hour. The music is performed in two parts, being tenor and treble; the men and boys composing the former, and the women and girls the latter. The several instruments were used with such accurate time and motion, and so blended with the vocal music, that it rendered the performance far superior to anything I had anticipated. The burthen of the song was the same throughout, consisting of a single stanza, and, as near as I can remember, as follows:

> Ho, hoa, ho;
> Ho, al, hoa;
> Hoa, ho, ho;
> Ho, hoa, ho.

II

Flush Times

NOW began a middle era lasting from about 1815 through 1860, when the South surged swiftly in prosperity, took a changed role in American life and developed an outlook in contrast with that of the rest of the United States.

The flush days had arrived. The future of the South, and that of much of America as well, altered dramatically as cotton took a new, greatly enlarged part in the nation's affairs. Because the cotton engine (or "gin") proved workable, that minor crop came suddenly to dominance, and vast new areas found themselves in an agricultural revolution.

As never before, the fleecy growth thrived in Georgia, in North and South Carolina. Then at once it proved that it could succeed even more magnificently in the long lowlands of the Deep South, in area after area within reach of the Gulf and the Atlantic. By this time the nation had been enlarged overnight as a result of the momentous Louisiana Purchase, doubling its area, adding the fecund Mississippi—heartland of the continent—to its possessions. And after the War of 1812 the new South advanced by giant steps, giving to the region a stronger coloration as well as a more piquant accent.

Men had an all-year-round river outlet to the world. Cotton sprang up astonishingly in the long, steaming summers of this lowest South, from the red soil or the waxy black alluvial land, in the river bottoms, along lakes and coasts and marsh edges. New territories formed: Louisiana, Mississippi, Alabama and eventually Texas and Arkansas would be in the Union. For tens of thousands of miles cotton would be king.

The crop demanded ever-increasing thousands of workers to fill the new fields, planting and picking the staple through a season of many months. In Virginia and other parts of the earlier South, slavery had been dwindling, with decaying plantation houses and neglected fields. Having used up much of the available soil, the system was in decline, and men of Jefferson's school predicted that the institution of bondage would fall away as an archaic, outmoded thing. Now, however, they watched as slavery obtained a firm new lease on life.

Virginia and the rest of the upper South became breeding grounds from which Negro men, women and children were sold to the later territories. Among the older Virginians some looked askance at the process, but others were ready to take their part in the trade. The proceeds at least enabled them to keep their own properties intact.

In brickwork, iron and ornamental detail, the rear gate of the reconstructed Governor's Palace at Williamsburg is an essay in grace.

In eighteenth-century style, surrounded by flowers, is this colonial summerhouse in the Benjamin Waller garden of Williamsburg.

The mahogany horseshoe-shaped central staircase of Berry Hill estate has long been celebrated in Halifax County. The exterior was imposing Greek Revival.

These were years of another manner, another emphasis, in the South, one rather different from the stately style of Williamsburg and Charleston and the isolated estates along the Chesapeake. In the new lands life was lived more vigorously, more robustly. The new cotton area lay close to the frontier or was part of the frontier itself; inevitably there would be, for the time at least, less emphasis on punctilio, on rigid rules of behavior.

Fresh wealth poured out of the earth, in a flow greater than the region had ever known. For those who managed to hold their own on the shifting scene, there was a greater means and a greater opulence—bigger plantings, longer lines of men and women in the Negro quarters, bigger dwelling places. The era was that of the Greek Revival, when white-pillared establishments rose along the banks of the rivers, in the gardens at the edges of the fields, and at Natchez, Memphis, Montgomery and scores of other points about the South.

Men of all sections joined in the cotton rush. There were New Yorkers and New Englanders, growers from Ohio and Pennsylvania. Yet Southerners had the leading role in the settlement, using methods and principles which they had learned in handling other crops. Virginians or Carolinians arrived with lines of slaves and work animals, or purchased them when they located themselves along the Mississippi or the Tombigbee or a short way from the Gulf. This new South had much of the look of the old, and the new Southerners set to work to establish systems as similar to the older ones as they could achieve.

As ever, of course, the number of small farmers was greater than that of the large ones, and they occupied, as elsewhere, less desirable lands, smaller strips closer to the swamps or on less accessible ridges. Yet again the big growers continued to control the scene, establishing their dominance over most of what they surveyed.

During these decades more and more Southerners, like Northerners, had the ballot, and to national office there came an individual who represented the newer, most bustling areas as Jefferson and Washington represented the original South. He was the riproaring Andrew Jackson of Tennessee, a hot-tempered, impulsive man on the economic make, who spoke for a rather different element than the aristocrats of the Atlantic age.

The new Southerner thought differently, acted differently from his predecessors. Often he had greater wealth, for this cotton kingdom brought higher returns to the plantation growers, and it encouraged a still more authoritative manner. He had little patience with the liberal ideas of the Jeffersonians, with their belief that all men were created equal. His leaders sniffed at the great Virginian's opinions, calling them mere generalities, meaningless words. To them slaves were property like bureaus and plows; they reasoned with firm practicality that their future was tied tightly to that of bondage.

Ever more steadily the South turned from apology for slavery to defense of it. Bondage became, as the term had it, a "necessary evil," and then, as later commentators said, so "necessary" a thing that it lost any suggestion of evil. A "positive good," the cotton growers cried out. Ministers stepped forward to assert that the good book itself sanctioned the enslavement of one man by another. With the 1830's, tension grew ever tighter over the issue. When New England reform elements attacked the institution directly, bitterly, Southern tempers broke as never before.

When slave uprisings threatened, or were rumored, men of the region became ever more anxious to protect slavery, ever more determined not to give way to reproaches from other sections. One by one, the last of the Southern movements to end the institution, to "colonize" Negroes in Africa or other places, fell away. In the South dissent became unfashionable, then dangerous— and still there remained men and women who did not hesitate, as natives of the region, to stand against slavery and protest that it was an evil.

In these years John Calhoun became the advocate of Southern resistance to all criticism. He rose to a place as prime spokesman against efforts to keep slavery from spreading to new territories and as author of a plan of "nullification" by which a state could override or disregard a Federal law. Eventually there came, in one of the most significant power clashes in America, the issue of Andrew Jackson for the Union against Calhoun for South Carolina. Calhoun lost, but some Southerners were to continue to maintain his views.

Americans differed more and more drastically over slavery. Was it a beneficent agency, or a cruel misuse of human power? People of all shades of opinion, from all sections and from abroad, debated the matter, and testimony from several points of view is offered in some of the pages that follow.

Yet, whatever their opinions, natives of the South lived on in this physically most lavish of American regions, and strangers visited it and told of what they saw there: the calming hours in the great houses, the bustle and luxury of the steamboats gliding down the Mississippi, the elegance of style at Charleston, the semitropic ease of New Orleans behind its levees. . . . For the planters and their friends it was a place of breeze-swept expanses, of balls and races, of hunting in the woods and bright gatherings on the porches and galleries. And more and more steadily the shadow of Walter Scott and the other spokesmen for chivalry and romance extended over the land.

Queen Dolly of Montpelier

DOROTHY TODD PAYNE MADISON

Beloved of men and women in many ranks, for years the warmhearted Dolly Madison exercised a benevolent rule over Washington. Friend of the great, generous in her meetings with thousands of lesser individuals, she enjoyed life and she enjoyed people. Her grandniece, in Memoirs and Letters of Dolly Madison, *published in 1887, told of Dolly primarily against the background of James Madison's handsome Montpelier estate in Virginia. She was a worthy assistant to her husband, "Father of the Constitution," fourth President of the country and a steady participant in the work of building an earlier America.*

MR. Madison's second term having expired, and his Secretary of State, James Monroe, being installed in the Presidency, he gladly retired to his dearly-beloved Montpelier, where with a few congenial friends around him, he could still give a large proportion of his time to his favorite studies. He was a silent, grave man, whose nature was relieved by a vein of quaint, quiet humor, which, in his moments of relaxation, gave an inexpressible charm to his presence.

His style of dress was never altered: plain black cloth coat and knee breeches with buckles, the hair powdered and worn in a queue behind; the daily task of dressing it devolved upon his wife, who would not think his body-servant capable of doing it justice. He was a decided contrast to Mrs. Madison, who was still blooming, and showed little sign of the forty-five years she was entitled to. Always handsomely and becomingly dressed, her matronly figure had not yet outgrown the grace and dignity so much admired. . . .

Like her husband, Mrs. Madison was devoted to Montpelier, and led a busy life among her household of guests, and the many interests of gardens and poor people. Mr. Madison senior, and his eldest son Ambrose had both passed away, leaving the property, which comprised 2500 acres, to James, who enlarged the house to make room for friends, without interfering at all with his mother's household. The older Mrs. Madison lived to the age of ninety-eight years, retaining the use of all the original part of the old homestead, and keeping up the old-fashioned hours; waited upon by servants who had grown old in her service. One old negro at ninety, with a halo of gray hair about his head, refused to allow any one to take his place behind his mistress's chair, though sleeping sometimes made him totter in a most alarming manner.

General Lafayette, when he visited Montpelier in his last journey to this country in 1825, enjoyed going about with Mrs. Dolly Madison to all the different cabins occupied by the negroes, one of whom, Granny Milly, a hundred and four years old, lived with her daughter and granddaughters, the youngest seventy years of age, all retired from their labors. These became great friends of his, and he would stroll down to the "Walnut Grove" for a little chat, coming back with a fresh egg, or a nosegay presented by the old people.

The house of Montpelier lay on a very pretty slope of land, surrounded by the Blue Ridge Mountains, which extended as far as the eye could reach, with little vistas of country roads winding in and out; roads eagerly scanned with a telescope, which was part of the portico furniture, when carriages were almost daily seen, bringing friends, or even strangers, who wished to pay their respects to the host and hostess. . . .

A contemporary writer says: "There are few houses in Virginia that gave a larger welcome, or made it more agreeable than that over which 'Queen Dolly,' the most gracious and beloved of all our female sovereigns, reigned, and wielding as skillfully the do-

Romantics of a robust constitution could enjoy sights such as the Bullard Rock and other formations in the New River, Giles County, Virginia.

Decade by decade, the Capitol at Washington City grew in importance in this town which was essentially Southern in air and intonation.

mestic as she had done worthily and popularly the public, sceptre; everything that came beneath her immediate and personal sway, the care and entertainment of visitors, the government of servants, the whole policy of the interior, was admirably managed with equal grace and efficacy."

The house had a very large, wide portico in front, supported by pillars, where Mr. Madison exercised in stormy weather, walking his allotted number of miles. In the center of the gravel walk to the first gate, a large tin cup was imbedded to show the amount of rain fallen, which was carefully measured and brought to him after a shower, and on the right hand a path bordered with silver pine led to a little building in the form of a temple surmounted by a statue of Liberty, and intended for his study; from this, groups of trees—silver poplar and weeping willow—concealed the numerous out-buildings so essential to a southern country-house.

Back of the house was another large portico, opening on an extensive lawn, bounded by a ha-ha hedge, and with two large tulip-trees in the center, so exactly alike that Mr. Madison named them "the twins"; they were still standing a few years ago in a field, surrrounded by a quantity of tiger-lilies, the product of seed sent from France by General Lafayette. . . . At some distance was a garden laid out in the form of a large horse-shoe, and kept in perfect order by a French gardener, named Beazée. This Beazée and his wife came to Virginia at the time of the French Revolution, and made themselves very popular with the slaves, taking the trouble to teach some of the more enlightened ones to speak French, much to the amusement of their mistress, who laughed very heartily over the jargon. . . .

From a letter written by a Virginia lady, once an inmate of the White House, we take the following: "My recollections of Mrs. Madison . . . were formed from a long and intimate acquaintance, beginning in my childhood and ending only with her life. She had a sweet natural dignity of manner, which attracted while it commanded; a proper degree of reserve without stiffness in company with strangers; and a stamp of frankness and

sincerity, which, with her intimate friends, became gayety and playfulness of manner.

"There was, too, a cordial, genial sunny atmosphere surrounding her which won all hearts—and was one of the secrets of her popularity. She was said to be, during Mr. Madison's administration, the most popular person in the United States, and she certainly had a remarkable memory for names and faces. No person introduced to Mrs. Madison at one of the crowded levees at the White House required a second presentation on meeting her again, but had the gratification of being recognized and addressed by name. . . ."

Until the close of Mr. Madison's troubled administration in 1817, Mrs. Madison had continued to dispense her hospitalities in the same hearty, simple manner, having among her guests from time to time many distinguished men, among whom were Thomas Moore, Talleyrand, Chateaubriand, Volney, General Moreau, Joseph and Jerome Bonaparte, Dr. Priestly, the celebrated philosopher and polemical divine, and others.

It had been said by a foreigner that "her table was more like a harvest home supper than the entertainment of a high official." These and similar remarks came to her ears, and she observed with a smile, "that to her, abundance was preferable to elegance; that circumstances formed customs, and customs formed taste; and as the profusion so laughed at by foreigners arose from the happy circumstance of the superabundance and prosperity of our country, she did not hesitate to sacrifice the delicacy of European taste for the less elegant, but more liberal, fashion of Virginia."

Two plain ladies from the West, passing through Washington, determined not to leave without seeing Mrs. Madison; and having but little time, they were much puzzled how to accomplish it. Meeting an old gentleman in the street early next morning, who happened to be a friend of Mrs. Madison's, they timidly explained their wish, and requested him to show them the way to the President's house. Pleased with their simplicity, he took pleasure in conducting them himself, where he found the family at breakfast. Mrs. Madison good-naturedly went in to the parlor to be inspected, and put the old ladies quite at their ease by her cordial welcome.

Their astonishment, however, at seeing so great a personage in a dark gray stuff dress, with a white apron, and kerchief pinned across her breast was unbounded, but so reassuring, that when the time came for leaving, one of them said: "P'r'aps you wouldn't mind if I just kissed you, to tell my girls about." Mrs. Madison, not to be outdone by her guests' politeness, gracefully embraced them both, and after many expressions of admiration and friendliness the delighted old ladies departed.

.   .   .

At Montpelier fruits of all kinds, including figs, flowers and plants, many of them rare and delicate, sent by admiring friends, made the grounds most attractive to guests. Roses and white jessamine entwined the pillars of the south portico, creeping up to the terraces and making the summer air rich with perfume, as it stole in through the long drawing-room windows.

The "old lady," as she was called (the older Mrs. Madison) had her own separate garden, laid out in the most prim, old fashioned manner by her own gardener. No innovation of any kind was allowed in her domain. She was a woman of strong mind and good education, active and bright up to the last days of her life, taking a great interest and pride in the friends visiting her son and daughter, who were brought to see her and her quaint surroundings at two o'clock, the hour set apart for receiving.

At this hour she was to be found seated upon a couch in the centre of a large room, with a table by her side, containing her Bible and prayer book, which, with her knitting, divided her time; the innumerable gloves and stockings made by her, with the names knitted in, were presented to those whom she fancied among the guests.

The long hall, with its highly polished floor, connecting the old wing with the main part of the house, was hung with pictures, and led into the large dining room in which there were many portraits. Napoleon in his ermine robes, Louis the Fourteenth, Con-fucius, several members of the family, and faithful slaves, together with a water-color painting of Mr. Jefferson by his enthusiastic admirer Kosciusko,—these with the many medallions and other testimonials of respect and admiration from crowned heads as well as friends, covered the walls, while the large, polished mahogany table and sideboard were bright with silver, the accumulation of three families. Out of this opened Mr. Madison's sitting-room, furnished with chairs and bed of iron, brought by Mr. Monroe from the dismantled palace of the Tuileries; the last with very high posts, and a heavy canopy of crimson damask.

Here, with his own desk and papers around him, he spent much time, and towards the latter years of his life, he dined at a small table, placed sufficiently near the door of the dining room to permit conversation with his guests. Another door opened into a room filled with statuary, called the "clock-room," out of respect to an old-fashioned English clock, which regulated the household for many years. There were some fifty statues and busts, including those of Washington, Jefferson and the elder Adams. . . . The drawing room was carpeted with Persian rugs, the walls were quite covered with mirrors and pictures, six of which last were by Stuart, and the framed Declaration of Independence; while many pretty bits of furniture and china made the room look cheerful and homelike, as one glanced through the glass doors leading in from the lawn.

From the front hall the carved oaken staircase led upstairs to the bedrooms and the library, the latter not only lined with bookcases but the center so filled with them that there was only just room enough to pass among them. Books and pamphlets were piled up everywhere, on every available chair and table, accumulated by Mr. Madison and his father, who shared the same literary tastes. . . .

Much as she graced her public station, Mrs. Madison has not been less admirable in domestic life. Neighborly and companionable among her country friends, as if she had never lived in a city; delighting in the society of young people, and promoting their pleasure by her participation and enjoyment of it; she

No less Southern was the President's House, occupied in early years by a succession of Virginians. The Old Dominion had the name of "Mother of Presidents."

The "Monumental City" was Baltimore, thriving port and shipbuilding center, known for the Washington Monument in foreground and other works. On a dividing line, Baltimore still shared many Southern ways.

still proved herself a most affectionate and devoted wife during the years of suffering before Mr. Madison's death. Without neglecting the duties of a kind hostess, a faithful friend and relative, she soothed, occupied and amused the tiresome hours of his long confinement.

Never, in the midst of a drawing-room, surrounded on all sides by everything that was brilliant and courtly,—the center of attraction, the object of admiration,—never was she so interesting, so attractive as in her loving attendance on her venerable mother-in-law, who said, "Dolly is my mother now, and cares most tenderly for all my wants," and later on, in filling the same office to her husband in his declining years.

Governor James Barbour, a warm friend and neighbor, gives a touching description of his burial, where friends of all classes, from far and near, flocked to do honor to his memory, and the hundred slaves, as they turned to leave the newly-made grave, could control themselves no longer, and gave vent to their lamentations in one violent outburst of grief that rent the air.

When at last the great bereavement and separation came upon Mrs. Madison, she did not dare give way to her grief. The feeling that there was something still to do for him, something that required all her energies, kept her up for several months, until the nervous strain produced its consequences, and her health gave way so completely, that during the following autumn and winter she was confined almost entirely to her bed.

Left sole executrix, and with the responsibility of the unpublished manuscript her husband had worked upon so long and so faithfully in her hands, hundreds of letters and resolutions coming in from every side, expressive of grief and sympathy, there was no time to give way to her sense of utter loneliness in a separation from one with whom she had lived so happily for forty years. The replies were all written by herself. . . .

"The Brink of Insurrection and Treason"

ANDREW JACKSON

Far different from Calhoun was Andrew Jackson, forthright, free-slashing advocate of a greater democracy for America. Though he was a self-made enterpriser in farm lands and other holdings, Jackson gathered under his banners thousands of Southern and Southwestern farmers as well as town and city workmen of all sections. He had violent likes and dislikes; he ordered acts of great harshness to the Indians, whom he helped push farther and farther from their lands. One of the great dramas of Jackon's life was his clash in 1832 with Calhoun over the Federal tariff, when a Carolina convention ruled the levies "unconstitutional" and ordered the creation of a state army. Responding, Jackson threatened to hang leaders of the "infatuated" Carolinians, called for Federal guns to subdue them. Other Southern states declined to follow Calhoun's lead, and Jackson carried the day. But the issue was somewhat blunted when the tariff was lowered.

THIS, then, is the position in which we stand: A small majority of the citizens of one State in the Union have elected delegates to a State convention: that convention has ordained that

Alexandroffsky was the ornate Baltimore home of Thomas Winans. After building rail equipment for Czar Nicholas I of Russia, he built the house with statuary around its gardens. When Baltimoreans professed horror at the uncovered shapes, Winans put up a twelve-foot wall.

all the revenue laws of the United States must be repealed, or that they are no longer a member of the Union. The Governor of that State has recommended to the Legislature the raising of an army to carry the secession into effect, and that he may be empowered to give clearances to vessels in the name of the State.

No act of violent opposition to the laws has yet been committed, but such a state of things is hourly apprehended. And it is the intent of this instrument to *proclaim*, not only that the duty imposed on me by the Constitution "to take care that the laws be faithfully executed" shall be performed to the extent of the powers already vested in me by law, or as such others as the wisdom of Congress shall devise and entrust to me for the purpose, but to warn the citizens of South Carolina who have been deluded into an opposition to the laws of the danger they will incur by the illegal and disorganizing ordinance of the con-

vention; to exhort those who have refused to support it to persevere in their determination to uphold the Constitution and laws of their country; and to point out to all the perilous situation into which the good people of that State have been led, and that the course they are urged to pursue is one of ruin and disgrace to the very State whose rights they affect to support.

Fellow-citizens of my native State, let me not only admonish you as the First Magistrate of our common country, not to incur the penalty of the laws, but use the influence that a father would over his children whom he saw rushing to a certain ruin. In that paternal language, with that paternal feeling, let me tell you, my countrymen, that you are deluded by men who are either deceived themselves or wish to deceive you. Mark under what pretences you have been led on to the brink of insurrection and treason on which you stand.

First, a diminution of the value of your staple commodity, lowered by overproduction in other quarters, and the consequent diminution in the value of your lands were the sole effects of the tariff laws. The effect of those laws was confessedly injurious, but the evil was greatly exaggerated by the unfounded theory you were taught to believe—that its burthens were in proportion to your exports, not to your consumption of imported articles. Your pride was aroused by the assertion that a submission to those laws was a state of vassalage and that resistance to them was equal in patriotic merit to the opposition your fathers offered to the oppressive laws of Great Britain. You were told that this opposition might be peaceably, might be constitutionally, made; that you might enjoy all the advantages of the Union and bear none of its burthens.

Eloquent appeals to your passions, to your State pride, to your native courage, to your sense of real injury, were used to prepare you for the period when the mask which concealed the hideous features of *disunion* should be taken off. It fell, and you were made to look with complacency on objects which not long since you would have regarded with horror. Look back to the arts which have brought you to this state; look forward to the consequences to which it must inevitably lead! Look back to what was first told you as an inducement to enter into this dangerous course.

The great political truth was repeated to you that you had the revolutionary right of resisting all laws that were palpably unconstitutional and intolerably oppressive. It was added that the right to nullify a law rested on the same principle, but that it was a peaceable remedy. This character which was given to it made you receive with too much confidence the assertions that were made of the unconstitutionality of the law and its oppressive effects. Mark, my fellow-citizens, that by the admission of your leaders the unconstitutionality must be *palpable* or it will not justify either resistance or nullification.

What is the meaning of the word *palpable* in the sense in which it is here used? That which is apparent to everyone, that which no man of ordinary intellect will fail to perceive. Is the unconstitutionality of this law of that description? Let those among your leaders who once approved and advocated the principle of protective duties answer the question; and let them choose whether they will be considered as incapable then of perceiving that which must have been apparent to every man of common understanding, or as imposing upon your confidence and endeavoring to mislead you now.

In every case they are unsafe guides in the perilous path they urge you to tread. Ponder well on these circumstances, and you will know how to appreciate the exaggerated language they address to you. They are not champions of liberty, emulating the fame of our Revolutionary fathers, nor are you an oppressed people, contending, as they repeat to you, against worse than Colonial vassalage. You are free members of a flourishing and happy Union. There is no settled design to oppress you. You have indeed felt the unequal operation of laws which may have been unwisely, not unconstitutionally, passed; but that inequality must necessarily be removed. At the very moment when you were madly urged on to the unfortunate course you have taken, a change in public opinion had commenced.

The nearly approaching payment of the public debt and the consequent diminution of duties had already produced articles of general consumption in your State. The importance of this change was underrated, and you were authoritatively told that no further alleviation of your burthens was to be expected at the very time when the condition of the country imperiously demanded such a modification of the duties as should reduce them to a just and equitable scale. But, as if apprehensive of the effect of this change in allaying your discontents, you were precipitated into the fearful state in which you now find yourselves.

I have urged you to look back to the means which were used to hurry you on to the position you have now assumed and forward to the consequences it will produce. Something more is necessary. Contemplate the condition of that country of which you still form an important part. Consider its Government, uniting in one bond of common interest

Charles Carroll of Carrollton, great landowner and patriot, was the last surviving signer of the Declaration of Independence. Of Irish Catholic family, he became a revered figure in Maryland.

Charles Carroll's granddaughter Mary married the Marquess Wellesley, brother of the Duke of Wellington. The other two of these "Three American Graces" married to high rank, helping rule over the world of Europe from which their grandfather had turned.

and general protection so many different States, giving to all their inhabitants the proud title of *American citizen*, protecting their commerce, securing their literature and their arts, facilitating their intercommunication, defending their frontiers, and making their name respected in the remotest parts of the earth. Consider the extent of its territory, its increasing and happy population, its advances in arts which render life agreeable, and the sciences which elevate the mind!

See education spreading the lights of religion, morality, and general information into every cottage in this wide extent of our Territories and States. Behold it as the asylum where the wretched and the oppressed find a refuge and support. Look at this picture of happiness and only say, *We are citizens of America.* Carolina is one of these proud states; her arms have defended, her best blood has cemented, this happy Union. And then add, if you can, without horror and remorse, This happy Union we will dissolve; this picture of peace we will interrupt; these fertile fields we will deluge with blood; the protection of that glorious flag we renounce; the very name of American we discard.

And for what, mistaken men? For what would you exchange your share in the advantages and honor of the Union? For the dream of a separate independence—a dream interrupted by bloody conflicts with your neighbors and a vile dependence on a foreign power. If your leaders could succeed in situation? Are you united at home? Are you free from the apprehension of civil discord, with all its fearful consequences? Do your neighbor republics, every day suffering some new revolution or contending with some new insurrection, do they excite your envy?

But the dictates of a high duty oblige me solemnly to announce that you cannot succeed. The laws of the United States must be executed. I have no discretionary power on the subject; my duty is emphatically pronounced in the Constitution. Those who told you that you might peaceably prevent their execution deceived you; they could not have been deceived themselves. They know that a forcible opposition could alone prevent the execution of the laws, and they know that such opposition must be repelled. Their object is disunion. But be not deceived by names. Disunion by armed force is *treason.*

Are you really ready to incur its guilt? If you are, on the heads of the instigators of the act be the dreadful consequences; on their heads be the dishonor. But on yours may fall the punishment. On your unhappy State will inevitably fall all the evils of the conflict you force upon the Government of your country. It cannot accede to the mad project of disunion, of which you would be the first victims. Its First Magistrate cannot, if he would, avoid the performance of his duty. The consequences must be fearful for you, distressing to your fellow-citizens here and to the friends of good government throughout the world. Its enemies have beheld our prosperity with a vexation they could not conceal; it was a standing refutation of their selfish doctrines, and they will point to our discord with the triumph of malignant joy.

It is yet in your power to disappoint them. There is yet time to show that the descendants of the Pinckneys, the Sumters, the Rutledges, and of the thousand other names which adorn the pages of your Revolutionary history will not abandon that Union to support which so many of them fought and bled and died. I adjure you, as you honor their memory, as you love the cause of freedom, to which they dedicated their lives, as you prize the peace of your country, the lives of its best citizens, and your own fair fame, to retrace your steps. . . .

The Jacksons at Home

HENRY A. WISE

The Nashville area in Tennessee and Andrew Jackson's Hermitage provide the setting of this firsthand description of the man, about to assume the Presidency in the 1840's, and of his tragic wife, Rachel, who did not survive to enter the White House. Henry Wise, member of a vigorous Virginia clan, went to the Hermitage with his Nashville bride. Later, Wise became Governor of Virginia, Minister to Brazil and a Confederate officer.

AND here the author of these pages must be indulged in an episode which connects himself with the great men of this narrative. . . . In the month of August, 1828, with a law license in hand, we left our native Eastern Shore of Virginia for Baltimore, on our way to Nashville to be married and settled for life. . . . In a month or more we were at Nashville, and married the daughter of the Reverend Dr. O. Jennings, the Presbyterian pastor of Andrew Jackson, who honored him with tender reverence and respect. The general tendered his daughter the hospitalities of the Hermitage, and ordered our attendance there, the day after the wedding, to make his house the home of our honey-moon. The marriage was on the 8th of October, and our whole wedding-party was punctually at the Hermitage on the day appointed. We desired to study General Jackson in his slipshod ways at home. The weather had been wet, and the roads were exceedingly bad in that soil of unbroken limestone. . . .

Escape from all disasters in a travel of eight hundred and fifty miles had made us too confident for a drive of only twelve miles, the distance to the Hermitage from Nashville. On the way we noticed a narrow defile of rock and mud-holes on one side, and stumps on the Murfreesborough road on the other side of the track, which required a nice eye, good light, a steady rein, and a strong horse, quick to obey every touch of the rein.

We arrived at the Hermitage to dinner, and were shown to a bridal chamber magnificently furnished with articles which were the rich and costly presents of the city of New Orleans to its noble defender.

Had we not seen General Jackson before, we would have taken him for a visitor, not the host of the mansion. He greeted us cordially, and bade us feel at home, but gave us distinctly to understand that he took no trouble to look after any but his lady guests; as for the gentlemen, there were the parlor, the dining-room, the library, the sideboard and its refreshments; there were the servants, and, if anything was wanting, all that was necessary was to ring. He was as good as his word. He did not sit at the head of his table, but mingled with his guests, and always preferred a seat between two ladies, obviously seeking a chair between different ones at various times.

He was very easy and graceful in his attentions; free, and often playful, but always dignified and earnest, in his conversation. He was quick to perceive every point of word or manner, was gracious in approval, but did not hesitate to dissent with courtesy when he differed. He obviously had a hidden vein of humor, loved aphorism, and could politely convey a sense of smart travesty. If put upon his mettle, he was very positive, but gravely respectful. He conversed freely, and seemed to be absorbed in attention to what the ladies were saying; but if a word of note was uttered at any distance from him audibly, he caught it by a quick and pertinent comment, without losing or leaving the subject about which he was talking to another person—such was his ease of sociability, without levity or lightness of activity, and without being oracular or heavy in his remarks. He had great power of attention and concentration, without being prying, curt, or brusque. Strong good sense and warm kindness of manner put every word of his pleasantly and pointedly in its right place. He conversed wonderfully well, but at times pronounced incorrectly and misused words; and it was remarkable, too, that when he did so it was with emphasis on the error of speech, and he would give it a marked prominence in diction.

To illustrate him in a scene, the Hermitage house was a solid, plain, substantial, commodious country mansion, built of brick, and two stories high. The front was south. You entered through a porch, a spacious hall, in which the stairs ascended, airy and well lighted. It contained four rooms on the lower floor, each entering the passage and each on either side opening into the one adjoining. The northwest room was the dining-room, the southeast and southwest rooms were sitting-rooms, and the northeast room had a door entering into the garden. The house was full of guests. There were visitors from all parts of the United States, numbering from twenty to fifty a day, constantly coming and going, all made welcome, and all well attended to.

The cost of the coming Presidency was even then very great and burdensome; but the general showed no signs of impatience, and was alive and active in his attention to all comers and goers. He affected no style, and put on no airs of greatness, but was plainly and simply, though impulsively, polite to all. Besides his own family he had his wife's relatives, Mr. Stokely and Andrew J. Donelson, around him every day, and his adopted son, Andrew Jackson, relieved him of all the minuter attentions to guests.

Henry Lee, of Virginia, was, we may say, resident for the time with him, as he was engaged in writing for his election some of the finest campaign papers even penned in this country.

He was not handsome as his half-brother, General Robert E. Lee, but rather ugly in face,—a mouth without a line of the bow of Diana about it, and nose not clean and classic, but rather meaty and, if we may make a word, "bloody-beety;" but he was one of the most attractive men in conversation we ever listened to. He, Harry Lee, who was so severe upon Mr. Jefferson and his writings because of his "Arcana" about his father, Light-Horse Harry Lee of the Revolution, was then, in fact, the entertaining host of the Hermitage, and attracted the crowd of visitors around his glowing words of commentary on the election.

The first or second evening of our stay, Mr. Lee had drawn around him his usual crowd of listeners; but we were the more special guests of Mrs. Jackson. She was a descendant of Colonel Stokely, of our native county, Accomack, Virginia, and we had often seen his old mansion, an old Hanoverian hip-roofed house, standing on the seaside, not far above Metompkin; and she had often heard her mother talk of old Assawaman Church, not very far above Colonel Stokely's house. Thus she was not only a good Presbyterian, whose pastor's daughter was the bride, and she a Presbyterian too, but the groom was from the county of her ancestors, in Virginia, and could tell her something about traditions she had heard of the family from which she sprung. . . .

First on our right near the window was old Judge Overton, one of General Jackson's earliest and best friends. He was a man who had made his mark in law and politics, but was not pious, and was a queer-looking little old man. Small in stature, and cut into sharp angles at every salient point, a round, prominent, gourd-like, bald cranium, a peaked, Roman nose, a prominent, sharp, but manly chin, and he had lost his teeth and swallowed his lips. "There was danger," as Mr. Philip Doddridge once said of his own chin and nose, "of their coming together, for many sharp words had passed between them!" . . . Judge Overton had thrown over his head a bandanna handkerchief, and sat all the time muttering or "mounching, mounching, mounching" on his toothless gums, looking like the Witch of Endor.

Mrs. Jackson was a lady who, doubtless, was once a form of rotund and rubicund beauty, but now was very plethoric and obese, and seemingly suffered from what was called phthisis, and talked low but quick, with a short and wheezing breath, the very personation of affable kindness and of a welcome as sincere as it was simple and tender. . . .

Concord, old-time Governor's Mansion at Natchez, Mississippi, had a Creole air, with long hipped roof, galleries on four sides, many columns and a double flight of stairs beneath the portico.

After several days of delightful delay, we moved to leave the Hermitage, but day after day were detained by the entreaty of General Jackson and his lady. At last we were resolved positively to start; still, we were not allowed to leave until after dinner, and the hour for dining was as late as 4 P.M. We apprehended anxiously the danger of the defile of stumps and mud-holes on the Murfreesborough road, on the way back to Nashville. The road was not paved, and it would certainly be dark when we arrived at the point of danger. We urged this necessity for early departure but in vain. After dinner the general insisted it was too late, but ordered the horses, and whilst awaiting their being brought to the door, he took his pipe, sat on the sill of the front door, and with a group in the porch around him, consisting of several of the family and guests, repeatedly warned us that it would be dark before we could travel half the way, that the road was unsafe, and that we would certainly meet with disaster. This led to tales by one and another of the group of "hairbreadth 'scapes." In every instance narrated of disaster we noticed that he pointedly and oracularly said, "Ah! young man, you did not trust in Providence." This was repeatedly said, adding, "Never encounter danger if you can avoid it: if inevitable, meet it more than half way; but whether to avoid or encounter it, trust altogether in Providence." We were struck by his repeated remarks of this sort, so much so that we could not but think, "Is this real faith, or is it not like an affected Napoleonic belief and trust in Fate?"

The gig came to the door. He rose to wait on the bride; and in handing her up the step, he said to her, "I have tried my best to protect you, madam, but your chosen one seems too self-reliant to heed your safety or my admonitions; I fear he don't trust in Providence, and will meet with disaster on the way. . . ."

We drove off, and hurried on faster than the saddle-horses traveled, in order to reach the "stumps and holes" before dark; but darkness overtook us; and, on approaching the place, the road was scrutinized; we drove slowly and steadily, but vision was perfectly

At St. Augustine, oldest permanent settlement in the United States, the weather-beaten cathedral has called the faithful through the centuries.

THE JACKSONS AT HOME   101

deceived. The wagon-wheels, daubed with the mortar of stiff clay, had to pass so close to an inclined stump that the dripping mud had fallen on the stump and colored it precisely like the bed of the road and the offal on the stump on the opposite side of the road looked black, and was taken for the stump itself; and this led the left wheel directly up and over it, overturning the gig to the right in the mortar of clay in the road. The horse was a generous lion of draught, and, though spirited, perfectly broken. The right shaft was broken, and the fragments pricked his right hind leg and made him restive; but we remained perfectly still, steadily grasping the reins until the bride could creep out into the road, and then, gradually relaxing the rein, we too crawled into the mud.

The breeching and traces were immediately undone and slipped out, and we found a dry spot of leaves on the roadside to stand on. So far was the bride from being put out or frightened, that she joined in the proposition to tie the horse in the woods and hide ourselves behind a large tree until the cavalcade escort should come up. In a short time they arrived at the spot, and, finding the gig upset and broken in the road, and no sign of the horse, or harness, or ourselves, they set up a wail of agony most distressing. Dr. Thomas R. Jennings was so shocked that we could conceal ourselves no longer, but ran out and relieved the party. Fortunately a four-horse wagon soon drove up, and the driver having an axe and other tools with which to cut a pole and straps to lash on the broken shaft, it was repaired, and we reached Nashville safe, but very muddy, in the wedding fine clothes.

The next Sabbath General Jackson and his lady came into Mr. John C. McLemore's, and, calling at the house of Dr. Jennings, at once inquired for our safety; when told of our "escape" from hurt, again he repeated, "Ah, young man, you did not trust in Providence! You would not be advised to avoid danger when you could. But for your trusting wife, it would have been worse for both." We then began to perceive what he meant by trusting in Providence. It was no inactive belief, no blind faith; but it was to do what was prudent, careful, and obviously most safe, and leave the "whole care" of the result to God.

It was to do every little thing necessary to be observed by human foresight and precaution, however inapt, apparently, to the end, as the mother of Moses did with the preparation of bulrushes and slime and pitch, and then put the basket on the waters, however much exposed to the crocodile and the Nile, and leave the whole care for conjunction of causes and effects to the goodness and wisdom of God!

"I Have No Where to Sleep at Night"

EDGAR ALLAN POE

Beyond much question, the greatest nineteenth-century writer who rose from the South, and one of America's authentic geniuses, was Edgar Allan Poe of Richmond, Baltimore, and other places. A tragic, almost a doomed figure, he had turbulent relations with his foster father, John Allan of Virginia. A gambler at an early age, a heavy drinker, Poe quarreled steadily with Allan, joined the Army, then went to West Point, from which he was discharged. He married a girl of thirteen, who soon died.

At times during his career the brilliant Poe faced starvation. To those around him, he could be as exasperating as he was gifted; his greatest admirers often found him impossible to bear. Sometimes a victim of injustices, Poe did much to cause his own sufferings. Yet meanwhile he created a series of poetic

Richmond, Monday (March 19, 1827)

SIR,

After my treatment on yesterday and what passed between us this morning, I can hardly think you will be surprised at the contents of this letter. My determination is at length taken to leave your house and endeavour to find some place in this wide world, where I will be treated—not as you have treated me. This is not a hurried determination, but one on which I have long considered—and having so considered my resolution is unalterable. You may perhaps think that I have flown off in a passion, & that I am already wishing to return; But not so—I will give you the reasons which have actuated me, and then judge—

Since I have been able to think on any subject, my thoughts have aspired, and they have been taught by you to aspire, to eminence in public life—this cannot be attained without a good Education, such a one I cannot obtain at a Primary school—

A collegiate Education therefore was what I most ardently desired, and I had been led to expect that it would at some future time be granted—but in a moment of caprice you have blasted my hope—because forsooth I disagreed with you in an opinion, which opinion I was forced to express—

Again, I have heard you say (when you little thought I was listening and therefore must have said it in earnest) that you had no affection for me—

You have moreover ordered me to quit your house, and are continually upbraiding me with eating the bread of idleness, when you yourself were the only person to remedy the evil by placing me to some business—

You take delight in exposing me before those whom you think likely to advance my interest in this world—

You suffer me to be subjected to the whims & caprice, not only of your white family, but the complete authority of the blacks—these grievances I could not submit to; and I am gone—

I request that you will send me my trunk containing my clothes & books—and if you still have the least affection for me, as the last call I shall make on your bounty, to prevent the fulfillment of the Prediction you this morning expressed—send me as much money as will defray the expences of my passage to some of the Northern cities & then support me for one month, by which time I shall be enabled to place myself in some situation where I may not only obtain a livelihood, but lay by a sum which one day or another will support me at the University. Send my trunk &c. to the Court-House Tavern. Send me I entreat you some money immediately, as I am in the greatest necessity. If you fail to comply with my request—I tremble for the consequences.

Yours, &c.

EDGAR. A. POE

Richmond, Tuesday (March 20, 1827)

DEAR SIR,

Be so good as to send me my trunk with my clothes. I wrote you on yesterday explaining my reasons for leaving. I suppose by my not receiving either my trunk, or an answer to my letter, that you did not receive it. I am in the greatest necessity, not having tasted food since yesterday morning. I have no where to sleep at night, but roam about the streets. I am nearly exhausted—I beseech you as you wish not your prediction concerning me to be fulfilled—to send me without delay my trunk containing my clothes, and to lend if you will not give me as much money as will defray the expence of my passage to Boston ($12) and a little to support me there until I shall be enabled to engage in some

Above the harbor and rooftops of Charleston, a temporary monarch scans the sunny city from his balustraded vantage point.

Among the Deep Delta canefields below New Orleans, the French-Spanish houses had a look of the West Indies.

business. I sail on Saturday. A letter will be received by me at the Court House Tavern, where be so good as to send my trunk.

Give my love to all   I am yours, &c
at home   EDGAR. A. POE
I have not one cent in the
world to provide any food.

West Point, Jan'y 3d, 1831

SIR,

I suppose, (altho' you desire no further communication with yourself, on my part,) that your restriction does not extend to my answering your final letter.

Did I, when an infant, solicit your charity and protection, or was it of your own free will, that you volunteered your services in my behalf? It is well known to respectable individuals in Baltimore, and elsewhere, that my Grandfather (my natural protector at the time you interposed) was wealthy, and that I was his favourite grand-child. But the promises of adoption, and liberal education which you held forth to him in a letter which is now in possession of my family, induced him to resign all care of me into your hands. Under such circumstances, can it be said that I have no right to expect anything at your hands? You may probably urge that you have given me a liberal education. I will leave the decision of that question to those who know how far liberal educations can be obtained in 8 months at the University of Va. Here you will say that it was my own fault that I did not return.

You would not let me return because bills were presented you for payment which I never wished nor desired you to pay. Had you let me return, my reformation had been sure—as my conduct the last 3 months gave every reason to believe—and you would never have heard more of my extravagances. But I am not about to proclaim myself guilty of all that has been alledged against me, and which I have hitherto endured, simply because I was too proud to reply. I will boldly say that it was wholly and entirely your own mistaken parsimony that caused all the difficulties in which I was involved while at Charlottesville. The expenses of the institution at the lowest estimate were $350 per annum. You sent me there with $110. Of this $50 were to be paid immediately for board—$60 for attendance upon 2 professors—and you even then did not miss the opportunity of abusing me because I did not attend 3. Then $15 more were to be paid in advance with $110—$12 more for a bed—and $12 more for room furniture. I had of course, the mortification of running in debt for public property—against the known rules of the institution, and was immediately regarded in the light of a beggar. You will remember that in a week after my arrival I wrote to you for some more money, and for books. You replied in terms of the utmost abuse—if I had been the vilest wretch on earth you could not have been more abusive than you were. . . .

I had enclosed to you in my letter (according to your express commands) an account of the expenses incurred amounting to $149—the balance to be paid was $39—you enclosed me $40, leaving me one dollar in pocket. In a short time afterwards, I received a packet of books consisting of *Gil Blas,* and the Cambridge *Mathematics* in 2 vols: books for which I had no earthly use since I had no means of attending the mathematical lectures. But books must be had, if I intended to remain at the institution—and they were bought accordingly upon credit. In this manner debts were accumulated, and money borrowed . . . for I was obliged to hire a servant, to pay for wood, for washing, and a thousand other necessaries. It was then that I became dissolute, for how could it be otherwise? I could associate with no students, except those who were in a similar situation with myself—altho' from different causes—they from drunkenness, and extravagance—I, because it was my crime to have no one on Earth who cared for me, or loved me. I call God to witness that I have never loved dissipation. Those who know me know that my pursuits and habits are very far from anything of the kind. But I was drawn into it by my companions. Even their professions of friendship—hollow as they were—were a relief. Towards the close of the session you sent me $100—but it was too late—to be of any service in extricating me from my difficulties. I kept it for some time—thinking that if I could obtain more I could yet retrieve my character. I applied to James Galt—but he, I believe, from the best of motives refused to lend me any. I then became desperate and gambled—until I finally involved myself irretrievably. If I have been to blame in all this—place yourself in my situation, and tell me if you would not have been equally so. But these circumstances were all unknown to my friends when I returned home. They knew that I had been extravagant—but that was all. I had no hope of returning to Charlottesville, and I waited in vain in expectation that you would, at least, obtain me some employment. I saw no prospect of this—and I could endure it no longer. Every day threatened with a warrant &c. I left home—and after nearly 2 years conduct with which no fault could be found—in the army, as a common soldier—I earned, myself, by the most humiliating privations—a Cadet's warrant which you could have obtained at any time for asking. It was then that I thought I might venture to sollicit your assistance in giving me an outfit. I came home, you will remember, the night after the burial. If she had not have died while I was away there would have been nothing for me to regret. Your love I never valued—but she I believe loved me as her own child. You promised me to forgive all—but you soon forgot your promise. You sent me to W. Point like a beggar. The same difficulties are threatening me as before at Charlottesville—and I must resign.

As to your injunction not to trouble you with further communication, rest assured, Sir, that I will most religiously observe it. When I parted from you—at the steam-boat—I knew that I should never see you again. As regards Sergt. Graves—I did write him that letter. As to the truth of its contents, I leave it to God, and your own conscience.—The Time in which I wrote it was within a half hour after you had embittered every feeling of my heart against you by your abuse of my family, and myself, under your own roof—and at a time when you knew that my heart was almost breaking.

I have no more to say—except that my future life (which thank God will not endure long) must be passed in indigence and sickness. I have no energy left, nor health. If it was possible to put up with the fatigues of this place, and the inconveniences which my absolute want of necessaries subject me to, and as I mentioned before it is my intention to resign —For this end it will be necessary that you (as my nominal guardian) enclose me your written permission. It will be useless to refuse me this last request—for I can leave the place without any permission—your refusal would only deprive me of the little pay which is now due as mileage.

From the time of this writing I shall neglect my studies and duties at the institution. If I do not receive your answer in ten days, I will leave the Point without—for otherwise I should subject myself to dismission.

E. A. POE

Baltimore, April 12th, 1833

It has now been more than two years since you have assisted me, and more than three since you have spoken to me. I feel little hope that you will pay any regard to this letter, but still I cannot refrain from making one more attempt to interest you in my behalf. If you will only consider in what a situation I am placed you will surely pity me—without friends, without any means, consequently of obtaining employment, I am perishing—absolutely perishing for want of aid. And yet I am not idle—nor addicted to any vice—nor have I committed an offence against society which would render me deserving of so hard a fate. For God's sake pity me, and save me from destruction.

E. A. POE

"At Home and Abroad"

JOHN P. KENNEDY

A happy nostalgia permeated the recollections in John P. Kennedy's At Home Abroad, *published in 1872. The Baltimore of which he told was one of the first important cities of the country, center of many traditions of the Calverts, Catholic founders of the original colony. A bustling port, a city of graceful homes, of good cuisine and good living for its leading elements, Baltimore has been called the most northerly of Southern capitals, but it has long maintained a certain Southern look and Southern outlook as well. Fondly Mr. Kennedy re-created the appearances on the narrow streets of wide-skirted ladies with proud family names and "weather-beaten gallants" who required the full width of a sidewalk to make their bows.*

MY most salient memory comes up from the old Play-House. We had not got into the euphuism of calling it "the theatre" in those days, or, at least, that elegance was patronized only by the select few who in that generation, like the select few of the present, were apt to be caught by the fancy of a supposed refinement in the substitution of Greek for the Anglo-Saxon. The Spectator and Rambler and the Vicar of Wakefield supplied the vocabulary of that era, and I think Addison, Johnson and Goldsmith generally followed Ben Jonson and Shakespeare, and taught people to call it the Play-House.

I dare say the actors—especially the young ones who were proud of their calling and were inclined to strut in speech as well as on the boards—had, even then, began to naturalize the new word. But there is such a perfume lingering about the old vernacular,—the aroma of flowers planted by it when all the world was fragrant to me—that I cannot give it up without risk of dulling the husbandry which yet keeps these fine odors alive.

"The theatre" would bring me to a later period, when the foot-lights were no longer fed with oil, when the glass diamonds and tinsel had lost their reality, and the stage had begun to reveal its tawdry secrets, to the disenchantment of that beautiful school-boy faith with which I plunged into this weird world. . . . This Play-House stood in Holiday street just where the present "theatre" now stands. What a superb thing it was!—speaking now as my fancy imagined it then. It had something of the splendor of a great barn, weatherboarded, milk white, with many windows and, to my conception, looked with a hospitable, patronizing, tragicomic greeting down upon the street.

It never occurred to me to think of it as a piece of architecture. It was something above that—a huge, mystical Aladdin lamp that had a magic to repel criticism, and filled with wonderful histories. There Blue Beard strangled his wives and hung them on pegs in the Blue Chamber; and the glorious Valentine overcame his brother Orson, by the clever trick of showing him his own image in a wonderful shield of looking-glass, which, of course, we believed to be pure burnished silver; and there the Babes in the Wood went to sleep under the coverlet provided for them by the charitable robins that swung down upon wires, —which we thought was even superior to the ordinary manner of flying; and the ghost of Gaffer Thumb came up through the floor, as white as a dredge-box of flour could make

him—much more natural than any common ghost we had seen.

Alas, what has become of Orcobrand's Cave and the Wood Demon and the Castle Spectre, and all the rest of those delightful old horrors which used to make our hair stand on end in delicious ecstasy in those days? . . . Young America is evidently not so easily scared as old America was; it has a sad propensity toward fast trotters and to that wretched business of driving buggies, which has spoiled the whole generation of young gentlemen, and made a good cavalry officer, just now, an impossibility, or at least, a virtuous exception, in one half of the country. The age is too fast for the old illusions, and the theatre now deals in respectable swindlers, burglars and improper young ladies as more consonant with the public favor than our old devils, ghosts and assassins, which were always shown in their true colors, and were sure to be severely punished when they persecuted innocence.

The players were part and parcel of the play-house, and therefore shared in the juvenile admiration with which it was regarded. In fact, there was a misty confusing of the two which destroyed the separate identity of either. The play-house was a compound idea of a house filled with mountains, old castles and cities and elderly gentlemen in wigs, brigands. fairies and demons. . . . Of course, there was but one play-house and one company of actors. Two or more would have destroyed that impression of the super-natural, or rather the extra-natural. . . . A cheap and common illusion soon grows stale. . . . Even Lady Macbeth, I believe, would become an ordinary sort of person in "a run"—such as is common now. The players understood this, and, therefore, did not allow themselves to grow too familiar. . . .

There was a universal gladness in this old Baltimore when the word was passed round— "the players are come." It instantly became every body's business to give them a good reception. They were strange creatures in our school-boy reckoning—quite out of the common order of humanity. We ran after them in the street as something very notable to be looked at. It was odd to see them dressed like gentlemen and ladies: almost incongruous, we sometimes thought, as if we expected to see them in slashed doublet and hose, with embroidered mantles and a feather in their caps.

"There goes *Old* Francis," was our phrase; not that he was *old*, for he was far from it, but because we loved him. It was a term of endearment. And as to Jefferson! Is there any body now who remembers that imp of ancient fame? I cannot even now think definitely of him as a man—except in one particular, that he had a prominent and rather arching nose. In regard to every thing else he was a Proteous —the nose always being the same. He played every thing that was comic and always made people laugh till tears came to their eyes. Laugh! Why, I don't believe he ever saw the world doing any thing else. Whomsoever he looked at laughed.

Before he came through the side scenes, when he was about to enter O.P. or P.S., he would pronounce the first words of his part to herald his appearance, and instantly the whole audience set up a shout. It was only the sound of his voice. He had a patent right to shake the world's diaphragm which seemed to be infallible.

When our players came, with their short seasons, their three nights in a week, and their single company, they were received as public benefactors, and their stay was a period carnival. The boxes were engaged for every night. Families all went together, young and old. Smiles were on every face; the town was happy. The elders did not frown on the drama, the clergy levelled no cannon against it, the critics were amiable. The chief actors were invited into the best company, and I believe their personal merits entitled them to all the esteem that was felt for them. But, among the young folks the appreciation was far above all this. With them it was a kind of hero worship prompted by a conviction that the player was that manifold creature which every night assumed a new shape, and only accidentally fell into the category of a common mortal. And therefore, it seemed so interesting to us to catch one of them sauntering on the street looking like other people. . . .

In the days I speak of, Baltimore was fast emerging from its village state into a thriving commercial town. . . . We had our seven hills then, which have been rounded off since, and

that locality, which is now described as lying between the two parallels of North Charles street and Calvert street, presented a steep and barren hill-side, broken by rugged cliffs and deep ravines washed out, by the storms of winter, into chasms which were threaded by paths of toilsome and difficult ascent. The rain-washed ravines supplied an amusement to the boys, which seems to have been the origin of a sport that has now descended to their grandchildren in an improved and more practical form. These same hills are now cut down into streets of rapid descent, which in winter, when clothed in ice and snow, are filled with troops of noisy sledders. . . .

As communities grow in density and aggregation, the individuality of men diminishes. . . . Society had a more aristocratic air than now—not because the educated and wealthy assumed more, but because the community itself had a better appreciation of personal worth, and voluntarily gave it the healthful privilege of taking the lead in the direction —a bustling, ambitious, I might say, rollicking of manners and in the conducting of public affairs. . . .

Our ancestors saw Baltimore just after the war of the Revolution, giving its first promise young aspirant for municipal honors. Market street (obsolete now—they call it Baltimore street) had shot like a snake out of a toy box, with its variegated range of low-browed, hiproofed wooden houses, standing forward and back, out of line, like an ill-dressed regiment. . . . Some houses were painted blue, some yellow, some white, and here and there, a more pretending mansion of brick, with windows after the pattern of a multiplication table, square and many-paned, and great wastes of wall between the stories; some with courtyards in front, and trees in whose shade truant boys and ragged negroes "skyed coppers" and played at marbles.

This avenue was enlivened with matrons and damsels; some with looped-up skirts, some in brocade luxuriantly displayed over hoops, with comely bodices supported by stays disclosing perilous waists, and with sleeves that clung to the arm as far as the elbow, where they were lost in ruffles that stood off like the feathers of a bantam. The whirligig of time has played its usual prank and brought these ghosts of the past back into the very same avenue. And then, such faces! so rosy, spirited and sharp;—with the hair drawn over a cushion—(they called it neither "cat" nor "rat", my dear young lady, but simply by the name I give it—tight enough to lift the eyebrows into a rounder curve, giving a pungent, supercilious expression to the countenance; and curls that fell in "cataracts" upon the shoulders (much prettier, my pretty friend, than those netted "beaver tails" you fancy.) Then, they stepped away in such a mincing gait, in shoes of so many colors with formidable points at the toes and high tottering heels delicately cut in wood, and in towering peaked hats, garnished with feathers that swayed aristocratically backward and forward at each step, as if they took pride in the stately paces of the wearers.

In the train of these goodly groups came the gallants who upheld the chivalry of the age;—cavaliers of the old school, full of starch and powder; most of them the iron gentlemen of the Revolution, with leather faces—old campaigners, renowned for long stories,—not long enough from the camp to lose their military *brusquerie* and dare-devil swagger. . . . And they walked with such a stir, striking their canes upon the pavement till it rang again. I defy all modern coxcombry to produce anything equal to it. It was a sight worth seeing, when one of these weather-beaten gallants accosted a lady on the street. There was a bow which required the whole width of the pavement, a scrape of the foot and the cane thrust with a flourish under the left arm and projecting behind in a parallel line with the cue. And nothing could be more piquant than the lady's return of this salutation, in a courtesy that brought her, with bridled chin and a most winning glance, half way to the ground. And such a volume of dignity!

Even the seasons were on a scale of grandeur unknown to the present time. There were none of your soft Italian skies and puny affectation of April in December. But winter strutted in, like a peremptory bandit of the stage, as one who knew his power and wasn't to be trifled with, and took possession of sky and field and river, flinging his snowy cloak upon the ground as a challenge to all comers, determined that it should lie there until he chose to take it up. . . . And the nights seemed to be made on purpose for frolics—they were so bright and crisp, and so inviting to the jovial spirits of the time who, crowded in sleighs, sped like laughing phantoms over every highway, echoing back the halloos of groups of boys that, at every street corner greeted them with volleys of snowballs. And the horse-bells jingling the music of revelry from many a near and many a distant quarter told of the universal mirth that followed upon the track of the old-fashioned winter.

John Randolph Always Had a Word For It

WILLIAM CABELL BRUCE

Fantastic, sometimes ingratiating, more often repellant, John Randolph was a Southern figure without a counterpart, and thousands rejoiced that there was only one of his kind. His mind was brilliant, his body misshapen, his mind shadowed; from time to time he seemed close to madness. In politics he followed an erratic course; now and then he spoke with quiet reason, but again his lips poured out gall and malevolence. Senator from Virginia, Congressman, sent to Russia on a mission by Andrew Jackson, Randolph at several points found himself in a strategic place. But his violent tempers, his churlish disposition, vitiated his influence. He is remembered for his undirected excesses of disposition, and some of the most sulphurous speeches in American history. He could, perhaps, have thrived only against his Southern background of privileged position. Some of Randolph's remarks, eloquent or vituperative, are summarized by his biographer, William Cabell Bruce, author of John Randolph of Roanoke, *published in 1922 by G. P. Putnam's Sons, New York.*

NEVER did a man have a cleverer gift of minting phrases that passed into general circulation.

Governor James H. Pleasants, Randolph asserted on one occasion, was like some of his blooded horses: "too weak for the plow, and too strong for the turf."

When Richard Rush was appointed to the office of Secretary of the Treasury, he said: "Never were abilities so much below mediocrity so well-rewarded; no, not when Caligula's horse was made Consul."

Of an ambitious man, with little native ability, Randolph said that his mind was like the lands at the headwaters of the Monongahela; naturally poor and made still poorer by excessive cultivation.

The wavering Edmund Randolph was "the chameleon on the aspen, always trembling, always changing."

The politic and secretive Van Buren "rowed to his object with muffled oars."

Yes, Thomas Ritchie, (the distinguished editor of the Richmond Enquirer) did have seven principles, but they were the five loaves and the two fishes.

"Clay's eye is on the Presidency; and my eye is on him."

Turning away from a lady who had been pouring her sympathy with the struggling Greeks into his ear, Randolph pointed to a group of ragged little Negroes near the steps of her home and exclaimed: "Madam, the Greeks are at your door!"—words that soon winged their way to every part of the United States.

"An English noble has but one son, all the rests are bastards."

"I am an aristocrat; I love liberty, I hate equality."

"Asking one of the states to surrender part of her sovereignty is like asking a lady to surrender part of her chastity."

"It is a turnstyle; it is in everybody's way but it stops no one."

"Stick to a friend a *little* in the wrong."

"That most delicious of privileges—spending other people's money."

His violent prepossession in favor of the Virginian *vice voce* mode of voting hurried him into the assertion that the ballot box was Pandora's box.

"Denouncing me! That is strange! I never did him a favor."

"No man was ever satisfied to be half a king."

The Northern Democrats with Southern principles were "doughfaces"; another phrase which was soon on the tip of every tongue in every country.

From Adlai E. Stevenson's "Something of Men I Have Known":

"A colleague from 'The Valley' probably remembered him well to the last. That colleague, recently elected to fill a vacancy caused by the death of a member of long service, signalized his entrance into the House by an unprovoked attack upon Mr. Randolph. The latter, from his seat nearby, listened with apparent unconcern to the fierce personal assault. To the surprise of all, no immediate reply was made to the speech, and the new member flattered himself, no doubt, that the 'grim sage' was for once completely unhorsed.

"A few days later, however, Randolph, while discussing a bill of local importance, casually remarked: 'This bill, Mr. Speaker, lost its ablest advocate in the death of my lamented colleague, whose seat is still vacant.'"

A similar story is told by W. H. Sparks:

"I remember, upon one occasion . . . when Mr. Randolph was in the habit of almost daily addressing the House, that a Mr. Beecher of Ohio, who was very impatient with Randolph's tirades, would, in the lengthy pauses made by him, rise from the place and move the previous question. The speaker would reply: 'The member from Virginia has the floor.'

"The first and second interruption were not noticed by Randolph, but, upon the repetition a third time, he slowly lifted his head from contemplating his notes, and said, 'Mr. Speaker, in the Netherlands, a man of small capacity, with bits of wood and leather will in a few moments construct a toy that, with the pressure of the finger and thumb, will cry "Cuckoo! Cuckoo!"

"'With less of ingenuity and with inferior materials, the people of Ohio have made a toy that will, without much pressure, cry "Previous question, Mr. Speaker! Previous question, Mr. Speaker!"'—at the same time designating Beecher by pointing at him with

his long skeleton-like finger. In a moment the House was convulsed with laughter, and I doubt if Beecher ever survived the sarcasm."

But, after all, Randolph's best epigram was this golden sentence: "Life is not so important as the duties of life."

A good pendant to this is that other pithy observation of his: "We all know our duty better than we discharge it." Nor should we overlook two other weighty utterances of his, notable for their sententious conciseness, if for nothing else: "Time is at once the most valuable and the most perishable of all our possessions." "All of us have two educations: one which we receive from others; another, and the most valuable, which we give ourselves."

Mr. Calhoun, "Wonder of the World"

ALBERT G. BROWN

John Calhoun of South Carolina is one of the most controversial, one of the most puzzlesome, figures of the South—a man of high private character, who inspired an astonishing personal devotion in his state, who began his career as a strong nationalist, then ended as a rigid sectionalist. In his later years he worked steadily, relentlessly, in a defensive-offensive movement in behalf of strong state rights, as opposed to broader interpretations of the Constitution. Born on a small farm, he married a cousin, member of the South Carolina elite, with whom he became identified. An unbending legalist, Calhoun is supposed once to have written a poem in which he used the word "whereas." Eventually he urged the doctrine of a "state veto" against an act of the national government, and at one point favored a scheme providing two presidents, a Southern and a Northern one, each to protect his section against the other. Here is a strong eulogy of Calhoun, spoken by Representative Albert G. Brown of Mississippi, from the Congressional Globe *of April 17, 1840.*

AND how—how, sir, shall I speak of him—he who is justly esteemed the wonder of the world, the astonisher of mankind? Like the great Niagara, he goes dashing and sweeping on, bidding all created things give way, and bearing down, in his resistless course, all who have the temerity to oppose his onward career.

He, sir, is indeed the cataract, the political

Niagara of America; and like that noblest work of nature and of nature's God, he will stand through all after time no less the wonder than the admiration of the world. His was the bright star of genius that in early life shot madly forth, and left the lesser satellites that may have dazzled its blaze to that impenetrable darkness to which nature's stern decree

A planter's house and sugar plantation on the Mississippi River

Dueling Oaks: The famous New Orleans dueling grounds

had destined them; his the mighty magazine of mind, from which his country clothed herself in the armor of defence; his the broad expansive wing of genius, under which his country sought political protection; his the giant mind, the elevated spotless mien, which nations might envy, but worlds could not emulate.

Such an one needs no eulogium from me, no defence from human lips. He stands beneath a consecrated arch, defended by a lightning shut up in the hearts of his countrymen— by a lightning that will not slumber, but will leap forth to avenge even a word, a thought, a look, that threatens him with insult.

The story of his virtuous frame is written in the highest vault of your political can-opy, far above the reach of grovelling speculation, where it can alone be sought upon an eagle's pinions and gazed at by an eagle's eye. His defence may be found in the hearts of his countrymen; his eulogium will be heard in the deep toned murmurs of posterity, which, like the solemn artillery of heaven, shall go rolling along the shores of time until it is ingulfed in the mighty vortex of eternity.

Little minds may affect to despise him; pigmy politicians may raise the war cry of proscription against him; be it so; insects buzz around the lion's mane, but do not arouse him from his lair. Imprecations will add but other links to the mighty chain that binds him to his countrymen; and each blast of your war trumpet will but awaken millions to his support.

An Underside of North Carolina Life

Old newspapers, official records and manuscripts of the old North State reveal a harsher underside of the state's affairs. These graphic excerpts are from the scholarly North Carolina History, Told by Contemporaries, *compiled by Hugh T. Lefler, University of North Carolina Press, 1956.*

FIFTY DOLLARS REWARD. Ran away from the subscriber, living in Franklin County, North Carolina on the 12th of January, 1817, a Negro man named Randol about 26 or 27 years of age, between 5 and 6 feet high, rather yellow complected; appears humble when spoken to. It is expected he has some marks of shot about his hips, thighs, neck and face, as he has been shot at several times. His wife belongs to a Mr. Henry Bridges, formerly of this country, who started with her about the 14th instant, to South-Carolina, Georgia or Tennessee. It is supposed he will attempt to follow her. This is to caution all persons harbouring or trading for said Negro. And all masters of vessels are forbid having anything to do with him at the penalty of the law. The above reward and all reasonable charges will be paid to any person who will secure the said negro, so that I may get him.

Dec. 23, 1817   WOOD TUCKER
Raleigh Register, Feb. 20, 1818

.   .   .

Outlawing of Runaway Slaves . . .
"Without Accusation . . ."

It shall be lawful for any Person or Persons whatsoever to kill and destroy such Slave or Slaves by such Ways and Means as he or she shall think fit, without Accusation or Impeachment of any Crime for the same. Provided always . . . That for every Slave Killed in Pursuance of this Act, or put to death by Law, the Master or Owner of such Slave shall be paid by the Public.—State Records of North Carolina, XXIII, 202-3

.   .   .

39 Lashes—and No Ears

Punishment for Perjury . . . To be ordered by Court "to have one Ear nailed to

Interior of a country store

the Pillory, and there stand for the space of One Hour, and the said Ear to be cut off, and thereafter the other Ear nailed in like manner, and cut off at the Expiration of one other Hour; and moreover, to order every such Offender Thirty Nine Lashes well laid, on his or her bare Back, at the Common Whipping Post.—Laws of 1741, Chap. XXIV

"Burned at the Stake"

Whereupon the Court doth pass this Sentence . . . that the said Negro man Darby be immediately committed to Gaol under a good Guard and that on Tomorrow between the Hourse of one and Four o'clock in the afternoon he be taken out thence and tied to a Steak on the Court House Lott and there burned to Death and to Ashes and his ashes strewed upon the Ground.—Manuscript Records of Duplin County Court, March 15, 1787

More for the Head Than for the Man

Ran away last November from the subscriber, a negro fellow, named Zeb; aged 36. As he is outlawed, I will pay twenty pounds currency to any person who shall produce his head severed from his body, and five pounds if brought home alive.—John Moseley, North Carolina Gazette, 1774.

Christmas Night in the Quarters

IRWIN RUSSELL

Through the years, thousands of Southerners have smiled or nodded happily to themselves over this white version of Negro holiday festivities. The dialect is heavy and the characters tend toward the overconventional. But many have found a warming satisfaction in the underlying sentiment, the mirroring of some of the earlier Negro moods and attitudes. Irwin Russell of Port Gibson, Mississippi, is the author. Born in the early 1850's, Russell contributed to newspapers and magazines, spent a short time in the postwar North, returned to his native region and died when he was only twenty-six. The long poem, "Christmas Night in the Quarters," comes from Poems by Irwin Russell, *published in New York, 1888.*

When merry Christmas-day is done,
And Christmas-night is just begun;
While clouds in slow procession drift,
To wish the moon-man "Christmas gift,"
Yet linger overhead, to know
What causes all the stir below;
At Uncle Johnny Booker's ball
The darkies hold high carnival.
From all the country-side they throng,
With laughter, shouts, and scraps of song,—
Their whole deportment plainly showing
That to the Frolic they are going.
Some take the path with shoes in hand,
To traverse muddy bottom-land;
Aristocrats their steeds bestride—
Four on a mule, behold them ride!
And ten great oxen draw apace
The wagon from "de oder place,"
With forty guests, whose conversation
Betokens glad anticipation.
Not so with him who drives: old Jim
Is sagely solemn, hard, and grim,
And frolics have no joys for him.
He seldom speaks but to condemn—
Or utter some wise apothegm—
Or else, some crabbed thought pursuing,
Talk to his team, as now he's doing:

———————

Come up heah, Star! Yee-bawee!
  You alluz is a-laggin'—
Mus' be you think I's dead,
  An' dis de huss you's draggin'—
You's 'mos' too lazy to draw yo' bref,
  Let 'lone drawin' de waggin.

Dis team—quit bel'rin', sah!
  De ladies don't submit 'at—
Dis team—you ol' fool ox,
  You heah me tell you quit 'at?
Dis team's des like de 'Nited States;
  Dat's what I's tryin' to git at!

De people rides behin',
  De pollytishners haulin'—
Sh'u'd be a well-bruk ox,
  To foller dat ar callin'—
An' sometimes nuffin won't do dem steers,
  But what dey mus' be stallin'!

Woo bahgh! Buck-kannon! Yes, sah,
  Sometimes dey will be stickin';
An' den, fus thing dey knows,
  Dey takes a rale good lickin'.
De folks gits down: an' den watch out
  For hommerin' an' kickin'.

Dey blows upon dey hands,
  Den flings 'em wid de nails up,
Jumps up an' cracks dey heels,
  An' pruzently dey sails up,
An' makes dem oxen hump deysef,
  By twistin' all dey tails up!

———————

In this our age of printer's ink
'Tis books that show us how to think—
The rule reversed, and set at naught,
That held that books were born of thought.
We form our minds by pedants' rules,
And all we know is from the schools;

Cotton, of such overarching importance as to deserve the title "King," made work for the entire slave family.

The first cotton gin

And when we work, or when we play,
We do it in an ordered way—
And Nature's self pronounce a ban on,
Whene'er she dares transgress a canon.
Untrammeled thus the simple race is
That "wuks the craps" on cotton places.
Original in act and thought,
Because unlearned and untaught.
Observe them at their Christmas party:
How unrestrained their mirth—how hearty!
How many things they say and do
That never would occur to you!
See Brudder Brown—whose saving grace
Would sanctify a quarter-race—
Out on the crowded floor advance,
To "beg a blessin' on dis dance."

———

O Mahsr! let dis gath'rin' fin' a blessin' in yo'
sight!
Don't jedge us hard fur what we does—you knows
it's Chrismus-night;
An' all de balunce ob de yeah we does as right's
we kin.
Ef dancin's wrong, O Mahsr! let de time excuse
de sin!

We labors in de vineya'd, wukin' hard an' wukin'
true;
Now, shorely you won't notus, ef we eats a grape
or two,
An' takes a leetle holiday,—a leetle restin'-spell,—
Bekase, nex' week, we'll start in fresh, an' labor
twicet as well.

Remember, Mahsr,—min' dis, now,—de sinfulness
ob sin
Is 'pendin' 'pon de sperret what we goes an' does
it in:
An' in a righchis frame ob min' we's gwine to
dance an' sing,
A-feelin' like King David, when he cut de pigeon-
wing.

It seems to me—indeed it do—I mebbe mout be
wrong—
That people raly *ought* to dance, when Chrismus
comes along;
Des dance bekase dey's happy—like de birds hops
in de trees,
De pine-top fiddle soundin' to de bowin' ob de
breeze.

We has no ark to dance afore, like Isrul's prophet
king;
We has no harp to soun' de cords, to holp us out
to sing;
But 'cordin' to de gif's we has we does de bes' we
knows,
An' folks don't 'spise de vi'let-flower bekase it
ain't de rose.

You bless us, please, sah, eben ef we's doin' wrong
to-night;

Kase den we'll need de blessin' more'n ef we's
doin' right;
An' let de blessin' stay wid us, untel we comes to
die,
An' goes to keep our Chrismus wid dem sheriffs
in de sky!

Yes, tell dem preshis anguls we's a-gwine to jine
'em soon:
Our voices we's a-trainin' fur to sing de glory
tune;
We's ready when you wants us, an' it ain't no
matter when—
O Mahsr! call yo' chillen soon, an' take 'em
home! Amen.

———

The rev'rend man is scarcely through,
When all the noise begins anew,
And with such force assaults the ears,
That through the din one hardly hears
Old fiddling Josey "sound his A,"
Correct the pitch, begin to play,
Stop, satisfied, then, with the bow,
Rap out the signal dancers know:

———

Git yo' pardners, fust kwattillion!
Stomp yo' feet, an' raise 'em high;
Tune is: "Oh! dat water-million!
Gwine to get to home bime-bye."
S'lute yo' pardners!—scrape perlitely—
Don't be bumpin' gin de res'—
Balance all!—now, step out rightly;
Alluz dance yo' lebbel bes'.
Fo'wa'd foah!—whoop up, niggers!
Back ag'in!—don't be so slow!—

Swing cornahs!—min' de figgers!
When I hollers, den yo' go.
Top ladies cross ober!
Hol' on, till I takes a dram—
Gemmen solo!—yes, I's sober—
Cain't say how de fiddle am.
Hands around!—hol' up yo' faces,
Don't be lookin' at yo' feet!
Swing yo' pardners to yo' places!
Dat's de way—dat's hard to beat.
Sides fo'w'd!—when you's ready—
Make a bow as low's you kin!
Swing acrost wid opp'site lady!
Now we'll let you swap ag'in:
Ladies change!—shet up dat talkin';
Do yo' talkin' arter while!
Right an' lef'!—don't want no walkin'—
Make yo' steps, an' show yo' style!

———

And so the "set" proceeds—its length
Determined by the dancers' strength;
And all agreed to yield the palm
For grace and skill to "Georgy Sam,"
Who stamps so hard, and leaps so high,
"Des watch him!" is the wond'ring cry—
"De nigger mus' be, for a fac',
Own cousin to a jumpin'-jack!"

On, on the restless fiddle sounds,
Still chorused by the curs and hounds;
Dance after dance succeeding fast,
Till supper is announced at last.
That scene—but why attempt to show it?
The most inventive modern poet,
In fine new words whose hope and trust is,
Could form no phrase to do it justice
When supper ends—that is not soon—
The fiddle strikes the same old tune;
The dancers pound the floor again,
With all they have of might and main;
Old gossips, *almost* turning pale,
Attend Aunt Cassy's gruesome tale
Of conjurors, and ghosts, and devils,
That in the smoke-house hold their revels;
Each drowsy baby droops its head,
Yet scorns the very thought of bed:—
So wears the night, and wears so fast,
All wonder when they find it passed,
And hear the signal sound to go
From what few cocks are left to crow.
Then, one and all, you hear them shout:
"Hi! Booker! fotch de banjo out,
An' gib us *one* song 'fore we goes—
One ob de berry bes' you knows!"
Responding to the welcome call,
He takes the banjo from the wall,
And tunes the strings with skill and care,
Then strikes them with a master's air,
And tells, in melody and rhyme,
This legend of the olden time.

————

Go 'way, fiddle! folks is tired o' hearin' you
a-squawkin'.
Keep silence fur yo' betters!—don't you heah de
banjo talkin'?
About de 'possum's tail she's gwine to lecter—
ladies, listen!—
About de ha'r whut isn't dar, an' why de ha'r
is missin':

"Dar's gwine to be a' oberflow," said Noah,
lookin' solemn—
Fur Noah tuk the "Herald," an' he read de
ribber column—
An' so he sot his hands to wuk a-cl'arin' timber-
patches,
An' 'lowed he's gwine to build a boat to beat de
steamah *Natchez.*

Ol' Noah kep' a-nailin' an' a-chippin' an'
a-sawin';
An' all de wicked neighbors kep' a-laughin' an'
a-pshawin';
But Noah didn't min' 'em, knowin' whut wuz
gwine to happen:
An' forty days an' forty nights de rain it kep'
a-drappin'.
Now, Noah had done cotched a lot ob ebry sort
o' beas'es—

Ob all de shows a-trabbelin', it beat 'em all
to pieces!
He had a Morgan colt an' sebral head o'
Jarsey cattle—
An' druv 'em 'board de Ark as soon's he heered
de thunder rattle.

Den sech anoder fall ob rain!—it come so awful
hebby,
De ribber riz immejitly, an' busted troo de
lebbee;
De people all wuz drownded out—'cep' Noah
an' de critters,
An' men he'd hired to work de boat—an' one
to mix de bitters.

De Ark she kep' a-sailin' an' a-sailin' *an'* a-sailin';
De lion got his dander up, an' like to bruk de
palin';
De sarpints hissed; de painters yelled; tell, whut
wid all de fussin',
You c'u'dn't hardly heah de mate a-bossin'
'roun' an' cussin'.

Now, Ham, de only nigger whut wuz runnin'
on de packet,
Got lonesome in de barber-shop, an' c'u'dn't
stan' de racket;
An' so, fur to amuse he-se'f, he steamed some
wood an' bent it,
An' soon he had a banjo made—de fust dat
wuz invented.

He wet de ledder, stretched it on; made bridge
an' screws an' aprin;
An' fitted in a proper neck—'twuz berry long
an' tap'rin';
He tuk some tin, an' twisted him a thimble
fur to ring it;
An' den de mighty question riz: how wuz he
gwine to string it?

De 'possum had as fine a tail as dis dat I's
a-singin';
De ha'r's so long an' thick an' strong,—des fit
fur banjo-stringin';
Dat nigger shaved 'em off as short as wash-day-
dinner graces;
An' sorted ob 'em by size, f'om little E's to basses.

He strung her, tuned her, struck a jig,—
'twuz "Nebber min' de wedder"—
She soun' like forty-lebben bands a-playin'
all togedder;
Some went to partin'; some to dancin': Noah
called de figgers;
An' Ham he sot an' knocked de tune, de happiest
ob niggers!
Now, sence dat time—it's mighty strange—dere's
not de slightes' showin'

Ob any ha'r at all upon de 'possum's tail a-growin';
An' curi's, too, dat nigger's ways: his people
    nebber los' 'em—
For whar you finds de nigger—dar's de banjo an'
    de 'possum!

———————

The night is spent; and as the day
Throws up the first faint flash of gray,
The guests pursue their homeward way;
And through the field beyond the gin,
Just as the stars are going in,
See Santa Claus departing—grieving—

His own dear Land of Cotton leaving.
His work is done; he fain would rest
Where people know and love him best.
He pauses, listens, looks about;
But go he must: his pass is out.
So, coughing down the rising tears,
He climbs the fence and disappears.
And thus observes a colored youth
(The common sentiment, in sooth):
"Oh! what a blessin' 'tw'd ha' been,
Ef Santa had been born a twin!
We'd hab two Chrismuses a yeah—
Or p'r'aps *one* brudder'd *settle* heah!"

Even the Ministers Liked the Races

CHARLES FRASER

Mellow-ripe recollections of older days in South Carolina were provided in 1854 by Charles Fraser, with his Reminiscences of Charleston. *In love with the rice capital as were many of its people, Mr. Fraser sighed over the light-hearted atmosphere, the town's indulgent spirit, its occasionally rigid etiquette and its French element, which has given its names and its identities to various aspects of the special Southern culture at the meeting place of the Ashley and Cooper rivers.*

(MR. Fraser recalled the height of the races:)

They made Charleston the great center for all who could afford to travel, even from distant parts of the state. The enthusiasm produced by their recurrence pervaded all classes of the community to such a degree as scarcely could be now conceived. Schools were dismissed. The judges, not unwillingly, adjourned the courts, for they were deserted by lawyers, suitors and witnesses. Clergymen thought it no impropriety to see a well-contested race; and if grave physicians played truant, they were sure to be found in the crowd on the race ground.

Every stable in the city was emptied—every saddle and bridle put into requisition, and those who could produce neither horse, saddle nor bridle enlisted as pedestrians. The course itself presented quite a showy and animated spectacle, from the number of well-dressed and well-mounted horsemen, and from the display of equipages and liveries.

The whole week was devoted to pleasure and the interchanges of conviviality; nor were the ladies unnoticed, for the Race ball, given to them by the Jockey Club, was always the most splendid of the season. But, in all this round of gaiety and enjoyment, business was not neglected. For throughout the country, its engagements were generally postponed to the race week in Charleston, where the planter came to settle accounts with his factor, or to receive the proceeds of his crops, as well as to pay off the annual bills of the merchant who had supplied him with groceries and other articles throughout the past year; for before the days of banks, all credits were annual, and dependent upon crops. The circulation of money thus produced had its effect, no doubt, in enhancing the general good humor.

(Mr. Fraser, recalling the tea tables of earlier days in Charleston, mused over the contrasting life of the ancient Romans:)

But what more need we say than that their most magnificent houses wanted that focus of social and personal comfort, a fireside; and that they were strangers to the attractions of the *tea table*, that great engine, by whose well-regulated steam, more has been done for the humanizing of modern society, than all the contrivances of art, or than all the ceremonious courtesies of chivalry. Indeed, what production of the earth . . . has been more profuse and universal in its blessings than the Tea-plant?

How often have I reflected upon the unfortunate privations to which our Mothers of the Revolution were subjected, by that odious tax which abridged their evening enjoyment, and banished from their parlors that little household altar, whose incense and libations were so grateful and exhilarating. But this was their first lessons in that course of suffering which, as they became familiar with it, exhibited their powers of endurance, and

that public spirit which made the name of a Carolina matron one of honour and distinction.

I remember when a tea-table was the center of polished intercourse, and the great attraction of elegant society in Charleston. Its *reunions* were not only a bond of domestic harmony, but often drew neighbours together. It was a common custom for ladies to send their compliments to a friend early after breakfast, saying that if not engaged in the evening, they would take tea with her. An agreeable party was thus often unexpectedly made up, and, however large, it did not exempt the lady of the house from performing the duties of the tea-table, which, in those times, with its rich display of china and plate, was an object of no ordinary interest in a drawing-room, and in every respect worthy of the fair hands that dispensed its honours.

In regard to their intellectual improve-

Slave auctions were held in most seaport towns of the old South.

ment, the ladies who grew up with the Revolution laboured, as we may well conceive, under great disadvantages. Their education was interrupted and their personal accomplishments necessarily much neglected. But the books placed in their hands were judiciously selected from the shelves of the domestic library, and better calculated to improve their minds than those trashy novels and romances which afterwards became so popular.

(Mr. Fraser's mind returned to earlier days of hoops, brocades, laced ruffles and high-heeled shoes:)

But one thing I do remember, which is that the ladies did not give up gay society as early as we do now. The matronly appearance of the elder proportion of them gave dignity to the gayest assemblies of the young, without being any restraint upon their enjoyment.

I remember once, as a row of them sat together in a ball-room, hearing them compared to a Roman Senate, and I have often since thought how sternly they would have frowned upon those graceless and exceptionable dances which the corrupt fashions of Europe are recommending to our imitation....

Dancing is now exclusively the amusement of the young. But not so formerly. An elderly lady once told me that at the first public assembly she attended after the (Revolutionary) war, the ball was opened by a minuet between General Multrie, in full regimentals, and a lady of suitable years, whom he afterwards married.... It was very common for both married gentlemen and married ladies to enter into the spirit of a country dance....

Fashion is that unwritten law which regulates the intercourse of society. Those who are independent in everything else, yield it almost an unconditional obedience. . . . I have seen instances of display in our ball-rooms, in the days of low-necked dresses and sleeveless robes, which would shock a young lady of the present time; and yet, what would have been thought *then* of a young lady who would have dared to exhibit in public, as an appendage to her person, such a monstrosity of form as that produced by a well-stuffed bustle, attracting all eyes to a point where they could not meet the reproof of her own.

In no part of female fashions do I remember a greater variety than in the head-dress. When I was a boy, the hair was suffered to hang over the shoulders in all its native length and profusion, and the longest tresses were always most admired. After that, and until the year 1800, no lady ever appeared in grand costume without first submitting to the operations of the hair-dresser; and those artists were in such demand upon the occasion of a great public ball, that they had to commence their important labours the day before it; and it was not uncommon for a lady, after having had her hair frizzed up into a grand *coiffure*, to pass a whole night in an upright position, for fear of disturbing it. In addition to this, powder, either brown or white, as best suited the complexion, was used, and patches, also, which history informs us, was a very common custom amongst the sex.

But in 1800, wigs and turbans became fashionable, and were thought just as essential to beauty as any style of dress that had preceded it. Neither brown, nor black, nor auburn, nor flaxed locks could escape the inexorable decree of fashion. And the scissors, like those of the fates, triumphed over all their beauty and luxuriancy. The custom of wearing wigs is supposed to have proceeded from the quantities of beautiful hair cut off from the victims of the guillotine. Hair became even an article of commerce. A merchant in extensive business once told me that during the prevalence of that fashion, he had received a consignment of a case or trunk of beautiful tresses that had come from France.

(The start of the Revolution in France, Mr. Fraser noted, drew a warm response in Charleston, with its many Gallic ties:)

The period . . . exhibited the most extravagant and enthusiastic sympathy in behalf of the French Revolution. The tri-colored cockade was generally worn. The American and French colors waved together at public entertainments. Civic feasts were given by the privateermen, and patronized by some of our most distinguished inhabitants, who did not hesitate, when the *bonnet rouge* was circulated round the table, to put it on, and then pass it to their neighbour. The cognomen of *citoyen* was the order of the day. Their cards of invitation were always addressed to Citizen *such a one*. On occasion of one of these civic festivals, given by Citizen Boutelle, captain of the little privateer *Sanspareille*, a guinea was placed under each plate as a pledge of fraternity.

But, finding that this offering was unpalatable to his guests, on the next occasion he changed it for a play ticket. I remember the privateermen parading our streets with long sabres at their sides, and assuming quite an ascendency in our community. They even had rendezvous opened in Charleston for volunteers, which the Governor, by an order of April, 1793, directed to be closed. They had also their Jacobin Clubs and public gambling houses. . . .

(Mr. Fraser found a newspaper account of a "grand civic pageant" of January, 1793, in which Charleston leaders honored the National Assembly of revolutionary France:)

. . . So great was the public enthusiasm that on the eve of that day, the bells of St. Michael's were chimed, and a salute of thirteen guns fired by the artillery. The same honours were repeated on the morning following, and in the course of the day a procession of French and American citizens paraded the streets of Charleston, headed by the Governor, the Chief Justice, Consul Mangourit, in full costume, the orator of the day, the Rev. Mr. Coste, pastor of the French Church, the Judges, Chancellors, Speaker and all other public officers. . . . In passing before the French Protestant Church, the Consul, as an expiation for the persecutions of Louis XIV against that church, halted the procession, took off his hat and saluted it with the national colours. . . . In the afternoon a grand fete was given at Williams Coffee-house, prepared for 250 persons. Two sets of toasts, French and English, were drunk. . . . It was truly a day of fraternization, and ended harmoniously. . . .

I remember a little French hair-dresser.

Dubard was a violent Sansculotte, and went to France upon a short visit at the height of the Revolution, to feast his eyes upon the sanguinary scenes that were then daily enacted there. The guillotining of Marie Antoinette was the climax of his enjoyment; and he returned to Charleston full of the interesting theme and used to entertain his customers with it, whilst sitting under the operation of his frizzing and his powder-puff, for everybody (both ladies and gentlemen) was powdered in those days, and never ventured into company without a grand *coiffure*. . . .

I remember that the French Revolution and that of St. Domingo occasioned the removal of many individuals to our community, who taught dancing, music and drawing and other accomplishments which before that time could only have been obtained abroad. It was computed in the year 1807 that there were in our city thirteen teachers of the several branches of female accomplishments, all of whom were French. . . .

The awful tragedy of St. Domingo threw on our shores a crowd of miserable and destitute French, with every claim that humanity could recognize to commiseration and relief. These claims were promptly and honourably answered by the people of Charleston. All who could afford to shelter them admitted them into their families; whilst all who could not do that, relieved them otherwise, readily and cheerfully, to the very extent of their means. And it is a recollection, personally gratifying to myself, that I was employed, then a boy, upon errands of charity to these unfortunate beings.

The great increase of French population in Charleston, and their national fondness for theatrical amusements, led to the establishment of a French theatre, which was opened on the 12th April, 1794, with a good company of comedians, pantomimists, rope dancers, etc. My liveliest recollection of it is the frantic enthusiasm with which the privateermen used to accompany the orchestra when playing the *Marseillaise* or *Ça ira*. It continued popular for some little time and then fell through, for want of encouragement.

"Mr. Washington, Dressed in Hannah's Short Gown and Petticoat"

EDMUND S. MORGAN

From diaries, letters or related accounts comes the following lively material which reflects the humor, the occasional charm and zestful amusements of plantation Virginians of the 1700's. I know of few more skillful presentations of the private life of the upper South. It is taken from Edmund S. Morgan's Virginians at Home, *Colonial Williamsburg, 1952.*

THERE were plenty of opportunities for the children of the first families to meet each other at the balls and entertainments which formed part of the high life of colonial Virginia. Probably many a match began in the formal banter which passed between couples engaged in the steps of a minuet or a country dance. The gentleman would pour out a string of extravagant compliments while the lady blushed and protested. Soon perhaps the gentleman would come visiting the lady at her father's plantation, and if his character and financial qualifications were in order, might eventually ask for her hand.

At this point both he and the lady were obliged to follow a ritual which required considerable dramatic skill. Though everyone agreed that marriage must be a union of properly proportioned worldly fortunes, nevertheless convention demanded that the actual proposal take place in an atmosphere of almost religious formality. The lady must be approached with fear and trembling as a kind of saint, the lover prostrating himself either literally or figuratively before her, while she betrayed great surprise and distress at the whole idea of marriage and agreed to consider the proposition only after much protestation. Sometimes a lover could not bring himself to undertake so excruciating a performance in person and would commit his proposal to writing, but even then the lady must go through the form of protest before agreeing.

A charming letter, from Anne Blair of Williamsburg to her sister Mrs. George Braxton, describes a young Virginia belle's reaction to a letter of proposal:

"She was in a little Pett, but it was a very becoming one, let me tell you. A glowing blush suffused o'er her face attended with a trembling, insomuch that in extending her arm to reach me *the creature's insolence* I thought the Paper would have fallen from her Hand. The emotions I saw her in did not fail of exciting the curiosity in me natural to all our Sex, so that a dog would not have caught more eagerly at a bone he was likely to lose than I did at the fulsome stuff (as she call'd it) tho' must own on perusal was charmed with the elegance of his stile: and I dare say he might with truth declare his love for her to equal that of Mark Anthony's for Cleopatra. She thought proper to turn his letter back again with just a line or two signifying the disagreeableness, &c. &c. of the subject. . . . There are several others Dancing and coopeeing about her, may they scrape all the skin off their shins stepping over the benches at Church in endeavoring who sho'd be first to hand her in the Chariot."

.   .   .

Virginians enjoyed hospitality so much that they spent a great deal of time simply in visiting one another, quite apart from the large-scale get-togethers at barbecues, balls and fish-feasts. Usually the visit was only a morning or afternoon call. Virginians liked to ride, and often they would make a visit to a neighboring plantation the excuse for a

"Rounding a Bend" on the Mississippi

A home on the Mississippi

canter. Sometimes they made longer visits to friends and relations who lived at some distance. The wealthier families were almost all related in some way by blood or marriage, and it was thought proper to keep in communication with all one's aunts, uncles and cousins. . . . Young people who were not yet troubled with the responsibilities of running a plantation . . . might go off on a round of visits lasting for several weeks. One of the most delightful documents that has survived from colonial Virginia is the journal of a young lady who with several companions made a tour of her friends' homes in 1782, staying a few days with each, gossiping, flirting and dancing.

The most entertaining visit was that which she paid to the Washingtons (relatives of the General), who were fond of practical jokes. "About sunset," she writes, "Nancy, Milly and myself took a walk in the Garden (it is a most butifull place.) We were mighty busy cutting thistles to try our sweethearts, when Mr. Washington caught us; and you can't conceive how he plagued us—chased us all over the Garden, and was quite impertinent." After they went to bed, the girls got hungry and decided to raid the larder: "We took it into our heads to want to eat; well, we had a large dish of bacon and beaf; after that, a bowl of Sago cream; and after that, an apple pye. While were were eating the apple pye in bed—God bless you, making a great noise—in came Mr. Washington, dressed in Hannah's short gown and petticoat, and seazed me and kissed me twenty times, in spite of all the resistance I could make; and then Cousin Molly. Hannah soon follow'd dress'd in his Coat. They joined in eating the apple pye, and then went out. After this we took it into our heads to want to eat oysters. We got up, put on our rappers, and went down in the Seller to get them: do you think Mr. Washington did not

follow us and scear us just to death. We went up tho, and eat our oysters. We slept in the old Lady's room too, and she sat laughing fit to kill herself at us."

.   .   .

Families living in town . . . could enjoy familiar visits in the afternoon and evening without having to make an expedition. Groups would gather informally to gossip and sing songs and discuss the latest news from London. An enchanting episode that occurred in Williamsburg in the year 1769 was recorded by Anne Blair:

"Mrs. Dawson's Family stay'd the Evening with us, and the Coach was at the door to carry them Home by ten o'clock; but every one appearing in great spirits, it was proposed to set at the Step's and Sing a few Song's which was no sooner said than done; while thus we were employ'd, a Candle & Lanthorn was observed to be coming up Street; (except Polly Clayton censuring their ill taste, for having a Candle such a fine Night) no one took any notice of it—till we saw, who ever it was, stopt to listen to our enchanting Notes—each Warbler was immediately silenced; whereupon, the invader to our Melody, call'd out in a most rapturous Voice, Charming! Charming! proceed for God sake, or I go Home directly—no sooner were those words utter'd, then all as with one consent sprung from their Seats, and the Air eccho'd with 'pray, Walk in my Lord;' No—indeed, he would not, he would set on the Step's too; so after a few ha, ha's, and being told what we all knew—that it was a delightfull Evening, at his desire we strew'd the way over with Flowers &c. &c. till a full half hour was elaps'd, when all retir'd to their respective Homes."

The visitor, Lord Botetour, was one of the most popular royal governors Virginia ever had. Yet it was only a few years later that the last royal governor, Lord Dunmore, fled from Virginia, taking with him the cordial hatred of the inhabitants and the last shred of British authority in the colony.

The Opportunity to Choose His Own Name

BOOKER T. WASHINGTON

Not until the post-Confederate period could Southerners and other Americans learn of many phases of another side of Southern life from the writings of former slaves such as Booker T. Washington. This early Negro leader in his Up From Slavery, *published in 1901, wrote simply and persuasively of the difficulties before the emancipated men and women of his day. There is conviction and pathos in the following passages from the book. The first head of Tuskegee Institute—formed about 1880 by a onetime slave master and a former bondsman—was less liberal than later Negro spokesmen of their people. Before his death in 1915 Booker Washington made appearances in many parts of the United States before whites and Negroes, emphasizing trades training for members of the race.*

I KNOW nothing of my ancestry beyond my mother. My mother was a slave on a plantation near Hale's Ford, in Franklin County, Virginia, and she was, as I now remember it, the cook for her owners as well as for a large part of the slaves on the plantation. The first time that I got a knowledge of the fact that my mother and I were slaves, was by being awakened by my mother early one morning, while I was sleeping in a bed of rags, on a clay floor of our little cabin.

She was kneeling over me, fervently praying as was her custom to do, that some day she and her children might be free. The name of my mother was Jane. She, to me, will always remain the noblest embodiment of womanhood with whom I have come in contact. She was wholly ignorant, as far as books were concerned, and, I presume, never had a book in her hands for two minutes at a time. But the lessons in virtue and thrift which she instilled into me during the short period of my life that she lived will never leave me. Some people blame the Negro for not being more honest, as judged by the Anglo-Saxon's standard of honesty; but I can recall many times when, after all was dark and still, in the late hours of the night when her children had been without sufficient food during the day, my mother would awaken us, and we would find that she had gotten from somewhere something in the way of eggs or chickens and had cooked them during the night for us.

These eggs and chickens were gotten without my master's permission or knowledge. Perhaps, by some code of ethics, this would be classed as stealing, but deep down in my heart I can never decide that my mother, under such circumstances, was guilty of theft. Had she acted thus as a free woman she would have been a thief, but not so, in my opinion, as a slave. After our freedom no one was stricter than my mother in teaching and observing the highest rules of integrity.

Who my father was, or is, I have never been able to learn with any degree of certainty. I only know that he was a white man. As nearly as I can get at the facts, I was born in the year 1858 or 1859. At the time I came into the world no careful registry of births of people of my complexion was kept. My birth place was near Hale's Ford . . . about as near to Nowhere as any locality gets to be. . . .

I remember very distinctly the appearance of the cabin in which I was born and lived until freedom came. It was a small log cabin about 12 x 16 feet, and without windows. There was no floor, except a dirt one. There was a large opening in the center of the floor, where sweet potatoes were kept for my master's family during the winter. In this cabin my mother did the cooking, the greater part of the time, for my master's family. Our bed, or "pallet," as we called it, was made every night on the dirt floor. Our bed clothing consisted of a few rags gathered here and there.

One thing I remember more vividly than any other in connection with the days when I was a slave was my dress, or, rather, my lack of dress. The years that the war was in progress between the States were especially trying to the slaves, so far as clothing was concerned. The Southern white people found it extremely hard to get clothing for themselves during that war, and, of course, the slaves underwent no little suffering in this respect. The only garment that I remember receiving from my owners during the war was a "tow shirt." When I did not wear this shirt I was positively without any garment. In Virginia, the tow shirt was quite an institution during slavery. This shirt was made of the refuse flax that grew in that part of Virginia, and it was a veritable instrument of torture. It was stiff and coarse. Until it had been worn for about six weeks it made one feel as if a thousand needle points were pricking his flesh.

I suppose I was about six years old when I was given one of these shirts to wear. After repeated trials the torture was more than my childish flesh could endure and I gave it up in despair. To this day the sight of a new shirt revives the recollection of the torture of my first new shirt. In the midst of my despair, in connection with this garment, my brother John, who was about two years older than I, did me a kindness which I shall never forget. He volunteered to wear my new shirt for me until it was "broken in." After he had worn it for several weeks I ventured to wear it myself, but not without pain. . . .

As soon as I was old enough I performed what, to me, was important service, in holding the horses and riding behind the white women of the household on their long horseback rides, which were very common in those days. At one time, while holding the horses and assisting quite a party of visiting ladies to mount their horses, I remember that, just before the visitors rode away a tempting plate of ginger cakes was brought out and handed around to the visitors. This, I think, was the first time that I had ever seen any ginger cakes, and a very deep impression was made upon my childish mind. I remember I said to myself that if I could ever get to the point where I could eat ginger cakes as I saw those ladies eating them the height of my ambition would be reached.

When I grew to be still larger and stronger the duty of going to the mill was intrusted to me; that is, a large sack containing three or four bushels of corn was thrown across the back of a horse and I would ride away to the mill, which was often three or four miles distant, wait at the mill until the corn was turned into meal, and then bring it home. More than once, while performing this service, the corn or meal got unevenly balanced on the back of the horse and fell off into the road, carrying me with it. This left me in a very awkward and unfortunate position. I, of course, was unable, with my small strength, to lift the corn or meal upon the horse's back, and, therefore would have to wait, often for hours, until someone happened to be passing along the road strong enough to replace the burden for me.

My owner's name was Jones Burroughs, and I am quite sure he was above the average in the treatment of his slaves. That is, except in a few cases they were not cruelly whipped. Although I was born a slave, I was too young to experience much of its hardships. The thing in connection with slavery that has left the deepest impression on me was the instance of seeing a grown man, my uncle, tied to a tree early one morning, stripped naked and someone whipping him with a cowhide. As each blow touched his back the cry, "Pray, master! Pray, master!" came from his lips, and made an impression upon my boyish heart that I shall carry with me to my grave.

When I was still quite a child, I could hear the slaves in our "quarters" whispering in subdued tones that something unusual—the war—was about to take place, and that it meant their freedom. These whispered conferences continued, especially at night, until the war actually began. While there was not a single slave on our plantation that could read a line, in some way we were kept informed of the progress of the war almost as accurately as

Framed by massive trees, Spanish dagger plants and palmettos, Oak Alley along the Mississippi is a pink Doric temple in the sunlight.

the most intelligent person. The "grapevine" telegraph was in constant use. When Lee surrendered all of the plantation people knew it, although all of them acted as if they were in ignorance of the fact that anything unusual had taken place.

Early one morning, just after the close of the war, word was sent around to the slave cabins that all the slaves must go to the "big house," the master's house; and in company with my mother and a large number of other slaves, including my sister Amanda and brother John, I went to the "big house," and stood by the side of my mother, and listened to the reading of some papers and a little speech made by the one who read the papers. This was the first public address I had ever heard, and I need not add that it was the most effective one to which it had ever been my privilege to listen. After the reading of the paper and the speech, my mother leaned over and whispered, "Now, my children, we are free." This act was hailed with joy by all the slaves, but it threw a tremendous responsibility upon my mother, as well as upon the other slaves. A large portion of the former slaves hired themselves to their owners, while others sought new employment; but, before the beginning of the new life, most of the ex-slaves left the plantation for a few days at least, so as to get the "hang" of the new life, and to be sure that they were free. My mother's husband, my stepfather, had in some way wandered into West Virginia during the war, and had secured employment in the salt furnace near Malden, in Kanawha county. Soon after freedom was declared he sought out my mother and sent a wagon to bring her and her children to West Virginia. After many days of slow, tiresome traveling over the mountains, during which we suffered much, we finally reached Malden, and my mother and her husband were united after a long enforced separation.

The trip from Franklin county to Malden, West Virginia, was the first one that had taken me out of the county where I was born, and, of course, it was quite an event, especially to the children of the family, although the parting from the old homestead was to my mother a very serious affair. All of our household and other goods were packed into a small wagon drawn by two horses or mules. I cannot recall how many days it took us to make this trip, but it seems to me, as I recall it now, that we were at least ten days. Of course we had to sleep in the wagon, or what was more often true, on the ground. The children walked a great portion of the distance.

. . .

Soon after we reached West Virginia a school teacher, Mr. William Davis, came into the community, and the colored people induced him to open a school. My stepfather was not able to spare me from work, so that I could not attend this school when it first opened, and this proved a sore disappointment to me.

I remember that soon after going to Malden, West Virginia, I saw a young colored man among a large number of colored people, reading a newspaper, and this fired my ambition to learn to read as nothing had done before. Although I could not attend the school, I remember that, in some way, my mother secured a book for me, and although she could not read herself, she tried in every way possible to help me to do so. In some way, I cannot now recall how, I learned my letters while working in the salt furnace and coal mines.

As time went on, after considerable persuasion on my part, my stepfather consented to permit me to attend the public school half of the day, provided I would get up very early in the morning and perform as much work as possible before school time. This permission brought me great joy. By four o'clock in the morning I was up and at my work, which continued until nearly nine o'clock.

The first day I entered school, it seems to me, was the happiest day that I have ever known. The first embarrassment I experienced was in the matter of finding a name. I had always been called "Booker" and had not known that one had use for more than one name. Some of the slaves took the surnames of their owners, but after freedom there was a prejudice against doing this. When the teacher called the roll, I noticed that he called each pupil by two names, a given one and a surname.

When he came to me I told him to put

Slowly filling up, Washington City of 1834 gave hint of the transformation that would occur
in this onetime vista of "magnificent distances" and not much else.

The neat, half-somnolent village of Georgetown stands in relief in this lithograph of about 1855.

me down as "Booker Washington," and that name I have borne ever since. In introducing me to an audience in Essex Hall, London, during my visit to Europe in the summer of 1899, Honorable Joseph H. Choate, the American Ambassador, said that I was one of the few Americans that had had the opportunity of choosing his own name, and in exercising the rare privilege I had very naturally chosen the best name there was on the list.

There Is Charm in a Pretty Foot

J. C. GUILD

There is love of the ladies, but of a kind far different from that of the chivalric tournaments, in the following words by Judge J. C. Guild of Nashville, regarding pre-war days in the rural South. Very much sui generis *was the judge, who conducted his court in a forthright and highly personal way and otherwise indulged in a strong individualism. As time passed, His Honor formed the habit of expressing his views without much regard for Dame Fashion, Mrs. Grundy or anybody else. These passages from his* Old Times in Tennessee, *published in 1878 in Nashville, have a refreshingly unconventional flavor.*

WE are fallen upon evil times—carrying pistols—dress and parade—giving entertainments attended with extraordinary expenditures, such as no honest calling can afford. Too much extravagance and too little work, are the fruitful causes of most of the evils of our time. . . .

Whenever young men put on broadcloth, silks, kid-gloves, and "prunellas," attend upon gambling houses and saloons and idle away their precious time, they are sure to fall into vicious habits; such characters as those who loiter about whisky shops and attend regularly upon gambling hells think themselves disgraced if they have not "killed their man." . . .

In writing about lovely women, we should always use a pen made of a quill plucked from an eagle's wing, dipped in the hues of the rainbow, upon rose-tinted paper, sprinkled with the dust from the wings of the beautiful butterfly—but I am constrained to notice the present extravagance in dress. Six yards of calico in ancient times made a dress that copied nature and displayed the comeliness of form and beautiful figure of lovely woman. Now it takes *twenty!* and, if silks are used, forty yards;

they carry on their backs from ten to fifteen yards, puckered, pinned and cruppered up so tight that they cannot step more than six inches at a time.

The other day I was at the depot at Nashville and two beautiful girls endeavored to raise their feet high enough to get upon the steps which lead into the cars; after repeated efforts and as many failures, I saw the dilemma and stepped up and *lifted* them into the car. . . . In earlier times families were clothed at home by their honest labor; the boys in their jeans and copperas cotton, and the girls in their beautiful strips of cotton and linsey. . . . One cannot tell now which is the girl and which is the dress. I have looked about over this vast assembly to see if I could not find one of those beautiful striped dresses, setting off the rosy mountain pinks of the present day, but the ancient customs have disappeared since I've been gone.

In those days but few mothers or daughters ever had a calico dress, to say nothing of the silks, cashmeres, muslins, crepes and poplins of the present. When a lady went to Dover or Palmyra, our commercial cities in those days, and bought a calico dress, it aroused and excited the whole community more than the killing of a bear, caught in the cowpen. When a calico dress was purchased, it spread like a wildfire. It was "norated" abroad. . . .

We had meeting houses made of logs and clapboards. We called it going to meeting. The elegant phrase now is to attend church, and we go in buggies and carriages. Then we walked from three to five miles in going to meeting, playing with the girls all the way. I have seen not further than five miles from this place, from fifty to one hundred ladies walking barefooted to meeting, carrying their shoes and stockings in their hands, and on arriving near the meeting house, sit down along the branch, wash their beautiful feet, and put on their stockings and shoes. There is a charm in a pretty foot. . . .

In those days our women did not deform their persons with artificial works about the head in the form of rats, chignons and waterfalls. There was no rouge, bespattering the rosy cheek, marring its natural beauty; nor were their beautiful forms destroyed by the hoop or bustle. There was no one taken in by false appearances. The match was a fair one upon both sides. . . .

The fair sex are now so disguised by art and dress, that the natural beauty of the person is lost in the polonaise, the redingote, the overskirt, the basque, the jacket, the false calves. . . . I would as soon put my hand on a muskrat as on one of those artificial things used to disguise the person.

Man can do nothing in the correction of these abuses, but must work himself to death and foot the bills. It is for the fair women of the land, who alone have the power and can successfully move in this great work. Man in his nature is unfit to govern himself or control the destinies of the world. They are the instruments, however, in the hands of women, by which great revolutions and reforms are made. We can do nothing without lovely woman. She fires the heart and nerves the arm to great and glorious deeds. Who would live without a woman? her beauty and heaven-born influence? If there is such a man, he is a Comanche, and should be made to join his tribe in the far distant West. . . .

In nice, striped homespun dresses a fair daughter would look more lovely, more beautiful, and carry captive the heart of a man worth having, much sooner and more effectually than could the woman who appeared at Washington lately covered with jewels and diamonds costing from $50,000 to $100,000. No wonder the government is robbed and plundered. . . . I would as lief be bit by a rattlesnake as have such a woman for my wife.

How changed the times! The country dance, the old-fashioned reel, has long since disappeared, and in its place we have the entree and quadrille, lancers, waltz, polka, redows, schottische, galop and the mazurka, all of which consist in bowing and trotting about, no display of the person or its charms. It is an artistic abandonment of the ancient dance, in which the young girls and young men distinguished themselves. . . .

The music of the wheel and the playing of the loom are rarely heard; the piano and the organ have taken their places. Instead of the old sentimental songs, that moved the heart and stirred the soul, we have the operatic thing that they call music, for the learned, and what is called the chaste and cultivated ear. When I hear a man say that he is not moved by our ancient and sentimental songs, but has a learned and chaste ear for the opera, I put him down as an ass, as a man fit for stratagem, treason, and spoils.

How to Insure an Election

DAVY CROCKETT

The redoubtable Crockett, part hunter, part Indian fighter, part politician, part legend, epitomizes a Southern era and area. A "coonskin Congressman," some called him when he arrived in Washington as a frontiersman of the late 1820's, representing the Western part of Tennessee. Self-educated and only lightly educated at that, he was loud, brash, opinionated, but when he played jokester for a crowd at a meeting or in an inn, hundreds slapped knees and roared over Davy's homespun (and definitely virile) humor, his frequently wild tales of doings in the woods and small settlements of the South and South-west. Enemies of Andrew Jackson used the shrewd Davy in fighting that democratic spokesman; after several years, running again, he opposed a wooden-legged candidate, whom he described caustically as "Old Timbertoes." Losing the race, he expressed his revulsion at political doings by going to Texas. There, in 1836, Crockett joined the defense of the Alamo and went down heroically under Mexican fire. Some writings credited to him were set down or at least "edited" by others. The following speech, believed to be authentic in essence, was delivered by Davy on his trip to the West. It appears in The Life of David Crockett, *published in Philadelphia in 1865. The scene was Little Rock, Arkansas.*

"ATTEND all public meetings," says I, "and get some friends to move that you take the chair; if you fail in this attempt, make a push to be appointed secretary; the proceedings of course will be published, and your name introduced to the public. But should you fail in both undertakings, get two or three acquaintances, over a bottle of whiskey, to pass some resolutions, no matter on what subject; publish them even if you pay the printer—it will answer the purpose of breaking the ice, which is the main point in these matters. Intrigue until you are elected an officer of the militia; this is the second step towards promotion, and can be accomplished with ease, as I know an instance of an election being advertised, and no one attending, the innkeeper at whose house it was to be held, having a military turn, elected himself colonel of his regiment." Says I, "You may not accomplish your ends with as little difficulty, but do not be discouraged—Rome wasn't built in a day.

"If your ambition or circumstances compel you to serve your country, and earn three dollars a day, by becoming a member of the legislature, you must first publicly avow that the constitution of the state is a shackle upon free and liberal legislation; and is, therefore, of as little use in the present enlightened age, as an old almanac of the year in which the instrument was framed. There is policy in this measure, for by making the constitution a mere dead letter, your headlong proceedings will be attributed to a bold and unshackled mind; whereas, it might otherwise be thought they arose from sheer mulish ignorance. 'The Government' has set the example in his attack upon the constitution of the United States, and who should fear to follow where 'the Government' leads?

"When the day of election approaches, visit your constituents far and wide. Treat liberally, and drink freely, in order to rise in their estimation, though you fall in your own. True, you may be called a drunken dog by some of the clean shirt and silk stocking gentry, but the real rough necks will style you a jovial fellow, their votes are certain, and frequently count double. Do all you can to appear to advantage in the eyes of the women. That's easily done—you have but to kiss and slabber their children, wipe their noses, and pat them on the head; this cannot fail to please their mothers, and you may rely on your business being done in that quarter.

'Promise all that is asked," said I, "and more if you can think of anything. Offer to build a bridge or a church, to divide a county, create a batch of new offices, make a turnpike, or anything they like. Promises cost nothing, therefore deny nobody who has a vote or sufficient influence to obtain one.

"Get up on all occasions, and sometimes on no occasion at all, and make long-winded speeches, though composed of nothing else than wind—talk of your devotion to your country, your modesty and disinterestedness, or on any such fanciful subject. Rail against taxes of all kinds, office-holders, and bad harvest weather; and wind up with a flourish about the heroes who fought and bled for our liberties in the times that tried men's souls. To be sure you run the risk of being considered a bladder of wind, or an empty barrel, but never mind that, you will find enough of the same fraternity to keep you in countenance.

"If any charity be going forward, be at the top of it, provided it is to be advertised publicly; if not, it isn't worth your while. None but a fool would place his candle under a bushel on such an occasion.

"These few directions," said I, "if properly attended to, will do your business; and when once elected, why a fig for the dirty children, the promises, the bridges, the churches, the taxes, the offices, and the subscriptions, for it is absolutely necessary to forget all these before you can become a thoroughgoing politician, and a patriot of the first water."

Fools, Fops and Men's Faces Remembered

L. J. BIGELOW

During the last century, dozens of older Southern lawyers drew on their well-packed memories for tales of their day regarding deeds and foibles of their friends of the legal profession or the judiciary. In his Bench and Bar, *published in New York in 1871, L. J. Bigelow offered a wide range of recollections about men of several states. They reflect a taste for the pricking of the stuffed shirt, the confounding of the self-important, and the prodigal deeds of well-known characters. Such stories are characteristic of Southerners' liking for anecdotal material.*

IT is known that Henry Clay was remarkable for his recollection of faces. A curious incident of this wonderful power is told of his visit to Jackson, Mississippi. . . . The cars stopped at Clinton for a few moments, when an eccentric but strongminded old man made his way up, exclaiming, "Don't introduce me, for I want to see if Mr. Clay will know me."

"Where did I know you?" said Mr. Clay.

"In Kentucky."

Mr. Clay struck his long, bony finger upon his forehead, as if in deep thought. "Have you lost that eye since I saw you, or had you lost it then?"

"Since," said the man.

"Then turn the sound side of your face to me, that I may get your profile."

Mr. C. paused for a moment, his thoughts running back many years. "I have it!" said he. "Did you not give me a verdict as juror, at

Frankfort, Kentucky, in the great case of the United States *vs.* Innis, twenty one years ago?"

"I did! I did!" said the overjoyed man.

"And is not your name," said Mr. Clay, "Hardwicke?"

"It is, it is," replied Dr. Hardwicke, bursting into tears. "Did I not tell you," he said to his friends, "that he knew me, even though I have not seen him from that time to this? Great men never forget faces."

.   .   .

Judge Underwood of Georgia, had a supreme contempt for fops. A dandy remarked of a gentlemanly planter who was passing that it would be a fine speculation to buy that man for what he *was* worth, and sell him for what he *thought* he was worth.

"Well," says the judge, "I have often seen men selling jackasses, but this is the first time I ever heard of a jackass offering to sell a gentleman."

The judge was a staunch Clay Whig, but his son, J. W. H. Underwood, was continually changing his politics. A friend asked, "What are John's politics?" "Really," said the judge, "I can't tell you; I haven't seen the boy since breakfast."

John applied to the old gentleman for a letter of recommendation to his friend, then Governor Crawford of Georgia. It was immediately given and John put off for Milledgeville. But, knowing his father's eccentricities, he thought it prudent to open his credentials, and, to his astonishment, read the following:

"My dear friend,—this will be handed to you by my son John. He has the greatest thirst for an office, with the least capacity to fill one, of any boy you ever saw. Yours truly, William H. Underwood."

The judge had a great dislike to the town of Marietta, Georgia. While presiding in court at Marietta, he remarked to General Hamsell: "When my time comes, I am coming to Marietta to die."

"Ah! I'm glad you think so much of our little town."

"It is not that," replied the judge. "It's because I can leave it with less regret than any other place on the face of the earth."

Singularly enough, he did die there eventually. He arrived there about twelve o'clock,

was taken suddenly ill about one, and in half an hour was dead.

.   .   .

The Honorable Thomas F. Marshall of Kentucky, a prince of good fellows, was once, in a wild fever of dissipation, taken by a friend to a room in the Mansion House in Lexington. When there, Marshall found the old schoolboy warning that "what goes up must come down" entirely reversed, and his friend, hearing the upheavings, said:

"Are you unwell, Mr. Marshall?"

"Oh, no," was the reply. "Only throwing up for fun."

.   .   .

Governor Giles of Virginia once addressed a note to Patrick Henry, demanding satisfaction:

"Sir, I understand that you have called me a 'bob-tail' politician. I wish to know if it be true; and if true, your meaning. William B. Giles."

To which Mr. Henry replied in this wise: "Sir, I do not recollect having called you a bob-tailed politician at any time, but think it probable I have. Not recollecting the time or occasion, I can't say what I did mean, but if you will tell me what you think I meant, I will say whether you are correct or not. Very respectfully, Patrick Henry."

.   .   .

Seargent S. Prentiss, the great Southern orator, received a challenge from a wretched creature who lived in Vicksburg. Once respectable, the man had lost every thing but a certain physical courage that made him willing to take the chances of a duel with one of brilliant character who had never fired a pistol. The following morning Mr. Prentiss made up a bundle, with a letter neatly tied on the outside, and by the hands of his servant sent it to the challenger.

The principal and friends were confounded at such a proceeding. "Certainly," said they, "Mr. Prentiss must be profoundly ignorant of the 'laws of honor,' else he would not send an answer to a challenge by the hands of a nigger;" but the reading of the note set the matter at rest. It read as follows:

"Mr. —, I have received your challenge to

Changing slowly through the years is this Charleston scene, with St. Michael's long-familiar spire at the right and columned, galleried houses on both sides.

FOOLS, FOPS AND MEN'S FACES 137

mortal combat; before I can accept it, I insist that you shall have at least one quality of a gentleman, viz., be habited in a clean shirt, which desirable article I send you by the honest bearer of this note. Thus strengthened in your social position by a single quality that makes you worthy of my notice, I will then proceed to arrange farther preliminaries."

It is useless to say that the duel did not take place.

On Spitting and Other Topics

CHARLES DICKENS

Charles Dickens, widely popular among Americans as among English-men, came to the United States in 1842, to be lionized wherever he went. In Washington, D. C., Maryland, parts of Virginia, Kentucky and Missouri, Dickens looked about himself, found things for which he felt admiration and other things that repelled him. On subjects from the prevalence of crude spitting habits to slavery and back, Dickens wrote directly, incisively. Ending his trip, the English-man set down his famous American Notes, *which angered and hurt many people of the United States, including Southerners. (Through the years both natives and visitors commented on the extreme sensitivity of Americans to even the faintest of questions raised about their perfection or their perfectibility.) But when Dickens returned in 1867 the country welcomed him easily. The following passages are from the* American Notes, *London, 1842, and* The Life of Charles Dickens, *John Forster, London, 1872–74.*

AS Washington may be called the head quarters of tobacco-tinctured saliva, the time is come when I must confess, without any disguise, that the prevalence of those two odious practices of chewing and expectorating began about this time to be anything but agreeable, and soon became most offensive and sickening. In all the public places of America, this filthy custom is recognised. In the courts of law, the judge has his spittoon, the crier his, the witness his, and the prisoner his; while the jury-men and spectators are provided for, as so many men who in the course of nature must desire to spit incessantly. . . . In public buildings, visitors are implored, through notices, to squirt the essence of their quids, or "plugs," as I have heard them called by gentlemen learned in this kind of sweetmeat, into the national spittoons, and not about the bases of the marble columns. But in some parts this custom is inseparably mixed up with every meal and morning call, and with all the transactions of social life. . . .

On board this steamboat, there were two young gentlemen . . . who planted two seats in the middle of the deck, at a distance of some four paces apart; took out their tobacco-boxes; and sat down opposite each other, to chew. In less than a quarter of an hour's time, these hopeful youths had shed about them on the clean boards, a copious shower of yellow rain; clearing, by that means, a kind of magic circle, within whose limits no intruder dared to come. . . . This being before breakfast rather disposed me, I confess, to nausea; but looking attentively at one of the expectorators, I plainly saw that he was young in chewing and felt inwardly uneasy, himself. As I marked his face turn paler and paler . . . I could have fallen on his neck and implored him to go on for hours.

With wooden porches facing the locks, and chickens, ducks and children near the water,
this Virginia canal scene evokes the spirit of an earlier day.

I was surprised to learn that even steady old chewers of great experience, are not always good marksmen, which has rather inclined me to doubt that general proficiency with the rifle, of which we have heard so often in England. Several gentlemen called upon me, who in the course of conversation, frequently missed the spittoon at five paces; and one (but he was certainly short-sighted) mistook the closed sash for the open window, at three. On another occasion, when I dined out, and was sitting with two ladies and some gentlemen round a fire before dinner, one of the company fell short of the fire-place, six distinct times. I am disposed to think, however, that this was occasioned by his not aiming at that object, as there was a white marble hearth before the fender, which was more convenient, and may have suited his purpose better.

. . .

We stopped to dine at Baltimore, and being now in Maryland, were waited on, for the first time, by slaves. The sensation of exacting any service from human creatures who are bought and sold, and being, for the time, a party as it were to their condition, is not an enviable one. The institution exists, perhaps, in its least repulsive and most mitigated form in such a town as this; but it *is* slavery; and though I was, with respect to it, an innocent man, its presence filled me with a sense of shame and self-reproach. . . .

Here is Washington, fresh in my mind and under my eye. Take the worst parts of the City Road and Pentonville . . . preserving all their oddities, but especially the small shops and dwellings, occupied in Pentonville (but not in Washington) by furniture-brokers, keepers of poor eating-places, and fanciers of birds. Burn the whole down; build it up again in wood and plaster; widen it a little; throw in part of St. John's Wood; put green blinds outside all the private houses, with a red curtain and a white one in every window; plough up all the roads; plant a great deal of coarse turf in every place where it ought *not* to be; erect three handsome buildings in stone and marble, anywhere, but the more entirely out of everybody's way the better; call one the Post Office, one the Patent Office, and one the Treasury; make it scorching hot in the morn-

ing, and freezing cold in the afternoon, with an occasional tornado of wind and dust; leave a brick-field without the bricks, in all central places where a street 'may naturally be expected: and that's Washington.

The hotel in which we live, is a long row of small houses fronting on the street, and opening at the back upon a common yard, in which hangs a great triangle. Whenever a servant is wanted, somebody beats on this triangle from one stroke up to seven, according to the number of the house in which his presence is required; and as all the servants are always being wanted, and none of them ever come, this enlivening engine is in full performance the whole day through. Clothes are drying in this same yard; female slaves, with cotton handkerchiefs twisted round their heads, are running to and fro on the hotel business; black waiters cross and recross with dishes in their hands; two great dogs are playing upon a mound of loose bricks in the centre of the little square; a pig is turning up his stomach to the sun, and grunting "that's comfortable"; and neither the men, nor the women, nor the dogs, nor the pig, nor any created creature, takes the smallest notice of the triangle, which is tingling madly all the time. . . .

It is sometimes called the City of Magnificent Distances, but it might with greater propriety be termed the City of Magnificent Intentions; for it is only on taking a bird's-eye view of it from the top of the Capitol, that one can at all comprehend the vast designs of its projector, an aspiring Frenchman. Spacious avenues, that begin in nothing, and lead nowhere; streets, mile-long, that only want houses, roads, and inhabitants; public buildings that need but a public to be complete; and ornaments of great thoroughfares, which only lack great thoroughfares to ornament—are its leading features. One might fancy the season over, and most of the houses gone out of town for ever with their masters. . . .

Such as it is, it is likely to remain. . . . It has no trade or commerce of its own; having little or no population beyond the President and his establishment; the members of the legislature who reside there during the session; the Government clerks and officers employed in the various departments; the keepers of the

Along tree-grown Bull Street, central axis of Savannah, natives stroll in the afternoon along a series of five squares. In the original plans these were defense points against Indians or Spanish enemies.

ON SPITTING AND OTHER TOPICS 141

hotels and boarding-houses; and the tradesmen who supply their tables. It is very unhealthy. Few people would live in Washington, I take it, who were not obliged to reside there. . . .

I was sometimes asked . . . whether I had not been very much impressed by the *heads* of the lawmakers at Washington . . . literally their individual and personal heads, whereon their hair grew . . . and I almost as often struck my questioner dumb with indignant consternation by answering, "No, that I didn't remember being at all overcome." . . . I do not remember having ever fainted away . . . at sight of any legislative body. I have borne the House of Commons like a man, and have yielded to no weakness, but slumber, in the House of Lords. . . .

It was but a week since an aged, grey-haired man, a lasting honour to the land [United States] that gave him birth, who has done good service to his country . . . and who will be remembered scores upon scores of years . . . stood for days upon his trial before this very body, charged with having dared to assert the infamy of that traffic, which has for its accursed merchandise, men and women, and their unborn children. Yes. And publicly exhibited in the same city all the while—gilded, framed and glazed; hung up for general admiration; shown to strangers not with shame, but pride; its face not turned towards the wall, itself not taken down and burned—is the Unanimous Declaration of The Thirteen United States of America, which solemnly declares that All Men are Created Equal; and are endowed by their Creator with the Unalienable Rights of Life, Liberty, and the Pursuit of Happiness!

It was not a month, since this same body had sat calmly by, and heard a man, one of themselves, with oaths which beggars in their drink reject, threaten to cut another's throat from ear to ear. . . . There was but a week to come, and another of that body, for doing his duty to those who sent him there; for claiming in a Republic the Liberty and Freedom of expressing their sentiments, and making known their prayer; would be tried, found guilty, and have strong censure passed upon him by the rest. His was a grave offence indeed; for years before, he had risen up and said, "A gang of

male and female slaves for sale, warranted to breed like cattle, linked to each other by iron fetters, are passing now along the open street beneath the windows of your Temple of Equality! Look!" . . .

[*On the railway to Richmond*] The tract of country through which it takes its course was once productive; but the soil has been exhausted by the system of employing a great amount of slave labour in forcing crops, without strengthening the land; and it is now little better than a sandy desert overgrown with trees. . . . In this district, as in all others where slavery sits brooding, (I have frequently heard this admitted, even by those who are its warmest advocates): there is an air of ruin and decay abroad, which is inseparable from the system. The barns and outhouses are mouldering away; the sheds are patched and half roofless; the log cabins (built in Virginia with external chimneys made of clay or wood), are squalid in the last degree. . . .

In the negro car belonging to the train in which we made this journey, were a mother and her children who had just been purchased; the husband and father being left behind with their old owner. The children cried the whole way, and the mother was misery's picture. The champion of Life, Liberty, and the Pursuit of Happiness, who had bought them, rode in the same train; and, every time we stopped, got down to see that they were safe. . . .

The next day, and the next, we rode and walked about the town, which is delightfully situated on eight hills, overhanging James River; a sparkling stream, studded here and there with bright islands, or brawling over broken rocks. . . .

[*At a planter's house which Dickens visited*] The day was very warm, but the blinds being all closed, and the windows and doors set wide open, a shady coolness rustled through the rooms, which was exquisitely refreshing after the glare and heat without. Before the windows was an open piazza, where, in what they call the hot weather—whatever that may be—they sling hammocks, and drink and doze luxuriously. I do not know how their cool refections may taste within the hammocks, but, having experience, I can report that, out of them, the mounds of ice and the bowls of mint-julep and sherry-cobbler they make in these latitudes, are refreshments never to be thought of afterwards, in summer, by those who would preserve contented minds. . . .

It is all very well to say "be silent on the subject" of slavery. They won't let you be silent. They *will* ask you what you think of it; and *will* expatiate on slavery as if it were one of the greatest blessings of mankind. "It's not," said a hard, bad-looking fellow to me the other day, "it's not the interest of a man to use his slaves ill. It's damned nonsense that you hear in England." I told him quietly that it was not a man's interest to get drunk, or to steal, or to game, or to indulge in any other vice, but he *did* indulge in it for all that. That cruelty, and the abuse of irresponsible power, were two of the bad passions of human nature, with the gratification of which, considerations of interest or of ruin had nothing whatever to do; and that, while every candid man must admit that even a slave might be happy enough with a good master, all human beings knew that bad masters, cruel masters, and masters who disgraced the form they bore, were matters of experience and history, whose existence was as undisputed as that of slaves themselves.

He was a little taken aback by this, and asked me if I believed in the Bible. "Yes," I said, "but if any man could prove to me that it sanctioned slavery, I would place no further credence in it." "Well then," he said, "by God, sir, the niggers must be kept down, and the whites have put down the coloured people wherever they have found them." "That's the whole question," said I. . . .

What words shall describe the Mississippi, great father of rivers, who (praise be to Heaven) has no young children like him! An enormous ditch, sometimes two or three miles wide, running liquid mud, six miles an hour; its strong and frothy current choked and obstructed everywhere by huge logs and whole forest trees; now twining themselves together in great rafts, from the interstices of which a sedgy, lazy foam works up, to float upon the water's top; now rolling past like monstrous bodies, their tangled roots showing like matted hair; now glancing singly by like giant leeches; and now writhing round and round the vortex

of some small whirlpool, like wounded snakes. . . .

The decline of day here was very gorgeous, tinging the firmament deeply with red and gold, up to the very keystone of the arch above us. As the sun went down behind the bank, the slightest blades of grass upon it seemed to become as distinctly visible as the arteries in the skeleton of a leaf; and when, as it slowly sank, the red and golden bars upon the water grew dimmer, and dimmer yet, as if they were sinking too; and all the glowing colours of departing day paled, inch by inch. . . . We drank the muddy water of this river while we were upon it. It is considered wholesome by the natives, and it is something more opaque than gruel. . . .

[*In St. Louis*] We went to a large hotel, called the Planter's House. . . . As many lights sparkled and glistened from the windows down into the street below, when we drove up, as if it had been illuminated on some occasion of rejoicing. It is an excellent house, and the proprietors have most bountiful notions of providing the creature-comforts. Dining alone with my wife in our own room, one day, I counted fourteen dishes at the table at once.

In the old French part of the town, the thoroughfares are narrow and crooked, and some of the houses are very quaint and picturesque: being built of wood, with tumble-down galleries before the windows, approachable by stairs, or rather ladders, from the street. There are queer little barber's shops and drinking-houses too, in this quarter; and abundance of crazy old tenements with blinking casements, such as may be seen in Flanders. Some of these ancient habitations, with high garret gable-windows perking into the roofs, have a kind of French shrug about them; and being lop-sided with age, appear to hold their heads askew, besides, as if they were grimacing in astonishment at the American improvements. . . .

It is not six years ago since a slave in this very same St. Louis, being arrested (I forget for what), and knowing he had no chance of a fair trial, be his offence what it might, drew his bowie knife and ripped the constable across the body. A scuffle ensuing, the desperate Negro stabbed two others with the same weapon. The mob who gathered round (among whom were men of mark, wealth and influence in the place) overpowered him by numbers; carried him away to a piece of open ground beyond the city; and *burned him alive* . . . in a city with its courts, lawyers, tipstaffs, judges, jail and hangman; and not a hair on the head of one of these men has been hurt to this day.

Two Innocents, and the Minstrels of St. Louis

MARK TWAIN

In a way that is sometimes not stressed, Samuel Clemens (Mark Twain) had a strong Southern element in his background. In and about Hannibal, Missouri, his childhood home on the Mississippi, there lived a number of Southern families. His father and mother were of the South, and during most of his early years Sam Clemens was in contact with the life of the old region. During his river pilot days, of course, the lower Mississippi bounded his existence. In this account, less well known than his river material, he tells of his forthright mother and aunt and the time he introduced them to blackface minstrels in St. Louis. The selection is from Bernard De Voto's Mark Twain in Eruption, *published by Harper and Brothers, New York, copyright 1922; copyright 1940 by the Mark Twain Company.*

WHERE now is Billy Rice? He was a joy to me and so were the other stars of the "nigger show"—Billy Birch, David Wambold, Backus and a delightful dozen of their brethren who made life a pleasure to me. . . . With them departed to return no more forever, I suppose . . . the show which to me had no peer and whose peer has not yet arrived, in my experience. We have the grand opera; and I have witnessed and greatly enjoyed the first act of everything which Wagner created. . . . But whenever I have witnessed two acts I have gone away physically exhausted; and whenever I have ventured an entire opera the result has been the next thing to suicide.

I remember the first negro musical show I ever saw. It must have been in the early 1840s. . . . It burst upon us as a glad and stunning surprise. Church members did not attend shows. . . . The minstrels appeared with coal-black hands and faces and their clothing was a loud and extravagant burlesque of the clothing worn by the plantation slaves; not that the rags of the poor slave were burlesqued, for that would not have been possible; burlesque could have added nothing in the way of extravagance to the sorrowful accumulation of rags and patches which constituted his costume; it was the form and color of his dress that was burlesqued.

Standing collars were in fashion in that day and the minstrel appeared in a collar which engulfed and hid half of his head and projected so far forward that he could hardly see sideways over its points. His coat was sometimes made of curtain calico with a

---

Set back from broad St. Charles Avenue in uptown New Orleans stands this "raised cottage" pillared residence. Of Greek Revival style, it was built by architect Henry Howard.

swallowtail that hung nearly to his heels and had buttons as big as a blacking box. His shoes were rusty and clumsy and cumbersome and five or six sizes too large for him.

The minstrel used a very broad negro dialect; he used it competently and with easy facility and it was funny—delightfully and satisfyingly funny. However, there was one member of the troupe who was not extravagantly dressed and did not use the negro dialect. He was clothed in the faultless evening costume of the white society gentleman and used a stilted, courtly, artificial and painfully grammatical form of speech, which the innocent villagers took for the real thing as exhibited in high and citified society, and they vastly admired it and envied the man who could frame it on the spot without reflection and deliver it in this easy and fluent and artistic fashion.

"Bones" sat at one end of the row of minstrels, "Banjo" sat at the other end, and the dainty gentleman just described sat in the middle. This middleman was the spokesman of the show. The neatness and elegance of his dress, the studied courtliness of his manners and speech and the shapeliness of his undoctored features made him a contrast to the rest of the troupe and particularly to "Bones" and "Banjo." "Bones" and "Banjo" were the prime jokers and whatever funniness was to be gotten out of paint and exaggerated clothing they utilized to the limit. Their lips were thickened and lengthened with bright red paint to such a degree that their mouths resembled slices cut in a ripe watermelon.

The original ground plan of the minstrel show was maintained without change for a good many years. There was no curtain to the stage in the beginning; while the audience waited they had nothing to look at except the row of empty chairs back of the footlights; presently the minstrels filed in and were received with a wholehearted welcome; they took their seats, each with his musical instrument in his hand; then the aristocrat in the middle began with a remark like this:

"I hope, gentlemen, I have the pleasure of seeing you in your accustomed excellent health and that everything has proceeded prosperously with you since last we had the good fortune to meet."

"Bones" would reply for himself and go on and tell about something in the nature of peculiarly good fortune that had lately fallen to his share; but in the midst of it he would be interrupted by "Banjo," who would throw doubt upon his statement of the matter; then a delightful jangle of assertion and contradiction would break out between the two; the quarrel would gather emphasis, the voices would grow louder and louder and more and more energetic and vindictive, and the two would rise and approach each other, shaking fists and instruments and threatening bloodshed, the courtly middleman meantime imploring them to preserve the peace and observe the proprieties—but all in vain, of course.

Sometimes the quarrel would last five minutes, the two contestants shouting deadly threats in each other's faces with their noses not six inches apart, the house shrieking with laughter all the while at this happy and accurate imitation of the usual and familiar negro quarrel, then finally the pair of malignants would gradually back away from each other, each making impressive threats as to what was going to happen the "next time" each should have the misfortune to cross the other's path; then they would sink into their chairs and growl back and forth at each other across the front of the line until the house had had time to recover from its convulsions and hysterics and quiet down.

The aristocrat in the middle of the row would now make a remark which was surreptitiously intended to remind one of the end men of an experience of his of a humorous nature and fetch it out of him—which it always did. It was usually an experience of a stale and moldy sort and as old as America. One of these things, which always delighted the audience of those days until the minstrels wore it threadbare, was "Bones's" account of the perils which he had once endured during a storm at sea. The storm lasted so long that in the course of time all the provisions were consumed. Then the middleman would inquire anxiously how the people managed to survive.

"Bones" would reply, "We lived on eggs."

"You lived on eggs! Where did you get eggs?"

"Every day, when the storm was so bad, the Captain laid *to*."

During the first five years that joke convulsed the house, but after that the population of the United States had heard it so many times that they respected it no longer and always received it in a deep and reproachful and indignant silence, along with others of its caliber which had achieved disfavor by long service.

The minstrel troupes had good voices and both their solos and their choruses were a delight to me as long as the negro show continued in existence. In the beginning the songs were rudely comic, such as "Buffalo Gal," "Camptown Races," "Old Dan Tucker," and so on; but a little later sentimental songs were introduced, such as "The Blue Juniata," "Sweet Ellen Bayne," "Nelly Bly," "A Life on the Ocean Wave," "The Larboard Watch," etc.

The minstrel show was born in the early forties and it had a prosperous career for about thirty-five years; then it degenerated into a variety show and was nearly all variety show with a negro act or two thrown in incidentally. . . .

Ten or twelve years later the minstrel show was as common in America as the Fourth of July but my mother had never seen one. She was about sixty years old by this time and she came down to St. Louis with a dear and lovely lady of her own age . . . Aunt Betsey Smith . . . aunt to the whole town. . . . She and my mother were very much alive; their age counted for nothing; they were fond of excitement, fond of novelties, fond of anything going that was of a sort proper for members of the church. . . . They were always up early to see the circus procession enter the town and to grieve because their principles did not allow them to follow it into the tent; they were always ready for Fourth of July processions, Sunday-school processions, lectures, conventions, camp meetings, revivals in the church—in fact, for any and every kind of dissipation that could not be proven to have anything

irreligious about it—and they never missed a funeral.

In St. Louis they . . . wanted something exciting and proper. I told them I knew of nothing in their line except a Convention which was to meet in the great hall of the Mercantile Library and listen to an exhibition and illustration of native African music by fourteen missionaries who had just returned from that dark continent. . . . If they actually and earnestly desired something instructive and elevating, I would recommend the Convention, but if at bottom they really wanted something frivolous I would look further. But no, they were charmed with the idea of the Convention and eager to go. I was not telling them the strict truth, but . . . it is not worth while to strain one's self to tell the truth to people who habitually discount everything you tell them, whether it is true or isn't.

The alleged missionaries were the Christy minstrel troupe . . . one of the best. We went early and got seats in the front bench. . . . When the grotesque negroes came filing out on the stage . . . the old ladies were almost speechless with astonishment. I explained to them that the missionaries always dressed like that in Africa.

But Aunt Betsey said, reproachfully, "But they're niggers."

I said, "That is no matter; they are Americans in a sense, for they are employed by the American Missionary Society."

Then both the ladies began to question the propriety of their countenancing the industries of a company of negroes, no matter what their trade might be, but I said that they could see by looking around that the best people in St. Louis were present and that certainly they would not be present if the show were not a proper sort.

They were comforted and also quite shamelessly glad to be there. They were happy now and enchanted with the novelty of the situation; all that they had needed was a pretext of some kind or other to quiet their consciences, and their consciences were quiet now, quiet enough to be dead. They gazed on that long curved line of artistic mountebanks with devouring eyes. The middleman began.

Presently he led up to that old joke which I was telling about. . . . Everybody in the house except my novices had heard it a hundred times; a frozen and solemn and indignant silence settled down upon the sixteen hundred, and poor "Bones" sat there in that depressing atmosphere and went through with his joke.

It was brand new to my venerable novices and when he got to the end and said, "We lived on eggs," and followed it by explaining that every day during the storm the Captain "laid *to*," they threw their heads back and went off into heart-whole cackles and convulsions of laughter that so astonished and delighted that great audience that it rose in a solid body to look and see who it might be that had not heard that joke before. The laughter of my novices went on and on till their hilarity became contagious and the whole sixteen hundred joined in and shook the place with the thunders of their joy.

Aunt Betsey and my mother achieved a brilliant success for the Christy minstrels that night, for all the jokes were as new to them as they were old to the rest of the house. They received them with screams of laughter and passed the hilarity on, and the audience left the place sore and weary with laughter and full of gratitude to the innocent pair that had furnished to their jaded souls that rare and precious pleasure.

.   .   .

My mother had a slender, small body but a large heart—so large that everybody's grief and everybody's joys found welcome in it. . . . The rest of the people whom I have known felt a strong interest in a few things, whereas to the very day of her death she felt a strong interest in the whole world and everything and everybody in it. . . . She always found something to excuse, and as a rule to love, in the toughest of them—even if she had to put it there herself. She was the natural ally and friend of the friendless. It was believed that, Presbyterian as she was, she could be beguiled into saying a soft word for the devil himself, and so the experiment was tried.

The abuse of Satan began; one conspirator after another added his bitter word, his malign reproach . . . till at last the unsus-

An enormous plantation bed has a *prie-dieu* at its foot for the devout worshiper.

pecting subject walked into the trap. She admitted that the indictment was sound, that Satan was utterly wicked and abandoned; *but* would any claim that he had been treated fairly? A sinner was but a sinner; Satan was just that, like the rest. . . . But who prays for Satan? Who, in eighteen centuries, has had the common humanity to pray for the one sinner that needed it most . . . the one who most needed a friend yet had not a single one, the one who had the highest and clearest *right* to every Christian's prayers?

. . . One day in St. Louis this friend of Satan walked out into the street and greatly surprised a burly cartman who was beating his horse over the head; for she took the whip away from him and then made such a persuasive appeal that he was tripped into saying he was to blame; and also into volunteering a promise which of course he couldn't keep, for he was not built that way—a promise that he wouldn't ever abuse a horse again.

. . . The town's population had come from the slave states and still had the institution of slavery with them. Yet, kind-hearted and compassionate as she was, I think my mother was not conscious that slavery was a bald, grotesque and unwarrantable usurpation. She had never heard it assailed in any pulpit but had heard it defended and sanctified in a thousand; her ears were familiar with Bible texts that approved it but if there were any that disapproved it they had not been quoted by her pastors; as far as her experience went, the wise and the good and the holy were unanimous in the conviction that slavery was right, righteous, sacred, the peculiar pet of the Deity and a condition which the slave himself ought to be daily and nightly thankful for. Manifestly, training and association can accomplish strange miracles. . . .

However, there was nothing about the slavery of the region to rouse one's dozing humane instincts to activity. It was the mild domestic slavery, not the brutal plantation article. Cruelties were very rare and exceedingly and wholesomely unpopular. To separate and sell the members of a slave family to different masters was a thing not well liked by the people and so it was not often done, except in the settling of estates. . . . I vividly remember seeing a dozen black men and women chained to one another, once, and lying in a group on the pavement . . . the saddest faces I have ever seen.

The "nigger trader" was loathed by everybody. He was regarded as a sort of human devil who bought and conveyed poor helpless creatures to hell—for to our whites and blacks alike the Southern plantation was simply hell. If the threat to sell an incorrigible slave "down the river" would not reform him, nothing would. Yet I remember that once when a white man killed a negro man for a trifling little offense everybody seemed indifferent about it—as regarded the slave—though considerable sympathy was felt for the slave's owner, who had been bereft of valuable property by a worthless person who was not able to pay for it.

Uncle Remus and the Animals

JOEL CHANDLER HARRIS

Joel Chandler Harris, a small man with a large good will toward the world and his fellows, spent his earliest years at or near Eatonton, Georgia. His dressmaker mother worked to support the family; the gentle Joel listened to Negroes of the vicinity as they told tales about animals, Brer (Brother) Fox, Brer Tarrypin (Terrapin) and the like. In the post-Confederate years Mr. Harris turned to newspaper work, holding jobs in Macon, Savannah, New Orleans and eventually Atlanta, where he became a widely known member of the Constitution *staff. In time he was composing plantation sketches in which Uncle Remus figured, telling the white children shrewd stories of the doings of animals. From them came the first of a number of books which made Joel Chandler Harris a national figure. Generations of the young grew up hearing the naïve-wise yarns. Certain modern-day observers have suspected that in such tales the Negroes, identifying themselves with, for instance, the humble rabbit, often get the better of the lumbering whites. The following is from* Uncle Remus, His Songs and His Sayings, *New York, 1888.*

"DE animils en de creeturs," said Uncle Remus, shaking his coffee around in the bottom of his tin-cup, in order to gather up all the sugar, "dey kep' on gittin' mo' en mo' familious wid wunner nudder, twel bimeby, 'twan't long 'fo' Brer Rabbit, en Brer Fox, en Brer Possum got ter sorter bunchin' der perwishuns tergedder in de same shanty. Atter w'ile de roof sorter 'gun ter leak, en one day Brer Rabbit, en Brer Fox, en Brer Possum, 'semble fer ter see ef dey can't kinder patch her up. Dey had a big day's work in front un um, en dey fotch der dinner wid um. Dey lump de vittles up in one pile, en de butter w'at Brer Fox brung, dey goes en puts in de spring-'ouse fer ter keep cool, en den dey went ter wuk, en 'twan't long 'fo' Brer Rabbit stummuck 'gun ter sorter growl en pester 'im. Dat butter er Brer Fox sot heavy on his mine, en his mouf water eve'y time he 'member 'bout it. Present'y he say ter hisse'f dat he bleedzd ter have a nip at dat butter, en den he lay his plans, he did. Fus' news you know, w'ile dey wuz all wukkin' 'long, Brer Rabbit raise his head quick en fling his years forrerd en holler out:

"'Here I is. W'at you want wid me?' en off he put like sump'n wuz atter 'im.

"He sallied 'roun', ole Brer Rabbit did, en atter he make sho dat nobody ain't foller'n un 'im, inter de spring-'ouse he bounces, en dar he stays twel he git a bait er butter. Den he santer on back en go to wuk.

"'Whar you bin?' sez Brer Fox, sezee.

"'I hear my chilluns callin' me,' sez Brer Rabbit, 'en I hatter go see w'at dey want. My ole 'oman done gone en tuck mighty sick,' sezee.

"Dey wuk on twel bimeby de butter tas'e so good dat ole Brer Rabbit want some mo'. Den he raise up his head, he did, en holler out.

"'Heyo! Hole on! I'm a comin'!' en off he put.

"Dis time he stay right smart w'ile, en w'en he git back Brer Fox ax him whar he bin.

"'I been ter see my ole 'oman, en she's a sinkin',' sezee.

"Dreckly Brer Rabbit hear um callin' 'im ag'in en off he goes en dis time, bless yo'

soul, he gits de butter out so clean dat he kin see hisse'f in de bottom er de bucket. He scrape it clean en lick it dry, en den he go back ter wuk lookin' mo' samer dan a nigger w'at de patter-rollers bin had holt un.

"'How's yo' ole 'oman dis time?' sez Brer Fox, sezee.

"'I'm oblije ter you, Brer Fox,' sez Brer Rabbit, sezee, 'but I'm fear'd she's done gone by now,' en dat sorter make Brer Fox en Brer Possum feel in moanin' wid Brer Rabbit.

"Bimeby, w'en dinner-time come, dey all got out der vittles, but Brer Rabbit keep on lookin' lonesome, en Brer Fox en Brer Possum dey sorter rustle roun' fer ter see ef dey can't make Brer Rabbit feel sorter splimmy."

"What is that, Uncle Remus?" asked the little boy.

"Sorter splimmy-splammy, honey—sorter like he in a crowd—sorter like his ole 'oman aint dead ez she mout be. You know how fokes duz w'en dey gits whar people's a moanin'."

The little boy didn't know, fortunately for him, and Uncle Remus went on:

"Brer Fox en Brer Possum rustle roun', dey did, gittin out de vittles, en bimeby Brer Fox, he say, sezee:

"'Brer Possum, you run down ter de spring en fetch de butter, en I'll sail 'roun' yer en set de table,' sezee.

"Brer Possum, he lope off atter de butter, en dreckly here he come lopin' back wid his years a trimblin' en his tongue a hangin' out. Brer Fox, he holler out:

"'W'at de matter now, Brer Possum?' sezee.

"'Yo all better run yer, fokes,' sez Brer Possum, sezee. 'De las' drap er dat butter done gone!'

"'Whar she gone?' sez Brer Fox, sezee.

"'Look like she dry up,' sez Brer Possum, sezee.

"Den Brer Rabbit, he look sorter sollum, he did, en he up'n say, sezee:

"'I speck dat butter melt in somebody mouf,' sezee.

"Den dey went down ter de spring wid Brer Possum, en sho nuff de butter done gone. W'iles dey wuz sputin' over der wunderment, Brer Rabbit say he see tracks all 'roun' dar, en he p'int out dat ef dey'll all go ter sleep, he

"Echoes of Old Plantation Melodies" is the title of this good-humored drawing, with three generations on the scene.

kin ketch de chap w'at stole de butter. Den dey all lie down en Brer Fox en Brer Possum dey soon drapt off ter sleep, but Brer Rabbit he stay 'wake, en w'en de time come he raise up easy en smear Brer Possum mouf wid de butter on his paws, en den he run off en nibble up de bes' er de dinner w'at dey lef' layin' out, en den he come back en wake up Brer Fox, en show 'im de butter on Brer Possum mouf. Den dey wake up Brer Possum, en tell 'im 'bout it, but c'ose Brer Possum 'ny it ter de las'. Brer Fox, dough, he's a kinder lawyer, en he argafy dis way—dat Brer Possum wuz de fus one at de butter, en de fus one fer ter miss it, en mo'n dat, der hang de signs on his mouf. Brer Possum see dat dey got 'im jammed up in a cornder, en den he up en say dat de way fer ter ketch de man w'at stole

de butter is ter b'il' a big bresh-heap en set her afier, en all han's try ter jump over, en de one w'at fall in, den he de chap w'at stole de butter. Brer Rabbit en Brer Fox dey bofe 'gree, dey did, en dey whirl in en b'il' de bresh-heap, en dey b'il' her high en dey b'il' her wide, en den dey totch her off. W'en she got ter blazin' up good, Brer Rabbit, he tuck de fus turn. He sorter step back, en look 'roun' en giggle, en over he went mo' samer dan a bird flyin'. Den come Brer Fox. He got back little fudder, en spit on his han's, en lit out en made de jump, en he come so nigh gittin' in dat de een' er his tail kotch afier. Ain't you never see no fox, honey?" inquired Uncle Remus, in a tone that implied both conciliation and information.

The little boy thought probably he had, but he wouldn't commit himself.

"Well, den," continued the old man, "nex' time you see one un um, you look right close en see ef de een' er his tail ain't w'ite. Hit's des like I tell you. Dey b'ars de skyar er dat bresh-heap down ter dis day. Dey er marked—dat's w'at dey is—dey er marked."

"And what about Brother Possum?" asked the little boy.

"Ole Brer Possum, he tuck a runnin' start he did, en he come lumberin' 'long, en he lit—

kerblam!—right in de middle er de fier, en dat wuz de las' er ole Brer Possum."

"But, Uncle Remus, Brother Possum didn't steal the butter after all," said the little boy, who was not at all satisfied with such summary injustice.

"Dat w'at make I say w'at I duz, honey. In dis worril, lots er fokes is gotter suffer fer udder fokes sins. Look like hit's mighty on-wrong; but hit's des dat away. Tribbalashun seems like she's a waitin' roun' de cornder fer ter ketch one en all un us, honey."

Epitaph to a Dead Slave

VIRGINIUS DABNEY

Virginius Dabney, editor of the Richmond Times-Dispatch, *is a member of a band of informed Southern leaders of opinion whose view is toward the road ahead. Here, in a passage from Mr. Dabney's* Liberalism in the South, *published in 1932 by the University of North Carolina Press, is a balanced statement of ante-bellum race relations.*

IN the Old South the family was the unit about which much of the life of the section revolved. Since most planters lived in comparative isolation, often miles from the nearest habitation and usually a great distance from anything remotely resembling a city, the family circle occupied a place which it could not have occupied under different conditions.

In summer the head of the household and his wife and children whiled away many a long hour together on the verandah or under the trees which almost invariably surrounded the home, while during the winter months they gathered in close communion about the family fireside. Unfortunately, however, this idyllic picture was in many instances seriously marred by the fact that while the planter was rearing a large brood of children in the "big house," he was rearing another brood of mulattoes in the slave quarters.

Northern abolitionists frequently adverted to the clandestine relationships on Southern plantations between white men and black women. If these relationships were not as widespread as unfriendly critics contended,

there was a firmer basis for charges of miscegenation than for the accusations of cruelty which were hurled at heads of the planters with such regularity by the Garrisonians. Cruelty existed, of course, more, indeed, than many Southerners cared to admit, but a majority of modern scholars agree that it was the exception rather than the rule. . . .

There was, in fact, in many instances a feeling of profound attachment between master and slave in the Old South, a feeling which transcended racial barriers and frequently lasted until death intervened. This is beautifully exemplified in the following inscription, placed over the grave of a faithful Negro by the Southern family he had served:

JOHN:

A FAITHFUL SERVANT

AND TRUE FRIEND:

KINDLY AND CONSIDERATE:

LOYAL AND AFFECTIONATE:

THE FAMILY HE SERVED

HONORS HIM IN DEATH:

BUT IN LIFE, THEY GAVE HIM LOVE:

FOR HE WAS ONE OF THEM

Glory That Was, Grandeur That Wasn't

HOWARD W. ODUM

In his many writings, balanced, stimulating, brilliantly informed, Howard W. Odum did as much as almost any Southerner of the past few decades to encourage a comprehension of the complex influences which have made the South. Leader of an important North Carolina school of thought, he was a native of Georgia, who studied there, in Mississippi, Massachusetts and New York, and eventually became director of the Institute for Research in Social Sciences at the University of North Carolina. His works include Rainbow Round My Shoulder, The Negro and His Songs, An American Epoch *and the widely acclaimed* Southern Regions of the United States *and* American Regionalism. *This selection is from* The Way of the South, *Macmillan and Company, New York, 1947.*

THE Glory That Was the South. The old Major, much given to philosophizing on political and moral issues, strolled along before the White House in springtime on one of his few visits to Washington, enjoying its southern columns and plantings. . . . There must surely be, he thought, a place through the years for some of the enduring values inherent in the glory that was the South. The thought was particularly fascinating when he contemplated the democratic principles of Jefferson, well wrought out into a practical society and dominated by his high standards for agriculture, science, education and architecture. Speculation on this day was the more encouraged by a recent rare visit to Monticello, which had left upon him vivid impressions of what was and what might have been, and by his thoughts of Abraham Lincoln's southern heritage and national greatness.

There came to his mind pictures of innumerable colonial homes with the glory that was theirs . . . the contrast of that first American epoch of independence in which the South had provided the occupants of the White House for nearly fifty of its first sixty years, and the barrenness of the South's contribution in a second similar epoch. . . . He recalled that, at the end of this first epoch and with two governments instead of one, both presidents were southerners, born within a hundred miles of each other, and that the wife of the northern republic had come from the South, and

the wife of the president of the southern confederacy had come from the North.[*] It was all very complex and mixed. . . .

How many of the big-columned houses had there been, and of what sort and variety, on the banks of the Potomac and the James and the Roanoke and down in the Carolinas? How many in Georgia, at Athens, LaGrange, Augusta, Columbus and Savannah? In Alabama, at Greensboro, Montgomery and Huntsville? In Mississippi, at Natchez, Vicksburg or Columbus? In old romantic Louisiana, and back again to Tennessee and Kentucky? And in the regions and land in between? Nobody has ever counted them; perhaps no one ever will. There have been notable samplings: Mount Vernon, Arlington, Shirley, Westover, Brandon, Sabine Hall. . . . What a variety of names and what range of character: Belle Grove, Seven Oaks, El Destino, Level Green, Gainswood, Snug Dale, Peach Point, Stratford, Tuckahoe, Montpelier . . . White Mast, the Shelter, Mount Airey, Bladenfield, Oaken Brown, Gaymount. . . .

[They were] as varied and different as were the personalities of the masters, and yet had the same sort of general similarity throughout. A big house on a hill by the river side or set far back from the road in the midst of great trees, white-framed with big columns, or a white-columned brick structure laid "in Flem-

---

[*]Actually, Varina Howell Davis was of Northern descent on her father's side, but born in the South.

The sport of kings flourished "before the war" and afterward as well, as word of the "great race at Baltimore" gives testimony.

ish bond of alternately glazed black leaders and dull pink broadsides which give the walls solidity, distinction and a rich beauty." Or another mansion "with four huge rooms downstairs and a like number above, stood upon a terraced plateau, with a bowling green in front and a 'little handsome street' at the rear leading to the kitchen, bakery, dairy and storehouses." . . . And another large rambling house "set in a magnificent grove of live oaks, the wide double gallery almost concealed by the luxurious vegetation."

Such were the plantation houses, while the colonial homes in the towns and cities had their marked characteristics scarcely less distinguished. They "stood back from the streets surrounded by heavily-scented gardens, almost hidden by the semitropical sweet gum and the

magnolia. . . . Voices, disembodied in the still air, floated into the street, as if the houses themselves had spoken."

. . . Whatever else they were, they were reflections of glory and grandeur, vivid, beautiful and distinctive. In these pictures one sees southern men and southern women as the perfect flowering of American personality, and the plantation life as the best of American culture. Even a Walter Hines Page with his keen criticism of southern deficiencies could see the romance and virtue of the big house. . . . There were the elegant house servants, coachmen, butlers dressed in broadcloth, and women servants so well dressed that Solomon in all his glory might find a new proverb, and so numerous that often, like the lilies of the field, they toiled not, neither did they spin. . . .

There were vivid pictures of hospitality, high living and fellowship within these physical bounds . . . single meals for more than fifty guests . . . days and weeks of entertaining . . . luxuries that came directly from abroad, silks, velvets, ribbons, jewelry and books . . . the contacts with London and Paris, with brilliant winters in New Orleans, Charleston, Mobile and other places where were produced plays of Shakespeare before ever they were given in New York or Boston or Philadelphia. And volumes of Shakespeare, Scott, George Eliot, Johnson, Goldsmith, Greek and Latin classics were often a part of the culture. . . .

The old plantation system was often likened unto a school in which society was molded into unerring patterns . . . a community in which there were teachers for the children of the house, their relatives and neighbors, and special instruction for the talented Negroes in crafts, in routine skill, and even in reading, writing and arithmetic. . . . What pageantry and variety: "the procession of plowmen at evening, slouched crosswise on their mules; the dance in the new sugarhouse, the bonfire with contests in clogs, cakewalks; the work songs in solo and refrain; the torchlight pursuit of 'possum and 'coon, with full-voiced halloo to baying houn' dawg and yelping cur. . . ."

The leading man in the big house and its drama was of course the old southerner . . . a gentleman and an aristocrat, whose character could be told at a glance by the measured dignity of his walking or riding or by the carriage in which he rode . . . proud, austere, impetuous, eloquent and sometimes over-irascible, loquacious of tongue and pen, so that he appeared domineering to many northerners and to many a common man of the South. Leading lady was the southern woman, grown from girlhood, full of larks and pranks, into serious, gracious woman competent to meet the tremendous demands upon her body and soul; mother of old statesmen and soldiers . . . remarkable for perfection in mastery and service, creating and guiding their own large families, and taking charge of and dividing fortunes with sundry subsidiary families of black folks. But perhaps the southern woman of all classes

best reflected her glory through fortitude and heroic devotion during the War and reconstruction. . . .

Not the least of all the pictures were those distinguished characters, the old slaves. . . . What artists in manners and serving and in skill of vocations, on special occasions equal to any demand . . . "the old negro clad in his blue swallow-tail coat with big brass buttons . . . carrying a silver tray filled with all the ingredients of his magic concoction. . . . Tender, fragrant mint, firmly pressed with the back of a spoon against the glistening inside of a sterling goblet; the bruised leaves gently removed and the cup half filled with cracked ice; mellow Bourbon, aged in oaken staves, bubbling from a brown jigger, percolated through the sparkling . . . slivers; in another receptacle, granulated sugar slowly stirred into chilled limestone water to a silvery mixture as smooth as some rare Egyptian oil, was poured on top of the ice; and then while beads of moisture gathered on the burnished exterior of the goblet, old Nelson garnished the frosted brim with choicest sprigs of mint and presented the tall cup, with a courtly bow, to the nearest guest."

This glory . . . was then of one pattern yet of many parts. The Kentucky glory was different from that of Virginia, the Virginia from that of Tennessee, and there was none like that of Charleston or New Orleans. The southern poetry of Edgar Allan Poe or Sidney Lanier was different from the oratory of John C. Calhoun or Henry Clay. Southern politics was different from southern philosophy. Southern statesmanship of a silver-tongued Benjamin Hill, a fire-eating Robert Toombs, was different from the force and drive of Andrew Johnson or the skill and artistry of Henry Clay. And thus one star differed from another star whether it were Washington, Madison, Patrick Henry, John Marshall, the Harrisons, the Lees and the other Virginians; Graham, Macon, Davie, Benton, Badger of North Carolina; Calhoun, Hayne, Laurens, Legaré, Lowndes, Pinckney, and the others from South Carolina; or Campbell, Jackson, Polk, White, of Tennessee; Houston of Texas; King of Alabama; Cobb, Forsyth, Stephens, Toombs of Georgia; Bibb, Breckinridge,

Henry Clay, Guyot, Johnson of Kentucky; Livingston, Slidell, Taylor of Louisiana; Prentiss and Walker of Mississippi. There were "giants" in the pictures of those days. . . . "Before the war" there were times when the sons of the South enrolled in its colleges were more than all the sons of New England; and its college endowments were more than all the regions of the "Big Three" and their lesser satellites. . . .

Perhaps no pictures were more characteristic of the glory than its military leaders, a veritable galaxy of stars, "picturesque individuals, flaming gentlemen at arms, who brought to this war sound military aptitude, and the color, also, of the age of chivalry." . . . Yet other pictures: A bride concealing a beautiful diamond in her mouth: to the enemy, looking dumb for fear; in reality, storing up resentments and transmitting them to her children. Soldiers pouring oil and turpentine on priceless furniture and setting it on fire . . . A grand old man with no word of bitterness, robbed of his Arlington and without a home, astride old Traveler looking for a small farm . . . Straggling processions of crippled men, torn, battered and gray . . . Arriving home, they found houses, barns, fences, supplies destroyed; no money, no farming implements, no seed, no labor. . . .

The Grandeur That Was Not. Both Uncle John and the old Major were enthusiastic followers of Jefferson and Jeffersonian democracy, but from different viewpoints. . . . The old Major had always doubted the efficacy of the old southern too-dominant autocracy. Part of this doubt had come from a fair reasoning about certain weaknesses of the southern economy, a certain theoretical study and considerable observations. But perhaps a considerable part came from natural rationalization, since he himself, like Jefferson Davis and many another late southern plantation man, had come to his status quickly, developing in a single generation from a family of insecure small farmers into a great planter. . . . He could see no aristocracy in the primitive days of the frontier, and he could think· of the whole South in no other terms than a series of frontier fringes, each great family at one time or another in its history having par-

ticipated in the great restless drive for wealth and progress and superior class development. . . . Thus the old Major was inclined to think of Uncle John, somewhat undeveloped and unlettered but highly honorable and energetic, as an earlier member of his own generation. . . .

Both Uncle John and the old Major were scornful of much of the false pride and hypocrisy of the Old South, and particularly of the remnants of proud folk on the one hand and the "strainers" and imitators on the other. There was much that was tragic and small alongside that which was tragic and glorious. It was difficult to decide whether pity or scorn was the predominant note in the conversations about the pathetic family of women in the neighborhood doing their washing in the attic and never hanging out the clothes lest the neighborhood might see the disgrace of their doing their own work. There was always this effect on southern standards and ideals of work, the lesser folk aping the bigger folk, the later generations imitating the old standards and old families. There was that pathetic case of another family having distinguished company from afar to dine, assigning one of the girls to blacken her face and hands and bring in the dinner in high fashion. And there was the family of unmarried men not knowing how to work, being too proud to work, aristocrats gone to seed, sometimes actually hungry, dressed in broadcloth, retaining fine dogs and horses. Sometimes they actually called on the common-folk neighbors at mealtime and accepted their hospitality in the guise of neighborly honors from aristocrats to common man. And ever there was some hidden tragedy in the big house on the hill or in the grove: shutters never open, dark mysterious pride and mourning inside; tragic womenfolks, veiled, slipping out to buy provisions; bitterness, tragedy, pride, old age, broken minds, broken bodies, degeneracy and decay.

The old Major had often maintained that the whole economic and cultural system of the South, although having many admirable features and at times approximating great possibilities, was neither well thought out nor well balanced. Just as the South could not and would not foresee the trend of events in its great embargo on cotton to England or the fallacy of its high-handed assumptions concerning the English attitude towards the war; and just as it could not or would not see the impossibility of slavery as a permanent institution in a rapidly changing social world, the South, instead of thinking out its economic problems and working out well balanced theories, had merely followed a temporary cycle, partly imitating English standards and partly following the same inclinations which looked to the present only.

There were many others than the old Major who thought that the developing social codes and practices of the plantation South would have undermined its own civilization sooner or later. An unthinking autocracy, a denial of education to the common folk and to women, an untenable attitude towards the Negro, a culture based on superficial acquaintances with the classics, an over-emphasis upon luxuries and physical life, hard drinking and duelling were all units in their count against that part of the old southern civilization. . . .

If the women of the South during the war and the tragic aftermath suffered beyond any man's estimate, there were also many who suffered much under the old system, where perchance they learned well a discipline which was to sustain them in the decades to come. There was the beautiful, heroic, and tragic case of several wives of one master, each taking up the load where the last one fell, each succeeding one bearing her quota of stalwart descendants of gentlemen. Thus rode forth a great master, married to a beautiful mistress, who begat near a score of children, some of whom died at birth or later. But even of those who remained there was still a large family. This mistress of the big house not only had her own family to look after, to supervise, to direct their nurture and education according to high standards, but also was called upon to supervise and direct the many industries of the great house and the large number of Negro families with children all about the place. In exchange for her efforts on behalf of these black folks she received of course much service, the nursing of her children, and many loyalties of the categorical sort. It may have been, too, however, that these servants were part and parcel of her family in other ways as

mothers of the great master's black children who, added to the score of her own, created a remarkable family indeed.

Thus to the glory and splendor and beauty of the mistress of the big house, with her remarkable mastery, was added much that was improper in any institutional order which claimed recognition for its glory and perfection. This woman, alongside the written and spoken eulogies of her beauty and grace, had little freedom of any sort. Her work, like the work of the woman among the common people, was never done. She was chaperoned and bound in by conventions and great tasks. Education of the broader sort was not for her, and she, mistress that she was in many ways, was not supposed to interest herself in social, intellectual, and political movements. Many things she was not supposed to see or, if seeing, to record or, if recording, to let it see the light either in her own consciousness or in the records for posterity. Thus this remarkable character became a symbol for a certain type of hypocrisy, superficialty, and rationalization wherever reality was concerned, and this symbolism carried over into the reconstruction period and far into the twentieth century. For decades white children had been turned over to colored mammies, some through genuine continuation of the old custom, some through imitation, some through general unfitness, and some through the grand rationalization that children needed this discipline to make them gentlefolk.

So also had the women of the Confederacy preserved mass pictures of the Old South based upon romantic developments from individual incidences of beauty and glory, pictures that never were on land or sea or earth or sky. The Old South had nothing save perfection; its men were gentlemen; its women, ladies all. Any who criticized the old order or brought to light facts not conducive to its glorification either were not patriots or else were so uncultured as not to understand that all this new generation was neither to the manner nor the manor born. . . .

There was the extrafamilial relationships of the master of the big house with the women slaves in violation of all codes of chivalry towards his own family and the utter lack of respect for the personalities of Negroes. . . . And husbands and wives among the slaves were sold to go into different parts of the country, sons and daughters were taken from family settings and distributed wherever the buyer might decide. There was here, also, then another striking case of unreality, so much so that many of the southerners never saw the rank inconsistency of their high morality for the purity of the women and the family in theory and their low morality in the practice of the opposite. . . . The tragedy of the South's immoral morality and moral immorality was to project itself far into the generations, into a South clamoring for purity of race, enforcing its clamor through technical legislation in the midst of an increasing mixed race of its own begetting. There were distinguished men of great families, handsome in bearing and powerful in influence, and their white sons alongside half-breeds. . . .

The magnificence of the old plantation life had its counterpart also in the stubborn individual, non-cooperative habits, violent tempers, feuds, duels, fighting and isolation. How much glory there was in the heroic pictures of a stalwart statesman seizing the dagger of an opponent, attacking him in public meeting, splitting his head wide open to the brains . . . depends upon the viewpoint and the standards of measurement. . . . And the carrying of this glory, reflecting fighting codes of honor, into national House and Senate, while providing plenty of liveliness and entertainment for the public, had left, nevertheless, a definite imprint not always an asset to the would-be southern statesman of the new day. . . . And there was cruelty to slaves, driving and beating and putting in chains. How much of this pattern remains today in the mob brutality and white-man defense of mob murder, no man can measure.

How a Model Planter Met His Troubles

SUSAN DABNEY SMEDES

In a loving book about her father and his plantation experiences at Burleigh in Hinds County, Mississippi, Mrs. Susan Dabney Smedes presented a frequently quoted account of the operations of an efficient cotton establishment. Thomas Dabney was a hard-working, good-spirited Virginian who took his family, slaves and other possessions to the Deep South, and prospered for years. Less attention has been given to the volume's later section, telling of the way troubles piled up for the high-minded Dabney, and the way he bore up under them. The selection is from Mrs. Smedes' Memorials of a Southern Planter, Baltimore, 1887.

AND now a great blow fell on Thomas Dabney. Shortly before the war he had been asked by a trusted friend to put his name as security on some papers for a good many thousand dollars. At the time he was assured that his name would only be wanted to tide over a crisis of a few weeks, and that he would never hear of the papers again. It was a trap set, and his unsuspicious nature saw no danger, and he put his name to the papers. Loving this man, and confiding in his honor as in a

son,'s, he thought no more of the transaction.

It was now the autumn of 1866. One night he walked upstairs with a paper in his hand to the room where his children were sitting. "My children," he said, "I am a ruined man. The sheriff is downstairs. He has served this writ on me. It is for a security debt. I do not even know how many more such papers have my name to them." His face was white as he said these words. He was sixty-eight years of age, with a large and helpless family on his hands, and the country in such a condition that young men scarcely knew how to make a livelihood.

The sheriff came with more writs. Thomas roused himself to meet them all. He determined to pay every dollar. But to do this he must have time. The sale of everything that he owned would not pay all these claims. He put the business in the hands of his lawyer, Mr. John Shelton, of Raymond, who was also his intimate friend. Mr. Shelton contested the claims, and this delayed things till Thomas could decide on some way of paying the debts.

A gentleman to whom he owed personally several thousand dollars courteously forbore to send in his claim. Thomas was determined that he should not on this account fail to get his money, and wrote urging him to bring a friendly suit, that, if the worst came, he should at least get his proportion. Thus urged, the friendly suit was brought, the man deprecating the proceeding, as looking like pressing a gentleman.

And now the judgments, as he knew they would, went against him one by one. On the 27th of November, 1866, the Burleigh plantation was put up at auction and sold, but the privilege of buying it in a certain time reserved to Thomas. At this time incendiary fires were common. There was not much law in the land. We heard of the gin-houses and cotton-houses that were burned in all directions. One day as Thomas Dabney came back from a business journey the smouldering ruins of his gin-house met his eye. The building was itself valuable and necessary. All the cotton that he owned was consumed in it. He had not a dollar. He had to borrow the money to buy a postage stamp, not only during this year, but during many years to come. It was a time of deepest gloom. . . .

Many honorable men in the South were taking the benefit of the bankrupt law. Thomas's relations and friends urged him to take the law. It was madness, they said, for a man of his age, in the condition the country was then in, to talk of settling the immense debts that were against him. He refused with scorn to listen to such proposals. But his heart was well-nigh broken. He called his children around him, as he lay in bed, not eating and scarcely sleeping. . . . "I shall have nothing to leave you but a fair name. But you may depend that I shall leave you that. I shall, if I live, pay every dollar that I owe. If I die, I leave these debts to you to discharge. Do not let my name be dishonored. . . ."

But he soon roused himself from this depression and set about arranging to raise the money needed to buy in the plantation. It could only be done by giving up all the money brought in by the cotton crop for many years. This meant rigid self-denial for himself and his children. He could not bear the thought of seeing his daughters deprived of comforts. He was ready to stand unflinchingly any fate that might be in store for him. But his tenderest feelings were stirred for them.

His chivalrous nature had always revolted from the sight of a woman doing hard work. General Sherman had said (or Thomas had read the assertion in a newspaper) that he would like to bring every Southern woman to the wash-tub. "He shall never bring my daughters to the wash-tub," Thomas Dabney said. "I will do the washing myself." And he did it for two years. He was in his seventieth year when he began to do it.

A curtain must be drawn over this part of the life of my lion-hearted father! . . . When the food was so coarse and so badly prepared that he could scarcely eat it, he never failed, on rising from the table, to say earnestly and reverently, "Thank the Lord for this much." During a period of eighteen months no light in summer, and none but a fire in winter, except in some case of necessity, was seen in the house. He was fourteen years in paying these debts that fell on him in his sixty-ninth year. He lived but three years after the last dollar was paid.

Pioneer Life in Kentucky

DR. DANIEL DRAKE

Writing with warmth, honesty and a certain charm of spirit, the well-loved Dr. Daniel Drake eventually looked back and recalled his earliest days in the newly settled Kentucky. Born in 1785, Daniel Drake died at sixty-seven, honored as a leading practitioner of his scene and day. This section is taken from his Pioneer Life in Kentucky, *edited by his son Charles, and published in 1870, after his death.*

NOW, fancy to yourself a log cabin . . . one story high, without a window, with a door opening to the south, with a half-finished wooden chimney, with a roof on one side only, without any upper or lower floor; and fancy, still further, a man and two women stepping from sleeper to sleeper (poles laid down to support the floor, when he should have time to split the puncheons), with two children sitting on the ground between them . . . and you will have the picture which constitutes *my first memory.*

For the next six years my father continued to reside at the same place, in the same original log cabin, which in due course of time acquired a roof, a puncheon floor below and a clap board floor above, a small square window without glass, and a chimney, carried up with "cats and clay" to the height of the ridge pole. These "cats and clay" were pieces of small poles, well imbedded in mortar. The rifle, indispensable for hunting and defense, lay on two pegs driven into one of the logs. The axe and scythe . . . were kept at night under the bed as weapons of defense, in case the Indians should make an attack.

In the morning the first duty was to ascend, by a ladder which always stood leaning behind the door, to the loft, and look out through the cracks for Indians, lest they might have planted themselves near the door, to rush in when the strong cross-bar should be removed, and the heavy latch raised from its resting place. . . .

The first and greatest labour after father had thus domiciliated his little family, was to clear sufficient land for a crop the following year, which was, of course, to consist of corn and a few garden vegetables. In this labour I was too young to participate, and he was too poor to hire; consequently his own hands had to perform the whole. At that time, and afterwards for more than 20 years, he was dyspeptic and by no means well fitted for the heavy task which lay before him. It was two or three years before his fields grew to any great extent. The soil, however, was highly productive and the autumn of 1789 would have brought forth a sufficient abundance but that on the night of the last day of August there came so severe a frost as to kill the unripe corn, and almost break the hearts of those who had watched its growth from day to day in joyous anticipation.

From the time of their arrival in Kentucky fourteen months before, they had suffered from want of bread, and now found themselves doomed to the same deficiency for another year. There was no fear of famine, but they cloyed on animal food, and sometimes almost loathed it, though of excellent quality. Deer were numerous and wild turkies numberless. The latter were often so fat that in falling from the tree when shot their skins would burst. There was no longing for the "*flesh* pots" of native land, but their hearts yearned for its neat and abounding *wheat-bread* trays. In this craving it seems I played no unimportant part (though I do not remember it) for my parents often told me afterwards that I would cry and beg for bread when we were seated round the table till they would have to leave it and cry themselves. . . .

About the same period the Indians one night attacked a body of travelers, encamped a mile from our village on the road to Washington. They were sitting quietly around their camp fire, when the Indians shot among them, and killed a man whose remains I remember to have seen brought, the next day, into the village on a rude litter. The heroic presence of mind of a woman saved the party. She broke open a chest in one of the wagons with an axe, got at the ammunition, gave it to the men and called upon them to fight. This, with the extinction of their Camp fires, led the Indians to retreat.

That night made an unfading impression on my mind. We went, with Uncle Abraham Drake's family, I think, to Uncle Cornelius' for concentration and greater safety. Several of the men of the village went to the relief of the travelers and one of them, a young married man, ran into the village and left his wife behind him!

Up to the victory of Wayne, in 1794, the danger from Indians still continued; that is, through a period of six years from the time of our arrival. I well remember that Indian wars, midnight butcheries ,captivities and horse stealings, were the daily topics of conversation. Volunteering to pursue marauding parties occasionally took place and sometimes men were drafted. . . . At that time as at present, there were many young men who delighted in war much more than work and, therefore, preferred the tomahawk to the axe. I remember that when a substitute for my father returned he had many wonderful tales to tell. . . .

In or near the year 1791, my aunt Lydia Shotwell was married. A number of Father's acquaintances in and around Washington were invited. They came armed, and while assembled in the house, report was brought that the Indians, about five miles up the road toward Lexington, had attacked a wagon. All the armed men mounted their horses and galloped off in a style so picturesque that I shall never forget it. . . .

I remember another calamitous event of those days. When about six years old, I was sent to borrow a little salt of one of the neighbors. Salt at that time was worth about $3 a bushel, or 12 times as much as at present. It was a small quantity, tied up in a paper, and when I had gotten about half way home, the paper tore, and most of the precious grains rolled out on the ground. As I write, the anguish I felt at the sight seems almost to be re-vived. I had not then learned that spilling of salt is portentous, but felt that it was a great present affliction, and apprehended that I should be blamed and scolded. Mother had, moreover, taught me to consider the waste of bread or anything that was scarce and could be used for food, as sinful. In this instance she thought, I believe, that the paper had not been been properly tied.

When I recur to this and other incidents, which I can not definitely relate, I discover that it was an original trait of character with me, to aim at a faithful execution of whatever was confided to me and feel unhappy if, through neglect or misfortune, I made a failure. To this hour I am more solicitous about that which is intrusted to me than that which is entirely my own. Hence I have given a great deal of time to public affairs (on a small scale to be sure) but often at the expense of my private interests. "But never mind."

The first money I ever had, as far as I can recollect, came to me in the following manner. A man had lodged all night with us, and the next morning lost a silver knee-buckle (at that time an indispensable article) in the snow, near the door of our cabin. I was set to hunt for it, and father at length came to my assistance with a rake. I do not recollect which found it, but I got the reward—a piece of cut money, at that time the circulating medium of Virginia and Kentucky. My joy was unbounded; and ever since I have had it reproduced by the receipt of money. Then, it was the mere possession that threw me into rapture. Since I grew up, it was the idea of appropriating it to the payment of some debt that gave me pleasure. . . .

The emigration into Kentucky was, at that period, immense and nearly the whole passed through Mayslick. Great quantities of merchandise, moreover, were hauled into the interior. My Uncle Abraham, who lived only across the Road from father's, kept both a store and tavern, at which many persons stopped. . . . It was during this period that I first tasted wine. Some travelers from Virginia had brought it out, and the taste seems still to dwell upon my tongue. Many of the travelers were wealthy; and as the Road did not well admit of carriages, they journeyed on horseback. Thus I often saw ladies and gentlemen riding side by side, and remember I thought the latter must be the happiest persons on earth; an estimate which nearly sixty years has not entirely overruled. . . . I find that an admiration for the sex was among the earliest sentiments developed in my moral nature. It has swayed me through life, and will, I suppose, continue to govern me to its close. When that solemn event shall come, I hope to see female faces round my bed,

> And wish a woman's hand to close
> My lids in death, and say—*Repose!*

In all the schools there was a custom never seen in cities, but still prevalent in remote places. The boys and girls were trained to take off their hats and bow and curtsy to all whom they met, either coming or going. Even during play hours, if a man or woman rode near the groups, it was regarded as a duty to give the salutation. Thus I have often run to the roadside with other boys to make my bow; and when a dozen of us, or more,

might be returning together, if a man overtook or met us, we all stepped aside, stopped in a row, took off our hats, and made our bows, as near as possible at the same time. This was that cultivation of reverence and good manners which I find so ominously neglected. . . .

My superstition, and that of the people of Mayslick, extended to other things than heaven and hell. It embraced omens, ghosts, and even the self-motion of dead men's bones. Some cabins were startled by strange sounds; a night or two before the death of my cousin Dr. John Drake, some member of the family heard the sound of a plane, as in preparing the boards for a coffin; the barking of dogs during the severe illness of a person was ominous of death; the inmates of a cabin, about a mile from father's, saw a piece of white drapery moving on the snow in the moonlight near their dwelling; and the arm or thigh-bone of a man who had been buried on a spot which was afterward cultivated, was exhumed. I do

Of all Southern racing centers, Louisville and the blue grass country claimed pre-eminence.

not remember how or why, but it was re-buried, and afterward appeared on the surface of the ground.

For myself, if not a firm believer in these specimens of the supernatural, they were so established in my imagination, that I was al-ways, when alone in the dark, in a kind of ex-pectation of fear that something would show itself from the world of mystery. That ap-prehension is gone; but darkness and solitude, in certain situations, by an association of ideas, still bring up images of that kind.

Everybody Called on New Year's Day
ELIZA RIPLEY

Writing in the later years of a full life, Mrs. Eliza Ripley cast a fond and musing look over earlier plantation and city days as she recalled the passing decades. Born in 1832, she lived until she was eighty; she knew the pre-Confederate days, the war era and many events that followed. In nostalgic fashion, in her book, Social Life in Old New Orleans, *published in 1912 by D. Appleton and Company, New York and London, Mrs. Ripley tells of a long-time custom which the city shared with many other places in the South. Although New Year's visits are not so general as in other years, they survive or have been revived in a number of towns and cities.*

IN the 1840s and for years thereafter, New Year's Day was the visiting day for the men, and receiving day for the ladies. All the fathers and grandfathers, in their newest rig, stick in hand, trotted or hobbled around, making the only calls they made from year to year. Before noon, ladies were in their parlors, prinked up, pomatumed up, powdered up, to "receive." Calling began as early as 11, for it was a short winter day, and much to be accomplished. A small stand in the hall held a card receiver, into which a few cards left from last year's stock were placed, so the first caller might not be embarrassed with the fact that he was the first. No one cared to be the very first, any more than now.

A table of generous dimensions occupied a conspicuous position in the parlor (we never said "drawing room") with a silver tray, an immense and elaborately decorated cake and a grand bowl of foaming eggnog. This was chiefly designed for the beaux. On the dining room sideboard (we did not say "buffet," either) a brandy straight or whisky straight was to be found for those walking-stick ones whose bones were stiff and whose digestion could not brook the fifty different concoctions of eggnog they were liable to find in the fifty different houses. Those varied refreshments, which every caller was expected to at least taste, often worked havoc on the young and spry, to say nothing of the halt and lame.

There were no flower decorations. It was the dead season for plants, and Boston green-houses were not shipping carloads of roses and carnations to New Orleans in the '40s. Rooms were not darkened, either, to be il-luminated with gas or electricity, but windows were thrown wide open to the blessed light of a New Year's Day. Little *cornets* of bon-bons and *dragées* were carelessly scattered about.

Those cornucopias, very slim and pointed, containing about a spoonful of French con-fections, were made of stiff, shiny paper, gaud-ily colored miniatures of impossible French damsels ornamenting them. I have not seen one of those pretty trifles for sixty years. It was quite the style for a swain to send his Dulcinea a *cornet* in the early morning. If the Dulcinea did not happen to receive as many as she wanted, she could buy a few more. One liked to be a belle!

Living in Canal Street, a little girl . . . enjoyed looking through the open window, onto the broad, unshaded street, watching an endless procession of callers. There were rows of fashionable residences in Canal Street to be visited, and the darting in and out of open doors, as though on earnest business bent, was a sight. The men of that day wore skin-tight pantaloons (we did not call them trousers), often made of light-colored materials. . . . Those tight-fitting pantaloons were drawn taut over the shoe; a strong leather strap extending under the foot buckled the garment down good and tight, giving the wearer as mincing a gait as the girl in the present-day hobble skirt. The narrow clawhammer coat with tails that hung almost to the knees behind and were scarcely visible in front, had to have the corner of a white handkerchief flutter from the tail pocket.

Military men like Gen. E. P. Gaines (he was in his zenith at that date) and all such who could sport a military record wore stiff stocks, which made their necks appear abnormally long. They were made of buckram (or sheet iron?) and must have been very trying, for the wearers could not turn their heads when buckled up, and, like the little boy with the broad collar, could not spit over them. I remember Major Waters had a bald spot on the top of his head and two long strands of sandy hair on each side, which he carefully gathered up over the bald spot and secured in place by the aid of a side comb! I used to wish the comb would fall out, to see what the major would do, for I was convinced he could not bend his head over that stiff, formidable stock.

All the men wore tall silk hats that shone like patent leather. They flocked in pairs to do their visiting. It would be a Mardi Gras nowadays to see one of those old-time processions. Men of business fulfilled their social duty by stepping into the dining room and taking a brandy straight, with a flourish of the hand and a cordial toast to the New Year. I remember a very original, entertaining beau of those days saying eggnog was good enough for him, and when he felt he was arriving at the brandy-straight age he meant to kill himself. How would he know when the time for hari-kari came? "When my nose gets spongy." . . . Not so many years ago I heard of him hobbling on crutches. Not only his nose, but his legs were spongy, but he gave no indication that life was not as dear to him as in his salad days.

The younger element rambled in all day long, hat in hand, with "A happy New Year," a quaff of eggnog, "no cake, thanks," and away like a flash, to go into house after house, do and say the same things, till night would find they had finished their list of calls and eggnog had about finished them. So the great day wore on. After the house doors were closed at the flirt of the last clawhammer coat tail, cards were counted and comments made as to who had called and who had failed to put in an appearance, the wreck of glasses, cake and tray removed, and it was as tired a set of ladies to go to bed as of men to be put to bed.

A Southern Gentleman Defends Southern Gentlemen

DANIEL R. HUNDLEY

In the gathering emotions over slavery, a number of Southerners made speeches or wrote books and essays which drew considerable attention. Like Northerners, some were tempered in their words, others hotheads who did much to bring on war. Daniel R. Hundley's Social Relations in Our Southern States,

"Harry of the West" was Henry Clay of Kentucky, who almost reached the Presidency. Hundreds of thousands liked him, but liking did not seem to be quite enough.

published in 1860 in New York, is a full-blown defense of his region, presenting a laudatory view of the slaveowner. While Hundley found faults in the system of bondage, his tone was heavily favorable, and many echoed him. He was an Alabama-born Unionist who married a Virginian. For a time Hundley looked after family business concerns in Chicago. Then, despite his Union feelings, he went back to Alabama as the war came close, and took a place as a colonel of the Alabama infantry.

SPREADING over a vast area of country, and boasting but few large cities or great commercial centres, the different phases presented by Southern society are almost as various as the extent of her territory is diversified; and while it must not be denied that she sometimes does shock our humaner sensibilities with brutal displays of one sort or another; still these, happily, are the exceptions to the generally pleasing character of the landscape—the shadows, if you will, whose very darkness only serves to render more conspicuous those heights of moral grandeur, and more gratefully pleasing those broad savannahs of genial hospitality, which stretch all the way from Little Delaware to the cactus-clad banks of the Rio Grande.

If the South has her Big Cypress, Okefenokee and Dismal Swamps, she can also point to her noble Blue Ridge, her graceful Cumberland and other mountain ranges, as well as to many a lovely river embowered in forests of magnolia, beechwood, hemlock, the wide-branching cedar, and the stately pine.

.   .

The Southern Gentleman comes of a good stock. Indeed, to state the matter fairly, he comes usually of aristocratic parentage; for family pride prevails to a greater extent in the South than in the North. In Virginia, the ancestors of the Southern Gentleman were chiefly English cavaliers, after whom succeeded the French Huguenots and Scotch Jacobites. In Maryland, his ancestors were in the main Irish Catholics—the retainers and associates of Lord Baltimore—who sought in the wilds of the New World religious tolerance and political freedom. In South-Carolina, they were Huguenots—at least the better class of them—those dauntless chevaliers, who, fleeing from the massacre of St. Bartholomew and the bloody persecutions of priests and tyrants, drained France of her most generous blood to found in the Western Hemisphere a race of heroes and patriots. In Florida, Louisiana, Texas, and other portions of the far South, the progenitors of the Southern Gentleman were chiefly Spanish Dons and French Catholics.

Thus it will be seen that throughout the entire extent of the South, (for the new Southern States have been settled almost wholly by emigrants from those named above,) wherever you meet with the Southern Gentleman, you find him *hijo dalgo*, as the Spaniards phrase it: however, there are many notable exceptions in every Southern State. For, owing to the repeal of the Law of Primogeniture, and the gradual decay of some of the old families, as well as the levelling effects of many of Mr. Jefferson's innovations, particularly the subsequent intermarriages between the sons and daughters of the gentry and persons of the middle class . . . there are . . . many gentlemen of the genuine Southern character, whose ancestry was only in part of the cavalier stock. Indeed, Mr. Jefferson himself was a fit representative of these; for, while his mother was a Randolph, his father was only a worthy descendant of the sturdy yeomanry of England.

Besides being of faultless pedigree, the Southern Gentleman is usually possessed of an equally faultless physical development. His average height is about six feet, yet he is rarely gawky in his movements, or in the least clumsily put together; and his entire *physique* conveys to the mind an impression of firmness united to flexibility. . . . The Northern people have been told so incessantly of the lazy habits of Southerners, that they honestly believe them to be delicate good-for-nothings, like their own brainless fops and nincompoops. . . . The gentlemen of the South owe their physical perfectness in part, doubtless, to those mailed ancestors who followed Godfrey and bold Coeur de Lion to the rescue of the Holy Sepulchre. . . .

Much more reasonably, however, we think we may attribute the good size and graceful carriage of the Southern Gentleman, to his out-of-doors and a-horseback mode of living. For we might as well here inform our readers, the genuine Southern Gentleman almost invariably lives in the country. But let them not conclude from this circumstance that he is nothing more than the simple-hearted, swearing, hearty, and hospitable old English or Virginia Country Gentleman, of whom we have all heard so repeatedly. The time has been when such a conviction could have been truthfully entertained; but that was long ago. In those good old times the Southern Gentleman had little else to do than fox-hunt, drink, attend the races, fight chicken-cocks, and grievously lament that he was owner of a large horde of savages whom he knew not how to dispose of.

But times change. . . . The new order of

things which succeeded the innovations of Mr. Jefferson made it necessary for the Gentlemen of the South, for all the old families who had before lived upon their hereditary wealth and influence, to struggle to maintain their position, else to be pushed aside by the thrifty middle classes, who thought it no disgrace to work by the side of their slaves, and who were, in consequence, yearly becoming more wealthy and influential. Besides, after the repeal of the Law of Primogeniture, the large landed estates, the former pride and boast of the first families, very soon were divided up into smaller freeholds, and the owners of these, of necessity, were frequently forced to lay aside the old manners and customs, the air and arrogance of the grand seignor, and to content themselves with the plain, unostentatious mode of life which at present characterizes most gentlemen in the South. The result of all which has been, that the Southern Gentleman of to-day is less an idler and dreamer than he was in the old days, is more practical, and, although not so great a lover of the almighty dollar as his Northern kinsman, still is far from being as great a spendthrift as his fathers were before him.

But, notwithstanding the old style of Southern Gentlemen has in a measure passed away, the young South is nurtured in pretty much the same school as formerly—at least so far as physical education is concerned—and participates more or less in all those rollicking out-door sports and amusements still common in England to this day. Scarcely has he gotten fairly rid of his bibs and tuckers, therefore, before we find him mounted a-horseback; and this not a hobby-horse either, (which the poor little wall-flower of cities is so proud to straddle,) but a genuine live pony—sometimes a Canadian, sometimes a Mustang, but always a pony. By the time he is five years of age he rides well; and in a little while thereafter has a fowling-piece put into his hands, and a little black boy of double his age put *en croupe* behind him, (or in case mamma is particularly cautious, his father's faithful servingman accompanies him, mounted on another horse,) and so accoutred, he sallies forth into the fields and pastures in search of adventures.

At first he bangs away at every thing indiscriminately, and the red-headed woodpeckers more often grace his game-bag than quail or snipe; but by degrees he acquires the art and imbibes the spirit of the genuine sportsman, and ever after keeps his father's hospitable board amply supplied with the choicest viands the woods or fields or floods afford. By floods, the reader will please understand rivers, creeks, and ponds; for our young Southerner is as much of a fisherman as a Nimrod. When he tires of his gun, he takes his fishing-rods and other tackle, and goes angling; and when he tires of angling, provided the weather is favorable, he denudes himself and plunges into the water for a swim, of which he tires not at all. Indeed, he will remain in the watery element until the sun blisters his back, and if thus forced to seek *terra firma*, he does it "upon compulsion," and under protest. As a general thing, the blue-noses of Nova Scotia, or the natives of South-America, are not greater lovers of the healthy exercise of swimming than the boys of the South, of all classes.

In his every foray, whether by flood or field, our young gentleman has for his constant attendant, Cuffee, junior, who sticks to him like his shadow. At the expiration of five years or so of this manner of living, (provided there is no family tutor, and in that case his mother has already learned him to read,) the master is sent to the nearest village, or district, or select school, returning home every night. Sometimes this school is from five to ten miles distant, and so he has to ride from ten to twenty miles every day, Saturdays and Sundays alone excepted. Again Cuffee is sent with his young master, and morning and evening the two are to be seen cantering to or from the school-house, the negro taking charge of their joint lunch for dinner, (to be eaten during "playtime,") and the master carrying on the pommel of his saddle or his arm the bag which contains his books and papers, and maybe a stray apple or peach to exchange with the village urchins for fishing-rods, or to present to some school-boy friend, who has a rosy-cheeked little sister, with a roguish black eye and a silvery laugh.

And although every day in the week, from Monday to Friday inclusive, is thus occupied, both master and slave sit up nearly

Liberty Street in Savannah was a busy thoroughfare with trains, wagons, horseback transportation on view—and also crinolines.

all of Friday night, cleaning guns, arranging fishing-lines, and discussing enthusiastically the sports to be followed on the morrow. These change very materially, as our young Southerner begins to get higher and higher in his teens. He very soon surfeits of the tame pastime of shooting squirrels and ducks, woodcock and plover, or chasing of hares; when for a short while, say a couple of years, his chief delight is to hunt wild turkeys—a rare sport where turkeys are abundant and when one has a well-trained dog. But even this soon ceases to be attractive, and is succeeded by fox-hunting. Preparatory to entering upon the latter rare old English sport, our young gentleman gets some one of the many dusky uncles on his father's plantation, to procure him a deep intoned horn; which procured, he proceeds immediately to exchange his pony for the fleetest and most active of his father's stud.

On a great many Southern plantations there are kept hunting horses, regularly trained for the sport as in England; and it is astonishing in what a little time they become as fond of the same as their riders. Even mules, after having been used a few times, will prick up their heavy ears at the sound of a merry horn, and will follow the hounds with all the eagerness of the best blooded of their sires. Having selected his steed, and mounted Cuffee on another, our young fox-hunter gives his horn a merry wind in the "wee sma' hours atween the twal" in the morning, answering to which well-known call, Ringwood, and Jowler, and Don, with all their yelping and barking mates, soon gather together and hasten after their master. . . .

But to proceed once more with our subject. When the Southern Gentleman has fully completed his academic labors—has honorably gone through the University Curriculum—if his means be ample, he seldom studies a profession, but gives his education a finishing polish by making the tour of Europe; or else marries and settles down to superintend his estates, and devotes his talents to the raising of wheat, tobacco, rice, sugar, or cotton; or turns his attention to politics, and runs for the State Legislature. Should, however, the patrimonial estate be small, or the heirs numerous, (and the generous clime of the South renders the latter supposition highly probable,) he then devotes himself to some one of the learned professions, or becomes an editor, or enters either the Army or the Navy. But of all things, he is most enamoured of politics and the Army; and it is owing to this cause, that the South has furnished us with all our great generals, from Washington to Scott, as well as most of our leading statesmen, from Jefferson to Calhoun. In order to attain either eminence or success, men must do whatever they undertake *con amore*. Hence the popular outcry against the undue political influence of the Slave Power, or the Southern Oligarchy, is just as senseless and absurd as if the little retail grocer, who sells brown sugar by the two-penny paper package, should denounce his fellow-citizens because they prefer "loaf" of the best quality. . . .

But to return. No matter what may be the Southern Gentleman's avocation, his dearest affections usually centre in the country. He longs to live as his fathers lived before him, in both the Old World and the New; and he ever turns with unfeigned delight from the bustle of cities, the hollow ceremonies of courts, the turmoil of politics, the glories and dangers of the battle-field, or the wearisome treadmill of professional routine, to the quiet and peaceful scenes of country life. The glare of gas and the glitter of tinsel, the pride, the pomp, the vanity, and all the grace and wit of *la bonne compagnie*, he surrenders without a sigh of regret, and joyfully retires to the seclusion of his own fireside, grateful for the auspicious and happy exchange. The old hall, the familiar voices of old friends, the trusty and well-remembered faces of the old domes-

tics—these all are dearer to the heart of the Southern Gentleman than the short-lived plaudits of admiring throngs, or the hollow and unsatisfactory pleasures of sense. Indeed, with all classes in the South the home feeling is much stronger than it is in the North; for the bane of hotel life and the curse of boarding-houses have not as yet extended their pernicious influences to our Southern States, or at best in a very small degree. Nearly every citizen is a landholder, and therefore feels an interest in the permanency of his country's institutions. This is one reason why the South has ever been the ready advocate of war, whenever the rights of the nation have been trampled on, or the national flag insulted. . . .

But to return. The natural dignity of manner peculiar to the Southern Gentleman, is doubtless owing to his habitual use of authority from his earliest years; for while coarser natures are ever rendered more savage and brutal by being allowed the control of others, refined natures on the contrary are invariably perfected by the same means, their sense of the responsibility and its incident obligations teaching them first to control themselves before attempting to exact obedience from the inferior natures placed under their charge. This is a fact which it were worth while to ponder thoughtfully, for herein lies the secret of the good breeding of the Gentlemen of the South, and the chief reason why they seldom evince that flurry of manner so peculiar to many of our countrymen; and why, also, they manifest on all occasions the utmost self-possession—that much coveted *savoir faire*, which causes a man to appear perfectly at home, whether it be in a hut or a palace. Hence in manners the Southern Gentleman is remarkably easy and natural, never haughty in appearance, or loud of speech —even when angry rarely raising his voice above the ordinary tone of gentlemanly conversation. Those boisterous good fellows, whom one meets constantly in the South, and sometimes even so far from home as New-York or Philadelphia, and whose wont is to monopolize all the talking, interlarding their speech with Southern provincialisms and Africanisms, are not in the remotest degree allied or akin to the real Southern Gentleman.

A Spokesman for Southerners Without Slaves

HINTON ROWAN HELPER

A slavery debater of far different persuasion from Daniel R. Hundley was Hinton Rowan Helper of North Carolina. Far from a misty-eyed advocate of bondage, Helper had a violent hatred of slavery, but a no less violent hatred of the Negro, and few more searing attacks have been published in the United States. Helper's sympathies were with the slaveless Southern whites; he argued bitterly that Negro bondage doomed the poorer whites to a permanent degradation. Southern officials, sympathetic with slavery, banned his book; Northerners printed it by the thousands of copies. When he was eighty, in post-Civil War times, the disheartened Helper took his own life. This selection is from Helper's Compendium of the Impending Crisis of the South, *New York, 1861, his best-known work, although later volumes contain yet more vitriolic material against Negroes.*

IN 1790, when the first census was taken, New York contained 340,120 inhabitants; at the same time the population of Virginia was 748,308, being more than twice the number of New York. Just sixty years afterward, as we learn from the census of 1850, New York had a population of 3,097,394; while that of Virginia was only 1,421,661, being less than half the number of New York.

In 1791, the exports of New York amounted to $2,505,465; the exports of Virginia amounted to $3,130,865. In 1852, the exports of New York amounted to $87,484,-465; the exports of Virginia, during the same year, amounted to only $2,724,657. . . . What says one of Virginia's own sons? Says Gov. Wise: ". . . At a period not very remote, Virginia stood pre-eminently the first commercial State in the Union; when her commerce exceeded in amount that of all the New England States combined; when the City of Norfolk owned more than one hundred trading ships, and her direct foreign trade exceeded that of the City of New York, now the centre of trade and the great emporium of North America. At the period of the war of independence, the commerce of Virginia was four time larger than that of New York."

The incontrovertible facts are . . . sufficient to bring conviction that there is something wrong, socially, politically and morally wrong, in the policy under which the South has so long loitered and languished. Else, how is it that the North, under the operations of a policy directly the opposite of ours, has surpassed us in almost everything great and good, and left us standing before the world, an object of merited reprehension and derision?

It is a fact well known to every intelligent Southerner that we are compelled to go to the North for almost every article of utility and adornment, from matches, shoepegs and paintings up to cotton-mills, steamships and statuary; that we have no foreign trade, no princely merchants, nor respectable artists; that, in comparison with the free states, we contribute nothing to the literature, polite arts and inventions of the age; that, for want of profitable employment at home, large numbers of our native population find themselves necessitated to emigrate to the West, whilst the free states retain not only the large proportion of those born within their own limits, but induce, annually, hundreds of thousands of foreigners to settle and remain amongst them; that almost everything produced at the North meets with ready sale, while, at the same time, there is no demand, even among our own citizens, for the productions of

In a setting of broad lawns and many flowers, Orton Plantation in North Carolina was originally owned by "King Roger" Moore. Once a plain single-storied house, it was later transformed into a neoclassic show place.

Southern industry; that, owing to the absence of a proper system of business amongst us, the North becomes, in one way or another, the proprietor and dispenser of all our floating wealth, and that we are dependent on Northern capitalists for the means necessary to build our railroads, canals and other public improvements; that if we want to visit a foreign country, even though it may lie directly south of us, we find no convenient way of getting there except by taking passage through a Northern port; and that nearly all the profits arising from the exchange of commodities, from insurance and shipping offices, and from the thousand and one industrial pursuits of the country, accrue to the North, and are there invested in the erection of those magnificent cities and stupendous works of art which dazzle the eyes of the South, and attest the superiority of free institutions!

The North is the Mecca of our merchants, and to it they must and do make two pilgrimages per annum—one in the spring and one in the fall. All our commercial, mechanical, manufactural, and literary supplies come from there. We want Bibles, brooms, buckets and books, and we go to the North; we want pens, ink, paper, wafers and envelopes, and we go to the North; we want shoes, hats, handkerchiefs, umbrellas and pocket knives, and we go to the North; we want furniture, crockery, glassware and pianos, and we go to the North; we want toys, primers, school-books, fashionable apparel, machinery, medicines, tombstones, and a thousand other things, and we go to the North for them all. Instead of keeping our money in circulation at home, by patronizing our own mechanics, manufacturers, and laborers, we send it all away to the North, and there it remains; it never falls into our hands again.

In one way or another we are more or less subservient to the North every day of our lives. In infancy we are swaddled in Northern muslin; in childhood we are humored with Northern gewgaws; in youth we are instructed out of Northern books; at the age of maturity we sow our "wild oats" on Northern soil; in middle-life we exhaust our wealth, energies and talents in the dishonorable vocation of entailing our dependence on our children and on our children's children, and, to the neglect of our own interests and the interests of those around us, in giving aid and succor to every department of Northern power; in the decline of life we remedy our eye-sight with Northern spectacles, and support our infirmities with Northern canes; in old age we are drugged with Northern physic; and, finally, when we die, our inanimate bodies, shrouded in Northern cambric, are stretched upon the bier, borne to the grave in a Northern carriage, entombed with a Northern spade, memorialized with a Northern slab!

But it can hardly be necessary to say more in illustration of the unmanly and unnational dependence, which is so glaring that it cannot fail to be apparent to even the most careless and superficial observer. All the world sees, or ought to see, that in a commercial, mechanical, manufactural, financial, and literary point of view, we are as helpless as babes; that, in comparison with the Free States, our agricultural resources have been greatly exaggerated, misunderstood and mismanaged; and that, instead of cultivating among ourselves a wise policy, of mutual assistance and coöperation with respect to individuals, and of self-reliance with respect to the South at large, instead of giving countenance and encouragement to the industrial enterprises projected among us, and instead of building up, aggrandizing and beautifying our own States, cities and towns, we have been spending our substance at the North. . . .

In our opinion, an opinion which has been formed from data obtained by assiduous researches, and comparisons, from laborious investigation, logical reasoning, and earnest reflection, the causes which have impeded the progress and prosperity of the South, which have dwindled our commerce and other similar pursuits, into the most contemptible insignificance; sunk a large majority of our people in galling poverty and ignorance, rendered a small minority conceited and tyrannical, and driven the rest away from their homes; entailed upon us a humiliating dependence on the Free States; disgraced us in the recesses of our own souls, and brought us under reproach in the eyes of all civilized and enlightened nations—may all be traced to one common source, and there find solution in the most hateful and horrible word, that was ever incorporated into the vocabulary of human economy—*Slavery!*

Reared amidst the institution of slavery, believing it to be wrong both in principle and in practice, and having seen and felt its evil influences upon individuals, communities and states, we deem it a duty, no less than a privilege, to enter our protest against it . . . and to use our most strenuous efforts to overturn and abolish it! Then we are an abolitionist? Yes! not merely a free-soiler, but an abolitionist, in the fullest sense of the term.

No conditional or half-way declaration will avail; no mere threatening demonstration will succeed. . . . Nothing short of the complete abolition of slavery can save the South from falling into the vortex of utter ruin. Too long have we yielded a submissive obedience to the tyrannical domination of an inflated oligarchy; too long have we tolerated their arrogance and self-conceit. . . . To say nothing of the sin and the shame of slavery, we believe it is a most expensive and unprofitable institution; and if our brethren of the South will but throw aside their unfounded prejudices and preconceived opinions, we feel confident that we can bring them to the same conclusion.

Sam Houston Seldom Missed a Trick

J. C. GUILD

Texas' great man of great men, Sam Houston, is seen in several behind-the-scenes episodes in J. C. Guild's Old Times in Tennessee, *Nashville, 1887. Onetime Governor of Tennessee, Houston figured in an unhappy domestic difficulty, retired for a time from public life, then came forth masterfully and magnificently during revolutionary days in Texas.*

ONE of the elements of General Houston's popularity was his constant study to know every man by name whom he happened to meet. If he did not know the name he would make the man believe he did, which accomplished the same end. In 1839, when between his first and second Presidency of the Republic of Texas he was spending the summer at Nashville, he was riding with a friend out on the Gallatin road on horseback, when they saw a man from Sumner approaching him, on his way to the city, when the General asked who he was.

And on being told that his name was Hall, and that his brother was killed at the battle of San Jacinto, the General, who had never seen him before, hastened towards him and exclaimed: "How are you, Mr. Hall? I am glad to see you again—how well you are looking." Remembering the General as Gov-

ernor of the state years before, Mr. Hall expressed his satisfaction at being recognized, and wondered that the General should have remembered him.

"Remember you," said Houston, "how can I ever forget you, sir, or any member of your family? Did not your gallant brother die in my arms on the bloody field of San Jacinto?"

When General Houston resigned the Governorship of Tennessee in consequence of some domestic infelicities, he went off to the Indian Nation and remained there two or three years. On his way back he crossed the Mississippi some thirty miles below Memphis and rode on horseback along the river until nightfall, when he stopped where a tavern sign told him there was entertainment for man and horse, and asked of the man who stood in the doorway if he could get quarters for the night. He was told that he could if he would be content with a little common hog and hominy and would sleep on his own blanket before the fire.

After retiring alongside of his host, stretched out before the fire, his feet toasting at the blaze of nearly a half cord of wood that the immense fireplace contained, he thought he would have a little conversation with the old tavern-keeper. So he asked . . . who was now Governor of Tennessee, and the reply was, "Governor Carroll." "And what sort of a Governor does he make, my friend?" asked the General. "He makes a pretty good Governor. . . ." Desiring to know how he stood himself in the estimation of his host, he asked: "And who was your Governor before Carroll?" "Houston—Sam Houston. He was all sorts of a fellow, was very much liked, made up an excellent Governor—*but he disgraced himself and the State and ran off amongst the Indians.*"

The General said he asked no more questions, drew his blanket closer around him, dropped to sleep and slept soundly till sunrise. He said he found he had made so good an impression upon the old tavern-keeper that when he rode away in the morning he would not spoil it by telling him that he had entertain Sam Houston.

Usually he made it a point, on his way North, to stop three or four days at Cairo to enjoy the fishing. On one occasion he had located himself on the stern guard of a wharf-boat, while a boy, bent on the same business, had taken position on a wood-boat moored a few feet away. Both were patiently awaiting results. At the interesting juncture of a bite at the boy's bait, Houston threw out his line, which became hopelessly entangled with that of the boy. There was a pause, and at last Houston broke the silence.

"Sonny, go elsewhere and fish, and then we'll avoid entangling alliances."

"You blasted old short-coat," retorted the bud of promise, "go elsewhere and fish."

"I apprehend that you are a very saucy boy," returned the Senator, "for whom there is by no means enough rods in pickle."

"Now look here, old Skeezicks," cried the boy, fully agitated, "I don't want to quarrel with you, nor nobody like you. Your name is Sam Dawson and you live in Texas; and like everybody else, you stole a hoss and had to go there; and now you're putting on a big shine, you old thief, and calling yourself Sam Houston." Saying which, this very amiable creature gave a sudden lurch, and pulled the honorable gentleman's rod from his hands, and threw it into the river.

In relating this in his characteristic style, Houston would say: "I have met men in debate at the bar, on the stump, and upon the floor of Congress, but never was I so completely discomfited. The boy had decidedly the best of me, and, from his looks, I know that when he said I stole a 'hoss,' in his heart of hearts he believed it."

A Former Plantation Lady Has Her Say

FANNY KEMBLE

A handsome woman who lived for a time as a Georgia plantation mistress delivered one of the strongest indictments of the Southern institution. Frances Anne Kemble began life as a member of a reigning British theatrical family. Her aunt was Mrs. Siddons, her father Charles Kemble, and in her teens Fanny Kemble became a much-acclaimed Juliet. Coming to America, she scored magnificently. Yet she did not like the life of an actress and after she fell in love with the plantation owner Pierce Butler, she married him in the 1830's. The plantation scene appalled her when, she said, she beheld the crudest of cruelties, physical degradation of women, separations or threats of separations of families. Writing simply, directly, Fanny Kemble eventually offered a devastating picture. When she took her children to England, Butler brought a divorce action. What follows, from her Journal of a Residence on a Georgia Plantation, *appeared in 1863. In the postwar years Fanny Kemble became a popular reader of Shakespeare on both sides of the Atlantic. And a grandson, Owen J. Wister, Jr., acquired his own fame as author of* The Virginian.

PURSUING my walk along the river's bank, upon an artificial dike, sufficiently high and broad to protect the fields from inundation by the ordinary rising of the tide—for the whole island is below high-water mark—I passed the blacksmith's and cooper's shops. At the first all the common iron implements of husbandry or household use for the estate are made, and at the latter all the rice barrels necessary for the crop, besides tubs and buckets, large and small, for the use of the people, and cedar tubs, of noble dimensions and exceedingly neat workmanship, for our own household purposes. . . .

After this I got out of the vicinity of the settlement, and pursued my way along a narrow dike—the river on the one hand, and, on the other, a slimy, poisonous-looking swamp, all rattling with sedges of enormous height, in which one might lose one's way as effectually as in a forest of oaks. Beyond this, the low rice-fields, all clothed in their rugged stubble, divided by dikes into monotonous squares, a species of prospect by no means beautiful to the mere lover of the picturesque. The only thing that I met with to attract my attention was a most beautiful species of ivy, the leaf longer and more graceful than that of the common English creeper, glittering with the highest varnish, delicately veined, and of a rich brown-green, growing in profuse garlands from branch to branch of some stunted evergreen bushes which border the dikes. . . .

On all sides of these lie either the marshy rice-fields, the brimming river, or the swampy patches of yet unreclaimed forest, where the huge cypress-trees and exquisite evergreen undergrowth spring up from a stagnant sweltering pool, that effectually forbids the foot of the explorer.

As I skirted one of these thickets to-day,

I stood still to admire the beauty of the shrubbery. Every shade of green, every variety of form, every degree of varnish, and all in full leaf and beauty in the very depth of winter. The stunted dark-colored oak; the magnolia bay (like our own culinary and fragrant bay), which grows to a very great size; the wild myrtle, a beautiful and profuse shrub, rising to a height of six, eight, and ten feet, and branching on all sides in luxuriant tufted fullness; most beautiful of all, that pride of the South, the magnolia grandiflora, whose lustrous dark green perfect foliage would alone render it an object of admiration, without the queenly blossom whose color, size, and perfume are unrivaled in the whole vegetable kingdom. This last magnificent creature grows to the size of a forest tree in these swamps. . . . Under all these the spiked palmetto forms an impenetrable covert, and from glittering graceful branch to branch hang garlands of evergreen creepers, on which the mocking-birds are swinging and singing even now. . . .

The profusion of birds here is one thing that strikes me as curious, coming from the vicinity of Philadelphia, where even the robin redbreast, held sacred by the humanity of all other Christian people, is not safe from the *gunning* prowess of the unlicensed sportsmen of your free country. The negroes (of course) are not allowed the use of firearms, and their very simply constructed traps do not do much havoc among the feathered hordes that haunt the rice-fields. Their case is rather a hard one, as partridges, snipes and the most delicious wild ducks abound here, and their allowance of rice and Indian meal would not be the worse for such additions. . . . Here our living consists very mainly of wild ducks, wild geese, wild turkeys, and venison. . . .

Hawks of every sort and size wheel their steady rounds above the rice-fields; and the great turkey-buzzards—those most unsightly carrion birds—spread their broad black wings, and soar over the river like so many mock eagles. . . .

Our servants—those who have been selected to wait upon us in the house—consist of a man, who is quite a tolerable cook (I believe this is a natural gift with them, as with Frenchmen); a dairy-woman, who churns for us; a laundry-woman; her daughter, our housemaid; and two young lads of from fifteen to twenty, who wait upon us in the capacity of footmen. . . . And here it may be well to inform you that the slaves on this plantation are divided into field hands and mechanics or artisans. The former, the great majority, are the more stupid and brutish of the tribe; the others, who are regularly taught their trades, are not only exceedingly expert at them, but exhibit a greater general activity of intellect, which must necessarily result from even a partial degree of cultivation.

There are here a gang (for that is the honorable term) of coopers, of blacksmiths, of bricklayers, of carpenters, all well acquainted with their peculiar trades. The latter constructed the wash-hand stands, clothes-presses, sofas, tables, etc., with which our house is furnished, and they are very neat pieces of workmanship—neither veneered or polished indeed, nor of very costly materials, but of the white pine wood planed as smooth as marble—a species of furniture not very luxurious perhaps, but all the better adapted therefore to the house itself, which is certainly rather more devoid of the conveniences and adornments of modern existence than anything I ever took up my abode in before.

It consists of three small rooms, and three still smaller, which would be more appropriately designated as closets, a wooden recess by way of pantry, and a kitchen detached from the dwelling—a mere wooden out-house, with no floor but the bare earth, and for furniture a congregation of filthy negroes, who lounge in and out of it like hungry hounds at all hours of the day and night, picking up such scraps of food as they can find about, which they discuss squatting down upon their hams,

in which interesting position and occupation I generally find a number of them whenever I have sufficient hardihood to venture within those precincts, the sight of which and its tenants is enough to slacken the appetite. . . .

The walls are plastered indeed, but neither painted nor papered; it is divided from our bedroom (a similarly elegant and comfortable chamber) by a dingy wooden partition covered all over with hooks, pegs, and nails, to which hats, caps, keys, etc., etc., are suspended in graceful irregularity. The doors open by wooden latches, raised by means of small bits of pack-thread—I imagine, the same primitive order of fastening celebrated in the touching chronicle of Red Riding Hood; how they shut I will not attempt to describe, as the shutting of a door is a process of extremely rare occurrence throughout the whole Southern country. The third room, a chamber with sloping ceiling, immediately over our sitting-room and under the roof, is appropriated to the nurse and my two babies.

Of the closets, one is Mr. ——, the overseer's, bedroom, the other his office or place of business; and the third, adjoining our bedroom, and opening immediately out of doors, is Mr. B.'s dressing-room and cabinet d'affaires, where he gives audiences to the negroes, redresses grievances, distributes red woolen caps (a singular gratification to a slave), shaves himself, and performs the other offices of his toilet.

Such being our abode, I think you will allow there is little danger of my being dazzled by the luxurious splendors of a Southern slave residence. Our sole mode of summoning our attendants is by a pack-thread bell-rope suspended in the sitting room. From the bedrooms we have to raise the windows and our voices, and bring them by power of lungs, or help ourselves. . . .

I had a most ludicrous visit this morning from the midwife of the estate—rather an important personage both to master and slave, as to her unassisted skill and science the ushering of all the young negroes into their existence of bondage is intrusted. I heard a great deal of conversation in the dressing-room adjoining mine while performing my own toilet, and presently Mr. B. opened my room door, ushering in a dirty, fat, good-humored looking old negress, saying, "The midwife, Rose, wants to make your acquaintance." "Oh massa!" shrieked out the old creature, in a paroxysm of admiration, "where you get this lilly alabaster baby!" For a moment I looked round to see if she was speaking of my baby; but no, my dear, this superlative apostrophe was elicited by the fairness of *my skin.* . . .

Soon after this visit, I was summoned into the wooden porch or piazza of the house, to see a poor woman who desired to speak to me. This was none other than the tall, emaciated-looking negress who, on the day of our arrival, had embraced me and my nurse with such irresistible zeal. She appeared very ill to-day, and presently unfolded to me a most distressing history of bodily afflictions. She was the mother of a very large family, and complained to me that, what with childbearing and hard field labor, her back was almost broken in two. With an almost savage vehemence of gesticulation, she suddenly tore up her scanty clothing, and exhibited a spectacle with which I was inconceivably shocked and sickened. The facts, without any of her corroborating statements, bore tolerable witness to the hardships of her existence. I promised to attend to her ailments and give her proper remedies; but these are natural results, inevitable and irremediable ones, of improper treatment of the female frame; and, though there may be alleviation, there can not be any cure. . . .

After the departure of this poor woman, I walked down the settlement toward the Infirmary or hospital, calling in at one or two of the houses along the row. These cabins consist of one room, about twelve feet by fifteen, with a couple of closets smaller and closer than the state-rooms of a ship, divided off from the main room and each other by rough wooden partitions, in which the inhabitants sleep. They have almost all of them a rude bedstead, with the gray moss of the forests for mattress, and filthy, pestilential-looking blankets for covering. Two families (sometimes eight and ten in number) reside in one of these huts, which are mere wooden frames. . . . A wide ditch runs immediately at the back of these dwellings, which is filled and emptied daily by the tide. Attached to each hovel is a small scrap of ground for a garden, which, however, is for the most part untended and uncultivated. . . . Such of these buildings as I visited today were filthy and wretched in the extreme, and exhibited that most deplorable consequence of ignorance and an abject condition. . . .

Firewood and shavings lay littered about the floors, while the half-naked children were cowering round two or three smouldering cinders. The moss with which the chinks and crannies of their ill-protecting dwellings might have been stuffed was trailing in dirt and dust about the ground, while the back door of the huts, opening upon a most unsightly ditch, was left wide open for the fowls and ducks, which they are allowed to raise, to travel in and out, increasing the filth of the cabin by what they brought and left in every direction. In the midst of the floor, or squatting round the cold hearth, would be four or five little children from four to ten years old, the latter all with babies in their arms, the care of the infants being taken from the mothers (who are driven afield as soon as they recover from child labor), and devolved upon these poor little nurses, as they are called, whose business it is to watch the infant, and carry it to its mother whenever it may require nourishment. . . .

I bade the elder boys and girls kindle up the fire, sweep the floor and expel the poultry. . . . When I began to sweep and make up the fire, they first fell to laughing, and then imitating me. . . . Thus I traveled down the "street," in every dwelling endeavoring to awaken a new perception. . . . The Infirmary is a large two-story building, terminating the broad orange-planted space between the two rows of houses which form the first settlement; it is built of whitewashed wood and contains four large-sized rooms. But how shall I describe the spectacle presented to me on entering the first of these? But half the casements, of which there were six, were glazed, and these were obscured with dirt, almost as much as the other windowless ones were darkened by the dingy shutters, which the shivering inmates had fastened to in order to protect themselves from the cold. In the enormous chimney glimmered the powerless embers of a few sticks of wood, round which, however, as many of the sick women as could approach were cowering, some on wooden settles, most of them on the ground, excluding those who were too ill to rise; and these last poor wretches lay prostrate on the floor, without bed, mattress, or pillow, buried in tattered and filthy blankets, which, huddled round them as they lay strewed about, left hardly space to move upon the floor. And there, in their hour of sickness and suffering, lay those whose health and strength are spent in unrequited labor for us. . . . I stood in the midst of them, perfectly unable to speak, the tears pouring from my eyes, myself and my emotion alike strange and incomprehensible to them. . . . I passed on to the other room on the ground floor, and to the two above, one of which is appropriated to the use of the men who are ill. . . . They were all in the same deplorable condition. . . .

I was glad to return to the house, where I gave vent to my indignation and regret at the scene I had just witnessed to Mr. B. and his overseer, who here is a member of our family. The latter told me that the condition of the hospital had appeared to him, from his first entering upon his situation, to require a reform and that he had proposed it to the former manager, Mr. K———, and Mr. B.'s brother, who is part proprietor, but, receiving no encouragement, had supposed that it was a matter of indifference to the owners. . . .

I forgot to tell you that in the hospital were several sick babies, whose mothers were permitted to suspend their field labor in order to nurse them. Upon addressing some remonstrances to one, who, besides having a sick child, was ill herself, about the horribly dirty condition of her baby, she assured me that it was impossible for them to keep their children clean; that they went out to work at daybreak, and did not get their tasks done till evening, and that then they were too tired and worn out to do anything but throw themselves down and sleep. This statement of hers I mentioned on my return from the hospital, and the overseer appeared extremely annoyed by it, and assured me repeatedly that it was not true. . . .

Dear E—— This morning I paid my second visit to the Infirmary, and found there had been some faint attempt at sweeping and cleaning, in compliance with my entreaties. The poor woman Harriet, however, whose statement with regard to the impossibility of their attending properly to their children had been so vehemently denied by the overseer, was crying bitterly. I asked her what ailed her, when, more by signs and dumb show than words, she and old Rose informed me that Mr. O—— had flogged her that morning for having told me. . . . Mr. O——'s visit had preceded mine but a short time only, or I might have been edified by seeing a man horsewhip a woman. . . .

.   .   .

My dearest E—— We have, as a sort of under nursemaid and assistant to my dear M—— . . . a young woman named Psyche, but commonly called Sack. . . . She can not be much over twenty, has a very pretty figure, a graceful, gentle deportment and a face which, but for its color (she is a dingy mulatto), would be pretty, and is extremely pleasing, from the perfect sweetness of its expression; she is always serious, not to say sad and silent. . . .

To my great astonishment, the other day M—— asked me if I knew to whom Psyche belonged, as the poor woman had inquired of her with much hesitation and anguish if she could tell her who owned her and her children. She has two nice little children under six years old, whom she keeps as clean and tidy, and who are sad and as silent as herself. My astonishment at this question was not small, and I forthwith sought out Psyche for an explanation. She was thrown into extreme perturbation at finding that her question had been referred to me, and it was some time before I could sufficiently reassure her to be able to comprehend, in the midst of her reiterated entreaties for pardon, and hopes that she had not offended me, that she did not know herself who owned her. She was, at one time, the property of Mr. K——, the former overseer who has just been paying Mr. B. a visit. He, like several of his predecessors in the management, has contrived to make a fortune upon it . . . and has purchased a plantation of his own in Alabama, I believe, or one of the Southwestern states. Whether she still belonged to Mr. K—— or not she did not know, and entreated me, if she did, to endeavor to persuade Mr. B. to buy her. Now you must know that this poor woman is the wife of one of Mr. B.'s slaves, a fine, intelligent, active, excellent young man. . . . I was so astonished at the (to me) extraordinary state of things revealed by poor Sack's petition, that I could only tell her that I had supposed all the negroes on the plantation were Mr. B.'s property, but that I would certainly inquire, and find out for her, if I could, to whom she belonged. . . .

Now, E——, just conceive for one moment the state of mind of this woman, believing herself to belong to a man who in a few days was going down to one of those abhorred and dreaded Southwestern states, and who would then compel her, with her poor little children, to leave her husband and the only home she had ever known, and all the ties and affections . . . of her former life; and this was so completely a matter of course that it was not even thought necessary to apprise her positively of the fact, and the only thing that interposed between her and this most miserable fact was the faint hope that Mr. B. *might have* purchased her and her children. . . .

I did not see Mr. B. until the evening; but, in the mean time, meeting Mr. O——, the overseer, I asked him about Psyche, and who was her proprietor, when, to my infinite surprise, he told me that *he* had bought her and her children from Mr. K——, who had offered them to him, saying that they would be rather troublesome to him than otherwise down where he was going; "and so," said Mr. O——, "as I had no objection to investing a little money that way, I bought them." With a heart much lightened, I flew to tell poor Psyche the news, so that, at any rate, she might be relieved from the dread of any immediate separation from her husband. You can imagine better than I can tell you what her sensations were; but she still renewed her prayer that I would, if possible, induce Mr. B. to purchase her, and I promised to do so.

Early the next morning, while I was still dressing, I was suddenly startled by hearing voices in loud tones in Mr. B.'s dressing-room, which adjoins my bedroom, and the noise increasing until there was an absolute cry of despair uttered by some man. I could restrain myself no longer, but opened the door of communication and saw Joe, the young man, poor Psyche's husband, raving almost in a state of frenzy, and in a voice broken with sobs and almost inarticulate with passion, reiterating his determination never to leave this plantation, never to go to Alabama, never to leave his old father and mother, his poor wife and children, and dashing his hat, which he was wringing like a cloth in his hands, upon the ground, he declared he would kill himself if he was compelled to follow Mr. K——. I glanced from the poor wretch to Mr. B., who was standing, leaning against a table with his arms folded, occasionally uttering a few words of counsel to his slave to be quiet and not fret, and not make a fuss about what there was no help for. I retreated immediately from the horrid scene, breathless with surprise and dismay, and stood for some time in my own room, with my heart and temples throbbing to such a degree that I could hardly support myself.

As soon as I recovered myself I again sought Mr. O——, and inquired of him if he knew the cause of poor Joe's distress. He then told me that Mr. B., who is highly pleased with Mr. K——'s past administration of his property, wished, on his departure for his newly-acquired slave plantation, to give him some token of his satisfaction, and *had made him a present* of the man Joe. . . .

You will not wonder that the man required a little judicious soothing under such circumstances, and you will also, I hope, admire the humanity of the sale of his wife and children by the owner who was going to take him to Alabama, because *they* would be encumbrances rather than otherwise down there. If Mr. K—— did not do this after he knew that the man was his, then Mr. B. gave him to be carried down to the South after his wife and children were sold to remain in Georgia. I do not know which was the real transaction, for I have not had the heart to ask; but you will easily imagine which of the two cases I prefer believing.

When I saw Mr. B. after this most wretched story became known to me in all its details, I appealed to him, for his own soul's sake, not to commit so great a cruelty. Poor Joe's agony while remonstrating with his master was hardly greater than mine while arguing with him upon this bitter piece of inhumanity —how I cried, and how I adjured, and how all my sense of justice, and of mercy, and of pity for the poor wretch, and of wretchedness at finding myself implicated in such a state of things, broke in torrents of words from my lips and tears from my eyes! It seemed to me that I was imploring Mr. B. to save himself more than to spare these wretches. He gave me no answer whatever, and I have since thought that the intemperate vehemence of my entreaties and expostulations perhaps deserved that he should leave me as he did without one single word of reply; and miserable enough I remained.

Toward evening, as I was sitting alone, my children having gone to bed, Mr. O—— came into the room. As he sat down looking over some accounts, I said to him, "Have you seen Joe this afternoon, Mr. O——?"

"Yes, ma'am; he is a great deal happier than he was this morning."

"Why, how is that?" asked I, eagerly.

"Oh, he is not going to Alabama. Mr. K—— heard that he had kicked up a fuss about it, and said that if the fellow wasn't willing to go with him, he did not wish to be bothered with any niggers down there who were to be troublesome, so he might stay behind."

"And does Psyche know this?"

"Yes, ma'am, I suppose so."

I drew a long breath; and whereas my needle had stumbled through the stuff I was sewing for an hour before, as if my fingers could not guide it, the regularity and rapidity of its evolutions were now quite edifying. The man was for the present safe, and I remained silently pondering his deliverance and the whole proceeding, and the conduct of every one engaged in it, and, above all, Mr. B.'s share in the transaction, and I think, for the first time, almost a sense of horrible personal responsibility and implication took hold of my mind, and I felt the weight of an unimagined guilt upon my conscience; and yet, God knows, this feeling of self-condemnation is very gratuitous on my part, since when I married Mr. B. I knew nothing of these dreadful possessions of his, and even if I had I should have been puzzled to have formed any idea of the state of things in which I now find myself plunged, together with those whose well-doing is as vital to me almost as my own.

With these agreeable reflections I went to bed. Mr. B. said not a word to me upon the subject . . . the next day. . . . In the evening I was again with Mr. O—— alone in the strange, bare, wooden-walled sort of shanty which is our sitting-room, and revolving in my mind the means of rescuing Psyche from her miserable suspense . . . I suddenly accosted Mr. O——.

"Mr. O——, you will never sell Psyche and her children without first letting me know of your intention to do so, and giving me the option of buying them."

Mr. O—— is a remarkably deliberate man, and squints, so that, when he has taken a little time in directing his eyes to you, you are still unpleasantly unaware of any result in which you are concerned; he laid down a book he was reading, and directed his head and one of his eyes toward me and answered. "Dear me, ma'am, I am very sorry—I have sold them." My work fell down on the ground, and my mouth opened wide, and surprised; and he deliberately proceeded: "I didn't know, ma'am, you see, at all, that you entertained any idea of making an investment of that nature; for I'm sure, if I had, I would willingly have sold the woman to you; but I sold her and her children this morning to Mr. B." . . .

I jumped up and left Mr. O—— still speaking, and ran to find Mr. B., to thank him for what he had done. . . . Think, how it fares with slaves on plantations where there is no crazy Englishwoman to weep, and entreat, and implore, and upbraid for them, and no master willing to listen to such appeals.

Does the Bible Favor Bondage?

REV. T. STRINGFELLOW

Yet another voice in the rising debate over bondage was that of the Rev. Thornton Stringfellow of Virginia, whose Scriptural and Statistical Views in Favor of Slavery, *published in 1856 in Richmond, impressed many who were on his side. In these days, as tempers cracked in South and North, ministers and non-ministers drew on history, economics and "science" (quoted by all elements) to justify their varying views. Thousands, in pulpits and out of them, echoed Mr. Stringfellow's words.*

MY reader will remember that the subject in dispute is, whether involuntary and hereditary slavery was ever lawful in the sight of God, the Bible being judge.

I have shown by the Bible, that God decreed this relation between the posterity of Canaan, and the posterity of Shem and Japheth.

I have shown that God executed this decree by aiding the posterity of Shem, (at a time when "they were holiness to the Lord,") to enslave the posterity of Canaan in the days of Joshua.

I have shown that when God ratified the covenant of promise with Abraham, he recognized Abraham as the owner of slaves he had bought with his money of the stranger, and recorded his approbation of the relation, by commanding Abraham to circumcise them.

I have shown that when he took Abraham's posterity by the hand in Egypt, five hundred years afterwards, he publicly approbated the same relation, by permitting every slave they had bought with their money to eat the passover, while he refused the same privilege to their *hired servants.*

I have shown that God, as their national lawgiver, ordained by express statute, that they should buy slaves of the nations around them, (the seven devoted nations excepted,) and that these slaves and their increase should be a perpetual inheritance to their children.

I have shown that God ordained slavery by law for their captives taken in war, while he guaranteed a successful issue to their wars, so long as they obeyed him.

I have shown that when Jesus ordered his gospel to be published through the world, the relation of master and slave existed by law in every province and family of the Roman Empire, as it had done in the Jewish commonwealth for fifteen hundred years.

I have shown that Jesus ordained, that the legislative authority, which created this relation in that empire, should be obeyed and honored as an ordinance of God, as all government is declared to be.

I have shown that Jesus has prescribed the mutual duties of this relation in his kingdom.

And lastly, I have shown, that in an attempt by his professed followers to disturb this relation in the Apostolic churches, Jesus orders that fellowship shall be disclaimed with all such disciples, as seditious persons—whose conduct was not only dangerous to the State, but destructive to the true character of the gospel dispensation.

This being the case, as will appear by the recorded language of the Bible, to which we have referred you, reader, of what use is it to argue against it from moral requirements?

They regulate the duties of this and all other lawful relations among men—but they cannot abolish any relation, ordained or sanctioned of God, as is slavery.

Knights and Court Ladies: The Romantic Ultimate

JAMES B. AVIRETT

The ultimate in Southern romanticism arrived in the 1840's and '50's when in state after state ring tournaments occurred—first in Virginia, then in other states along the Atlantic, eventually in the lower South and in Texas. Those competing were "knights" in costume, mounted on horses and tilting at rings as did legendary figures of the medieval days. The tournaments had "courts" with "Queens of beauty," maids seated about them, poems recited to the populace, and other trappings of the middle ages. Orators waved their arms in praise of the glory of knighthood and womankind (or ladyhood, as some of the more florid speakers put it). A similar vogue had started about the same time, or earlier, in England; some attributed its popularity in the South to the influence of Walter Scott and other writers in the chivalric mood. This selection is from the Norfolk Herald *of September 5, 1857.*

IT is a mistake to say that the age of chivalry has passed. It is true that in our lowland country, where we have, or think we have, a greater variety of amusements of a refined character, we never attempt even the semblance of a tournament, as it is practised in the mountains of our State. But a recent visit to the upper counties has convinced us that this once martial exercise, which had its origin in Roman or perhaps in Trojan times, and was so common in the feudal ages, still exists, and although *armes à outrance* are superseded by the rockets, yet the chivalric spirit of the descendants of the knights of the olden time is the same which stimulated the latter to deeds of greater danger.

It is fashionable to sneer at these imitations of the amusements of the middle ages; but when it is remembered that they are done in the daytime, and bring together from distant places the young and old of both sexes, and excite to courtly emulation, whilst they perfect our young men in the elegant accomplishment of horsemanship, they are far more worthy of commendation than the midnight revels of the ballroom, and other such like recreations (?) of our silken knights and faded damsels of the cities.

It was our good fortune to be present at a recent display of the kind, near Markham,

in the County of Fauquier, which was held in honor of the nuptials of Miss ——, of Morven. All the beauty and bravery of that region seemed to have assembled on the occasion, if one might judge from the number of ladies who were ranged along the side of the mountain to witness the feats of the Knights, who were present, not to do battle as in the more barbarous times, but to prove their ability to bear the sword and lance in their behalf, if such necessity should ever arise.

Nothing can be more simple than the preparation as it appeared to us. In a dry meadow, or plain, at the foot of the mountain, two high posts were planted, about ten feet apart, from which was suspended a cord fastened to the top of each, and from the middle of this cord was hung a ring about six inches in diameter, slightly held by a hook. To dash at full speed from a point of some two hundred yards, and passing between the posts, to bear off the ring upon the point of a lance of six feet length, was one of the mysteries of the joust, and it would seem to be of easy accomplishment; but to do it all, and to do it gracefully, is a feat of horsemanship requiring fearlessness and hard practice.

In the present instance, we were struck with the whole of the arrangements. It was

One of the ultimates in Southern romanticism was the custom of the ring tournament, which continued until after the Confederate war.

In more remote parts of North Carolina, as elsewhere, the law had its troubles with homespun moonshiners.

announced in the beginning that six young married ladies were to be the judges of the tournament and, beginning with the bride, they were successively called to their seats, which overlooked the field. A band of music, high up above the lady judges, sounded the approach of the Knights, who were then for the first time seen filing through the rocks and trees, and in good order soon displayed in line a few yards below where the ladies were seated. The Knights were nobly mounted, and dressed in the gay fashion and coloring which the fancy of each had selected. Richard Ashby, the Herald, one of the most manly-looking persons we ever beheld, then introduced the Knights, calling the roll as it were, thus: "The Knight of Avon"—"of Avenel"—"of the Lancet"—"of Aldenburg"—"of Frederick"—"Ali Pascha"—"Rob Roy"—"Roderick Dhu"—"McIvor"—"Knight of Markham"—and so on to the end of the list. A short address followed, stating the rules of the tilt, the duties of the contestants, and expressing confidence in their endeavors to win by their bravery the rewards which beauty was ready to bestow. The music sounded again, and the troop turned and passed along and away, until they were entirely concealed from view among the trees. And now the Herald, Mr. A. ——, of Markham, called to the Knight of Avon to come forth, and in an instant he was seen emerging from the forest and bounding upon his horse as fleetly as the spirited animal could bear him toward the ring, and, as gracefully as only he could do the deed, bore away the ring in triumph, amidst the shouts of the spectators and the strains of music. After, came one and another of the Knights, as well trained, and managing their horses as if they were centaurs, but with various success,—each successful one receiving the applause of the spectators in his turn.

There was one, however, who was a stranger, calling himself the Knight of Aldenburg, of moderate stature, simply attired, and indifferently mounted, who in spite of all his efforts, and he freely used his spurs, could not force his steed to the lists, so that he was ruled out after three baffled attempts. The lady judges, however, overruled the rules, and admitted him to another trial, which he modestly accepted; and mounted upon another charger

he came thundering along the plain, and bore away the prize from all competitors, having taken the ring seven times in succession.

The Knight of Avon, Rob Roy and Roderick Dhu were decided to be next in skill to him of Aldenburg, and entitled, after the victor had selected the Queen, to name the Maids of Honor—or, we believe, of love and beauty. This decree being announced, the Knights, with their Herald, rode up and again deployed before the judges, when the Knight of Aldenburg dismounted, and handing his bridle to his Esquire, knelt before Miss M. of Markham, and crowned her Queen. In quick succession the Knights of Avon, Rob Roy, and Roderick Dhu bowed lowly before Miss C. M. of Fauquier, Miss C. of Winchester, and Miss S. of Fredericksburg, as the selected Maids of Honor. Each lady replied with ease and fitly to the complimentary speeches of their respective knights. While this was being done, the echoes of the hills around were waked up by the trumpets of the musicians, and a most charming excitement prevailed among all—unless we except, perhaps, the Knights who had failed in the contest and the ladies to whom these Knights had vowed to do homage in case of success—for each Knight had knelt at his especial shrine that day, not excepting the turbaned representative of Ali Pascha.

The sun was setting behind the hill which made the western boundary of the lists, just as the act of coronation was finished—and so we might let the curtain drop upon them; but there was one incident that might have found fitting place even at the "passage of arms at Ashby." During the contest, a horseman rode up in the full costume of an Indian chief, painted and feathered, and calling himself Hiawatha. He rode an unbroken colt, without saddle or bridle; and without noticing the music or the crowd, he uttered the war-cry of his race, and passing like a flash along the line, he lifted the ring from its rest as if it were child's play, and continuing at full speed to the outer extremity of the plain, bounded over a high stone wall, and disappeared. This man of the forest, by the rules of the tournament, was not permitted to select and crown the Queen of Love and Beauty, nor was it his wish to do so, as it seemed; but in the judgment of the bride, tribunal, or ladies'-court, and of all who looked upon that scene, no Christian Knight was ever more fully entitled than he to the highest honors of Chivalry.

We have omitted much of this amusing spectacle, and incidents perhaps worthy of a place in the foreground of the picture; nor have we expatiated on the superb scenery of valley and mountain, embellished by the fine mansion of Mr. Marshall, (one of the sons of the late Chief Justice), which looked over upon the field of the tournament; nor of the surpassing beauty of the ladies, without whose smiles the gallant knights would not have toiled for their spurs;—but we have said enough to show that "peace hath its triumphs as well as war," and to inspire our lowland youth with an honest desire to emulate their highland brethren in feats of manhood.

III

Ever Southward, Ever Westward

NEW ORLEANS near the Gulf of Mexico, the Mississippi River country up to Natchez and Memphis and beyond, the lands of Mississippi and Alabama . . . of the various sub-regions within the South, they formed a subtropical tier, most Southerly of all, with a life that often appeared more fervent than any other, and the least Puritanical. This lowest-lying of the several Souths had an additional flourish, an intensity beyond that of the rest.

To some the scene presented a somber note—the gloom of many swamps, their wine-dark waters and Spanish moss that hung like tattered gray garments in the still air, and the forests that thrust their way to the shore. Others accepted the many contrasts: glinting water, dazzling light over plains and fields, heavy shadows in the foreground. Few things in Louisiana and Mississippi and adjoining areas were temperate, or muted in look or mood; between velvety dark and a sunlight that could hurt the eye, gradations were slight. And there was no long, slowly descending dusk as in Virginia or Maryland; night dropped quickly, and dawn broke with no less speed.

For mile after mile, estates were lonely settlements, more separated than those in the earlier South, which had filled up to a degree. More than in Virginia and Georgia and the Carolinas, the clusters of whites and blacks and brown-skinned people became villages all but swallowed by a wilderness. Here crops grew swiftly, vines almost advancing before the eyes, with a junglelike insect and parasite life. During a nine-month period new small crops might thrust themselves up three times a year. Great bushes splashed violet reds and yellows and more delicate gradations against the sides of a hill and at river landings, in the shadow of fences or the corners of neat circles of growth set out by a plantation family. Everything about the land had an added vigor, a greater concentration.

Under these conditions the people sometimes showed a passionate mood that made newcomers stare. These Deep Southerners fluctuated between calm weeks in the shade and outbursts of sudden energy or equally sudden temper. Social life had a quicker tempo; life was to be enjoyed, to be savored to the last drop. Only a bluenose would reject its offerings, its lively cotillions and ceremonial processions, its marches about the ballrooms or hotel porches and, at New Orleans and Mobile and other places of French heritage, the Mardi Gras about which much of the life centered through the years.

For hundreds of miles, forests enveloped the separate plantations, but within the brightly lighted circle of town or country center, couples moved in the perfumed air, in the softened light of the candles. Shoulders shrugged and fans hid the lower face while women's eyes widened and flickered at a question or a compliment. And to Natchez or Port Gibson, Vicksburg or New Orleans or Baton Rouge, whole families went often in a chattering cluster for several weeks of balls and suppers, hunt breakfasts and receptions.

Not least diverting were the events in which riders urged on their steeds in matches that drew hundreds to tracks at New Orleans or other river cities. At annual meetings vast sums were bet, and families rode down from Natchez or more distant points to be part of history-making competitions. Contests were in the Southerners' blood, and repeatedly the steamboats engaged in impromptu races. As sparks flew and throngs screamed from the decks and the banks, lives were endangered—and forfeited.

In other ways among these Deep Southerners, emotions were close to the surface, and men struck out in anger. Thus it was that planters and town lawyers, cotton dealers and merchants dueled over the slightest of imputations, the faintest shadow of a reflection. New Orleans, with combinations of many nationalities, of French and Spanish, Americans and others, became the major point of formal encounters in the early morning. In the great hotels other individuals collided in less stately manner, exchanging gunfire while onlookers dodged.

There were other, still less lustrous aspects of the life. As the years passed, the prospect of quick returns drew men to parts of the lower South in a rush of land-grabbing, manipulation and the piling up of overnight fortunes, with all that sudden wealth, gained under such conditions, makes possible. Politics became brash, uninhibited and, while often funny, had little of the feeling of inherited obligation that had once marked the Virginians.

In these days, as memoirs make clear, lawless ones rode high, as card cheats, cutthroats and assorted other rascals thrived magnificently. Slave traders enticed dark people to escape with them, promising freedom a short way off; then they callously sold the men and women to the first bidder. On the Mississippi and other rivers, adept scoundrels rode like any other passengers, fleecing strangers, then slipping away. Certain individuals fled from state to state, bilking victims as they went. For years desperadoes lurked along roads and at river landings, terrorizing bands of travelers or even whole towns, until civilians at Vicksburg and other towns rose against them with knife, gun and rope.

Prices rose high, higher; a likely Negro might fetch $1,800 or more. As the saying went, planters had a mania to buy more Negroes to plant more cotton so as to buy still more Negroes to plant still more cotton. And in lower Louisiana a second great crop competed with cotton; sugar cane proved a vast potential source of wealth, yet one that required even greater outlay of cash. . . . The spirit of this semitropic South was contagious; men of Illinois or New England settled here as growers or town lawyers, to become the warmest spirits of all, acquiring an art of oratory, a love of the dance, an inclination to resort to the duel as the arbiter of issues.

There were small plantation houses and enormous ones, simple and elaborate, some slovenly, others gleaming with a polish of fanlighted doorways and shining knobs. A general pattern developed: the central house at the best point of land, the top of a slow rise from the shore or the dominant bend along the river, with side buildings for offices, overseer's house, bachelor's quarters, smokehouse, a separate kitchen and, in a double line at the back, the huts of the slaves.

Big porches or galleries had a functional use, holding the sunlight from the rooms, providing a steady shade throughout the day. In most cases a wide central hallway extended from the front of the house to the back, and it might be as large as the biggest of rooms, to permit an unimpeded sweep of air. Ornamented ceilings were high, windows long and wide, and the plantation houses often had fewer rooms than strangers expected, in order to provide the maximum of breezes through the passageways.

At times a gardener looked after the many plantings about the residence, with a hothouse and sheds for experimentation with imported plants. A schoolhouse often stood at a distance, and at another point an icehouse might await, its cover extending slightly above the ground, in the coolest part of the estate. And smokehouses, shadowed, redolent, held hams and other produce, the special pride of host or hostess.

Whenever possible, these Deep Southerners occupied chairs or hammocks on the galleries, fanning themselves through part of the day, sipping mild drinks or not so mild ones. And in the evenings they and their guests might take places under the punkahs or hanging fans which a servant, holding a string, drew back and forth. Later they waltzed in the drawing rooms beneath chandeliers whose prisms tinkled lightly in the reverberations of the dance.

During the more florid 1840's and '50's larger houses acquired ballrooms, all white or with walls painted in elaborate designs, or tinted in pastel green or other shadings of the rainbow. Hand-painted doorknobs, marble mantels, silver locks at the doors . . . and four-poster beds became monumental in size, with room for four or five, and trundle beds stored beneath them in the day hours.

In the distance, with lines of trees around it, was the family cemetery; because of the usual inaccessibility of the estate, the distance to the nearest town, the plantation buried its own people in a shadowed place of retreat and meditation. . . . In many things the pattern of this life was large and also graceful.

Yet, in a way that some did not realize, then or now, such an existence might be a hazardous one. A great house could disappear in a matter of hours, by fire, or suffer drastic damage in a flood. More irretrievably, a planter would lose everything in a bad crop, or two or three. A large plantation might have a steady succession of masters; as an old, tight-lipped one left, a smiling newcomer took his place. Tenure in planterdom could be brief and tragic.

Under the Poetic Oaks

THOMAS McCALEB

As the vogue for dueling spread itself over most of the South, there were few places in which men followed it so enthusiastically as in Louisiana. Now and then New Orleans was called the dueling capital of America. The clashes involved Creoles, Americans, "Frenchmen from France," old residents, newcomers, guns, swords and occasionally weird weapons not recognized by the official code. Perhaps it was the semitropical climate, or the careless life of the lower delta, the rivalries of contrasting civilizations. . . . Whatever the explanation, the Crescent City had duels every day, often several a day, and the favorite spot was under the oaks of what is now City Park. Here is an authoritative account from Thomas McCaleb's The Louisiana Book, *published in 1894.*

A SHORT walk from the terminus of the Bayou Road street-car line brings the visitor in front of a magnificent little forest of gigantic live oaks. It is the Lower City Park, in former times a wooded plantation belonging to Louis Allard, a man of letters and a poet. During the latter portion of his life, crippled in health and fortune, Allard saw his land sold but was permitted to continue his occupation. There he spent his days, reclining in an armchair under his beloved oaks, reading his favorite authors and dreaming of what might have been. In compliance with his dying wish he lies buried in the old place under the very oak where the last years of his life had been spent. From its site the legendary trees rear their majestic heads in solemn grandeur.

A terrible war between two sections of our country has revolutionized the social system of the South. But the great oaks are still the same, solemnly brooding over memories of the past. The lights and shades of their leafy arcades, typical of a state of society where tragedy and gayety walked side by side in chivalrous converse, take back our memories to a period scarcely fifty years remote, when it was an everyday occurrence to see under these branches a meeting of adversaries in mortal combat, with rapier or pistol, sabre or shotgun.

At that time New Orleans, though even then to a degree cosmopolitan, was essentially a Creole city, and under the full influence of the traditions which governed that high-strung and chivalrous race. The world and society were of courtly brilliance. Merchants and lawyers were incidentally poets and wits, and the ladies accomplished musicians. Over all this, over men and women there ruled a supreme sense of dignity and honor, maintained by the strictest public opinion. Bankrupts committed suicide, and women fallen from virtue disappeared and were never heard from. . . .

The punctilio among men was strict even to exaggeration. The least breach of etiquette, the most venial sin against politeness, the least suspicion thrown out of unfair dealing, even a bit of awkwardness, were causes sufficient for a cartel, which none dared refuse. The acceptance, however, did not mean that the quarrel must inevitably be settled on the field. The seconds, two on each side, discussed the quarrel dispassionately, sometimes with the assistance of mutual friends, and often arrived at an amicable and honorable settlement. . . . Experienced friends, well versed in the law and precedents of the code, settled beforehand every nice point, so that the adversaries met under the oaks in full equality, morally and socially.

How many a bloody combat originated in a ballroom, where the cause of the difficulty passed unnoticed by all. Said a gentleman to a much-courted lady: "Honor me with half of this dance?"

Pre-eminent among Southern figures who explored the early West was Daniel Boone, brave, adventuresome, but eventually a victim of the scheming of other men.

"Ask monsieur," answered the lady; "it belongs to him."

"Never," spoke the dancer, whirling past in the waltz, and just caught the words softly spoken by smiling lips as he passed by: "*Ah, vous êtes mal élevé.*" ("Ah, you are badly reared.") Not a word more was said that night between the two gentlemen, though they subsequently met and bowed; but early the next morning the flippant talker received a challenge, and in the evening a neat *coup droit* under the oaks. . . .

So well recognized was the code by all who had any pretensions to good breeding that even judges on the bench would resent an insult from lawyers at the bar. While on the bench Judge Joachim Bermudez, father of the Chief Justice of the State, made a ruling against a certain lawyer, who objected in rather unbecoming terms. Ordered to sit down, he refused; whereupon the judge ordered the sheriff to take him into custody for contempt. Taking a pistol, the lawyer defied the sheriff, who feared to advance. The judge, leaping from his bench, seized the lawyer by the arm and handed him to a police officer, who led him to prison. The judge soon afterward ordered his release. That evening he received a challenge from the lawyer, which was promptly accepted. On the field the lawyer offered to apologize, but that was not permitted by the code. Never, on the field. The judge absolutely refused any apology, and the lawyer had to leave the country. He could not have practiced, after this, before the courts of the State.

It is true that there existed a law against duelling, but the practice was so strongly welded in the customs of the people that the statute served only to add the glamour of mystery and the flavor of forbidden fruit to the other fascinations of the deadly game, and might as well not have existed. Things being so, it is not astonishing that New Orleans should have been a favorite resort for professors of fence or *maîtres d'armes*. Most of these, having no further personal value than their skill with the foils, lived in blood, wine and profligacy their circumscribed lives between the *cafés* and *salles d'escrime*. Others, who pursued their callings as an honored profession, acquired a certain standing in society, and old residents love to talk over their skill and their other lovable and manly traits. Others, again, have acquired fame for having killed or having been killed in duels.

Among the latter were Marcel Dauphin, who was killed by A. Nora in a duel with shotguns; Bonneval, who was killed by Reynard, also a professional swordsman; L'Alouette, who killed Shubra, another professor, and who was Pepe Llulla's teacher of fence and subsequently his associate; Thimécourt, who killed Poulaga, and others. There were also E. Baudoin, a Parisian, very popular and well esteemed; Émile Cazère, who had quite an aristocratic clientele, and Gilbert Rosière, familiarly called by his pupils "Titi" Rosière, perhaps the most popular among all the masters. I must not forget Basile Croquère, who, though a mulatto, was such a fine blade that many of the best Creole gentlemen did not hesitate, notwithstanding the strong prejudice against color, to frequent his *salle d'armes*, and even cross swords with him in private *assauts*.

All of us who were young before the Confederate war, remember the gay, whole-souled though irascible Rosière, whose son, himself an admirable swordsman, followed the *Gardes d'Orléans* to the plains of Shiloh at General Beauregard's call. A native of Bordeaux, he came to New Orleans when very young to make his fortune at the bar. But he fell in with a wild set; he dropped the Code Napoléon for the Code of Honor, became a leader in the devil-may-care adventures of the youth of that time and turned fencing master. He was everybody's friend, and, contradictory as it may seem, this hero of seven duels in one week was, in some respects, of womanly tenderness. He would fight with men to the bitter death, but would not have hurt a defenceless thing, woman, child or fly.

A great frequenter of the opera, his superb head could be seen almost every night in the parquette. On one occasion, deeply touched, he wept audibly. An impudent neighbor laughed, but his amusement was of short duration. The next day a flesh wound taught the man that it is not always good to laugh.
. . .

In the spring of 1840 there was a grand *assaut d'armes* between professors at the old Salle St. Philipe, which was filled with the gilded youth. None but brevetted experts, who could show a diploma, were allowed to participate. An Italian professor of counterpoint, Poulaga, a man of magnificent physique and herculean strength, held his own with the broadsword and bade defiance to all comers. Captain Thimécourt, a former cavalry officer, opposed and defeated him. The humiliation was too much for the Italian's pride and he made a sneering remark. At once the soldier exclaimed: "Let us advance to the field." Without further parley, they took rendezvous for the oaks, and there Thimécourt cut his adversary to pieces.

The same *assaut d'armes* was the cause of Pepe Llulla's challenging a French professor named Grand Bernard, who had insisted on his producing a diploma before crossing swords with him in the *salle d'armes*. They fought with broadswords and Pepe, though he had no diploma, opened the master's flank in two places.

Another well-known professor was a German swordsman, Monthiach. He was tall, fleshy and muscular, and at the same time the best-natured fellow in the world, but of course always ready for a duel, particularly with a professor. Professors of all kinds have always been more or less jealous of each other, but the *maîtres* of that period were peculiarly and aggressively so. Well, Thimécourt and Monthiach had some slight difference about a *coup*, and, naturally, as they disagreed completely, the only way to come to an understanding was to fight it out.

They fought with broadswords, because it was about that weapon that they had disagreed. The duel was short, sharp and decisive. At the first pass, Monthiach made a terribly vicious cut at his adversary, evidently intended to cut off his head at one blow. The *coup* was admirably conceived and executed. Thimécourt, who had his own idea, did not parry with the sword, but dodged. His hat was cut clear in two, Monthiach's blade grazing his scalp. At the same time the Frenchman, passing under his adversary's sword, opened his breast with a splendid *coup de pointe*. The seconds interfered. The gash was a frightful one, and the blood flowed freely, yet the German professor insisted upon going on with the fight. The seconds would not permit it.

They had taken no surgeon with them, and Monthiach, to the horror of the bystanders, pulled out some tow which he had in his pocket, and packing his wound with it to stop the flow of blood, walked home in a frenzy of anger, cursing at the seconds, for, as he said, it was a beautiful *coup*, and he would have assuredly chopped off Thimécourt's head if he had had a chance to renew it. Three days later he was on parade in a military company.

There was not a day passed without one or two encounters at the oaks or elsewhere.

Old citizens in the neighborhood of the oaks say that for a time it was a daily procession of pilgrims to this bloody Mecca. Some walked or rode back, others were carried home for burial, but once on the field, honor required that some blood should be spilt. Sometimes it was a drop only, sometimes a draining of the veins.

Hugues Pedesclaux had a quarrel with a retired French cavalry officer and the Frenchman selected broadswords, on horseback. An eyewitness says: "It was a handsome sight. The adversaries were mounted on spirited horses and stripped to the waist. As they rode up to each other, nerved for the combat, their respective muscular development and the confidence of their bearing gave promise of an interesting fight. The Frenchman was heavy and somewhat ungainly, but his muscles looked like whip-cord, and his broad, hairy chest gave evidence of remarkable strength and endurance. Pedesclaux, somewhat lighter, was admirably proportioned, and his youthful suppleness seemed to more than counterbalance his adversary's brawny but somewhat rigid manhood. An eyewitness said:

"A clashing of steel, which drew sparks from the blades, and the two adversaries crossed and passed each other by unhurt. In a moment the enemies met again. A terrible head blow from the Frenchman would now have cleft Pedesclaux to the shoulder-blade, if his quick sword had not warded off the death stroke. It was then that, with lightning rapidity, before his adversary could recover his guard, which had been disturbed by the momentum of his blow, the Creole, by a rapid half-circle, regained his and plunged his blade through the body of the French officer, who reeled in his saddle, fell, and was picked up senseless and bleeding. . . . He died soon afterward."

Mother Always Regulated the Terms

THOMAS ASHE

Through many years, surprised or amused visitors to the French-American New Orleans put down their impressions of the semiformal arrangements by which white men of the city met handsome, light-skinned women at the balls, then set them up as "placées" in little cottages, generally on the city's outskirts. Not many wrote so carefully, with less gilding of the basic situation, than did Thomas Ashe, in his Travels in America, *published in London in 1808.*

THE Americans, since their arrival here, have been so occupied by politics and legislation that their minds have never been sufficiently unbent to form a course of pleasures for themselves; therefore the indulgence of the table, cards and billiards, are the principal fountain of the enjoyments of the men. It is not so with the French gentlemen: their pleasures are forever varied, and of a nature to be participated in by the most delicate of the female sex. This casts over them a considerable degree of refinement, and the concert, dance, promenade, and *petit souper*, are conducted with as much attention as at Paris or Rome. At times, the limits of the French entertainments extend from a partial circle and pervade the whole town.

Besides the French and American amusements of the men, I can still trace some old Spanish recreations. On returning to my lodging late at night, I have more than once heard the guitar under the windows of a sleeping beauty, or the harp delicately touched under a *corridore* over which some charming girl attentively reclined. Songs, too, are often heard in the silence of the night. They sometimes assume the form of a duet, and are repeated by the lover and the confidential friend who accompanies him as a guard.

It could be wished that the Spanish character were only to be discerned by their empassioned songs and innocent amours: unfortunately it often breaks out in sanguinary stabs of the stiletto and frequent assassinations. Several Americans who have interrupted their midnight serenades have already fallen. The remainder go armed and have also learned to correct their conduct towards the Spaniards, whom they now find they cannot trample upon with impunity or scorn.

The women, who in point of manners and character have a very marked superiority over the men, are divided into two ranks—the white and the brown. They have two separate ballrooms in the city. At the white ballroom no lady of colour is admitted. Those called the whites are principally brunettes with deep black eyes, dark hair, and good teeth. Their persons are eminently lovely and their movements indescribably graceful, far superior to anything I ever witnessed in Europe. The dress of the white ladies is very plain and simple. The robe white, fastened under the breast with a diamond pin, and the hair in the form of a coronet, connected by small bands of precious stones and pearls.

The principal amusement of the young women of this class is to ride out after sunset in small cabriolets, which they drive themselves with great ease and dexterity. A Negro boy or girl, elegantly dressed, stands behind. In these excursions they are never attended by gentlemen; the loss of reputation being dreaded here beyond the loss of every thing else beside. Their public amusements are balls and concerts, which are generally well attended; their private entertainment consists of music-parties at home, and conversations around the door.

The "Women of Colour" stand next to the white in society. They are very beautiful, of a light copper colour, and tall and elegant persons. Their dress is widely different in general from that of the white ladies; their

A pathway of empire for men and women of the older South was the Cumberland Gap, over which thousands of families trudged or rode in a never-ending file.

petticoats are ornamented at the bottom with gold lace or fringe richly tasselled; their slippers are composed of gold-embroidery, and their stockings interwoven with the same metal, in so fanciful a manner as to display the shape of the leg to the best advantage.

A kind of jacket made of velvet, fitted tight to the shape and laced or buttoned in front, with long points hanging down quite round the petticoat and trimmed at the end with pearl tassels, is also worn; and on the shoulders of the jacket is fastened a cloak made of gauze, or some such light materials, which hangs as a loose train to the ground, or is occasionally fastened to the side by a clasp of jewels. Their most general head-dress is either a handkerchief of gold-gauze braided in with diamonds, or else chains of gold and pearls twisted in and out through a profusion of fine black hair, which produces a pleasing effect.

Notwithstanding the beauty and wealth of these women, they are not admitted, as I before remarked, to the white assemblies. They have therefore a ballroom of their own, which is well attended, and where as beautiful persons and as graceful dancing is witnessed as in any other assemblies of the sort whatever. A distinction exists between ladies of colour of a very singular sort. Those who are but one remove from the African cast are subordinate to those who are from two to three, or more, and are interdicted, by custom, from inter-marrying with the whites; but they are al-lowed, by the same authority, to become mistresses of the whites without being dis-honoured in the eyes of society: that is, they are esteemed honourable and virtuous while faithful to one man; but if, in their amours, they at any time become indiscriminate, they lose the advantage of ranking among the virtu-ous and are classed in the city-books among prostitutes and slaves.

This, or a native disposition to conti-nence, has such a dominion over them, that the instances of their infidelity are very rare, though they are extremely numerous, and are mistresses to the married and unmarried, and nearly to all the strangers who resort to the town. For though infidelity is punished among them, they are no sooner disengaged from one attachment than they are at liberty to form another.

The introduction of strangers to them is attended with some ceremony and must al-ways be through the means of the mother, or [some other] female adopted to supply her place. The inhabitants of the town never break down their regulations, or treat them abruptly, and strangers are instructed by their acquaintance how to proceed. The levee, at sunset, is the principal market for all this traffic *de coeur*. There all the beauties assem-ble, and there all those who need a kind companion joyfully repair: all walk up and down for a considerable time, or sit under orange-trees with the objects of their separate choice. Such an expression of reserve, morals, and decency reigns over the women of every sort, that a stranger passes and repasses, before he can assume sufficiently to tell the one he admires the most *qu'elle est belle comme une ange*, and so forth.

To an Englishman, this timid, bashful, silent demeanour opposes difficulties which require his utmost resolution to surmount, and he walks the levee many a pensive evening before the sense of virtue is sufficiently con-sumed by the new passion of his breast to permit him to speak, or to offer terms to a parent, from which his soul shrinks, from the conviction of their being base and dishonor-able. Some mothers now, on becoming ac-quainted with the English timidity, begin to alter their line of conduct, and suffer their daughters to remove their veil *en passant un Anglais*, or flirt their fan, or drop a handker-chief, which they receive with such gracious accents of gratitude, that a conversation may easily succeed.

The mothers always regulate the terms and make the bargain. The terms allowed the parents are generally fifty dollars a month: during which time the lover has the exclusive right to the house, where fruit, coffee, and refreshments may at any time be had, or where he may entirely live with the utmost safety and tranquility. Many do live in this manner, notwithstanding which, I have never heard a complaint against these interesting females. In proportion as they advance in age they enter into service, etc., and are respected as much as when in their virgin state.

The Old - Time Mardi Gras

CHARLES LYELL

Among many descriptions, early and late, of New Orleans' Mardi Gras—part folk festival, part a series of private social events—few have the appeal of Sir Charles Lyell's version of the doings of 1846. A well-recognized geologist, Sir Charles did not confine himself to rock formations when he traveled about the United States. He set down most of New Orleans' variegated sights and sounds —"grand processions," masked figures on horseback, people in open carriages, the throwing of flour, the French Opera with its layer-cake arrangement of races and castes. This section appeared in his A Second Visit to the United States, published in London in 1849.

Feb. 23, 1846. THE distance from Mobile to New Orleans is 175 miles by what is called the inland passage, or the channel between the islands and the mainland. . . . We sailed out of the beautiful bay of Mobile in the evening, in the coldest month of the year, yet the air was warm, and there was a haze like that of a summer's evening in England. Many gulls followed our ship, enticed by pieces of bread thrown out to them by the passengers, some of whom were displaying their skill in shooting the birds in mere wantonness. . . .

Next morning at daylight we found ourselves in Louisiana. We had already entered the large lagoon, called Lake Pontchartrain, by a narrow passage, and, having skirted its southern shore, had reached a point six miles north of New Orleans. Here we disembarked and entered the cars of a railway built on piles, which conveyed us in less than an hour to the great city, passing over swamps in which the tall cypress, hung with Spanish moss, was flourishing, and below it numerous shrubs just bursting into leaf. In many gardens of the suburbs, the almond and peach trees were in full blossom. In some places the blue-leaved palmetto and the leaves of a species of iris (*iris cuprea*) were very abundant. We saw a tavern called the Elysian Fields Coffee House, and some others with French inscriptions. There were also many houses with porte-cochères, high roofs, and volets, and many lamps suspended from ropes attached to tall posts on each side of the road, as in the French capital. We might indeed have fancied that we were approaching Paris, but for the Negroes and mulattoes, and the large verandahs reminding us that the windows required protection from the sun's heat.

It was a pleasure to hear the French language spoken and to have our thoughts recalled to the most civilized parts of Europe by the aspect of a city, forming so great a contrast to the innumerable new towns we had lately beheld. The foreign appearance, moreover, of the inhabitants made me feel thankful that it was possible to roam freely and without hindrance over so large a continent—no bureaus for examining and signing of passports, no fortifications, no drawbridges, no closing of gates at a fixed hour in the evening, no waiting till they are opened in the morning, no custom houses separating one state from another, no overhauling of baggage by *gens d'armes* for the octroi; and yet as perfect a feeling of personal security as I ever felt in Germany or France.

The largest of the hotels, the St. Charles, being full, we obtained agreeable apartments at the St. Louis, in a part of the town where we heard French constantly spoken. Our rooms were fitted up in the French style, with muslin curtains and scarlet draperies. There was a finely proportioned drawing room, furnished *à la Louis Quatorze*, opening into a large dining room with sliding doors, where the boarders and the 'transient visitors,' as they are called in the United States, met at meals. The mistress of the hotel, a widow, presided at dinner, and we talked French with her and some of the attendants; but most of the servants of the house were Irish or German. There was a beautiful ballroom, in which preparations were making for a grand masked ball to be given the night after our arrival.

It was the last day of the Carnival. From the time we landed in New England to this hour, we seemed to have been in a country where all, whether rich or poor, were labouring from morning till night, without ever indulging in a holiday. I had sometimes thought that the national motto should be, "All work and no play." It was quite a novelty and a refreshing sight to see a whole population giving up their minds for a short season to amusement. There was a grand procession parading the streets, almost every one dressed in the most grotesque attire, troops of them on horseback, some in open carriages, with bands of music, and in a variety of costumes—some as Indians, with feathers in their heads, and one, a jolly fat man, as Mardi Gras himself.

All wore masks, and here and there in the crowd, or stationed in a balcony above, we saw persons armed with bags of flour, which they showered down copiously on any one who seemed particularly proud of his attire. The strangeness of the scene was not a little heightened by the blending of Negroes, quadroons, and mulattoes in the crowd; and we were amused by observing the ludicrous surprise, mixed with contempt, of several unmasked, stiff, grave Anglo-Americans from the north, who were witnessing for the first time what seemed to them so much mummery and tomfoolery. One wagoner, coming out of a cross-street, in his working-dress, drove his team of horses and vehicle heavily laden with cotton bales right through the procession, causing a long interruption.

The crowd seemed determined to allow nothing to disturb their good humour; but although many of the wealthy Protestant citizens take part in the ceremony, this rude intrusion struck me as a kind of foreshadowing of coming events, emblematic of the violent shock which the invasion of the Anglo-Americans is about to give to the old _régime_ of Louisiana. A gentleman told me that, being last year in Rome, he had not seen so many masks at the Carnival there; and, in spite of the increase of Protestants, he thought there had been quite as much "flour and fun" this year as usual. The proportion, however, of strict Romanists is not so great as formerly, and tomorrow, they say, when Lent begins, there will be an end of the trade in masks; yet the butchers will sell nearly as much meat as ever. During the Carnival, the greater part of the French population keep open house, especially in the country.

New Orleans, February, 1846. Walking first over the most ancient part of the city . . . we entered the Place d'Armes and saw on one side of the square the old Spanish Government House, and opposite to it the Cathedral, or principal Catholic church, both in an antique style of architecture, and therefore strikingly unlike anything we had seen for many months. Entering the church, which is always open, we found persons on their knees, as in Catholic countries, although it was not Sunday, and an extremely handsome quadroon woman coming out.

February 26. In the evening we went to the French opera, and were much pleased with the performance, the orchestra being the best in America. The audience was very quiet and orderly, which is said not to be always the case in some theatres here. The French Creole ladies, many of them descended from Norman ancestors, and of pure unmixed blood, are very handsome. They were attired in Parisian fashion, not overdressed, usually not so thin as the generality of American women; their luxuriant hair tastefully arranged, fastened with ornamental pins, and adorned simply with a coloured ribbon or a single flower. My wife learnt from one of them afterward, that they usually pay, by the month, a quadroon female hairdresser, a refinement in which the richest ladies of Boston would not think of indulging.

The word Creole in Louisiana . . . never means persons of mixed breed. . . . The frequent alliances of the Creoles, or Louisianians of French extraction, with lawyers and merchants from the Northern States help to cement the ties which are every day binding more firmly together the distant parts of the Union. Both races may be improved by such connection, for the manners of the Creole ladies are, for the most part, more refined; and many a Louisianian might justly have felt indignant if he could have overheard a conceited young bachelor from the North telling me "how much they were preferred by the fair sex to the hard-drinking, gambling, horse-racing, cock-fighting, and tobacco-chewing Southerners."

If the Creoles have less depth of character and are less striving and ambitious than the New Englanders, it must be no slight source of happiness to the former to be so content with present advantages. They seem to feel, far more than the Anglo-Saxons, that if riches be worth the winning, they are also worth enjoying. . . .

Some part of the feeling prevailing in New England, in regard to the immorality of New Orleans, may be set down to the fact of their theatres being open every Sunday evening, which is no indication whatever of a disregard of religion, on the part of the Catholics. The latter might, with as much reason, reflect on the Protestants for not keeping the doors of their churches open on weekdays. . . .

The quadroons, or the offspring of the whites and mulattoes, sat in an upper tier of boxes appropriated to them. When they are rich, they hold a peculiar and very equivocal position in society. As children, they have often been sent to Paris for their education, and, being as capable of improvement as any whites, return with refined manners, and not unfrequently with more cultivated minds than the majority of those from whose society they are shut out. By the tyranny of caste they are driven, therefore, to form among themselves a select and exclusive set.

Among other stories illustrating their social relation to the whites, we were told that a young man of the dominant race fell in love with a beautiful quadroon girl, who was so light-coloured as to be scarcely distinguishable from one of pure breed. He found that, in order to render the marriage legal, he was required to swear that he himself had Negro blood in his veins, and, that he might conscientiously take the oath, he let some of the blood of his betrothed into his veins with a lancet. The romance of this tale was, however, greatly diminished, although I fear that my inclination to believe in its truth was equally enhanced, when the additional circumstance was related, that the young lady was rich.

The tombs in the cemeteries on the outskirts of the town are raised from the ground, in order that they may be above the swamps, and the coffins are placed in bins like those of a cellar. The water is seen standing on the soil at a lower level in many places; there are often flowers and shrubs round the tombs, by the side of walks made of shells of the Gnathodon. Over the grave of one recently killed in a duel was a tablet, with the inscription—"Mort, victime de l'honneur!" Should anyone propose to set up a similar tribute to the memory of a duelist at Mount Auburn, near Boston, a sensation would be created, which would manifest how widely different is the state of public opinion in New England from that in the "First Municipality." . . .

The desertion of the city for five months by so many of the richer residents causes the hotels and the prices of almost every article in shops to be very dear during the remainder of the year. "Goods selling at Northern prices" is a common form of advertisement, showing how high is the usual cost of all things in this city. The Irish servants in the hotel assure us that they cannot save, in spite of their high wages, for whatever money they put by soon goes to pay the doctor's bill, during attacks of chill and fever. . . .

I asked an Irishman if the summer heat was intolerable. "You would have something else to think of in the hot months," said he, "for there is one set of mosquitoes who sting you all day, and when they go in toward dusk, another kind comes out and bites you all night."

A few days after the Carnival we had another opportunity of seeing a grand procession of the natives, without masks. The corps of all the different companies of firemen turned out in their uniform, drawing their engines dressed up with flowers, ribbons, and flags, and I never saw a finer set of young men. We could not help contrasting their healthy looks with the pale, sickly countenances of "the crackers," in the pine-woods of Georgia and Alabama, where we had been spending so many weeks. These men were almost all of them Creoles, and thoroughly acclimatized; and I soon found that if I wished to ingratiate myself with natives or permanent settlers in this city, the less surprise I expressed at the robust aspect of these young Creoles the better. The late Mr. Sydney Smith advised an English friend who was going to reside some years in Edinburgh to praise the climate: —"When you arrive there it may rain, snow, or blow for many days, and they will assure you they never knew such a season before. If you would be popular, declare you think it the most delightful climate in the world." . . .

One morning we rose early to visit the market and found the air on the bank of the Mississippi filled with mist as dense as a London fog, but of a pure white instead of yellow color. Through this atmosphere the innumerable masts of the ships alongside the wharf, were dimly seen. Among other fruits in the market we observed abundance of bananas, and good pineapples, for 25 cents each, from the West Indies. There were stalls where hot coffee was selling in white china cups, reminding us of Paris. Among other articles exposed for sale were brooms made of palmetto leaves, and wagonloads of the dried Spanish moss, or *Tillandsia*. The quantity of this plant hanging from the trees in the swamps surrounding New Orleans and everywhere in the delta of the Mississippi might suffice to stuff all the mattresses in the world. The Indians formerly used it for another purpose—to give porosity or lightness to their building materials. When at Natchez, I saw some bricks dug out of an old Indian mound, in which the tough woody fiber of the *Tillandsia* was still preserved. When passing through the stalls, we were surrounded by a population of Negroes, mulattoes, and quadroons, some talking French, others a patois of Spanish and French, others a mixture of French and English, or English translated from French, and with the French accent. They seemed very merry, especially those who were jet black. Some of the Creoles also, both of French and Spanish extraction, like many natives of the south of Europe, were very dark.

Amid this motley group, sprung from so many races, we encountered a young man and woman, arm-in-arm, of fair complexion, evidently Anglo-Saxon, and who looked as if they had recently come from the north. The Indians, Spaniards, and French standing round them, seemed as if placed there to remind us of the successive races whose power in Louisiana had passed away, while this fair couple were the representatives of a people whose dominion carries the imagination far into the future. However much the moralist may satirize the spirit of conquest, or the foreigner laugh at some vain-glorious boasting about "our density," none can doubt that from this stock is to spring the people who will supersede every other in the northern, if not also in the southern continent of America.

The "Dearest" of All Institutions

WILLIAM MAKEPEACE THACKERAY

The amiable, urbane English commentator, William Makepeace Thackeray, had a happy time and embraced everything, or nearly everything, that came before him when he made a famous trip to the United States during the years before the Confederacy. Thackeray liked people, and the Southerners decided that they liked him in return. The following genial lines, typical of his good will, only slightly restrained at some points, are from his Roundabout Papers, 1862. *In his travels Thackeray made a notable remark after eating an oyster much larger than those to which he was accustomed. He felt, he said, as if he had just swallowed a baby.*

HOW they sang; how they laughed and grinned; how they scraped, bowed and complimented you and each other, those negroes of the cities in the Southern parts! . . . I witnessed a curious gaiety; heard amongst the black folk endless singing, shouting and laughter; and saw on holy-days black gentlemen and ladies arrayed in such splendor and comfort as freeborn workmen in our towns seldom exhibit. . . . I am not going into the slavery question, I am not an advocate of "the institution," as I know, madam, by that angry toss of your head, you are about to declare me to be. For domestic purposes, my dear lady, it seemed to me about the dearest institution that can be devised.

In a house in a Southern city you will find fifteen negroes doing the work which John, the cook, the housemaid and the help, do perfectly in your own comfortable London house. And these fifteen negroes are the pick of a family of some eighty or ninety. Twenty are too sick, or too old for work, let us say; twenty too clumsy; twenty are too young, and have to be nursed and watched by ten more. This was an account given by a gentleman of Richmond of his establishment. Six European servants would have kept his house and stables well. "His farm," he said, "barely sufficed to maintain the negroes residing on it."

Old Sol "Breaks a Bank"

"Old Sol" everybody called Sol Smith, who was for years a leading comedian of the South and Southwest. He was known affectionately throughout the area; year after year he moved about with varying troupes, enjoying adventures disturbing, peculiar or fantastic. At times Sol wrote sketches for newspapers and eventually collected them in a highly readable volume. The tale presented here is a good example of the type. It appeared in the volume A Quarter Race in Kentucky, *edited by William T. Porter in 1846.*

CAPTAIN Summons is a very clever fellow—and the "Dr. Franklin" *was* a very superb boat, albeit inclined to rock about a good deal, and nearly turn over on her side when visited by a breath of air in the least resembling a gale. Capt. Summons is a clever fellow. All steamboat captains are clever fellows—or *nearly* all; but what I mean to say is, Captain Summons is a *particularly* clever fellow!—A clever fellow in the widest sense of the term—a fellow that is clever in every way—anxious that his passengers shall be comfortably bestowed, well fed and well attended to—and *determined* that they shall amuse themselves "just as they d—n please," as the saying is. If he happens to have preachers on board, he puts on a serious countenance of a Sunday morning—consents that there shall be preaching—orders the chairs to be set out, and provides Bibles and hymnbooks for the occasion—himself and officers, whose watch is below, taking front seats and listening attentively to the discourse. Likely as not, at the close of the service, he will ask the reverend gentleman who has been officiating, with his back in close proximity to a hot fire in a Franklin furnace, to accompany him to the bar and join him in some refreshments! If there are passengers on board who prefer to pass the time away in playing poker, ucre, brag, or whist, tables and chairs are ready for *them*, too,—poker, brag, ucre and whist be it! All sorts of passengers are accommodated on the "Dr. Franklin"—the rights of none are suffered to be infringed;—all are free to follow such employments as shall please themselves.

It sometimes happens that, at the commencement of a voyage, it is found somewhat difficult to reconcile *all* the passengers to the system of Capt. Summons, which is founded on the broad principle of equal rights to all. On the occasion of my voyage in the "Doctor," in December, 1844, I found myself surrounded by a crowd of passengers who were *entire strangers* to me—a very rare occurrence to one who travels so often on the western rivers as I do. . . .

I don't know how it is, or *why* it is, but by strangers I am almost always taken for a PREACHER. It was so on this voyage. There were three Methodist *circuit* riders on board; and it happened that we got acquainted, and were a good deal together—from which circumstances I was supposed to be *one of them;* which supposition was the means of bringing me into an acquaintance with the lady passengers, who, for the most part, were very pious, religiously inclined souls. We had preaching every day, and sometimes at night; and I must say, in justice to brothers Twichell and Switchell, that their sermons were highly edifying and instructive.

In the mean time, a portion of the passengers "at the other end of the hall" continued to play sundry games with cards, notwithstanding the remonstrances of the worthy followers of Wesley, who frequently requested the captain to interfere and break up such unholy doings. The captain had but one answer—it was something like this: "Gentlemen, amuse yourselves as you like; preach and pray to your hearts' content—none shall interfere with your pious prayers; some like that sort of thing—*I* have not objection to it. These men prefer to amuse themselves with cards; let them—they pay their passage as well as you, gentle*men,* and have as much right to their amuse*ments* as you have to *yours;* and they shall not be disturbed. Preach, play cards, dance cotillions—do what you like, *I* am agreeable; only understand that *all games (preaching among the rest) must cease at ten o'clock.*" So *we* preachers got very little comfort from Captain Summons.

Up—up, up,—up he went. Christmas day arrived. All the *other* preachers had holden forth on divers occasions, and it being ascertained that it was my intention to leave the boat on her arrival at Cairo, a request was presented, that I *should preach the Christmas sermon!* The LADIES (God bless them all!) were *very* urgent in their application to me. "Oh *do,* brother Smith! we *want* to hear you preach! All the others have contributed their share to our spiritual comfort—you *must* oblige us—indeed you must." I endeavoured to excuse myself the best way I could, alleging the necessity of my leaving the boat in less than an hour—my baggage was not ready—I had a terrible cold, and many other good and substantial reasons were given; but all in vain—preach I must. "Well," thinks I, "if I must, I must." At this crisis, casting my eyes down towards the Social Hall, and seeing an unusual crowd assembled around a table, I asked one of the brethren what might be going on down there? The fattest of the preaching gentlemen replied—"The poor miserable sinners have filled the measure of their iniquity by opening a FARO BANK!" "Horrible!" exclaimed I, holding up my hands—and "horrible!" echoed the ladies and missionaries in full chorus. "Cannot such doings be put a stop to?" asked an elderly lady, addressing the pious travellers. "I fear not," groaned my Methodist contemporary (the fat one). "We have been trying to convince the captain that some dreadful accident will inevitably befall the boat, if such proceedings are permitted—and what do you think he answered?" "What?" we all asked, of course. "Why, he just said, that, inasmuch as he permitted *us* to preach and pray, he should let other passengers dance and play, if they chose to do so; and that if I didn't like the 'proceedings' I complained of *I might leave the boat!* Yes—he did; and, moreover, he mentioned that it was eleven o'clock, and asked me if I wouldn't 'liquor.'" This announcement of the captain's stubbornness and impiety was met with a general groan of pity and sorrow, and we resumed the conversation respecting the unhallowed faro bank. "It is much to be regretted," remarked the elderly lady who had spoken before, "that *something* can't be done—Brother Smith," she continued, appealing directly to me, and laying her forefinger impressively upon my arm, "cannot *you* break up that bank?" "Dear Madam," I answered, "you know not the difficulty of the task you impose upon me—FARO BANKS ARE NOT SO EASILY BROKEN UP as you may imagine; however, as you all appear so anxious about it, if you'll excuse me from the sermon, I'll see what can be done." "Ah, that's a dear soul!"—"I knew he would try."—"He'll be sure to succeed!"—"Our prayers shall not be wanting!" Such were the exclamations that greeted me, as I moved off towards the faro bank. Elbowing my way into the crowd, I got near the table in front of the dealer, and was for a time completely concealed from the view of my pious friends near the door of the ladies' cabin. I found the bank was a small affair. The betters were risking trifling sums, ranging from six to twenty-five cents.

A log cabin of the mountain folk of the old South

Lookout Mountain, Tennessee, and the Chattanooga Rail Road

"Mr. Dealer," I remarked, "I have come to break up this bank." "The deuce you have!" replied the banker—"let's see you do it." "What amount have you in bank?" I inquired. "Eleven dollars," was his answer. "What is your limit?" asked I. "A dollar," he replied. "Very well," said I, placing a ragged Indian dollar behind the queen—"turn on." He turned, and the king won for me. I took the two dollars up and let him make another turn, when I replaced the bet, and the queen came up in my favour; I had now four dollars, which I placed in the square, taking in the 5, 6, 7, and —and it won again! Here were seven dollars of the banker's money. I pocketed three of them, and bet four dollars behind the queen again; the Jack won, and the BANK WAS BROKEN! The crowd dispersed in all directions, laughing at the breaking up of the petty bank, and I made my way towards the ladies' cabin, where my new friends were anxiously awaiting the result of my bold attempt. "Well, well, well," they all exclaimed—"What success?—have you done it? Do let us hear all about it!" I wiped the perspiration from my brow, and putting on a very serious face, I said solemnly: "I HAVE BROKEN THAT BANK!" "You have?" they all exclaimed.— "Yes, I'll be d—d if he hasn't," muttered the disappointed gamester, the keeper of the late bank, who was just going into his state-room. In the midst of the congratulations which were showered upon me, I received a *summons* from the captain to come forward with my baggage —we were at Cairo.

Cougar Hunt

JOHN JAMES AUDUBON

John James Audubon, the superlative naturalist, learned about the South as did few men, by long travels through the region, during which he studied birds, animals and people with an eager and comprehending eye. Louisiana, Mississippi, the Kentucky and Tennessee areas, and dozens of other places . . . Audubon knew them from many viewpoints. The natural son of a lieutenant and a French colonial, he was born in Santo Domingo, went to France, attempted one field of work after another until he turned to the world of natural objects. Audubon had a taste for the primitive or semiprimitive; the frontier South drew him and stirred him. In his Ornithological Biography, *published in 1831 in Philadelphia, he gave the following magnificent account of a hunt.*

THERE is an extensive Swamp in the section of the State of Mississippi which lies partly in the Choctaw territory. It commences at the borders of the Mississippi, at no great distance from a Chickasaw village, situated near the mouth of a creek known by the name of Vanconnah, and partly inundated by the swellings of several large bayous, the principal of which, crossing the swamp in its whole extent, discharges its waters not far from the mouth of the Yazoo River. This famous bayou is called False River. The Swamp follows the windings of the Yazoo, until the latter branches off to the north-east, and at this point forms the stream named Cold Water River. . . .

In the course of one of my rambles, I chanced to meet with a squatter's cabin on the banks of the Cold Water River. In the owner of this hut, like most of the adventurous settlers in the uncultivated tracts of our frontier districts, I found a person well versed in the chase, and acquainted with the habits of some of the larger species of quadrupeds and birds.

. . . I entered the squatter's cabin, and immediately opened a conversation with him respecting the situation of the swamp. . . . He told me he thought it the very place I ought to visit, spoke of the game which it contained, and pointed to some bear and deer skins, adding that the individuals to which they belonged formed but a small proportion of the number of those animals which he had shot within it.

My heart swelled with delight, and on asking if he would accompany me through the great morass, and allow me to become an inmate of his humble but hospitable mansion, I was gratified to find that he cordially assented to all my proposals. So I immediately unstrapped my drawing materials, laid up my gun, and sat down to partake of the homely but wholesome fare intended for the supper of the squatter, his wife, and his two sons.

The quietness of the evening seemed in perfect accordance with the gentle demeanor of the family. The wife and children, I more than once thought, seemed to look upon me as a strange sort of person, going about, as I told them I was, in search of birds and plants; and were I here to relate the many questions which they put to me in return for those which I addressed to them, the catalogue would occupy several pages. The husband, a native of Connecticut, had heard of the existence of such men as myself, both in our own country and abroad, and seemed greatly pleased to have me under his roof. Supper over, I asked my kind host what had induced him to remove to this wild and solitary spot. "The people are growing too numerous now to thrive in New England," was his answer. I thought of the state of some parts of Europe, and calculating the denseness of their population compared with that of New England, exclaimed to myself, "How much more difficult must it be for men to thrive in those populous countries!" The conversation then changed, and the squatter, his sons and myself, spoke of the hunting and fishing, until at length

"Loading Cotton on the Mississippi." The great river was America's biggest roadway, a spectacle, a way of life for passengers, crew and riverbank dwellers.

tired, we laid ourselves down on the pallets of bear skins, and reposed in peace on the floor of the only apartment of which the hut consisted.

Day dawned, and the squatter's call to his hogs, which, being almost in a wild state, were suffered to seek the greater portion of their food in the woods, awakened me. Being ready dressed, I was not long in joining him. The hogs and their young came grunting at the well known call of their owner, who threw them a few ears of corn and counted them, but told me that for some weeks their number had been greatly diminished by the ravages committed upon them by a large *Panther*, by which name the Cougar is designated in America, and that the ravenous animal did not content himself with the flesh of the pigs, but now and then carried off one of his calves, notwithstanding the many attempts he had made to shoot it.

The *Painter*, as he sometimes called it, had on several occasions robbed him of a dead deer; and to these exploits the squatter added several remarkable feats of audacity which it had performed, to give me an idea of the formidable character of the beast. Delighted by his description, I offered to assist him in destroying the enemy, at which he was highly pleased, but assured me that unless some of his neighbours should join us with their dogs and his own, the attempt would prove fruitless. Soon after, mounting a horse, he went off to his neighbours, several of whom lived at a distance of some miles, and appointed a day of meeting.

The hunters, accordingly, made their appearance, one fine morning, at the door of the cabin, just as the sun was emerging from beneath the horizon. They were five in number, and fully equipped for the chase, being mounted on horses, which in some parts of Europe might appear sorry nags, but which in strength, speed and bottom, are better fitted for pursuing a cougar or bear through the woods and morasses than any in that country. A pack of large ugly curs were already engaged in making acquaintance with those of the squatter. He and myself mounted his two best horses, whilst his sons were bestriding others of inferior quality.

Few words were uttered by the party until we had reached the edge of the Swamp, where it was agreed that all should disperse and seek for the fresh track of the Painter, it being previously settled that the discoverer should blow his horn, and remain on the spot until the rest should join him. In less than an hour, the sound of the horn was clearly heard, and, sticking close to the squatter, off we went through the thick woods, guided only by the now and then repeated call of the distant huntsman. We soon reached the spot, and in a short time the rest of the party came up. The best dog was sent forward to track the Cougar, and in a few moments the whole pack were observed diligently trailing, and bearing in their course for the interior of the Swamp. The rifles were immediately put in trim, and the party followed the dogs, at separate distances, but in sight of each other, determined to shoot at no other game than the Panther.

The dogs soon began to mouth, and suddenly quickened their pace. My companion concluded that the beast was on the ground, and putting our horses to a gentle gallop, we followed the curs, guided by their voices. The noise of the dogs increased, when all of a sudden their mode of barking became altered, and the squatter, urging me to push on, told me that the beast was *treed*, by which he meant that it had got upon some low branch of a large tree to rest for a few moments, and that should we not succeed in shooting him when thus situated, we might expect a long chase of it. As we approached the spot, we all by degrees united into a body, but on seeing the dogs at the foot of a large tree, separated again and galloped off to surround it.

Each hunter now moved with caution, holding his gun ready, and allowing the bridle to dangle on the neck of his horse, as it advanced slowly towards the dogs. A shot from one of the party was heard, on which the Cougar was seen to leap to the ground, and bound off with such velocity as to show that he was unwilling to stand our fire longer. The dogs set off in pursuit with great eagerness and a deafening cry. The hunter who had fired came up and said that his ball had hit the monster, and had probably broken one of his fore-legs near the shoulder, the only place at which he could aim. A slight trail of blood was discovered on the ground, but the curs proceeded at such a rate that we hardly noticed this, and put spurs to our horses, which galloped on towards the centre of the Swamp.

One bayou was crossed, then another still larger and more muddy; but the dogs were brushing forward, and as the horses began to pant at a furious rate, we judged it expedient to leave them and advance on foot. These determined hunters knew that the Cougar being wounded, would shortly ascend another tree, where in all probability he would remain for a considerable time, and that it would be easy to follow the track of the dogs. We dismounted, took off the saddles and bridles, set the bells attached to the horses' necks at liberty to jingle, hoppled the animals, and left them to shift for themselves. . . .

After marching for a couple of hours, we again heard the dogs. Each of us pressed forward, elated at the thought of terminating the career of the Cougar. Some of the dogs were heard whining, although the greater number barked vehemently. We felt assured that the Cougar was treed, and that he would rest for some time to recover from his fatigue. As we came up to the dogs, we discovered the ferocious animal lying across a large branch, close to the trunk of a cotton-wood tree. His broad breast lay toward us; his eyes were at one time bent on us and again on the dogs beneath and around him; one of his forelegs hung loosely by his side, and he lay crouched, with his ears lowered close to his head, as if he thought he might remain undiscovered.

Three balls were fired at him, at a given signal, on which he sprang a few feet from the branch, and tumbled headlong to the ground. Attacked on all sides by the enraged curs, the infuriated Cougar fought with desperate valor; but the squatter advancing in front of the party, and almost in the midst of the dogs, shot him immediately behind and beneath the left shoulder. The Cougar writhed for a moment in agony, and in another lay dead.

The sun was now sinking in the west. Two of the hunters separated from the rest, to procure venison, whilst the squatter's sons were ordered to make the best of their way home, to be ready to feed the hogs in the morning. The Cougar was despoiled of its skin, and its carcass left to the hungry dogs. Whilst engaged in preparing our camp, we heard the report of a gun, and soon one of our hunters appeared with a small deer. A fire was lighted, and each hunter displayed his *pone* of bread, along with a flask of whisky. The deer was skinned in a trice, and slices placed on sticks before the fire. These materials afforded us an excellent meal, and as the night grew darker, stories and songs went round, until my companions, fatigued, laid themselves down, close under the smoke of the fire, and soon fell asleep.

A Good Cheat and Card Stealer at Eleven

GEORGE H. DEVOL

There is a disarming candor in the confessions of the flamboyant George H. Devol in his Forty Years a Gambler on the Mississippi, *published in Cincinnati in 1887. What others might have charged against him, Devol admitted and boasted about. This is a side of Southern affairs—blowhard passengers, yokels who invited deception, deft tricks on land and water—about which few were so qualified to write. Perhaps the gambler drew a long bow here and there, but in the main his narratives seem accurate. Running away from home at ten, George became a cabin boy on a steamboat; worked his way upward to keno*

Baton Rouge, eventually the capital of Louisiana, occupied a favored spot on the twisting Mississippi above New Orleans.

and faro dealer, then went on his own to fleece Southerners as far west as the Mexican border. At eleven, he said proudly, he could steal cards and cheat the boys; within only two more years he could stack a deck with the best of them.

I WAS on a boat coming from Memphis one night, when my partner beat a man out of $600, playing poker. After the game broke up, the man went into the ladies' cabin and told his wife. She ran into his room and got his pistol, and said, "I will have that money back, or kill the man."

I saw her coming, pistol in hand, and stepped up to the bar and told the barkeeper to hand me that old gun he had in the drawer, which I knew had no loads in it. She came on, frothing at the mouth, with blood in her eyes. I saw she was very much excited, and I said to her: "Madame, you are perfectly right. You would do right in shooting that fellow, for he is nothing but a gambler. I don't believe your pistol will go off; you had better take my pistol, for I am a government detective, and have to keep the best of arms."

So I handed her the pistol, and took hers. Just a moment later out stepped the man who had won the money, and she bolted up to him and said: "You won my husband's money, and I will just give you one minute to hand it to me, or I will blow your brains out in this cabin."

Well, you ought to have seen the passengers getting out of the cabin when she pulled down on him; but he knew the joke and stood pat, and showed what a game fellow he was. He told the woman her husband lost the money gambling, and he could not get a cent back. Then she let go; but the pistol failed to go off, and he got her to go back into the cabin, and pacified her by giving her $100. After taking the charges out of her pistol, I returned it to her. So, reader, you can see what a gay life there is in gambling.

.   .   .

Another time I was coming up on the steamer *Fairchild* with Captain Fawcett, of Louisville. When we landed at Napoleon, there were about twenty-five of the "Arkansas Killers" came on board, and I just opened out and cleaned the party of money, watches, and all their valuables. Things went along smoothly for a while, until they commenced to drink pretty freely.

Finally one of them said: "Jake, Sam, Ike, get Bill and let us kill that d——d gambler who got our money."

"All right," said the party, and they broke for their rooms to get their guns. I stepped out of the side door, and got under the pilot-house, as it was my favorite hiding place. I could hear every word downstairs, and could whisper to the pilot. Well, they hunted the boat from stem to stern—even took lights and went down into the hold—and finally gave up the chase, as one man said I had jumped overboard.

I slipped the pilot $100 in gold, as I had both pockets filled with gold and watches, and told him at the first point that stood out a good ways to run her as close as he could, and I would jump. He whispered, "Get ready," and I slipped out and walked back, and stood on the top of the wheelhouse until she came, as I thought, near enough to make the jump, and away I went.

But it was farther than I expected, so I went down about thirty feet into the river,

and struck into the soft mud clear up to my waist. Some parties who were standing on the stern of the boat saw me, and gave the alarm, when the "killers" all rushed back and commenced firing at me, and the bullets went splashing all around me. The pilot threw her into the bend as quick he could, and then let on she took a sheer on him, and nearly went to the other side. The shooting brought the Negroes from the fields to the bank of the river. I hallooed to them to get a long pole and pull me out, for I was stuck in the mud. They did so, and I got up on the bank and waited for another boat.

.   .   .

Bluff is a good game, and sometimes it will turn a trick when everything else fails. I boarded Morgan's Railroad, as it was called, upon one occasion at Algiers (opposite New Orleans.) Trains on that road were generally full of suckers, as the road connected with the Galveston steamers at Berwick's Bay. Tom Brown and Holly Chappell, my partners, were both along; and as game was plenty along the road, we carried our shotguns along, and in the event of no bigger game were accustomed to get off and shoot snipe, catching the return train to the city in the evening.

Sure enough, there was a party of traders aboard, and Brown lost no time in making their acquaintance and opening out. One of them commenced to cut his clothes the minute he got a glimpse of the corner after Chappell made one cap. To make matters more binding, I came up and lost $1200.

Then the ball opened, and it was not more than half an hour before we had downed the party. Then the devil was to pay. One of the party said: "Look here; I must have my money back, or h——l will flop around here mighty quick." Then they all joined in and made a big kick; and as I saw fun brewing, I slipped into the baggage-car, changed hats and coats with the baggage-master, got his badge and my double-barreled shotgun.

Then I rushed into the car and drew the bead on the party who had collected around the boys, giving a war-whoop and demanding in stentorian tones, "Who has been playing cards in this car?"

"I have," said Brown.

"Get off this train mighty quick"; and I pulled the rope. My partners lost no time in getting off. Pulling the rope again, the train started; and when the conductor came back, I explained that somebody would have been hurt, had I not acted as I did. This was satisfactory, and going back, he told the party that gambling on the road was against the rules, and that he could have them all arrested when the bay was reached, if he wished.

This had the effect of quieting them down, especially as they knew that the man who had won their money was off the train.

I was not long in reaching the baggage-car and returning the borrowed articles, and quietly slipping off at the first station, not forgetting my shotgun. Hunting was good that day, and I bagged ten snipe and thirteen robins, which the boys helped me eat at our old friend Cassidy's restaurant, on Gravier street opposite the St. Charles Hotel. The boys all agreed that my conduct was all that saved the boodle, which consisted of $3300 and two gold watches. Thus it is that a little management, backed by a double-barreled shotgun and an official badge, is oftentimes a powerful persuader.

Every Vote Counted

HENRY S. FOOTE

One of the raciest memoirists of the day and region was little Henry S. Foote, a high-tempered, mercurial fellow, a criminal lawyer who mixed in many affairs throughout a crowded lifetime. Foote had at least four duels; he traded slaps and punches with assorted men, including his enemy Jefferson Davis. Born of Virginia heritage, he went to Alabama and then to Mississippi. For a long time Henry Foote opposed Southern secessionists; he scored in one court case after another, one personal exchange on top of another. Meanwhile he stored up a treasury of observations of men's foibles, which he put to use in his Bench and Bar of the South and Southwest, *published in 1876.*

JUDGE HARRIS reached his hotel on a bright Sunday evening. He asked to be shown the room he was to occupy, and learning the number thereof, he proceeded to it without delay. On reaching the door and opening it, he found a gentleman and lady in it, and immediately returned and asked to be shown another room. Some little delay occurred before this was done, and when he reached the second room he found that also occupied.

He then came back to the bar and rather indignantly addressed the host upon this irritating subject: "Pray, sir, are you keeping a bawdy-house? I found the first room you di-

rected me to occupy already in the possession of a man and woman—the latter of whom I understand to be your wife—who were lying together upon the bed. On opening the door of the second room, I found the same woman lying on the bed there, but attended by another man. I wish to know what all this means."

"My dear Judge," exclaimed the good-natured tavern-keeper, "I beg you will be composed. It is not possible that I can for the present say a single word concerning the matter of which you complain. You see, my dear Judge, I am a candidate for constable in this

Through the years Brulatour Courtyard, with fanlights, arches, stairway and flagstones, has remained a favored spot in New Orleans' Royal Street.

beat, and very hard run for votes. Were I to make any parade of my wrongs before the election . . . I should inevitably be beaten. The election will come off tomorrow, after which I promise you that there shall be no similar cause of complaint."

.   .   .

Judge Child's mind was agile and vigorous; he always expressed himself . . . with an aversion to long and flatulent speeches, to turgid exclamation, or the copious citation of books of authority. He exclaimed from the bench of the circuit court in Port Gibson, once, when a lawyer of some standing had, after reading in the Judge's hearing the whole of quite a long judicial opinion, announced with an air of pleasant exultation, that he had lying before him at least *seventeen* decisions of various respectable courts precisely to the effect, to all of which he proposed to invite his honor's attention.

"What! Do you say that these authorities are all to the same effect?"

"Yes, sir," answered the delighted and learned advocate, "I do. They are all to the same effect, precisely."

"I am really rejoiced to hear it," said the sneerful judge, "and will you please have the goodness to read again the decision I have already heard read with such exquisite pleasure, as I thought it read very well; and if you will read it over again sixteen times, we shall all understand it perfectly, and be able to give it such application as may be right, to the case now to be decided."

.   .   .

Judge James C. Mitchell is reported to have been especially careful in preserving the dignity of the court. He was one day presiding in the trial of a civil case of much importance, when he was subjected to annoyance. A genteel-looking, well-dressed young man walked through the court room, once or twice, wearing boots whose creaking resounded through the hall of justice in a manner which could not but attract general attention.

"Mr. Sheriff," exclaimed the judge, "bring that young man with the creaking boots immediately before the court." This having been done, and the young man coming forward with striking signs of perturbation, the judge thus addressed him: "Pray, how much did your boots cost you?"

"Ten dollars."

"Well," said the judge, "you will never be able to reply thus again; the boots shall cost you twenty dollars. Enter a fine of ten dollars," said the irritated judge to the clerk of the court, "against this young man for striding through this court room in creaking boots"; which was done according.

.   .   .

(On one occasion, Henry S. Foote declares, the remarkable Judge Mitchell told friends how he had been in a Tennessee town when a native returned from a mission abroad, and the residents prepared to honor their friend. Because Judge Mitchell was so familiar with all the established rules of etiquette, according to Judge Mitchell himself, he was asked to give the address of welcome. A grand ball was to be held, and, in Mitchell's words:)

I was formally requested to accompany the beautiful and charming daughter of our returned friend and be her partner in the first dance: to which arrangement I could not but accede, not being able to deny that I was quite as well-versed in the mysteries of the dancing art as in the business of public speaking. Well, the first dance happened to be a contra-dance. There were at least fifty couples upon the floor. My partner and myself had, of course, taken our stations at the head, where, for a minute or two, we were the 'observed of all observers.'

And well we might be, for a better-looking and more splendidly-dressed couple had, I am sure, never before been seen on *terra firma* since the days of our first parents in Paradise. The music struck up and I whisked my graceful partner through the mazes of the dance with a vivacity and elegance which I am quite sure has never been surpassed—whispering in her ears as we moved along such words of soft and winning complaisance as men of genuine gallantry have ever at their command, and which ladies of taste and sensibility never fail to appreciate.

When we reached the foot of the set the

captivated fair exclaimed in tones of thrilling pathos: "Oh, Judge Mitchell, how I wish that you were not a *married man!*" To this I promptly responded: "Most adorable lady, I assure you that at least one thousand of your sex have expressed the same wish." On uttering these last words, seeing a vacant space to my right, I leaped from the side of my partner, full ten feet, turned a graceful and impressive somersault, and, lighting firmly upon my feet, I faced the astonished lady, and, waving my hand in token of respect, I said: "Miss, pray tell me what you think of that?" To which reply she responded:

"That is positively the most wonderful exploit I ever witnessed, and I feel that it is my duty to apply to you the words of Lord Byron when describing George the Fourth:

"Without the least alloy of fop or beau,
A perfect gentleman from top to toe."

. . .

The Hon. John I. Guion was always more successful in addressing juries than he was in the argument of mere legal questions. In the defence of criminals he sometimes spoke in a manner calculated to elicit much commendation. I heard him in the defence of a man called William A. Hardwicke, who was charged with having committed a most atrocious murder.

Hardwicke had in some way managed to enlist the sympathies of Judge Guion very deeply, and in his defence all his powers as an advocate were fully put in requisition. The case was one of the greatest difficulty, and the alleged outrage had called forth much popular indignation.

The victim of Hardwicke's ruffianly malevolence was a colored man whom I knew very well, and who was under excellent character. For some reason Hardwicke had conceived for him a strong feeling of hatred and had, apparently, without any reliable evidence of the fact, charged him with having stolen some articles of personal property of no considerable value. Hardwicke appears to have gone to the man's cabin at midnight, dragged him forth from his bed where he was lying by the side of a sick wife—after which, with the aid of several miscreants of his own stamp, he tied him across a barrel, and inflicted upon his bare back more than a thousand stripes.

When the poor creature was released he was found to be in a dying condition, and only survived a few seconds. In the intenseness of his agony, he had bitten his tongue in two. An honest and enlightened justice of the peace, sitting as a court of inquiry, had sent Hardwicke to jail; an application for his discharge on bail had been denied; an indictment had been regularly found against him, and after a few month's delay, Hardwicke's trial came on in the Circuit Court of Hinds County, and in the town of Raymond.

The offender was prosecuted by a very able district attorney, and with as much of rigor as the law allowed; but when Judge Guion entered upon the defence of his client, he very soon convinced many of his listeners that in no case should negro evidence be allowed to prevail against a member of the proud Caucasian race; and, as the evidence against the accused was mainly of that character, he insisted that it should be altogether thrown out of the case.

After this, when the plausible and captivating advocate suggested the extreme *impolicy*, in the then existing condition of the country, of having a *white man hanged for punishing a negro for theft*, the case was well nigh won. Then came an animated and touching peroration, under which both judge and bystanders were melted to tears, and the *oppressed* and *persecuted* Hardwicke was in a few minutes strutting forth from the court-house, and hurrying towards a neighboring tippling-shop, purse in hand, for the purpose of *treating* to liquor all who were willing to drink in honor of his deliverance.

Chita, Last Island on the Gulf

LAFCADIO HEARN

America has had few writers of a background and capacity so exotic as those of Lafcadio Hearn. Born in 1850 on an island of the Ionian Archipelago, he was the son of a Greek mother and an Irish father. He spent his early years in Dublin, then went to France and England for a mixed education. Arriving in New York before he was twenty, the dreamy, impractical Hearn found trouble in supporting himself; in Cincinnati he gave five or six years to newspaper work. Picking up a presentation of Louisiana plantation life, he decided that he had to see the place, and persuaded an editor to retain him for dispatches from New Orleans. He was supposed to send political accounts; instead he composed brilliant descriptions of the multicolored Creole life. Hearn found himself absorbed by the rich, semitropic air and manner. Here was one of the major influences of his life. But such material was hardly what the editor wanted, and soon he was out of work. There followed months of scraping for a living, and then for about ten years Hearn worked on the New Orleans newspapers, contributing vivid pictures of scenes and people. Later he went to Japan, where he married, taught and wrote. His Chita, *published in 1889 in New York, deserves a place in the front rank of all writings about the Gulf South.*

TRAVELLING south from New Orleans to the Islands, you pass through a strange land into strange sea, by various winding waterways. You can journey to the Gulf by lugger if you please; but the trip may be made much more rapidly and agreeably on some one of those light, narrow steamers, built especially for bayou-travel, which usually receive passengers at a point not far from the foot of old Saint-Louis Street, hard by the sugar-landing, where there is ever a pushing and flocking of steam-craft—all striving for place to rest their white breasts against the levee, side by side,—like great weary swans. But the miniature steamboat on which you engage passage to the Gulf never lingers long in the Mississippi: she crosses the river, slips into some canal-mouth, labors along the artificial channel awhile, and then leaves it with a scream of joy, to puff her free way down many a league of heavily shadowed bayou. Perhaps thereafter she may bear you through the immense silence of drenched rice-fields, where the yellow-green level is broken at long intervals by the black silhouette of some irrigating machine;—but, whichever of the five different routes be pur-

sued, you will find yourself more than once floating through sombre mazes of swamp-forest,—past assemblages of cypresses all hoary with the parasitic *tillandsia*, and grotesque as gatherings of fetich-gods. Ever from river or from lakelet the steamer glides again into canal or bayou,—from bayou or canal once more into lake or bay; and sometimes the swamp-forest visibly thins away from these shores into wastes of reedy morass where, even of breathless nights, the quaggy soil trembles to a sound like thunder of breakers on a coast: the storm-roar of billions of reptile voices chanting in cadence,—rhythmically surging in stupendous *crescendo* and *diminuendo*,—a monstrous and appalling chorus of frogs! . . .

Panting, screaming, scraping her bottom over the sand-bars,—all day the little steamer strives to reach the grand blaze of blue open water below the marsh-lands; and perhaps she may be fortunate enough to enter the Gulf about the time of sunset. For the sake of passengers, she travels by day only; but there are other vessels which make the journey also by night—threading the bayou-labyrinths winter and summer: sometimes steering by the North

Star,—sometimes feeling the way with poles in the white season of fogs,—sometimes, again, steering by that Star of Evening which in our sky glows like another moon, and drops over the silent lakes as she passes a quivering trail of silver fire.

Shadows lengthen; and at last the woods dwindle away behind you into thin bluish lines;—land and water alike take more luminous color;—bayous open into broad passes;—lakes link themselves with sea-bays;—and the ocean-wind bursts upon you,—keen, cool, and full of light. For the first time the vessel begins to swing,—rocking to the great living pulse of the tides. And gazing from the deck around you, with no forest walls to break the view, it will seem to you that the low land must have once been rent asunder by the sea, and strewn about the Gulf in fantastic tatters. . . .

Sometimes above a waste of wind-blown prairie-cane you see an oasis emerging,—a ridge or hillock heavily umbraged with the rounded foliage of evergreen oaks:—a *chênière*. And from the shining flood also kindred green knolls arise,—pretty islets, each with its beach-girdle of dazzling sand and shells, yellow-white,—and all radiant with semi-tropical foliage, myrtle and palmetto, orange and magnolia. Under their emerald shadows curious little villages of palmetto huts are drowsing, where dwell a swarthy population of Orientals,—Malay fishermen, who speak the Spanish-Creole of the Philippines as well as their own Tagal, and perpetuate in Louisiana the Catholic traditions of the Indies. There are girls in those unfamiliar villages worthy to inspire any statuary,—beautiful with the beauty of ruddy bronze,—gracile as the palmettoes that sway above them. . . . Further seaward you may also pass a Chinese settlement: some queer camp of wooden dwellings clustering around a vast platform that stands above the water upon a thousand piles;—over the miniature wharf you can scarcely fail to observe a white sign-board painted with crimson ideographs. The great platform is used for drying fish in the sun; and the fantastic characters of the sign, literally translated, mean: "*Heap—Shrimp—Plenty*." . . . And finally all the land melts down into desolations of sea-marsh, whose stillness is seldom broken, except by the melancholy cry of long-legged birds, and in wild seasons by that sound which shakes all shores when the weird Musician of the Sea touches the bass keys of his mighty organ. . . .

Beyond the sea-marshes a curious archipelago lies. If you travel by steamer to the sea-islands to-day, you are tolerably certain to enter the Gulf by Grande Pass—skirting Grande Terre, the most familiar island of all, not so much because of its proximity as because of its great crumbling fort and its graceful pharos: the stationary White-Light of Barataria. Otherwise the place is bleakly uninteresting: a wilderness of wind-swept grasses and sinewy weeds waving away from a thin beach ever speckled with drift and decaying things,—worm-riddled timbers, dead porpoises. Eastward the russet level is broken by the columnar silhouette of the light-house, and again, beyond it, by some puny scrub timber, above which rises the angular ruddy mass of the old brick fort, whose ditches swarm with crabs, and whose sluiceways are half choked by obsolete cannon-shot, now thickly covered with incrustation of oyster shells . . . Around all the gray circling of a shark-haunted sea. . . .

Sometimes of autumn evenings there, when the hollow of heaven flames like the interior of a chalice, and waves and clouds are flying in one wild rout of broken gold,—you may see the tawny grasses all covered with something like husks,—wheat-colored husks,—large, flat, and disposed evenly along the lee-side of each swaying stalk, so as to present only their edges to the wind. But, if you approach, those pale husks all break open to display strange splendors of scarlet and seal-brown, with arabesque mottlings in white and black: they change into wondrous living blossoms, which detach themselves before your eyes and rise in air, and flutter away by thousands to settle down farther off, and turn into wheat-colored husks once more . . . a whirling flower-drift of sleepy butterflies!

Southwest, across the pass, gleams beautiful Grande Isle: primitively a wilderness of palmetto *(latanier)*;—then drained, diked, and cultivated by Spanish sugar-planters; and now familiar chiefly as a bathing-resort. Since the war the ocean reclaimed its own;—the cane-fields have degenerated into sandy plains, over which tramways wind to the smooth beach;—the plantation-residences have been converted into rustic hotels, and the Negro-quarters remodelled into villages of cozy cottages for the reception of guests. But with its imposing groves of oak, its golden wealth of orange-trees, its odorous lanes of oleander, its broad grazing-meadows yellow-starred with wild camomile, Grande Isle remains the prettiest island of the Gulf; and its loveliness is exceptional. For the bleakness of Grande Terre is reiterated by most of the other islands,—Caillou, Cassetête, Calumet, Wine Island, the twin Timbaliers, Gull Island, and the many islets haunted by the gray pelican,—all of which are little more than sand-bars covered with wiry grasses, prairie-cane, and scrub-timber.

Last Island (L'Île Dernière),—well worthy a long visit in other years, in spite of its remoteness, is now a ghastly desolation twenty-five miles long. Lying nearly forty miles west of Grand Isle, it was nevertheless far more populated a generation ago: it was not only the most celebrated island of the group, but also the most fashionable watering-place of the aristocratic South;—to-day it is visited by fishermen only, at long intervals. Its admirable beach in many respects resembled that of Grand Isle to-day; the accommodations also were much similar, although finer: a charming village of cottages facing the Gulf near the western end. The hotel itself was a massive two-story construction of timber, containing many apartments, together with a large dining-room and dancing-hall. In rear of the hotel was a bayou, where passengers landed—"Village Bayou" it is still called by seamen;—but the deep channel which now cuts the island in two a little eastwardly did not exist while the village remained.

The sea tore it out in one night—the same night when trees, fields, dwellings, all vanished into the Gulf, leaving no vestige of former human habitation except a few of those strong brick props and foundations upon which the frame houses and cisterns had been raised. One living creature was found there after the cataclysm—a cow! But how that solitary cow survived the fury of a storm-flood that actually rent the island in twain has ever remained a mystery.

On the Gulf side of these islands you may observe that the trees—when there are any trees—all bend away from the sea; and, even on bright, hot days when the wind sleeps, there is something grotesquely pathetic in their look of agonized terror. A group of oaks at Grande Isle I remember as especially suggestive: five stooping silhouettes in line against the horizon, like fleeing women with streaming garments and wind-blown hair,—bowing grievously and thrusting out arms desperately northward as to save themselves from falling. And they are being pursued indeed;—for the sea is devouring the land. Many and many a mile of ground has yielded to the tireless charging of Ocean's cavalry: far out you can see, through a good glass, the porpoises at play where of old the sugar-cane shook out its million bannerets; and shark-fins now seam deep water above a site where pigeons used to coo. Men build dikes; but the besieging tides bring up their battering-rams—whole forests of drift —huge trunks of water-oak and weighty cypress. Forever the yellow Mississippi strives to build; forever the sea struggles to destroy;—and amid their eternal strife the islands and the promontories change shape, more slowly, but not less fantastically, than the clouds of heaven.

And worthy of study are those wan battle-grounds where the woods made their last brave stand against the irresistible invasion,—usually at some long point of sea-marsh, widely fringed with billowing sand. Just where the waves curl beyond such a point you may discern a multitude of blackened, snaggy shapes protruding above the water,—some high enough to resemble ruined chimneys, others bearing a startling likeness to enormous skeleton-feet and skeleton-hands,—with crustaceous white growths clinging to them here and there

---

Delicacy in iron lacework is the mark of this often-studied, much admired balcony structure at Royal and St. Peters streets in New Orleans.

like remnants of integument. There are bodies and limbs of drowned oaks,—so long crowned that the shell-scurf is inch-thick upon parts of them. Farther in upon the beach immense trunks lie overthrown.

Some look like vast broken columns; some suggest colossal torsos imbedded, and seem to reach out mutilated stumps in despair from their deepening graves;—and besides these are others which have kept their feet with astounding obstinacy, although the barbarian tides have been charging them for twenty years, and gradually torn away the soil above and beneath their roots. The sand around,—soft beneath and thinly crusted upon the surface,—is everywhere pierced with holes made by a beautifully mottled and semi-diaphanous crab, with hairy legs, big staring eyes, and milk-white claws;—while in the green sedges beyond there is a perpetual rustling, as of some strong wind beating among reeds: a marvellous creeping of "fiddlers," which the inexperienced visitor might at first mistake for so many peculiar beetles, as they run about sideways, each with his huge single claw folded upon his body like a wing-case. Year by year that rustling strip of green land grows narrower; the sand spreads and sinks, shuddering and wrinkling like a living brown skin; and the last standing corpses of the oaks, ever clinging with naked, dead feet to the sliding beach, lean more and more out of the perpendicular. As the sands subside, the stumps appear to creep; their intertwisted masses of snakish roots seem to crawl, to writhe,—like the reaching arms of cephalopods. . . .

. . . Grande Terre is going: the sea mines her fort, and will before many years carry the ramparts by storm. Grande Isle is going,—slowly but surely: the Gulf has eaten three miles into her meadowed land. Last Island has gone! How it went I first heard from the lips of a veteran pilot, while we sat one evening together on the trunk of a drifted cypress which some high tide had pressed deeply into the Grande Isle beach. The day had been tropically warm; we had sought the shore for a breath of living air. Sunset came, and with it the ponderous heat lifted,—a sudden breeze blew,—lightnings flickered in the darkening horizon,—wind and water began to strive to-

gether,—and soon all the low coast boomed. Then my companion began his story; perhaps the coming of the storm inspired him to speak! And as I listened to him, listening also to the clamoring of the coast, there flashed back to me recollection of a singular Breton fancy: that the Voice of the Sea is never one voice, but a tumult of many voices—voices of drowned men,—the muttering of multitudinous dead,—the moaning of innumerable ghosts, all rising, to rage against the living, at the great Witch-call of storms. . . .

The charm of a single summer day on these island shores is something impossible to express, never to be forgotten. Rarely, in the paler zones, do earth and heaven take such luminosity: those will best understand me who have seen the splendor of a West Indian sky. And yet there is a tenderness of tint, a caress of color, in these Gulf-days which is not of the Antilles,—a spirituality, as of eternal tropical spring. It must have been to even such a sky that Xenophanes lifted up his eyes of old when he vowed the Infinite Blue was God;—it was indeed under such a sky that De Soto named the vastest and grandest of Southern havens Espiritu Santo,—the Bay of the Holy Ghost. There is a something unutterable in this bright Gulf-air that compels awe,—something vital, something holy, something pantheistic: and reverentially the mind asks itself if what the eye beholds is not the Πνεύμα indeed, the Infinite Breath, the Divine Ghost, the great Blue Soul of the Unknown. All, all is blue in the calm,—save the low land under your feet, which you almost forget, since it seems only as a tiny green flake afloat in the liquid eternity of day. Then slowly, caressingly, irresistibly, the witchery of the Infinite grows upon you: out of Time and Space you begin to dream with open eyes,—to drift into delicious oblivion of facts,—to forget the past, the present, the substantial,—to comprehend nothing but the existence of that infinite Blue Ghost as something into which you would wish to melt forever. . . .

And this day-magic of azure endures sometimes for months together. Cloudlessly the dawn reddens up through a violet east: there is no speck upon the blossoming of its

Along the quiet Bayou St. John of New Orleans a line of semitropical villas extends near the water line.

Mystical Rose,—unless it be the silhouette of some passing gull, whirling his sickle-wings against the crimsoning. Ever, as the sun floats higher, the flood shifts its color. Sometimes smooth and gray, yet flickering with the morning gold, it is the vision of John,—the apocalyptic Sea of Glass mixed with fire;— again, with the growing breeze, it takes that incredible purple tint familiar mostly to painters of West Indian scenery;—once more,

under the blaze of noon, it changes to a waste of broken emerald. With evening, the horizon assumes tints of inexpressible sweetness,—pearl-lights, opaline colors of milk and fire; and in the west are topaz-glowings and wondrous flushings as of nacre. Then, if the sea sleeps, it dreams of all these,—faintly, weirdly,— shadowing them even to the verge of heaven.

Beautiful, too, are those white phantas-magoria which, at the approach of equinoctial days, mark the coming of the winds. Over the rim of the sea a bright cloud gently pushes up its head. It rises; and others rise with it, to right and left—slowly at first; then more swiftly. All are brilliantly white and flocculent, like loose new cotton. Gradually they mount in enormous line high above the Gulf, rolling and wreathing into an arch that expands and advances,—bending from horizon to horizon. A clear, cold breath accompanies its coming. Reaching the zenith, it seems there to hang poised awhile,—a ghostly bridge arching the empyrean,—upreaching its measureless span from either underside of the world. Then the colossal phantom begins to turn, as on a pivot of air,—always preserving its curvilinear symmetry, but moving its unseen ends beyond and below the sky-circle. And at last it floats away unbroken beyond the blue sweep of the world, with a wind following after. Day after day, almost at the same hour, the white arc rises, wheels, and passes. . . .

. . . Never a glimpse of rock on these low shores;—only long sloping beaches and bars of smooth tawny sand. Sand and sea teem with vitality;—over all the dunes there is a constant susurration, a blattering and swarming of crustacea;—through all the sea there is a ceaseless play of silver lightning,—flashing of myriad fish. Sometimes the shallows are thickened with minute, transparent, crablike organisms,—all colorless as gelatine. There are days also when countless medusae drift in—beautiful veined creatures that throb like hearts, with perpetual systole and diastole of their diaphanous envelopes; some, of translucent azure or rose, seem in the flood the shadows or ghosts of huge campanulate flowers;—others have the semblance of strange living vegetables,—great milky tubers, just beginning to sprout. But woe to the human skin grazed by those shadowy sproutings and spectral stamens!—the touch of glowing iron is not more painful. . . . Within an hour or two after their appearance all these tremulous jellies vanish mysteriously as they came.

Perhaps, if a bold swimmer, you may venture out alone a long way—once! Not twice!—even in company. As the water deepens beneath you, and you feel those ascending wave-currents of coldness arising which be-

speak profundity, you will also begin to feel innumerable touches, as of groping fingers—touches of the bodies of fish, innumerable fish, fleeing towards shore. The farther you advance, the more thickly you will feel them come; and above you and around you, to right and left, others will leap and fall so swiftly as to daze the sight, like intercrossing fountain-jets of fluid silver. The gulls fly lower about you, circling with sinister squeaking cries;—perhaps for an instant your feet touch in the deep something heavy, swift, lithe, that rushes past with a swirling shock. Then the fear of the Abyss, the vast and voiceless Nightmare of the Sea, will come upon you; the silent panic of all those opaline millions that flee glimmering by will enter into you also. . . .

From what do they flee thus perpetually? Is it from the giant sawfish or the ravening shark?—from the herds of the porpoises, or from the *grande-écaille*,—that splendid monster whom no net may hold,—all helmed and armored in argent plate-mail?—or from the hideous devil-fish of the Gulf,—gigantic, flat-bodied, black, with immense side-fins ever outspread like the pinions of a bat,—the terror of luggermen, the uprooter of anchors? From all these, perhaps, and from other monsters likewise—goblin shapes evolved by Nature as destroyers, as equilibrists, as counterchecks to that prodigious fecundity, which, unhindered, would thicken the deep into one measureless and waveless ferment of being. . . . But when there are many bathers these perils are forgotten,—numbers give courage,—one can abandon one's self, without fear of the invisible, to the long, quivering, electrical caresses of the sea. . . .

Thirty years ago, Last Island lay steeped in the enormous light of even such magical days. July was dying;—for weeks no fleck of cloud had broken the heaven's blue dream of eternity; winds held their breath; slow wavelets caressed the bland brown beach with a sound as of kisses and whispers. To one who found himself alone, beyond the limits of the village and beyond the hearing of its voices,—the vast silence, the vast light, seemed full of weirdness. And these hushes, these transparencies, do not always inspire a causeless apprehension: they are omens sometimes—omens of coming tempest. Nature,—incomprehensible Sphinx!—before her mightiest bursts of rage, ever makes more manifest her awful beauty....

But in that forgotten summer the witchery lasted many long days,—days born in rose-light, buried in gold. It was the height of the season. The long myrtle-shadowed village was thronged with its summer population; —the big hotel could hardly accommodate all its guests;—the bathing-houses were too few for the crowds who flocked to the water morning and evening. There were diversions for all,—hunting and fishing parties, yachting excursions, rides, music, games, promenades. Carriage wheels whirled flickering along the beach, seaming its smoothness noiselessly, as if muffled. Love wrote its dreams upon the sand. . . .

. . . Then one great noon, when the blue abyss of day seemed to yawn over the world more deeply than ever before, a sudden change touched the quicksilver smoothness of the waters—the swaying shadow of a vast motion. First the whole sea-circle appeared to rise up bodily at the sky; the horizon-curve lifted to a straight line; the line darkened and approached,—a monstrous wrinkle, an immeasurable fold of green water, moving swift as a cloud-shadow pursued by sunlight. But it had looked formidable only by startling contrast with the previous placidity of the open: it was scarcely two feet high;—it curled slowly as it neared the beach, and combed itself out in sheets of woolly foam with a low, rich roll of whispered thunder. Swift in pursuit another followed—a third—a feebler fourth; then the sea only swayed a little, and stilled again. Minutes passed, and the immeasurable heaving recommenced—one, two, three, four . . . seven long swells this time; —and the Gulf smoothed itself once more. Irregularly the phenomenon continued to repeat itself, each time with heavier billowing and briefer intervals of quiet—until at last the whole sea grew restless and shifted color and flickered green;—the swells became shorter and changed form. Then from horizon to shore ran one uninterrupted heaving—one vast green swarming of snaky shapes, rolling in to hiss and flatten upon the sand. Yet no single cirrus-speck revealed itself through all the violet heights: there was no wind!—you might have fancied the sea had been upheaved from beneath. . . .

And indeed the fancy of a seismic origin for a windless surge would not appear in these latitudes to be utterly without foundation. On the fairest days a southeast breeze may bear you an odor singular enough to startle you from sleep,—a strong, sharp smell as of fish-oil; and gazing at the sea you might be still more startled at the sudden apparition of great oleaginous patches spreading over the water, sheeting over the swells. That is, if you had never heard of the mysterious submarine oilwells, the volcanic fountains, unexplored, that well up with the eternal pulsing of the Gulf-Stream. . . .

But the pleasure-seekers of Last Island knew there must have been a "great blow" somewhere that day. Still the sea swelled; and a splendid surf made the evening bath delightful. Then, just at sundown, a beautiful cloud-bridge grew up and arched the sky with a single span of cottony pink vapor, that changed and deepened color with the dying of the iridescent day. And the cloud-bridge approached, stretched, strained, and swung round at last to make way for the coming of the gale,—even as the light bridges that traverse the dreamy Têche swing open when luggermen sound through their conch-shells the long, bellowing signal of approach.

Then the wind began to blow, with the passing of July. It blew from the northeast, clear, cool. It blew in enormous sighs, dying away at regular intervals, as if pausing to draw breath. All night it blew; and in each pause could be heard the answering moan of the rising surf,—as if the rhythm of the sea moulded itself after the rhythm of the air,— as if the waving of the water responded precisely to the waving of the wind,—a billow for every puff, a surge for every sigh.

The August morning broke in a bright sky;—the breeze still came cool and clear from the northeast. The waves were running now at a sharp angle to the shore: they began to carry fleeces, an innumerable flock of vague green shapes, wind-driven to be despoiled of their ghostly wood. Far as the eye could follow

Reflected in a nearby pool is the Hermitage, happy example of Louisiana's version of the Greek Revival.

the line of the beach, all the slope was white with the great shearing of them. Clouds came, flew as in a panic against the face of the sun, and passed. All that day and through the night and into the morning again the breeze continued from the northeast, blowing like an equinoctial gale. . . .

Then day by day the vast breath freshened steadily, and the waters heightened. A week later sea-bathing had become perilous: colossal breakers were herding in, like moving leviathan-backs, twice the height of a man. Still the gale grew, and the billowing waxed mightier, and faster and faster overhead flew the tatters of torn cloud. The gray morning of the 9th wanly lighted a surf that appalled the best swimmers: the sea was one wild agony of foam, the gale was rending off the heads of the waves and veiling the horizon with a fog of salt spray. Shadowless and gray the day remained; there were mad bursts of lashing rain. Evening brought with it a sinister apparition, looming through a cloud-rent in the west—a scarlet sun in a green sky. His sanguine disk, enormously magnified, seemed barred like the body of a belted planet. A moment, and the crimson spectre vanished; and the moonless night came.

Then the Wind grew weird. It ceased being a breath; it became a Voice moaning across the world,—hooting,—uttering nightmare sounds, — *Whoo!—whoo!—whoo!*—and with each stupendous owl-cry the mooing of the waters seemed to deepen, more and more abysmally, through all the hours of darkness. From the northwest the breakers of the bay began to roll high over the sandy slope, into the salines;—the village bayou broadened to a bellowing flood. . . . So the tumult swelled and the turmoil heightened until morning,—a morning of gray gloom and whistling rain. Rain of bursting clouds and rain of wind-blown brine from the great spuming agony of the sea.

The steamer *Star* was due from St. Mary's that fearful morning. Could she come? No one really believed it,—no one. And nevertheless men struggled to the roaring beach to look for her, because hope is stronger than reason. . . .

Even to-day, in these Creole islands, the advent of the steamer is the great event of the week. There are no telegraph lines, no telephones: the mail-packet is the only trustworthy medium of communication with the outer world, bringing friends, news, letters. The magic of steam has placed New Orleans nearer to New York than to the Timbaliers, nearer to Washington than to Wine Island, nearer to Chicago than to Barataria Bay. And even during the deepest sleep of waves and winds there will come betimes to sojourners in this unfamiliar archipelago a feeling of lonesomeness that is a fear, a feeling of isolation from the world of men,—totally unlike that sense of solitude which haunts one in the silence of mountain-heights, or amid the eternal tumult of lofty granitic coasts: a sense of helpless insecurity.

The land seems but an undulation of the sea-bed: its highest ridges do not rise more than the height of a man above the salines on either side;—the salines themselves lie almost level with the level of the flood-tides;—the tides are variable, treacherous, mysterious. But when all around and above these ever-changing shores the twin vastnesses of heaven and sea begin to utter the tremendous revelation of themselves as infinite forces in contention, then indeed this sense of separation from humanity appals. . . . Perhaps it was such a feeling which forced men, on the tenth day of August, eighteen hundred and fifty-six, to hope against hope for the coming of the *Star*, and to strain their eyes towards far-off Terrebonne. "It was a wind you could lie down on," said my friend the pilot.

. . . "Great God!" shrieked a voice above the shouting of the storm,—*"she is coming!"*
. . . It was true. Down the Atchafalaya, and thence through strange mazes of bayou, lakelet, and pass, by a rear route familiar only to the best of pilots, the frail river-craft had toiled into Caillou Bay, running close to the main shore;—and now she was heading right for the island, with the wind aft, over the monstrous sea. On she came, swaying, rocking, plunging,—with a great whiteness wrapping her about like a cloud, and moving with her moving,—a tempest-whirl of spray;—ghost-white and like a ghost she came, for her smoke-stacks exhaled no visible smoke—the

wind devoured it! The excitement on shore became wild;—men shouted themselves hoarse; women laughed and cried. Every telescope and opera-glass was directed upon the coming apparition; all wondered how the pilot kept his feet; all marvelled at the madness of the captain.

But Captain Abraham Smith was not mad. A veteran American sailor, he had learned to know the great Gulf as scholars knew deep books by heart: he knew the birthplace of its tempests, the mystery of its tides, the omens of its hurricanes. While lying at Brashear City he felt the storm had not yet reached its highest, vaguely foresaw a mighty peril, and resolved to wait no longer for a lull. "Boys," he said, "we've got to take her out in spite of Hell!" And they "took her out." Through all the peril, his men stayed by him and obeyed him. By mid-morning the wind had deepened to a roar,—lowering sometimes to a rumble, sometimes bursting upon the ears like a measureless and deafening crash. Then the captain knew the *Star* was running a race with Death. "She'll win it," he muttered;—"She'll stand it . . . Perhaps they'll have need of me to-night."

She won! With a sonorous steam-chant of triumph the brave little vessel rode at last into the bayou, and anchored hard by her accustomed resting-place, in full view of the hotel, though not near enough to shore to lower her gang-plank. . . . But she had sung her swan-song. Gathering in from the northeast, the waters of the bay were already marbling over the salines and half across the island; and still the wind increased its paroxysmal power.

Cottages began to rock. Some slid away from the solid props upon which they rested. A chimney tumbled. Shutters were wrenched off; verandas demolished. Light roofs lifted, dropped again, and flapped into ruin. Trees bent their heads to the earth. And still the storm grew louder and blacker with every passing hour.

The *Star* rose with the rising of the waters, dragging her anchor. Two more anchors were put out, and still she dragged—dragged in with the flood,—twisting, shuddering, careening in her agony. Evening fell; the sand began to move with the wind, stinging

faces like a continuous fire of fine shot; and frenzied blasts came to buffet the steamer forward, sideward. Then one of her hog-chains parted with a clang like the boom of a big bell. Then another! . . . Then the captain bade his men to cut away all her upper works, clean to the deck. Overboard into the seething went her stacks, her pilot-house, her cabins,—and whirled away. And the naked hull of the *Star*, still dragging her three anchors, labored on through the darkness, nearer and nearer to the immense silhouette of the hotel, whose hundred windows were now all aflame. The vast timber building seemed to defy the storm. The wind, roaring round its broad verandas,—hissing through every crevice with the sound and force of steam,—appeared to waste its rage. And in the half-lull between two terrible gusts there came to the captain's ears a sound that seemed strange in that night of multitudinous terrors . . . a sound of music!

. . . Almost every evening throughout the season there had been dancing in the great hall;—there was dancing that night also. The population of the hotel had been augmented by the advent of families from other parts of the island, who found their summer cottages insecure places of shelter: there were nearly four hundred guests assembled. Perhaps it was for this reason that the entertainment had been prepared upon a grander plan than usual, that it assumed the form of a fashionable ball. And all those pleasure-seekers,—representing the wealth and beauty of the Creole parishes,—whether from Ascension or Assumption, St. Mary's or St. Landry's, Iberville or Terrebonne, whether inhabitants of the multicolored and many-balconied Creole quarter of the quaint metropolis, or dwellers in the dreamy paradises of the Têche,—mingled joyously, knowing each other, feeling in some sort akin—whether affiliated by blood, connaturalized by caste, or simply interassociated by traditional sympathies of class sentiment and class interest. Perhaps in the more than ordinary merriment of that evening something of nervous exaltation might have been discerned,—something like a feverish resolve to oppose apprehension with gayety, to combat uneasiness by diversion. But the hours passed

With the passing years New Orleans gave America its biggest-scaled folk festival, the Mardi Gras, ranging from parades and formal masking to balls and impromptu street merrymaking.

in mirthfulness; the first general feeling of depression began to weigh less and less upon the guests; they had found reason to confide in the solidity of the massive building; there were no positive terrors, no outspoken fears; and the new conviction of all had found expression in the words of the host himself,— *"Il n'y a rien de mieux à faire que de s'amuser!"* Of what avail to lament the prospective devastation of cane-fields,—to discuss the possible ruin of crops? Better to seek solace in choregraphic harmonies, in the rhythm of gracious motion and of perfect melody, than hearken to the discords of the wild orchestra of storms; —wiser to admire the grace of Parisian toilets, the eddy of trailing robes with its fairyfoam of lace, the ivorine loveliness of glossy shoulders and jewelled throats, the glimmering of

satin-slippered feet,—than to watch the raging of the flood without, or the flying of the wrack. . . .

So the music and the mirth went on: they made joy for themselves—those elegant guests; —they jested and sipped rich wines;—they pledged, and hoped, and loved, and promised, with never a thought of the morrow, on the night of the tenth of August, eighteen hundred and fifty-six. Observant parents were there, planning for the future bliss of their nearest and dearest;—mothers and fathers of handsome lads, lithe and elegant as young pines, and fresh from the polish of foreign university training;—mothers and fathers of splendid girls whose simplest attitudes were witcheries. Young cheeks flushed, young hearts fluttered with an emotion more puissant than the excitement of the dance;—young eyes betrayed the happy secret discreeter lips would have preserved. Slave-servants circled through the aristocratic press, bearing dainties and wines, praying permission to pass in terms at once humble and officious,—always in the excellent French which well-trained house-servants were taught to use on such occasions.

... Night wore on: still the shining floor palpitated to the feet of the dancers; still the piano-forte pealed, and still the violins sang, —and the sound of their singing shrilled through the darkness, in gasps of the gale, to the ears of Captain Smith, as he strove to keep his footing on the spray-drenched deck of the *Star*.

—"Christ!" he muttered,—"a dance! If that wind whips round south, there'll be another dance! . . . But I guess the *Star* will stay." . . .

Half an hour might have passed; still the lights flamed calmly, and the violins trilled, and the perfumed whirl went on . . . And suddenly the wind veered!

Again the *Star* reeled, and shuddered, and turned, and began to drag all her anchors. But she now dragged away from the great building and its lights,—away from the voluptuous thunder of the grand piano,—even at that moment out-pouring the great joy of Weber's melody orchestrated by Berlioz: *l'Invitation à la Valse*,—with its marvellous musical swing!

—"Waltzing!" cried the captain, "God help them!—God help us all now! . . . *The Wind waltzes to-night, with the Sea for his partner!*" . . .

. . . Some one shrieked in the midst of the revels;—some girl who found her pretty slippers wet. What could it be? Thin streams of water were spreading over the level planking,—curling about the feet of the dancers . . . What could it be? All the land had begun to quake, even as, but a moment before, the polished floor was trembling to the pressure of circling steps;—all the building shook now; every beam uttered its groan. What could it be? . . .

There was a clamor, a panic, a rush to the windy night. Infinite darkness above and beyond; but the lantern-beams danced far out over an unbroken circle of heaving and swirl-ing black water. Stealthily, swiftly, the meas-ureless sea-flood was rising.

—"*Messieurs—mesdames, ce n'est rien.* Nothing serious, ladies. I assure you. . . . *Mais nous en avons vu bien souvent, les inon-dations comme celle-ci; ça passe vite!* The water will go down in a few hours, ladies;—it never rises higher than this; *il n'y a pas le moindre danger, je vous dis! Allons! il n'y a—* My God! what is that?" . . .

For a moment there was a ghastly hush of voices. And through that hush there burst upon the ears of all a fearful and unfamiliar sound, as of a colossal cannonade—rolling up from the south, with volleying lightnings. Vastly and swiftly, nearer and nearer it came, —a ponderous and unbroken thunder-roll, terrible as the long muttering of an earth-quake.

The nearest mainland,—across mad Cail-lou Bay to the sea-marshes,—lay twelve miles north; west, by the Gulf, the nearest solid ground was twenty miles distant. There were boats, yes!—but the stoutest swimmer might never reach them now! . . .

Then rose a frightful cry,—the hoarse, hideous, indescribable cry of hopeless fear,—the despairing animal-cry man utters when suddenly brought face to face with Nothing-ness, without preparation, without consola-tion, without possibility of respite . . . *Sauve qui peut!* Some wrenched down the doors; some clung to the heavy banquet-tables, to the sofas, to the billiard-tables:—during one terrible instant,—against fruitless heroisms, against futile generosities,—raged all the frenzy of selfishness, all the brutalities of panic. And then—then came, thundering through the blackness, the giant swells, boom on boom! . . . One crash!—the huge frame building rocks like a cradle, seesaws, crackles. What are human shrieks now?—the tornado is shriek-ing! Another!—chandeliers splinter; lights are dashed out; a sweeping cataract hurls in; the immense hall rises,—oscillates,—twirls as upon a pivot,—crepitates,—crumbles into ruin. Crash again!—the swirling wreck dissolves into the wallowing of another monster billow; and a hundred cottages overturn, spin in sudden eddies, quiver, disjoint, and melt into the seething.

. . . So the hurricane passed,—tearing off the heads of the prodigious waves, to hurl them a hundred feet in air,—heaping up the ocean against the land,—upturning the woods. Bays and passes were swollen to abysses; rivers regorged; the sea-marshes were changed to raging wastes of water. Before New Orleans the flood of the mile-broad Mississippi rose six feet above highest water-mark. One hundred and ten miles away, Donaldsonville trembled at the towering tide of the Lafourche. Lakes strove to burst their boundaries. Far-off river steamers tugged wildly at their cables,—shivering like tethered creatures that hear by night the approaching howl of destroyers. Smoke-stacks were hurled overboard, pilot-houses torn away, cabins blown to fragments.

And over roaring Kaimbuck Pass,—over the agony of Caillou Bay,—the billowing tide rushed unresisted from the Gulf,—tearing and swallowing the land in its course,—ploughing out deep-sea channels where sleek herds had been grazing but a few hours before,—rending islands in twain,—and ever bearing with it, through the night, an enormous vortex of wreck and vast wan drift of corpses. . . .

But the *Star* remained. And Captain Abraham Smith, with a long, good rope about his waist, dashed again and again into that awful surging to snatch victims from death,—clutching at passing hands, heads, garments, in the cataract-sweep of the seas,—saving, aiding, cheering, though blinded by spray and battered by drifting wreck, until his strength failed in the unequal struggle at last, and his men drew him aboard senseless, with some beautiful half-drowned girl safe in his arms. But well-nigh twoscore souls had been rescued by him; and the *Star* stayed on through it all.

Long years after, the weed-grown ribs of her graceful skeleton could still be seen, curving up from the sand-dunes of Last Island, in valiant witness of how well she stayed.

Day breaks through the flying wrack, over the infinite heaving of the sea, over the low land made vast with desolation. It is a spectral dawn: a wan light, like the light of a dying sun.

The wind has waned and veered; the flood sinks slowly back to its abysses—abandoning its plunder,—scattering its piteous waifs over bar and dune, over shoal and marsh, among the silences of the mango-swamps, over the long low reaches of sand-grasses and drowned weeds, for more than a hundred miles. From the shell-reefs of Pointe-au-Fer to the shallows of Pelto Bay the dead lie mingled with the high-heaped drift;—from their cypress groves the vultures rise to dispute a share of the feast with the shrieking frigate-birds and squeaking gulls. And as the tremendous tide withdraws its plunging waters, all the pirates of air follow the great white-gleaming retreat: a storm of billowing wings and screaming throats.

And swift in the wake of gull and frigate-bird the Wreckers come, the Spoilers of the dead,—savage skimmers of the sea,—hurricane-riders wont to spread their canvas-pinions in the face of storms; Sicilian and Corsican outlaws, Manila-men from the marshes, deserters from many navies, Lascars, marooners, refugees of a hundred nationalities,—fishers and shrimpers by name, smugglers by opportunity,—wild channel-finders from obscure bayous and unfamiliar *chênières*, all skilled in the mysteries of these mysterious waters beyond the comprehension of the oldest licensed pilot. . . .

There is plunder for all—birds and men. There are drowned sheep in multitude, heaped carcasses of kine. There are casks of claret and kegs of brandy and legions of bottles bobbing in the surf. There are billiard-tables overturned upon the sand;—there are sofas, pianos, footstools and music-stools, luxurious chairs, lounges of bamboo. There are chests of cedar, and toilet-tables of rosewood, and trunks of fine stamped leather stored with precious apparel. There are *objets de luxe* innumerable. There are children's playthings: French dolls in marvellous toilets, and toy carts, and wooden horses, and wooden spades, and brave little wooden ships that rode out the gale in which the great *Nautilus* went down. There is money in notes and in coin—in purses, in pocket-books, and in pockets: plenty of it! There are silks, satins, laces, and fine linen to be stripped from the bodies of the drowned,—and necklaces, bracelets, watches, finger-rings and fine chains, brooches and trinkets. . . . "*Chi bidizza! —Oh! chi bedda mughieri! Eccu, la bidizza!*" That ball-dress was made in Paris by— But you never heard of him, Sicilian Vicenzu . . . "*Che bella sposina!*" Her betrothal ring will not come off, Giuseppe; but the delicate bone snaps easily: your oyster-knife can sever the tendon . . . "*Guardate! chi bedda picciota!*" Over her heart you will find it, Valentino— the locket held by that fine Swiss chain of woven hair—"*Caya manan!*" And it is not your quadroon bondsmaid, sweet lady, who now disrobes you so roughly; those Malay hands are less deft than hers,—but she slumbers very far away from you, and may not be aroused from her sleep. "*Na quita mo! dalaga!—na quita maganda!*" . . . Juan, the fastenings of those diamond ear-drops are much too complicated for your peon fingers: tear them out! —"*Dispense, chulita!*" . . .

. . . Suddenly a long, mighty silver trilling fills the ears of all: there is a wild hurrying and scurrying; swiftly, one after another, the overburdened luggers spread wings and flutter away.

Thrice the great cry rings rippling through the gray air, and over the green sea, and over the far-flooded shell-reefs, where the huge white flashes are,—sheet-lightning of breakers,—and over the weird wash of corpses coming in. It is the steam-call of the relief-boat, hastening to rescue the living, to gather in the dead. . . .

The Marshes of Glynn

SIDNEY LANIER

For thousands of readers, Sidney Lanier wrote the finest poetry to appear in the postwar South. Although generally florid in style, it shows a rare imagery, a romantic identification with nature, and Lanier's work has often been reprinted and admired by readers who have "discovered" him since the war and in the present century. Member of a musical family, he was a gifted flutist and appeared professionally for a time. But his life was a series of tragedies. As a Confederate, Lanier was captured and spent many months in Federal prisons. His health shattered, he traveled to Texas and Florida in an effort to find some cure for his tuberculosis. At various times he worked as a teacher, a hotel clerk, a legal assistant. He was thirty-nine when death came.

Glooms of the live-oaks, beautiful-braided and woven
With intricate shades of the vines that myriad-cloven
Clamber the forks of the multiform boughs,—
Emerald twilights,—
Virginal shy lights,
Wrought of the leaves to allure to the whisper of vows,
When lovers pace timidly down through the green colonnades
Of the dim sweet words, of the dear dark woods
Of the heavenly woods and glades
That run to the radiant marginal sand-beach within
The wide sea-marshes of Glynn;—

Beautiful glooms, soft dusks in the noon-day fire,—
Wildwood privacies, closets of lone desire,
Chamber from chamber parted with wavering arras of leaves,—
Cells for the passionate pleasure of prayer to the soul that grieves,
Pure with a sense of the passing of saints through the wood,
Cool for the dutiful weighing of ill with good;—

O braided dusks of the oak and woven shades of the vine,
While the riotous noon-day sun of the June-day long did shine
Ye held me fast in your heart and I held you fast in mine;

But now when the noon is no more, and riot is
    rest,
And the sun is a-wait at the ponderous gate of
    the West,
And the slant yellow beam down the wood-aisle
    doth seem
Like a lane into heaven that leads from a dream,—
Ay, now, when my soul all day hath drunken
    the soul of the oak,
And my heart is at ease from men, and the
    wearisome sound of the stroke
Of the scythe of time and the trowel of trade
    is low,
And belief overmasters doubt, and I know that
    I know,
And my spirit is grown to a lordly great compass
    within,
That the length and the breadth and the sweep
    of the marshes of Glynn
Will work me no fear like the fear they have
    wrought me of yore
When length was fatigue, and when breadth was
    but bitterness sore,
And when terror and shrinking and dreary un-
    namable pain
Drew over me out of the merciless miles of the
    plain,—

Oh, now, unafraid, I am fain to face
The vast sweet visage of space.
To the edge of the wood I am drawn, I am
    drawn,
Where the gray beach glimmering runs, as a belt
    of the dawn,
For a mete and a mark
To the forest-dark:—
So:
Affable live-oak, leaning low,—
Thus—with your favor—soft, with a reverent
    hand,
(Not lightly touching your person, Lord of the
    land!)
Bending your beauty aside, with a step I stand
On the firm-packed sand,
Free
By a world of marsh that borders a world of sea.
Sinuous southward and sinuous northward the
    shimmering band
Of the sand-beach fastens the fringe of the marsh
    to the folds of the land.
Inward and outward to northward and southward
    the beach-lines linger and curl
As a silver-wrought garment that clings to and
    follows the firm sweet limbs of a girl.
Vanishing, swerving, evermore curving again into
    sight,
Softly the sand-beach wavers away to a dim gray
    looping of light,
And what if behind me to westward the wall of
    the woods stands high?

The world lies at ease: how ample, the marsh
    and the sea and the sky!
A league and a league of marsh-grass, waist-high,
    broad in the blade,
Green, and all of a height, and unflecked with a
    light or a shade,
Stretch leisurely off, in a pleasant plain,
To the terminal blue of the main.

Oh, what is abroad in the marsh and the terminal
    sea?
Somehow my soul seems suddenly free
From the weighing of fate and sad discussion
    of sin,
By the length and the breadth and the sweep
    of the marshes of Glynn.

Ye marshes, how candid and simple and nothing-
    withholding and free
Ye publish yourselves to the sky and offer
    yourselves to the sea!
Tolerant plains, that suffer the sea and the rains
    and the sun,
Ye spread and span like the catholic man who
    hath mightily won
God out of knowledge and good out of infinite
    pain
And sight out of blindness and purity out of a
    stain.

As the marsh-hen secretly builds on the watery
    sod,
Behold I will build me a nest on the greatness
    of God:
I will fly in the greatness of God as the marsh-
    hen flies
In the freedom that fills all the space 'twixt the
    marsh and the skies:
By so many roots as the marsh-grass sends in
    the sod
I will heartily lay me a-hold on the greatness
    of God:
Oh, like to the greatness of God is the greatness
    within
The range of the marshes, the liberal marshes
    of Glynn.

And the sea lends large, as the marsh: lo, out of
    his plenty the sea
Pours fast: full soon the time of the flood-tide
    must be:
Look how the grace of the sea doth go
About and about through the intricate channels
    that flow
Here and there,
Everywhere,
Till his waters have flooded the uttermost creeks
    and the low-lying lanes,

And the marsh is meshed with a million veins,
That like as with rosy and silvery essences flow
In the rose-and-silver evening glow.

Farewell, my lord Sun!
The creeks overflow: a thousand rivulets run
'Twixt the roots of the sod; the blades of the
    marsh-grass stir;
Passeth a hurrying sound of wings that westward
    whirr;
Passeth, and all is still; and the currents cease
    to run;
And the sea and the marsh are one.

How still the plains of the waters be!
The tide is in his ecstasy.

The tide is at his highest height;
And it is night.
And now from the Vast of the Lord will the
    waters of sleep
Roll in on the souls of men,
But who will reveal to our waking ken
The forms that swim and the shapes that creep
Under the waters of sleep?
And I would I could know what swimmeth below
    when the tide comes in
On the length and the breadth of the marvelous
    marshes of Glynn.

Two Girls Visit a Gentleman

GRACE KING

*Among the most graceful writers of the region about the Gulf Coast was
an Anglo-Saxon with a French Huguenot connection on one side of her family,
Miss Grace King of New Orleans. Among her many works, including* New
Orleans: The Place and the People, *various short stories and biographies, she published* Memories of a Southern Woman of Letters, *Macmillan, New York, 1932.
Looking back over a long life, she gave a precise evocative recollection of her
first visit to Judge Charles Gayarré, the historian whose work had a great influence upon hers.*

"THE Judge," as we called him familiarly,
passed his summers at his little country place,
coming to New Orleans at frequent intervals.
. . . He expected to return to Ronçal at the
end of the week, and my sister May and I
were made ready to go with him. We had
never seen him, although he was my father's
most intimate friend. But besides his amusing
foreign peculiarities, we knew that he was the
historian of Louisiana, and that my father, our
supreme judge, pronounced him one of the
most distinguished men in the United States,
a judgment that my mother warmly echoed;
but in truth she always echoed his opinions
and seemed to have a horror of forming her
own.

The day came slowly and surely, like the
day of execution to a criminal. . . . May was
fourteen, I a year older. This was our first
parting from home. At the station we found
the Judge awaiting us. He was an impressive
figure, very tall; our father, a tall man, appeared short beside him. Our father was handsome; but the judge was majestic, in his high
satin stock that held his head inflexibly erect.
He was dressed in a long black broadcloth
coat and tall top hat. His beard was clipped
close, to a point, beneath his chin. He smiled
cordially and shook each of us by the hand,
dismissed "King's" further attendance, and assisted us up the tall steep steps of the car.

As we had never been in a steamcar before, we cowered in our seats. When the train
started, our hearts started too, and dismay
seized us. . . . If we did not weep, it was because of our shyness and instinctive obedience
to our father's standard of cold, stern repres-
sion of feeling as a measure of good breeding.
Soon we were on a high railroad trestle, crossing a wide lake. We "stepped across" several
bayous. Great pine and cypress forests in all
their savage force filled the intervening country like a defiant army.

Innumerable stops were made at minute

Rex parades on Canal Street, passing by Henry Clay's statue.

stations swarming with white, black and yellow men, women and children. The Judge told us the name of each station as we gazed with wondering eyes out of our window. Amite, Tickfaw, Tangipahoa were fine stations, and offered with their pretty names glimpses of a fine country. We tried to fix the names in our memory so that we should never forget them. "The next stop will be ours," said the Judge at length, and he proceeded to gather up his bundles, which were spread over two seats. "Ronçal! Ronçal!" called the conductor, and in great trepidation of haste the two new travelers followed the Judge and were helped down the steps.

We walked along a path cut in the pine forest, our feet slipping and sliding over the pine straw that covered it. At the end of the path, or avenue as the Judge called it, we entered the park, which was indeed a park, according to the descriptions we had read. For in our little experience we had never seen one before. It was beautifully cleared of underbrush; the trees were well trimmed. At the far end stood the house, rising out of an encircling row of flower beds, thick with roses in bloom.

The house! ... We had expected a stately white marble mansion. ... The house was a little, low, brown cottage. On the steps stood Mrs. Gayarré. She was of ordinary height, slight of figure, her ever-bright face radiant with pleasure. She was, as all ladies of her age dressed then, in a skirt of calico and a loose *sacque*, or *peignoir*, of fine white cambric, with a fine lace edging at the neck.

Her husband kissed her on the forehead, and she, with her girlish, elastic step, preceded us into the house, directing the shabby, awkward Negro man who had met us at the station where to place our trunk. When we had refreshed ourselves, we went out and found the Judge and Mrs. Gayarré waiting to show us around the park. We walked for an hour, looking at the trees—magnolia, hickory, chestnut, hackberry, crab apple, holly—which they presented to us by name with the tender sentiment of old and loved companions. . . . We began to perceive dimly that Ronçal held something grander and more precious to its owners than a marble mansion, and that what we saw was indeed a more fitting place of residence for a great man than what we had so ignorantly expected—the perfect silence broken only by the singing of the birds; the majestic solitude, the heavenly peace that overspreads even the skies.

The cottage stood on a little ridge just large enough to hold it. The kitchen and domestic buildings were in a declivity at a haughty distance beyond. . . . It all looked French and foreign and different from the usual American country place, although the visitors were too young and inexperienced to appreciate this. The only remark they made was that they saw no chickens. Mrs. Gayarré explained, "The Judge will have no chickens about him, with roosters crowing in the morning to disturb sleep, and hens with their noisy cackling around the house!"

The dinner was simplicity itself—a soup, a dish of chicken, brown and appetizing, rice and sweet potatoes, a dish of preserves, cheese and soda biscuits. Instead of water, we drank full goblets of Spanish wine. We lingered around the table until the light began to fade. Then Mrs. Gayarré arose, lighted the coal-oil lamp and put it on the sideboard, and we went out on the gallery in front. Two large wicker chairs were placed opposite one another, evidently for Mrs. Gayarré and the Judge. May and I took our seats on the steps, where we could look at our hosts and see the park at the same time.

Soon the air began to cool, and the soft shadows descended; the trees of the park seemed to advance upon us, black and huge. Above their branches the evening stars appeared, glistening and bright. Homesickness followed the thought of home, and dear Mrs. Gayarré, knowing our hearts intuitively, suggested that we were tired and invited us to go to bed. She conducted us to our room, lighted our lamp and left us, warning us not to wake too early, as the Judge was not an early riser and breakfast would not be served before nine o'clock.

Oh, the quiet of that first night. At the beginning we could not sleep in spite of our fatigue. The rustling of the leaves over the roof, the hum of the droning insects, the barking of a dog in the far distance, the consciousness that we were at Ronçal with the famous Gayarrés, kept our eyes open. The night air through the open casements was fragrant of the woods, and in a fainter degree of the roses around the house. . . .

The morning was just turning gray as we opened our eyes. It was a strange world, with great trees standing close to our windows, a forest of silence surrounding us. . . . At last a mocking-bird burst out impatiently with defiant song. We started at its boldness, daring to disobey the Judge's orders, to flaunt its impudence. But finally, with whispers and stealthy tread, we coaxed open the fastened door that closed our room, and like thieves or murderers slipped through a narrow crack. We never had been in the wide world before in our lives. How still, how beautiful it was! . . .

We walked upon the grass fearfully, then timidly, then boldly, in full consciousness of our new rapture. We went as far as the little creek, running on into daylight, it seemed, so cool, so cool and silver gray, the moss hanging low over it like a veil over a face. We lingered, enjoying with greed our pleasure.

A bell rang from the house. "So the Judge permits bells," we exclaimed, and hurried back to our room. It was merely the bell to summon the cook, who lived in a cabin apart from the kitchen. While she cooked the breakfast, we sat down and waited for it, sitting on the step outside our door. After a faint, very faint, rustling, Mrs. Gayarré knocked at the door.

We followed her into the hall, where the table was set for breakfast. Not an American breakfast, by any means. A foaming pot of chocolate for the Judge, and one of tea for Mrs. Gayarré, home-made bread (cold) and butter constituted the menu. No coffee, upon which we ultra Americans had been brought up! But the Judge gave us each a cup of his chocolate. The Judge's cup was an immense one, as large as three ordinary tea cups. He bought his own chocolate in New Orleans from old Limongi, the historic chocolate purveyor, as he may be called, to the fine gourmets of the city, and made according to a recipe brought from France. Through a long life the memory of it has lasted. . . . We did not drink it, but following our host's example, dipped our buttered bread into it, and thus made a meal of it.

It was the first time my sister and I realized what conversation was. . . . Could anyone converse better than the Judge? In a long memory his rival in conversation is not found. Mrs. Gayarré was a good partner, following her husband's lead with ready fluency and skill, in a bright, cheery voice, very sweet and musical. The Judge spoke English with the perfection of an artist in language, each word given its full completeness of sound and significance, betraying thus the speaker's foreignness. His talk was enchantment pure and simple to his auditors, and he too must have been enchanted by the rapt attention paid by the brown-eyed young girls looking at him with naïve admiration and appreciation.

Selecting from his bookcase a book for each of us: *The Memoirs of a Femme de Chambre* by Lady Blessington for May, and *Napoleon in Exile* by O'Meara for me, and advising us to "read them yonder, sitting under the trees," we all separated, to meet again at the early dinner. This followed always the same menu as the day before—soup, chicken, vegetables from the garden, a piece of fruit for dessert, and plenty of good Spanish wine, which the Judge served from great, tall, cut-glass decanters, with tall steeple-shaped stoppers.

In the afternoon there was a walk, across the railroad, into the woods on the other side, to the great stream of this part of the country —the Tangipahoa River. The sumach leaves were like a red cloth thrown over the bushes; the purple pokeberries clung like barnacles to their stalks. . . . After supper we sat on the gallery as usual. Mrs. Gayarré would sometimes bring out her beautiful little guitar of young-ladyhood days, and tinkle upon it, accompanying the songs that she had learned in her youth. And in a voice still sweet, but slightly weakened by age, she would sing "Oft in the Stilly Night" and "Believe Me If All Those Endearing Young Charms." Alas, these always seem to sound sweeter when sung in after-youth, when the voice is not fresh!

The Judge would listen for a while—he who had listened to Malibran and Garcia—but soon he would jump up. "Come, it is time for us to go to bed!" Mrs. Gayarré would say gayly and with her guitar would follow him.

Through the house from front to back ran a hall large enough to hold the dining table with chairs around it, a sideboard and bookcases along the walls. On the right side of the house was the Judge's office, its distinguishing mark a tall desk, at which he stood to write. Back of this was his bedroom, small, square and simply furnished, whose glass door and window opened on to a side gallery, with a view of the old "quarters," of course now emptied of its slaves. Mrs. Gayarré's bedroom was dainty and elegant, with a handsome toilette of carved rosewood. By her bed stood a *table de nuit* bearing its carafe and sugar bowl on a glass tray, all of pink and white Bohemian glass.

Never, surely, has the forest of the Tangipahoa surrounded a parlor like unto Judge Gayarré's. It was the salon of a Paris apartment. It remains bright and complete in memory, a corner of France. The walls were papered in white, with delicate gold traceries. Over the mantel hung the beautiful life-size portrait of the Judge, painted when he was in Paris—when he was a young man, and handsome, with life before him. He was dressed in the fashion of 1830, in formal black broadcloth, high satin stock, and black satin waistcoat over a fine-pleated cambric shirt, holding his eyeglasses in his hand. His face was of great intellectual beauty, with high forehead,

The Krewe of Mystic, with Egyptian theme, turns a corner.

clear blue eyes, slightly thinning dark, a mouth of slightly ironic lips.

The four sides of the room held in central places four paintings by Gérard, small-size replicas of those in the Louvre—"Peace," "War," "Gallic Courage" and "Plenty." They were bought in Paris thirty years before, when the portrait on the mantel was painted, when he knew Baron Gérard and was himself known of the great social and political world of Paris. Around these were hung smaller canvases, the "Heads of the Apostles," and bits of French scenery, executed with the finished fineness and beauty of French art. On the mantel was a superb bronze clock, with tall bronze candelabra at either side. . . . The furniture was of rosewood inlaid with brass filature, and the chairs covered with dark-blue damask. The center table held a great brass-stemmed carcel lamp, daguerreotypes, paper cutters and a papier-mâché writing desk glittering with the mother-of-pearl ornaments of its period.

On rainy days when we could not walk out-of-doors, we sat snugly ensconced in the delicious soft fauteuils, reading in the comfort we had never known in our big family life in a house too small for us. Sometimes the Judge would walk in, leaving his workroom on the other side of the house, and while the rain poured down through the trees outside, he seemed glad to gossip cheerfully with us of the time when he was the elegant man of the world of his portrait, when he lived in an apartment in Paris, and enjoyed the counterpart of the little salon at Ronçal.

He was growing old now and wore a *toupet*. His face was wrinkled, his short pointed beard was almost white, and his mouth was disfigured by age; but his short-sighted eyes were bright and clear, and his voice, fine and strong. We were too young and inexperienced to make the comparison between him and the portrait and indulge in reflections upon it. These came during the long years afterwards when the handsome gentleman of the portrait and the little brown house was traversing the long road before him, the road leading through poverty, neglect, privation, obscurity, to the end of it all. . . .

At a shy question from us about a remarkably vivid portrait of a man's head, he told us that it was evidently the work of a great master; that Charles Lanusse, his cousin, had given it to him in Paris, telling him not to part with it, as it was valuable, and to take good care of it. Lanusse had bought it for a trifle from a ragged old veteran of Napoleon's army who had come to great misery. He had obtained the painting in the loot of a studio in some town of the Low Country. Lanusse, himself, had taken it from its hook on the wall. . . .

The room next to the salon was the winter dining room. It also was small and square. Here hung the family portraits, in bright, glittering frames: Don Estevan Gayarré, the *Contador Real*, who came to Louisiana with Ulloa; his grandson, Don Carlos Gayarré, the father of the Judge; and the best loved of all, Etienne de Boré, the grandfather on whose plantation Gayarré had passed his childhood, whose fine, shrewd, old face with a kindly smile on his lips bespoke the affection of all. . . .

The little villa had been built according to the plans and under the supervision of the Judge. At the time he was possessed of a large fortune and was contemplating another long sojourn in Europe. He needed a place of deposit for his pictures, books, and furniture, and a home for his slaves. This beautiful tract of land was found, well wooded, well watered, and at just the distance from the city required for convenience. . . . He named his place "Ronçal," after the region in Spain where the family of Gayarré had lived for centuries, and where they had been ennobled because of the famous stand made by them against the Arabs, or Moors. . . .

But when everything was completed, and all arrangements had been made for the sojourn in Europe, the departure did not take place. . . . The Confederate War broke out. The Judge . . . was beyond the fighting age, but he invested his fortune, that was to have been taken to Europe, in Confederate bonds, and thus he went the way to poverty. But fortunately he had prepared a home for himself and could retire to it.

"The Power of the Voudoo Is Still Feared by Many"

CHARLES DUDLEY WARNER

While a great deal of poppycock has been written about voodooism in the South, by whites and Negroes as well, remnants of the old religion-superstition-folk-beliefs have lingered through the years here and there, in rural areas and in towns and cities. One of the more dependable nineteenth-century descriptions of it, on which many later individuals have drawn for material, is in Charles Dudley Warner's Studies in the South and West, *published in New York in 1889.*

THERE was nothing mysterious about it. The ceremony took place in broad day, at noon in the upper chambers of a small frame house in a street just beyond Congo Square and the old Parish prison in New Orleans. It was an incantation rather than a dance—a curious mingling of African voudoo rites with modern "spiritualism" and faith-cure. . . .

In its origin it is serpent worhip. The Voudoo signifies a being all-powerful on the earth, who is, or is represented by, a harmless species of serpent (*coulevre*), and in this belief the sect perform rites in which the serpent is propitiated. In common parlance, the chief actor is called the Voudoo—the Voudoo King or Queen.

Some years ago Congo Square was the scene of the weird midnight rites of this sect, as unrestrained and barbarous as ever took place in the Congo country. All these semi-public performances have been suppressed, and all private assemblies for this worship are illegal, and broken up by the police when discovered.

It is said in New Orleans that Voudooism is a thing of the past. But the superstition remains, and I believe that very few of the colored people in New Orleans are free from it —that is, free from it as a superstition. Those who repudiate it, have nothing to do with it, and regard it as only evil, still ascribe power to the Voudoo, to some ugly old woman or man, who is popularly believed to have occult power (as the Italians believe in the "evil-eye"), can cast a charm and put the victims under a spell, or by incantations relieve them from it. The power of the Voudoo is still feared by many who are too intelligent to believe in it intellectually. . . .

Although very few white people in New Orleans have ever seen the performance I shall try to describe, and it is said that the police would break it up if they knew of it, it takes place every Wednesday at noon at the house where I saw it; and there are three or four other places in the city where the rites are celebrated sometimes at night. Our admission was procured through a friend who had, I suppose, vouched for our good intentions.

We were received in the living-rooms of the house on the ground-floor by the "doctor," a good looking mulatto of middle age, clad in a white shirt with gold studs, linen pantaloons, and list slippers. He had the simple-minded, shrewd look of a "healing medium."

The interior was neat, though in some confusion. . . . There were several negroes about the door, many in the rooms and in the background, and all had an air of expectation and mild excitement. After we had satisfied the scruples of the doctor, and signed our names to his register, we were invited to ascend by a narrow, crooked stairway in the rear. This led to a small landing where a dozen people might stand, and from this a door opened into a chamber perhaps fifteen feet by ten, where the rites were to take place; beyond this was a small bedroom. Around the sides of these rooms were benches and chairs, and the close quarters were already well filled.

The assembly was perfectly orderly, but a motley one, and the women largely outnumbered the men. There were coal-black negroes, porters and stevedores, fat cooks, slender chamber-maids, all shades of complexion, yellow girls and comely quadroons, most of them in common servant attire, but some neatly dressed. And among them were, to my surprise, several white people.

On one side of the middle room where we sat was constructed a sort of buffet or bureau, used as an altar. On it stood an image of the Virgin Mary in painted plaster, about two feet high, flanked by lighted candles and a couple of cruets, with some other small objects. On a shelf below were two other candles, and on this shelf and the floor in front were various offerings to be used in the rites— plates of apples, grapes, bananas, oranges; dishes of sugar, of sugar-plums; a dish of powdered orris root, packages of candles, bottles of brandy and of water. Two other lighted candles stood on the floor, and in front an earthen bowl. The clear space in front for the dance was not more than four or five feet square.

Some time was consumed in preparations, or in waiting for the worshippers to assemble. From conversation with those near me, I found that the doctor had a reputation for healing the diseased by virtue of his incantations, of removing "spells," of finding lost articles, of ministering to the troubles of lovers, and, in short, of doing very much what clairvoyants and healing mediums claim to do in what are called civilized communities. But failing to get a very intelligent account of the expected performance from the negro woman next me, I moved to the side of the altar and took a chair next a girl of perhaps twenty years old, whose

About 1825, New Orleans seemed on its way to rank as America's greatest, as well as its most flamboyant, city.

complexion and features gave evidence that she was white.

Still, finding her in that company, and there as a participant in the Voudoo rites, I concluded that I must be mistaken, and that she must have colored blood in her veins. Assuming the privilege of an enquirer, I asked her questions about the coming performance, and in doing so carried the impression that she was kin to the colored race. But I was soon convinced, from her manner and her replies, that she was pure white. She was a pretty, modest girl, very reticent, well-bred, polite and civil. None of the colored people seemed to know who she was, but she said she had been there before.

She told me, in the course of the conversation, the name of the street where she lived (in the American part of the town), the private school at which she had been educated (one of the best in the city), and that she and her parents were Episcopalians. . . . She did not communicate her difficulties to [this Voudoo doctor] or speak to him, but she evidently had faith that he could discern what every one present needed, and minister to them. When I asked her if, with her education, she did not think that more good would come to her by confiding in known friends or in regular practitioners, she wearily said that she did not know. After the performance began, her intense interest in it, and the light in her eyes, were evidences of the deep hold the superstition had upon her nature. In coming to this place she had gone a step beyond the young ladies of her class who make a novena at St. Roch.

While we still waited, the doctor and two other colored men called me into the next chamber, and wanted to be assured that it was my own name I had written on the register, and that I had no unfriendly intentions in being present. Their doubts at rest, all was ready.

The doctor squatted on one side of the altar, and his wife, a stout woman of darker hue, on the other. "*Commençons*," said the woman, in a low voice. All the colored people spoke French, and French only, to each other and in the ceremony.

The doctor nodded, bent over, and gave three sharp raps on the floor with a bit of wood. (This is the usual opening of Voudoo rites.) All the others rapped three times on the floor with their knuckles. Any one coming in to join the circle afterwards, stopped and rapped three times. After a moment's silence, all kneeled and repeated together in French the Apostles' Creed, and still on their knees, they said two prayers to the Virgin Mary.

The colored woman at the side of the altar began a chant in a low, melodious voice. It was the weird and strange "Dansez, Calinda." A tall negress, with a bright, good-natured face, entered the circle with the air of a chief performer, knelt, rapped the floor, laid an offering of candles before the altar, with a small bottle of brandy, seated herself beside the singer, and took up in a strong, sweet voice the bizarre rhythm of the song. Nearly all those who came in had laid some little offering before the altar. The chant grew, the single line was enunciated in stronger pulsations, and other voices joined in the wild refrain,

"Dansez, Calinda, boudoum, boudoum!
Dansez, Calinda, boudoum, boudoum!"

Bodies swayed, the hands kept time in soft patpatting, and the feet in muffled accentuation.

The Voudoo arose, removed his slippers, seized a bottle of brandy, dashed some of the liquid on the floor on each side of the brown bowl as a libation, threw back his head and took a long pull at the bottle, and then began in the open space a slow measured dance, a rhythmical shuffle, with more movement of the hips than of the feet, backward and forward, round and round, but accelerating his movement as the time of the song quickened and the excitement rose in the room.

The singing became wilder and more impassioned, a strange minor strain, full of savage pathos and longing, that made it almost impossible for the spectator not to join in the swing of its influence, while the dancer wrought himself up into the wild passion of a Cairene dervish. Without a moment ceasing his rhythmical steps and his extravagant gesticulation, he poured liquid into the basin, and dashing in brandy, ignited the fluid with a match.

The liquid flamed up before the altar. He seized then a bunch of candles, plunged them into the bowl, held them up all flaming with the burning brandy, and, keeping his step to the maddening "Calinda," distributed them lighted to the devotees. In the same way he snatched up dishes of apples, grapes, bananas, oranges, deluged them with burning brandy, and tossed them about the room to the eager and excited crowd. His hands were aflame, his clothes seemed to be on fire; he held the burning dishes close to his breast, apparently inhaling the flame, closing his eyes and swaying his head backward and forward in an ecstasy, the hips advancing and receding, the feet still shuffling to the barbaric measure.

Every moment his own excitement and that of the audience increased. The floor was covered with the débris of the sacrifice— broken candy, crushed sugar-plums, scattered grapes—and all more or less in flame. The wild dancer was dancing in fire! In the height of his frenzy he grasped a large plate filled with lump-sugar. That was set on fire. He held the burning mass to his breast, he swung in round, and finally, with his hand extended under the bottom of the plate(the plate only adhering to his hand by the rapidity of his circular motion), he spun around like a dancing dervish, his eyes shut, the perspiration pouring in streams from his face, in a frenzy. The flaming sugar scattered about the floor, and the devotees scrambled for it.

In intervals of the dance, though the singing went on, the various offerings which had been conjured were passed around—bits of sugar and fruit and orris powder. That which fell to my share I gave to the young girl next me, whose eyes were blazing with excitement, though she had remained perfectly tranquil, and joined neither by voice or hands or feet in the excitement. She put the conjured sugar and fruit in her pocket, and she seemed grateful to me for relinquishing it to her.

Before this point had been reached the chant had been changed for the wild *canga,* more rapid in movement than the *chanson africaine:*

"Eh! eh! Bomba, hen! hen!
Canga bafio té

To millions of Southerners and other Americans, Andrew Jackson was a great man, a great democrat; to others, he was simply that fellow in the White House—or on his way to it.

Canga moune dé lé
Canga do ki la
Canga li."

At intervals during the performance, when the charm had begun to work, the believers came forward into the open space, and knelt for "treatment." The singing, the dance, the wild incantation, went on uninterruptedly; but amid all his antics the dancer had an eye for business. The first group that knelt were four stalwart men, three of them white laborers. All of them, I presume, had some disease which they had faith the incantation would drive away. Each held a lighted candle in each hand. The doctor successively extinguished each candle by putting it in his mouth, and performed a number of antics of a saltatory sort.

During his dancing and whirling he frequently filled his mouth with liquid, and discharged it in spray, exactly as a Chinese laundryman sprinkles his clothes, into the faces and on the heads of any man or woman within reach. Those so treated considered themselves specially favored. Having extinguished the candles of the suppliants, he scooped the liquid from the bowl, flaming or not as it might be, and with his hands vigorously scrubbed their faces and heads, as if he were shampooing them. While the victim was still sputtering and choking he seized him by the right hand, lifted him up, spun him round half a dozen times, and then sent him whirling.

This was substantially the treatment that all received who knelt in the circle, though sometimes it was more violent. Some of them were slapped smartly upon the back and the breast, and much knocked about. Occasionally a woman was whirled until she was dizzy, and perhaps swung about in his arms as if she had been a bundle of clothes. . . .

Nearly all those present knelt, and were whirled and shaken, and those who did not take this "cure" I suppose got the benefit of the incantation by carrying away some of the consecrated offerings. Occasionally a woman in the whirl would whisper something in the doctor's ear, and receive from him doubtless the counsel she needed. But generally the doctor made no inquiries of his patients, and they said nothing to him.

While the wild chanting, the rhythmic movement of hands and feet, and barbarous dance, and the fiery incantations were at their height, it was difficult to believe that we were in a civilized city of an enlightened republic. Nothing indecent occurred in word or gesture, but it was so wild and bizarre that one might easily imagine he was in Africa or in hell.

As I said, nearly all the participants were colored people; but in the height of the frenzy one white woman knelt and was sprayed and whirled with the others. She was a respectable married woman from the other side of Canal street. I waited with some anxiety to see what my modest little neighbor would do. She had told me that she should look on and take no part. I hoped that the senseless antics, the mummery, the rough treatment, would disgust her.

Towards the close of the séance, when the spells were all woven and the flames had subsided, the tall, good-natured negress motioned to me that it was my turn to advance into the circle and kneel. I excused myself. But the young girl was unable to resist longer. She went forward and knelt, with a candle in her hand. The conjurer was either touched by her youth and race, or he had spent his force. He gently lifted her by one hand, and gave her one turn around, and she came back to her seat.

The singing ceased. The doctor's wife passed round the hat for contributions, and the ceremony, which had lasted nearly an hour and a half, was over. . . .

In the breaking up I had no opportunity to speak further to the interesting white neophyte; but as I saw her resuming her hat and cloak in an adjoining room there was a strange excitement in her face, and in her eyes a light of triumph and faith. We came out by the back way, and through an alley made our escape into the sunny street and the air of the nineteenth century.

Louisiana Folklore

ALCéE FORTIER

*Throughout the South, men and women of all colors and shades have long
held traditional beliefs of many sources. Some are Anglo-Saxon in origin—English,
Scottish; a number are of African origin, or East European, or of a universal nature.
This neat collection is from Alcée Fortier's* Louisiana Studies, *published in 1894,
the work of a brilliant folklorist and historian who studied in Paris, wrote exten-
sively of the New World and its people, and was highly honored as a teacher
and authority on Louisiana.*

When a woman whistles, it makes the
Virgin Mary weep.

Put nails in the shape of a cross in the
nest of a goose, that thunder should not spoil
the eggs and prevent them from hatching.

A person must come out of a room by
the same door through which he came in;
otherwise there will be a misfortune.

When little children in their sleep put
their arms on their heads we must put them
down, for they are calling misfortune on their
heads.

When the palate falls, we must tie very
tight a lock of hair in the middle of the head,
and the palate will resume its natural position.

A dog that howls at night announces the
death of some one.

A horse that neighs where there is a dead
body, announces the death of some one else.

When a hearse stops before your door,
it is a sign of misfortune.

To kneel on the threshold is an omen
of misfortune.

When one eats a sweet potato one must
eat first a piece of the peel in order that the
potato should not be too heavy on the
stomach.

If in walking your right ankle turns, you
will have a pleasant surprise; if it is the left
ankle, a disappointment.

If your right ear is hot, some one is speaking well of you; if it is the left ear, some one
is speaking badly of you.

To pass a child through a window makes
a thief of him.

To pass over a child lying down will
pevent him from growing.

You must always burn and not throw
away your hair, because the birds will pick
it up to make their nest, and that will make
you crazy.

If you make a child who stammers eat
in the same dish as a little dog, that will cure
the child.

If your nose itches an old bachelor is
going to kiss you, and a young man is crazy
to do so.

If you strike your "crazy bone," you will
be disappointed.

If a child teething looks at himself in a
mirror, his teething will be painful.

To pass in front of a carriage at a funeral
is a bad omen.

When a fly bothers you, it is a sign that
you are going to receive a letter.

When a snake is cut to pieces, its friends
come to get it to put the pieces together.

When in taking leave four persons cross
hands it is a sign of marriage.

To dream of death is a sign of marriage;
to dream of a marriage is a sign of death.

It is a sign of misfortune to pass the loaf
of bread turned down.

When you cut a banana you cut the cross
of Christ.

If you have a sore on the tip of the
tongue, it is a sign that you have lied.

If you forget what you were going to
say, it is a sign that you were going to lie.

It was his almost incredible victory over the British in the Mississippi River Delta, at the end of the War of 1812, that made Jackson, the gaunt Tennessean, a hero to his fellow Americans.

If you sweep the feet of a child with a broom, it will make him walk early.

To turn a chair on one leg is a bad omen.

If scissors fall down with one point in the floor, you will receive a visit, and it will come in the direction in which the other point lies.

If you plough on Good Friday, the ground will bleed.

If you carry an Irish potato in your pocket it will cure your rheumatism.

To cure a wart take a green pea, cut it, rub it on the wart, then take the pea and wrap it in a piece of paper and throw it away. The person who will pick it up will get the wart.

To open an umbrella in the house chases away the lovers.

To put an umbrella on the bed causes disputes.

To throw black pepper on a table is a sign of marriage.

It cures rheumatism to tie an eel's skin on the leg or the arm.

You must watch for a full moon if you want to make soap.

It makes the hair healthier to cut the ends of it at the time of the new moon.

If you cut your nails on Monday you will secure a present during the week.

Jackson crowned in ceremonies after the Battle of New Orleans

If you wear green garters you will often receive presents.

If you walk on the tail of a cat you will not marry during the year.

It is a sign of misfortune to light a candle in a room when there is already another light.

It is a sign of good luck to meet a person who squints.

It is a sign that you will hear good news if you see a white butterfly.

If a girl wears on her left leg a yellow garter which has been worn by a bride, she will marry within the year.

Houston—on its way, with a look that was both Southern and Western, and its eye on the future.

IV

On to the Brazos

"TEXAS, a world in itself . . ." So wrote that land's gifted interpreter, George Sessions Perry, in an especially meaningful phrase. Texas, of course, whether it had the name or not, was known to the explorers and the early settlers of the Gulf, from the days of the original probings by the Spanish adventurers.

Toward this immense and also immensely variegated scene, the *conquistadores* marched or dragged themselves from Louisiana and Florida and the edges of the Mississippi River. For generations it served as a kind of no man's land between Louisiana, the Spanish-French colony which ultimately became American, and Spain's sparsely settled colonial stretches which bore the name of Mexico. Slowly the earth merged with that of the nearest South, about the green-grown eastern valleys of Texas, and along the route men from several North American states advanced in uncertain, sometimes hesitant files, into the territory of His Hispanic Majesty.

These first men—eventually to be dubbed *gringos*—met varying reactions: gunfire, uneasy questions, long delays. While such invaders were suspect, they talked of vague cattle-hunting plans, or an intention to settle down and become good subjects of Spain. Mexico's upper provinces needed settlement, and certain of the strangers gave solemn pledges of peaceful intent. They would even become Catholics, they said.

In the early 1820's the pioneer Stephen Austin brought his colonists to the vicinity of the Brazos and Colorado rivers, which flowed into the Gulf not far from the future sites of several large towns. Along the Sabine—border of Texas and Louisiana—the productive soil drew still others. The silty southeast part of the area was its best farm terrain, and the Anglo-Saxons recognized it as the closest to the kind of land they had known, with opportunities for the crop that they knew best, and liked best as an investment—cotton.

A modified version of the South had sprung up near the Brazos. New Orleans, great port of entry and exit, lay only three or four days' sailing to the east, and the Gulf Coast, especially the vicinity of old Galveston Island, became the favored point of emigration into Texas. With them, many of Austin's colonists and those who followed brought their slaves, to set up plantations which quickly widened and improved.

But soon Mexico declared itself independent of its Spanish rulers across the Atlantic, and it forbade slavery and declared that any children of slaves must be freed at fourteen. By one means or another various Anglo-Saxons tried to hide their plantings in the canebrake or the woods, and some located themselves near the Sabine River line, so that they could slip over to Louisiana and hide when Mexican officials made inspections.

By the time the *gringo* Texans were ready to rise in their own revolution against the Mexicans, this South in somewhat Western garb was thriving. Clear lines of division developed between sections. The woodlands toward the north became a land of small farmers with little in the way of cash crops, producing mainly what they needed for their families. By contrast the plantation men erected their big houses, the subordinate buildings, the huts of their slaves. On the more open land near the Gulf, the scale of growing began large and was to continue large.

From that South-in-Texas came many of the leaders of the Texas uprising, and they set their stamp on the official proceedings and much of the Lone Star life that would follow. Dallas, Austin and Waco started with fair-sized slave populations; beyond them bondage quickly slackened, and the more traditional West began.

In many of its public affairs, Texas would long keep its Southern slant. Its giants were men like Sam Houston of Tennessee, who came here to carve out a new existence after years of achievement, followed by tragedy and hurt in other parts of the South; and Jim Bowie of Bowie knife fame in Louisiana; William Travis, the fire-eating South Carolina lawyer; and not least, Davy Crockett, one-time coonskin officeholder, disgusted with politics of the older places. From them and others of the earlier South, the new "world in itself" offered opportunity for a wider scope, a new excitement in life.

Through the years Texans were to debate their precise geographical identity, while Lone Star types like Three-Legged Willie, a jurist who will figure in these pages, thrived in a fashion that can best be described as plain Texan, unlike any other.

Missions, old churches, trails dating from the Spanish days . . . they are all part of the state's Latin background which lingers in places like San Antonio, Corpus Christi and other points in the longer-settled sections. Old mines, lost or half-forgotten, nourish legends, taboos and superstitions. And tall tales, tall deeds, achievements by towering figures, are an integral part of the Texans' story. But the best of all Texas stories, that of the Alamo, was a tragic drama in which men suddenly touched greatness in the climactic hours of their lives.

Meanwhile, early and late, cotton moved steadily into Texas. Here was the South's, and America's, future capital of the staple. By 1850 the crop was doubling itself every year or so. And long before then the lands draining into the Gulf produced more cotton than the states along the Atlantic. In these last years of the prewar South, King Cotton spoke with an unmistakable Texas twang.

A Hard Land to Win

PAUL HORGAN

In eloquent language Paul Horgan, one of the leading present-day voices of the Southwest, analyzes the region and the struggle that man has waged to conquer it through the centuries. Mr. Horgan, who has spent much of his life in and about this land, is author of the prize-winning The Great River: The Rio Grande in North American History, *published in 1954. The following selection is from the* Southwest Review, *July 1933.*

THE Southwest is large enough to include the widest varieties of terrain, and thus of weather and of human pursuits. It is a country of one of two characters: either there are immense plains, flats alike to the tempests and the endless days of sunlight, or there are mountains that challenge the zenith with the power of a legend. Only in the littlest local sense are there pastoral regions, with bounding green hills and sustained valleys. This meant that, looking for natural securities and havens, the early people found none; and the resultant exercise of human ingenuity and faith produced that crew of pioneers whose philosophy so often seemed almost geological in its simplicity and its strength.

The great river Rio Grande went slowly and widely down to the Gulf of Mexico, hardly oozing enough water in summer to slake a traveled animal train, going brown and reedy in the winter under its red banks, tearing away from the course of mountains in the spring, and changing the face of deserts through which it went with the high breast of flood. So, either sleepy and endlessly peaceful, or sudden and terrible with storm and change, the life in the valley of the Rio Grande affords an easy figure for the life of the entire region.

In a land where gold was the temptation from the first rumors of the cities of Cíbola, water was immensely more valuable. Its only sources were the mountain streams that made the rivers, and the heavy thunderheads that gathered like a doom in El Greco. When the clouds broke and the plains were harried by the quick passing lines of the rain, the water sheeted down the brown spotted hills into the low runs where the arroyos were cut; and the sandy walls of the arroyos were dragged and broken by the red water as it flowed. A party of travelers, crossing such an arroyo to the south, where it might be sunny and dry, could hear a roar of mysterious quality; and suddenly perceive the flood wall, dirt-red, advancing between the blue shadowed walls of the bed upon their fording party.

The foam on the water would be light tan, whipped up from the surface mud. Yet the whisper of gravel, rolling under the pour, the scamper of prairie animals, the hurry of the travelers to mount the firm ground while the flood went by, the wait for the fall of the water, and the final seep of the red earth under the sun—these things marked the land but rarely. For the rest of the time, there was the sun overhead, and there lay the distance, changing in the heat and never dropping its challenge.

The surface of the ground was hard and resistant, with unfriendly plants and stones. The salty white of alkali was exposed, and the chalky sharp stone of gypsum. Under the shadow of the mountains, wherever they might be encountered, lay hills that offered protection. Safer from sunlight, they were neither baked nor blinding. Farms might be set up in such places, if the river country was too insecure with flood and shift.

To the south, near Mexico, the wild plants blossomed with furious color, scarlets and whites, high yellows and flashing greens. Over the whole of the territory when the spring had been soaked by the skies, the white and lavender verbena came to purfle the ground. It was one of the few times when a

Just outside Baltimore, on a typical day at the Fairview Inn on the Franklin Road, farmers paused with their cattle and owners of Conestoga wagons talked over their prices. Europe, the West Indies, the emerging American West, New England . . . Maryland traded with them all.

sense of something intimate, like a little wild flower, pervaded the land, and gave it, besides its terrible beauty and its mysterious wonder of distance and newness, some friendly aspect, much needed by men in a place where the only change from a flat brown plain was a sudden butte, hard and disdainful in its abrupt walls and unseen top.

The things that lived there required no conditions that were not common. Up the river valleys lived the Indians in houses built of the earth. Wild animals found their food in the endless life-process of stalking and killing, with the high vultures sailing until the feast was done and the refuse abandoned. Snakes dwelt with the secrecy of plants, and in the mountains, the cat watched for the antelope, and the coyote whimpered after dark on the desert.

Buffalo wandered under the changing months, governed by solstices and the species of food. Their paths were never constant; nothing charted the huge spaces for the pioneers but the courses of rivers and the steadfast sign of stars. The interruption of a northward course by a canyon, long ago eaten down by an irresistible water, would cause weeks of search for a crossing or a ford. A mountain range, with flanks rearing back from miles of approach, must have been resistant to the search for a pass, over or around. There were dangers from everything, from the very distance, from the very passage of time. A young man could easily die from natural causes before a mission was completed.

A climate, tropical in the daytime and cold at night because of the steady rise of the ground with the advance away from the sea, could of itself produce a need for a new philosophy. To the European eye, the eloquent strangeness of this country of Nueva Granada must have offered first fancy, and then fact, as a basis for legend. Travelers that return from new lands bring exactly enough information and have suffered exactly enough terror and hardship and excitement to let the several kinds of experience mingle in their reports.

And so legend is born, is transmuted in passing from person to person, and a social force too strong to be resisted is put in motion. The quality of this sort of legend that makes it both dangerous and splendid is its constant change: while the serene legend from which myth grows, the legend that is devised without author and accepted without apostasy, is so slow to change that dogma seems really safe and the gods reliable.

Though men put upon a new country at once bring about marvels too exciting for silence, it is the land which is supreme in Nueva Granada. From its rusty earth must grow the grasses for the range on which the red cows rove, when winter withdraws before the southern breath of spring, when the young rains come sweeping across the plains . . . into the scrubby pine hills and leonine mountains and westward to the deserts . . . where the scarlet and the white flowers, monster-glorious, blossom under the sun.

It is the cattle, feeding on the nourished ground, that still establish the economics of the region, if no longer that legendary character of it. And any people that must depend so directly on the rain to bring food is still subservient to the land and its tempers and its conditions. The Southwest still exists upon realities, instead of symbols of realities like urban systems of commerce and finance and machines. It exists upon realities because the land is so tremendous, so bare of human life in so many million acres, because there are so many plains rising sharply to mountainhood, so much communication between sky and earth with great slow-sailing clouds and stars that watch the night like near eyes; because to go from one place to another it is necessary so very often to drive in cars along lonely roads with nothing in sight but the gently lifting and falling horizons of low hills; because the conditions of natural life raise no clamor like that sustained daily by tiring nerves in other regions. . . . And because, though the survivals are only travesties to be noticed amidst the developments of our time, the color of past splendors of race and deed is mixed with the land by the agency of our imaginations; and we pay it tribute, as it nourishes us.

Year after year, Americans went southward and westward in their search for new lands along the ever-extending frontier of Dixie.

"Three-Legged Willie" Knew His Law

L. J. BIGELOW

During most of its history, Texas has been notable for untrammeled characters, including judges of high individuality and low boiling point. Whether or not he was typical, one redoubtable jurist, known as "Three-Legged Willie," did his part in building up the lore and folklore of the region. The following selection is from L. J. Bigelow's Bench and Bar, *published in New York in 1871.*

JUDGE Williamson, or "Three-Legged Willie," as he was familiarly called, was one of the early judges of Texas. In his court a lawyer by the name of Charlton stated a point of law, and the court refused to admit the counsel's statement as sufficient proof.

"Your law, sir," said the judge. "Give us the book and page, sir."

"This is my law, sir," said Charlton, pulling out a pistol, "and this, sir, is my book," drawing a bowie-knife, "and that is the page," pointing the pistol toward the court.

"Your law is not good, sir," said the unruffled judge. "The proper authority is *Colt on Revolvers*," and he brought a six-shooter instantly to bear on the head of the counsel, who dodged the point of the argument and turned to the jury.

On another occasion this same judge concluded the trial of a man for murder by sentencing him to be hung that very day. A petition was immediately signed by the bar, jury and people, praying that longer time might be granted the poor prisoner.

The judge replied to the petition "that the man had been found guilty, the jail was very unsafe, and besides, it was so very uncomfortable that he did not think any man ought to be required to stay in it any longer than was necessary." The man was hung!

The Men of the Alamo

America has known few tales so stirring or so touching as that of the Alamo and its brave defense by a band of doomed but unfrightened men. The documents which follow, unembellished because there is scant need for embellishment of the facts, present the story simply and vividly. Travis' Appeal has been called one of the most heroic messages in the history of North America. It and the others are from Texas History, *edited by Eugene C. Barker, published in 1929 by the Southwest Press of Dallas.*

Travis Appeals . . .

COMMANDANCY OF THE ALAMO

Bexar, Feb'y 24th, 1836

To the People of Texas and all Americans in the World

Fellow Citizens and Compatriots: I am besieged, by a thousand or more of the Mexicans under Santa Anna. I have sustained a continual bombardment and cannonade for 24 hours and have not lost a man. The enemy has demanded a surrender at discretion, otherwise, the garrison are to be put to the sword, if the fort is taken. I have answered the demand with a cannon shot, and our flag still waves proudly from the walls. *I shall never surrender or retreat.* Then, I call on you in the name of Liberty, of patriotism and everything dear to the American character, to come to our aid with all dispatch. The enemy is receiving reinforcements daily and will no doubt increase to three or four thousand in four or five days. If this call is neglected I am determined to sustain myself as long as possible and die like a soldier who never forgets what is due to his own honor and that of his country. VICTORY OR DEATH.

WILLIAM BARRETT TRAVIS, Lt. Col. Comdt.

P.S. The Lord is on our side. When the enemy appeared in sight we had not three bushels of corn. We have since found in deserted houses 80 or 90 bushels and got into the walls 20 or 30 head of beeves.   TRAVIS

. . .

Governor Smith Appeals . . .

Fellow Citizens and Countrymen: The foregoing official communication from Col. Travis, now in command at Bexar, needs no comment. The garrison, composed of only 150 Americans, engaged in a deadly conflict with 1,000 of the mercenary troops of the Dictator, who are daily receiving reinforcements, should be a sufficient call upon you without saying more. However secure, however fortunate, our garrison may be, they have not the provisions nor the ammunition to stand more than a thirty days' siege at farthest.

I call upon you as an officer, I implore you as a man, to fly to the aid of your besieged countrymen and not permit them to be massacred by a mercenary foe. I slight none! The call is upon ALL who are able to bear arms, to rally without one moment's delay, or in fifteen days the heart of Texas will be the seat of war. This is not imaginary. The enemy from 6,000 to 8,000 strong are on our border and rapidly moving by forced marches for the colonies. The campaign has commenced. We must promptly meet the enemy or all will be lost. Do you possess honor? Suffer it not to be insulted or tarnished! Do you possess patriotism? Evince it by your bold, prompt and manly action! If you possess even humanity you will rally without a moment's delay to the aid of your besieged countrymen!

. . .

Santa Anna Reports His Victory . . .

Most Excellent Sir: Victory belongs to the army, which at this very moment, 8 o'clock A.M., achieved a complete and glorious triumph that will make its memory imperishable.

. . . I awaited the arrival of the first brigade of infantry to commence active operations against the fortress of the Alamo. However, the whole brigade having been delayed beyond my expectation, I ordered that three of its battalions, viz., the Engineers, Aldama and Toluca, should force their march to join me. These troops together with the Battalions of Matamoros, Ximenes, and San Luis Potosi, brought the force at my disposal, recruits excluded, up to 1400 Infantry. This force, divided into four columns of attack, and a reserve, commenced the attack at 5 o'clock A.M. They met with a stubborn resistance, the combat lasting more than one hour and a half, and the reserve having to be brought into action.

The scene offered by this engagement was extraordinary. The men fought individually, vieing with each other in heroism. Twenty-one pieces of artillery, used by the enemy with the most perfect accuracy, the brisk fire of musketry, which illuminated the interior of the fortress and its walls and ditches, could not check our dauntless soldiers, who

are entitled to the consideration of the Supreme Government, and to the gratitude of the nation.

The Fortress is now in our power, with its artillery, stores, etc. More than 600 corpses of foreigners were buried in the ditches and intrenchments, and a great many, who had escaped the bayonet of the infantry, fell in the vicinity under the sabres of the cavalry. I can assure Your Excellency that few are those who bore to their associates the tidings of their disaster.

Among the corpses are those of Bowie and Travis, who styled themselves Colonels, and also that of Crockett, and several leading men, who had entered the fortress with dispatches from their Convention. We lost about 70 men killed and 300 wounded, among whom are 25 officers. The cause for which they fell renders their loss less painful, as it is the duty of the Mexican soldier to die for the defense of the rights of the nation; and all of us were ready for any sacrifice to promote this fond object; nor will we hereafter suffer any foreigners, whatever their origin may be, to insult our country and to pollute its soil . . . God and Liberty!

ANTONIO LOPEZ DE SANTA ANNA
Headquarters, Bexar, March 6, 1836
To His Excellency, the Secretary of War and Navy, General José Maria Tornel

. . .

Alcalde Ruiz Reports . . .

On the north battery of the fortress convent lay the lifeless body of Col. Travis on the gun carriage, shot only through the forehead. Towards the west, and in a small fort opposite the city, we found the body of Col. Crockett. Col. Bowie was found dead in his bed in one of the rooms on the south side.

Santa Anna, after all the Mexican bodies had been taken out, ordered wood to be brought to burn the bodies of the Texans. He sent a company of dragoons with me to bring wood and dry branches from the neighboring forests. About three o'clock in the afternoon of March 6, we laid the wood and dry branches upon which a pile of dead bodies were placed, more wood was piled on them and another pile of bodies was brought, and in this manner they were all arranged in layers. Kindling wood was distributed through the pile and about 5 o'clock in the evening it was ignited.

The dead Mexicans of Santa Anna were taken to the graveyard, but not having sufficient room for them, I ordered some to be thrown into the river, which was done on the same day.

The gallantry of the few Texans, who defended the Alamo was really wondered at by the Mexican army. Even the generals were astonished at their vigorous resistance and how dearly victory was bought. . . .

FRANCISCO ANTONIO RUIZ

Begun in Defeat, Ended in Resurrection

LON TINKLE

With moving simplicity Lon Tinkle, editor, author and aficionado of Texas writing, here pronounces a final word in celebration of those who sacrificed their lives at the Alamo. The passage is from Mr. Tinkle's re-creation of the Alamo story in his Thirteen Days to Glory, *published in 1959 by McGraw-Hill Company of New York.*

THERE remained now on March 6 at the Alamo only the matter of burning the enemy dead. By three o'clock in the afternoon the bodies had been sorted and the fires made ready. Alcalde Ruiz of San Antonio had been in charge of bringing in wood and dry branches from the neighboring "forests," and had supervised the laying down of the alter-

A true original, Davy Crockett fought red men, drawled backwoods wisdom and kept a countryside in chuckles. Going to Congress, he was seen here as he made his political fellows roar like anyone else.

nating layers of wood and dry twigs and bodies of the fallen. There were three or four stacks, rising several layers high. Grease and oil had been used to soak the bodies.

The tradition of burning the enemy dead was an old one, going back to Homer's heroes at Troy and beyond. In carrying it out now, Santa Anna was not merely reliving the cruelty he had learned from General Arredondo twenty-three years before. He was giving an example to all revolutionists in North America and throughout the world of what would happen to those who followed their "manifest destiny."

The example was made, but not in the way Santa Anna intended it. Travis, Bowie, Crockett, Bonham and the others were to become supreme examples throughout the world of how a man can live on by dying. In the words of Frank Dobie, the men crossing Travis's line had the choice between life and immortality. Perhaps it is history's lesson that they chose well.

Now, as the torch was applied and the flames rose, their names were being carried to Gonzales, to Goliad, to San Jacinto. Fourteen of the burning dead, it is said, were unknown soldiers, unidentified, unmourned, unsung, lost. But the name "Alamo" was not. It became a battle cry that brought to defeat the men who thought they had defeated it.

In the late afternoon sky the flames rose and disappeared. The wind was rising. The Alamo that began in defeat ended in resurrection.

Albert Sidney Johnston

WILLIAM PRESTON JOHNSTON

There is a different kind of courage, a different kind of bravery, in the efforts of a man from the older South to set up a plantation in Texas. He was Albert Sidney Johnston of Kentucky, who had begun to make a name for himself in the Texas Army of the 1830's. In time Johnston felt discouragement in his prospects, and resigned to attempt farming at China Grove plantation in Brazoria County. Here he labored steadily, doggedly against obstacles; once he wrote sadly that "a man in my situation is not likely to be overburdened by his friends." At last, however, he had to give up, and he returned to army affairs. When the Confederacy formed, Johnston made the long trip from California to Virginia to join it. Many considered him one of the finest, if not the finest, of Southern generals. The Confederacy suffered a bad blow when he died at Shiloh in April of 1862. This selection is from William Preston Johnston's The Life of General Albert Sidney Johnston, New York, 1879.

GENERAL Johnston returned to Galveston and was received with enthusiasm by its citizens. . . . But he had come back from the army with a heavy heart. When the war broke out, rank and celebrity seemed to await him, but his brief career had ended in disappointment. He had seen the regiment, which he had converted into a powerful engine of war, dissolved before his eyes, and his services were not such as his Government chose to acknowledge. . . . His wife, moreover, insisted upon a fulfillment of his promise not to rejoin the army against her consent.

. . . He possessed a life-estate in the property inherited from his first wife by her children. Considering the avails not more than sufficient for their education, maintenance and start in life, he divested himself of his life-estate, and surrendered it for the benefit of these children. With the small means now at his command, he bought the simple furniture, utensils, and supplies, required in the humble home to which he was retiring, and such stock, farm-implements, and seed, as were absolutely necessary. His housekeeping was in a style as primitive as any of the pioneers. A double log-cabin, covered with clapboards, and fronted with a wide porch, gave a rude shelter; and the pine tables, hickory chairs and other household effects, might have suited a camp better than a permanent establishment.

The China Grove plantation was situated partly in the alluvial bottomlands of Oyster Creek, a stream nearly parallel with the Brazos River, and partly in the flat and rather sandy prairie that stretched toward Galveston Bay. Three or four hundred acres, constituting "the plantation" proper, had been cleared of the dense timber and undergrowth of the primeval forest, which still shaded nearly a thousand acres more; while toward the south and east a square league of prairie, waving with the luxuriant grasses of the coastlands, afforded ample pasture for herds of cattle which ranged at will.

A belt of thick woods, eight or ten miles wide, almost pathless, filled with all manner of wild beasts and game, thick set with jungle, and concealing miasmatic swamps caused by the annual overflow of the river, reached almost to the doors. A fever-breeding malaria exhaled from these marshes and crept toward the prairies, where it was met by the salt sea-breeze, which, sweeping steadily across the broad savanna, mastered it with a doubtful victory. The open friend was always gladly welcomed; the secret foe sometimes laid its poisonous finger on an unsuspecting household.

From the front porch, the view extended as far as the eye could reach over a grassy plain, unbroken except by an occasional fringe or *mot* of distant timber. . . . Everywhere were the evidences of fertility; and Nature offered to the observant eye all the beauty that a level surface, unaided by art, could afford. In early spring an emerald sward, embroidered with the blue lupin, the crimson phlox, the fragrant and flossy mimosa, and a thousand flowers of varied perfume and hue, invited great herds of deer to browse, while the long-horned cattle, scarcely less wild, watched with startled eyes the infrequent traveler. Innumerable flights of wild-fowl circled and settled in the shallow ponds left by the winter rains. Cranes, herons, wild-geese, brants, ducks and sea birds, gulls, curlews and others, made this their feeding-ground.

Summer saw the tall, yellow grass waving like a sea of gold, and the transforming power of a Southern sun and moist atmosphere working the marvels of the mirage. In winter came the long rains, driving slant, or the air cleared by the bracing norther, or the midnight sky lit by a distant or nearer circle of flame that marked the movement of the prairie-fire. Over all was solitude. . . . General Johnston's family consisted of his wife and infant son, a negro man and his wife, two negro boys and a girl. . . . In this secluded spot he was buried for three years. His chief business was to make a crop of Indian-corn, for bread for his family and forage for his work-animals; a crop of cotton, for the purchase of supplies; a small crop of sugar cane; and an ample supply of all sorts of vegetables. To these ends he gave a good deal of hard labor in the field and garden, but he did not neglect the simple but delightful recreation of the flower-garden. . . .

His letters were written under great mental strain. A heavy, increasing and seemingly hopeless burden of debt taxed his energies, his pride and his patience. He heard the sound of arms afar off. . . . Rare greetings came from old friends, and in the mighty sweep of events he was passing out of memory. . . . Yet he never dreamed of succumbing to poverty, privation, debt and solitude.

TO THE SON, WILLIAM PRESTON JOHNSTON:
China Grove, August 3, 1847
Dear Preston: . . . I will effect all or more than I expected in coming here, without encountering the dangers from the climate, with which the apprehensions of our friends threatened us. If by any good fortune I can obtain the capital to cultivate my plantation in sugar cane, I feel sure that I will accumulate wealth.

Following the near-tropical banks of the upper St. Johns River in Florida, the crew of a small, rickety steamboat takes aim at birds, 'gators and other objects.

Like the poor, imprisoned abbé of the Castle d'If, I am sure that, in the ownership of this beautiful estate, I possess a great treasure; but I fear I shall not be able to make it manifest to any capitalist. . . . Fifteen years ago yesterday we fought the Sacs and Foxes, and defeated them at Bad Axe on the Upper Mississippi. . . .

TO GEORGE HANCOCK

China Grove, February 28, 1847

Dear Hancock: You have long since, I fear, condemned me for neglect, and appearances are so much against me that I would not blame you; but I had a reasonable excuse in the un-

remitted labor I had to encounter in repairing my farm and preparing for a crop. I may say with truth that I have scarcely taken time to rest since we came here. The plantation has quite a renovated appearance, and I hope by next winter to have it in complete reparation, with a comfortable house to live in, and everything farmer-like about it. I hoped to be able to return in the autumn in time to make you a visit, but I was detained so much later than I expected that I was compelled to come here at once and go to work. . . .

The successful cultivation of the cane here is no longer a problem. Everywhere it has

No Southerner and no American had a life like that of the vivid-tempered Sam Houston. As Governor of Tennessee, he saw his career destroyed there because of an unhappy domestic situation; he returned to friends among the Indians, then went to Texas, where he became its hero, its governor, its great man.

been tried in this neighborhood it has succeeded excellently well. The yield has been great; and the quality Mr. Kenner, I understand, says equal, if not superior, to Louisiana sugar made by the most improved means. Mr. Caldwell, fifteen miles from here, on the same kind of soil as mine (peach-land), made 104 hogsheads (or thousands of pounds) of sugar, besides molasses, with sixteen hands, which is selling from eight to ten cents per pound. Sweeney has been quite as successful, and others that I have heard from. . . . Your kind

invitation and offers to us will be long gratefully remembered. . . .

TO GEORGE HANCOCK

China Grove, October 21, 1847

. . . We have been blessed with excellent health since we came here, and everything has prospered with us better than we had any right to anticipate. I have *cribbed* 900 bushels of corn, and will send enough cotton to market to pay all of our expenses of every kind, besides considerable repairs and improvements.

This, I think, is as much as could have been expected from so small a force. I esteem it also of great importance to me to have acquired some practical knowledge as a farmer; and mine has been truly so, for I have often lent a hand in the work.

My object in coming here with a force so inadequate was to repair the dilapidations which rented property always suffers, and to keep the place until I could sell it, or make such an arrangement for the cultivation of the whole of the cleared land as to enable me to pay the remainder of my debt. The latter arrangement I would prefer, as I still regard this as a splendid estate, which, if possible, I would like to hold. If I had it paid for, I would be satisfied to live here with the little force I have, with the confidence of supporting myself, but it would be a pity to let so large a place lie idle, when its cultivation in sugar-cane would, without doubt, produce abundant wealth in a few years. . . .

TO GEORGE HANCOCK
March 22, 1848

We like our residence here, although entirely secluded from the world and from all society whatever. If we lose the pleasures and sweets of society, we are free from all the drawbacks, which themselves form a numerous catalogue. Happy contentment reigns under our humble roof. We both industriously endeavor to do our part in our own sphere, and the result of our efforts is never the subject of complaint. We have been married nearly five years and the first unkind word or look has never passed between us. If this is true—and it is so, *for I have said it*—have we not sufficient indemnity for the loss of society and the absence of wealth? There are those who, not comprehending the object of life, would sneer at our humble and satisfied views of it, but experience will in the end convince. . . . Our little crop will need my constant supervision, and the expense of the journey [a visit to Kentucky, suggested by Mr. Hancock] would go far toward building a comfortable residence for us. Our expense is very little for we manage to raise almost everything we want.

We are now in the midst of spring. Every-thing is very beautiful around us. The grounds around our cabin are filled with China-trees in full bloom; large monthly roses, also blooming; the Cherokee-rose hedge, its dark green spangled with large white roses; the Quasatchee, a species of acacia, "waving its yellow hair;" and the air redolent of sweets. Tell Aunt Mary I am reaping the fruits of my apprenticeship under her as a gardener; my horticultural knowledge is very respectable. We have fine strawberries and Irish potatoes, tomatoes in bloom, and many other vegetables. My corn all came up in February, and the stand is excellent and growing finely. I had a time of it to save it from the birds. "The price of *corn* is eternal vigilance" here.

TO WILLIAM PRESTON JOHNSTON
China Grove, May 16, 1849

My crops are small, but since I have become a farmer I have the gratification of success in everything I have attempted; and in gardening I have succeeded as well. We have had a great abundance of strawberries; and at this time we have a good variety of excellent vegetables—artichokes, pie-plants, fine heads of early York cabbage, squash, tomatoes, Irish potatoes and your favorite yams of last year's crop, which we have never been without since we came here. Our cantaloupes will soon be ripe, and in a short time we will have plenty of figs and watermelons.

The statistics of the poultry-yard and dairy are still more creditable to the industry and attention of your mother. She boasts of her flock of 100 turkeys, with prospects of as many more, besides swarms of chickens and ducks, and as many eggs as we want. . . . All these things, with butter and milk and a good appetite gained by some toil, enable us to live, so far as these matters are concerned, as well as rich folk; and these are the things within the reach of the industrious poor from the St. Lawrence to San Francisco. This is the mystery which foreigners cannot unveil. They do not perceive that the well-being of our population flows from a fostering government, which does not meddle much with private pursuits, and taxes with great moderation—always excepting the municipal tyrannies of our land. . . .

TO EDWARD HOBBS

China Grove, June 10, 1849

. . . The life of seclusion and obscurity in which I have lived accounts for your not having heard from me. On my return from Mexico after the campaign of Monterey, I found that all the proceeds of the Louisville property would scarcely suffice for the education of Will and his sister, and that it was necessary to go to work at once with small means for the support of my family. It was a question of bread. My own personal labor (this is no figure of speech—I don't mean head-work) was necessary in conducting my small farming operations; and I have yielded it with cheerfulness, and have thus, after three years' toil, become a rugged farmer, with good habits.

We have been away from home but about three or four times to visit a neighbor since we came here. So you can see our habits conform to the humbleness of our position; and, as for correspondence, a man in my situation is not likely to be overburdened by his friends. In this "battle of life" such ammunition so aimed would be uselessly expended. A series of adverse circumstances have, with me, disappointed expectations most justly founded; and, although I am still confident of a final extrication, the effect has been to throw me beyond the sphere of motion of friends and acquaintances to a distance, I fear, at which sympathy languishes. . . .

Jim Bowie and the Lost San Saba Mine

J. FRANK DOBIE

J. Frank Dobie, dean of Texas writers, has had an influence in the Southwest matched by few modern literary men. Over several generations he has contributed a series of meaningful works in folklore, the daily life of his people, the past and present history of Texas. At the same time Frank Dobie has spurred and prodded others to fresh study of the many aspects of the Southwestern scene. In his Coronado's Children, *published in 1930 by the Southwest Press of Dallas, Mr. Dobie presented the following passages.*

WHAT the golden fleece was to the Greeks or what El Dorado—the Gilded Man—has been to South Americans, the lost mines on the San Saba and Llano rivers have been to that part of the United States once owned by Spain. . . .

Sometimes the name of the fabled source of wealth is Los Almagres; sometimes, Las Amarillas; again, La Mina de las Iguanas, or Lizard Mine, from the fact that the ore is said to have been found in chunks called *iguanas* (lizards); oftener the name is simply the Lost San Saba Mine or the Lost Bowie Mine. In seeking it, generations of men have disemboweled mountains, drained lakes, and turned rivers out of their courses. It has been found—and lost—in many places under many conditions. . . .

Only the land that hides it does not change. Except that it is brushier, groomed down in a few places by little fields, and cut across by fences, it is today essentially as the Spaniards found it. A soil that cannot be plowed under keeps its traditions—and its secrets. Wherever the mine may be, however it may appear, it has lured, it lures and it will lure men on. . . .

The preface to this cycle of a thousand cantos goes back to a day of the seventeenth century when a Spanish conquistador set out from Nueva Viscaya "to discover a rumored Silver Hill (Cerro de la Plata) somewhere to the north." At a later date La Salle's Frenchmen, wandering forth, from Saint Louis Bay on the Texas coast, listened to Indians tell of "rivers where silver mines are found." Like most great legends, the legend of the San Saba Mine is a magnification of historical fact. . . .

. . .

Flaming above all the other searchers is the figure of James Bowie. It is a great pity that we have no biography of him such as we have of Davy Crockett. This biography would tell—often with only legend for authority—how he rode alligators in Louisiana; how, like Plains Indians chasing the buffalo, he speared wild cattle; how, with the deadly bowie knife, he fought fearful duels in dark rooms; how he trafficked for black ivory with the pirate Lafitte on Galveston Island; and then how he came to San Antonio and married the lovely Ursula de Veramendi, daughter of the vice-governor of Texas.

Bowie was a master of men and a slave to fortune. He was willing to pawn his life for a chance at a chimerical mine, and he asked no odds. Out on the Nueces and Frio rivers, far beyond the last outpost of settlement, he prospected for gold and silver. In his burning quest for the fabled Spanish mines on the San Saba he engaged in one of the most sanguinary and brilliant fights of frontier history.

Four years later, at San Antonio, he mistook some bundles of hay loaded on Mexican mules for bags of silver, and led in the so-called Grass Fight. Then on March 6, 1836, leaving not one "messenger of defeat," he and one thousand eighty-odd other Texans died in the Alamo. Thousands of men have believed and yet believe that he died knowing the location of untold riches. At any rate, dying there in the Alamo, he carried with him a secret. . . .

The story of Bowie's adventures with the Indians . . . has no support from history. What follows is on record. On November 2, 1831, Bowie set out to find the Spanish mine. His brother, Rezin P. Bowie, was in the company and was perhaps the leading spirit. It has been claimed that he had made a previous trip of exploration into the San Saba country. Both of the brothers were remarkable men and both left accounts of the expedition. With them were nine other men, the name of one of whom, Cephas (or Caiaphas)

K. Ham, will weave into odd patterns through the long Bowie Mine story.

If James Bowie knew exactly where he was going, he coursed in a strange manner. In fact, he took so much time in "examining the nature of the country," to use his own words, that three weeks after setting out from San Antonio he had not yet arrived at the abandoned presidio on the San Saba only a hundred and fifty miles away. Yet the San Saba fort was a chief, if not the chief, objective of the expedition, for the Bowies were certain that it had protected the Spaniards "while working the silver mines, which are a mile distant." Why then did the Bowies not go directly to the fort and the mine? Did Jim Bowie know —from a Lipan's confidence—of some other place? Where had he spent the three weeks in scouting before he stopped? *Quien sabe?*

On the nineteenth of November a friendly Comanche warned him that hostile Indians were out. Whether Tres Manos was among them is not recorded; they were mostly Caddos, Wacos, and Tehuacanas. About daylight on the twenty-first, one hundred and sixty-four hostiles—fifteen against one—swooped down upon the Bowie camp. The Texans were not unready. They had the advantage of a thicket and of being near water in a creek. The fight lasted all day. One man was killed; three others were wounded. The Indians had fifty dead and thirty-five wounded. . . .

Without exception, one might say, the men of that highly individualized class who called themselves Texians knew about the Bowie Mine. Most of them who left any kind of chronicle make mention of it. . . . "Old Rip" Ford gave a sequel to the Bowie expedition from Cephas K. Ham, who survived "the Calf Creek Fight" for many, many years and became a veritable high priest to the Bowie Mine tradition.

According to Ham's story, he (and not Bowie) was adopted by the Indians and was —almost—shown the mine. His warrior brothers were a band of Comanches under the leadership of Chief Incorroy. In 1831 he was wandering around with these Comanches, trading for horses and catching mustangs in order to make up a bunch to drive to Louisiana. One pint of powder, eight balls of lead, one plug of tobacco, one butcher knife, and two brass rings made the price of a good horse. "A certain fat warrior," Ham relates, "was frequently my hunting companion. One day he pointed to a hill and said: 'There is plenty of silver on the other side. We will go out by ourselves, and I will show it to you. If the other Indians find I have done so, they will kill both of us.' " But camp was hurriedly moved next day and the fat warrior never fulfilled his promise.

Not long afterward Bowie sent a message to Ham advising him that, as the Mexicans were about to make war on the Comanches, he had better cut loose from them. He came into San Antonio, only to find that Bowie's real motive in sending a warning was to get him to join an expedition in search of the San Saba Mine.

Rezin P. Bowie, Ham's story goes on, had already visited the mine. "It was not far from the fort. The shaft was about eight feet deep." Rezin P. Bowie went down to the bottom of it "by means of steps cut in a live oak log" and hacked off some ore "with his tomahawk." He carried the ore to New Orleans and had it assayed. "It panned out rich." He came back to San Antonio. . . .

Here Rezin P. Bowie drops out of the story, but Jim Bowie did not give up the quest. Ham and other like authorities agree that he raised a second expedition of thirty men. This time, according to Ham, Bowie reached the San Saba but could not find the shaft, as it had been filled up either by rains or by Indians. Others say that about the time Bowie got ready to exploit the mineral riches he had located, the Texan war for independence broke out. Among many Texans the legend is persistent that Bowie's chief motive in searching for the San Saba treasure was to secure means for financing the Texas army— a view hardly tenable to anyone who knows anything about the real Bowie. Thus Bowie's name lives on. . . .

"Till You Get It in the Neck"

CHARLES J. FINGER

Highly individual in method, Charles J. Finger's essay, "I Remember Another Texas," appears to me to have an approach and mood matched by few others who have written of Texas. It reflects a fine friendliness and capacity for appreciation of an adopted region. A native of England, Mr. Finger resided for a long time in the Southwest. A magazine editor and book author, he died in 1941. This selection is from the Southwest Review *of April 1927.*

THIS is a note about Texas—Texas prior to the Galveston flood; Texas when business was conducted in great measure before the bar, with one foot on the brass rail and the bar-keeper present by way of witness or arbiter or court of appeal, diagrams and helpful calculations being drawn on the counter with spilled beer, and a well-cooked free-lunch provided to sustain men in their commercial activities.

It is of a Texas when the name of Leonard Doughty, who lived in Goldthwaite, was being hailed, by those fitted to express an opinion, as that of a poetic genius, because of his newly-published songs which Nevin had set to music; when the son of the author of *David Harum* cut a dash in San Angelo, driving a brilliantly painted Stanhope and a black horse with hoofs polished by the shoe-shiner; and when out of a single Sunday School class in Knickerbocker came a covey of outlaws such as Black Jack, Barry Ketchum, Laura Bullion —a school teacher who turned burglar, an enterprising gentleman who for the first time in history held up a train single-handed.

It is of the Texas . . . when Haberkorn, now a sedate Kansas violinist, got off a freight train and made his way to Sonora, where he played Mozart, and Viotti, and Beethoven to an audience of cowboys who encored him nine times for his rendition of a Mozart minuet; and of a Texas which rang with the daring of the Iconoclast Brann who made the simplest statement look astonishing by the use of sesquipedalianisms, and had a Shaw-Chesterton trick of turning a platitude into a plaything.

This is of Texas when men talked about sixteen-to-one without the slightest knowledge of what they meant; when Paderewski was taken to Dallas by the enterprising Mr. Watkin during a reunion, and played bravely and brilliantly, in spite of the fact that many of the old fellows the worse for liquor and enthusiasm were whooping and rebel-yelling all through the program; and when there were buggies, and freight wagons, and surreys, and stylish saddle horses, and—an innovation— bicycles.

It is to be a note about Texas before moving pictures and phonographs; when, in the west, the Santa Fé ended at San Angelo and before there was any Orient; and when the dramatic event of the year in counties Tom Green and Irion and Crockett and Presidio and El Paso and Schleicher and Runnels was the coming of Mollie Bailey's show. For Mollie's exhibition was of the heavy conventional kind, and the company supporting her had no artistic prejudices: mingling with the audience, turning their hands to matters connected with transportation, using the circus horses for draft animals, putting up and taking down the tent, rushing from ticket stand to ring with trained expertness, outshining their competitors (the medicine man and the traveling mesmerist and the peripatetic merry-go-round, for these made their circuits, too), outshining in effect and originality by advertising the singing of The Newest Song from New York.

And Mollie herself was the singer, irresistible in her tragic power when she sang,

"George Collins rode home one cold winter night,
George Collins rode home so fine,
George Collins rode home one cold winter night,
And taken sick and died."

because there were appropriate motions of dramatic significance and virtuosity of execution, and a trombone obligato with the player far off in a vacant lot—so that it was all very soothing to the ear, although baffling and exasperating to those who wanted to know what it was all about. And never did it fail to come to pass but that Mollie—carried away with enthusiasm and quite regardless of the applause— accepting the very slightest noise as homage to the delicacy of her performance, with elaborate bows and curtseys, swept into a thirty-stanza ballad about Jeff Davis, commencing—

"Jeff Davis built a wagon and on it put his name,
And Beauregard was driver, too, Secession was
the same.
The horses they got hungry, as horses always do;
They had to keep the collars tight to stop them
getting through—"

which was interrupted every third or fourth stanza by volumes of noise—ironic, patriotic, originating from dramatic perspicacity, humor, chivalry, or from sheer lightheartedness.

It is to be a note about Texas when David Guion, a musician I uphold as the most original and sparklingly clever of those native composers who reveal America, was a little lad with bright and shining eyes, in the town of Ballinger, and sometimes gave performances to which we listened with ever fresh pleasure, doing what he had set out to do with grace, dignity, and repose.

And his sister was herself a pianist, a dainty little slip of a girl with a taste for dramatics, getting up Floradora entertainments and surmounting difficulties wonderfully, such as mere accidents of the stage, and lighting without lamps, and mastering the bashful young men from the plains that she had pressed into service, who stumbled over their feet and showed a tendency to retire from their roles in abashed despair.

Alamo—shrine of Texas liberty. Present building is the old chapel of Mission San Antonio de Valero, founded in 1718 by the Franciscan padres.

It is to be a note about Texas that talked about Clay McGonegal, who broke the roping record and was lionized by Joaquin Miller, the poet of the Sierras; and about Boogher Red who cared nothing for the color line, and so became impresario for Dick the Demon Negro Who Threw a Steer with His Teeth—by riding alongside the animal, taking it by the horns as it ran, getting on its back, and leaning over until, with his legs about the steer's neck, he was far enough forward to catch the animal's upper lip with his teeth—and we, who sat in the reserved seats in the fair grounds, broke into frantic applause at the Unique Moral Entertainment—as Boogher Red advertised it on bilious green handbills.

And it is to tell about Texas when on the Concho River sheepmen remembered a strange fellow who herded sheep, with a book close at hand, one named Morley Roberts, of whom the most optimistic never expected much, let alone the writing of such books as *The Western Avernus* and *Time and Thomas Waring*. It is the Texas of the time when men trusted one another, and when the affair of Nick Hughes and Loop Reed caused no comment. Reed was a drifter with some 4,000 sheep, and Hughes was a fellow of no occupation who happened to wander into the Devil's River country looking for a job; so Reed, having finished shearing and having sold his wool, employed Hughes to take charge of his Mexican herder and his chuck wagon—instructing him to drift west to Pecos City, where in the space of six weeks, between Pecos and Carlsbad, he proposed to meet him—for Reed had planned a high-hearted time in Chicago, spending his wool money.

So Hughes drifted, made the Pecos and went up and down as long as he dared, expecting Reed, until at last it became a nice point whether it was safe for him to drift thereabouts any longer because of the objections made by the cattlemen. Whereupon he drifted up the Penasco, then south and over to the Guadalupe country, leaving messages everywhere, then down to the Rio Grande country, then down to Maxon Springs, north to Fort Stockton and east to Menardville, lambing and shearing in season, selling his wool and banking the money, until three seasons passed with no sign of Reed and with the landless shepherd still tied to his flock.

So, when he met one named Stanton, owner of a merry-go-round—one of the old-fashioned sort, the motive power of which was furnished by energetic boys who were willing to make ten complete circuits pushing the contrivance for five cents—and when Stanton, hearing the sad tale of Hughes' having the responsibility of property for which he didn't care at all, set before Hughes the advantages of the ownership of the merry-go-round, and further told him that there was an unexploited field for such a machine in South America, then and there a vision appeared to Hughes; so that he made a rough and ready exchange, accepting the merry-go-round, lock, stock and barrel, and delivering flocks and herds to Stanton. And to cut a long story short, both men entered into Old Mexico, crossing the border at Fort Hancock, and what further is to be told of their adventures has not yet been recorded in history.

. . . It is about the time when down in the Rio Grande Valley men talked about Jim B. Gillett, who kidnaped Raca out of Mexico, and El Paso people had not forgot Neal Nuland's saloon where Stoudemire killed Johnson, who had threatened to kill Stoudemire; when men still remembered Victorio, who ran amuck and was shot by Mexicans in the Ysleta country; when down at Round Rock you could still read the lettering over a grave:

SAMUEL BASS
Born July 21st, 1851
Died July 21st, 1878

A brave man reposes in death here. Why was he not true?

It was Texas when no one dreamed of oil until that first Beaumont business, when with others, the goodhearted Judge John I. Guion tried his luck at Spindletop and turned over some $800 on his first deal, then thinking that sufficient, turned his face homeward, but passing through Dallas, remembered his gifted son David, when he saw a handsome piano in a store window; so bought the piano then and there, had it expressed to Ballinger, wired ahead for men to carry it; and like the high-

For many years, the Military Plaza at San Antonio kept its old-time look, with many
Latin overtones.

hearted fellow he was, entered into his own home with his profits safely invested for the benefit of all who chose to enjoy them, for the Judge's home was a place of open-handed hospitality.

As for Fredericksburg, it was then a long street, white and clean and sharp-edged against a clear sky; and there was no Port Arthur; and Beaumont was a ramshackle village. And Galveston was as picturesque as the streets in the neighborhood of St. Louis Cathedral in New Orleans are today, with Spanish scissors-and-knife grinders with their little pushcarts and their velvet jackets and their quaint tunes played on a piece of serrated steel; and sheepskin coated peasants from Russia; and

dark-eyed, patient-looking Armenians and dockhands who were Negroes, bright in colors and singing as they worked.

For it was in Galveston that I first landed from South America, and I recall distinctly being greeted on a street running parallel with the Mallory docks by a man who seemed interested in my welfare, for he catechized me as to my business, my place of abode, my destination. And when I told him something—more for the sake of friendliness than for information—saying that I knew something of seamanship, he was all for shipping me out on a barque bound for Belize. But when I spoke of leading a land life, he led me away, down a business street (which I could not recognize the other day)—a place of many awnings which expressed their owners' taste in color, shape, and design—and so took me to a saloon, where he introduced me to a jolly-looking bartender who, without a word of invitation, set two huge glasses of beer before us.

And these being emptied, we went upstairs to a gambling hall—a long room crowded with men of many nationalities—where were in progress many games of poker, keno, roulette, dice, rouge-et-noir, and a large toy race course on a green baize table with metal horses which flew around at the release of a spring. And everywhere else, in chili-joints, and barrooms, and tobacco stores, and newsstands, and places of common resort where men drop in and out, there were other machines into which you dropped money from a dime to a dollar, wagering against wheels as it were, and sometimes—with fortune smiling—received returns

up to the sum of ten silver dollars which clattered pleasantly into a little cup at which moments the dial of the mechanical gambler took on a beneficent look, jolly and good-humored and liberal. And some of these machines had music inside of them, so that you won or lost to the tune of "Lou, Lou, I Love You" or the more doleful air of "You Never Know What's Coming, Till You Get It in the Neck."

So that locates the time of this note about Texas, and sets a sort of vast background for what I intended to say. But the background has overshadowed the figure in the foreground as any man with a healthy sense of proportion may see. And when I sat down to write, all these things came in perfectly natural sequence. But I was in Texas in those days, and remembering them, I find myself glad and grateful to have been there.

Tale of Two Cities

GEORGE SESSIONS PERRY

The big-formed, seemingly nerveless George Sessions Perry was born in 1910 in Rockdale, Texas, a town he admired and loved. He attended Houston University, Purdue and other colleges but, as he said, he never finished freshman class at any of them. After a term as deck boy on a freighter, he sailed as a passenger on a liner, worked hard on unpublished novels and began to make a success as a magazine writer. His novels, Hold Autumn in Your Hand *and* Wall Rise Up, *books of warm feeling and natural humor, won considerable praise. For some years George Perry traveled America, doing municipal profiles for the* Saturday Evening Post. *From his* Cities of America, *published by Whittlesey House in 1947, this selection is taken. In ill health, he died tragically in 1956.*

THE most dangerous man that ever lived in Texas was named Jim Bowie. He rode alligators bareback, and when he fought a knife fight he liked to hold one corner of a handkerchief in his teeth while his opponent bit into it and held the opposite corner. When either duelist got enough, he could stop the fighting by turning loose the handkerchief.

But in the long fight between Dallas and

Fort Worth, the thirty-mile strip of land that inadequately separates these cities can't be turned loose. Both towns are built immovably into the earth, tightly entangled in each other's hair. Thus they stand belligerently facing each other at close quarters, like two bull chickens in a pit with hackles blooming. And nothing so enraptures either combatant as to plunge his gaff into his neighbor.

More often than not it has been a healthy, actually a profitable, rivalry. Just as two pigs in the same pen will gobble more corn and gain more weight than if they lived separately, so have these cities extended themselves to extraordinary degree, spurred, even after their own self-interest had been served, by a gnawing, wagon-green jealousy. Certainly this brawl has been carried on so noisily that the Southwest has been made more conscious of these cities than it otherwise might have been.

. . . However, according to Tom Gooch, a Dallas coffin manufacturer once had to ship his wares for Fort Worth via St. Louis because people in Fort Worth wouldn't be caught dead in anything from Dallas. In later times there could have been a great airport halfway between Dallas and Fort Worth, and convenient to both. But once a squabble developed over whose side the administration should be located on, negotiations were broken off, and each city had to supply its own facilities.

Much of this conflict undoubtedly derives from the antipathetic natures of the two cities themselves, as in the case of Sparta and Athens. Down in his secret heart, the zealous Fort Worth citizen thinks of his Dallas neighbor as a pallid, money-changing, road-show Texan, and the particularly sophisticated Dallasite may admit to the belief that his Fort Worth brother is a barbarian.

There are natural reasons why Fort Worth, along the old Chisholm Trail, should have a Western flavor and why a man in Eastward-looking Dallas can wear spats in comparative safety. Fort Worth, "Where the West begins," is a cow town, a big-hearted, loudmouthed, "Howdy, stranger" town. It is the capital city of that magnificent realm of Western ranch lands that stretch west to New Mexico and northward almost to Kansas and Colorado. In much of this land rain is a curiosity and everything either "sticks, stings or stinks." And the sturdy Western folk with the rawhide hands and the high-heeled boots rub off on a town where they bank and buy and frolic. In its efforts to make a hit with the outside world, its problem is simple: it has simply to be itself, exuberant and whooping and friendly, since nearly everybody loves a Western story.

Dallas has a much more complex problem. "Big D," as it likes to be called, reflects an altogether different region and way of life. In earlier times it was shut off, even shielded, from the frontier by the outpost city lying just to the west. Dallas grew up in a more orderly fashion into a town with a metropolitan population of a half-million plus, and where the natural emphasis was upon the virtues of the account book instead of those of the open range. It became the happy hunting ground of the farmers of North Texas who, with tame mule rather than fiery bronc, processed the fertility of the great ribbon of black land that stripes the state from north to south.

Dallas has undertaken to become the Athens of the alfalfa fields, the cultural capital of the Southwest. For a new Texas business town, that was a big order. This municipal aspiration was bound to be confusing to many a hitherto poor family that had got rich on East Texas oil or who had happened to snag the wholesale agency for a good line of farm equipment. But in a way that's really amazing, they all pitched in and played the game, even if some of them had no very definite idea of what the score was. They just knew that, culture-wise, Dallas had climbed into the saddle, and they meant to keep it there. For though Dallas is, in essence, a Southern city, rather than a Western one, still it is bathed with the rampant emotional juices of Texas and is, therefore, Southern in a more than ordinarily virile way. And when Dallas puts on a concert or an art show, it does it in precisely the same way its sister city stages a rodeo. It's playing for keeps. A few musicians or painters may get trampled in the rush, but everybody will know he's been somewhere.

Whether Dallas culture results from a yearning in the souls of the people for the higher things of life or, as some skeptics charge, from a desire on the part of the local Medici to show their muscle, its achievements are actual and real. Those who think of Texans with a six-gun in one hand and a chili bowl in the other, both smoking, may be surprised to learn that Dallas is one of the biggest book towns in the nation. While the average percapita expenditure for books in the United States is about $1.50 a year, that of the average

By 1840, Austin had become Texas' new capital—a small settlement with a future before it, and room for growth.

Fort Worth, "where the West began," but still a Texas town sharing many Southern habits and attitudes.

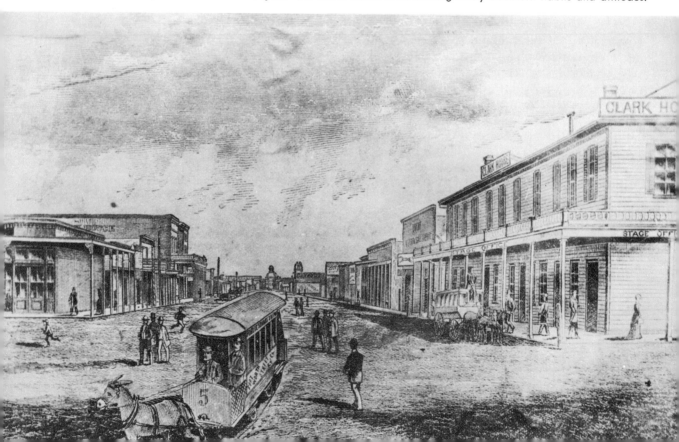

Dallasite is six dollars. Dallas' Cokesbury book-store, from a standpoint of elegance and size, need take a back seat to none on earth. Annually this store sells one and a quarter million dollars' worth of books, which is said to be more than any other American store dealing exclusively in books. . . . Not only is Dallas a town that visiting authors love, because it makes such a pleasing fuss over them, but it's downright sympathetic to struggling young artists in a way that Paris and London, San Francisco and New York, have been at varying stages of these cities' careers. . . .

The town is rabid about all branches of the arts. It turns out in force for such exotic spectacles as the ballet and the opera. However, Dallas' detractors enjoy pointing out that desperadoes Bonnie Parker and Clyde Barrow were both manifestations of Dallas' vaunted culture, as is the "East Dallas Special," a kind of curving blade with which to treat thy neighbor to sudden evisceration. Some Texans also charge Dallas' elite with an inordinate love of expensive display, particularly in regard to raiment.

It is the conviction of many qualified observers that Dallas has, on the whole, the best-groomed women in America. . . . It has what even New York and Paris haven't got: a single style dictator, Stanley Marcus, of internationally famous Neiman-Marcus. To show the length to which this influence spreads, chain-store buyers buy one class of goods for their other Texas stores, but a simpler line for Dallas, so that their customers can look as if they bought their clothes from Neiman-Marcus.

But all this wealth and power and flamboyance does not even dent Fort Worth's brashness or its determination to get the jump on Dallas. In some respects it can move faster, since it's pretty much of a one-man town. Indeed, the three principal historical events in the Fort Worth story are (1) when the Texas and Pacific railroad came to town in 1876, (2) when the stockyards were built at the turn of the century and (3) a dozen or so years later when the late Amon Carter moved in.

Amon Carter was Mr. Fort Worth. He was its dynamo for so long that he came to resemble the town and it to resemble him.

They both wore good Justin boots and Stetson hats. For years Amon Carter gave visiting firemen these big Western hats as a token of Fort Worth hospitality—in two sizes: three-inch brims to medium shots, and five-inch brims to thoroughgoing big shots. His newspaper, the *Star-Telegram*, is a highly vocal spokesman for the Fort Worth cause (as, for that matter, is the Forth Worth Press), and when Mr. Carter had to go to Dallas on business, he carried his own lunch, in order to avoid making so small a purchase as a hamburger from the Philistines.

There is one fundamental trend which nobody can stop, and which plays straight into Fort Worth's hand. That is the continuing movement in Texas away from cotton and corn and toward cow, sow and hen. The first two things a man wants to know when he is buying a ranch are: (1) the annual local rainfall and (2) the distance to Fort Worth's one hundred acres of stockyards, where, daily, a thousand truckloads of livestock arrive at their last roundup. Fort Worth's Western tendencies are expressed in the way the town itself is built. Its city limits are of the wide-ranging Los Angeles type, and it's not too unusual to find a cow pasture or a copse of scrub oak woods here and there. The city's 10,400 acres of rambling parks is said to be the largest per-capita park acreage of any principal city in the United States. . . .

In the early 'Thirties, the Texas legislature was trying to decide where to hold the state's official Centennial Exposition in 'Thirty-Six. But Banker Bob Thornton got it for Dallas when he said, "We've got the plant, we've got the money, and, to show our pride in Texas, we've got the guts to spend it." When he promised the committee that Dallas could get up $12,000,000 in public and private funds, he'd bought himself a centennial exposition. Amon Carter, who had been out of the state at the time, rallied Fort Worth's business people. Fort Worth, he declared, would stage a centennial celebration on its own, and one that would make Dallas' look like a Sunday school picnic. Long distance phone lines began crackling like a Chinese celebration. Mr. Carter got hold of Billy Rose and offered him a thousand dollars a day for a hundred days if he would come and put on a show that not only couldn't be beat but couldn't be tied.

In Dallas Bob Thornton and his cohorts stood at the Rubicon. The question was whether to make their show cultural and dignified, thereby inviting grave risks at the box-office, or whether to seize onto the sure-fire old carnival maxim of "kewpies, curiosity and sex." Uplift won. Bill Kittrell of Dallas brought big-time industrial exhibitors and also organized a five-alarm pageant, *Cavalcade of Texas*. He persuaded D. W. Griffith, who'd done all right with *The Birth of a Nation*, to come to Dallas and lend a hand. Both cities stumped the nation. Amon Carter plastered the state with billboards: "Go to Dallas for education. Come to Forth Worth for entertainment." . . . Texas ruled that it was a draw. And both sides came out bloody but unbowed.

Today there are many citizens in Fort Worth and Dallas, which together form the South's largest population pool, more interested in future co-operation than in past throat-cutting rivalry. Their attitude has been summed up by North-Texan Dr. George W. Truett when he gave the toast: "Hats off to the past! Coats off to the future!"

"Oil Is Like That"

GEORGE FUERMANN

An adopted Texan, George Fuermann is a close student of the state, its people and their ways, oil-style or otherwise. A popular columnist for the Houston Post, Mr. Fuermann is an anecdotist and lively reporter of the Houston scene. Thus far he has written two nonfiction Texas books, Reluctant Empire, *and* Houston: Land of the Big Rich, *published by Doubleday and Company in 1951, from which this selection is taken.*

A State of Never Mind A Scottish newspaperman found Houston the point in the United States "where the traveler can no longer rationalize or explain what he sees." To most Americans this Houston effect has something to do with money. They are flabbergasted by the fact that Houston is the one place in the world where a man with only four or five million dollars is not considered noticeably wealthy. To them, there is a goofy unreality in the fact that to get attention as a moneyed man a Houstonian needs at least twenty-five million dollars. Houstonians, who are tired of hearing about it, have the highest per capita wealth in the world.

The city's money is overemphasized, but no more so by others than by Houstonians themselves. Though the external features of the city's magic are business and finance, stoutly based on the dollar miracles of oil and gas, it is the citizens' roaring we-can-do-anything spirit that is father and mother to all this magic. Money is the golden by-product of the spirit. Reckless speculation, grim work, and tradition-junking are the superhighways leading to the magic. A Yankee once tritely described Houston as a State of Mind. It would be appropriate only to call it a State of Never Mind.

The New Houstonian, the one who came during and after World War II, has been raised on the city's superlatives and is so accustomed to them that nothing astonishes him. But the Old Houstonian, particularly the one who came before the Great Depression, is often as bewildered by the city's unrestrained zip as are visitors who have merely paused in Houston for an hour or a day or a week.

The evidence is relentless. Along the banks of the Houston Ship Channel is a crop even more impressive than oil—a billion dollars' worth of the world's greatest concentration of newly built industry. A downtown corner was sold in 1940 for $1,150,000; seven years later Woolworth bought it for $3,050,-000—or at the rate of $2000 a front *inch*. Since 1940 the Houston area's oil, gas, salt, sulphur, oyster shells, forests, and cash have built the world's greatest concentration of chemical and petrochemical industries. The value of the area's industrial products increases by almost half a billion dollars a year. Within the city limits are more oil companies and allied industries than in any other community anywhere. Though fifty miles inland, Houston has the nation's second port; only New York's port handles more tonnage.* Within a two-hundred-mile radius of Houston more wealth is taken from the soil than from any other equivalent area on earth.

When a school had an auction to raise money for a new gym, one of the citizens bid $1500 for a collie pup. Next day, because the students complained that the bidding was too steep for them to have a chance, another dog was auctioned. As expected, the bidding started at a nickel. It stopped when a twelve-year-old girl bid $115 and wrote a check for it herself. The check was good. In Houston, a champion steer has been auctioned for a world record $72,500; a basket of tomatoes has been auctioned for $600, and a single bale of cotton has been auctioned for $2528.

Naturally, Houston uses dollars as Niagara Falls uses water. And there is no mistaking the avenues of most of the wealth. Planted helter-skelter in the downtown area are the signposts: skyscrapers called the Gulf Building, the Humble Building, the Texas Company Building, the Shell Building, the Petroleum Building, the Oil and Gas Building, the Commerce Building. Signposts of an older but still burgeoning thoroughfare is the Cotton Exchange Building, where Anderson, Clayton & Company, incomparably the world's largest

cotton merchant, is headquartered, and where work the men who have made Houston the world's leading spot cotton market.

Houston is the focus of the Land of the Big Rich. It is the pivot of what may be the last frontier of great new fortunes: the Golden Coast, a crescent that sweeps the Gulf of Mexico from New Orleans on the east to Brownsville on the west. The hypnotic fascination of gushering dollars, the abnormal and sensational whoosh of oil riches, and the Wizard of Oz-like fantasy of whizzing real estate values have not made Houston's magic either impermanent or unreal. Oddly, even the city-slicking promoters, the schemers and the get-rich-quick artists who have swirled into Houston have been useful in forming the city's strapping economy.

Houstonians, most of them, are aware that their city is an astonishing phenomenon as it sprays its frisky wealth in a dozen directions at once. They have not the depth of historic color and tradition that the people of Atlanta and New Orleans like to talk about; they have not the utopian climate that the people of Florida and California like to brag about; they have not the olden roots of intellectual culture that New Englanders like to gush about. But in Houston they are creating a new kind of culture, one that is already distressingly colorful and one that will eventually be impressively deep in historical tradition. They also have an independence of spirit—it has been called a mind-your-own-business spirit—which implies that they are merely warming up. Walter Kuttner, an immigrant who came to Houston from Germany in 1938, once tried to describe Houston to a Houstonian. "Maybe you've seen an adolescent tell his first girl that he loves her, mincing unhappily from one foot to the other," he said. "That's Houston." For most of the hundreds of thousands who have merged from everywhere to form Houston, though they may never have thought much about it, Kuttner had hit the nail on its head. Most of them, if they could only air-condition their hell-hot, humid climate, would not change any other important aspect of their throbbing city.

Hubert Mewhinney of the Houston *Post* once called Houston a whisky-and-trombone town. He did this in the late forties—the 1940s, not the 1840s—yet his irreverence was partly as true of the twentieth century as it was wholly true of the nineteenth. Though Houston was 115 years old in 1951, which is considered an age of municipal maturity in the Southwest, it was still shiny new, partly because its population had doubled every twelve years since it was started in 1836, partly because the sophisticating influences of latter-day civilization had never prospered much in Houston, but mostly because its citizens had always been far more interested in where they were going than in where they had been.

Oil: Two and Two are Five An oilman and a promoter, meeting in the Rice Hotel one afternoon in 1950, made a $330,000,000 gas deal in twenty minutes. Same year, a Houston oilman sent a new Cadillac to Europe to have a $5000 custom body put on its chassis. He sent instructions to "throw the old body away."

If such unrestrained, forthright dollar spending is not commonplace in Houston, it is also not unusual enough to cause much comment. Most Houstonians have never even heard of Robert A. Welch, a slender, shy Houston oilman who wears a Vandyke and tips his barber a dime. In his eighties, he is reportedly worth at least a hundred million dollars. Through 1947, the King Ranch's Robert Kleberg had received $3,250,000 in oil royalties from Houston's Humble Oil and Refining Company. Yet Kleberg does not even call himself an oilman. He is a rancher.

Oil is like that. It is the Southwest's Cinderella legend. It is to Houston what green is to grass, what women are to Hollywood. Without oil, Houston would be important but not conspicuous. Without oil, a Houstonian with a million dollars would undoubtedly be considered wealthy. But whiffling through the city's spewing prosperity with Arabian Nighted magic and an adolescent prince's awkward majesty, oil is everybody's business in Houston. Everybody—stenos, insurance salesmen, bartenders—daydreams of getting a piece of an oil deal. At one time or another, at least a tenth of the citizens get a piece. But only a handful are lucky. Luckier than most were

the twenty Houston doctors who, in 1950 in what oilmen call a "poor-boy" deal, took a chance and invested in some oil property. They got a strike and speedily sold out. Though gambling is illegal in Texas, oil, the biggest gamble in the universe, is the state's fairy godmother, guardian, and chief topic of conversation.

It got started deep in East Texas, just outside Beaumont, where there is a gently rounded dome rising a dozen feet above the flat Gulf Coastal Plain. It is a salt dome, and it is the most important of Texas' many geological freaks. There, on January 10, 1901, Captain Anthony Lucas, a retired Austrian naval officer, put a rotary drill down through the salt and quicksand and brought in the famed Lucas Gusher. In no time at all the Spindletop field was a jungle of drilling rigs and derricks. It was said that you could walk across Spindletop without touching the ground, merely stepping from one derrick floor to another.

Lucas tried to sell his production to the Standard Oil Company, but a Standard official shook his head. "Too big. Too big," he said. "There's more oil there than the whole world will need for the next century." Because he was wrong, Texas became the world's Promised Land, the Land of the Big Rich, a land that proved Horatio Alger to be a man with faint, slipshod imagination.

Texas has almost two thirds of the nation's proven oil reserves. It has so far produced more than twenty-five billion dollars' worth of oil and gas. In 1950, Texas alone completed 10,600 new producing wells. Texas has also produced a separate race. Oilmen. Their distinguishing characteristics include a homespun honesty that is not understood in any other business, a forthright and salt-tongued disposition that is often mistaken for poor breeding but is simply a bold new culture, and a staggering number of dollars. Add to these characteristics whisky drinking and violence, these because most oilmen move up from the iron-fisted caste system of the oil fields—roughnecks, roustabouts, tool pushers—where a man has to be tough.

To others, oilmen often seem to be oddly eccentric, sometimes unbelievable subhumans or super-humans, depending on the incident concerned.

Like Houston's West family. J. M. West was an old-type tycoon, a man who made an immense fortune in cattle and timberlands and then multiplied it in oil. Tough and taciturn, he wore his Stetson hat indoors or out, and he had a genius for making people uneasy. It would have embarrassed him had he ever stopped to consider it, but he was also kind and generous. Once when Glenn McCarthy needed cash in a hurry, he called on West, whom he barely knew, to try to interest him in some leases that later proved to be good. West was not interested, and McCarthy started to leave. "Hear you've been having some financial troubles," West said. McCarthy admitted that he needed about $30,000 to satisfy some small but troublesome creditors. West snorted and McCarthy left. An hour later, when McCarthy had returned to his office, a messenger gave him an envelope. In it was a check for $50,000 and a note, "Pay me when you can. Jim West."

When Big Jim died he left his sons, Marion and Wesley, his wife and his daughter about seventy million dollars' worth of oil and lumber property and other land. The sons, Marion, as eccentric as his father, and Wesley, as civilized as it is considered appropriate for Texans to become, have expanded the fortune. In 1938 the Humble Oil and Refining Company bought 30,000 acres from the West estate for $8,500,000 cash.

The actions of the Brothers West are among the most spellbinding of those of all Houstonians. Wesley once bought a ranch because he liked an "old-timey" house that was on it. He then proceeded to build additions that largely covered the original structure and thereafter had valleys dug around the house so that it would stand on a hill. Finally, he had a small lake bed scooped out near the house and a pipe line constructed to bring in the water.

To save himself time and trouble, Wesley once parked his Cadillac in a bus zone in front of his office and cheerfully paid a daily $5.00 fine. By the time his total fines were more than $1000, newspapers raised sufficient fuss to cause Wesley to park his car somewhere else.

But such extroverted conduct is uncommon in Wesley's life. His beautiful River Oaks home is not only in good taste but is one of the city's show places. In the home are murals showing the history of the West family and more murals lampooning thirty-odd of Wesley's friends. Like other oilmen, Wesley is in a position to entertain with a lavish sweep. He does so. To entertain guests at a Christmas party he gave in 1950, he hired and had flown to Houston singers Mel Tormé and Evelyn Knight and Henry King's orchestra.

Compared to his brother Marion, Wesley is as sedate as a violet. In a land where eccentricity is considered a normal, healthful condition, Marion West has set a bewildering though harmless pace that even astounds other oilmen.

Marion is called Silver Dollar West. He uses only silver dollars for tipping, often twenty and twenty-five at a time. In one otherwise orderly Houston restaurant he once threw handfuls of silver dollars on the floor, then watched the Negro waiters scramble for them. Dallas citizens, who advertise themselves as deeply cultured and thus above such doings, are fascinated by Marion's arrivals and departures from their city of learning. When he lands at Dallas' Love Field, he tosses from fifty to a hundred silver dollars among porters and limousine drivers, and he is equally generous when he arrives at a downtown hotel.

Marion also likes to have recipients play hide-and-seek with the cartwheels. When he and Wesley were building their fabulous garage and utility building not far from downtown Houston, Marion threw handfuls of silver dollars into arriving gravel trucks. Finding them was at least as hard as finding needles in a haystack. To delight guests at swimming parties he used to give for his two daughters, he threw huge handfuls of the dollars into his pool, then watched the youngsters dive to retrieve them. When riding taxis, he often lets a few silver dollars slip down behind the seat. Whenever a doorman delivers one of Marion's Cadillacs to the front of the Shamrock, he is regularly tipped three silver dollars—unless he permits the white sidewall tires to touch the curb, in which case he is fined a dollar and gets only two cartwheels.

Marion's love of radio can only be compared with the love most men have for women. He owns a tremendously powerful private radio station and he has as many as eight aerials on some of his personal cars. Once, when he was driving to Houston from an oil lease, he tuned in his radio station but encountered some ear-shattering static. He directed one of his men to find out what was causing the static. Turned out it was a station in France that had the same frequency as Marion's station. Reportedly, Marion directed his man to "buy the French station and take it off the air."

. . . Consider J. Collier Hurley. In most cities he would be one of the wealthiest of men. In Houston he is not even widely known. He wears nothing but black shoes, rarely wears a pair more than five or six times and buys a dozen pairs at once. Also, he wears nothing but black suits. For twenty years he has saved friends' birth and anniversary dates and sends cards and sometimes gifts to more than two thousand every year, buying, addressing, and mailing the cards and gifts himself. Neither his secretary nor his wife are permitted to help with this personal function. Besides wearing a new tie every two or three days, he gives an expensive tie to every man who calls at the Hurley home on New Year's Eve. In between New Year's Eves, he gives friends almost a thousand ties a year and figures this hobby costs between five and ten thousand dollars annually.

Frank Champion, a tough, friendly oilman who is built like a small size bear, is the city's Glad Hatter. He buys a dozen hats at a time and more than fifty hats every year. Because he wants them where they can all be seen at a glance, he keeps them where most people keep books—on library shelves in his den. There is also a house rule that none can be put in closets. Some years he gives away as many as twenty-five hats to friends and celebrities. They are white-on-white ten-gallon western hats that cost Champion $100 each. Once, to prove that he was the city's foremost hat enthusiast, he got a haircut without taking off his hat.

Houstonians, like everyone else, rarely tire of the legends of the oil race. Joseph S. Cullinan was one of the founders of the now mighty Texas Company. Until he died in 1937 he flew a pirates' skull-and-crossbones flag atop the twenty-two-story Petroleum Building "as a warning . . . that liberty is a right and not a privilege." Jim Abercrombie, one of the quietest and one of the most respected of Houston oilmen, sold only a part of his holdings for $54,000,000 in 1946. In a single visit to Dallas' Neiman-Marcus store once, a Houston oilman spent $8700 just buying clothes for his back. Another oilman, in eleven years, sent 406 men through college, paying all their expenses and giving them jobs in the summer. All they had to do was agree to take petroleum engineering. By the time he died, the hobby had cost him $1,218,000.

Early in 1951, when a Houston oilman bought a lease in Southwest Texas priced at $77,000, he insisted that the price be boosted to $77,777. "All those sevens," he explained to the amazed seller, "are bound to be lucky."

V

Banners in a High Wind

At last we are
A nation among nations; and the world
Shall soon behold in many a distant port
Another flag unfurled . . . .

THESE deeply felt words came from the pen of Henry Timrod, as romantic-minded an individual as ever lived in the South. He spoke for hundreds of thousands who saw the conflict of the 1860's as the inevitable result of decades of events, some disheartening, some inspiring. For years they had thought and talked of themselves as a people separated by background, by conviction, by basic interest, from the population of the North.

Such Southerners considered themselves victims of malevolent attacks by a lesser people, money-grabbers without ideals. As those of the North worked to confine slavery to its existing borders, many Southerners conceived of slavery as an advancing force, spreading to the new territories of the United States, taking in much or all of Mexico and Cuba as well. Unless the South expanded in such fashion, they insisted, it would be overshadowed forever by a North that grew ever more swiftly, ever more efficiently.

Arrayed against the South, perhaps beyond remedy by Southerners, were the census tables, the indices of Northern wealth, the surge of an ever more modern business-industrial civilization, linked to a system of free labor. Various Southerners, foreseeing a lessened future, marshaled forces for counterattacks, for improvement in their own economy, better agricultural methods to replace the wasteful ones of their traditional past, and altered trading with Europe—if possible, without the intervention of Northern agents.

More and more often Southern zealots cried out for the annexation of Mexico and islands in the Caribbean, to form a slave empire and grow its major staples for the world—cotton, tobacco, sugar. It would be a new Rome with a great role, a breath-taking one, in international affairs. A number of enthusiasts began an organization, Knights of the Golden Circle, which actually made attacks across the Mexican border, and there were assaults on Cuba which did not succeed.

For years, the more romantic among the Southerners spoke of their side, specifically, as "the Chivalry." In speeches, magazines, newspapers, the word stood out as a term of simple description. One of the Confederate or post-

Confederate songs, not so well known as others, but familiar to thousands, had the title of "Chivalrous C.S.A.":

> I'll sing you a song of the South's sunny clime,
> Chivalrous C.S.A. !
> Which went to housekeeping once on a time.
> Bully for C.S.A. !
> Like heroes and princes they lived for a time;
> Chivalrous C.S.A. !
> And routed the Hessians in most gallant style.
> Bully for the C.S.A. !

Chorus:
> Chivalrous, chivalrous people are!
> Chivalrous, chivalrous people are!
> In C.S.A. ! In C.S.A. !
> Aye, in chivalrous C.S.A. !

To the average present-day man or woman of the Northern states, the conflict may seem a distant one, marked by a few sad family recollections, stories of a great-uncle or grandfather lost at Shiloh or Gettysburg or Petersburg. To the Southerner it is generally more than that—a conflagration on the home scene, battles that occurred in the very streets, along a creek within a few minutes' walk, and, too, memories that followed the end of the fighting: the greatest dislocation that any part of the United States was to know, the chaos of broken public buildings, of levees wrecked in floodtime, of former lawyers and brokers who hunted odd jobs to provide food for their families.

In the South the war meant still more: harsh attacks of the kind common in conflict, yet hard to forget when inflicted upon the homes, and hurtful descriptions passed on by the women: the dying words of a man who succumbed to ailments brought on by the fighting, and tales of lost cotton or sugar or tobacco fields, of houses burned without clear military reason. And here and there today, along the Mississippi or one of its many tributaries, a notable flight of stairs lifts proudly from a weed-grown patch, and ends in nothing. The residence is gone, lost in a fire, or a victim of the slow rot of the years.

Again, eight columns rise at the front, the same number extending backward at each side—and that is all. Walls have fallen, the high portico and the roof behind it have collapsed. Long ago the last vandal or frugal farmer has pulled away bits to be set up elsewhere: half of a white marble mantel, an intact chandelier, a pair of doorknobs painted with roses, that stand out oddly against the drab gray of a weather-worn cottage door.

At its start, for thousands of Northerners the war might have appeared needless, one which could well have been avoided. Simply let the South go, and see what happens. . . . So some had argued, caring little about the issue of slavery, the ideologies of the situation. Then, as tensions grew and the fighting became ever more violent, more searing, motives altered, and Northerners debated in strengthening conviction over the matter of preservation of the Union. And with his Emancipation Proclamation, Abraham Lincoln gave the conflict a new dimension, another meaning. World opinion shifted; from ministers in the pulpit, from the throats of tired soldiers in blue, the words arose: They were giving their means, perhaps their lives, for liberty in their nation.

In the South men rode out from the beginning under other banners and other slogans. The yeomen farmers, although without slaves, echoed the words of the plantation owner. They were struggling for the homeland, for the place in which they were born. Robert E. Lee put it best when, although he had questioned secession as a legal right and frowned at the "arrogance" of the cotton South, he said simply that he could not turn his back upon his family, his neighbors, his friends.

Whether consciously or not, the Confederates made a romantic fight, under romantic impulse or conviction. One element might admit, sadly, wryly, that they stood for an archaic system, one which they would concede—as had their forefathers—must eventually drop away of its own dead weight. And yet they were ready to die for their side.

Some planters' sons arrived in camp booted, spurred, feather-capped like figures out of Sir Walter's novels. A number did not neglect to bring along body servants, and a few bristled furiously that fellow officers (perhaps superiors as well) had sought to "insult" or degrade them by giving them orders. Therefore the grandiloquent ones issued challenges to duels. Nevertheless, after such notions worked themselves out, the Southerner of the cotton and sugar and rice estates usually made his mark as a fighter. After all, he had been trained for war; he rode well, he knew how to use firearms with skill, he had already served in the military or the local militia. . . . He might not be able to lick seven Yankees in every case, but under fire he could account for himself, and do it well.

Often the Confederate labored with heavy odds against him, and his knowledge of the margin spurred him to achieve feats that might have seemed impossible. Here and there his romantic inclinations had harmful effect, when he waged all too individual a foray. At times officers turned pending successes into failure because they struck, not like modern soldiers, but in the style of another age, ignoring the demands of discipline, forgetting instructions as they fought furiously onward.

As has often been noted, this war ranked in many ways as the first of the modern ones, with balloons in the air, primitive submarines in the water, mass armies, powerful guns, amphibious operations. It was also in other respects the last of the romantic ones. Brothers in opposing armies did meet on or near the battlefield; a man who had beaten down a lean opponent would discover that it was one of his cousins. Bits of chivalric mercy tempered the rage of enemies. Under a flag of truce a Southerner encountered an old schoolmate in blue garb, and they talked excitedly, then sadly, of their families, and the last picnic they had all enjoyed at Louisville or Nashville or Knoxville. . . .

With women spies ("female agents" was the preferred term, because many considered "spy" too hard a word for a lady), colonels and generals might be convinced that such an individual was a deadlier enemy than a resolute brigade commander, and still they permitted her to go. Would it have been gentlemanly to execute a lady, who clearly came from a good family?

The pages that follow are intended primarily to reflect some of the attitudes of the Southerners. A modern-day Virginian, living in the heart of the Confederacy, appraises the leading figures and their attitudes, including Robert E. Lee, Stonewall Jackson, Jefferson Davis. Then we see each of them at a vital moment, a happy or a tragic hour. An observer, greatly touched, recalls Lee as his head sank in weariness at a religious rite in camp, and distant guns thundered on the battle grounds. The Confederate military men and civilians sing songs that express a sad hope or a casual jibe, and Southerners thumb noses, as have all soldiers at all times, in the direction of a self-sure ass in uniform. And in verse two Southerners give their emotions, one in the restraint of the twentieth century, his predecessor with the pounding rhythms, the declamatory gesture of an earlier time.

Slaves leaving Hampton to go to Fortress Monroe

"If We Succeed . . ."

HUDSON STRODE

With these words from Jefferson Davis' inaugural address as leader of the Confederacy, Hudson Strode closed Volume 1 of his biography, Jefferson Davis, *published in 1955 by Harcourt, Brace and Company, New York, with a subtitle,* American Patriot. *Written from the point of view of a warm admirer of Mr. Davis, the work is to be a three-volume one. Mr. Strode's first effort in this field, it follows his travel books and was prepared while the author continued his well-known creative writing classes at the University of Alabama.*

THE morning of Monday, February 18, 1861, was as fine a day for the birth of a nation as the heavens could provide. The sun shone full in a cloudless sky, making the atmosphere balmy and invigorating; more like a rare June day in Maine than one which the calendar claimed for February. Ladies had no apprehension in risking their best garden-party costumes, and some got out silken parasols to shade their complexions. By ten o'clock a crowd, white and black, had gathered on the sidewalks of Dexter Avenue, which led from the public fountain and the Exchange Hotel up to the white-domed Capitol crowning the hill at the top of the thoroughfare. Tennant Lomax, one of Montgomery's leading citizens, had lent his handsome new carriage to take the President-elect to his inauguration. Today, this elegant equipage, lined with white and yellow hangings, was drawn by four white horses.

Just before the stroke of noon, when Arnold's Band and the First Alabama Regiment were already in line, Jefferson Davis and Alexander Stephens took their seats in the carriage, along with the Reverend Basily Manly and an army officer, who sat facing them. As the President's carriage swung into position, Herman Arnold led his musicians up the avenue in a tune that had never been played anywhere before by a band, for he had orchestrated it himself only a week before. It was a minstrel piece called "I Wish I Was in Dixie's Land," just published the preceding

June as sheet music arranged for pianoforte. It proved to be stirring, as well as catchy. The soldiers marched briskly; the horses pricked up their ears, lifted their feet proudly, and held their heads high. The music helped to excite the crowd to rousing cheers. But no one dreamed then that "Dixie" was to become the Southern "Marseillaise." [1]

As Mr. Davis's carriage passed, the crowd cheered lustily and fell in behind the procession in its slow progress up the gently rising street. The "important" people were already assembled on the green-sod terraces of the Capitol to witness the ceremony. Within the building, members of the Confederate Congress sat waiting to greet their leader. When the carriage halted, Robert Barnwell Rhett received Mr. Davis, gave him his arm in the grand manner, and escorted him to the congressional chamber. Dwarfish Alexander Stephens walked on the other side of the President-elect. As Allen Tate observed, "Had Davis known it, he was at that moment between the upper and nether millstone." For this chief begetter of secession and this "mite of a man" who had opposed it came to be bitter enemies of the Chief Executive and sought to mangle his authority, and in the end effectively helped to wreck the Confederacy.

In presenting the President-elect, Rhett announced courteously but with laconic formality, "Gentlemen of the Congress, allow me to present to you the Honorable Jefferson Davis, who in obedience to your choice has come to assume the important trust you have confided to his care."

After making a brief speech of greeting, Mr. Davis was escorted back outside to a stage arranged on the front portico between the

towering white pillars of the western façade. The members of the Congress filed out to seats set up on the top terrace facing the speaker's stand. As the clock struck one, Jefferson Davis rose and stood before a table on which lay a wreath of red, white and blue flowers cradling a Bible. Howell Cobb administered the simple oath of office. The President delivered his inaugural address. Its tone was tempered and calm. The natural music of his voice charmed his hearers.

"Our present political position," the President affirmed, "has been achieved in a manner unprecedented in the history of nations. It illustrates the American idea that governments rest on the consent of the governed, and that it is the right of all those to whom we would sell, and from whom we would buy, that there should be the fewest practicable restrictions upon the interchange of these commodities. . . .

"There can be, however, but little rivalry between ours and any manufacturing or navigating community, such as the Northeastern States of the American Union. It must follow, therefore, that mutual interests will invite to goodwill and kind offices on both parts."

Then, with an expression in which pain and resolution mingled, he spoke out over the heads of the crowd. "If, however, passion or lust of dominion should cloud the judgment or inflame the ambition of those States, we must prepare to meet the emergency and maintain, by the final arbitrament of the sword, the position which we have assumed among the nations of the earth.

"We have entered upon the career of independence, and it must be inflexibly pursued. . . . As a necessity, not a choice, we have resorted to the remedy of separation, and henceforth our energies must be directed to the conduct of our own affairs, and the perpetuity of the Confederacy which we have formed. If a just perception of mutual interest shall permit us peaceably to pursue our separate political career, my most earnest desire will have been fulfilled. But if this be denied to us, and the integrity of our territory and jurisdiction be assailed, it will but remain for us with firm resolve to appeal to arms and invoke the blessing of Providence on a just cause. . . ."

[1] Few in the crowd had ever heard "Dixie," though it had been sung in Bryant's Traveling Minstrel Show since 1859, when, purportedly, Dan Emmett, one of the minstrels, had composed it hurriedly for an opening "walk around" during a New York engagement. As Arnold, a naturalized German musician who had married a Montgomery girl, searched for something new and exciting to play for the inauguration, his wife suggested, "Why don't you play that minstrel piece about Dixie's Land? It's lively and catchy and would make a good band number." So Arnold had hurriedly orchestrated the score and rehearsed his band vigorously in a room of the Capitol provided for the purpose. Now for the first time a band played "Dixie," composed by Dan Emmett, a showman from Ohio. As the Baltimore *Sun* declared, even if written by the son of an Abolitionist, "Dixie" is essentially a plantation song supposedly sung by slaves.

Retreat of the Confederates from Shiloh

He warned the incoming Washington administration that war would be a policy so detrimental to the civilized world, including the Northern states, that he did not see how it could be dictated by even "the strongest desire to inflict injury upon us." But if the North *should* make war, he emphasized the terrible responsibility that would rest upon it. "The suffering of millions will bear testimony to the folly and wickedness of our aggressors."

As he drew to his conclusion, he humbly asked the people of the Confederacy to bear

with him in the responsibilities he faced. "Experience in public stations . . . has taught me that toil and care and disappointment are the price of official elevation. You will see many errors to forgive, many deficiencies to tolerate; but you shall not find in me either want of zeal or fidelity to the cause that is to me the highest in hope, and of most enduring affection. . . ."

As his glance swept the throng from left to right, a heart-lifting smile lighted his countenance. "It is joyous in the midst of perilous times to look around upon a people united in heart, where one purpose of high resolve animates and actuates the whole; where the sacrifices to be made are not weighed in the balance against honor and right and liberty and equality. . . ." Then he ended his brief address with an invocation to divinity: "Reverently let us invoke the God of our fathers to guide and protect us in our efforts to perpetuate the principles which by His blessing they were able to vindicate, establish, and transmit to their posterity. With the continuance of His favor ever gratefully acknowledged, we may hopefully look forward to success, to peace, and to prosperity."

Like a gigantic spotlight the sun of half-past one fell full upon Jefferson Davis, illuminating the thin chiseled features, the gray-gold hair, the blue-gray eyes. He stood there like some handsome ascetic, congenial to sacrificial fastings, dedicated to a righteous cause, and, for this particular moment, blessed with a special grace. Before the South, as well as this immediate audience, he stood, a leader to inspire confidence, admiration, and a certain devotion. It was the high hour of his career, and Varina [his wife] was not there to share in it.

The men on the portico surged about him to grasp his hand. To attract his attention, Mrs. Kilpatrick, the beautiful wife of the one-time Alabama Senator, in an oddly democratic gesture, poked him in the back with her parasol. Arnold's Band again struck up "Dixie," a tumultuous shout arose, and ladies began tossing flowers at their President. The ceremony of birthing a nation was over.

"To Die We Would Prefer . . ."

Of all the Confederate songs, Southerners had a particular reverence for "The Bonnie Blue Flag," which celebrated the first banner of the Southern side, with a single star. A number of sources declared that General Ben F. ("Spoons" to New Orleans, "Beast" to others) Butler promised swift punishment if he so much as heard a man whistling or humming it. Butler supposedly destroyed plates of the song when they fell into his hands.

We are a band of brothers, and native to the soil,
Fighting for our liberty, with treasure, blood and toil;
  And when our rights were threatened, the cry rose near and far:
  Hurrah for the Bonnie Blue Flag that bears a Single Star!

Chorus
  Hurrah! Hurrah! for Southern rights, Hurrah!
  Hurrah for the Bonnie Blue Flag that bears a Single Star!

As long as the Union was faithful to her trust,
Like friends and like brethren kind were we and just;
  But now when Northern treachery attempts our rights to mar,
  We hoist on high the Bonnie Blue Flag that bears a Single Star.

First gallant South Carolina nobly made the stand;
Then came Alabama, who took her by the hand;
  Next, quickly Mississippi, Georgia, and Florida,
  All raised on high the Bonnie Blue Flag that bears a Single Star.

Ye men of valor, gather round the banner of the right,
Texas and fair Louisiana, join us in the fight:
  Davis, our loved President, and Stephens, statesman rare,
  Now rally round the Bonnie Blue Flag that bears a Single Star.

And here's to brave Virginia! The Old Dominion State
With the young Confederacy at length has linked her fate;
  Impelled by her example, now other States prepare
  To hoist on high the Bonnie Blue Flag that bears a Single Star.

Rebels moving south from Atlanta

Then cheer, boys, cheer, raise the joyous shout,
For Arkansas and North Carolina now have both
    gone out;
  And let another rousing cheer for Tennessee be
    given—
  The Single Star of the Bonnie Blue Flag has
grown to be eleven.

Then, here's to our Confederacy; strong we are
  and brave,

Like patriots of old, we'll fight our heritage to
    save;
  And rather than submit to shame, to die we
    would prefer—
So cheer again for the Bonnie Blue Flag that
  bears a Single Star!
Chorus
  Hurrah! Hurrah! for Southern rights, Hur-
    rah!
  Hurrah! for the Bonnie Blue Flag has gained
    the Eleventh Star.

Hadn't Hugged for So Long, He Was Out of Practice

BELL IRVIN WILEY

Out of concentrated research, the meticulous reading and careful judgment of uncounted thousands of letters, reports and documents, Bell Irvin Wiley has achieved the best study of the average Southern man in uniform, with his The Life of Johnny Reb, *published in 1943 by Bobbs-Merrill, Indianapolis. In this appraisal of the common soldier of the Confederacy, judicious inquiry is substituted for eulogy, realism for sentimentality, and yet the book has many moments of pathos as well as some hilarious ones.*

"I BELIEVE the biggest half of our Study here is about Something to eat and the other part is about wives and sweethearts," wrote a lonely Reb from camp in December, 1862.

His statement was not exaggerated, for woman was of tremendous moment in the life of the ordinary soldier. . . . When exhaustion transported him to the realm of dreams he luxuriated in her fancied presence, and he resented the blatant morning call that took her away. . . . More romantically disposed Rebs saw the war as a composite of individual combats, with each soldier playing the knight for his particular lady. One wore a sprig of palmetto in his hat as a lover's token; others called their guns by their sweethearts' names. Even the thoroughfares of camp were given such feminine designations as "Maiden Lane."

"Kiss all . . . for me," wrote an unattached soldier in 1862, "and tell them I shall be back some of these days and not one of them shall go uncourted." Another sent this message: "Tell . . . Miss Mollie when I come home if she wants to Marrie me all she has to do is to say so"; and a third said: "I am tired of camp life and thank God all Mighty if I live through this war I will be stoped roving. I intend to come home and marry Miss Lizzie Kemp."

"I have not seen a gal in so long a time that I would not know what to do with myself if I were to meet up with one," wrote a disconsolate Virginian, "though I recon I would learn before I left her. . . . I would be glad to [see] one more gal before the Yankees kill me." Another wrote: "I havent hug a girl for so long I am out of practice."

Some soldiers sought relief for their insatiable yearning by making long and reminiscent entries in their diaries. Others took to verse. Of the latter class was an unsophisticated Tar Heel named Malone.

> You are a charming little dandy
> Sweeter than the sweetest candy
>   Candy is sweet
> It is very dear
> But not half so sweet
> As you my dear . . .

The arrival of an officer's wife—or even a comely washerwoman—would set a whole camp to gawking. Henry Kyd Douglas told of a visit to the army of the beauteous Hettie Cary shortly after her marriage to General Pegram. As Douglas escorted this lady from the parade ground after a review, an enraptured Reb was almost knocked down by her horse. When she began to apologize the awestruck veteran lifted his shabby hat and said, "Never mind, Miss. You might have rid all over me, indeed you might."

When soldiers on the march encountered a group of girls there was invariably a painful straining of necks, and if the gentle creatures were so thoughtful as to present pails of water, an overpowering thirst was sure to play havoc with the ranks. A young soldier who was thus refreshed wrote the next day to his sister:

One of them was a perfect wayside lily. . . .
I could not help taking off my hat & bowing
low to her as the bugle call forward was heard.
I dont know her name & shall never see her
again, but I am indebted to her for much more
than a can of water.

Femininity was regarded as the supreme
attribute in women. Robustness was definitely
objectionable, and big feet were almost dis-
qualifying—"They are all too tremendous,"
complained one soldier of Kentucky girls, and
another said disgustedly of backwoods Arkansas women who visited camp: "I have not seen
one that would wear less than a number eight
pair of shoes." Affectionate disposition and
accomplishment in aesthetics were held very
desirable. A Tennesseean described a girl:

"She is a regular beauty, sings like an
angel, dances like a sylph, talks like an author-
ess and . . . the English language is inadequate
to express how much she does love. . . . Life
has been but one dream of her since first I
beheld her. The other night she came to the
dance gaudy with *nature's* ornaments. She
wore no jewels. Every gem she might have
worn would but have hid a charm. Nature
has completed for her a toilet which art can
never rival. She seems to move in a halo of
glory. She has a dowry of pearls but they
are in her mouth . . . she possesses a mind enriched with the gems of intellect, and a conversation brilliant with thought, repartee, and
wit. She is indeed an angel on earth and no
doubt will be an angel in heaven."

Private W. C. McClellan boasted of having found a "shore nuff Sweetheart" who was
"worth $50 thousand dollers, a lady a fine
sence and education" who lived "in a fine
house surrounded by a fine plantation and innumerable slaves and hates the Yankees very
much."

Another Reb who aspired to the affection
of a wealthy girl wrote in dejection to his
sister that he had been "thrust through the
little end of the horn with such violence as
to almost cause contusion." His valedictory
was as follows:

Depth of mercy, can there be
Mercy yet reserved for me
And I could say to that same woman

Of all the etts
I love Brunets
Therefore you I adore
But of all the Etts
I hate coquets
Therefore you I abhor.

Men who wore the gray had an eye for
shapeliness, and some were confessedly over-
whelmed by voluptuousness. But the great
majority considered modesty an indispensable
attribute. Rebs classed as forwardness the
opening of conversation by girls to whom
they had not been properly introduced. There
was one who took exception to the conduct
of an officer's wife on the ground that she
was "a perfect fidget." Another had his faith
in feminine virtue terribly jarred by a woman
presenting him this conundrum: "If a Tumble
Bug can role an ounce ball up a hill perpendicular how much can he sholder on a levell?"

Amorous dalliance was deemed very
gauche—one correspondent observed with disgust that he had "yet to find a lady about
Fredericksburg that will not let a man kiss
and hug them"—but formal betrothal was considered to sanction osculation. "I would have
nothing to do with a young lady that would
not kiss me . . . after we are engaged," remarked an Alabamian; "kissing is the truest
[indication] of love, nothing more so, even
tears," he said, but before engagement "it is
illegal."

Other forms of conduct held in disrepute
were noted by a South Carolinian who was
quartered for a while with a private citizen
having two daughters. The girls were pretty,
he said, but "decidedly fast; the younger about
16, speaks of giving the dogs h-ll & slaps our
faces when we *kiss* her; this same 'gal' climbs
the trees for peaches, rides to mill on a horse
bare back & not with both legs on the same
side but one on each-astraddle."

. . . Some Rebel suitors attempted to en-
hance their prestige among the ladies by thinly
veiled references to the old wounds received
at Bull Run. A few would boast openly of
gallant actions in sundry battles. . . . Suitors
often made pretenses of great wealth and high
social standing. One Reb of ordinary background had the girls all addressing him by the
title of doctor. A Tar Heel private, who

boasted of winning fifteen Virginia sweethearts, wrote thus of his technique:

They thout I was a saint I told thim som sweete lies and they Believed it all for they love a North Carolinian. I will tell you how I talk a round them After I got acquainted with them I would tell them I got a letter from home stating that five of my negroes had runaway and ten of Pappies But I wold say I recond he did not mind it for he had plenty more left and then they would lean to me like a sore eyd kitten to a Basin of Milk.

. . . Some gay youngsters had sweethearts on every hill surrounding camp, and a few extras scattered in the valleys. Harry St. John Dixon, a Mississippi cavalryman who entered the service shortly after leaving the University of Virginia, was among wooers of exceptional prowess. While at Pulaski, Tennessee, in 1863 he listed on a leaf of his diary "the girls I know here" as follows: "Miss Emma Rose, Celest Rose, Amanda Kenery *le belle*, Manella Mosely, Ida Caldwell, Ala Petaway, Eugenia McCord &c."

This tabulation was postscribed with the comment: "O-o-o-o-o-how I lub you gals!!!—You sweet little criters." Dixon had one romance after another of youthful fire and brevity. His journal, covering four years of war, is, in fact, little more than a cataloging of his *affaires du coeur*. At intervals he chided himself for his susceptibility to feminine wiles: "I wish I was not such a fool about women. They have so much influence with me—it is so easy for them to gain the mastery over me." He recorded in his diary:

"Jan. 2, 1864 . . . attended a 'storm' [dance] at Miss Cuny's last evening. . . . Took the 'little humming bird'—the little thing was chattering & smelling camphor all evening—Waltzed with Miss Annie Cozart till my right arm ached. What makes men so impure? Why cannot he have the manhood to resist temptation?—Her little bosom rested pantingly upon mine need I confess that I squeezed a little—just a little bit—soft, convulsive! And something else—our knees—*Diable!*"

. . . In cases when officers refused to grant leaves without tangible proof of forthcoming marriage, Rebs sometimes secured written commitments from their brides-to-be. One such statement, addressed to an Alabamian, was as follows:

If you come home, I'll marey you any time you come home. Love has pierced me with his never erring dart, I yield to you my hart most willingly in wedlock. I with you would gladly jine, and know fer [you] that I never shall repine.

A few who took war brides were not legally entitled to them. "Lit Dooley was married last weak to a Miss Bailey," wrote a Reb from camp in 1864; "he has a wife at home." A Richmond paper in 1863 cited a recent case of bigamy. A young lieutenant had on the same day written a long and affectionate letter to his wife in Louisiana and another of even greater endearment to his Virginia bride of a few weeks who lived near camp. By accident he put the letter of each in the envelope addressed to the other.

. . . Illiterate Rebs sometimes carried on correspondence with sweethearts through amanuenses. Private W. C. McClellan wrote love letters for several comrades in Company F of the Fourth Alabama Regiment. He also read to the suitors the answers which the letters received. McClellan must have been much in demand as a composer and scribe for according to his own statement he succeeded in getting three men engaged in the space of one month. Unfortunately he left no record of his magic formula.

. . .

Certain random types that appeared in Rebel ranks require special notice. Almost every regiment had a braggart who regaled his comrades at every opportunity with tales of his magnificent doings from early childhood. . . . Closely akin was the self-seeker—the man who in private life had perhaps made a splash as a petty politician, and who in the army became hell bent for promotion. . . . Occasionally there was a snob, such as a youngster from Natchez who refused to join one company because it was composed of commoners and who, when he finally joined another, looked down his nose at most of his associates.

"We are two distinct parties," he said on one occasion, "the Aristocrats and the demo-

Union troops enter Richmond after its surrender

crats," and he professed nothing but disdain for the latter. He took offense at his colonel for "putting on airs," ceased saluting him and swore to call him to task after the war for failure to proffer the recognition due one of his high social standing. Another wrote: "It is galling for a gentleman to be absolutely and entirely subject to the orders of men who in private life were so far his inferiors, & who when they met him felt rather like taking off their hats to him than giving him law & gospel."

. . . Eccentrics of various sorts were scattered among the rank and file. An old country gentleman who enlisted in the Twenty-first Virginia took an umbrella to camp, and in sun or rain, on the march and in the field, he insisted on seeking shelter beneath this canopy. . . . Some of the troops who hailed from the West were very rough in appearance. A Louisianian who watched a group of four hundred Texans ride by his plantation reported that they bore no resemblance to soldiers. "If the Confederacy has no better soldiers than those we are in A bad roe for stumps," he said; "they looke more like Baboons mounted on gotes than anything else." . . .

But the average Rebel private belonged to no special category. He was in most respects an ordinary person. He came from a middle-class rural society, made up largely of non-slaveholders, and he exemplified both the defects and the virtues of that background. He was lacking in polish, in perspective and in tolerance, but he was respectable, sturdy and independent. . . .

He complained of the shortcomings of officers, the scantiness of clothing, the inadequacy of rations, the multiplicity of pests and numerous other trials that beset him, but there was little depth to his complaints, and his cheerfulness outweighed his dejection. Adaptability and good-nature, in fact, were among his most characteristic qualities. He was a gregarious creature, and his attachment to close associates was genuine.

He had a streak of individuality and of irresponsibility that made him a trial to officers during periods of inactivity. But on the battlefield he rose to supreme heights of soldierhood. He was not immune to panic, nor even to cowardice, but few if any soldiers have had more than he of *élan*, of determination, of perserverance, and of the sheer courage which it takes to stand in the face of withering fire. He was far from perfect, but his achievement against great odds in scores of desperate battles through four years of war is an irrefutable evidence of his prowess and an eternal monument to his greatness as a fighting man.

"Wearing Out Your Grinders, Eating Goober Peas"

Perhaps the happiest and most carefree of Confederate songs was the famous "Goober Peas." Although eventually published just after the war, it was seemingly a folk creation, which grew up here and there during the hostilities, with varying lines composed at different points and added by individuals or groups.

GOOBER PEAS
Sitting by the roadside on a summer day,
Chatting with my messmates, passing time away,
Lying in the shadow underneath the trees,
Goodness, how delicious, eating goober peas!

Chorus
  Peas! peas! peas! eating goober peas!
  Goodness, how delicious, eating goober peas!

When a horseman passes, the soldiers have a rule,

Jefferson Davis

To cry out at their loudest, "Mister, here's your
    mule,"
But another pleasure enchantinger than these,
Is wearing out your grinders, eating goober peas!

Just before the battle the General hears a row,
He says, "The Yanks are coming, I hear their
    rifles now,"
He turns around in wonder, and what do you
    think he sees?

The Georgia militia eating goober peas!

I think my song has lasted almost long enough,
The subject's interesting, but the rhymes are
    mighty rough,
I wish this war was over, when free from rags
    and fleas,
We'd kiss our wives and sweethearts and gobble
    goober peas!

Antique Harvesters

JOHN CROWE RANSOM

*A native of Pulaski, Tennessee, born in 1888, John Crowe Ransom has won
a high place as a critic and poet of the South, and leader of an important critical
school of poetry. After schooling at Vanderbilt, Mr. Ransom went to England
as a Rhodes Scholar. Returning to the States, he taught at Vanderbilt, then sailed
for France a few years later to fight in World War I as a field artillery lieutenant.
Following the war, he remained in France until 1929, and taught a year at
Saumur Artillery School. Eventually Mr. Ransom became professor of poetry
at Kenyon College, and editor of the* Kenyon Review. *In 1951 he received the
Bollingen prize in poetry. He was one of the original group of Southern agrarians
of the late 20's and early 30's, and a founder of the "I'll Take My Stand" movement. This selection is from his* Selected Poems, *published by Alfred A. Knopf,
Inc., in 1945.*

(Scene: Of the Mississippi the bank sinister,
and of the Ohio the bank sinister.)

Tawny are the leaves turned but they still hold,
And it is harvest; what shall this land produce?
A meager hill of kernels, a runnel of juice;
Declension looks from our land, it is old.
Therefore let us assemble, dry, grey, spare,
And mild as yellow air.

"I hear the croak of a raven's funeral wing."
The young men would be joying in the song
Of passionate birds; their memories are not long.
What is it thus rehearsed in sable? "Nothing."
Trust not but the old endure, and shall be older
Than the scornful beholder.

We pluck the spindling ears and gather the corn.
One spot has special yield? "On this spot stood
Heroes and drenched it with their only blood."
And talk meets talk, as echoes from the horn
Of the hunter—echoes are the old men's arts,
Ample are the chambers of their hearts.

Here come the hunters, keepers of a rite;
The horn, the hounds, the lank mares coursing by
Straddled with archetypes of chivalry;
And the fox, lovely ritualist, in flight
Offering his unearthly ghost to quarry;
And the fields, themselves to harry.

Resume, harvesters. The treasure is full bronze
Which you will garner for the Lady, and the
    moon
Could tinge it no yellower than does this noon;
But grey will quench it shortly—the field, men,
    stones.
Pluck fast, dreamers, prove as you amble slowly
Not less than men, not wholly.

Bare the arm, dainty youths, bend the knees
Under bronze burdens. And by an autumn tone
As by a grey, as by a green, you will have known
Your famous Lady's image; for so have these;
And if one say that easily will your hands
More prosper in other lands.

Stonewall Jackson

Angry as wasp-music be your cry then:
"Forsake the Proud Lady, of the heart of fire,
The look of snow, to the praise of a dwindled
   choir,
Song of degenerate specters that were men?
The sons of the fathers shall keep her, worthy of
What these have done in love."

True, it is said of our Lady, she ageth.
But see, if you peep shrewdly, she hath not
   stopped;
Take no thought of her servitors that have
   dropped,
For we are nothing; and if one talk of death—
Why, the ribs of the earth subsist frail as a breath
If but God wearieth.

The Ode of a Latter-Day Poet

ALLEN TATE

Poet, critic, editor, biographer, essayist, Allen Tate has had a long and rewarding career, and much, although not all, of his work has centered about the South. Born in Kentucky, Mr. Tate attended Vanderbilt University at Nashville and there became a leader of the Agrarian group which produced the much-discussed volume of the 1930's, I'll Take My Stand. *Over a period of many years his influence upon others—students, colleagues, co-workers—has been marked. Of Mr. Tate's many poems particular attention has been drawn by his* "Ode to the Confederate Dead," *from* Poems, 1922–1947, *published by Charles Scribner's Sons, New York, 1948.*

ODE TO THE CONFEDERATE DEAD

Row after row with strict impunity
The headstones yield their names to the element,
The wind whirrs without recollection;
In the riven troughs the splayed leaves
Pile up, of nature the causal sacrament
To the seasonal eternity of death;
Then driven by the fierce scrutiny
Of heaven to their election in the vast breath,
They sough the rumor of morality.

Autumn is desolation in the plot
Of a thousand acres where these memories grow
From the inexhaustible bodies that are not
Dead, but feed the grass row after rich row.
Think of the autumns that have come and gone!—
Ambitious November with the humors of the
    year,
With a particular zeal for every slab,
Staining the uncomfortable angels that rot
On the slabs, a wing chipped here, an arm there:
The brute curiosity of an angel's stare
Turns you, like them, to stone,
Transforms the heaving air
Till plunged to a heavier world below
You shift your sea-space blindly
Heaving, turning like the blind crab.

    Dazed by the wind, only the wind
    The leaves flying, plunge

You know who have waited by the wall
The twilight certainty of an animal,
Those midnight restitutions of the blood
You know—the immitigable pines, the smoky
    frieze
Of the sky, the sudden call: you know the rage,
The cold pool left by the mounting flood,
Of muted Zeno and Parmenides.
You who have waited for the angry resolution
Of those desires that should be yours tomorrow,

You know the unimportant shrift of death
And praise the vision
And praise the arrogant circumstance
Of those who fall
Rank upon rank, hurried beyond decision—
Here by the sagging gate, stopped by the wall.

    Seeing, seeing only the leaves
    Flying, plunge and expire

Turn your eyes to the immoderate past,
Turn to the inscrutable infantry rising
Demons out of the earth—they will not last.
Stonewall, Stonewall, and the sunken fields of
    hemp,
Shiloh, Antietam, Malvern Hill, Bull Run.
Lost in that orient of the thick-and-fast
You will curse the setting sun.

    Cursing only the leaves crying
    Like an old man in a storm

You hear the shout, the crazy hemlocks point
With troubled fingers to the silence which
Smothers you, a mummy, in time.
                    The hound bitch
Toothless and dying, in a musty cellar
Hears the wind only.
                    Now that the salt of their blood
Stiffens the saltier oblivion of the sea,
Seals the malignant purity of the flood,
What shall we who count our days and bow
Our heads with a commemorial woe
In the ribboned coats of grim felicity,
What shall we say of the bones, unclean,
Whose verdurous anonymity will grow?
The ragged arms, the ragged heads and eyes
Lost in these acres of the insane green?
The gray lean spiders come, they come and go;
In a tangle of willows without light
The singular screech-owl's tight

Invisible lyric seeds the mind
With the furious murmur of their chivalry.

We shall say only the leaves
Flying, plunge and expire

We shall say only the leaves whispering
In the improbable mist of nightfall
That flies on multiple wing:
Night is the beginning and the end
And in between the ends of distraction
Waits mute speculation, the patient curse

That stones the eyes, or like the jaguar leaps
For his own image in a jungle pool, his victim.

What shall we say who have knowledge
Carried to the heart? Shall we take the act
To the grave? Shall we, more hopeful, set up the
    grave
In the house? The ravenous grave?
                  Leave now
The shut gate and the decomposing wall:
The gentle serpent, green in the mulberry bush,
Riots with his tongue through the hush—
Sentinel of the grave who counts us all!

A Priest Honors the Confederate Flag

ABRAM JOSEPH RYAN

Among the more remarkable followers of the Southern flag was Father Abram Joseph Ryan, originally of Norfolk, Virginia, a churchman of strong emotion and rare skill in declamation—a favorite postwar figure to thousands of audiences. Long-haired, spectacular in look and manner, Father Ryan withstood bad health during the war to serve continuously as a Southern chaplain. Since his death many have echoed his words as they recited one of his best-known works, "The Conquered Banner."

Furl that Banner, for 'tis weary;
Round its staff 'tis drooping dreary;
  Furl it, fold it, it is best;
For there's not a man to wave it,
And there's not a sword to save it,
And there's not one left to lave it
In the blood which heroes gave it;
And its foes now scorn and brave it;
  Furl it, hide it—let it rest.

Take that banner down! 'tis tattered;
Broken is its staff and shattered;
And the valiant hosts are scattered
  Over whom it floated high.
Oh! 'tis hard for us to fold it;
Hard to think there's none to hold it;
Hard that those who once unrolled it
  Now must furl it with a sigh.

Furl that Banner! furl it sadly!
Once ten thousands hailed it gladly,
And ten thousands wildly, madly,
  Swore it should forever wave;
Swore that foeman's sword should never
Hearts like theirs entwined dissever,
Till that flag should float forever
  O'er their freedom or their grave!

Furl it; for the hands that grasped it,
And the hearts that fondly clasped it,
  Cold and dead are lying low;
And that Banner—it is trailing!
While around it sounds the wailing
  Of its people in their woe.

For, though conquered, they adore it!
Love the cold, dead hands that bore it!
Weep for those who fell before it!
Pardon those who trailed and tore it!
But, oh! wildly they deplore it,
  Now who furl and fold it so.

Furl that Banner! True, 'tis gory,
Yet 'tis wreathed around with glory,
And 't will live in song and story,
  Though its folds are in the dust:
For its fame on brightest pages,
Penned by poets and by sages,
Shall go sounding down the ages—

  Furl its folds though now we must.
Furl that banner, softly, slowly!
Treat it gently—it is holy—
  For it droops above the dead.
Touch it not—unfold it never,
Let it droop there, furled forever,
  For its people's hopes are dead!

A Meeting at Appomattox

DOUGLAS SOUTHALL FREEMAN

A masterly re-enactment of a fateful hour for the Confederacy was achieved by Dr. Douglas Southall Freeman in one of the climactic passages of his monumental R. E. Lee, a Biography, *Charles Scribner's Sons, New York, 1935–47. Basing his pages on meticulous research, official records and reports of witnesses, Dr. Freeman told of Lee's painful hours of final decision which led to Appomattox Courthouse. His passages here have been often discussed, often quoted. Dr. Freeman also wrote the massive* Lee's Lieutenants *and a full biography of George Washington.*

GRANT already had offered, it will be remembered, to have the surrender arranged through officers designated for that purpose, in order that the Confederate leader might be spared humiliation, but Lee probably never thought of passing on to others this unpleasant task. He meant literally what he had said . . . that he would go to General Grant and surrender himself and take the consequences of his act. Marshall thought that Lee subconsciously was impelled to this personal surrender by reason of his father's unfavorable reference in his *Memoirs* to Cornwallis's failure to appear on the day of the surrender at Yorktown. . . .

On such a mission as he was now about to begin, Lee naturally would be accompanied by his adjutant general and by his military secretary, but Colonel Taylor had no heart for being present at a surrender. He begged off on the ground that he already had ridden twice through the lines that morning. Lee excused him with his usual consideration for the feelings of others. In the company of Marshall, Babcock and Tucker, the daring orderly, Lee started up the hill, and beyond the thin and silent line of battle on the hillside. At the stream, Traveller wanted to drink. Lee waited until his faithful mount had his fill. Then he went on.

How often he had ridden that strong steed and in scenes how various! Up Malvern Hill, when the very earth seemed alive with the crawling wounded; over Thoroughfare Gap while "Stonewall's" guns were growling, and after the spinning wheels of the pursuing guns at Second Manassas; across South Mountain; among the bloody ridges of the Antietam; with the mists enveloping him at Fredericksburg; confident and calm when the cheering thousands acclaimed him in the woods of Chancellorsville; out on the hill at Gettysburg; along the mournful byways of the Wilderness; down the Telegraph road toward Cold Harbor; over the James and over that same Appomattox, sullen and tawny, at Petersburg. Jackson had ridden with him, the battle light in his eyes, the laughing Stuart, the nervous Hill, the diligent Pender, the gallant Rodes—all of them dead now, and he alone, save for those silent companions, was on his last ride as commander of the Army of Northern Virginia. Thirty-nine years of devotion to military duty had come to this . . . and this, too, was duty.

As the little cavalcade passed toward the village of Appomattox, Lee had to arouse himself and arrange the details: Grant had left it to him to select the place of meeting. Would Marshall go ahead and find a suitable house? Obediently, the colonel trotted off. Lee remained with Babcock. They did not talk—how could they?

After a while the orderly returned to say that Colonel Marshall had found a room for the conference. Lee went on and, under the soldier's guidance, drew rein beyond the courthouse in the yard of a house on the left-hand

Robert E. Lee

side of the road to Lynchburg. The residence belonged to Major Wilmer McLean, who, by the oddest chance, had owned the farm on Bull Run where, in the first battle of that name, the initial clash had occurred. Major McLean had removed from that exposed position and had purchased a property at Appomattox—only to find that the march of the armies he had sought to avoid was now about to end, as it had begun, at his door.

Lee dismounted in the yard and after the orderly took Traveller, he walked toward the wide steps that led to the covered porch which ran the whole width of the house. Entering the central hall, at the top of the steps, he turned into the front room on his left, a typical parlor of a middle-class Virginia home. Colonel Marshall went with him. Colonel Babcock accompanied Lee, also, with the explanation that as General Grant would soon arrive, the orderly could easily direct him to the place. Lee walked diagonally across the room and sat down close to a small table in the corner beyond the front window and farthest from the hall. He put his hat and gauntlets on the table, and there he waited. Babcock and Marshall remained in the room and, no doubt, seated themselves at his invitation.

Town-burning marked Sherman's passage from Atlanta to Raleigh.

Half an hour passed, perhaps the longest half hour in Lee's whole life. If there was any conversation, it was in snatches and was slow, labored, and vague. About 1:30 o'clock there was a clatter in the road, the sound of the approach of a large body of mounted men. They drew nearer, they halted, they dismounted. Some of them climbed the steps. Babcock went to the door and opened it. A man of middle height, slightly stooped and heavily bearded, came in alone. He was dressed for the field,

with boots and breeches mud-bespattered. He took off his yellow thread gloves as he stepped forward.

Lee had never seen him to remember him but he knew who he was and, rising with Marshall, he started across the room to meet General Grant. They shook hands quietly with brief greetings. Then Grant sat down at the table in the middle of the room, and Lee returned to his place. Marshall stood to the left and somewhat behind him. Babcock had a few whispered words with Grant, then went from the room and out on the porch. He soon was back, followed by a full dozen Federal officers, Sheridan and Ord among them. These new-comers arranged themselves behind Grant and in sight of Lee as quietly as boots and spurs and clanking swords permitted. Grant made no reference to their coming. Lee showed no sign of resentment at their presence.

The conversation began: "I met you once before, General Lee," Grant said in his normal tones, "while we were serving in Mexico, when you came over from General Scott's headquarters to visit Garland's brigade, to which I then belonged. I have always remembered your appearance, and I think I should have recognized you anywhere."

"Yes," answered Lee quietly, "I know I met you on that occasion, and I have often thought of it and tried to recollect how you looked, but I have never been able to recall a single feature."

Mention of Mexico aroused many memories. Grant pursued them with so much interest and talked of them so readily that the conversation went easily on until the Federal was almost forgetting what he was about. Lee felt the weight of every moment and brought Grant back with words that seemed to come naturally, yet must have cost him anguish that cannot be measured.

"I suppose, General Grant," he said, "that the object of our present meeting is fully understood. I asked to see you to ascertain upon what terms you would receive the surrender of my army."

Grant did not change countenance or exhibit the slightest note of exultation in his reply. "The terms I propose are those stated substantially in my letter of yesterday—that is, the officers and men surrendered are to be paroled and disqualified from taking up arms again until properly exchanged, and all arms, ammunition and supplies to be delivered up as captured property."

Lee nodded an assent that meant more than his adversary realized. The phantom of a proud army being marched away to prison disappeared as Grant spoke, and the hope Lee had first expressed to Taylor that morning was confirmed. "Those," said he, "are about the conditions I expected would be proposed."

"Yes," Grant answered, "I think our correspondence indicated pretty clearly the action that would be taken at our meeting; and I hope it may lead to a general suspension of hostilities and be the means of preventing any further loss of life."

That, of course, was a theme that Lee's conception of his duty as a soldier would not permit him to discuss. It was his to obey orders and to direct the forces in the field. The civil authorities had the sole power, he held, to make peace of the sort General Grant had in mind. So he merely inclined his head again.

Grant talked on of peace and its prospects. Lee waited and then, courteously, but in a manifest desire to finish the business in hand, he said: "I presume, General Grant, we have both carefully considered the proper steps to be taken, and I would suggest that you commit to writing the terms you have proposed, so that they may be formally acted upon."

"Very well, I will write them out."

Lee sat in silence and looked straight ahead as Grant called for his manifold order-book, opened it, lit his pipe, puffed furiously, wrote steadily for a while with his pencil, paused, reflected, wrote two sentences and then quickly completed the text. Grant went over it in an undertone with one of his military secretaries, who interlined a few words. Lee did not follow any of this. He sat as he was until Grant rose, crossed to him, and put the manifold book in his hands, with the request that he read over the letter.

Lee probably was at his tensest then, for he busied himself with little mechanical acts as though to master his nerves. He placed the book on the table. He took his spectacles from his pocket. He pulled out his handkerchief. He wiped off the glasses, he crossed his legs, he set his glasses very carefully on his nose, and then he took up the order book for a slow, careful reading:

Appomattox C. H. Va.
April 9th, 1865

"Gen. R. E. Lee,

"Comd. C. S. A.

"Gen.

"In accordance with the substance of my letter to you of the 8th instant I propose to receive the surrender of the Army of N. Va. on the following terms, to-wit:

"Rolls of all the officers and men to be made in duplicate, one copy to be given to an officer designated by me, the other to be retained by such officer or officers as you may designate. The officers to give their individual paroles not to take up arms against the"

—At this point Lee turned the page and read on—

"Government of the United States until properly and each company or regimental sign a like parole for the men of their command."

Lee stopped in his reading, looked up, and said to Grant: "After the words 'until properly,' the word 'exchanged' seems to be omitted. You doubtless intended to use that word."

"Why, yes," answered Grant, "I thought I had put in the word 'exchanged.'"

"I presumed it had been omitted inadvertently, and with your permission I will mark where it should be inserted."

"Certainly."

Lee felt for a pencil, but could not find one. Colonel Horace Porter stepped forward and offered his. Lee took it, thanked him, placed the book on the table, inserted the caret, and resumed his reading:

"The arms, artillery and public property to be parked and stacked and turned over to the officer appointed by me to receive them.

"This will not embrace the side arms of the officers, nor their private horses or baggage. This done, each officer and man will be allowed to return to their homes not to be disturbed by the United States authority so long as they observe their paroles and the laws in force where they may reside.

Very respectfully,

U. S. GRANT, Lt. Gl."

There was a slight change in Lee's expression as he read the closing sentences, and his tone was not without warmth as now he looked up at Grant and said: "This will have a very happy effect on my army."

"Unless you have some suggestions to make in regard to the form in which I have stated the terms," Grant resumed, "I will have a copy of the letter made in ink and sign it."

Lee hesitated: "There is one thing I would like to mention. The cavalrymen and artillerists own their own horses in our army. Its organization in this respect differs from that of the United States. I would like to understand whether these men will be permitted to retain their horses."

"You will find," answered Grant, "that the terms as written do not allow this. Only the officers are allowed to take their private property."

Lee read over the second page of the letter again. For months he had agonized over his field transportation and cavalry mounts. He knew what the army's horses would mean to the South, stripped as it had been of all draft animals, and he wanted those of his men who owned mounts to have them for the spring ploughing. His face showed his wish. His tongue would not go beyond a regretful "No, I see the terms do not allow it; that is clear."

Grant read his opponent's wish, and, with the fine consideration that prevailed throughout the conversation—one of the noblest of his qualities, and one of the surest evidences of his greatness—he did not humiliate Lee by forcing him to make a direct plea for a modification of terms that were generous. "Well, the subject is quite new to me. Of course, I did not know that any private soldiers owned their animals, but I think this will be the last battle of the war—I sincerely hope so—and that the surrender of this army will be followed soon by that of all the others, and I take it that most of the men in the ranks are small farmers, and as the country has been so raided by the two armies, it is doubtful whether they will be able to put in a crop to carry themselves and their families through the next winter without the aid of the horses they are now riding, and I will arrange it this way: I will not change the terms as now written, but I will instruct the officers I shall appoint to receive the paroles to let all the men who claim to own a horse or mule to take the animals home with them to work their little farms."

It could not have been put more understandingly or more generously. Lee showed manifest relief and appreciation. "This will have the best possible effect upon the men," he said, "it will be very gratifying and will do much toward conciliating our people."

While Grant set about having his letter copied, Lee directed Marshall to draft a reply. In the wait that followed, Grant brought up and introduced the officers who had remained silent in the background. Lee shook hands with those who extended theirs and bowed to the others, but he spoke only to General Seth Williams, a warm friend during his superintendency at West Point. He talked to Williams without apparent effort, but when that officer introduced a pleasantry of the old days, Lee had no heart for it. He could not jest as his army was surrendering and his country dying. He only inclined his head ever so little at Williams' joke, and he did not smile. When Colonel Parker was presented, it seemed to Horace Porter that General Lee looked at him longer than at the others. It was Porter's belief that General Lee thought the Indian a negro and was surprised to find an African on Grant's staff.

When the introductions were over, Lee turned again to Grant. "I have a thousand or more of your men as prisoners, General Grant, a number of them officers whom we have required to march along with us for several days. I shall be glad to send them into your lines as soon as it can be arranged, for I have no provisions for them. I have, indeed, nothing for my own men. They have been living for the last few days principally upon parched corn, and are badly in need of both rations and forage. I telegraphed to Lynchburg, directing several train loads of rations to be sent on by rail from there, and when they arrive I should be glad to have the present wants of my men supplied from them."

There was a stir among the listeners at this remark, and they looked at Sheridan, for, unknown to Lee, he had the previous night captured at Appomattox Station the rations that had come down from Lynchburg. Those that had been sent up from Farmville had been found by the Federals farther down the road. Grant did not add to Lee's distress by a recountal of these seizures. He merely said, "I should like to have our men within our lines as soon as possible. I will take steps at once to have your army supplied with rations, but I am sorry we have no forage for the animals. We have to depend upon the country for our supply of forage. Of about how many men does your present force consist?"

Lee reflected for a moment: "Indeed, I am not able to say. My losses in killed and wounded have been exceedingly heavy, and besides, there have been many stragglers and some deserters. All my reports and public papers, and indeed, my own private letters, had to be destroyed on the march to prevent them from falling into the hands of your people. Many companies are entirely without officers, and I have not seen any returns for several days; so that I have no means of ascertaining our present strength."

Grant had estimated Lee's numbers at 25,000 and he asked, "Suppose I send over 25,000 rations, do you think that will be a sufficient supply?"

"I think it will be ample," Lee is said by Horace Porter to have replied. "And it will be a great relief, I assure you," he added instantly. Colonel Marshall's memory of Lee's answer was that he said 25,000 rations would be "more than enough."

General Sheridan then came forward and requested that he might copy two dispatches he had sent Lee that day, in such a hurry that he had not written them out for his records. These dispatches were protests against alleged violations of the truce. Lee took out the dispatches from his pocket and said he was sure that if the truce had been violated it was through a misunderstanding.

By this time, Marshall had finished his draft of Lee's acceptance of Grant's terms of surrender. It began with a sentence that would indicate that the agreement had been reached by correspondence. Lee modified this because he thought it would create a false impression. He made, perhaps, a few other changes, and

An on-the-scene sketch of Confederates capturing disabled guns at Gaines Mills

Union troops entering the mined streets of Fredericksburg on December 11, 1862,
looking for anything still left to pillage

then he had Marshall copy the document. The Federals had borrowed Marshall's ink in order to write their answer, and now, Marshall, having no paper with him, had to procure some from their stock.

The finished letter was now brought Lee and was read over by him:

"Lieut-Gen. U. S. Grant,

"Commanding Armies of the United States.

"General: I have received your letter of this date containing the terms of surrender of the Army of Northern Virginia as proposed by you. As they are substantially the same as those expressed in your letter of the 8th instant, they are accepted. I will proceed to designate the proper officers to carry the stipulations into effect.

Very respectfully, your obedient servant."

Lee put his signature to this without a quiver. Marshall signed it and went over to Parker, who already had Grant's letter waiting for him, duly signed and in an addressed envelope. They made the exchange and the surrender was complete. It was then about 3:45 P.M.

The rest was casual and brief. Grant explained why he was without his sword. Lee is said to have remarked that he usually wore his when with the army in the field. Then Lee requested that Grant notify Meade of the surrender, so that firing might not break out and men be slain to no purpose. He requested also, that pending the actual surrender, the two armies be kept separate, so that personal encounters would be avoided. Grant acquiesced immediately and suggested that time might be saved if two of his officers rode to Meade through the Confederate lines.

Lee thereupon rose, shook hands with General Grant, bowed to the spectators and passed from the room. He went through the hall to the porch, where several Federal officers at once sprang to their feet and saluted. Putting on his hat, Lee mechanically but with manifest courtesy returned their salute and with measured tread crossed the porch. At the head of the steps he drew on his gauntlets, and absently smote his hands together several times as he looked into space—across the valley to the hillside where his faithful little army lay. In a moment he aroused himself and, not seeing his mount, called in a voice that was hoarse and half-choked, "Orderly! Orderly!" Quickly Tucker answered from the corner of the house, where he was holding Traveller's rein as the steed grazed. Lee walked down the steps and stood in front of the animal while the man replaced the bridle. Lee himself drew the forelock from under the brow band and parted and smoothed it. Then, as Tucker stepped aside, Lee mounted slowly and with an audible sigh. At that moment General Grant stepped down from the porch on his way to the gate, where his horse was waiting. Stopping suddenly, Grant took off his hat, but did not speak. The other Federals followed the courteous example of their chief. Lee raised his hat, without a word, turned his horse and rode away to an ordeal worse than a meeting with Grant—the ordeal of breaking the news to his soldiers and of telling them farewell.

By no means all the men were prepared for the surrender. The rapidity of the retreat, the failure of rations, and the dwindling of brigades to companies had spelled disaster in the minds of the intelligent. The circle of fire reflected on the clouds the night of the 8th had convinced the discerning that the army was virtually surrounded. The halt of the morning and the frequent passage of flags of truce had confirmed their fears of capitulation. Yet such was the faith of the army in itself and in its commander that many were unwilling to believe the end had come.

Lee came toward them, down from the ridge, across the little valley, up the hillside through the pickets, and into the line. He was as erect as ever, but he was staring straight ahead of him, with none of the cheerfulness and composure that usually marked his countenance even in the most dreadful moments of his hardest battles. The men started to cheer him, as they often did when he rode among them, but somehow their cheers froze in their throats at the sight of him. They hesitated a moment as he rode fixedly on, and then without a word they broke ranks and rushed toward him.

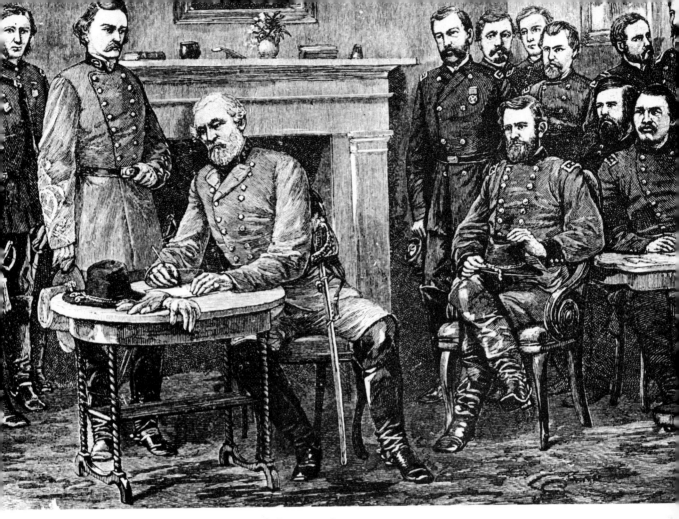

Lee and Grant at Appomattox

"General," they began to cry, "are we surrendered?"

The question was like a blow in the face. He tried to go on, but they crowded about him, bareheaded. He removed his hat in acknowledgment and attempted once more to proceed. The road was too full of frenzied, famished faces. He had to halt and answer his loyal old soldiers. "Men," he said, "we have fought the war together, and I have done the best I could for you. You will all be paroled and go to your homes until exchanged." Tears came into his eyes as he spoke. He attempted to say more but even his amazing self-mastery failed him. Moving his lips in a choking "good-bye," he again essayed to ride on to the orchard from which he had come.

"General, we'll fight 'em yet," they answered.

"General, say the word and we'll go in and fight 'em yet."

Everywhere, as the news spread, each soldier reacted to it in his own fashion. Some wept, openly and without abashment. Others were dazed, as though they did not understand how the Army of Northern Virginia, Lee's army, could surrender. To Field's division, which had suffered little on the retreat, it seemed incomprehensible. To others, it was as the very end of the world. "Blow, Gabriel, blow!" cried one man, and threw down his musket as General Grimes told him what had happened. "My God, let him blow. I am ready to die!"

Some blasphemed and some babbled, but all who could do so crowded to say farewell to Lee. Catching hold of his hands, they looked up at him and cried the more. They touched his uniform or his bridle rein, if they could not grasp his hand, and if they could not reach him they smoothed Traveller's flank or patted his neck. And in a confused roar, half-sob, half-acclamation, they voiced their love for him, their faith in him, their good-bye to him as their commander. . . .

The sun was now near its setting. The immediate duties were done. Lee mounted Traveller and started toward his headquarters, which were under a large white oak, about a mile to the rear. As he went, the scenes of his return from the interview with General Grant were repeated in heightened pathos. For now the whole army knew that the surrender had occurred, and most of the intelligent men had been given time to reflect what that act meant to him who was, in their eyes, both cause and country. "There was," Blackford wrote, "a general rush from each side of the road to greet him as he passed, and two solid walls of men were formed along the whole distance. Their officers followed, and behind the lines of men were groups of them, mounted and dismounted, awaiting his coming. . . . As soon as he entered this avenue of these old soldiers, the flower of the army, the men who had stood to their duty through thick and thin in so many battles, wild, heartfelt cheers arose which so touched General Lee that tears filled his eyes and trickled down his cheeks as he rode his splendid charger, hat in hand, bowing his acknowledgments. This exhibition of feeling on his part found quick response from the men whose cheers changed to choking sobs as, with streaming eyes and many evidences of affection, they waved their hats as he passed. Each group began in the same way, with cheers, and ended in the same way, with sobs, all along the route to his quarters. Grim, bearded men threw themselves on the ground, covering their faces with their hands, and wept like children. Officers of all ranks made no attempt to conceal their feelings, but sat on their horses and cried aloud. . . . Traveller . . . took as much pleasure in applause as a human being, and acknowledged the cheers of the troops by tosses of his head and the men frequently cheered him for it, to which he would answer back as often as they did. On this, Traveller's last appearance before them, his head was tossing a return to the salutes all along the line. . . . One man . . . extended his arms, and with an emphatic gesture said, "I love you just as well as ever, General Lee!"

They thronged about him when he reached his headquarters, and when he dismounted all who were in sight of his camp hastened up.

"Let me get in," they began to cry. "Let me bid him farewell."

Lee stood with Long and Stevens and a few other old personal friends, and he sought to keep his composure, but as man after man crowded around him, each with warm words, his eyes filled anew with tears. In broken phrases he told his veterans to go home, to plant a crop and to obey the law, and again and again he tried to say farewell. But they would not have it so. One handsome private, a gentleman in bearing, for all his dirt and rags, shook hands and said, "General, I have had the honor of serving in this army since you took command. If I thought I were to blame for what has occurred today, I could not look you in the face, but I always try to do my duty. I hope I have the honor of serving under you again. Good-bye, General; God bless you."

On the instant another gripped his fingers. "Farewell, General Lee," he said, "I wish for your sake and mine that every damned Yankee on earth was sunk ten miles in hell!" This forthright profession relieved the strain. In the stir that followed, Lee lifted his hat once more in salute and went to his tent . . . to be alone.

A Time of Family Trouble After Shiloh

STARK YOUNG

For the delicacy of its writing, an almost luminous quality that permeates it, Stark Young's novel, So Red the Rose, *has won praise in many circles. It had a nationwide reception when it was published in 1942 by Charles Scribner. In this rich, intricately patterned work, Mr. Young's pictures of pre-war and wartime life, characters and also "characters" are intimate and sympathetic. A native of Mississippi, Mr. Young taught English there, in New York and in Texas. Mr. Young is the author of poems, dramatic and critical works and a short story. He may be remembered longest, however, for this work and for his* Heaven Trees. *The passage which follows is taken from a scene after the Battle of Shiloh, when the bodies of three Confederates are returned to Mississippi.*

WHEN Valette, with the two children, reached Montrose in the evening, they saw three coffins on the front gallery. The stench had made that necessary. On the floor stood saucers of charcoal. The ends of the coffins rested on chairs. Mrs. Bedford had left Portobello soon after daylight and Valette saw her with Mrs. Quitman, Mr. Balfour and another gentleman who had his back turned her way as she came up to the steps. They were watchers with the dead.

The two children at the sight of the coffins clung to Valette's skirts. "Lette, which is Cousin Edward?" Middleton whispered, drawing her down to his little ears.

"Hush, precious, you must keep quiet. Lette doesn't know, Cousin Edward's not there—that's only— Come, let's sit over here." She led them to a seat at the far end of the gallery, partly to keep them from seeing the men standing inside the graveyard wall. There were three men, two of them Negroes, and Black Dave was waiting outside the gate with a spade on his shoulder. The children on each side of her put their arms through Valette's, shutting their lips tight, and sat looking around them, and then into each other's eyes. Their mother left the other watchers and tiptoed over to that end of the gallery with her finger on her lips.

"You must be good chillun," she said, "do what Valette tells you."

Middleton slid off the bench and put up his arms to embrace her. "Aunt Sallie, which is Cousin Edward?" he whispered, "which is Cousin Edward, Aunt Sallie?"

"Sh! He's the one at this side. You mustn't talk—"

"No, m'am." He took away his arms and sat down on the bench again, never taking his eyes off the coffin that she had spoken of. She watched him a moment and then, brushing her hand across her cheek, leaned down and kissed his brow. "Yes, my darlin'."

Valette learned that the second coffin was the Hammond boy from West Feliciana Parish, the other was from that parish also and of the same company; but there was no trace of his name on the coffin. Charlie Taliaferro had never been found; in the confusion, the tents being destroyed, the retreat, nobody knew what had happened to him.

When Valette heard that, tears sprang into her eyes and began to run down her cheeks. She caught Mrs. Bedford's hand.

"Charlie Taliaferro, My Dumplin'?"

"Yes, poor thing! But you hardly knew him, honey. It's just the way war is."

"But if he were alive they would know it."

"We're talking about your cousin Charlie Taliaferro, honey," Valette said to Middleton. She laid her hand on his.

"I know you are," said the little boy, looking at her strangely, as if to say that he knew more than she thought.

"Valette, you haven't heard how 'twas, I reckon," Mrs. Bedford said. "Well, they wouldn't let Agnes go on the field, 'twas night already. But old William Veal stole out there. And he went over the field, feeling all the hair of all the dead till he found Edward, he knew him by his hair. You know how fine it was. Yes, so that's it. And then, after they left Jackson last night, it was so dark that they stopped at a house and got one of those piny woods people to ride ahead of them on a white horse. So they could follow along the road. That's how dark it was. So the man rode ahead on those blind roads and they followed."

Mary Hartwell, hearing this and seeing the expression on Valette's face, began to sob, making almost no sound; and Valette took her on her knees, pressing the child to her bosom and whispering to her; and then looking up at Mrs. Bedford as if to say they should not have brought the children.

"If Mary Hartwell cries," her mother said, patting the little shoulder, "we'll have to take her home, do you hear, Hartie, hear what Mamma says? But I think 'twas right to bring them. They ought to be here and see—they ought to see it with us."

"My Dumplin', do you know where Lucy is?"

"No, I haven't seen her. But I'm going in now, I ought to."

"If you see her—everybody'll be with Aunt Agnes and Uncle Hugh. My Dumplin', if you see Lucy, you talk to her."

A number of people arrived in carriages or on horseback, and came up the steps and indoors. A few remained on the lawn and presently went down to wait at the cemetery. After a few minutes some one opened a window, and Valette could see into the parlor where Agnes and Hugh McGehee were with their friends. Valette gazed into the room and thought it seemed older and sadder there than it was on the gallery, where the dead men lay in their coffins, heaped with flowers. The air stirred the leaves, the sun shone bright over the lawns and fields.

The two children leaned against Valette, talking in low tones about their Cousin Edward. She could feel their little heads pressed against her, like birds. But she did not hear quite what they were saying. She sat looking vaguely in front of her. "Blessed are they that die in the Lord—" She had heard that often, but now for the first time, she said to herself, she understood it. To die in the Lord meant to die young, tender, beautiful, all that love is.

Making a Yankee Out of Him

J. BRYAN, III

J. Bryan, III, a member of a leading Richmond family, is a superlative anecdotist, a descendant of Confederates with a bright glint of humor in his typewriter. One of his most successful stories is this one from his The Sword Over the Mantel, *published in 1960 by McGraw-Hill Company of New York.*

THE scene is Charlottesville, the seat of Albemarle County, Virginia; the time is early in the Reconstruction; the occasion is the first election after The War.

A veteran of Old Jack's "foot cavalry" came down from the hills to vote, and was dismayed to learn that under a new law, he would first have to swear allegiance to the Union.

He protested, but the registrar was firm: no oath, no vote. Grudgingly, he took the oath. Disconsolately, he asked, "Does that make me a Yankee?"

"If you want to look at it that way."

His face brightened. He slapped the registrar's shoulder. "Boy, didn't Old Jack beat hell out of us in the Valley of Virginia?"

"The Antique Earth Returned Out of the Past"

SIDNEY LANIER

Sidney Lanier, the poet, spoke these words at memorial services for Robert E. Lee, at Macon, Georgia, on October 12, 1870.

SIR, the last time that I saw him with mortal eyes—for, with spiritual eyes, many, many times have I contemplated him since,—the scene was so beautiful, the surroundings were so rare, nay, time and circumstances did so fitly frame him as it were, that I think the picture should not be lost. There was nothing melodramatic in the circumstances, nothing startling, nothing sensational: which was all the more particularly in accord with his character, for this was one of those grand but modest, sweet souls that love simplicity and shrink from all that is loud and vulgar.

It was at fateful Petersburg on one glorious Sunday morning, whilst the armies of Grant and Butler were investing our last stronghold there. It had been announced, to those who happened to be stationed in the neighborhood of General Lee's headquarters, that religious services would be conducted on that morning, by Major General Pendleton, of the artillery. At the appointed hour I strolled over to Dunn's Hill, where General Lee's tent was pitched, and found General Pendleton ensconced under a magnificent tree, and a small party of soldiers with a few ladies from the dwellings nearby, collected about him.

In a few moments, General Lee appeared, with his camp chair, and sat down. The services began. That terrible battery number five was firing, very slowly, each report of the great guns making the otherwise profound silence still more profound. Even Hoke's line was quiet. I sat down on the grass, and gazed, with such reverence as I had never given to mortal man before, upon the grand face of General Lee.

He had been greatly fatigued by loss of sleep. As the sermon progressed, and the immortal words of Christian doctrine came to our hearts and comforted us, sweet influences born of the liberal sunlight that lay warm upon the grass, of the waving leaves and trembling flowers, seemed to steal over the General's soul. Presently his eyelids gradually closed, and he fell gently asleep.

Not a muscle of him stirred, not a nerve of his grand countenance twitched, there was no drooping of the head, nor bowing of the figure, and I could not have been sure that he really slept had I not observed that a venturesome fly crawled unheeded upon his brow. As he slumbered so, sitting erect with arms folded upon his chest in an attitude of majestic repose such as I never saw assumed by mortal man before: as the large and comfortable words fell from the preacher's lips; as the lazy cannon of the enemy anon hurled a screaming shell to within a few hundred yards of where we sat, as finally a bird flew into the tree overhead and sat and piped small blissful notes in unearthly contrast with the roar of the war machines; it seemed to me as if the present earth floated off through the sunlight, and the antique earth returned out of the past, and some majestic god sat on a hill, sculptured in stone, presiding over a terrible yet sublime contest of human passions. . . .

"The Losers Always Remember Longer..."

HODDING CARTER

Of a Louisiana-Mississippi background, Hodding Carter has contributed writings over a wide field—analyses of the South, appraisals of race relations, history, a novel. A well-recognized speaker, Mr. Carter has addressed many groups on themes relating to the South and the liberal faith. In 1959 Doubleday and Company published his The Angry Scar, *in the Mainstream of America Series, edited by Lewis Gannett. A part of the book appears here.*

EIGHTY years have gone by since the white Democrats of Louisiana and South Carolina traded off austere Samuel Tilden for Republican surrender of control of state, county, and community governments in those states; and it is nearly seventy years since the careful Southern legalists began fashioning the state constitutions which would insure in perpetuity, so they believed, white political rule no matter how greatly the white citizenry might be outnumbered by the challenging Negro.

Since then our nation has fought two major and two lesser wars and has become inextricably involved in a world revolution of ideology and of race. Experimental man has produced the ultimate tools for the destruction or the transformation of life on his planet. So much has almost every aspect of American life been altered that many of us, in fear or hope for tomorrow, forget today the crises of yesterday.

But the memory of Reconstruction endures meaningfully among nearly thirty million white Americans in the South and, to a considerably less extent, among the ten million Southern Negroes. The yet livid scar of Reconstruction also affects, if indrectly, one hundred and twenty million other Americans and, most certainly, many other people elsewhere who have never heard of Thaddeus Stevens of Pennsylvania or of South Carolina's Wade Hampton or of Louisiana's White Leagues. Millions of distant, dark-skinned folk have been continuously aroused against the United States by contemporary incidents within our borders which have their remote origins in Reconstruction itself.

In our day the scar's outline may have seemed to grow fainter. But with the crucial decision of the United States Supreme Court to reverse all earlier related rulings, and so make illegal the continuance of racially separate public school systems, old specters took menacing shape again, and so quickly that we know surely that they had never really vanished. The same resolutions offering resistance to national authority are being adopted today as if time since 1876 had stood still. Let the rest of the nation speak in indignation to the South for an unpunished racial murder or in protest against the denial of the ballot or in rebuke for disobedience of the Supreme Court's edict, and the voices of most of the South's politicians, much of its press, and even some among its educators and churchmen, sound the grim echoes from the unforgotten past.

Leave us alone . . . It's our problem and

we know how to handle it . . . Clean up your own backyard first . . . This is a white man's country . . . Interposition . . . Nullification . . . Go to Hell . . .

Despite historical re-evaluations—and how soon or how often have the records of history altered folklore?—the cherished tales and convictions and stereotypes have persisted. *We were needlessly humiliated, men still say in the South as if they were talking of yesterday; Yankee retaliation after the surrender violated all civilized conduct, for never before had the foot of the ignorant slave been placed by white hands upon the necks of a defeated enemy who was also white . . . All thieving is evil but the thief who steals from the hungry and the helpless, with a policeman at his side and the government urging him on, is the worst of all thieves . . . The education of the ignorant is a worthy objective, but not a policy of education which abandons to the spoilsmen the established institutions and concentrates upon an educational revolution . . . The Southern white man who linked his fortune with the Northern interloper was a Scalawag, a predatory renegade to caste and race or a poor white hating his betters. The Northerner who came down hungrily was a graceless adventurer with all that he owned packed in a carpetbag, his single piece of luggage; and his only purpose was to enrich himself and to debase the South by forcing racial intermingling and even intermarriage . . . The Negro politician was an ignorant buffoon, a stupid tool, a defiant savage, intent only upon getting what he could, lusting for the women of his former masters and ready to sell his vote and his soul itself for anything but a Confederate dollar . . . The Yankee churchmen knew only the God of wrath and came to desecrate and to offer a spurious Christianity to the Negro and to destroy their white brothers in Christ . . . The Ku Klux Klan of Reconstruction and all who turned to the rifle and the faggot, the rope and the lash in the name of white supremacy were the South's saviors; heroic, consecrated men whose ghostly riding alone kept alive the hope of white survival . . .*

The proportion of fact to fable varies with the purposes of the narrators and the severity of the old or new experience about which the tales revolve. The former Confederate soldier might have confided to a crony over a tall julep, seventy-five years ago, that he had had an odd sort of liking for the Yankee who settled down on the next farm to his after the war. But this he would not shout from the hustings. A minister in an Alabama church of Reconstruction might have admitted privately that the invading Yankee Methodists had a sincere if misguided sense of divine mission. He could not say this to his congregation, then or even now, without furious challenge.

A story about two young American college students who were on a bicycle tour of Ireland one summer during the troubles of the 1920s is applicable here. The unhappy island was wracked by assassinations, executions, and guerilla warfare between the Irish Republican Army and the British-directed constabulary, the Black and Tans. One day the travelers halted in a small village not far from Dublin for a mug of beer. They were soon in conversation with an old Irish woman who had recognized them as Americans and had inquired about her kinsman in Boston. Soon she was telling tales of British perfidy and tyranny.

"And do ye know what was done to three hundred poor Irish lads only a stone's throw from this very place?" she demanded. The Americans said they did not know.

"They were burned to death at the stake, poor lads, every mother's son of them!"

"My God," answered one of the listeners, wondering how they had missed such a story in the newspapers. "And when did this awful thing take place?"

The old woman's voice quivered with rage. "Cromwell did it," she shrilled, "the dirty, murdering dog."

And that's that. The losers always remember strife and ruin and abuse far longer and more imaginatively than do the victors, whether they dwell in Ireland or India or Georgia; and eighty years do not seem so long when we consider that men presently in their prime and occupying places of political leadership in the South today were born no later than midway between the beginning of Reconstruction and now. As boys and young men they heard the patriarchal—and matriarchal—tales told and believed by teller and hearers as unchallenged proof of Yankee avarice and vengeance and Southern suffering and heroism. And no matter how filmy the stuff of which some of the tales are spun, they cannot be laughed away.

There are other reasons for the survival of Reconstruction memories. Military disaster dealt a profound psychological blow to a people who had produced and followed the nation's only warrior caste and had believed themselves militarily invincible. And in the wake of Appomattox came the enormous complications and chaos attendant upon the need to revise a slave-based agricultural economy which no longer existed as such. The freeing of the slaves had wiped out more than two billion dollars in once negotiable investments. The destruction of the South's railways and rolling stock and much of its scant industry, and the prewar neglect of its industrial potential in favor of cotton, left the South no other road to recovery than agriculture. The lack of a continuing national program to rehabilitate the former slave, and to aid the dispossessed master, the small non-slaveholding farmer, and the urban worker retarded the region's economic recovery.

The Freedmen's Bureau which sought to provide the Negro with employment and food and medical and hospital care and to resettle the wandering masses was staffed too much by ambitious political mediocrities, by incompetents, and by some thieves, and it failed to win support from the affronted whites. Instead the Bureau was added to the wrathful legend.

More important than these material stimuli to the South's long memory was the political convulsion which enfranchisement of the Negro brought about. To military chastisement and economic chaos were joined a revolutionary political realignment and an ultimatum to the South. Never before had a nation or a people been put into political irons concurrently with the unshackling of an imprisoned multitude, different in race, culturally disparate, and untrained for freedom.

Moreover, some of the aggravations that accompanied the beginning of the Reconstruction era were needlessly petty, stupid, shortsighted, or cruel. The removal of the proscribed military buttons from uniforms which were all so many had to wear . . . The seizure of Southern churches for the use of ministers of Northern denominations . . . The requirement of the loyalty oath from Southern women when they appeared at a military headquarters to seek rations or assistance. These things were remembered. Forgotten were the generosity with which Northern charitable groups soon aided destitute Southerners; the generally good relations between white federal occupation troops and the people, and the selflessness of the Yankee schoolteachers whose efforts to educate the Negroes had, in time, beneficial results. The wrath and the shame of the white Southerners were heightened by the knowledge that their fellow white men, their very brothers, were elevating the black men to political equality. The South was not so much galled by the political corruption of Reconstruction as it was by the fact of Negro participation, free of Southern direction, in the region's political life. Even had the neophyte Negro lawmakers been uniformly honest and capable, they would have been resented almost as much; for such honesty contradicted the white man's concept of the Negro in politics. What was basically intolerable was the knowledge that the white Radical Republicans in Washington and in the Southern states were principally responsible for the Negro on the bench, in the legislature, and in Washington itself, and especially so since the Southerner read into the demands for Negro suffrage and political acceptance a social meaning which was unacceptable to him.

The negation of the Radical philosophy of Negro political equality thus became and remained the first consideration of Southern white leadership which emerged in reaction to Radical Reconstruction policies. The restoration of white domination—which had been threatened seriously in its political aspects but hardly at all in the economic or social spheres —took precedence over all else, over material needs, basic political cleavages within the white group, and even honesty in government itself.

The racial aspect of the Reconstruction struggle doomed all programs of the Radicals and left tragic legacies which have not yet been expended or likely will be in our time. The legacies are fourfold—political, cultural, economic, and moral. . . .

The South in its bitterness and the North in its disinterest are alike unaware of the temporary or lasting achievements of the Reconstruction invaders. The Carpetbag administration did assure free school systems to both races, the first to be provided not only for Negroes but for many of the whites. Their record in public school expansion was, in general, and despite accompanying corruption, better than were the performances of the Redemptionist administrations which followed Reconstruction, and, for that matter, better than the public educational achievements of the prewar South where the novel idea of free, mass education had not caught on. The Reconstruction administrations also sought, with at least temporary success, to widen the democratic base. The constitutions which they adopted provided for efficient changes in the taxing systems and the judiciary, and some of their reforms were kept intact in the constitutions of the white Redemptionists. They introduced new social services to an area chronically lacking in them. Their efforts to rebuild war-destroyed roads, schools and public buildings were commendable.

This is not to say that on balance the good outweighed the bad. It did not; but had the constructive record been far better, Radical Reconstruction would nevertheless have failed. The refusal of the white South to accept the new status of the Negro was the principal and the only needful reason.

What were the other reasons for the failure? High among these was the watering down of initial Radical idealism. The zealots gave way to the practical politicians and the plunderers, so that in time the nation, no less than the South, began to sicken of the looting that was as marked in the North, dur-

ing the Grant administration, as it was anywhere in the Southern states.

Another reason, and a telling one, was the absence of a lasting program for the material rehabilitation of the freed Negro. His benefactors were chiefly concerned with him as a political force, and eventually he found this out. Republican manipulation of the Negro voter ultimately aroused Northern sympathy for the Southerners and strengthened the resurgent Democratic party. The roughshod tactics of the Carpetbaggers made it impossible for them to enlist any appreciable support from the Southern white leadership. In time thousands of Negro voters in the South also became wary of their Republican bosses; and, because of their disillusion or through Democratic coercion and bribery, they entered the party of their former masters. . . .

More often than not the middle-aged and older Southerner—the son or grandson of Confederate and Redeemer—is aggressively regional-minded about almost everything. He looks upon himself as a citizen of a nation within a nation and acts accordingly. His near single-minded concentration upon his problems and his biases cannot be ascribed solely to Reconstruction, but the period provided its most durable motivation. He has inherited and retained his Reconstruction forebears' suspicion of the critical stranger, the inquisitive writer, the agent of a central government, and the visiting student of his affairs. He is distrustful of the younger generation's talk of "moderation" of his insistence upon racial separateness.

His solidarity is at the same time healthy and disruptive. In his self-conscious homogeneity he gives his strongest loyalties to the family, the clan, the community and the region; and in a day of centralization of regulatory functions and of metropolitan anonymity, these localized and individualistic concerns often make for a needed balance. When he dwells upon his past, which is rather often, he prefers folklore to fact if fact is unpalatable; and when reason goes against his convictions he is likely to discard reason. In his loyalties and his hatreds he is an extremist. He is acutely sensitive to criticism even when he denies that he is even attentive to it; and he is convinced, and with considerable reason, that his region is misunderstood, his problems minimized, and his good intent doubted elsewhere. His homeland has produced more than its share of creative folk, but few have escaped the confines of regionalism. He has been diverted by his racial concerns from broader and more purposeful considerations. He suffers still from the intellectual impoverishment experienced during Reconstruction because of necessary preoccupation with political and economic survival.

Even though his region peculiarly reflects a political genius, his political legacy has not enriched him. Save for the relatively brief period of Populist-Bourbon conflict over yet unresolved issues, his politics mirror primarily the factionalism inevitable in a one-party society, the racial compartmentalization within which his leaders work, and a unity based on race, without reference to economic goals and needs.

Yet social consciousness, which survives today, was characteristic of most of the new breed of demagogues of the post-Reconstruction period. They were aware of the plain people and of the need for social reform. But they struck brutally at the Negro, either from actual distaste or for fear of being tarred as "nigger lovers" and disrupters of white unity. Of all the notable Southern demagogues only Huey P. Long of Louisiana did not make the Negro a whipping boy. So the Southerner continues to insist upon one-party conformity —at least on state and local levels—for the very logical reason that should the Southern whites be divided, the Negro could hold the balance of power within the region just as he does in a half dozen or more Northern states. The white South regained political control during Reconstruction in great part through bloodshed and corruption, and it has remained relatively indifferent to corruption and inefficiency in its political life so long as its white Democratic foundations are not threatened.

The economic impact of Reconstruction has also persisted. Since the North devised no alternate program, the Southerner of Reconstruction had no other choice at Reconstruction's outset than to make the new relationship between freed black worker and impoverished landowner as nearly like the old system as possible. He usually wanted it that way anyhow, if only because of a preference for the familiar. In his traditional indifference to other commercial pursuits than the raising of cotton, tobacco, rice, and sugar, he permitted his forests to be destroyed and much of his other natural resources appropriated by the Northern financier and speculator. Because of his political peonage and the long national dominance of the Republican party he could do nothing against the high tariffs which further disadvantaged him. He accepted and even encouraged the idea that the lower the wage scale the better, primarily because he was unwilling for the Negro to receive in other competitive pursuits the wages that he was both reluctant and unable to pay him in the cotton field. The plantation system and the competitive presence of the landless white and the Negro discouraged the immigrant who could have brought new talents and determination. Post-Reconstruction's small farm owner and poor white submitted to economic exploitation by the bankers, the lawyers, and the generals, the planter aristocracy, partly because these had been their wartime leaders and mostly because, before and after the Populist lapse, they became convinced again that salvation lay in racial solidarity.

How long will the memory of the Reconstruction periods affect the South and the nation? There can be no certain answer. The South is reacting in predictable fashion to old and new racial pressures. The doctrine of nullification has been advanced as fervently as it was ever propounded by John C. Calhoun. Today the Southern moderate is as suspect as were his Reconstruction prototypes. Today a more determined Negro is again faced by a nearly unified white South no less determined than in 1868 to circumvent the intent of the Federal government. Today the singing of "Dixie," the waving of a Confederate flag, and the stump orator's passionate appeal to the past are as sure fire as in the 1870s. And the end is not in sight.

VI

"An Era Had Ended, An Era Had Begun"

IT SEEMS only a few years ago that H. L. Mencken, with a perceptible sniff, made his often-quoted remark: "Alas for the South! Her books have grown fewer—She never was much given to literature." As a matter of fact, the Baltimorean Mr. Mencken could himself be classified as a Southerner, and others have observed that he did a generous service to various Southerners by calling attention to the work of James Branch Cabell and others. But the point is that if such a statement as his were remotely applicable at the time, only a fool would concur in it today.

In the past fifteen or twenty years the South has become—suddenly, as some view the matter—the "writingest part of America," producing a remarkable quality and quantity of works. By almost general agreement among appraisers of books, it has in William Faulkner America's most powerful novelist of today and one of the great writers of the current century. In Robert Penn Warren it presents a commentator of brilliant stature; in Eudora Welty, Katharine Anne Porter and a few others, a group of the nation's rare stylists. With Douglas Southall Freeman the South has provided the nation with a biographer-historian of major stature. With Erskine Caldwell the region has given the world a novelist-short story writer who has the greatest international readership of any American of today. And there are others, many others. . . .

The number of such generally applauded literary figures is such that, as the saying has gone, more Southerners may appear to be writing books than are reading them. This statement, like Mr. Mencken's, does not hold water; Richmond and Atlanta, Dallas and Houston, Memphis and a half dozen others are good book cities; with its Cokesbury organization, for instance, Dallas can claim the country's biggest book agency under one roof.

How has this come about? Even the most chauvinistic individual must admit that the pre-1860 South was not notable for literary works. There may have been a few good reasons for that fact. Largely the region was rural, with only a few cities advancing slowly to true size. It may be argued that rural civilizations do not tend to nurture book writing or writing of other varieties. As has many times been observed, the earlier Southerners gave their energies to speechmaking, to oratory and debate.

The traditional Southerner grew crops or joined the military (or did both things in turn). In the 1800's, as war with the North came gradually nearer, men who might have produced books were directed toward politics, and those who did write were pressed by others, or by their own impulses, into defenses of slavery against free labor, agrarianism against business and industry.

Literary activity was, also, an even less fashionable or acceptable calling than in most other parts of America. Even in recent years the tale is repeated of a Richmond figure whose picture appeared with an account of his first volume. Sadly a dowager spoke: Wasn't it a shame about so-and-so composing a book? And he came from such nice people, too. . . .

To be sure, the earlier South did produce or help produce some admirable literary figures: Poe, Sidney Lanier, eventually Mark Twain, and also a well-filled school of humorous writers of the robust frontier or close-to-the-frontier area: Joseph G. Baldwin of *The Flush Times of Alabama and Mississippi*, Augustus B. Longstreet and a good-sized group of similarly vigorous observers of the less elegant folk.

In the beginning years, a number of on-the-scene settlers or explorers had recorded their impressions with zest or in simple good reporting. At a later period William Byrd did much astringent writing; yet a major part of his output was never published during his lifetime. Men like Jefferson set down their views and philosophies in works of a general political interest. A number of naturalists described the South in volumes of value—William Bartram's travels, for instance, and John James Audubon's notations on animals and men.

Largely, however, Southern writing of the pre-1860 period tended toward angry defenses or saccharine, oversentimental fiction, in clear (but also pale) imitation of Walter Scott. Even in such cases the average Southerner who read failed even to glance at the works of his fellow natives. There was more than a handful of hard-working individuals like William G. Simms, who died impoverished, in spiritual defeat.

During much of the last century America's literary development centered about New England. Then for a time it seemed that New York was the focus of the nation's writing. Today it might be demonstrated that the South produces a heavy share of America's most-applauded literary work.

Yet why would states with low general rates of literacy, low economic standing and other cultural ratings to match, achieve the distinction of such a writing group? No one can give a certain answer, a completely convincing explanation. The evolution of a perceptive, penetrating mind may be an eternal, ever-individual mystery. And still the environment, the physical, emotional, psychic setting, has an inevitable part in the creation of any writer or school of writers.

Whatever other qualities the twentieth-century South has as a background, it may well possess assets for writers which grow out of the scenes and events of the sort outlined in previous passages of this book. For the South has long been a locale of clash and conflict, the meeting, often with abrasive effect, of classes and nationalities and races, of cabin owner and proprietor of the big house. It has been part of a frontier, but one upon which a certain culture had been imposed in places. It had people who lived remote, isolated lives in swampside huts a few miles from others who enjoyed luxury or at least an impressive plenty, who went twice a year to New Orleans or Memphis or Savannah, and to Europe for an occasional six-month period. And at their side, as always, were the Negroes, influencing the masters and themselves influenced during every waking hour.

Then, too, as C. Vann Woodward has pointed out in a notable essay, of all parts of America the South is the only one which has known defeat in war, the consequences of military loss, the grimness of slow, long-lived-out poverty. Perhaps alone among the people of the world, he notes, those of the United States enjoy "illusions of innocence" drawn from their national childhood, leading to sometimes "impetuous" and "naïve" assumptions about national and international matters. By contrast, the Southerners through many years have tasted tragedy, sick disappointment, gnawing uncertainty.

For other Americans the past seldom comes so close. From their first days, Southerners have lived a simpler existence, a generally rural one, with less constant contact with people of different experiences, other beliefs. "Primitive," some may have called their life; it was not quite that, but it was carried on against the background of more ancient ways, less changing scenes and settings. For the Southerner his history has been close at hand, so that it could almost be touched with the fingers, like ornate wallpaper in a fading living room, or a painted panel in a hallway along the Tennessee or the Tombigbee River. Whatever he does, whatever he thinks, perhaps, will be influenced by the quiet voices of earlier times, by the memory, however dim, of acts performed in another century, by a half-forgotten grandfather laboring over a rude cabin in the pine barrens, by an eccentric aunt in Pensacola or Mobile.

Today, as in past years, the South is a place of stories, the Southerner a man or woman who can tell a tale with skill. Anecdotes, yarns ridiculous or pathetic or of several possible implications . . . the average literate, and not necessarily only the book-literate person, has a store of stories to make the head of a newcomer spin. A man who cannot read can still fill out a masterful tale. All such recollections, all such stories, are part of the hidden heritage, the folk experience, of the native of the South.

It is also a place of considerable humor—heavy, delicate, making its point with a belly laugh or a light implication. Oratory remains on the Southerner's tongue or in his pen. And—in a way that some strangers think most phenomenal of all—the Southerner still talks at full tilt, full command, with raging energy and something approaching dedication. In the words of a Philadelphian who moved to Baton Rouge, Louisiana: "The conversation! I've never heard anything like it. Sometimes my forehead hurts, but it hurts in a nice way."

Such has been the scene, such the influences which may have helped create such diverse Southern writers as Thomas Wolfe, Jesse Stuart, Ellen Glasgow, Tennessee Williams, Elizabeth Spencer, John Gould Fletcher, Julia Peterkin, DuBose Heyward, Paul Green, Marjorie Rawlings, T. S. Stribling, Ben Burman, John Crowe Ransom, Allen Tate, John Peale Bishop, Flannery O'Connor, Caroline Gordon, Shelby Foote, Gerald Johnson, Ralph McGill, Calder Willingham, Harper Lee, Ovid Pierce, Lyle Saxon, Robert Tallant, Shirley Grau, Harriette S. Arnow, Roark Bradford, R. Emmett Kennedy, Hubert Creekmore, Archibald Henderson, James Street, Frances Newman, Donald Davidson, Herman Clarence Nixon, Andrew Nelson Lytle, John Donald Wade, Frank L. Owsley, Lon Tinkle, David Westheimer, and others.

In one twenty-four-hour period a caller may find the earlier South and another South struggling to be born; a plain, casual-mannered farmer and a graceful plantation woman in riding costume; a dusty, riverside landing unchanged from that of a century ago; a frontier-style scene, with men around a stove, preparing for a hunt near the marsh; accounts of mass brutalities of seventy-five years past, and also of colossal family rivalries and rages; evidences of a shattering hurricane or another catastrophe of nature; an eccentric whose mind is halted at a day a quarter century earlier; a group of semi-outcasts living near a marsh, their coloration an odd one, supposedly part white, part Indian, part Negro. Often the place is one of tensions, of frustrations revolving about a family clan or an explosive individual. Always, through the years, the crops thrust unendingly above the ground, are unendingly harvested and replanted again. Howard Odum* summed it up in terms of the present century:

An era had ended. An era had begun. Old golden pages of history, shining parchment records of culture, then yellow and faded, scorched and seared with years of embattled conflict, and epic struggle. . . . Gallant figures on black horses and white . . . and crude, simple folk, sore with the footfall of time, passing across an epoch which was to be destroyed by physical and cultural conflagration and to rise up again in another American Epoch. . . . Cultures in the making, social processes at work, portraiture descriptive of how civilizations grow. All the South's yesterdays, with their brilliant episodes and their sordid pictures receding, giving way to the South's tomorrows. . . .

Both the old and the new culture abounded in sharp contrasts and logical paradoxes. There were many Souths yet *the* South. It was pre-eminently national in backgrounds, yet provincial in its processes. There were remnants of European culture framed in intolerant Americanism. There were romance, beauty, glamor, gayety, comedy, gentleness, and there were sordidness, ugliness, dullness, sorrow, tragedy, cruelty. There were wealth, culture, education, generosity, chivalry, manners, courage, nobility, and there were poverty, crudeness, ignorance, narrowness, brutality, cowardice, depravity. The South was American and un-American, righteous and wicked, Christian and barbaric. It was a South getting better, a South getting worse. It was strong and it was weak, it was white and it was black, it was rich and it was poor. . . .

*An American Epoch, New York, Henry Holt Company, 1930.

Red Neck, Burr Head

JONATHAN DANIELS

Immediate best-sellerdom greeted A Southerner Discovers the South, *by Jonathan W. Daniels, on its publication in 1938, establishing the basis of a long literary career for the editor of the Raleigh, North Carolina,* News and Observer. *A trenchant but also a graceful author, a student of men and issues, Mr. Daniels has written, among other books,* Tarheels, *a portrait of his state;* A Southerner Discovers New England; The Man of Independence. *He has been assistant director of the Office of Civil Defense, press secretary and also administrative assistant to the President of the United States. The selection is from* A Southerner Discovers the South, *published by the Macmillan Company, New York.*

WE Southerners are, of course, a mythological people. Supposed to dwell in moonlight or incandescence, we are in part to blame for our own legendary character. Lost by choice in dreaming of high days gone and big house burned, now we cannot even wish to escape. We may not even be found. Certainly the land called South is no realm for geographers. I know. There are two old ladies in Sussex County, Delaware, who are as certain that they are Southerners on Southern soil as are any four persons who live on Bull Street in Savannah. There is a dirt farmer deep in Texas who preserves the plantation pattern with a fidelity impossible in Virginia.

And I have talked with men and women fixed in big houses on Red Mountain at Birmingham and on Paces Ferry Road in Atlanta who never in any true sense could be Southern. They make the land Yankee by stepping on it. The Gulf and Atlantic are fairly dependable borders. But the Potomac and the Mississippi cannot with the slightest accuracy bound a Dixie which, if it contains anything Southern, must include a yellow fellow who roasts oysters on the Eastern Shore of Maryland, the Boston Club in New Orleans and a well-advanced case of pellagra which I had the privilege of observing in southeastern Arkansas. . . .

Such a South as I found! Mountain and Piedmont and Coastal Plain. I rode it. I ate Oysters Rockefeller in New Orleans on the very day old man John D. Rockefeller died in Ormond, Florida. I lay on my belly in the Arkansas dust and changed a tire on the hottest summer day. I waited at night, while the tree toads sang, for the ferry to come following the Mississippi up an avenue of forest through which the waters of the spring rise had spread. I talked with governors and professors, with male and female patriots, with labor leaders and industrialists, educators and uplifters, engineers and chemists, and foresters and physicians.

They told me solemn things, true things maybe. But I also talked to hitch-hikers and tenant farmers, to filling station operators, hill billies and Delta planters, to poets, and bartenders, to Syrians in Vicksburg and Cajuns in Louisiana, to a lovely, starry-eyed, aristocratic young woman in love with a liquor salesman, to a drunkard who lives and buys his liquor on the quarter-dollars which tourists give him for seeing the big house which his ancestors built, and everywhere to the Negroes. . . . There are as many Souths, perhaps, as there are people in it. Maybe the only certain South is the addition of all the Southerners. . . .

For good or for ill, being a Southerner is like being a Jew. And, indeed, more needs to be written about the similarity of the minds and the emotions of the Jew, the Irishman, the Southerner, and perhaps the Pole, as a basis for the better understanding of each of them and of them all. There is, of course, the sense of exile; homesickness is entirely possible to those who remain on the homeland. All of them have mastered the art of breast beating. All of them hold up history between the world and their personal deficiencies. And all of them have succeeded in making themselves fascinating to other folk. . . .

The South naturally, like each of the others, deviates in details from the common pattern. The South is two races. Uncle Tom is as essential as the Colonel; burr head is as indispensable as redneck. The South would not be anywise what we feel and mean when we say the round word "South" without the Negro. Without the white man it might be Africa. The white Southerner without the Negro would certainly be different. Perhaps a warm Kansan. Fortunately, I think, both of them are what they are, though each of them is a long way from perfection. Like Siamese twins they can be cut apart only with the possibility of killing.

A Southerner Probes the South's Mind

W. J. CASH

A book of powerful impact, W. J. Cash's The Mind of the South *is one of the most sustained and most penetrating critiques of the region's attitudes which has yet appeared in America. While many did not concur in its conclusions, they have read it, debated it at length, and cited it. Born in 1901 in South Carolina, Mr. Cash was reared in North Carolina and served on college papers there. As a youth, he said, he often daydreamed that he carried a Confederate battle banner. Assigned to write of a textile mill strike during the depression of the 1930's, he reported that his experiences changed his earlier conservatism. At various times he worked on farms, drove a truck and fired boilers. Eventually he became associate editor of the Charlotte* News. *His death in 1941, the same year his book was published, was a tragedy to the South. The volume was published by Alfred A. Knopf of New York.*

WHOLLY apart from the strict question of right and wrong, it is plain that slavery was inescapably brutal and ugly. Granted the existence, in the higher levels, of genuine humanity of feeling toward the bondsman; granted that, in the case of the house-servants at least, there was sometimes real affection between master and man; granted even that, at its best, the relationship here got to be gentler than it has ever been elsewhere, the stark fact remains: It rested on force. The black man occupied the position of a mere domestic animal, without will or right of his own. The lash lurked always in the background. Its open crackle could often be heard where field hands were quartered. Into the gentlest houses drifted now and then the sound of dragging chains and shackles, the bay of hounds, the report of pistols on the trail of the runaway. And, as the advertisements of the time incontestably prove, mutilation and the mark of the branding iron were pretty common.

Just as plain was the fact that the institution was brutalizing—to white men. Virtually unlimited power acted inevitably to call up, in the coarser sort of master, that sadism which lies concealed in the depths of universal human nature—bred angry impatience and a taste for cruelty for its own sake, with a strength that neither the kindliness (it continued frequently to exist unimpaired side by side, and in the same man, with this other) nor notions of honor could effectually restrain. And in the common whites it bred a savage and ignoble hate for the Negro, which required only opportunity to break forth in relentless ferocity; for all their rage against the "white-trash" epithet concentrated itself on him (the Negro) rather than on the planters. . . .

With all these characteristics established, we are in a position to turn to the examination of the South's claim to a superior culture. Or, more correctly . . . to that claim so far as it relates to culture in the narrow sense—to intellectual and aesthetic attainments. And in this respect it may be said without ceremony that it was perhaps the least well founded of the many poorly founded claims which the Southerners so earnestly asserted to the world and to themselves and in which they so warmly believed.

I know the proofs commonly advanced by apologists—that at the outbreak of the war the section had more colleges and students in those colleges, in proportion to population, than the North; that many planters were ready and eager to quote you Cicero or Sallust; that Charleston had a public library before Boston, and its famous St. Cecilia Society from the earliest days; that these Charlestonians, and with them the older and wealthier residents of Richmond and Norfolk and New Orleans, regularly imported the latest books from London, and brought back from the grand tour the paintings and even the statuary of this or that fashionable artist of Europe; that, in the latest days, the richest among the new planters of the deep South began to imitate these practices; that in communities like those of the Scotch Highlanders in the Cape Fear country there were Shakespeare libraries and clubs; that Langdon Cheves of South Carolina is reported by Joseph LeConte to have discussed the idea of evolution in private conversation long before *The Origin of Species;* and so on *ad infinitum.*

But such proofs come to little. Often, as they are stated, they are calculated to give a false picture of the facts. Thus, the majority of the colleges were no more than academies. And of the whole number of them perhaps the University of Virginia alone was worthy to be named in the same breath with half a dozen Yankee universities and colleges, and as time went on, even it tended to sink into a hotbed of obscurantism and a sort of fashionable club, propagating dueling, drinking, and gambling.

Thus again, the general quoting of Latin, the flourish of "Shakespeare says," so far from indicating that there was some profound and esoteric sympathy with the humanities in the South, a deliberate preference for the Great Tradition coming down from the ancients, a wide and deep acquaintance with and understanding of the authors quoted, really means only this, it seems to me: that the great body of men in the land remained continuously under the influence of the simple man's almost superstitious awe for the classics, as representing an arcanum beyond the reach of the ordinary.

And over and behind these considerations lies the fact that the South far overran the American average for (white) illiteracy—that not only the great part of masses but a considerable number of planters never learned to read and write, and that a very great segment of the latter class kept no book in their houses save only the Bible.

But put this aside. Say that the South is entitled to be judged wholly by its highest and its best. The ultimate test of every culture is its productivity. What ideas did it generate? Who were its philosophers and artists? And—perhaps the most searching test of all—what was its attitude toward these philosophers and artists? Did it recognize and nurture them when they were still struggling and unknown?

One almost blushes to set down the score of the Old South here. If Charleston had its St. Cecilia and its public library, there is no record that it ever added a single idea of any notable importance to the sum total of man's stock. If it imported Mrs. Radcliffe, Scott, Byron, wet from the press, it left its only novelist, William Gilmore Simms, to find his reputation in England, and all his life snubbed him because he had no proper pedigree. If it fetched in the sleek trumpery of the schools of Van Dyck and Reynolds, of Ingres and Houdon and Flaxman, it drove its one able painter, Washington Allston (though he was born an aristocrat), to achieve his first recognition abroad and at last to settle in New England.

And Charleston is the peak. Leaving Mr. Jefferson aside, the whole South produced, not only no original philosopher but no derivative one to set beside Emerson and Thoreau; no novelist but poor Simms to measure against the Northern galaxy headed by Hawthorne and Melville and Cooper; no painter but Allston to stand in the company of Ryder and a dozen Yankees; no poet deserving the name save Poe—only half a Southerner. And Poe, for all his zeal for slavery, it despised in life as an inconsequential nobody; left him, and with him the *Southern Literary Messenger*, to starve, and claimed him at last only when his bones were whitening in Westminster churchyard.

Certainly there were men in the Old South of wide and sound learning, and with a genuine concern for ideas and, sometimes, even the arts. There were the old Jeffersons and Madisons, the Pinckneys and the Rutledges and the Henry Laurenses, and their somewhat shrunken but not always negligible descendants. Among both the scions of colonial aristocracy and the best of the newcomers, there were men for whom Langdon Cheves might stand as the archetype and Matterhorn—though we must be careful not to assume, what the apologists are continually assuming, that Cheves might just as well have written *The Origin of Species* himself, if only he had got around to it. For Darwin, of course, did not launch the idea of evolution, nor yet of the struggle for existence and the survival of the fittest. What he did was laboriously to clarify and organize, to gather and present the first concrete and convincing proof for notions that, in more or less definite form, had been the common stock of men of superior education for fifty years and more. . . .

To be sure, there were such men in the South: men on the plantation, in politics, in the professions, in and about the better schools, who, in one degree or another, in one way or another, were of the same general stamp as Cheves. There were even men who made original and important contributions in their fields, like Joseph LeConte himself, one of the first of American geologists; like Matthew Fontaine Maury, author of *Physical Geography*

of the Sea, and hailed by Humboldt as the founder of a new science; like Audubon, the naturalist. And beneath these were others: occasional planters, lawyers, doctors, country schoolmasters, parsons, who, on a more humble scale, sincerely cared for intellectual and aesthetic values and served them as well as they might.

But in the aggregate these were hardly more than the exceptions which proved the rule—too few, too unrepresentative, and, above all, as a body themselves too sterile of results very much to alter the verdict.

In general, the intellectual and aesthetic culture of the Old South was a superficial and jejune thing, borrowed from without and worn as a political armor and a badge of rank; and hence (I call the authority of old Matthew Arnold to bear me witness) not a true culture at all.

This is the fact. The reason for it is not too far to seek. If we were dealing with the cotton South alone, one might be tempted to think, indeed, that it resides wholly in the question of time, in the consideration I have emphasized, that there were but seventy years between the invention of the cotton gin and the outbreak of the Civil War. But even here the answer is hardly adequate; in view of the wealth and leisure ultimately afforded the master class, in view of the fact that the second generation had largely grown up in this wealth and leisure, one might have expected, even though this cotton South had stood quite alone, to find a greater advance, something more than the blank in production we actually find.

But we are not dealing with the cotton South alone, of course. As we have sufficiently seen, it was the Virginians, too. Here was the completed South, the South in flower—a South that, rising out of the same fundamental conditions as the great South, exhibiting, with the obvious changes, the same basic pattern, and played upon in the first half of the nineteenth century by the same forces, had enjoyed riches, rank, and a leisure perhaps unmatched elsewhere in the world, for more than a hundred years at least; a South, therefore, which, by every normal rule, ought to have progressed to a complex and important intellectual culture, to have equaled certainly, probably to have outstripped, New England in production, and to have served as a beacon to draw the newer South rapidly along the same road. And if it did none of these things, why, then, we shall have to look beyond the factor of time for a satisfactory explanation, not only of its barrenness but, to a considerable extent, of that of the great South also.

In reality, the reason is immanent, I think, in the whole of Southern life and psychology. Complexity in man is invariably the child of complexity in environment. The desire for knowledge when it passes beyond the stage of being satisfied with the most obvious answer, thought properly so called, and, above all, aesthetic concern, arise only when the surrounding world becomes sufficiently complicated to make it difficult or impossible for human energies to escape on a purely physical plane, or, at any rate, on a plane of direct activity. Always they represent, among other things, a reaching out vicariously for satisfaction of the primitive urge to exercise of muscle and nerve, and achievement of the universal will to mastery. And always, too, they feed only upon variety and change. Whence it is, no doubt, that they have never reached any notable development save in towns, and usually in great towns.

But the Southern world, you will remember, was basically an extremely uncomplex, unvaried, and unchanging one. Here economic and political organization was reduced to its simplest elements. Here were no towns to rank as more than trading posts save New Orleans, Charleston, Richmond, and Norfolk; here, perhaps, were no true towns at all, for even these four (three of which were scarcely more than overgrown villages) were rather mere depots on the road to the markets of the world, mere adjuncts to the plantation, than living entities in their own right, after the fashion of Boston and New York and Philadelphia. Here was lacking even that tremendous ferment of immigration which was so important in lending variety to the rest of the American scene. And here everywhere were wide fields and blue woods and flooding yellow sunlight. A world, in fine, in which not a single factor operated to break up the old pattern of outdoor activity laid down on the frontier, in which, on the contrary, everything conspired to perpetuate it; a world in which even the Virginian could and inevitably did discharge his energies on the purely physical plane as fully as his earliest ancestor in the land; a world in which horses, dogs, guns, not books, and ideas and art, were his normal and absorbing interests.

And if this was not enough? If his energies and his ambition demanded a wider field of action? He went, in this world at battle, inescapably into politics. To be a captain in the struggle against the Yankee, to be a Calhoun or a Brooks in Congress, or, better still, to be a Yancey or a Rhett ramping through the land with a demand for the sword—this was to be at the very heart of one's time and place, was, for the plantation youth, full of hot blood, the only desirable career. Beside it the pursuit of knowledge, the writing of books, the painting of pictures, the life of the mind, seemed an anemic and despicable business, fit only for eunuchs. "Why," growled a friend of Philip Pendleton Cooke, Virginia aristocrat and author of the well-known lyric, *Florence Vane*, "why do you waste your time on a damned thing like poetry? A man of your position could be a useful man"—and summed it up exactly.

But it was not only the consumption of available energy in direct action. The development of a considerable intellectual culture requires, in addition to complexity of environment, certain predisposing habits of mind on the part of a people. One of these is analysis. "*L'état de dissociation des lieux communs de la morale semble en corrélation assez étroite avec le degré de la civilization intellectuelle,*" says Remy de Gourmont—and says truly. Another is hospitality to new ideas. Still another is a firm grip on reality; and in this connection I am not forgetting the kind of art which is called romantic and the more fanciful varieties of poetry; in so far as they are good, in so far as they are truly art, they also must rise ultimately from the solid earth. And, finally, there is the capacity, at least, for detachment, without which no thinker, no artist, and no scholar can do his work.

But turn back now and examine the South

in the light of this. Analysis is largely the outcome of two things: the need to understand a complex environment (a consideration already disposed of) and social dissatisfaction. But, as we are aware, satisfaction was the hallmark of Southern society; masters and masses alike were sunk in the deepest complacency; nowhere was there any palpable irritation, any discontent and conflict, and so nowhere was there any tendency to question. Again, being static and unchanging, the South was, of course, an inherently conservative society— one which, under any circumstances, would have naturally been cold to new ideas as something for which it had no need or use. As for the grip on reality, we know that story fully already. Imagination there was in plenty in this land with so much of the blood of the dreamy Celt and its warm sun, but it spent itself on puerilities, on cant and twisted logic, in rodomontade and the feckless vaporings of sentimentality. And as for detachment, the South, you will recall, was, before all else, personal, an attitude which is obviously the negation of detachment. Even its love of rhetoric required the immediate and directly observable satisfactions of speech rather than the more remote ones of writing.

There is still more here. As well as having nothing to give rise to a developed intellectual culture, as well as having much that was implicitly hostile, much that served as a negative barrier, the Old South also had much that was explicitly hostile and served as a quite positive barrier. The religious pattern will come to mind at once. Theologians have everywhere been the enemies of analysis and new ideas, and in whatever field they have appeared—feeling, quite correctly, that, once admitted, there is no setting limits to them. And in this country in which the evangelical ministers had already won to unusual sway, in which they had almost complete control of the schools, in which they had virtually no opposition, they established their iron wall with an effectiveness which went well beyond even its American average.

But the greatest force of all was the result of conflict with the Yankee. In Southern unity before the foe lay the final bulwark of every established commonplace. And the defense of

slavery not only eventuated, as we have seen, in a taboo on criticism; in the same process it set up a ban on all analysis and inquiry, a terrified truculence toward every new idea, a disposition to reject every innovation out of hand and hug to the whole of the *status quo* with fanatical resolution. Detachment? In a world in which patriotism to the South was increasingly the first duty of men, in which coolness about slavery was accounted treason, it was next to impossible.

In sum, it was the total effect of Southern conditions, primary and secondary, to preserve —but let Henry Adams tell it, in the pages of the *Education,* from direct observation of Roony Lee, the son of Robert E. Lee, and other young Southerners he knew at Harvard between 1854 and 1858, who had behind them two hundred years of shaping in the pattern, and who are to be taken, as Adams infers, as the typical flower of the Old South at its highest and best:

"Tall, largely built, handsome, genial, with liberal Virginia openness toward all he liked, he [Lee] had also the Virginian habit of command. . . . For a year, at least . . . was the most popular and prominent man in his class, but then seemed slowly to drop into the background. The habit of command was not enough, and the Virginian had little else. He was simple beyond analysis; so simple that even the simple New England student could not realize him.

". . . Strictly, the Southerner had no mind; he had temperament. He was not a scholar; he had no intellectual training; he could not analyze an idea, and he could not even conceive of admitting two. . . ."

There it is, then. We return to the point with which we began. It was the total effect of Southern conditions, primary and secondary, to preserve the Southerner's original simplicity of character as it were in perpetual suspension. From first to last, and whether he was a Virginian or a *nouveau*, he did not (typically speaking) think; he felt; and discharging his feelings immediately, he developed no need or desire for intellectual culture in its own right—none, at least, powerful enough to drive him past his taboos to its actual achievement.

"Is It True What They Say About Dixie?"

WILLIAM T. POLK

> Southern Accent, *the only book by the late William T. Polk, published in 1953 by William Morrow and Company of New York, is a witty, wise and sometimes eloquent commentary on his native area as this former associate editor of the Greensboro, North Carolina,* Daily News *saw it. Born in North Carolina, Mr. Polk was an enlisted man and also a second lieutenant in World War I, and studied law at Harvard, where at one time he occupied an attic with a fellow student named Thomas Wolfe. Legal practice, trips to Europe and eventually his editorship occupied his later years. He wrote poems, articles, "deeds, mortgages, charters and wills."*

WHAT is the South? It is not what people say it is—and never has been.

From the time of the landing of Amadas and Barlowe on Roanoke Island "in Virginia" to the time of Thomas Nelson Page, say from 1584 to 1884, the region was, by its own admission, "the goodliest land under the cope of heaven," peopled by angels in human form, with a few foreign devils from "up North" thrown in by way of contrast. From the time of Page to that of Erskine Caldwell, William Faulkner and Lillian Smith, the South has somehow become transformed into a never-never, Krafft-Ebing land of psychopathia sexualis, peopled by sadists, masochists, rapists, satyrs, nymphomaniacs, and necrophiles, to mention a few of the better known types, together with assorted murderers, arsonists and lynchers, although it seems to draw the line at cannibalism, even during a failure of the turnip crop.

The notion that the South is a geographical region of the United States of America, populated by rather easy-going people of various shades of complexion, who live rather ordinary lives . . . is too fantastic a thought to be entertained seriously by writers or readers of modern Southern literature. . . . The South has become a cross between a Gothic romance and a Greek tragedy rewritten by Freud. . . .

The South is largely responsible for the queer notions that people have of it. It has from the beginning fostered extravagant views of itself abroad, and the credulousness of Southerners regarding themselves and their land is as broad as the region itself. There is a tall tale from Warrenton, North Carolina about how a poker game, which was instituted there prior to the Civil War, has been going on continuously ever since, with the eldest sons taking their fathers' places at the gaming table from generation to generation.

Of course there is not a scrap of truth or sense in it, but there is a good deal of belief in it. One of the syndicated "believe-it-or-not" newspaper features once wrote me begging for details of the immortal poker game, and I, feeling that such faith should not go unrewarded, supplied it with a long, circumstantial and purely imaginary account of the legendary game, stating that the only interruption in its history was when General Lee visited it, causing the players to stand at attention and salute, but that on his taking a hand, play was immediately resumed.

This bit of foolery, which appeared in various papers, was never challenged, but was taken seriously by a number of people, some of whom wrote me asking whether it was still strictly limited to lineal descendants by primogeniture. I wrote them that unfortunately it was.

.   .   .

Southern fiction really got to work rose-coloring a quarter of a continent in 1832, when Kennedy's *Swallow Barn* fixed the popular conception of the South as one great plantation, "open as an inn and as rich as a castle." Fertilized by William Gilmore Simms, this tradition reached full flower in the 1850's, bathing the South in its balmy and unearthly sweetness.

Northern abolitionists contended that all was not perfect in Dixie; *Uncle Tom's Cabin* was published in 1851, and a flood of literature from the self-righteous North was directed against the slavery-propped South. Southern writers, indignantly springing to their pens in defense of their beloved Southland, categorically denied the presence of any imperfection whatsoever. . . .

Southern fiction half a century ago was a fearful and wonderful work of the unfettered imagination. . . . The most amateurish novel written in the most excruciating style would, as likely as not, have a foreword ending thus: "This is such as Shakespeare or Macaulay might have dashed off in a happy hour of literary excitement. (Signed) Critic."

The following . . . is a sample of the Southern fiction of some fifty years ago.

My Day in the Old South

In the orthodox Southern novel of the time, Earl Barringer, the *beau ideal* of manly beauty and the scion of the wealthy and aristocratic Colonel Barringer, who would rather die than brook an insult to himself or friend, is awakened by the rosy beams of Aurora and springs from his couch as he recalls his matutinal tryst with Camilla Montrose, the blooming ward of Col. Fitzhugh Fairfax, his father's ancient enemy.

Camilla has already reached the trysting place, an oak in a glade. As she reclines there on the moss in amorous reverie, listening to the warbling of the feathery choir overhead, she is hypnotized by a rattlesnake. The reptile charms her with his basilisk eye. Coiled, he is ready to spring upon the hapless maiden.

But Earl Barringer suddenly appears on the scene, and, throwing his body between the lady and snake, receives the mortal venom that was meant for his betrothed.

Meanwhile a plot has been hatched by Leopold Cottonmouth Stowe, a disguised ex-overseer, to obtain the fortune of Colonel Barringer, father of our hero, Earl. Today is the day of the Camptown races, and Leopold has wagered a fabulous sum with Colonel Barringer that the colonel's mare Firefly will not win the race. By way of precaution Leopold has given knockout drops to Snowball, the only jockey who can ride the fiery Firefly.

This is not the only plot that Leopold has laid today. He has also laid one against the lovely Camilla. She has rejected his addresses, spurned his suit. Repaying scorn with vengeance, Leopold has forged documents to show that Camilla's parentage is tainted with Negro blood. "We shall see, my proud beauty!" he mutters over and over to himself between clenched teeth.

The forged documents, together with the instruments whereby he committed the forgery, he has concealed behind a secret panel in the room he occupies as a guest in Colonel Barringer's mansion.

The hour approaches. All is ready for the Camptown race. But no. Snowball cannot be found. Earl Barringer is having delirium tremens from the gallon of liquor he took to cure the snake bite. Who but the brave and buxom Camilla, disguised somewhat ineffectually as a jockey, volunteers to ride Firefly and save her beloved's father's fortune? 'Tis done! They're off! Nose and nose at the finish! Firefly wins! By a nostril! Camilla doffs her disguise, or so much as is proper. Colonel Barringer, reconciled, takes his enemy's ward to his breast. Leopold Cottonmouth Stowe is foiled.

But not for long. Silently gritting his teeth behind a forced smile, he slinks to the secret panel and opens it to exhibit the forged papers which will wreck Camilla's life.

Zip! A flash of lightning illumines the cloud-darkened room. But Leopold secures the papers and takes them to the parlor where Colonel Barringer, Colonel Fairfax, Camilla and Earl are gathered together.

All are dumbfounded at the news of the terrible taint. Colonel Barringer is about to drive Camilla out into the storm when Earl stops him.

"Hold!" cries he with an imperious gesture. "She is the star of my hope and my future intended."

"My son," says Colonel Barringer, "if you persist in this insane resolve you are no son of mine. I would cut you off as cleanly as I would yon cuspidor."

"Father," retorts young Barringer, "mistake me not. The die is cast. Wealth would be poverty without her love. Poverty would be wealth, if we but shared it together. I would rather marry her, though she worked in a sewing house in New York, than wed the proudest daughter of the highest nobleman of all England, though her brow were decked with a jeweled diadem."

"Boy, you are mad!"

"Follow me," is all young Barringer says.

Leading the way to Leopold's room with the secret panel, he points suddenly to the window on the opposite side. There, mysteriously printed on the pane, is a perfect photograph of Leopold in the act of taking the papers from their hiding place. Earl opens the panel and discloses the instruments of the forgery.

"Curse you!" hisses Leopold. "How did you get that picture?"

Earl, turning to the astounded company, explains how, knowing that Leopold was using the secret panel, he had coated the window opposite with a mixture of quicksilver and buttermilk. The quicksilver acted as a mirror, and the lightning flash, at the same time it revealed Leopold in the act of securing the papers, curdled the milk, thus rendering the reflection permanent.

"We shall meet again, Barringer," snarls Leopold, reaching for his hat.

Earl is tempted to pollute the earth with his vile heart's blood, but stays his hand for the nonce, remembering that there is a lady present.

The storm suddenly subsides, the chants of the mammies and pickaninnies dancing on the levee can be heard above the whistle of the *Robert E. Lee* coming around the bend, and Earl and Camilla are left alone at last.

Earl, beside himself with passion, presses a kiss on the not reluctant cheek of his betrothed. At first blush she is overcome with remorse at her unmaidenly forwardness.

"Oh, God," she cries, "pardon the weakness of woman!" and, burying her face in his bosom, her lachrymal lakes overflowed and anointed his garments with drops which were to him the myrrh of the soul.

"It is pursuit," she sobs, "and not possession that man enjoys, and now therefore the tender regard you have for me is about to be cremated upon the pyre of my broken spirit and naught but an urn of ashes left for its memory."

"Never," replies Barringer, "never until God himself is buried and the dark mantle of oblivion is erected for his tombstone shall my person or my angel forsake the fair Camilla Montrose."*

Let us here leave them.

But Hell is More Amusing. It took Southern writers a century—say, from Kennedy's *Swallow Barn* in 1832 to Faulkner's *Light in August* in 1932—to wake up to the fact that there is more human nature and drama, and therefore better materials for fiction, to be found in hell than in heaven, a lesson they could have learned from Dante at any time. But once they caught on to it, they went to town. . . . No longer did Southern writers fly off to the ends of the earth as if driven by some centrifugal force—Lafcadio Hearn had removed himself to a Japanese fairyland, Poe had taken up his abode in the "misty, mid-region of Weir," and James Branch Cabell had, by Poictesme, got as far as hell. . . .

The life thus brought to life was more rough and robust, yet more varied, subtle and profound than that which had passed for the South in books. Some of these writers, notably William Faulkner, made a desperate attempt to show men and women in their erratic gyrations through this life, throwing off, by their collisions with one another, sparks which would light for an enduring instant some wrinkle of the divinely darkened countenance of truth.

What, No Likeness? Does this mean that a recognizable likeness or portrait of the South

---

*This concluding dialogue is borrowed practically verbatim from *The Balsam Groves of Grandfather Mountain* by Shepherd M. Dugger, the only book I know of that is not like any other book.

is emerging at last? Not at all. Take two Southern novelists—Erskine Caldwell, the most widely read, and William Faulkner, the most highly esteemed—and ask: "Is it true what they say about Dixie?"

A great many people must think so. As early as 1950 a total of 23,000,000 of Caldwell's books had been sold, mostly in drugstores, and their number is increasing like the national debt. There is much realistic detail in them, as there is in the paintings of Hieronymus Bosch or Salvador Dali and the stories of the Grimm brothers. Millions of readers doubtless believe that they present an accurate picture of the South, but they do not.

It is true that there are Tobacco Roads in the South, as there are Jeeter Lesters, Dudes, Ellie Mays, Mollies, and Ty Ty Waldens. But the gargoyle is not the building.

In one of Erskine Caldwell's novels, *Journeyman*, a preacher comes uninvited into Clay Horvey's house, "seduces his Negro cook, shoots her husband, and finally wins Clay's wife in a crooked crap game, along with his car and his farm." These are not typical results of a pastoral visitation, even in the South. In another Caldwell work, *A Place Called Estherville*, a virtuous Negro boy, after successfully attempting to preserve his chastity "from the wily seductions of a beautiful, rich, white girl," falls prey to "a sultry white widow who tackles him and rapes him while he is making his deliveries on his bicycle." Negro boys are not all that popular in Southern society.

Faulkner's novels do not reach nearly as many people as Caldwell's, but they win critics and influence people in the upper intellectual brackets. The high praise which critics and the intelligentsia accord them is fairly won. He is one of the most effective narrative writers this country has ever produced.

Honest Southern readers would have to admit that his pictures of life in the South are accurate in minutest detail. Anyone who has ever been in the store of what is known in the South as a "supply man" knows that Faulkner wrote photographically when he noted that his character's books recorded "that slow trickle of molasses and meal and meat,

of shoes and straw hats and overalls, of plowlines and collars and heelbolts and clevises, which returned each fall as cotton."

Furthermore, Faulkner knows his people, and he gets the three main classes—the aristocrats, the up-and-coming former poor whites and the Negroes—into his books with amazing success. He knows and tells how they look, think, talk and feel. He sees them with clarity, humor and compassion, and, like any genuine artist, he searches for the truth behind them and the land they live in.

It is, of course, his privilege and business as a novelist to specialize in matricide, patricide, infanticide, incest, rape and plain and fancy murder for the same reason that Aeschylus and Sophocles did. These crimes make good copy. They provide plot fables evocative of "pity and terror." They supply levers for prying into human nature. But Faulkner's fables are no more representations of Mississippi than the *House of Atreus* trilogy and *Oedipus Rex* were accounts of typical days in the life of the ancient Greeks. . . .

A fairly typical representation of the South in modern fiction would run somewhat as follows:

A Scythe For Mother. Maj. Earl Barringer on his return home from the First World War suspects his bride Camilla (supposedly descended from the fine old Montrose family who moved from Virginia to the Deep South after the death of old Colonel Barringer —not the *first* Colonel Barringer but the one before him—commonly referred to in genealogical records as "Minus One") of being unfaithful to him with her mulatto half-brothers Simeon and Samuel. Earl has, in fact, been rather suspicious of her since learning that she spent her teens in a sporting house in Natchez-Under-The-Hill.

Awakening early after a fitful sleep on his first night home, Earl gazes at the pure and placid countenance of his fiery-haired Camilla on the lace pillow slip in the ancestral four-poster, until he can stand it no longer.

Jumping from bed and grabbing a scythe, which he habitually kept beside the bedside table for purely personal reasons, he strides across the dewy grass to Simeon's and Samuel's cabin, neatly beheads them and sews each one's head to the other's body to make identification more difficult. With a giant's strength he carries their bodies on his shoulders to the decaying mansion where he dumps them in a large vat of maturing moonshine in an abandoned snake pit under the front porch.

Next day he places the corpses in the old four-poster, separating them by a bolster because the bed has a tendency to sag in the middle.

Camilla comes home the next day from a business trip to Natchez-Under-The-Hill, drinks a few gourdfuls of the white lightning from the vat, and goes to bed in place of the bolster between Sim and Sam without thinking twice about it. But soon her confusion is pitiable. Earl, who has been watching the proceedings through the closet keyhole, rushes out intending to kill her in a jealous rage, but chivalrously changes his mind and hands her the scythe instead, begging her to kill him.

Always obliging, Camilla separates him at the neck, leaves his body on the floor, kicks his head under the bed, and goes to sleep.

She has been asleep only a couple of days when her son (by a former friend) Ramon who had just failed his mid-term examinations at Harvard Law School (where he had been sent by Camilla to wean him away from Darling Jean Jitters, the albino daughter of a tenant on the place who was not a fit character for Ramon to associate with) rushes into the room.

More intoxicated than a Southern gentleman should be (because he had generously sampled the moonshine in the vat, which seemed to him to have a better color and bead than ever before) and seeing his mother (of whom he was, alas! too, too fond) in bed between two dark men (who were after all his half-uncles) and also his father's decapitated body on the floor, he requests an explanation.

Camilla jumps from bed in a state of nature (nothing unusual with her), clasps her son to her bosom and tells him he is the only man she ever really loved.

Strangely revolted by all this (a clear victory for Harvard over heredity), Ramon cuts off his mother's head as she kneels in supplication before him. He does it with the scythe. Pitching her body on the bed and jumping in after it, he lights a Murad and burns up the whole shebang.

Mobile: Harmonious Through the Mellowing of Time

CARL CARMER

Carl Carmer's Stars Fell on Alabama, *published in 1934 by Farrar and Rinehart, New York, opened a crowded writing career for this gifted folklorist and student of American history and ways. A native New Yorker, Mr. Carmer has lived in the South and also visited there on many occasions. He has dealt frequently with the region in books, magazine articles, poems and other works. Among his volumes are* Listen for a Lonesome Drum, The Hudson *and* Dark Trees to the Wind; *he has edited or co-edited the* Rivers of America *series. The following is from* Stars Fell on Alabama.

MOBILE stays in the heart, loveliest of cities. I have made many journeys down the Black Warrior and I have always found happiness at its mouth. And so I summarize my impressions rather than tell the story of a visit.

Few travelers "pass through" Mobile. The old city rests apart, remembering the five flags that have flown over her. Spain and France and England and the Old South, grown harmonious through the mellowing of time, are echoes in the streets. But since only people who "are going to Mobile" are her visitors, her charms have been less exploited than those of any of the other sea cities of the South.

Whether you come by train or by boat, you arrive in the same part of town. There is a smell of hemp and tar about it. Long low two-story buildings, their intricate iron balconies interrupted here and there by signs—"Sailors' Supplies," "The Army and Navy Store," line the narrow streets. Sometimes the balcony overhangs the sidewalk and makes a roofed passage for pedestrians, ornate iron pillars supporting it at the street's edge. These buildings once housed a roistering assembly. The crews of ocean windjammers found liquor here in gilded saloons. They lined up at the mirrored bar with the bully-boys of North Alabama—keel-boatmen on the Black Warrior, planters' sons arrived by side-wheel steam packet from the wide estates on the Tombigbee, badman gamblers in extravagant apparel. One of these squalid doorways was the entrance to Madame Valerie's, where in chandeliered brilliance a soft-voiced Creole dowager conducted her salon of culture and lechery, her ladies advertised as educated, refined, charming, all sisters in profession, however, of the sloe-eyed ivory-colored quadroons in the "houses" near the water. The waterfront itself is no longer as picturesque as it was in the days of the clipper ships or the river packets. The gay welter of colorful types has disappeared. Where it once reveled you may sometimes meet a strange woman, ragged and unkempt—a small hat set on the top of her wide profusion of yellow hair. "Floating Island," the Mobilians call her, and they will tell you she waits for a sailor lover who embarked fifty years ago and was drowned. Each day she looks out over the tossing horizon for signs of his returning boat—mumbling to herself.

Or, tottering along the cobbles on a sunny morning, Cudjo may greet you—a wizened black man who must be treated with respect. The boat that brought Cudjo to America was the last of the slavers to run the Federal Blockade. Hardly had he and his companions been delivered to the slave-dealers when the end of the war made them free men in an alien country. Huddling in a terrified group, they built their cabins close together—cabins that are now all empty save one—and in their little community they continued to use their native tongue. Cudjo is very old now. But he haunts the shores of the ocean over which he was brought, a frightened prisoner, so many years ago. He says he was the son of a king in Africa. Only a few words of the strange primitive language he once spoke so fluently remain in his memory. He repeats them slowly, knowing there is a reward. Where he stands, all is businesslike that was once picturesque. The bustle of the quai has been supplanted by the silence of great warehouses. Above their dark massive screen, white gulls circle and dip out of sight toward the waters of Mobile Bay.

It seems that almost any street of downtown Mobile will lead to Bienville Square—most revealing symbol of the city's quality. With modern business buildings completely surrounding it, the gnarled old oaks spread grotesquely, making sharp patterns of sunlight and shadow on this dreaming acre.

Business may be briskly American on one side of the street, but the Mobilian need only look to the other to feel the serene influence of time's passing over land and trees, in wind and sun and rain. The events that Bienville Square has seen, moreover, emanate a magic—a distilled essence of history which even the ignorant cannot help but feel. De Soto was here, Bienville and Iberville, General Andrew Jackson, Admiral Farragut.

It was near this square, the legend goes, that a German colony settled a little over two hundred years ago. Among them was a Russian woman whose beauty and prideful bearing were such that all Mobile wondered. The town's curiosity was soon satisfied. For with eyes flashing more brilliantly even than the gorgeous jewels she wore, the lady stated that she was the wife of Alexis, son of Peter the Great. Her husband, she said, had been so cruel to her that she had fled from him to the refuge of a new world, and his pride had been so great that he had announced that she was dead. The story aroused such a storm of emotion in the breast of an aristocratic French officer that he offered his name to her, and there was a wedding full of pomp and ceremony as befitted a princess and her noble consort. They sailed for France soon and lived happily ever after—so the story is told—even though it was discovered that she was only a servant to the princess she impersonated, and had stolen the jewels. So Mobile provided America with a mystery of a Russian princess long before the days of Anastasia.

The air is soft in Mobile—filled with sea moisture. The tropics reach toward the town from the south. Palms raise straight trunks to the greening tufts that cap them. Fig trees and oleanders, magnolias and Cape Jasmine, Cherokee roses and azaleas make the breezes heavy with sweet odor through the long warm season. It is a gentle air Like the atmosphere that the people of Mobile create among themselves, it is friendly and easy-going. It folds with equal warmth about the white pillars lifted by a retired Black Belt planter and the wrought-iron patterns of a façade conceived by a French immigrant. Unlike the New Orleans Creoles, with their enclosed patios, Mobile's Latin colonists chose to build homes that looked out on the world. The lawns on which the French and Spanish houses rest have been green for almost two centuries. Outside the commercial streets down by the waterfront, Mobile is a city of leisured space. The old part of the town is a honeycomb of exquisite design. Fleurs-de-lis in formal grace adorn a balcony that faces a wild profusion of grape clusters across the street. The bees of Napoleon, were they to take flight from their iron frame, might light upon the roses of Provence that clamber over the railings of both upper and lower galleries next door. At the city market, once the Spanish government buildings, the iron curves have a cleaner, freer

sweep and they turn more delicately against the white stone.

Mobile has not always been a city on a byway. In the days of her glory the big-hatted, bright-waistcoated planter brought his wife and daughters down the Black Warrior for the theater, the horse racing, the shopping. Perhaps they embarked at Wetumpka on the famous *St. Nicholas*, its calliope tooting out *Life on the Ocean Wave* to the panic of negroes along the shore. Or they may have come from Gainesville down the Tombigbee on that gorgeous packet *Eliza Battle*, fated to be consumed in flame with a loss of forty lives. In a bayou up the Warrior, a few miles from Mobile, lie many of the sisters of these ships. In that graveyard of the steamboats few names are discernible now. Perhaps the *Southern Belle* rests there, and the *Orline St. John*, the *Ben Lee*, stern-wheeler, the *Allen Glover* (named for her planter owner). . . .

Paris gowns went back up the river. So did memories of Charlotte Cushman as Rosalind and Chanfran Booth as Shylock, of Parisian ballet, of Jenny Lind, of the race between the famous horses, Louisiana's *Ricardo* owned by W. S. Minor, and Alabama's *Brown Dick*, who belonged to Colonel Goldsby.

Though these days are memories now, the city has not forgotten. With all its outward semblance of calm, Mobile is gayest of American cities. Its free spirit, less commercialized than that of New Orleans, has kept its Gallic love of the fantastic and amusing. Behind the ornate balconies and long French windows that sedately face the streets, live a people to whom carnival is a natural heritage.

While Mobile waited the coming new year, 1833, candles burning in the windows, the horses of dandies clopping daintily along the cobblestones of Dauphin Street, a band of young men in whom the liquors of many a bar rioted, descended upon a hardware store —accoutered themselves with rakes and cowbells—and turned the night into a bedlam. Thus the society of *Cowbellian de Rakin* was born. For a hundred years thereafter Mobile has had its mad, bad time of Carnival. Until the War Between the States, New Year's Eve witnessed its revels. Now the Cowbellians are no more; only the Strikers, a similar carnival organization, celebrate the birth of the year with a ball, and all the other social groups make merry on Shrove Tuesday at the annual Mardi Gras festival

It is difficult for most residents of America to understand the social processes of a Southern coast city. The rigid formality that was once natural to the aristocratic émigré has now become a game that must be played as strictly according to the rules as bridge or chess. The Strikers' Ball given annually in Mobile at the old Battle House is a revelatory example of the quality that makes the survivals of social rituals in American life so charming. The Strikers are the oldest mystic society in Mobile. It is a popular fiction that no one knows who its members are, though there is hardly a distinguished gentleman in the city who can truthfully deny membership. The origin of the name is explained variously. Some say that the first Strikers were markers of cotton bales; others that they were a group which broke away from the Cowbellian Society.

As New Year's Eve approaches, an atmosphere of tension and mystery settles over the homes on Government Street and its environs. Débutantes look anxious, though they know that they at least will be present and be danced with. The hearts of post-débutantes and wives grow lighter when an envelope bearing the cherished "call-out" card, a masker's request for the honor of a dance, appears. The men of the house disappear frequently to attend unexplained "conferences" over costumes, favors, procedure. The younger men and the male visitors in town importantly make engagements for the "black-coat" dances that maskers unselfishly allow them.

The lobby of the Old Battle House, as nine o'clock of New Year's approaches, is filled with an excited crowd in full evening dress. They enter the ballroom to discover that curtains have been hung from the balcony to shut off the dance floor and the stage at the far end. Four or five rows of chairs, close to the curtains, are occupied by ladies, happy ladies who carry big bouquets of flowers, débutantes, sweethearts, wives who have received the "call-out" cards. Behind them sit the other guests of the Strikers.

At nine o'clock the band strikes up a march and the curtains are drawn. On the stage, grouped in striking tableau, stand the maskers. They may be in the laces and knee breeches of the court of Louis XIV, in the regimentals of the American Revolution, in the buckskin and beads of Indians, in the attire of any one of countless picturesque periods. Suddenly from the back of the stage the Captain of the Ball, in more elaborate dress than any other, leads out to the center of the tableau the girl who has been chosen by the Strikers as the princess of the night's revel. She wears a white gown and her arms are filled with red roses. There is a burst of applause as the two bow and then the Captain leads the girl down the center of the floor. Spotlights play on the couple from the balcony, sequins sparkle from their costumes, the applause grows deafening, almost drowning the blare of the band. Marching in single file, the maskers follow the couple. At the end of the hall, while the Captain and his lady wait, they find their partners for the grand march—the first call-out. The Strikers' Ball has begun.

In the old days the guests were entertained at eleven o'clock with a champagne supper in the main dining room of the Battle House. The maskers had their supper in another room—a secret chamber where they might unmask without fear of being recognized. But prohibition brought the abandonment of a custom that may be revived.

Mardi Gras in Mobile is the most formal and elaborate function in modern America. Felix, Emperor of Joy, rules over the revels of this day of days. His identity and that of his queen are made known at a dinner in the Battle House on the preceding Saturday. They sit at the head of the central table. On Monday morning Felix proceeds once more to the Battle House wherein occurs a ritual entitled the Dressing of the King, during which he and his knights attain at least a slight degree of alcoholic stimulation while he is being invested with the royal robes of his office. Thence the royal party is spirited by devious route to a government revenue cutter down the bay. The royal vessel, pennants fluttering, then moves up to the wharf at the foot of Government Street. Here King Felix makes his formal entry to the city, mounts his throne, and is borne through the streets in a vast procession of colorful and elaborate floats. In her pavilion before the Athelstan Club in Bienville Square the Queen awaits his coming. The throne float stops at the pavilion and a cupbearer brings His Majesty a silver flagon brimming with champagne. The King lifts it high in honor of the Queen, drinks, and the procession moves on through the crowds of merrymakers that line its path.

That evening at the municipal wharf the coronation ceremony takes place. Thousands crowd the vast building to its doors as the King and his court enter along a raised platform, over a hundred yards long, that runs down the center. Each participant in the ritual walks beneath a battery of spotlights the full length of this passage to the stage at the other end, on which the throne is reared.

After the coronation is over, King and Queen and entire court in full costume appear at the ball of the Infant Mystics, their entrance heralded by massed trumpeters. This ceremonial visit at an end, they move on to other festivities throughout the city, ending their royal progress at a ball at the Athelstan Club where, regal robes discarded, they join in the dancing.

On the morning of the next day, Mardi Gras itself, the entire city is given over to masked merrymaking. Noon sees the parade of the Knights of Revelry and the Comic Cowboys, and the high float of the King sways through the streets again. The monarch's last appearance before the populace is in the flare of countless torches borne by strutting Negroes to light the parade of the Order of Myths. That organization, founded in 1868 for the express purpose of dispelling the gloom brought about by the War Between the States, chose as its emblem the figure of Folly belaboring Death with colored bladders. The first float in its parade is always a representation of this emblem, and its annual ball on Mardi Gras is always prefaced by Death's wild dash across the ballroom floor pursued by Folly, who mercilessly whacks him with the resounding bladders. This ball, similar to the Strikers' in formal ceremonies, brings the day's revels to a close and the city enters the solemn Lenten period fortified by gay memories.

Mobile is a city of intimacies that have stood the test of time. On Government Street the houses shaded by magnolias and Cape jasmines shelter families whose grandfathers and great-grandfathers were friends. Along the azalea-strewn road to Spring Hill, the old Catholic college, today as a hundred years ago, a black cook bears a gift of wine and jelly from her white folks' kitchen to the white folks next door. Affections are strong in this place, for they have been long depended on.

Even the heat of summer drives but few of the people of Mobile northward. Point Clear "across the bay" or Biloxi on the Gulf Coast a few miles away are pleasant enough for vacations. Country houses on the picturesque Dog River are usually filled with gay parties on week-ends throughout the year. At midday the city's homes are cool refuges and streets are empty. In the evening thousands of automobiles line Mobile Bay while a breeze from the moonlit waters blows inland and little sailboats scud about silhouetted against the shining surface.

It is easy to become adapted to the rhythm of this city. Acquaintances gradually become friends. The processes of earning a living are slow and comparatively unimportant to the living itself. Dignity and charm and gayety permeate life there. Mobile is a city of the lotus—bringing forgetfulness of everything except the pleasant passing of the hours.

The Increased Summer

JOHN PEALE BISHOP

With urbane, highly civilized philosophy, John Peale Bishop wrote a number of polished essays on traditional Southern values. Of old Virginia stock, he was born in Charles Town, West Virginia, went to a military academy, then Princeton, where F. Scott Fitzgerald was in the same class. He spent long periods in France, living near Paris, and writing fiction, short stories and poetry. He never formally joined the Southern agrarians of the "I'll Take My Stand" group, but was close to members of that school. He had a considerable influence as a reviewer-critic. What follows is from The Collected Essays of John Peale Bishop, *edited by Edmund Wilson, published in 1948 by Charles Scribner's Sons.*

IN the first small town of Maryland, the South is already there, to be seen in a street whose shade would anywhere else seem excessive, in a girl sweeping a porch, in an old Negro drooping half-asleep over the board of his wagon, to which is attached a drowsy and equally immobile mule. To cross the border is for me to proceed into the landscape of boyhood and youth. In this country I was reared, and the very smells have an air of memory; there is no other land in the world where the late summer ripens so redolently with sun, where in fall, orchards dispel so rich an odor of misty fruit. The fields are rolling; the hills, instead of confining the view, lead it on through fold after fold of fading blue, increasing the distance.

It is a land that has been loved, and not only by me; all that have lived here have had the feel of this earth. I talk to a blind man. It is the Blue Ridge whose sight he most regrets. "I miss just being able to ride out and look at those hills." But Tidewater Virginia is already strange, a land abandoned by time, largely despoiled by the voracity of the tobacco-plant, returning in many places to a wilderness of scrub-oak and dwarf pine. And the strangeness is increased by two encounters: a chance hyena being driven in a lonely cage over a sandy road; two boys dragging a raft ashore from a small inland lake, surrounded by the degradation of a poverty-stricken settlement. They and their parents are the last of the Chickahominy Indians.

State lines are real. I suppose I had never considered this before, but I can only say that, coming south, I was struck always at the change both in land and inhabitants that confronts the traveler as soon as he goes from one political division to another. In the passage from North to South Carolina, even the sky changes, becomes more spacious, and the clouds accumulate in the high heavens with the slow dignity, with the arrogance almost, of a Charleston planter. The division is as distinct as that between the French provinces, which are still realities of contour and custom, though the first emperor long ago cut them up into convenient administrative units. . . . To pass from Virginia to North Carolina is to remember the passage from the rich country of the Lyonnais to the dull baked plains of the Dauphiné.

There is another and beautiful North Carolina, but I do not see it; I am in the coastal plain. I must take Mr. Thomas Wolfe's word for the vigorous imagination, the argumentative virtues of the men of Old Catawba. The North Carolinians I see remind me only of William Byrd's account of their ancestors in the early eighteenth century. And, as I pass the thinly populated plains, the meagre cotton-patches, the poor cabins and untended garden-plots, the comparison returns to the Dauphiné . . . that province which never seems to have belonged either to the old domain of France

330   "AN ERA HAD ENDED, AN ERA HAD BEGUN"

nor yet to Provence. That ancient kingdom comes suddenly in plane trees dappling white roads. . . .

Not quite so suddenly are you in the Deep South of America; it is announced by scattered cotton-patches; you are aware of it in the first live oaks, in the swamps haunted by stilted blue herons, and hanging with Spanish moss, in the rivers of burnt umber, colored by the clay. Cheraw is a prelude to Charleston, but in the old part there is first the sense of a complete accommodation of the Southerner to his climate. About the Battery is a noble architecture, double galleries the length of the house, which is presented to an enclosed garden, access to the street being through a postern door in a projecting wall. There is that ostentation of privacy amid shade which the world over belongs to hot climates.

Savannah approaches through a land as monotonous as Provence. Its early nineteenth-century squares interlinked by shaded streets revive an impression of Nîmes with its summer gardens, where Louis XV remolded in stone the balustrades above the intricate shape of the Roman pool. (Incidentally, I wonder if Mr. Lewis Mumford, who is so interested in city-planning, has ever, even on the grandiose blueprints of the future, seen anything finer as an urban conception than this part of Savannah.)

The first glimpse of the Gulf of Mexico comes as blue as the Mediterranean, though seen not through gaps of the Maritime Alps but across piney barrens. But not even that most mythical of seas could show a beach so dazzling in loveliness as that crescent of white sand and sun beyond Pensacola, outlined by dunes, so that there is no sight save toward the brilliant expanse of water, whose lucid greens deepen and waver to darkest blue, then fade under the sun to blinding azure.

Marseilles is encountered at New Orleans, at least along the riverfront, a port of the extreme South opening upon an alien and still more Southern world. Cargoes and vice, the dusky and olive-skinned faces, in this case of African and Sicilian stevedores, and cranes grappling boatloads of bananas; open markets reeking with savors of the sea; drowsy and flyspecked barbershops in the hot afternoon,

sinister and mechanically musical salons at midnight, all combine to set Decatur Street in mind beside the Cannebière.

. . . In every country there is a South which feels itself alien to the North. Sorrentines will tell you that Italy begins at Rome and goes North; I have known a Gascon gardener who after years in the Île-de-France would let no one call him a Frenchman. And long after the Confederacy is lost in the national archives and the last old lady has forgotten in the grave that this was conquered territory, there will still be, regardless of the government, a deep division between the states that grow cotton and those which first manufactured it into cloth. . . .

The road from New England to the mouth of the Mississippi has often been taken. . . . Rather I should like to mark a little the difference between the upper South in which I was born and the Deep South into which I have come. It is for the first time. And I have but first impressions: the country is vast and varied; the very atmosphere seems more heavily saturated, just as there are evidences of greater if vanished wealth, the poor-whites poorer, the Negroes blacker and more primitive. It is with difficulty that I understand the small black street-boys of Charleston when they propose to dance for my pennies. Any morning one may awake in New Orleans to find the cook in a state of terror, having stepped over a voodoo charm left for her on the backdoor sill by the laundress.

It is no longer a land of moderate contours, hills gently rolling to receive and beneficently retain the rain; but flat, with pine barrens, sandy plains, or else rank with swamps, as dense in vegetation as the prehistoric forest. Even in the soil there is that constant meridional contrast presented by poor unfertile stretches which seem about to last forever, when suddenly they change into an excessive richness of alluvial deposit. It is a land where Protestantism becomes abased, belonging, as it does, as a code, to cold climates. But it also, in Louisiana, provides the rare instance in America of a country dominated by Catholicism, and not that puritanic Catholicism which here and there has been brought in by Irish peasant, but the rich and humane Catholicism of France.

Yes, the distinction is there between the Upper and Lower South—immediately sensed. I also remember a conversation with Allen Tate, in which he put it as his opinion that, even at the time of the War Between the States, the latent antagonism was so strong between the two sections that, even with the Confederacy victorious, they must have broken apart into disparate and perhaps separately governed regions.

The difference is first one of climate. In the Virginias, four seasons with more or less accuracy quarter the year. But in Louisiana winter is hardly more than a suspension of summer. Frost may be sure, but snow is rare, and when, once in a lifetime, it lies long and deep enough to mold into snowballs, little boys will carry them to school and ask the teacher to preserve them in glass. In January camellias will begin to bloom; petals so precisely whorled, so painted in color, that they recall those porcelain flowers with which the gardens of Louis XIV pricked the parterres of the Grand Trianon to make them gay all winter long for the old age of the king.

It is to the climate that must be attributed, in no small part, the increased respect for politeness, a greater attention to formal manners. And this is as it should be: In a climate as enervating as this, where it is comparatively easy to make a mere living, there is no natural discipline to insure decency, such as is derived from Connecticut snows or the sea off Cape Cod. One simply cannot let down. Some artifice must be imposed on conduct. No characteristic of the South has been so endlessly satirized; it has been shown, not only as provincial, pretentiously silly, which it often is, but as something much worse.

The planter who is such a perfect gentleman in the parlor can be a perfect reprobate once he has stepped down the stairs under the Roman portico. Where there is a supremacy of manners over morals, there is apt to be a disparity between them. And sometimes this is appalling. Long before the modern novelists, a half century indeed before Mrs. Stowe, Crèvecoeur had seen, in a swamp near Charles-

ton, a Negro suspended in a cage, his eyes pricked out by birds of prey. . . .

There is, then, the increased summer, the long heated air, which ripens citrus fruits, which once enriched Carolinians with indigo, which later grew and still grows cotton, rice and sugar-cane. That is, between the Upper and Lower South there is a difference in space; there is also, I suspect, a difference in time. Maryland and Virginia were settled a whole generation before the establishment of the Bank of England. Economy was a land economy; it could be nothing else. Though the Virginia planters were quick to discover that they had in tobacco what today must be called a money-crop, since their accumulations made them the first capitalists in the country, nevertheless it also happens to be well-known that even the richest of them seldom had the feel of money in their hands. . . .

The holdings in the border states were always comparatively small; Mr. Thomas J. Wertenbaker has made it clear that even in the seventeenth century the great landlords were few. Virginia society had as models the English country gentleman and the yeomen (who, though then dwindling in his native land, thought to revive his estate in the new.) Possibly the Scotch crofter should be included. The land had to be fought for before it was cleared, it was sometimes paid for in personal blood, often in money; sometimes it was granted for military services. . . . But the possibilities of credit, the continual American curse, were limited. And the land was there to be lived on, once acquired, and hence conserved; only later was its profit considered. There was, to be sure, a money-crop, and the first in America; but tobacco which created the Tidewater aristocracy (as well as a good many smaller people) at length despoiled the land and destroyed its owners.

These things are, of course, relative; but I think in general it is true that the planters of the Lower South lived on a far grander scale than anything that the Peninsula or the Piedmont could show. Their lands became immense domains, whose crop, whether cotton, rice or cane, could be—in fact, must be— turned into money, whether coin or credit. Where had they come from, these vast estates? Well, I think that almost the first glance reveals that, so large, so magnificently dominated, they came out of the tills of banks, out of the money-drawers of lenders. Swamps went down before credit, forests were felled by speculators; cotton and blacks amazingly spread over territory lately and forcibly deserted by the Cherokee.

That is certainly one of the distinctions between the border states and those of the Gulf. They were settled much later, and in that time the possibilities of credit had been continually enlarged. To be sure, there is something in the bright and optimistic air of the continent that abuses confidence and lightheartedly mortgages the future. Did not the town of Plymouth find itself at the end of King Philip's war pledged for an amount more than double the total holdings of the colony? Commodities were exchanged; tobacco-leaf was shipped to England, useful and luxurious objects returned, minus the factor's double commission.

In Louisiana the beginnings seem to have been very much the same: the wild swamp had to be cleared before it could be settled, the pine tree felled. Grants from the government, royal or colonial, often had still to be paid for in blood until the Indians were dispelled. The Creole plantations along the river were modest and conservative undertakings. But by the time the Americans came in, the way was clear for money. Royal Street was lined with banks, and out of their tills came forth bills of sale from the earlier owners, titles to vast domains, possibly uncleared but soon to be cultivated; from the cashiers' caged windows were shoved out boatloads of darkies, buck niggers and corn-fed negresses, machines perfected in Africa for use in the sun, and capable, amazingly, of reproducing themselves in all their parts.

We are now in the nineteenth century. No longer is the land there to be lived on (with profit a later, if perfectly proper, consideration), to be used, but also to be conserved as a form of wealth more nearly permanent than any other. No, the age is one of speculation. Gamblers are not all on the river, nor at Natchez-under-the-hill. The plantations on both sides of the Mississippi changed hands, passing into money and back again; there was as yet no boll weevil, the wilful degeneration of the sugar-cane was not evident until very late in the period; credit was easy to come at, and so were markets . . . the Lower South was soon committed to a capitalist agriculture. Its economy is still based on the money-crop, with disastrous results. . . .

The culture of the Deep South after 1830 was, I am convinced, far more commercial than it is commonly credited with being. The plantation was dependent upon this factor. And this, along with first the presence, and then the debris of slavery, which seems to have numbed the critical sense and not a little destroyed the realistic sense of politics, may have contributed to the failure of the governing classes accurately and effectively to rule. . . .

Why, then, was this not another Pittsburgh? The answer is to be found, I think, in the greater continuity of life in the South. The humane tradition was stronger. And how strong it was is shown in the architecture. In this region, as I say, the planters came comparatively late; but they were still able to build dwellings harmonious with human dignity, when this art had been lost in the rest of the Western world. And it is a living art, for it is in complete accord with the climate. . . .

The long double-galleried houses of Charleston were, I am told, derived in the first instance from a similar type of architecture in the Barbadoes. The plantation house of Louisiana, enclosed in double rows of columns, can be shown to have been devised out of the French manor-house with the hip-roof and small dormers. The Americans added magnificence, and in the raised cottage—elevated originally from fear of occasional floods and constant damp—created the last and loveliest instance of the classic revival. That architecture is gone in the decline of the class that created it, for it is essentially a social art. Already in 1857, Belle Grove of Louisiana shows an opulent decadence; the pink-washed walls, the unbalanced ornament are as depraved as a Grand Duke's villa at Nice. . . .

But that there was more vitality in this class than they are commonly given credit for is manifest in their survival. For survive they did, though depleted, not only by the war but even that ten year period . . . known as Reconstruction. . . . With the confiscation and freedom of slaves succeeded an arrangement of labor, including blacks and whites, not unlike that of the colonies of Italy in the second century, when agricultural slavery was likewise on the point of being turned into serfdom. The position of the sharecropper is hardly better than that of the serf—in some respects worse, for he is not, unfortunately for his family, permanently attached to the land. And his slovenliness, his poor knowledge of farming, his indifference to anything beyond a bare subsistence for himself and, if it is not too much trouble, his children, make him a destructive and unprofitable agent for the planter. As one of the larger members of his class, a man of energy, conscience and, as it happens, considerable capital, said to me, walking over land beyond the Fausse Rivière in Louisiana, "This plantation supports a hundred and seventy-five families; every one of them gets a living out of it except me." . . .

It is always difficult in speaking of the South not to seem to prefer the terms of the past, even when the real concern is the present. This country is backward; there are customs and attitudes that persist here which have long disappeared elsewhere; or to put the matter in a more favorable phrase, one can say that in the Deep South, more than anywhere else in America, better than in many parts of Europe, the humane tradition of living has outlasted the many attacks upon it. I am not pretending that there are not Southerners who do let us down, or that, when they do, the results are not pretty awful. I am not forgetting either Senator Bilbo or Senator Long. But even among the hill-billies there is continuity of a sort, a conservation of the ways of the first pioneers. It is too often ignored that in the South, scarcely less than in the West, there are remnants of an early frontier, unaltered, save in so far as the slovenliness of the frontiersman, his ruthless destruction of forest and game, his bad tillage of soil never understood, have mutilated his background and diminished his sustenance.

I have had but a glimpse of the Charleston drawing-room, shaded from the afternoon light, still golden in the street below, the walls showing the subdued colors of Audubon's mocking-birds in formal and terrified flight about the huge coils and darting head of a black snake—the plate composed from sketches made by the ornithologist on an ancestral plantation. I know that the forms of society are carefully preserved there, that the conversation is cultivated and aware.

And yet I have the impression of something wistful in the charm, even in the force, of the Charlestonian. It is a little as though one had strayed into some legitimist sect who are determined, perhaps, not so much to restore the present heirs of the Bourbons as to commemorate the martyrdom of Louis XVI with an appropriate emotion. It is not snobbery that one finds here, but an overwhelming sense of immense and heavy heritage. And I am obliged to notice that both Mr. DuBose Heyward and Mrs. Julia Peterkin, at least as literary figures, prefer to consort with the colored race, whether of city or remote country, rather than admit the existence of that huge, sprawling, tawdry expanse, white but vulgar, that is Charleston beyond Broad Street.

Though I am told that the youngest generation in New Orleans is not entirely uncorrupted, I have nowhere else in America seen such polite ease among youngsters. The influence of the Carnival balls is potent; their fantastical prodigality is more than a spectacle and the courts of mock kings and queens are not all a travesty; for they provide something of a center to the social life of the whole year, though they begin with Twelfth Night and are over with Mardi Gras, and, for all that they lack seriousness and even sobriety, they do succeed in imposing a code on their followers. Now that the old French Opera is gone, it is the balls more than anything else which give New Orleans its living and delightful air of a provincial capital.

They are, of course, Creole in origin. But if French is still frequently heard, conversation in New Orleans is essentially Southern; where there is wit, it is not, as usually in France, dictated by vanity; the desire is not to startle but to please. Domestic difficulties are not among the common topics, nor loss of money, nor even mishaps on the golf-course; politics may be, but the discussion of it will have a certain aloofness and will lack, amazingly to one recently from the East, the rancorousness of the opinionated intellectual, the fatuousness of the business man to whom politics has ever been a variation on his one theme of personal interests.

Comment on an emotional situation will be, as in the mid-century Natchez of Mr. Stark Young, oblique rather than straight. This last may lead at times to an alarming vagueness. But the Southerner at his best, like the French at their worst, has always known at least what manners were for, that they are not intended, as the Westerner with his broad handclasp and easy salutation supposes, to bring people together out of a loneliness as wide as the prairies, but to keep them comfortably apart, to pre-serve between them and you whatever distance is necessary both for their integrity and yours.

The families with French names have still a formidable unity. And it is perhaps the French sense of tradition that gives to social gatherings in New Orleans a meaning that, as far as I am aware, has been lost elsewhere, and that not only in American cities. For they are, as they should be everywhere, a school of manners. This demands a mingling of genera-tions. While in the other American cities with which I am familiar it is customary rigorously to separate those of various ages, it is by no means uncommon in New Orleans to find seventy-seven in conversation with seventeen. And this is as it should be. The young should not be admitted to society until they are pre-pared to adopt the conventions and behavior of adults.

What Folks Were Like at Cross Creek

MARJORIE KINNAN RAWLINGS

A literary career which was slightly late in blooming, yet nevertheless richly gratifying, was that of Marjorie Kinnan Rawlings. Born in 1896 in Washington, D. C., a graduate of the University of Wisconsin, she did publicity and magazine work for the national Y.W.C.A., joined the Louisville Courier; *wrote verse for United Features, became a Hearst woman reporter, and tackled the short story medium without result. Then, just before 1929, she turned her back on journalism to buy an orange grove at Cross Creek, Florida. All at once, as she began to write with a warm humanity of the Florida locale and people, her fortunes changed. Her short fiction sold; her book,* South Moon Under, *published in 1933, was a Book of the Month selection.* The Yearling, *1938, was chosen by the same organization and won the Pulitzer prize.* Cross Creek, *a vivid account of the Floridians of the swamp edges, was her third major book club selection. The selection here is from opening passages of* Cross Creek, *published in 1942 by Charles Scribner's Sons. She died in 1953.*

CROSS CREEK is a bend in a country road, by land, and the flowing of Lochloosa Lake into Orange Lake, by water. We are four miles west of the small village of Island Grove, nine miles east of a turpentine still, and on the other sides we do not count distance at all, for the two lakes and the broad marshes create an in-finite space between us and the horizon. We are five white families; "Old Boss" Brice, the Glissons, the Mackays and the Bernie Basses; and two colored families, Henry Woodward and the Mickenses. People in Island Grove consider us just a little biggety and more than a little queer. Black Kate and I between us once misplaced some household object, quite unreasonably.

I said, "Kate, am I crazy, or are you?"

She gave me her quick sideways glance that was never entirely impudent.

"Likely all two of us. Don't you reckon it take somebody a little bit crazy to live out here at the Creek?"

At one time or another most of us at the Creek have been suspected of a degree of madness. Madness is only a variety of mental nonconformity and we are all individualists here. I am reminded of Miss Malin and the Cardinal in the Gothic tale, "The Deluge at Norderney."

"But are you not," said the Cardinal, "a little—"

"Mad?" asked the old lady. "I thought that you were aware of that, My Lord."

The Creek folks of color are less suspect than the rest of us. Yet there is something a little different about them from blacks who live gregariously in Quarters, so that even if they did not live at the Creek, they would stay, I think, somehow aloof from the layer-cake life of the average Negro. Tom Glisson and Old Boss and I think anybody is crazy not to live here, but I know what Kate meant. We have chosen a deliberate isolation, and are enamored of it, so that to the sociable we give the feeling that St. Simon Stylites on top of his desert pillar must have given the folks who begged him to come down and live among them. He liked the pillar or he would not have been there. Something about it suited his nature. And something about Cross Creek suits us—or something about us makes us cling to it contentedly, lovingly and often in exasperation, through the vicissitudes that have driven others away.

"I wouldn't live any place else," Tom said, "if I had gold buried in Georgia. I tell you, so much happens at Cross Creek."

There is of course an affinity between people and places. "And God called the dry land Earth; and the gathering together of waters called He Seas; and God saw that it was good." This was before man, and if there be such a thing as racial memory, the con-sciousness of land and water must lie deeper in the core of us than any knowledge of our fellow beings. We were bred of earth before we were born of our mothers. Once born, we can live without mother or father, or any other kin, or any friend, or any human love. We cannot live without the earth or apart from it, and something is shrivelled in a man's heart when he turns away from it and concerns himself only with the affairs of men.

And along with our deep knowledge of the earth is a preference of each of us for certain kinds of it, for the earth is various as we are various. One man longs for the mountains, and does not even need to have been a child of the mountains to have this longing; and another man yearns for the valleys or the plains. A seaman I know said that he was making a great effort to assure himself of going to Hell, for the Bible says that in Heaven "there shall be no more sea," and Heaven for him is a place of great waters.

We at the Creek need and have found only very simple things. We must need flowering and fruiting trees, for all of us have citrus groves of one size or another. We must need a certain blandness of season, with a longer and more beneficent heat than many require, for there is never too much sun for us, and through the long summers we do not complain. We need the song of birds, and there is none finer than the red-bird. We need the sound of rain coming across the *hamaca*, and the sound of wind in trees—and there is no more sensitive Aeolian harp than the palm. The pine is good, for the needles brushing one another have a great softness, and we have the wind in the pines, too.

We need above all, I think, a certain remoteness from urban confusion, and while this can be found in other places, Cross Creek offers it with such beauty and grace that once entangled with it, no other place seems possible to us, just as when truly in love none other offers the comfort of the beloved. We are not even offended when others do not share our delight. Tom Glisson and I often laugh together at the people who consider the Creek dull, or, in the precise sense, outlandish.

"There was a fellow woke me up," he said, "was lost. I'd heard his car go by and hit the Creek bridge like cattle stampeding. I wondered if ary one in that big of a hurry knowed where he was going. Directly he come back and stopped and I heard him holler from the gate. I pulled on my breeches and went out to him. I said, 'Reckon you're lost.' 'Lost ain't the word for it,' he said. 'Is this the end of the world? Where in God's name am I?' I said, 'Mister, you're at Cross Creek.' 'That don't tell me a thing,' he said. 'I still ain't anywhere.' "

"People in town sometimes say to me when I start home at night," I said, " 'We hate to see you drive off alone to that awful place.' "

"Well," he said comfortably, "they just don't know the Creek."

We do. We know one another. Our knowledge is a strange kind, totally without intimacy, for we go our separate ways and meet only when new fences are strung, or some one's stock intrudes on another, or when one of us is ill or in trouble, or when woods fires come too close, or when a shooting occurs and we must agree who is right and who must go to jail, or when the weather is so preposterous, either as to heat or cold, or rain or drought, that we seek out excuses to be together, to talk together about the common menace. We get into violent arguments and violent quarrels, sometimes about stock, sometimes because we take sides with our favorites when the dark Mickens family goes on the warpath.

The village exaggerates our differences and claims that something in the Creek water makes people quarrelsome. Our amenities pass unnoticed. We do injustices among ourselves, and another of us, not directly involved, usually manages to put in a judicious word on the side of right. The one who is wrong usually ends by admitting it, and all is well again, and I have done my share of the eating of humble pie. And when the great enemies of Old Starvation and Old Death come skulking down on us, we put up a united front and fight them side by side, as we fight the woods fires.

Each of us knows the foibles of the others and the strength and the weaknesses, and who can be counted on for what. Old Aunt Martha Mickens, with her deceptive humility and her face like poured chocolate, is perhaps the shuttle that has woven our knowledge, carrying back and forth, with the apparent innocence of a nest-building bird, the most revealing bits of gossip; the sort of gossip that tells, not trivial facts, but human motives and the secrets of human hearts. Each of us pretends that she carries these threads only about others and never about us, but we all know better, and that none of us is spared.

A dozen other whites and a baker's dozen of other blacks have lived at one time or another among us, or in the immediate vicinity of the Creek, coming and going like the robins. We are clannish and do not feel the same about them as we feel about ourselves. It was believed in the beginning that I was one of these. Surely the Creek would drive me away. When it was clear that a freezing of the orange crop was as great a catastrophe to me as to the others, surely I would not be here long. It was when old Martha, who had set up the Brices as Old Boss and Old Miss, referred to me one day as Young Miss, that it was understood by all of us that I was here to stay.

For myself, the Creek satisfies a thing that had gone hungry and unfed since childhood days. I am often lonely. Who is not? But I should be lonelier in the heart of a city. And as Tom says, "So much happens here." I walk at sunset, east along the road. There are no houses in that direction, except the abandoned one where the wild plums grow, white with bloom in springtime. I usually walk halfway to the village and back again. No one goes, like myself, on foot, except Bernie Bass perhaps, striding firmly in rubber boots with his wet sack of fish over his shoulder.

Sometimes black Henry passes with a mule and wagon, taking a load of lighter'd home to Old Boss; sometimes a neighbor's car, or the wagon that turns off toward the turpentine woods to collect the resin, or the timber truck coming out from the pine woods. The white folks call "Hey!" and children wave gustily and with pleasure. A stranger driving by usually slows down and asks whether I want a lift. The Negroes touch a finger to their ragged caps or pretend courteously not to see me. Evening after evening I walk as far as the magnolias near Big Hammock, and home, and see no one.

Folk call the road lonely, because there is not human traffic and human stirring. Because I have walked it so many times and seen such a tumult of life there, it seems to me one of the most populous highways of my acquaintance. I have walked it in ecstacy, and in joy it is beloved. Every pine tree, every gallberry bush, every passion vine, every joree rustling in the underbush, is vibrant. I have walked it in trouble, and the wind in the trees beside me is easing. I have walked it in despair, and the red of the sunset is my own blood dissolving into the night's darkness. For all such things were on earth before us, and will survive after us, and it is given to us to join ourselves with them and to be comforted.

The Negro in the Well

ERSKINE CALDWELL

A writer of more limited range than Faulkner, and one whose later work has not held to the level of his earlier productions, Erskine Caldwell is nevertheless a man of considerable capacity. His themes in the main have been social ones; at his best, in his harsh humors, his tales of gross hatred and mistreatment, he has intensity and strength. A number of his stories—"The Negro in the Well," which is used here, and his "Kneel to the Rising Sun"—are near-classics, written with economy and a fierce directness. A native of Georgia, Mr. Caldwell has told of his limited formal schooling, although eventually he was a University of Virginia student for three years. Later a newspaperman, he held many odd jobs. While little of a stylist in the sense of a careful, perceptive selector of the best word, the most meaningful phrase, the author has a capacity for vigorous, purposeful dialogue—the language of the plain man, the words of the shifty-eyed individual on the rise in a small town. His manner of writing, as it has been said, often has fitted his intention with perfection—gaunt sentences, speeches that quickly advance the story. To millions of readers in many countries, Caldwell's words have meaning and also a vast readability.

Throughout his work there appears an element of caricature, of conscious use of the grotesque. Frequently the innocence of a plain man wins over guile; again the vicious individual triumphs. In Caldwell's work there is a more or less outspoken indictment of hard, destructive forces in the Southern world. He is also the author of a number of volumes of serious sociological comment on the population of the South.

JULE ROBINSON was lying in bed snoring when his foxhounds struck a live trail a mile away and their baying woke him up with a start. He jumped to the floor, jerked on his shoes, and ran out into the front yard. It was about an hour before dawn.

Holding his hat to the side of his head like a swollen hand, he listened to the trailing on the ridge above the house. With his hat to deflect the sound into his ear, he could hear the dogs treading in the dry underbrush as plainly as his own breathing. It had taken him only a few seconds to determine that the hounds were not cold-trailing, and he put his hat back on his head and stooped over to lace his shoes.

"Papa," a frightened voice said, "please don't go off again now—wait till daybreak, anyway."

Jule turned around and saw the dim outline of his two girls. They were huddled together in the window of their bedroom. Jessie and Clara were old enough to take care of themselves, he thought, but that did not stop them from getting in his way when he wanted to go fox-hunting.

"Go on back to bed and sleep, Jessie—you and Clara," he said gruffly. "Those hounds are just up on the ridge. They can't take me much out of hollering distance before sunup."

"We're scared, Papa," Clara said.

"Scared of what?" Jule asked impatiently. "There ain't a thing for two big girls like you and Jessie to be scared of. What's there to be scared of in this big country, anyway?"

The hounds stopped trailing for a moment, and Jule straightened up to listen in the silence. All at once they began again, and he bent down to finish tying his shoes.

Off in the distance he could hear several other packs of trailing hounds, and by looking closely at the horizon he could see the twinkle of campfires where bands of fox-hunters had stopped to warm their hands and feet.

"Are you going, anyway, Papa?" Clara asked.

"I'm going, anyway," he answered.

The two girls ran back to bed and pulled the covers over their heads. There was no way to argue with Jule Robinson when he had set his head on following his foxhounds.

The craze must have started anew sometime during the holidays, because by the end of the first week in January it looked and sounded as if everybody in Georgia were trading foxhounds by day and bellowing "Whoo-way-oh!" by night. From the time the sun went down until the next morning when it came up, the woods, fields, pastures, and swamps were crawling with beggar-liced men and yelping hound-dogs. Nobody would have thought of riding horseback after the hounds in a country where there was a barbwire fence every few hundred yards.

Automobiles roared and rattled over the rough country roads all night long. The fox-hunters had to travel fast in order to keep up with the pack. It was not safe for any living thing with four legs to be out after sundown, because the hounds had the hunting fever too, and packs of those rangy half-starved dogs were running down and devouring calves, hogs, and even yellow-furred bobcats. It had got so during the past two weeks that the chickens knew enough to take to their roosts an hour ahead of time, because those packs of gaunt hunt-hungry hounds could not wait for sunset any more.

Jule finished lacing his shoes and went around the house. The path to the ridge began in the back yard and weaved up the hillside like a cowpath through a thicket. Jule passed the well and stopped to feel in his pockets to see if he had enough smoking tobacco to last him until he got back.

While he was standing there he heard behind him a sound like water gurgling through the neck of a demijohn. Jule listened again. The sound came even more plainly while he listened. There was no creek anywhere within hearing distance, and the nearest water was in the well. He went to the edge and listened again. The well did not have a stand or a windlass; it was merely a twenty-foot hole in the ground with boards laid over the top to keep pigs and chickens from falling into it.

"O Lord, help me now!" a voice said.

Jule got down on his hands and knees and looked at the well-cover in the darkness. He felt of the boards with his hands. Three of them had been moved, and there was a black oblong hole that was large enough to drop a calf through.

"Who's that?" Jule said, stretching out his neck and cocking his ear.

"O Lord, help me now," the voice said again, weaker than before.

The gurgling sound began again, and Jule knew then that it was the water in the well.

"Who's down there muddying up my well?" Jule said.

There was no sound then. Even the gurgling stopped.

Jule felt on the ground for a pebble and

dropped it into the well. He counted until he could hear the *kerplunk* when it struck the water.

"Doggone your hide, whoever you are down there!" Jule said. "Who's down there?"

Nobody answered.

Jule felt in the dark for the water bucket, but he could not find it. Instead, his fingers found a larger pebble, a stone almost as big around as his fist, and he dropped it into the well.

The big rock struck something else before it finally went into the water.

"O Lord, I'm going down and can't help myself," the voice down there said. "O Lord, a big hand is trying to shove me under."

The hounds trailing on the ridge swung around to the east and started back again. The fox they were after was trying to back-trail them, but Jule's hounds were hard to fool. They had got to be almost as smart as a fox.

Jule straightened up and listened to the running.

"Whoo-way-oh!" he called after the dogs.

That sent them on yelping even louder than before.

"Is that you up there, Mr. Jule?" the voice asked.

Jule bent over the well again, keeping one ear on the dogs on the ridge. He did not want to lose track of them when they were on a live trail like that.

"This is me," Jule said. "Who's that?"

"This is only Bokus Bradley, Mr. Jule," the voice said.

"What you doing down in my well, mud-dying it up like that, Bokus?"

"It was something like this, Mr. Jule," Bokus said. "I was coming down the ridge a while ago, trying to keep up with my hounds, and I stumbled over your well-cover. I reckon I must have missed the path, somehow or other. Your well-cover wouldn't hold me up, or something, and the first thing I knew, here I was. I've been here ever since I fell in. I reckon I've been down here most of the night. I hope you ain't mad at me, Mr. Jule. I just naturally couldn't help it none at all."

"Where'd your dogs go to, Bokus?" Jule asked.

"I don't know, Mr. Jule. I haven't heard a sound of them since I fell in here. They was headed for the creek when I was coming down the ridge behind them. Can you hear them anywhere now, Mr. Jule?"

Several packs of hounds could be heard. Jule's on the ridge was trailing east, and a pack was trailing down the creek toward town. Over toward the hills several more packs were running, but they were so far away it was not easy to tell to whom they belonged.

"Sounds to me like I hear your dogs down the creek, headed for the swamp," Jule said.

"Whoo-way-oh!" Bokus called.

The sound from the well struck Jule like a blast out of a megaphone.

"Your dogs can't hear you from 'way down there, Bokus," he said.

"I know they can't, Mr. Jule, and that's why I sure enough want to get out of here. My poor dogs don't know which way I want them to trail when they can't hear me talk to them. Whoo-way-oh!" Bokus shouted. "O Lord, help me now!"

Jule's dogs sounded as if they were clos-ing in on a fox, and Jule jumped to his feet.

"Whoo-way-oh!" he shouted, cupping his hands around his mouth. "Whoo-way-oh!"

"Is you still up there, Mr. Jule?" Bokus asked. "Please, Mr. Jule, don't go away and leave me down here in this cold well. I'll do anything for you if you'll just only get me out of here. I've been standing neck-deep in this cold water near about all night long."

Jule threw some of the boards over the well.

"What are you doing up there, Mr. Jule?"

Jule took off his hat and held the brim like a fan to the side of his head. He could hear the panting of the dogs while they ran.

"How many foxhounds have you got, Bokus?" Jule asked.

"I got me eight," Bokus said. "They're mighty fine fox-trailers, too, Mr. Jule. But I'd like to get me out of this here well before doing much more talking with you."

"You could get along somehow with less than that, couldn't you, Bokus?"

"If I had to, I'd have to," Bokus said, "but I sure enough would hate to have fewer than my eight dogs, though. Eight is just naturally the right-sized pack for me, Mr. Jule."

"How are you figuring on getting out of there?" Jule said.

"I just naturally figured on you helping me out, Mr. Jule," he said. "Leastaways, that's about the only way I know of getting out of this here well. I tried climbing, but the dirt just naturally crumbles away every time I dig my toes into the sides."

"You've got that well so muddied up it won't be fit to drink out of for a week or more," Jule said.

"I'll do what I can to clean it out for you, Mr. Jule, if I ever get on top of the solid ground again. Can you hear those hounds of mine trailing now, Mr. Jule?"

"They're still down the creek. I reckon I could lower the water bucket, and I could pull a little, and you could climb a little, and maybe you'd get out that way."

"That just naturally would suit me fine, Mr. Jule," Bokus said eagerly. "Here I is. When is you going to lower that water bucket?"

Jule stood up and listened to his dogs trailing on the ridge. From the way they sounded, it would not be long before they treed the fox they were after.

"It's only about an hour till daybreak," Jule said. "I'd better go on up the ridge and see how my hounds are making out. I can't do much here at the well till the sun comes up."

"Don't go away and leave me now, Mr. Jule," Bokus begged. "Mr. Jule, please, sir, just lower that water bucket down here and help me get out. I just naturally got to get out of here, Mr. Jule. My dogs will get all balled up without me following them. Whoo-way-oh! Whoo-way-oh!"

The pack of fox-trailing hounds was coming up from the creek, headed toward the house. Jule took off his hat and held it beside his ear. He listened to them panting and yelping.

"If I had two more hounds, I'd be mighty pleased," Jule said, shouting loud enough for Bokus to hear. "Just two is all I need right now."

"You wouldn't be wanting two of mine, would you, Mr. Jule?" Bokus asked.

"It's a good time to make a trade," Jule said. "It's a mighty good time, being as how you are down in the well and want to get out."

"Two, did you say?"

"Two is what I said."

There was silence in the well for a long time. For nearly five minutes Jule listened to the packs of dogs all around him, some on the ridge, some down the creek, and some in the far-off hills. The barking of the hounds was a sweeter sound to him than anything else in the world. He would lose a night's sleep any time just to stay up and hear a pack of fox-hounds live-trailing.

"Whoo-way-oh!" he called.

"Mr. Jule!" Bokus shouted up from the bottom of the well.

Jule went to the edge and leaned over to hear what the Negro had to say.

"How about that there trade now, Bokus?"

"Mr. Jule, I just naturally couldn't swap off two of my hounds, I just sure enough couldn't."

"Why not?" Jule said.

"Because I'd have only just six dogs left, Mr. Jule, and I couldn't do much fox-hunting with just that many."

Jule straightened up and kicked the boards over the top of the well.

"You won't be following even so few as one hound for a while," he said, "because I'm going to leave you down in the bottom where you stand now. It's another hour, almost, till daybreak, and I can't be wasting that time staying here talking to you. Maybe when I get back you'll be in a mind to do some trading, Bokus."

Jule kicked the boards on top of the well.

"O Lord, help me now!" Bokus said. "But, O Lord, don't make me swap off no two hounds for the help I'm asking for."

Jule stumbled over the water bucket when he turned and started across the yard toward the path up the ridge. Up there he could hear his dogs running again, and when he took off his hat and held it to the side of his head he could hear Polly pant, and Senator snort, and Mary Jane whine, and Sunset yelp, and the rest of them barking at the head of the trail. He put on his hat, pulled it down hard all around, and hurried up the path to follow them on the ridge. The fox would not be able to. hold out much longer.

"Whoo-way-oh!" he called to his hounds. "Whoo-way-oh!"

The echo was a masterful sound to hear.

A Rose for Emily

WILLIAM FAULKNER

For William Faulkner of Mississippi, a towering success came slowly, after years of comparative neglect. His work is far from simple, with overlong sentences which stretch across pages, with sections which demand rereading, and often a presentation of shifting viewpoints. His writing has flaws and confusions, and yet it possesses a great strength, a vast compassion and powerful characters. Repeatedly Faulkner demonstrates contempt for the snide, the grabbers of the earth. He has achieved a remarkable presentation of his "Yoknapatawpha County," which exists in Mississippi but not under that name, and he has filled it with a swarming, often squirming people: with the long-aristocratic Sartoris clan; with the low white Snopeses who are the destroyers; with the Negroes for whom, in the main, the author seems to hold sympathy. Faulkner's work is a saga, a collection of sagas of what he regards as a doomed land, suffering under a weight of guilt for past wrongs and injustices. In his novels and short stories he offers an incident, jumps to another family and another era, then reintroduces earlier episodes and characters. His themes are many: the white man's harshness to the Indians; the launching of great estates, sometimes through trickery; race mixtures, violences of a dozen kinds, aberrations, slow degradations. And still Faulkner has shown a more affirmative side, a comprehension of men's hopes for a future. His earlier novels, tentative and uncertain in places, were largely passed over until the 1940's, when reviewers came to appreciate him. New recognition was swift. When he received the Nobel prize in 1950 he had approached a pinnacle for an American author. He is often an experimenter, a man who lavishes his gifts, writing with "cold ferocity" or "strained intensity" of a scene combining "civilization and savagery, like a colonial mansion in a cypress swamp." His remarkable short story, "A Rose for Emily," was written in 1924, and is used by permission of Random House. It is supposedly based on a true incident.

WHEN Miss Emily Grierson died, our whole town went to her funeral: the men through a sort of respectful affection for a fallen monument, the women mostly out of curiosity to see the inside of her house, which no one save an old manservant—a combined gardener and cook—had seen in at least ten years.

It was a big, squarish frame house that had once been white, decorated with cupolas and spires and scrolled balconies in the heavily lightsome style of the seventies, set on what had once been our most select street. But garages and cotton gins had encroached and obliterated even the august names of that neighborhood; only Miss Emily's house was left, lifting its stubborn and coquettish decay above the cotton wagons and the gasoline pumps—an eyesore among eyesores. And now Miss Emily had gone to join the representatives of those august names where they lay in the cedar-bemused cemetery among the ranked and anonymous graves of Union and Confederate soldiers who fell at the battle of Jefferson.

Alive, Miss Emily had been a tradition, a duty, and a care; a sort of hereditary obligation upon the town, dating from that day in 1894 when Colonel Sartoris, the mayor—he who fathered the edict that no Negro woman should appear on the streets without an apron —remitted her taxes, the dispensation dating from the death of her father on into perpetuity. Not that Miss Emily would have accepted charity. Colonel Sartoris invented an involved tale to the effect that Miss Emily's father had loaned money to the town, which the town, as a matter of business, preferred this way of repaying. Only a man of Colonel Sartoris' generation and thought could have invented it, and only a woman could have believed it.

When the next generation, with its more modern ideas, became mayors and aldermen, this arrangement created some little dissatisfaction. On the first of the year they mailed her a tax notice. February came, and there was no reply. They wrote her a formal letter, asking her to call at the sheriff's office at her convenience. A week later the mayor wrote her himself, offering to call or to send his car for her, and received in reply a note on paper of an archaic shape, in a thin, flowing calligraphy in faded ink, to the effect that she no longer went out at all. The tax notice was also enclosed, without comment.

They called a special meeting of the Board of Aldermen. A deputation waited upon her, knocked at the door through which no visitor had passed since she ceased giving china-painting lessons eight or ten years earlier. They were admitted by the old Negro into a dim hall from which a stairway mounted into still more shadow. It smelled of dust and disuse—a close, dank smell. The Negro led them into the parlor. It was furnished in heavy, leather-covered furniture. When the Negro opened the blinds of one window, they could see that the leather was cracked; and when they sat down, a faint dust rose sluggishly about their thighs, spinning with slow motes in the single sun-ray. On a tarnished gilt easel before the fireplace stood a crayon portrait of Miss Emily's father.

They rose when she entered—a small, fat woman in black, with a thin gold chain descending to her waist and vanishing into her belt, leaning on an ebony cane with a tarnished gold head. Her skeleton was small and spare; perhaps that was why what would have been merely plumpness in another was obesity in her. She looked bloated, like a body long submerged in motionless water, and of that pallid hue. Her eyes, lost in the fatty ridges of her face, looked like two small pieces of coal pressed into a lump of dough as they moved from one face to another while the visitors stated their errand.

She did not ask them to sit. She just stood in the door and listened quietly until the spokesman came to a stumbling halt. Then they could hear the invisible watch ticking at the end of the gold chain.

Her voice was dry and cold. "I have no taxes in Jefferson. Colonel Sartoris explained it to me. Perhaps one of you can gain access to the city records and satisfy yourselves."

"But we have. We are the city authorities, Miss Emily. Didn't you get a notice from the sheriff, signed by him?"

"I received a paper, yes," Miss Emily said. "Perhaps he considers himself the sheriff . . . I have no taxes in Jefferson."

"But there is nothing on the books to show that, you see. We must go by the—"

"See Colonel Sartoris. I have no taxes in Jefferson."

"But, Miss Emily—"

"See Colonel Sartoris." (Colonel Sartoris had been dead almost ten years.) "I have no taxes in Jefferson. Tobe!" The Negro appeared. "Show these gentlemen out."

So she vanquished them, horse and foot, just as she had vanquished their fathers thirty years before about the smell. That was two years after her father's death and a short time after her sweetheart—the one we believed would marry her—had deserted her. After her father's death she went out very little; after her sweetheart went away, people hardly saw her at all. A few of the ladies had the temerity to call, but were not received, and the only sign of life about the place was the Negro man—a young man then—going in and out with a market basket.

"Just as if a man—any man—could keep a kitchen properly," the ladies said; so they were not surprised when the smell developed. It was another link between the gross, teeming world and the high and mighty Griersons.

A neighbor, a woman, complained to the mayor, Judge Stevens, eighty years old.

"But what will you have me do about it, madam?" he said.

"Why, send her word to stop it," the woman said. "Isn't there a law?"

"I'm sure that won't be necessary," Judge Stevens said. "It's probably just a snake or a rat that nigger of hers killed in the yard. I'll speak to him about it."

The next day he received two more complaints, one from a man who came in diffident deprecation. "We really must do something about it, Judge. I'd be the last one in the world to bother Miss Emily, but we've got to do something." That night the Board of Aldermen met—three graybeards and one younger man, a member of the rising generation.

"It's simple enough," he said. "Send her word to have her place cleaned up. Give her a certain time to do it in, and if she don't . . ."

"Dammit, sir," Judge Stevens said, "will you accuse a lady to her face of smelling bad?"

So the next night, after midnight, four men crossed Miss Emily's lawn and slunk about the house like burglars, sniffing along the base of the brickwork and at the cellar openings while one of them performed a regular sowing motion with his hand out of a sack slung from his shoulder. They broke open the cellar door and sprinkled lime there, and in all the outbuildings. As they recrossed the lawn, a window that had been dark was lighted and Miss Emily sat in it, the light behind her, and her upright torso motionless as that of an idol. They crept quietly across the

lawn and into the shadow of the locusts that lined the street. After a week or two the smell went away.

That was when people had begun to feel really sorry for her. People in our town, remembering how old lady Wyatt, her great-aunt, had gone completely crazy at last, believed that the Griersons held themselves a little too high for what they really were. None of the young men were quite good enough to Miss Emily and such. We had long thought of them as a tableau; Miss Emily a slender figure in white in the background, her father a spraddled silhouette in the foreground, his back to her and clutching a horse-whip, the two of them framed by the back-flung front door. So when she got to be thirty and was still single, we were not pleased exactly, but vindicated; even with insanity in the family she wouldn't have turned down all of her chances if they had really materialized.

When her father died, it got about that the house was all that was left to her; and in a way, people were glad. At last they could pity Miss Emily. Being left alone, and a pauper, she had become humanized. Now she too would know the old thrill and the old despair of a penny more or less.

The day after his death all the ladies prepared to call at the house and offer condolence and aid, as is our custom. Miss Emily met them at the door, dressed as usual and with no trace of grief on her face. She told them that her father was not dead. She did that for three days, with the ministers calling on her, and the doctors, trying to persuade her to let them dispose of the body. Just as they were about to resort to law and force, she broke down, and they buried her father quickly.

We did not say she was crazy then. We believed she had to do that. We remembered all the young men her father had driven away, and we knew that with nothing left, she would have to cling to that which had robbed her, as people will.

She was sick for a long time. When we saw her again, her hair was cut short, making her look like a girl, with a vague resemblance to those angels in colored church windows—sort of tragic and serene.

The town had just let the contracts for paving the sidewalks, and in the summer after her father's death they began the work. The construction company came with niggers and mules and machinery, and a foreman named Homer Barron, a Yankee—a big, dark, ready man, with a big voice and eyes lighter than his face. The little boys would follow in groups to hear him cuss the niggers, and the niggers singing in time to the rise and fall of picks. Pretty soon he knew everybody in town. Whenever you heard a lot of laughing anywhere about the square, Homer Barron would be in the center of the group. Presently we began to see him and Miss Emily on Sunday afternoons driving in the yellow-wheeled buggy and the matched team of bays from the livery stable.

At first we were glad that Miss Emily would have an interest, because the ladies all said, "Of course a Grierson would not think seriously of a Northerner, a day laborer." But there were still others, older people, who said that even grief could not cause a real lady to forget *noblesse oblige*—without calling it *noblesse oblige*. They just said, "Poor Emily. Her kinsfolk should come to her." She had some kin in Alabama; but years ago her father had fallen out with them over the estate of old lady Wyatt, the crazy woman, and there was no communication between the two families. They had not even been represented at the funeral.

And as soon as the old people said, "Poor Emily," the whispering began. "Do you suppose it's really so?" they said to one another. "Of course it is. What else could . . ." This behind their hands; rustling of craned silk and satin behind jalousies closed upon the sun of Sunday afternoon as the thin, swift clop-clop-clop of the matched team passed: "Poor Emily."

She carried her head high enough—even when we believed that she was fallen. It was as if she demanded more than ever the recognition of her dignity as the last Grierson; as if it had wanted that touch of earthiness to reaffirm her imperviousness. Like when she bought the rat poison, the arsenic. That was over a year after they had begun to say "Poor Emily," and while the two female cousins were visiting her.

"I want some poison," she said to the druggist. She was over thirty then, still a slight woman, though thinner than usual, with cold, haughty black eyes in a face the flesh of which was strained across the temples and about the eye-sockets as you imagine a lighthousekeeper's face ought to look. "I want some poison," she said.

"Yes, Miss Emily. What kind? For rats and such? I'd recom—"

"I want the best you have. I don't care what kind."

The druggist named several. "They'll kill anything up to an elephant. But what you want is—"

"Arsenic," Miss Emily said. "Is that a good one?"

"Is . . . arsenic? Yes, ma'am. But what you want—"

"I want arsenic."

The druggist looked down at her. She looked back at him, erect, her face like a strained flag. "Why, of course," the druggist said. "If that's what you want. But the law requires you to tell what you are going to use it for."

Miss Emily just stared at him, her head tilted back in order to look him eye for eye, until he looked away and went and got the arsenic and wrapped it up. The Negro delivery boy brought her the package; the druggist didn't come back. When she opened the package at home there was written on the box, under the skull and bones: "For rats."

So the next day we all said, "She will kill herself"; and we said it would be the best thing. When she had first begun to be seen with Homer Barron, we had said, "She will marry him." Then we said, "She will persuade him yet," because Homer himself had remarked—he liked men, and it was known that he drank with the younger men in the Elks' Club—that he was not a marrying man. Later we said, "Poor Emily" behind the jalousies as they passed on Sunday afternoon in the glittering buggy. Miss Emily with her head high and Homer Barron with his hat cocked and a cigar in his teeth, reins and whip in a yellow glove.

Then some of the ladies began to say that it was a disgrace to the town and a bad example to the young people. The men did not want to interfere, but at last the ladies forced the Baptist minister—Miss Emily's people were Episcopal—to call upon her. He would never divulge what happened during that interview, but he refused to go back again. The next Sunday they again drove about the streets, and the following day the minister's wife wrote to Miss Emily's relations in Alabama.

So she had blood-kin under her roof again and we sat back to watch developments. At first nothing happened. Then we were sure that they were to be married. We learned that Miss Emily had been to the jeweler's and ordered a man's toilet set in silver, with the letters H. B. on each piece. Two days later we learned that she had bought a complete outfit of men's clothing, including a nightshirt, and we said, "They are married." We were really glad. We were glad because the two female cousins were even more Grierson than Miss Emily had ever been.

So we were not surprised when Homer Barron—the streets had been finished some time since—was gone. We were a little disappointed that there was not a public blowing-off, but we believed that he had gone on to prepare for Miss Emily's coming, or to give her a chance to get rid of the cousins. (By that time it was a cabal, and we were all Miss Emily's allies to help circumvent the cousins.) Sure enough, after another week they departed. And, as we had expected all along, within three days Homer Barron was back in town. A neighbor saw the Negro man admit him at the kitchen door at dusk one evening.

And that was the last we saw of Homer Barron. And of Miss Emily for some time. The Negro man went in and out with the market basket, but the front door remained closed. Now and then we would see her at a window for a moment, as the men did that night when they sprinkled the lime, but for almost six months she did not appear on the streets. Then we knew that this was to be expected too; as if that quality of her father which had thwarted her woman's life so many times had been too virulent and too furious to die.

When we next saw Miss Emily, she had grown fat and her hair was turning gray. During the next few years it grew grayer and grayer until it attained an even pepper-and-salt iron-gray, when it ceased turning. Up to the day of her death at seventy-four it was still that vigorous iron-gray, like the hair of an active man.

From that time on her front door remained closed, save for a period of six or seven years, when she was about forty, during which she gave lessons in china-painting. She fitted up a studio in one of the downstairs rooms, where the daughters and granddaughters of Colonel Sartoris' contemporaries were sent to her with the same regularity and in the same spirit that they were sent to church on Sundays with a twenty-five cent piece for the collection plate. Meanwhile her taxes had been remitted.

Then the newer generation became the backbone and the spirit of the town, and the painting pupils grew up and fell away and did not send their children to her with boxes of color and tedious brushes and pictures cut from the ladies' magazines. The front door closed upon the last one and remained closed for good. When the town got free postal delivery, Miss Emily alone refused to let them fasten the metal numbers above her door and attach a mailbox to it. She would not listen to them.

Daily, monthly, yearly we watched the Negro grow grayer and more stooped, going in and out with the market basket. Each December we sent her a tax notice, which would be returned by the post office a week later, unclaimed. Now and then we would see her in one of the downstairs windows—she had evidently shut up the top floor of the house—like the carven torso of an idol in a niche, looking or not looking at us, we could never tell which. Thus she passed from generation to generation—dear, inescapable, impervious, tranquil, and perverse.

And so she died. Fell ill in the house filled with dust and shadows, with only a doddering Negro man to wait on her. We did not even know she was sick; we had long since given up trying to get any information from the Negro. He talked to no one, probably not even to her, for his voice had grown harsh and rusty, as if from disuse.

She died in one of the downstairs rooms, in a heavy walnut bed with a curtain, her gray head propped on a pillow yellow and moldy with age and lack of sunlight.

The Negro met the first of the ladies at the front door and let them in, with their hushed, sibilant voices and their quick, curious glances, and then he disappeared. He walked right through the house and out the back and was not seen again.

The two female cousins came at once. They held the funeral on the second day, with the town coming to look at Miss Emily beneath a mass of bought flowers, with the crayon face of her father musing profoundly above the bier and the ladies sibilant and macabre; and the very old men—some in their brushed Confederate uniforms—on the porch and the lawn, talking of Miss Emily as if she had been a contemporary of theirs, believing that they had danced with her and courted her perhaps, confusing time with its mathematical progression, as the old do, to whom all the past is not a diminishing road but, instead, a huge meadow which no winter ever quite touches, divided from them now by the narrow bottle-neck of the most recent decade of years.

Already we knew that there was one room in that region above stairs which no one had seen in forty years, and which would have to be forced. They waited until Miss Emily was decently in the ground before they opened it.

The violence of breaking down the door seemed to fill this room with pervading dust. A thin, acrid pall as of the tomb seemed to lie everywhere upon this room decked and furnished as for a bridal: upon the valence curtains of faded rose color, upon the rose-shaded lights, upon the dressing table, upon the delicate array of crystal and the man's toilet things backed with tarnished silver, silver so tarnished that the monogram was obscured. Among them lay a collar and tie, as if they had just been removed, which, lifted, left upon the surface a pale crescent in the dust. Upon a chair hung the suit, carefully folded; beneath it the two mute shoes and the discarded socks.

The man himself lay in the bed.

For a long while we just stood there, looking down at the profound and fleshless grin. The body had apparently once lain in the attitude of an embrace, but now the long sleep that outlasts love, that conquers even the grimace of love, had cuckolded him. What was left of him, rotted beneath what was left of the nightshirt, had become inextricable from the bed in which he lay; and upon him and upon the pillow beside him lay that even coating of the patient and biding dust.

Then we noticed that in the second pillow was the indentation of a head. One of us lifted something from it, and leaning forward, that faint and invisible dust dry and acrid in the nostrils, we saw a long strand of iron-gray hair.

Intimate Secrets from a Stranger on a Bus
ROBERT TALLANT

Born in 1909 in New Orleans, Robert Tallant finished high school about the time of his father's death, became a bank runner, then a staff member of the Federal Writers' Project, and later a government censorship worker. Mr. Tallant's first book, Voodoo in New Orleans, *appeared in 1946, to be followed by a series of humorous novels,* Mrs. Candy and Saturday Night *and a number of sequels;*

Southern Territory, Mardi Gras, Ready to Hang, *and others. His books showed a lively humor and an unusual skill in the handling of dialogue. He died suddenly in 1957. This selection is from* The Romantic New Orleans, *published in 1950 by Dutton.*

THE day the International Trade Mart in New Orleans opened its doors to visitors a matron devoted to all the old, if curious ways of her city was among those calling. She did not remain inside long. After a quick glance around the first and second floors, she hastened to the street and shot a startled glance towards the outside of the handsome modern structure of concrete and glass brick. "This is perfectly absurd!" she snapped to a group emerging from the building. "There are no windows at all. How is anyone going to look out and see a parade?"

. . .

New Orleanians have always loved to open their world to properly identified visitors. For New Orleans is a world. . . . Here, they feel, is an opportunity to introduce a stranger to the only civilized city in the United States, if not in the world, the only place where people know how to eat and drink and live. . . . The native does feel that the outsider is fortunate to have arrived in New Orleans, and when the visitor leaves, the New Orleanian nearly, if not literally, weeps for him. "You will come back," he is likely to assure the departing guest. "Yes. Don't worry. You will come back!" This is said not only as an invitation to return. It is intended for consolation.

Woe to him who is so foolish as to say he does not like any part of it! No woman ever reacted to unrequited love as can a New Orleanian to hearing his city criticized. . . . The visitor may have somewhere tasted food he liked as well as that served him in one of the famous restaurants in New Orleans, he may have had a cocktail he liked better than a Sazerac, he may not have been gifted with the proper temperament for full enjoyment of the Mardi Gras, or he may not be able to discern the charm beneath the outer shabbiness of some house in the French Quarter. But he must keep these sad defects in his being to himself. The average New Orleanian

will think him either insulting or pathetically ignorant if he confesses any of them. After all, he has just come to New Orleans. What can he know of *true* civilization?

. . .

New Orleanians are, naturally, interested in what goes on beyond the willowy outlines of their city, but they are probably somewhat less interested than most other communities. This attitude has abated somewhat of late years, for both world wars thrust pins into it. Yet it is still true enough for a classically illustrative story of it to persist. It seems that two matrons met in a hotel lobby. Not having seen each other in a long time, they fell into each other's arms. When this was over and tears of joy were brushed away, one gasped to the other, "But, my dear, where *have* you been? I never see you any place these days!"

"Oh, I know, darling!" cried the other breathlessly. "My husband has been traveling, you know. We were in New York for a few months. Then we spent some time in Paris, and after that we were in Rome for a year. We've just come home, and I'm so excited."

"You poor thing!" shrieked the first lady, seizing her friend's arm and wheeling her around toward the cocktail lounge. "We must have a drink and a long talk. I have so much to tell you. I know you don't know a *thing!*"

. . .

New Orleanians love conversation. Practically everybody talks all the time. Even making a purchase in a store is usually preceded by some oral pleasantries. Most salesladies in the downtown stores are prone to call everybody "honey" and are likely to be called "honey" or "darling," or even "precious" in return. Waiters and grocers always have time for bits of conversation, and one seldom purchases a box of aspirin in a drugstore without genial comments upon the weather, the football season or the state of one's liver.

Now and then a visitor has a rather harrowing experience on a streetcar or bus when the occupant of the seat next to his begins to reveal the innermost secrets of his personal life in every vivid detail. It is commonplace for friends meeting on the most crowded of business streets to stop and form a group in the middle of the sidewalk and there hold a lengthy conversation, blithely unconscious of the fact that other pedestrians may have to take to the street to by-pass them.

Some Notes on River Country

EUDORA WELTY

A distinguished artist of a considerable range, with an informed sympathy for people of many elements and a humor sometimes astringent, again uproarious, Eudora Welty occupies a special niche among American writers. Born in 1909, daughter of a Mississippi insurance executive, she attended Mississippi State College for Women, University of Wisconsin, and Columbia, where she studied advertising. Almost at once Miss Welty gave up the latter calling, to launch a writing career which critics hailed from its start. While her scenes and people are generally of the South, she treats them with rare versatility. In her short stories she offers poor farmers, middle-class "nice ladies" seen in beauty parlors or doing good among neighbors; in The Robber Bridegroom *she essays fantasy; elsewhere she introduces Aaron Burr and Audubon and Murrell, nineteenth-century gangster, in strange, delicate tales. Her* Delta Wedding *is a quiet, evocative portrait of a Southern family. In* The Ponder Heart *she has written a masterpiece of comedy about some odd and wonderful folk. Her works have sadness, the quiet grins of fey characters, a delicate thread of drama, an occasional happy vulgarity. Less well known than some of her works are these meaningful "Notes on River Country" from Harper's Bazaar of 1944.*

A PLACE that ever was lived in is like a fire that never goes out. It flares up, it smolders for a time, it is fanned or smothered by circumstance, but its being is intact, forever fluttering within it, the result of some original ignition. Sometimes it gives out glory, sometimes its little light must be sought out to be seen, small and tender as a candle flame, but as certain.

I have never seen in this small section of old Mississippi River country and its little chain of lost towns between Vicksburg and Natchez anything so mundane as ghosts, but I have felt many times there a sense of place as powerful as if it were visible and walking and could touch me.

The clatter of hoofs and the bellow of boats have gone, all old communications. The Old Natchez Trace has sunk out of use, it is deep in leaves. The river has gone away and left the landings. Boats from Liverpool do not dock at these empty crags. The old deeds are done, old evil and old good have been made into stories, as plows turn up the river bottom, and the wild birds fly now at the level where people on boat deck once were strolling and talking of great expanding things, and of chance and money. Much beauty has gone, many little things of life. To light up the nights there are no mansions, no celebrations. Just as, when there were mansions and celebrations, there were no more festivals of an Indian tribe there; before the music, there were drums.

But life does not forsake any place. People live still in Rodney's Landing; flood drives them out and they return to it. Children are born there and find the day as inexhaustible and as abundant as they run and wander in their little hills as they, in innocence and rightness, would find it anywhere on earth. The seasons come as truly, and give gratefulness, though they bring little fruit. There is a sense of place there, to keep life from being extinguished, like a cup of the hands to hold a flame.

To go there, you start west from Port Gibson. This was the frontier of the Natchez country. Postmen would arrive here blowing their tin horns like Gabriel where the Old Natchez Trace crosses the Bayou Pierre, after riding three hundred wilderness miles from Tennessee, and would run in where the tavern used to be to deliver their mail, change their ponies, and warm their souls with grog. And up this now sand-barred bayou trading vessels would ply from the river. Port Gibson is on a highway and a railroad today, and lives on without its river life, though it is half-diminished. It is still rather smug because General Grant said it was "too pretty to burn." Perhaps it was too pretty for any harsh fate, with its great mossy trees and old camellias, its exquisite little churches, and galleried houses back in the hills overlooking the cotton fields. It has escaped what happened to Grand Gulf and Bruinsburg and Rodney's Landing.

A narrow gravel road goes into the West. You have entered the loess country, and a gate might have been shut behind you for the difference in the world. All about are hills and chasms of cane, forests of cedar trees, and magnolia. Falling away from your road, at times merging with it, an old trail crosses and recrosses, like a tunnel through the dense brakes, under arches of branches, a narrow, cedar-smelling trace the width of a horseman. This road joined the Natchez Trace to the river. It too was made by buffaloes, then used by man, trodden lower and lower, a few inches every hundred years.

Loess has the beautiful definition of aeolian—wind-borne. The loess soil is like a mantle; the ridge was laid down here by the wind, the bottom land by the water. Deep under them both is solid blue clay, embalming the fossil horse and the fossil ox and the great mastodon, the same preserving blue clay that was dug up to wrap the head of the Big Harp in bandit days, no less a monstrous thing when it was carried in for reward.

Loess exists also in China, that land whose plants are so congenial to the South; there the bluffs rise vertically for five hundred feet in some places and contain cave dwellings without number. The Mississippi bluffs once served the same purpose; when Vicksburg was being shelled from the river during the year's siege there in the War between the States, it was the daily habit of the three thousand women, children, and old men who made up the wartime population to go on their all-fours into shelters they had tunneled into the loess bluffs. . . .

Winding through this land unwarned, rounding to a valley, you will come on a startling thing. Set back in an old gray field, with horses grazing like small fairy animals beside it, is a vast ruin—twenty-two Corinthian columns in an empty oblong and an L. Almost seeming to float like lace, bits of wrought-iron balcony connect them here and there. Live cedar trees are growing from the iron black acanthus leaves, high in the empty air. This is the ruin of Windsor, long since burned. . . .

Immediately the cane and the cedars become more impenetrable, the road ascends and descends, and rather slowly, because of the trees and shadows, you realize a little village is before you. Grand Gulf today looks like a scene in Haiti. Under enormous dense trees where the moss hangs long as ladders, there are hutlike buildings and pale whitewashed sheds, most of the faces under the straw hats are black, and only narrow jungly paths lead toward the river. Of course this is not Grand Gulf in the original, for the river undermined that and pulled it whole into the river—the opposite of what it did to Rodney's Landing. A little corner was left, which the Federals burned, all but a wall, on their way to Vicksburg. After the war, the population built it back—and the river moved away. Grand Gulf was a British settlement before the Revolution and had close connection with England, whose ships traded here. It handled more cotton than any other port in Mississippi for about twenty years. The old cemetery is there still, like a roof of marble and moss overhanging the town and about to tip into it. Many names of British gentry stare out from the stones, and the biggest snakes in the world must have their kingdom in that dark green tangle.

Two miles beyond, at the end of a dim jungle track where you can walk, is the river, immensely wide and vacant, its bluff occupied sometimes by a casual camp of fishermen under the willow trees, where dirty children playing about and nets drying have a look of timeless roaming and poverty and sameness. . . By boat you can reach a permanent fishing camp, inaccessible now by land. Go till you find the hazy shore where the Bayou Pierre, dividing in two, reaches round the swamp to meet the river. It is a gray-green land, softly flowered, hung with stillness. Houseboats will be tied there among the cypresses under falls of the long moss, all of a color. Aaron Burr's "flotilla" tied up there, too, for this is Bruinsburg Landing, where the boats were seized, one wild day of apprehension. Bruinsburg grew to be a rich, gay place in cotton days. It is almost as if a wand had turned a noisy cotton port into a handful of shanty boats. Yet Bruinsburg Landing has not vanished: it is this.

Wonderful things have come down the current of this river, and more spectacular things were on the water than could ever have sprung up on shores then. Every kind of treasure, every kind of bearer of treasure has come down, and armadas and flotillas, and the most frivolous of things, too, and the most pleasure-giving of people.

Natchez, downstream, had a regular season of drama from 1806 on, attended by the countryside—the only one in English in this part of the world. The plays would be given outdoors, on a strip of grass on the edge of the high bluff overlooking the landing. With the backdrop of the river and the endless low marsh of Louisiana beyond, some version of Elizabethan or Restoration comedy or tragedy would be given, followed by a short farcical afterpiece, and the traveling company would run through a little bird mimicry, ventrilo-

quism and magical tricks in-between. Natchez, until lately a bear-baiting crowd, watched eagerly "A Laughable Comedy in 3 Acts written by Shakespeare and Altered by Garrick called Catherine & Petrucio," followed by "A Pantomime Ballet Called a Trip through the Vauxhall Gardens into which is introduced the humorous song of Four and Twenty Fiddlers concluding with a dance by the characters." Or sometimes the troupe would arrive with a program of "divertisements"—recitations of Lochinvar, Alexander's Feast, Cato's Soliloquy of the Soul, and Clarence's Dream, interspersed with Irish songs by the boys sung to popular requests and concluding with "A Laughable Combat between Two Blind Fiddlers."

The Natchez country took all this omnivorously to its heart. There were rousing, splendid seasons, with a critic writing pieces in the newspaper to say that last night's Juliet spoke just a *bit too* loudly for a girl, though Tybalt kept in perfect character to delight all, even after he was dead—signed "X.Y.Z."

But when the natural vigor of the day gave clamorous birth to the minstrel show, the bastard Shakespeare went; and when the showboat really rounded the bend, the theatre of that day, a child of the plantation and the river, came to its own. The next generation heard calliopes filling river and field with their sound, and saw the dazzling showboats come like enormous dreams up the bayous and the little streams at floodtime, with whole French Zouave troops aboard, whole circuses with horses jumping through paper hoops, and all the literal rites of the minstrel show, as ever true to expectations as a miracle play.

Now if you pick up the Rodney Road again, through twenty miles of wooded hills, you wind sharply round, the old sunken road ahead of you and following you. Then from a great height you descend suddenly through a rush of vines, down, down, deep into complete levelness, and there in a strip at the bluff's foot, at the road's end, is Rodney's Landing.

Though you walk through Rodney's Landing, it long remains a landscape, rather than a center of activity, and seems to exist altogether in the sight, like a vision. At first you think there is not even sound. The thick soft morning shadow of the bluff on the valley floor, and the rose-red color of the brick church which rises from this shadow, are its dominant notes—all else seems green. The red of the bricks defies their element; they were made of earth, but they glow as if to remind you that there is fire in earth. No one is in sight.

Eventually you see people, of course. Women have little errands, and the old men play checkers at a table in front of the one open store. And the people's faces are good. Theirs seem *actually* the faces your eyes look for in city streets and never see. There is a middle-aged man who always meets you when you come. He is like an embodiment of the simplicity and friendliness not of the mind—for his could not teach him—but of the open spirit. He never remembers you, but he speaks courteously. "I am Mr. John David's boy—where have you come from, and when will you have to go back?" He has what I have always imagined as a true Saxon face, like a shepherd boy's, light and shy and set in solitude. He carries a staff, too, and stands with it on the hill, where he will lead you—looking with care everywhere and far away, warning you of the steep stile. . . . The river is not even in sight here. It is three miles beyond, past the cotton fields of the bottom, through a dense miasma of swamp.

The houses merge into a shaggy fringe at the foot of the bluff. It is like a town some avenging angel has flown over, taking up every second or third house and leaving only this. There are more churches than houses now; the edge of town is marked by a little wooden Catholic church tiny as a matchbox, with twin steeples carved like icing, over a stile in a flowery pasture. The Negro church, weathered black with a snow-white door, has red hens in the yard. The old galleried stores are boarded up. The missing houses were burned—they were empty, and the little row of Negro inhabitants have carried them off winters for firewood.

You know instinctively as you stand here that this shelf of forest is the old town site, and you find that here, as in Grand Gulf, the cemetery has remained as the roof of the town. In a mossy wood the graves, gently tended here, send up mossy shafts, with lilies flowering in the gloom. Many of the tombstones are marked ."A Native of Ireland," though there are German names and graves neatly bordered with sea shells and planted in spring-flowering bulbs. People in Rodney's Landing won silver prizes in the fairs for their horses; they planted all this land; some of them were killed in battle, some in duels fought on a Grand Gulf sand bar. The girls who died young of the fevers were some of them the famous "Rodney heiresses." All Mississippians know descendants of all the names. I looked for the grave of Dr. Nutt, the man who privately invented and used his cotton gin here, previous to the rest of the world. The Petit Gulf cotton was known better in England than any, as superior to all cotton, and was named for the little gulf in the river at this landing, and Rodney too was once called Petit Gulf.

Down below, Mr. John David's boy opens the wrought-iron gate to the churchyard of the rose-red church, and you go up the worn, concave steps. The door is never locked, the old silver knob is always the heat of the hand. It is a little church, simply a little country church, upon whose calm interior nothing seems to press from the outer world, which, though calm itself here, is still "outer." (Even cannon balls were stopped by its strong walls, and are in them yet, though this church was carried down whole from hill to valley.) It is the kind of little church in which you might instinctively say prayers for your friends; how is it that both danger and succor, both need and response, seem intimately near in little country churches?

Something always hangs imminent above all life—usually claims of daily need, daily action, a prescribed course of movement, a schedule of time. In Rodney, the imminent thing is a natural danger—the town may be flooded by the river, and every inhabitant take to the hills. Every house wears a belt of ineradicable silt around its upper walls. I asked the storekeeper what his store would be like after the river had been over it, and he said, "You know the way a fish is?" Life threatened by nature is simplified, most peaceful in present peace, quiet in seasons of waiting and readiness. There are rowboats under all the houses.

Even the women in sunbonnets disappear and nothing moves at noon but butterflies, little white ones, large black ones, and they are like some flutter of heat, some dervishes of the midday hour, as in pairs they rotate about one another, ascending and descending, appearing to follow each other up and down some swaying spiral staircase invisible in the dense light. The heat moves. Its ripples can be seen, like the ripples in some vertical river running between earth and sky. It is so still at noon. I was never there before the river left, to hear the thousand swirling sounds it made for Rodney's Landing, but could it be that its absence is so much missed in the life of sound here that a stranger would feel it? The stillness seems absolute, as the brightness of noon seems to touch the point of saturation. Here the noon sun does make a trance; here indeed at its same zenith it looked down on life sacrificed to it and was worshiped.

It is not strange to think that a unique nation among Indians lived in this beautiful country and they were envied by the other in mystery. But their people, five villages in the seventeenth century, were unique in this country and they were envied by the other younger nations—the Choctaws helped the French in their final dissolution. In Mississippi they were remnants surely of medievalism. They were proud and cruel, gentle-mannered and ironic, handsome, extremely tall, intellectual, elegant, pacific, and ruthless. Fire, death, sacrifice formed the spirit of the Natchez' worship. They did not now, however, make war.

The women—although all the power was in their blood, and a Sun woman by rigid system married a low-caste Stinkard and bore a Sun child by him—were the nation's laborers still. They planted and they spun, they baked their red jugs for the bear oil, and when the men came from the forests, they would throw at the feet of their wives the tongues of the beasts they had shot from their acacia bows—both as a tribute to womanhood and as a command to the wives to go out and hunt on the ground for what they had killed, and to drag it home.

The town of Natchez was named after this nation, although the French one day, in a massacre for a massacre, slew or sent into slavery at Santo Domingo every one of its namesakes, and the history of the nation was done in 1773. The French amusedly regarded the Natchez as either "*sauvages*" or "*naturels, innocents*." They made many notes of their dress and quaint habits, made engravings of them looking like Cupids and Psyches, and handed down to us their rites and customs with horrified withholdings or fascinated repetitions. The women fastened their knee-length hair in a net of mulberry threads, men singed theirs short into a crown except for a lock over the left ear. They loved vermilion and used it delicately, men and women, the women's breasts decorated in tattooed designs by whose geometrics they strangely match ancient Aztec bowls. "*En été*," male and female wore a draped garment from waist to knee. "*En hyver*" they threw about them swan-feather mantles, made as carefully as wigs. For the monthly festivals the men added bracelets of skin polished like ivory, and thin disks of feathers went in each hand. They were painted fire-color, white puffs of down decorated their shorn heads, the one lock left to support the whitest feathers. As children, the Natchez wore pearls handed down by their ancestors—pearls which they had ruined by piercing them with fire.

The Natchez also laughed gently at the French. (Also they massacred them when they were betrayed by them.) Once a Frenchman asked a Natchez noble why these Indians would laugh at them, and the noble replied that it was only because the French were like geese when they talked—all clamoring at once. The Natchez never spoke except one at a time; no one was ever interrupted or contradicted; a visitor was always allowed the opening speech, and that after a rest in silence of fifteen or twenty minutes, to allow him to get his breath and collect his thoughts. (Women murmured or whispered, their game after labor was a silent little guessing game played with three sticks that could not disturb anyone.) But this same nation, when any Sun died, strangled his wife, and a great company of loyal friends and ambitious Stinkards to attend him in death, and walked bearing his body over the bodies of strangled infants laid before him by their parents. A Sun once expressed great though polite astonishment that a certain Frenchman declined the favor of dying with him.

Their own sacrifices were great among them. When Iberville came the Natchez had diminished to twelve hundred. They laid it to the fact that the fire had once been allowed to go out and that a profane fire burned now in its place. Perhaps they had prescience of their end—the only bit of their history that we really know.

TODAY Rodney's Landing wears the cloak of vegetation which has caught up this whole land for the third time, or the fourth, or the hundredth. There is something Gothic about the vines, in their structure in the trees—there are arches, flying buttresses, towers of vines, with trumpet flowers swinging in them for bells and staining their walls. And there is something of a warmer grandeur in their very abundance—stairways and terraces and whole hanging gardens of green and flowering vines, with a Babylonian babel of hundreds of creature voices that make up the silence of Rodney's Landing. Here are nests for birds and thrones for owls and trapezes for snakes, every kind of bower in the world. From earliest spring there is something, when garlands of yellow jasmine swing from tree to tree, in the woods aglow with dogwood and redbud, when the green is only a floating veil in the hills.

And the vines make an endless flourish in summer and fall. There are wild vines of the grape family with their lilac and turquoise fruits and their green, pink, and white leaves. Muscadine vines along the stream banks grow a hundred feet high, mixing their dull, musky, delicious grapes among the bronze grapes of the scuppernong. All creepers with trumpets and panicles of scarlet and yellow cling to the treetops. On shady stream banks hang lady's eardrop, fruits and flowers dangling pale jade. The passionflower puts its tendrils where it can, its strange flowers of lilac rays with their little white towers shining out, or its fruit, the maypop, hanging. Wild wistaria hangs its flowers like flower-grapes above reach, and the sweetness of clematis, the virgin's-bower which grow in Rodney, and of honeysuckle, must fill even the highest air. There is a vine that grows to great heights, with heart-shaped leaves as big and soft as summer hats, overlapping and shading everything to deepest jungle blue-green.

Ferns are the hidden floor of the forest, and they grow too in the trees, their roots in the deep of mossy branches.

All over the hills the beautiful white Cherokee rose trails its glossy dark green leaves and its delicate luminous-white flowers. Foliage and flowers alike have a quality of light and dark as well as color in Southern sun, and sometimes a seeming motion like dancing due to the flicker of heat, and are luminous or opaque according to the time of day or the density of summer air. In early morning or in the light of evening they become translucent and ethereal, but at noon they blaze, or darken opaquely, and the same flower may seem sultry or delicate in its little being, all according to when you see it.

It is not hard to follow one of the leapings of old John Law's mind, then, and remember how he displayed diamonds in the shop windows in France—during the organization of his Compagnie d'Occident—saying that they were produced in the cups of the wildflowers along the lower Mississippi. And the closer they grew to the river, the more nearly that might be true.

Deep in the swamps the water hyacinths make solid floors you could walk on over still black water, the Southern blue flag stands thick and sweet in the marsh. Lady's-tresses, greenish-white little orchids with spiral flowers and stems twisted like curls and braids, grow there, and so do nodding lady's-tresses. Water lilies float, and spider lilies rise up like little coral monsters.

The woods on the bluffs are the hardwood trees—dark and berried and flowered. The magnolia is the spectacular one with its heavy cups—they look as heavy as silver—weighing upon its aromatic, elliptical, black-green leaves, or when it bears its dense pink cones. I remember an old botany book, written long ago in England, reporting the magnolia by hearsay, as having blossoms "so large as to be distinctly visible a mile or more—seen in the mass, we presume." But I tested the visibility power of the magnolia, and the single flower can be seen for several miles on a clear day. One magnolia cousin, the cucumber tree, has long sleevelike leaves and pale green flowers which smell strange and cooler than the grandiflora flower. Set here and there in this country will be a mimosa tree, with its smell in the rain like a cool melon cut, its puffs of pale flowers settled in its sensitive leaves.

Perhaps the live oaks are the most wonderful trees in this land. Their great girth and their great spread give far more feeling of history than any house or ruin left by man. Vast, very dark, proportioned as beautifully as a church, they stand majestically in the wild or line old sites, old academy grounds. The live oaks under which Aaron Burr was tried at Washington, Mississippi, in this section, must have been old and impressive then, to have been chosen for such a drama. Spanish moss invariably hangs from the live oak branches, moving with the wind and swaying its long beards, darkening the forests; it is an aerial plant and strangely enough is really a pineapple, and consists of very, very tiny leaves and flowers, springy and dustily fragrant to the touch; no child who has ever "dressed up" in it can forget the sweet dust of its smell. It would be hard to think of things that happened here without the presence of these live oaks, so old, so expansive, so wonderful, that they might be sentient beings. W. H. Hudson, in his autobiography, *Far Away and Long Ago*, tells of an old man who felt reverentially toward the ancient trees of his great country house, so that each night he walked around his park to visit them one by one, and rest his hand on its bark to bid it good-night, for he believed in their knowing spirits.

Now and then comes a report that an ivory-billed woodpecker is seen here. Audubon in his diary says the Indians began the slaughter of this bird long before Columbus discovered America, for the Southern Indians would trade them to the Canadian Indians—

four buckskins for an ivory bill. Audubon studied the woodpecker here when he was in the Natchez country, where it lived in the deepest mossy swamps along the windings of the river, and he called it "the greatest of all our American woodpeckers and probably the finest in the world." The advance of agriculture rather than slaughter has really driven it to death, for it will not live except in a wild country.

This woodpecker used to cross the river "in deep undulations." Its notes were "clear, loud, and rather plaintive . . . heard at a considerable distance . . . and resemble the false high note of a clarinet." "Pait, pait, pait," Audubon translates it into his Frenchlike sound. It made its nest in a hole dug with the ivory bill in a tree inclined in just a certain way—usually a black cherry. The holes went sometimes three feet deep, and some people thought they went spirally. The bird ate the grapes of the swampland. Audubon says it would hang by its claws like a titmouse on a grapevine and devour grapes by the bunch—which sounds curiously as though it knew it would be extinct before very long. This woodpecker also would destroy any dead tree it saw standing—chipping it away "to an extent of twenty or thirty feet in a few hours, leaping downward with its body . . . tossing its head to the right and left, or leaning it against the bark to ascertain the precise spot where the grubs were concealed, and immediately renewing its blows with fresh vigor, all the while sounding its loud notes, as if highly delighted." The males had beautiful crimson crests, the females were "always the most clamorous and the least shy." When caught, the birds would fight bitterly, and "utter a mournful and very piteous cry." All vanished now from the earth—the piteous cry and all; unless where Rodney's swamps are wild enough still, perhaps it is true, a little pair of ivory-billed woodpeckers still exist in the world, in this safe spot, inaccessible to man.

Perhaps time, unpleaded with, does stand still here; and as when a human being becomes still all the impressions that surround him in place and time and memory—some fulfilled, some never fulfilled, but projected in dream—

can enter his soul then and saturate it with their full original powers, Rodney is filled with the winds of all these breaths blowing upon it while it seems to sleep.

Indians, Mike Fink the flatboatman, Burr, and Blennerhassett, John James Audubon, the bandits of the Trace, planters, and preachers —the horse fairs, the great fires—the battles of war, the arrivals of foreign ships, and the comings of floods: could not all these things still move with their true stature into the mind here, and their beauty still work upon the heart? Perhaps it is the sense of place that gives us the belief that passionate things, in some essence, endure. Whatever is significant and whatever is tragic in a place live as long as the place does, though they are unseen, and the new life will be built upon those things— regardless of commerce and the way of rivers and roads, and other vagrancies.

An Eccentric, Childlike Universe

TRUMAN CAPOTE

Born in 1924, Truman Capote has given New Orleans as his birthplace, and said that he once tap-danced on a showboat. His mother was from Alabama and he spent part of his youth there and in other sections of the South. After attending high schools in New York and Connecticut, he became an errand boy—his own description—for the New Yorker *magazine. His first book, in 1948,* Other Voices, Other Rooms, *was launched with a weird publicity photograph which showed him lounging, à la Madame Récamier, with bangs over his forehead. Here, as in later works, Capote presented a grotesque universe, seen through a child's eyes, with satanic touches, many eccentrics and decadent influences. With* The Grass Harp, *a play based on that book, and another play,* House of Flowers, *he achieved a greater critical praise, and in later works he has shown a rather broader talent. These impressions of New Orleans are from* Local Color, *published in 1950 by Random House.*

IN the courtyard there was an angel of black stone, and its angel head rose above giant elephant leaves; the stark glass angel eyes, bright as the bleached blue of sailor eyes, stared upward. One observed the angel from an intricate green balcony—mine, this balcony, for I lived beyond in three old white rooms, rooms with elaborate wedding-cake ceilings, wide sliding doors, tall French windows. On warm evenings, with these windows open, conversation was pleasant there, tuneful, for wind rustled the interior like fan-breeze made by ancient ladies. And on such warm evenings the town is quiet. Only voices: family talk weaving on an ivy-curtained porch; a barefoot woman humming as she rocks a sidewalk chair, lulling to sleep a baby she nurses quite publicly; the complaining foreign tongue of an irritated lady who, sitting on her balcony, plucks a fryer, the loosened feathers floating from her hands, slipping into the air, sliding lazily downward.

One morning—it was December, I think, a cold Sunday with a sad gray sun—I went up through the Quarter to the old market where, at that time of year, there were exquisite winter fruits, sweet satsumas, twenty cents a dozen, and winter flowers, Christmas poinsettia and snow japonica. New Orleans streets have long, lonesome perspectives; in empty hours their atmosphere is like Chirico, and things innocent, ordinarily (a face behind the slanted light of shutters, nuns moving in the distance, a fat dark arm lolling lopsidedly out some window, a lonely black boy squatting in an alley, blowing soap bubbles and watching sadly as they rise to burst), acquire qualities of violence. Now, on that morning, I stopped still in the middle of a block, for I'd caught out of the corner of my eye a tunnel-passage, an overgrown courtyard. A crazy-looking white hound stood stiffly in the green fern light shining at the tunnel's end, and compulsively I went toward it. Inside there was a fountain; water spilled delicately from a monkey-statue's bronze mouth and made on pool pebbles desolate bell-like sounds. He was hanging from a willow, a bandit-faced man with kinky platinum hair; he hung so limply, like the willow itself. There was terror in that silent suffocated garden. Closed windows looked on blindly; snail tracks glistened silver on elephant ears; nothing moved except his shadow. It swung a little, back and forth, yet there was no wind. A rhinestone ring he wore wrinkled in the sun, and on his arm was tattooed a name, "Francy." The hound lowered its head to drink in the fountain, and I ran. Francy—was it for her he'd killed himself? I do not know. N.O. is a secret place.

My rock angel's glass eyes were like sundials, for they told, by the amount of light focused on them, time: white at noon, they grew gradually dimmer, dark at dusk, black—nightfall eyes in a nightfall head.

The torn lips of golden-haired girls leer luridly on faded leaning house fronts: Drink Dr. Nutt, Dr. Pepper, NEHI, Grapeade, 7 Up, Koke, Coca-Cola. N.O., like every southern town, is a city of soft-drink signs; the streets of forlorn neighborhoods are paved with Coca-Cola caps and, after rain, they glint in the dust like lost dimes. Posters peel away, lie mangled until storm wind blows them along the street, like desert sage—and there are those who think them beautiful; there are those who paper their walls with Dr. Nutt and Dr. Pepper, with Coca-Cola beauties who, smiling above tenement beds, are night guardians and saints of the morning. Signs everywhere, chalked, printed, painted: Madame Ortega—Readings, Love-potions, Magic Literature, C Me; If You Haven't Anything to Do . . . Don't Do it Here; Are You Ready to Meet Your Maker?; B Ware, Bad Dog; Pity the Poor Little Orphans; I Am A Deaf & Dumb Widow With 2 Mouths to Feed; Attention; Blue Wing Singers At Our Church Tonight (signed) the Reverend.

There was once this notice on a door in the Irish Channel district, "Come In And See Where Jesus Stood."

"And so?" said a woman who answered when I rang the bell. "I'd like to see where Jesus stood," I told her, and for a moment she looked blank; her face, cut in razorlike lines, was marshmallow white; she had no eyebrows, no lashes, and she wore a calico kimono. "You too little, honey," she said, a jerky laugh bouncing her breasts, "you too damn little to see where Jesus stood."

In my neighborhood there was a certain café no fun whatever, for it was the emptiest café around N.O., a regular funeral place. The proprietress, Mrs. Morris Otto Kunze, did not, however, seem to mind; she sat all day behind her bar, cooling herself with a palmetto fan, and seldom stirred except to swat flies. Now glued over an old cracked mirror backing the bar were seven little signs all alike: Don't Worry About Life . . . You'll Never Get Out Of It Alive.

July 3. An "at home" card last week from Miss Y., so I made a call this afternoon. She is delightful in her archaic way, amusing, too, though not by intent. The first time we met, I thought: Edna May Oliver; and there is a resemblance most certainly. Miss Y. speaks in premeditated tones but what she says is haphazard, and her sherry-colored eyes are forever searching the surroundings. Her posture is military, and she carries a man's Malacca cane, one of her legs being shorter than the other, a condition which gives her walk a penguinlike lilt. "It made me unhappy when I was your age; yes, I must say it did, for Papa had to squire me to all the balls, and there we sat on such pretty little gold chairs, and there we sat. None of the gentlemen ever asked Miss Y. to dance, indeed no, though a young man from Baltimore, a Mr. Jones, came here one winter, and gracious!—poor Mr. Jones—fell off a ladder, you know—broke his neck—died instantly."

My interest in Miss Y. is rather clinical, and I am not, I embarrassedly confess, quite the friend she believes, for one cannot feel close to Miss Y.: she is too much a fairy tale, someone real—and improbable. She is like the piano in her parlor—elegant, but a little out of tune. Her house, old even for N.O., is guarded by a black broken iron fence; it is a poor neighborhood she lives in, one sprayed with room-for-rent signs, gasoline stations, jukebox cafés. And yet, in the days when her family first lived here—that, of course, was long ago—there was in all N.O. no finer place. The house, smothered by slanting trees, has a graying exterior; but inside, the fantasy of Miss Y.'s heritage is everywhere visible: the tapping of her cane as she descends birdwing stairs trembles crystal; her face, a heart of wrinkled silk, reflects fumelike on ceiling-high mirrors; she lowers herself (notice, as this happens, how carefully she preserves the comfort of her bones) into father's father's father's chair, a wickedly severe receptacle with lion-head handrests. She is beautiful here in the cool dark of her house, and safe. These are the walls, the fence, the furniture of her childhood. "Some people are born to be old; I, for instance, was an atrocious child lacking any quality whatever. But I like being old. It makes me feel somehow more—" she paused, indicated with a gesture the dim parlor, "—more suitable."

Miss Y. does not believe in the world beyond N.O.; at times her insularity results, as it did today, in rather chilling remarks. I had mentioned a recent trip to New York, whereupon she, arching an eyebrow, replied gently, "Oh? And how *are* things in the country?"

. . .

1. Why is it, I wonder, that all N.O. cabdrivers sound as though they were imported from Brooklyn?

2. One hears so much about food here, and it is probably true that such restaurants as Arnaud's and Kolb's are the best in America. There is an attractive, lazy atmosphere about these restaurants: the slow-wheeling fans, the enormous tables and lack of crowding, the silence, the casual but expert waiters who all look as though they were sons of the management. A friend of mine, discussing N.O. and New York, once pointed out that comparable meals in the east, aside from being considerably more expensive, would arrive elaborate with some chef's mannerisms, with all kinds of froufrou and false accessories. Like most good things, the quality of N.O. cookery de-

rived, he thought, from its essential simplicity.

3. I am more or less disgusted by that persistent phrase, "old charm." You will find it, I suppose, in the architecture here, and in the antique shops (where it rightly belongs), or in the minglings of dialect one hears around the French Market. But N.O. is no more charming than any other southern city—less so, in fact, for it is the largest. The main portion of this city is made up of spiritual bottomland, streets and sections rather outside the tourist belt.

. . .

(From a letter to R.R.) There are new people in the apartment below, the third tenants in the last year; a transient place, this Quarter, hello and goodby. A real bonafide scoundrel lived there when I first came. He was unscrupulous, unclean, and crooked—a kind of dissipated satyr. Mr. Buddy, the one-man band. More than likely you have seen him—not here of course, but in some other city, for he keeps on the move, he and his old banjo, drum, harmonica. I used to come across him banging away on various street corners, a gang of loafers gathered round. Realizing he was my neighbor, these meetings always gave me rather a turn. Now to tell the truth, he was not a bad musician—an extraordinary one, in fact, when, late of an afternoon, and for his own pleasure, he sang to his guitar, sang ghostly ballads in a grieving whisky voice: how terrible it was for those in love.

"Hey, boy, you! You up there . . ." I was *you*, for he never knew my name, and never showed much interest in finding it out. "Come on down and help me kill a couple."

His balcony, smaller than mine, was screened with sweet-smelling wistaria; as there was no furniture to speak of we would sit on the floor in the green shade, drinking a brand of gin close kin to rubbing alcohol, and he would finger his guitar, its steady plaintive whine emphasizing the deep roll of his voice. "Been all over, been in and out, all around; sixty-five, and any woman takes up with me ain't got no use for nobody else; yessir, had myself a lota wives and a lota kids, but christamighty if I know what come of any of 'em—and don't give a hoot in hell—'cept maybe about Rhonda Kay. There was a woman, man, sweet as swamp honey, was she hot on me! On fire all the time, and her married to a Baptist preacher, too, and her got four kids—five, countin' mine. Always kinda wondered what it was—boy or girl—boy, I spec. I always give 'em boys. Now that's all a long time ago, and it happened in Memphis, Tennessee. Yessir, been everywhere, been to the penitentiary, been in big fine houses like the Rockefellers' houses, been in and out, been all around."

And he could carry on this way until moonrise, his voice growing froggy, his words locking together to make a chant.

His face, stained and wrinkled, had a certain deceptive kindness, a childish twinkle, but his eyes slanted in an oriental manner, and he kept his fingernails long, knife-sharp and polished as a Chinaman's. "Good for scratching, and handy in a fight, too."

He always wore a kind of costume: black trousers, engine-red socks, tennis shoes with the toes slit for comfort, a morning coat, a gray velvet waistcoat which, he said, had belonged to his ancestor Benjamin Franklin, and a beret studded with Vote for Roosevelt buttons. And there is no getting around it—he *did* have a good many lady friends—a different one each week, to be sure, but there was hardly ever a time when some woman wasn't cooking his meals; and on those occasions when I came to visit he would invariably, and in a most courtly fashion, say, "Meet Mrs. Buddy."

Late one night I woke with the feeling I was not alone; sure enough, there was someone in the room, and I could see him in the moonlight on my mirror. It was he, Mr. Buddy, furtively opening, closing bureau drawers, and suddenly my box of pennies splattered on the floor, rolled riotously in all directions. There was no use pretending then, so I turned on a lamp, and Mr. Buddy looked at me squarely, scarcely fazed, and grinned. "Listen," he said, and he was the most sober I'd ever seen him. "Listen, I've got to get out of here in a hurry."

I did not know what to say, and he looked down at the floor, his face turning slightly red. "Come on, be a good guy, have you got any money?"

I could only point to the spilt pennies;

without another word he got down on his knees, gathered them, and, walking very erectly, went out the door.

He was gone the next morning. Three women have come around asking for him, but I do not know his whereabouts. Maybe he is in Mobile. If you see him around there, R., won't you drop me a card, please?

. . .

I want a big fat mama, yes yes! Shotgun's fingers, long as bananas, thick as dill pickles, pound the keys, and his foot, pounding the floor, shakes the café. Shotgun! the biggest show in town! Can't sing worth a damn, but man can he rattle that piano—listen: *She's cool in the summer and warm in the fall, she's a four-season mama and that ain't all* . . . There he goes, his fat mouth yawning like a crocodile's, his wicked red tongue tasting the tune, loving it, making love to it: jelly, Shotgun, jelly-jelly-jelly. Look at him laugh, that black, crazy face all scarred with bullet-shot, all glistening with sweat. Is there any human vice he doesn't know about? A shame, though . . . Hardly any white folks ever see Shotgun, for this is a Negro café. Last year's dusty Christmas decorations color the peeling arsenic walls; orange-green-purple strips of fluted paper, dangling from naked light bulbs, flutter in the wind of a tired fan; the proprietor, a handsome quadroon with hooded milk-blue eyes, leans over the bar, squalling, "Look here, what you think this, some kinda charity? Get up that two-bits, nigger, and mighty quick."

And tonight is Saturday. The room floats in cigarette smoke and Saturday-night perfume. All the little greasy wood tables have double rings of chairs, and everyone knows everyone, and for a moment the world is this room, this dark, jazzy, terrible room; our heartbeat is Shotgun's stamping foot, every joyous element of our lives is focused in the shine of his malicious eyes. *I want a big fat mama, yes yes!* He rocks forward on his stool, and, as he lifts his face to look straight at us, a great riding holler goes up in the night: *I want a big fat mama with the meat shakin' on her, yes!*

A Sad Café and Its Ballad

CARSON McCULLERS

Born in 1917 in Columbus, Georgia, Carson McCullers began to write before she was seventeen, and soon published stories to which critics gave heed. Not long after, while living in North Carolina, she received a Guggenheim Foundation award. Although her works—novels and shorter fiction—are infrequent, she has gained a considerable special following, with highly individual tales of half-lost, lonely people, young and old, bearing occasional psychiatric implications. In recent years she has lived abroad. Mrs. McCullers' writings have puzzled some, while many others have been warmly appreciative. They include Reflections in a Golden Eye, The Heart Is a Lonely Hunter, *and* Member of the Wedding, *which she turned into a glowing play. This selection is from the opening of her* Ballad of a Sad Café, *published by Houghton Mifflin in 1951.*

THE town itself is dreary; not much is there except the cotton mill, the two-room houses where the workers live, a few peach trees, a church with two colored windows, and a miserable main street only a hundred yards long. On Saturdays the tenants from the near-by farms come in for a day of talk and trade. Otherwise the town is lonesome, sad, and like a place that is far off and estranged from all other places in the world. The nearest train stop is Society City, and the Greyhound and White Bus Lines use the Forks Falls Road which is three miles away. The winters here are short and raw, the summers white with glare and fiery hot.

If you walk along the main street on an August afternoon there is nothing whatsoever to do. The largest building, in the very center of the town, is boarded up completely and leans so far to the right that it seems bound to collapse at any minute. The house is very old. There is about it a curious, cracked look that is very puzzling until you suddenly realize that at one time, and long ago, the right side of the front porch had been painted, and part of the wall—but the painting was left unfinished and one portion of the house is darker and dingier than the other. The building looks completely deserted. Nevertheless, on the second floor there is one window which is not boarded; sometimes in the late afternoon when the heat is at its worst a hand will slowly open the shutter and a face will look down on the town. It is a face like the terrible dim faces known in dreams—sexless and white, with two gray crossed eyes which are turned inward so sharply that they seem to be exchanging with each other one long and secret gaze of grief. The face lingers at the window for an hour or so, then the shutters are closed once more, and as likely as not there will not be another soul to be seen along the main street. These August afternoons—when your shift is finished there is absolutely nothing to do; you might as well walk down to listen to the chain gang.

However, here in this very town there was once a café. And this old boarded-up house was unlike any other place for many miles around. There were tables with cloths and paper napkins, colored streamers from the electric fans, great gatherings on Saturday nights. The owner of the place was Miss Amelia Evans. But the person most responsible for the success and gaiety of the place was a hunchback called Cousin Lymon. One other person had a part in the story of this café—he was the former husband of Miss Amelia, a terrible character who returned to the town after a long term in the penitentiary, caused ruin, and then went on his way again. The café has long since been closed, but it is still remembered.

The place was not always a café. Miss

Amelia inherited the building from her father, and it was a store that carried mostly feed, guano, and staples such as meal and snuff. Miss Amelia was rich. In addition to the store she operated a still three miles back in the swamp, and ran out the best liquor in the county. She was a dark, tall woman with bones and muscles like a man. Her hair was cut short and brushed back from the forehead, and there was about her sunburned face a tense, haggard quality. She might have been a handsome woman if, even then, she was not slightly cross-eyed. There were those who would have courted her, but Miss Amelia cared nothing for the love of men and was a solitary person. Her marriage had been unlike any other marriage ever contracted in this county—it was a strange and dangerous marriage, lasting only for ten days, that left the whole town wondering and shocked. Except for this queer marriage Miss Amelia had lived her life alone. Often she spent whole nights back in her shed in the swamp, dressed in overalls and gum boots, silently guarding the low fire of the still.

With all things which could be made by the hands Miss Amelia prospered. She sold chitterlins and sausage in the town near-by. On fine autumn days she ground sorghum, and the syrup from her vats was dark golden and delicately flavored. She built the brick privy behind her store in only two weeks and was skilled in carpentering. It was only with people that Miss Amelia was not at ease. People, unless they are nilly-willy or very sick, cannot be taken into the hands and changed overnight to something more worth-while and profitable. So that the only use that Miss Amelia had for other people was to make money out of them. And in this she succeeded. Mortgages on crops and property, a sawmill, money in the bank—she was the richest woman for miles around. She would have been rich as a congressman if it were not for her one great failing, and that was her passion for lawsuits and the courts. She would involve herself in long and bitter litigation over just a trifle. It was said that if Miss Amelia so much as stumbled over a rock in the road she would glance around instinctively as though looking for something to sue about it. Aside from

these lawsuits she lived a steady life and every day was very much like the day that had gone before. With the exception of her ten-day marriage, nothing happened to change this until the spring of the year that Miss Amelia was thirty years old.

It was toward midnight on a soft quiet evening in April. The sky was the color of a blue swamp iris, the moon clear and bright. The crops that spring promised well and in the past weeks the mill had run a night shift. Down by the creek the square brick factory was yellow with light, and there was the faint, steady hum of the looms. It was such a night when it is good to hear from faraway, across the dark fields, the slow song of a Negro on his way to make love. Or when it is pleasant to sit quietly and pick a guitar, or simply to rest alone and think of nothing at all. The street that evening was deserted, but Miss Amelia's store was lighted and on the porch outside there were five people. One of these was Stumpy MacPhail, a foreman with a red face and dainty, purplish hands. On the top step were two boys in overalls, the Rainey twins—both of them lanky and slow, with white hair and sleepy green eyes. The other man was Henry Macy, a shy and timid person with gentle manners and nervous ways, who sat on the edge of the bottom step. . . . One of the twins, who had been looking down the empty road, was the first to speak. "I see something coming," he said.

"A calf got loose," said his brother.

The approaching figure was still too distant to be clearly seen. The moon made dim, twisted shadows of the blossoming peach trees along the side of the road. In the air the odor of blossoms and sweet spring grass mingled with the warm, sour smell of the near-by lagoon.

"No. It's somebody's youngun," said Stumpy MacPhail.

Miss Amelia watched the road in silence. She had put down her rope, in which she had been patiently untying knots, and was fingering the straps of her overalls with her brown bony hand. . . . It was not until the figure was quite close, within the range of the yellow light from the porch, that they saw clearly what had come.

The man was a stranger, and it is rare that a stranger enters the town on foot at that hour. Besides, the man was a hunchback. He was scarcely more than four feet tall and he wore a ragged, dusty coat that reached only to his knees. His crooked little legs seemed too thin to carry the weight of his great warped chest and the hump that sat on his shoulders. He had a very large head, with deep-set blue eyes and a sharp little mouth. His face was both soft and sassy—at the moment his pale skin was yellowed by dust and there were lavender shadows beneath his eyes. He carried a lopsided old suitcase which was tied with a rope.

"Evening," said the hunchback, and he was out of breath.

Miss Amelia and the men on the porch neither answered his greeting nor spoke. They only looked at him.

"I am hunting for Miss Amelia Evans."

Miss Amelia pushed back her hair from her forehead and raised her chin. "How come?"

"Because I am kin to her," the hunchback said.

"That's me," she said. "How do you mean 'kin'?"

"Because—" the hunchback began. He looked uneasy, almost as though he was about to cry. He rested the suitcase on the bottom step, but did not take his hand from the handle. "My mother was Fanny Jesup and she come from Cheehaw. She left Cheehaw some thirty years ago when she married her first husband. I remember hearing her tell how she had a half-sister named Martha. And back in Cheehaw today they tell me that was your mother."

Miss Amelia listened with her head turned slightly aside. She ate her Sunday dinners by herself; her place was never crowded with a flock of relatives, and she claimed kin with no one. She had a great-aunt who owned the livery stable in Cheehaw, but that aunt was now dead. Aside from her there was only one double first cousin who lived in a town twenty miles away, but this cousin and Miss Amelia did not get on so well, and when they chanced to pass each other they spat on the side of the road. Other people had tried very hard, from time to time, to work out some kind of far-fetched connection with Miss Amelia, but with absolutely no success.

The hunchback went into a long rigmarole, mentioning names and places that were unknown to the listeners on the porch and seemed to have nothing to do with the subject. "So Fanny and Martha Jesup were half-sisters. And I am the son of Fanny's third husband. So that would make you and I—" He bent down and began to unfasten his suitcase. His hands were like dirty sparrow claws and they were trembling. The bag was full of all manner of junk—ragged cloths and odd rubbish that looked like parts out of a sewing machine, or something just as worthless. The hunchback scrambled among these belongings and brought out an old photograph. "This is a picture of my mother and her half-sister."

Miss Amelia did not speak. She was moving her jaw slowly from side to side, and you could tell from her face what she was thinking about. . . . It was a picture of two pale, withered-up little children of about two and three years of age. The faces were tiny white blurs, and it might have been an old picture in anyone's album. Stumpy MacPhail handed it back with no comment. "Where you come from?"

The hunchback's voice was uncertain. "I was traveling."

Still Miss Amelia did not speak. She just stood leaning against the side of the door, and looked down at the hunchback. Henry Macy winked nervously and rubbed his hands together. Then quietly he left the bottom step and disappeared. He is a good soul, and the hunchback's situation had touched his heart. Therefore he did not want to wait and watch Miss Amelia chase this newcomer off her property and run him out of town. The hunchback stood with his bag open on the bottom step; he sniffled his nose, and his mouth quivered. Perhaps he began to feel his dismal predicament. Maybe he realized what a miserable thing it was to be a stranger in the town with a suitcase full of junk, and claiming kin with Miss Amelia. At any rate he sat down on he steps and suddenly began to cry.

It was not a common thing to have an

unknown hunchback walk to the store at midnight and then sit down and cry. Miss Amelia rubbed back her hair from her forehead and the men looked at each other uncomfortably. All around the town was very quiet. At last one of the twins said: "I'll be damned if he ain't a regular Morris Finestein."

Everybody nodded and agreed, for that is an expression having a certain special meaning. But the hunchback cried louder because he could not know what they were talking about. Morris Finestein was a person who had lived in the town years before. He was only a quick, skipping little Jew who cried if you called him Christ-Killer, and ate light bread and canned salmon every day. A calamity had come over him and he had moved away to Society City. But since then if a man were prissy in any way, or if a man ever wept, he was known as a Morris Finestein.

"Well, he is afflicted," said Stumpy Mac-Phail. "There is some cause."

Miss Amelia crossed the porch with two slow, gangling strides. She went down the steps and stood looking thoughtfully at the stranger. Gingerly, with one long black forefinger, she touched the hump on his back. The hunchback still wept, but he was quieter now. The night was silent, and the moon still shone with a soft, clear light—it was getting colder. Then Miss Amelia did a rare thing; she pulled out a bottle from her hip pocket and after polishing off the top with the palm of her hand she handed it to the hunchback to drink. Miss Amelia could seldom be persuaded to sell her liquor on credit, and for her to give so much as a drop away free was almost unknown.

"Drink," she said. "It will liven your gizzard."

The hunchback stopped crying, neatly licked the tears from around his mouth, and did as he was told. When he was finished, Miss Amelia took a slow swallow, warmed and washed her mouth with it, and spat. Then she also drank. . . . The whisky they drank that evening (two big bottles of it) is important. Otherwise, it would be hard to account for what followed. Perhaps without it there would never have been a café. For the liquor of Miss Amelia has a special quality of its own. It is clean and sharp on the tongue, but once down a man it glows inside him for a long time afterward.

And that is not all. It is known that if a message is written with lemon juice on a clean sheet of paper there will be no sign of it. But if the paper is held for a moment to the fire then the letters turn brown and the meaning becomes clear. Imagine that the whisky is the fire and that the message is that which is known only in the soul of a man—then the worth of Miss Amelia's liquor can be understood. Things that have gone unnoticed, thoughts that have been harbored far back in the dark mind, are suddenly recognized and comprehended. . . . A man who has drunk Miss Amelia's liquor may suffer, or he may be spent with joy—but the experience has shown the truth; he has warmed his soul and seen the message hidden there.

They drank until it was past midnight, and the moon was clouded over so that the night was cold and dark. The hunchback still sat on the bottom steps, bent over miserably with his forehead resting on his knee. Miss Amelia stood with her hands in her pockets, one foot resting on the second step of the stairs. She had been silent for a long time. Her face had the expression often seen in slightly cross-eyed persons who are thinking deeply, a look that appears to be both very wise and very crazy. At last she said: "I don't know your name."

"I'm Lymon Willis," said the hunchback.

"Well, come on in," she said. "Some supper was left in the stove and you can eat."

Only a few times in her life had Miss Amelia invited anyone to eat with her, unless she were planning to trick them in some way, or make money out of them. So the men on the porch felt there was something wrong. Later they said among themselves that she must have been drinking back in the swamp the better part of the afternoon. At any rate she left the porch, and Stumpy MacPhail and the twins went on off home. She bolted the front door and looked all around to see that her goods were in order. Then she went to the kitchen, which was at the back of the store. The hunchback followed her, dragging his suitcase, sniffing and wiping his nose on the sleeve of his dirty coat.

"Sit down," said Miss Amelia. "I'll just warm up what's here."

It was a good meal they had together on that night. Miss Amelia was rich and she did not grudge herself food. There was fried chicken (the breast of which the hunchback took on his own plate), mashed rootabeggars, collard greens, and hot, pale golden, sweet potatoes. Miss Amelia ate slowly and with the relish of a farm hand. She sat with both elbows on the table, bent over the plate, her knees spread wide apart and her feet braced on the rungs of the chair. As for the hunchback, he gulped down his supper as though he had not smelled food in months. During the meal one tear crept down his dingy cheek —but it was just a little leftover tear and meant nothing at all. . . .

Having finished, Miss Amelia tilted back her chair, tightened her fist and felt the hard, supple muscles of her right arm beneath the clean, blue cloth of her shirtsleeves—an unconscious habit with her, at the close of a meal. Then she took the lamp from the table and jerked her head toward the suitcase as an invitation for the hunchback to follow after her.

Above the store there were the three rooms where Miss Amelia had lived during all her life—two bedrooms with a large parlor in between. Few people had even seen these rooms, but it was generally known that they were well-furnished and extremely clean. And now Miss Amelia was taking up with her a dirty little hunchbacked stranger, come from God knows where. Miss Amelia walked slowly, two steps at a time, holding the lamp high. The hunchback hovered so close behind her that the swinging light made on the staircase wall one great, twisted shadow of the two of them. Soon the premises above the store were dark as the rest of the town.

The Grave

KATHERINE ANNE PORTER

For years critical readers have recognized in Katherine Anne Porter one of the most craftsmanlike, and one of the most polished writers in the English language. She has completed only a small number of books, short-story collections or novellas; they rank among the best that twentieth-century America has produced. A native of Indian Creek, Texas, Miss Porter is of a family with roots deep in the South and has spent much of her life there. Ancestors are of Virginia, Kentucky and Louisiana; she was reared in Texas and Louisiana. A happy traveler, she has lived from time to time in Mexico, Paris, Berlin, Basel, and other places. She has looked with an appreciative eye on "foreign" groups such as Mexicans, Germans of Texas, French elements of the Gulf area. Many of her stories, told in a meditative, unexcited tone, conclude with devastating effect. Generally she holds aloof from the events she depicts, then concludes them with a shattering revelation, a vivid emphasis. Her volumes include Flowering Judas and Other Stories, *1935;* Pale Horse, Pale Rider, *1939;* The Days Before, *1952; and* The Leaning Tower and Other Stories, *published in 1944 by Harcourt, Brace and Company. From the last volume comes this tale, "The Grave."*

THE grandfather, dead for more than thirty years, had been twice disturbed in his long repose by the constancy and possessiveness of his widow. She removed his bones first to Louisiana and then to Texas as if she had set out to find her own burial place, knowing well she would never return to the places she had left. In Texas she set up a small cemetery in a corner of her first farm, and as the family connection grew, and oddments of relations came over from Kentucky to settle, it contained at last about twenty graves. After the grandmother's death, part of her land was to be sold for the benefit of certain of her children, and the cemetery happened to lie in the part set aside for sale. It was necessary to take up the bodies and bury them again in the family plot in the big new public cemetery, where the grandmother had been buried. At last her husband was to lie beside her for eternity, as she had planned.

The family cemetery had been a pleasant small neglected garden of tangled rose bushes and ragged cedar trees and cypress, the simple flat stones rising out of uncropped sweet-smelling wild grass. The graves were lying open and empty one burning day when Miranda and her brother Paul, who often went together to hunt rabbits and doves, propped their twenty-two Winchester rifles carefully against the rail fence, climbed over and explored among the graves. She was nine years old and he was twelve.

They peered into the pits all shaped alike with such purposeful accuracy, and looking at each other with pleased adventurous eyes, they said in solemn tones: "These were graves!" trying by words to shape a special, suitable emotion in their minds, but they felt nothing except an agreeable thrill of wonder: they were seeing a new sight, doing something they had not done before. In them both there was also a small disappointment at the entire commonplaceness of the actual spectacle. Even if it had once contained a coffin for years upon years, when the coffin was gone a grave was just a hole in the ground. Miranda leaped into the pit that had held her grandfather's bones. Scratching around aimlessly and pleasurably as any young animal, she scooped up a lump of earth and weighed it in her palm. It had a pleasantly sweet, corrupt smell, being mixed with cedar needles and small leaves, and as the crumbs fell apart, she saw a silver dove no larger than a hazel nut, with spread wings and a neat fan-shaped tail. The breast had a deep round hollow in it. Turning it up to the fierce sunlight, she saw that the inside of the hollow was cut in little whorls. She scrambled out, over the pile of loose earth that had fallen back into one end of the grave, calling to Paul that she had found something, he must guess what . . . His head appeared smiling over the rim of another grave. He waved a closed hand at her. "I've got something too!" They ran to compare treasures, making a game of it, so many guesses each, all wrong, and a final showdown with opened palms. Paul had found a thin wide gold ring carved with intricate flowers and leaves. Miranda was smitten at sight of the ring and wished to have it. Paul seemed more impressed by the dove. They made a trade, with some little bickering. After he had got the dove in his hand, Paul said, "Don't you know what this is? This is a screw head for a *coffin!* . . . I'll bet nobody else in the world has one like this!"

Miranda glanced at it without covetousness. She had the gold ring on her thumb; it fitted perfectly. "Maybe we ought to go now," she said, "maybe one of the niggers 'll see us and tell somebody." They knew the land had been sold, the cemetery was no longer theirs, and they felt like trespassers. They climbed back over the fence, slung their rifles loosely under their arms—they had been shooting at targets with various kinds of firearms since they were seven years old—and set out to look for the rabbits and doves or whatever small game might happen along. On these expeditions Miranda always followed at Paul's heels along the path, obeying instructions about handling her gun when going through fences; learning how to stand it up properly so it would not slip and fire unexpectedly; how to wait her time for a shot and not just bang away in the air without looking, spoiling shots for Paul, who really could hit things if given a chance. Now and then, in her excitement at seeing birds whizz up suddenly before her face, or a rabbit leap across her very toes, she lost her head, and almost without sighting she flung her rifle up and pulled the trigger. She hardly ever hit any sort of mark. She had no proper sense of hunting at all. Her brother would be often completely disgusted with her. "You don't care whether you get your bird or not," he said. "That's no way to hunt." Miranda could not understand his indignation. She had seen him smash his hat and yell with fury when he had missed his aim. "What I like about shooting," said Miranda, with exasperating inconsequence, "is pulling the trigger and hearing the noise."

"Then, by golly," said Paul, "whyn't you go back to the range and shoot at bulls-eyes?"

"I'd just as soon," said Miranda, "only like this, we walk around more."

"Well, you just stay behind and stop spoiling my shots," said Paul, who, when he made a kill, wanted to be certain he had made it. Miranda, who alone brought down a bird once in twenty rounds, always claimed as her own any game they got when they fired at the same moment. It was tiresome and unfair and her brother was sick of it.

"Now, the first dove we see, or the first rabbit, is mine," he told her. "And the next will be yours. Remember that and don't get smarty."

"What about snakes?" asked Miranda idly. "Can I have the first snake?"

Waving her thumb gently and watching her gold ring glitter, Miranda lost interest in shooting. She was wearing her summer roughing outfit: dark blue overalls, a light blue shirt, a hired-man's straw hat, and thick brown sandals. Her brother had the same outfit except his was a sober hickory-nut color. Ordinarily Miranda preferred her overalls to any other dress, though it was making rather a scandal in the countryside, for the year was 1903, and in the back country the law of female decorum had teeth in it. Her father had been criticized for letting his girls dress like boys and go careening around astride barebacked horses. Big sister Maria, the really independent and fearless one, in spite of her rather affected ways, rode at a dead run with only a rope knotted around her horse's nose. It was said the motherless family was running down, with the Grandmother no longer there to hold it together. It was known that she had discriminated against her son Harry in her will, and that he was in straits about money. Some of his old neighbors reflected with vicious satisfaction that now he would probably not be so stiffnecked, nor have any more high-stepping horses either. Miranda knew

this, though she could not say how. She had met along the road old women of the kind who smoked corn-cob pipes, who had treated her grandmother with most sincere respect. They slanted their gummy old eyes side-ways at the granddaughter and said, "Ain't you ashamed of yoself, Missy? It's aginst the Scriptures to dress like that. Whut yo Pappy thinkin about?" Miranda, with her powerful social sense, which was like a fine set of antennae radiating from every pore of her skin, would feel ashamed because she knew well it was rude and ill-bred to shock anybody, even bad-tempered old crones, though she had faith in her father's judgment and was perfectly comfortable in the clothes. Her father had said, "They're just what you need, and they'll save your dresses for school . . ." This sounded quite simple and natural to her. She had been brought up in rigorous economy. Wastefulness was vulgar. It was also a sin. These were truths; she had heard them repeated many times and never once disputed.

Now the ring, shining with the serene purity of fine gold on her rather grubby thumb, turned her feelings against her overalls and sockless feet, toes sticking through the thick brown leather straps. She wanted to go back to the farmhouse, take a good cold bath, dust herself with plenty of Maria's violet talcum powder—provided Maria was not present to object, of course—put on the thinnest, most becoming dress she owned, with a big sash, and sit in a wicker chair under the trees . . . These things were not all she wanted, of course; she had vague stirrings of desire for luxury and a grand way of living which could not take precise form in her imagination but were founded on family legend of past wealth and leisure. These immediate comforts were what she could have, and she wanted them at once. She lagged rather far behind Paul, and once she thought of just turning back without a word and going home. She stopped, thinking that Paul would never do that to her, and so she would have to tell him. When a rabbit leaped, she let Paul have it without dispute. He killed it with one shot.

When she came up with him, he was already kneeling, examining the wound, the rabbit trailing from his hands. "Right through the head," he said complacently, as if he had aimed for it. He took out his sharp, competent bowie knife and started to skin the body. He did it very cleanly and quickly. Uncle Jimbilly knew how to prepare the skins so that Miranda always had fur coats for her dolls, for though she never cared much for her dolls she liked seeing them in fur coats. The children knelt facing each other over the dead animal. Miranda watched admiringly while her brother stripped the skin away as if he were taking off a glove. The flayed flesh emerged dark scarlet, sleek, firm; Miranda with thumb and finger felt the long fine muscles with the silvery flat strips binding them to the joints. Brother lifted the oddly bloated belly. "Look," he said, in a low amazed voice. "It was going to have young ones."

Very carefully he slit the thin flesh from the center ribs to the flanks, and a scarlet bag appeared. He slit again and pulled the bag open, and there lay a bundle of tiny rabbits, each wrapped in a thin scarlet veil. The brother pulled these off and there they were, dark gray, their sleek wet down lying in minute even ripples, like a baby's head just washed, their unbelievably small delicate ears folded close, their little blind faces almost featureless.

Miranda said, "Oh, I want to *see*," under her breath. She looked and looked—excited but not frightened, for she was accustomed to the sight of animals killed in hunting—filled with pity and astonishment and a kind of shocked delight in the wonderful little creatures for their own sakes, they were so pretty. She touched one of them ever so carefully, "Ah, there's blood running over them," she said and began to tremble without knowing why. Yet she wanted most deeply to see and to know. Having seen, she felt at once as if she had known all along. The very memory of her former ignorance faded, she had always known just this. No one had ever told her anything outright, she had been rather unobservant of the animal life around her because she was so accustomed to animals. They seemed simply disorderly and unaccountably rude in their habits, but altogether natural and not very interesting. Her brother had spoken as if he had known about everything all along.

He may have seen all this before. He had never said a word to her, but she knew now a part at least of what he knew. She understood a little of the secret, formless intuitions in her own mind and body, which had been clearing up, taking form, so gradually and so steadily she had not realized that she was learning what she had to know. Paul said cautiously, as if he were talking about something forbidden: "They were just about ready to be born." His voice dropped on the last word. "I know," said Miranda, "like kittens. I know, like babies." She was quietly and terribly agitated, standing again with her rifle under her arm, looking down at the bloody heap. "I don't want the skin," she said, "I won't have it." Paul buried the young rabbits again in their mother's body, wrapped the skin around her, carried her to a clump of sage bushes, and hid her away. He came out again at once and said to Miranda, with an eager friendliness, a confidential tone quite unusual in him, as if he were taking her into an important secret on equal terms: "Listen now. Now you listen to me, and don't ever forget. Don't you ever tell a living soul that you saw this. Don't tell a soul. Don't tell Dad because I'll get into trouble. He'll say I'm leading you into things you ought not to do. He's always saying that. So now don't you go and forget and blab out sometime the way you're always doing . . . Now, that's a secret. Don't you tell."

Miranda never told, she did not even wish to tell anybody. She thought about the whole worrisome affair with confused unhappiness for a few days. Then it sank quietly into her mind and was heaped over by accumulated thousands of impressions, for nearly twenty years. One day she was picking her path among the puddles and crushed refuse of a market street in a strange city of a strange country, when without warning, plain and clear in its true colors as if she looked through a frame upon a scene that had not stirred nor changed since the moment it happened, the episode of that far-off day leaped from its burial place before her mind's eye. She was so reasonlessly horrified she halted suddenly staring, the scene before her eyes dimmed by the vision back of them. An Indian vendor had held up before her a tray of dyed sugar sweets, in the shapes of all kinds of small creatures: birds, baby chicks, baby rabbits, lambs, baby pigs. They were in gay colors and smelled of vanilla, maybe. . . . It was a very hot day and the smell in the market, with its piles of raw flesh and wilting flowers, was like the mingled sweetness and corruption she had smelled that other day in the empty cemetery

at home: the day she had remembered always until now vaguely as the time she and her brother had found treasure in the opened graves. Instantly upon this thought the dreadful vision faded, and she saw clearly her brother, whose childhood face she had forgotten, standing again in the blazing sunshine, again twelve years old, a pleased sober smile in his eyes, turning the silver dove over and over in his hands.

A Christian Education

ROBERT PENN WARREN

An ever-versatile man, poet, critic, essayist, dramatist, biographer, Robert Penn Warren is perhaps most notable as a novelist and short-story writer. Like Faulkner, Warren for years missed full recognition by reviewers or readers. Then in recent times both groups found in him a strong and original author, one of great conviction, and a storyteller of resource and universality. He has written with distinction of several parts of the South, in particular of the "border" state of Kentucky in which he was born. As much as any of his contemporaries, perhaps, Mr. Warren is concerned with ethics, with man's moral choices in a world of uncertainties and contradictions. Such issues have a large role in his Night Rider, *dealing with the tobacco wars of the early 1900's;* At Heaven's Gate, *with a character much like Luke Lea of Tennessee, hard-driving tycoon-politico;* All the King's Men, *a Huey Long-like figure, and* World Enough and Time, *drawn from a famous crime case of Kentucky. Mr. Warren has concerned himself often with the subject of violences in American and Southern life and history, though in less sensational style than some contemporaries. Grandson of a Confederate soldier, he was one of the Fugitive group and the agrarians of "I'll Take My Stand." While a number of judges have found ambiguity and overweighting of his themes, he is a Southerner with a still-growing general recognition. The selection here is from his* Circus in the Attic and Other Stories, *published in 1948 by Harcourt, Brace and Company.*

MR. Jim Nabb, who was a successful farmer and highly respected in our section, had about three hundred and fifty acres of first-rate land, a couple of big red barns, a big house painted red with the same kind of paint used on the barns, a big fat wife and a boy who wasn't right bright. He was a good man, everybody used to say, and from all reports I reckon he was. He was superintendent of the Sunday school at the Methodist church

in town, and I can recollect the time when I was a boy and used to go to church and recollect him there every Sunday up in front leading the singing or making the announcements about how the Epworth League would meet that night at seven o'clock and would all the members please come because it would be an interesting meeting. He was almost what you might call a little man, but he stood up straight in his Sunday suit and he had a wide face too big for his body, his face being smooth and pink like a boy's, even if his clean-looking mustache was getting grayish. He didn't have either the bullying kind of voice or the tearful kind of voice like most people have who get up and talk a lot in public to show off, especially in church, and when he led the singing his voice would get up mighty high like a woman's or get swallowed up in the noise the other people made. But when he talked or made his announcements everybody listened close, even if his voice wasn't very strong, because he was so well respected in the community.

Mr. Nabb never smiled, that is, to speak of, but always had a sort of sad look on his face. He didn't have a sour look, just sad and resigned like he was carrying his cross, as the saying goes. Looking back now, I reckon he had that sad look on account of his boy not being very bright, which must be enough to make a man sad, especially when you've got a good piece of land and a house like his and money in the bank, but nobody to leave it all to when you pass on to the better world. I guess he wanted another child mighty bad, somebody who could take up where he left off, so to speak, and protect the one who wasn't very bright. I can remember the ladies talking about how Mrs. Nabb just couldn't get in a family way no matter what she tried, and her health wasn't too good anyway like it frequently isn't with those big fat women who ail all the time and are inclined to cry if you look at them. Mrs. Nabb used to start getting tearful in church sometimes at the least little thing, and sometimes just for nothing you could notice. Anyway, it took Mr. Nabb eleven more years before he got any results and there was another baby, which was a boy, too. Mrs. Nabb told the ladies it was just an answer to prayer and was like a miracle, and my mother told my father, and my father, sitting there at the dinner table, told her not to go talking about him that way if she ever got another child because it wasn't very flattering to Mr. Nabb.

When the second baby came Mr. Nabb didn't lose that sad look like you might think, even if now he did have what he had been praying for for such a long time. His face had probably just grown that way by that time, or maybe he wasn't sure the new one would turn out to be right bright either, for you can't tell when they're little, and he didn't want to be counting his chickens before they hatched. And by the time the new one, Alec Nabb, had got any size on him and you could tell he had good sense, something else happened to make Mr. Nabb look sad again.

Everybody always felt sorry for Mr. Nabb because he was a good man and tried to practice what he preached. A Christian education, he said, was the greatest thing in the world. And he tried to give his boy, the one who wasn't bright, a good raising, and it must be pretty hard to try to give a nitwit a good Christian education, when they look at you that way and are liable to slobber. When they look at you that way, you must feel like you are just pouring something valuable down the drain.

Silas Nabb wasn't really an idiot, he just wasn't right bright. He was in the same Sunday school class I was in, and got promoted when the time came, even if he couldn't answer questions. He could say the Golden Text sometimes, though, if he got a little prompting from his mother, who taught the class. When he got it all out, she used to look mighty pleased, and when he didn't and began to stare off at something else, the tears would start running down her cheeks. But he didn't get promoted in school after the first year or two, and after he was in the second grade for about three years, his father took him out of school, which likely is the only advantage in being a nitwit.

But Silas learned one thing his people tried to teach him about being a good Christian. Mrs. Nabb used to try to teach us boys in Sunday school about a soft answer turning away wrath and about turning the other cheek when somebody was mean to you and about the meek inheriting the earth. That and about giving your money to the poor was what she tried hardest to hammer into us, but since we didn't have any money anyway, being just kids, we didn't have much trouble learning the second thing. What money our people gave us for Sunday school, we had to put in the collection anyway, for we would have caught hell if we hadn't. Silas always brought a dime to Sunday school, and he used to put it in his mouth and suck it until his mother made him stop. After a while she got so she would put it in his shirt pocket and pin up the pocket with a safety pin; then he would have trouble getting the pin out when the collection came and she would have to help him half the time. But he learned better than anybody about turning the other cheek.

The boys used to pester him a little bit just because they knew he wouldn't do anything about it or fight back. They never hit him or were real mean to him. They would just push him off the sidewalk out in front of the church when we were waiting for Sunday school to start; or maybe they would rub their knucks in his head a little, which if you ever had done to you, you know how unpleasant it is. It don't hurt, but it sure makes you mad. It is called the Dutch shampoo.

We used to get to Sunday school early because the only fun in going was to horse around outside before things got started. We would stand around out there in front in our good clothes, somebody sneaking up to pull somebody else's tie or mess somebody's hair up. Then somebody would see the Nabbs come driving up the street and everybody would straighten up and look innocent.

Mr. Nabb would be sitting in front holding the reins, with Mrs. Nabb by his side. Silas would be on the back seat, leaning against the back and looking behind at the dust they raised. Mrs. Nabb would say good morning to all of us, calling us by our names, and then she would say to Silas, "Silas, don't you want to play with the boys?" Then she would leave him out there.

The boys weren't really mean to Silas. They just pestered him. They would push him off the sidewalk and make him step in the deep dust and get his shoes full of dust, or full of mud, if it was muddy. He would just say, "Don't," and come back on the sidewalk, and somebody would push him off again. Even the little kids would push him and I remember kids not more than four or five years old going up to push Silas when he was ten or twelve and big for his age. That was the funniest. Then somebody would say,

"Silas, why don't you lam somebody for pushing you? I wouldn't let nobody push me like that." And maybe he would say, "God says not to fight." That is, if he said anything.

And somebody would say: "Did God say that? You know I didn't hear Him say nothing, or maybe I just misunderstood Him."

But nobody ever got any rise out of Siles, except maybe to make him cry. If he cried, everybody would get afraid he would tell and they would wipe his nose and comfort him to make him stop. I used to get plain disgusted sometimes, and after I got any size on me, I never pushed him myself because I got so I didn't approve of it somehow. But it was funny when the real little kids pushed him. But sometimes I used to wish Silas would knock hell out of somebody.

There used to be a big Sunday school picnic every summer. All the women would fix up stuff to eat, fried chicken and boiled ham and deviled eggs and beaten biscuits and lemon pie and chess pie and salt-rising bread and tea in fruit jars. And they would carry a lot of ice wrapped up in tow sacks to make iced tea and to keep the ice cream good.

The summer that Silas was about thirteen or fourteen years old, Mr. Nabb asked them to have the picnic out at his place, which for a matter of fact was a right good place for a picnic. There was a big pond or sort of lake on his place, not just a stock pond with mud and manure tramped around the edges, but one with nice trees and some thickets you could hide in, and there was good grass all around the pond. And there was a good rowboat people used for fishing, though Mr. Nabb himself didn't fish any. He just kept the boat there for people who liked to fish, which was one of the things that made Mr. Nabb so highly respected in the community.

We had the picnic out there under the trees. It was July and hot, but it was cool in the shade with a nice breeze. After the ladies got everything fixed out nice on the tables, we all came up and stood around while Mr. Nabb returned thanks for the blessings God had bestowed upon us. Then we got paper plates and paper napkins and the ladies gave us helpings of everything. We ate all we could hold, but there was always a lot left over, because no lady likes to have people think she's stingy. Mr. Nabb always suggested they ought to give what was left to the poor, which they did.

We ate all we could, and then we lay around a little letting it settle. But it don't take long for food to settle on a kid's stomach, and so pretty soon we got to horsing around and playing games, playing "high spy" in the thickets and behind the trees. Then somebody, Joe Sykes I believe it was, said to me, "Let's go out in that boat." So some of us pushed the boat out and got in. Then Silas Nabb came down and wanted to go too. Mrs. Nabb didn't want him to go, but Mr. Nabb came down and said it would do Silas good to go, and asked us very politely did we mind. It being Mr. Nabb's boat, what could we say? So we said, "Sure."

We rowed around out there in the pond some, but rowing around in a pond never is as much fun as you think it is before you start, unless you're fishing or something. And the sun was bearing down too. The trouble was there just wasn't anything to do sitting out there in a boat in the sun, so the boys got to telling Silas dirty jokes like they did sometimes or teaching him dirty words. They would ask him dirty questions and no matter what he said, whether he said yes or no or what, it would sound funny, coming from a nitwit that way. Then the smallest boy in the boat, Ben Tupper, who was about nine years old maybe, got to pestering Silas. He was sitting behind Silas in the boat and he would pull the short hair on the back of Silas' neck a little or take his shirttail out behind. We told him to stop, but it just made him worse. And all the time we were drifting around out there in the hot sun.

Little Ben Tupper wouldn't stop, so one of the bigger boys said, "Ben, I'm going to slap your teeth down your throat if you don't stop." But after a minute he kept right on. He would pull out Silas' shirttail and say, "Silas, what does God say?" But Silas never said anything the whole time.

I guess it was the sun bearing down and Silas being so crowded up with people in the boat that made him do it. And that boat was too full anyway. But Ben Tupper kept on pestering him, and saying, "Silas, what does God say?" All of a sudden I noticed Silas had a little pocketknife in his hand, which his father didn't have any better sense than to give him one Christmas. So I yelled, "Ben!" But it didn't do any good, for just that second Ben was jerking at the short hair on the back of Silas' neck again. And Silas swung around with that knife open to make a pass at Ben. One of the big boys up front near Silas made a grab for his arm, and got stabbed in the hand, and yelled, "God damn you!" And little Ben Tupper, just scared to death, jumped up and fell back to get out of the way. Mrs. Nabb way back on shore must have seen something was up, because I can remember hearing her voice coming across the water saying, "Silas! Silas!" Maybe she caught the sunshine on that knife. But one of the other boys made a grab for Silas and maybe hit him accidentally or something, or maybe it was because little Ben started the boat to rocking so bad, but all of a sudden Silas hit the water and splashed everybody in the boat wringing wet.

You know how it is when somebody dives out of a boat, it sends the boat away a piece, too. Well, Silas fell out of the boat the same way, and by the time we stopped the boat rocking we were more than fifteen feet away. Silas came back up to the top of the water and began to yell and splash, and I saw he couldn't swim. I was a pretty good swimmer, and I always figured I would like to save somebody's life sometime and be a hero, but when I saw him go down again, I just didn't move a muscle even if I did hear a voice in my head plain as day, saying, *He's going to drown.*

One of the oars was lost and was floating around near Silas, but he didn't see it or didn't have sense enough to grab it, though somebody yelled to him to grab it. We paddled with the other oar and with our hands trying to get to him, but the boat was heavy and we didn't make it. We just sat there looking at the place a minute. Then somebody said, "He's drowned." And the Tupper kid began to cry.

We got the other oar and started back to the shore. That was all we could do, and while we rowed in we could hear Mrs. Nabb's voice screaming, "Silas! Silas!" We didn't look at her as we rowed in.

By the time we got there she had fainted and they dragged her back from the shore a piece, and the ladies were working on her. But there was Mr. Nabb and the other men standing around him on the shore, watching us come. One of the men walked out in the water toward us and said: "Boys, get outer that boat." We got out, and the men climbed in, Mr. Nabb, too. Then one of the men said to me, "Get your pants and shirt off and get in here." And I did, though for just a minute I couldn't think what for. Then I knew I was going to have to dive for that body. That man knew I could swim and dive pretty good. So we rowed back out to the place as near as we could tell, Mr. Nabb sitting on the seat in the boat, gone mighty white in the face and not saying anything and not crying. One of the men said, "If we can get him up right quick maybe there's some breath in him." But Mr. Nabb said, "No, it's God will."

When we got out there, one of the men said: "Is this the place?"

I said, "I reckon so."

"All right," he said. He didn't say for me to dive, he just said, "All right." So I stood up, feeling the sun hitting me on the back of my neck and between my shoulder blades, and got ready to dive. I didn't look at Mr. Nabb. The men held the oars in the water to steady the boat, and I dived. I was so nervous or something I didn't get a good breath before I hit the water, and so I didn't get to the bottom before me climb in the boat. One of the men helped me climb in the boat. None of them said a word, just sitting there in the sun.

The next time I got bottom. I went down fast, swimming breast stroke down, and I felt my hand touch bottom, for it was so deep it was dark. The bottom of a pond is the softest place in the world and dark deep down, not water and not mud, just like velvet in the dark, only softer, and when my hand touched bottom that time, just for a split second I thought how nice it would be to lie there, it was so soft, and look up trying to see where the light made the water green.

Then I got scared, and I swam to the top and popped out of the water with my ears roaring and the light sudden like an explosion.

I kept on diving. I likely dived near fifty times, I guess, and I got bottom a lot of times. One time I touched the body on the face, and I made a grab for something to hold to, but I missed, and I couldn't see in the dark. When I touched that face, I felt like screaming, but you can't scream under water but once. When I missed, I came back on top.

After a while I got so tired out I couldn't get in the boat hardly. The last time, they had to pull me in and I couldn't move. I said I would dive again in a minute, but Mr. Nabb said, "No. And thank you, Son."

They rowed back in and took me out of the boat. Somebody had telephoned town, and some big boys and men had come on out to get the body. A young fellow named Spooner dived down and got it. He got it on his third try, but that was just luck to get it so soon. I was sick at my stomach and my head was about to pop open from diving so much. In a way I was glad I didn't get the body, for if I had been the one to get it up, Mr. Nabb might have thought I was good enough to save Silas when he fell in. I was so sick I didn't even see them carry the body to the house. I just heard voices, but I didn't care. After a while people wrapped me up in a blanket they got and carried me home.

It was mighty hard on Mr. and Mrs. Nabb having a tragedy like that in the family, I reckon. In some ways I reckon it is worse to have a nitwit die on your hands than somebody with good sense, because you feel more responsible. But some people said it was a blessing in the long run, Silas being afflicted like he was. And the Nabbs had Alec, who wasn't but about three years old then.

Alec turned out to have good sense, all right. And they never tried to teach him about turning the other cheek like they did Silas. Somebody must have told them how the boys imposed on Silas because Silas never hit back. Alec turned out to be a terror. He wasn't very big, taking after his father, but he was a terror. He wouldn't take anything off nobody, and he always had a chip on his shoulder. The older he got, the worse he got that way. And he kept fast company too. When he was about twenty-two he got in a row and shot a man with a .38. The man died. Alec is over in Nashville in the pen now, and I guess he'll be there a good long time.

Changed, Yet Eternally the Same

WILLIAM ALEXANDER PERCY

William A. Percy, a man of poetic sensitivity, wrote verse of high merit, but will be known longest for his Lanterns on the Levee, *from which passages appear here. It was published in 1941 by Alfred A. Knopf, Inc. Born in 1885, Mr. Percy was the son of a United States Senator, who greatly influenced his life. Attending the University of the South (Sewanee), he went on to Harvard Law School and took a place in his father's office. Of a slim, slight figure, he helped thrust back the Ku Klux Klan when it reached out anew for power in Mississippi. He did considerable flood control relief work in 1927, and served also with the Hoover Belgian Relief Commission. Many of these activities appear in* Lanterns on the Levee, *a literate statement of the creed of a wise conservative, with touches of humanity and liberalism.*

MY COUNTRY is the Mississippi Delta. . . . It lies flat, like a badly drawn half oval, with Memphis at its northern and Vicksburg at its southern tip. Its western boundary is the Mississippi River, which coils and returns on itself in great loops and crescents. Every few years it rises like a monster from its bed and pushes over its banks to vex and sweeten the land it has made. For our soil, very dark brown, creamy and sweet-smelling, without substrata of rock or shale, was built up slowly, century after century, by the sediment gathered by the river in its solemn task of cleansing the continent and deposited in annual layers of silt on what must once have been the vast depression between itself and the hills. . . .

The land does not drain into the river as most riparian lands do, but tilts back from it towards the hills of the south and east. Across this wide flat alluvial stretch run slowly and circuitously other rivers and creeks, also high-banked, with names pleasant to remember—Rattlesnake Bayou, Quiver River, the Bogue Falaya, the Tallahatchie, the Sunflower—pouring their tawny waters finally into the Yazoo, which in turn loses itself just above Vicksburg in the river . . . the great river, the shifting, unappeasable god of the country, feared and loved, the Mississippi.

In the old days this was a land of unbroken forests. The trees grew to enormous heights, with vast trunks and limbs, and between them spread a chaos of vines and cane and brush. . . . Wild flowers were few, the soil being too rich and warm and deep, and those, like the yellow-top of early spring, apt to be rank and weed-like. A still country it must have been, ankle-deep in water, mostly in shadow, with mere flickers of sunshine, and they motey and yellow and thick like syrup. The wild swans loved it; tides of green parakeets from the south and of gray pigeons from the north melted into its tree-tops and gave them sound; ducks—mallards, canvas-back, teal, and wood-duck—and Canadian geese, their wedges high in the soft air of autumn like winter's first arrows, have still not deserted it.

Such was my country hardly more than a hundred years ago. It was about then that slavery became unprofitable in the older

Southern states and slaveholders began to look for cheap fertile lands farther west. . . . So younger sons from Virginia, South Carolina, and Kentucky with their gear, livestock, and chattels, human and otherwise, started a leisurely migration into the Delta. Forests were cleared, roads constructed (such dusty or muddy roads!), soil shaped into fields, homes built.

The real highway was the river. All life, social and economic, centered there. The river steamers furnished transportation, relaxation, and information to the whole river people. In our town the *Pargaud* landed regularly on Sunday, usually between eleven o'clock and noon. Everybody would be at church, but when she blew, the male members of the congregation to a man would rise and, in spite of indignant glares from their wives and giggles from the choir, make their exits, with a severe air of business just remembered. With the *Pargaud* came the week's mail and gossip of the river-front from St. Louis to New Orleans and rumors from the very distant outside world.

They were a fine fleet, those old sidewheelers, which stopped on signal at the various plantations and river settlements—the *White*, the *Pargaud*, the *Natchez*, the *Robert E. Lee*. The last and least of them was the *Belle of the Bends*, which as a small boy I could never see steaming majestically through the sunset to the landing without a fine choky feeling. They had pleasant outside cabins opening on an enormous white dining-saloon, decorated in the most abandoned gingerbread style, which after supper became a ballroom. . . . Anybody who was anybody knew everybody else, and each trip was rather like a grand house-party, with dancing and gambling and an abundance of Kentucky whisky and French champagne. The ladies (who never partook of these beverages—maybe a sip of champagne) were always going to New Orleans for Mardi Gras or to shop or hear the opera (well established there before it was begun in New York) or to visit cousins and aunts in the Louisiana and Natchez territory; and as those were days of enormous families, cousins and aunts were plentiful. There never was a Southern family that was a Southern Family some member of which, incredibly beautiful and sparkling, had

not opened the ball with Lafayette. For years apparently his sole occupation was opening balls in New Orleans, Charleston, Natchez and St. Louis.

Memphis was hardly more than a country town. The commission merchants had their offices in New Orleans and it was they who supplied the planters with the cash for their extensive and costly operations. Here was an ever ready reason for the men to board the boat, and one that made unnecessary any reference to the lottery, the races, the masked balls, the fantastic poker games, the hundred and one amiable vices of that most European and sloe-eyed of American cities. . . .

We had few of those roomy old residences, full of fine woodwork and furniture and drapery, which excellent French or English architects built in the Natchez and Charleston neighborhoods and in the Louisiana sugar cane territory. The few we had have caved into the river or burned. But a library was as portable as a slave, and excellent ones abounded. . . . On the bottom shelf would be a fat Bible, the front pages inscribed with long lists of deaths and births in a beautiful flourishing hand. On the top shelf presumably beyond the reach of the young and impressionable, would be the novels of George Sand and, later, of Ouida. *Paul and Virginia* too was a favorite, but who can now recall that title, though no book ever had more warm and innocuous tears shed over it?

I recall one survivor of that generation, or rather of the one immediately following it. Aunt Fannie, my great-aunt by marriage, was in looks all that the *Surry of Eagle's Nest* and *Marse Chan* school of writers would have you believe elderly Southern gentlewomen invariably were. She had exquisite slender white hands, usually folded in idleness on her lap; upon her neat curly white hair, parted in the middle, reposed a tiny white thing of frills and lace which may have been a cap but which looked more like a doily; her face was small and white, with truly a faded flower look; her dress was black and fitted well and with a sort of chic but still slender figure; she smelled faintly of orris root, a bit of which she usually chewed with no observable cud-motion. (I don't know why old ladies abandoned orris root—it's the right smell for them. But, after all, there are no old ladies now.)

. . . Certain little personal eccentricities of Aunt Fannie's endeared her to me as a child. She would suddenly drop into a little nap, sitting bolt upright in her chair and with the animated company around her pretending not to notice it. Or, equally inexplicably and with equal disregard of surroundings, she would sob gently and delicately and wipe quite real tears from her eyes with her diminutive orris-scented handkerchief. I attributed this phenomenon to some old and overwhelming sorrow which she carried in her heart and was too proud and ladylike to reveal. Only years and years later I learned that these engaging little habits of hers arose from another little habit: Aunt Fannie took her grain of morphine every day. Being the only wicked thing she ever did, it must have been doubly consoling. . . .

The river is changed and eternally the same. The early settlers soon began to rebuff its yearly caress, that impregnated and vitalized the soil, by building small dikes around their own individual plantations. This was a poor makeshift and in time, not without ruction and bitter debate, was abandoned in favor of levee districts which undertook to levee the river itself at the cost of the benefited landowners. . . . Only within the last fifteen years has the government accepted the view urged for half a century by our people that the river's waters are the nation's waters and fighting them in the nation's fight.

But this work has not changed the savage nature and austere beauty of the river itself. Man draws near to it, fights it, uses it, curses it, loves it, but it remains remote, unaffected. . . . The gods on their thrones are shaken and changed, but it abides, aloof and unappeasable, with no heart except for its own task, under the unbroken and immense arch of the lighted sky where the sun, too, goes a lonely journey.

No longer the great white boats and their gallant companies ply to and fro on its waters. A certain glamour is gone forever. But the freighters and barge lines of today keep one reminder of the vanished elder packets—their deep-throated, long-drawn-out, giant voices. And still there is no sound in the world so filled with mystery and longing and unease as the sound at night of a river boat blowing for the landing—one long,, two shorts, one long, two shorts. . . . The sound of the river boats hangs inside your heart like a star.

Revolt of a Damnyankee

H. ALLEN SMITH

Thousands of Americans, North and South, have laughed in good-humored appreciation over H. Allen Smith's The Rebel Yell, *published by Doubleday and Company in 1954. A man with a twinkle as well as bright appraisal in his eye, Mr. Smith wrote the following passages with tongue in friendly cheek, and a large group of Southern friends applauded. He says that his early book,* Stranded on a Davenport, *was suppressed by a breathless justice of the peace in Huntington, Indiana. His other writings include* Low Man on a Totem Pole, Life in a Putty Knife Factory *and* Smith's London Journal. *Born in Illinois, Mr. Smith worked on newspapers in Louisville, Kentucky, in Florida, Oklahoma and other places, and then won attention as an interviewer-staff writer on the New York* World-Telegram.

I AM a Northerner, and proud of it. My father was a Northerner before me, and his father before him. My people fought and bled for the Union and since that awful day at Appomattox we have never faltered in our devotion to the ideals and traditions of the

North. We believed then as we believe now that right and justice were on our side; we have never been ashamed of the part we took in the War of the Rebellion.

There appears to be a notion abroad in the South that we of the North are a decadent people, that we are drenched in frustration and shame because of the humiliation we suffered at the hands of the South. I for one am going to stand like a stone wall against this relentless persecution. I believe that I speak for all the people of the North when I say that we're sick and tired of being pushed around and abused by Southerners. I'm not so foolhardy as to contend that we are better than they are. Certainly we have our grievous faults. Certainly there are symptoms of mildew and decadence among us.

But why, in the name of John Brown, can't they leave us alone? If they'd just cease their impertinent meddling they'd soon find out that we are capable of working out our problems by ourselves, without assistance from them. Haven't they ever heard of States' Rights?

The people of the South scrutinize us and assume, from the superficial aspects of our behavior—our tendencies toward steady work, our hard-going way of life, our frenetic dashing about, the way we bolt down our lunches —that we are incurably industrious and even ambitious. On that ridiculous assumption, the South inveighs against us, needles us, lampoons us, tries to reform us and, failing that, deliberately keeps the ancient animosities alive. I've had just about enough.

They act, sometimes, as if we were not aware of the fact that we have a Woman problem. Certainly we are aware of it and we'll learn how to cope with it from hard and practical experience, from *living with it*, and not from the flow of unsolicited advice that is coming across the Mason-Dixon line. Let them understand, once and for all, that we'll handle this problem the way the Lord, Yo-He-Wah, meant it to be handled.

The thing they are unable to grasp in the South is that we have some ennobling traditions behind us. Institutions which to them represent evil and degradation have, in fact, been a blessing to us. A Southerner is simply incapable of understanding the *Northern tradition*. Take this same matter of the Woman. They swarm around us and try to tell me how the problem can be handled. Good Lord! I was raised from the cradle by a faithful old Woman. Old Miss Martha she was, and still is, bless 'er big white heart!

She was like a mother to me, and today, at the age of a hundred and seventeen, she still frets over me whenever I'm at home, dragging her weary bones up the stair each night to tuck me in and make sure I've been a "good boy" and taken my phenobarbital tablets. I've known Old Miss and loved her for as long as I have memory and no kindlier soul ever lived on this earth. It seems only yesterday that she sat with me beneath the scraggly, beetle-infested elm in our back yard, softly crooning *Waiting for the Chester A. Arthur* while she fed me sips of delicious gin with a spoon (spoon-gin, we call it up North). Yet the Southerners howl about how we discriminate against the Woman.

They suffer delusions that we could end our Woman problem with a snap of the fingers, when any sensible person knows that it is going to take generations. They point the finger of scorn at us because we choose to segregate men from women, maintaining separate washrooms for them in public; compelling the women to go to one side of the shoe store and the men to the other; even sending them to separate colleges. They call attention to the fact that our Northern hotels retain detectives whose chief duty is to enforce segregation, telephoning male guests and saying, "Get that Woman out of your room!"

What a shallow view these Southerners hold! Can't they see that this is a deliberately constructive program? Through these seemingly cruel restrictions we are actually encouraging miscegenation, intermarriage between men and women, so that in the end—in seven or eight or thirty-five generations, perhaps—we shall have solved one of our most trying problems by absorbing the Woman into the male race. Granted it is a dangerous form of biological experimentation. I am well aware of the fact that the pendulum is swinging in the opposite direction in many cases —that there are instances in the North where it appears that the male is being absorbed into the female race.

The thing that makes me foaming mad is the accusation, peated and repeated by Southern agitators, that we refuse to forget about the Civil War—that it still rankles in our breasts. How *could* we ever forget it? We, who sacrificed the very flower of Northern manhood!

I contend that we of the North have tried to forget that war. Sometimes I'm tempted to believe that *they* are really the ones who are keeping the issue alive, taunting us about it. For years it has been a custom in my house, as well as in the homes of most Northerners, to say at the beginning of a party, "Please, everyone, let's not talk sex, religion or the Civil War."

Still they taunt us, charging us with placing Ulysses S. Grant on a pedestal; nay, even elevating him to sainthood. And if not Grant, they abuse us about Lincoln. What if he was a product of Tomato Road? What if he was, in boyhood, compelled to subsist on woodchuck jowl and unboiled hominy? We admit he was uncouth and had dirty fingernails and said "you" rather than "you-all." But he was able to rise above all that, we think, just as we would be able to rise above our unhappy condition if they'd just stay home and mind their own barbecue stands and leave us alone.

They needle and harpoon us constantly in their newspapers, giving the rank-and-file of the South a distorted picture of the North. The misguided Southerner honestly believes that we spend all our waking hours chasing dollars in the sultry shade of our Empire State buildings. He snickers at us because we put on shoes in the morning and wear them until we go to bed at night, and even because we do all our sleeping at night instead of in the afternoon and night. He mocks us for shooting off firecrackers on the Fourth of July instead of at Christmas time.

I would like to see a friendlier feeling between the South and the North, but we'll never have it if they continue their intolerant sniping at us. By what right do they set themselves up as a superior race? Just because they are so powerful in Washington, just because

they have all that cotton and all that tobacco and all that pellagra and all that grits and all that rubbery talk—that doesn't give them the right to look down their patrician noses at us as if we were hopelessly benighted and ignorant and addicted to dipping nutmeg.

They've got to understand that we are striving toward a culture that will stand alongside their own. We yearn for the same degree of civilization that they have achieved for themselves. It's a thing that can't be wrought overnight. Atlanta wasn't burned in a day (or was it?). I suspect that they actually don't want us to have that culture, that they are jealous of their own high degree of genteel living, and would like nothing better than to see us go on forever slaving and sweating in our steel mills, our auto plants, our banks, our publishing houses, our symphony halls, our movie studios and our universities.

Yet they forget that we have our pride. Ah, but we are a proud people! They'd better learn to reckon with *that*. For all their scorn, we have traditions that are imbedded deep in our souls. We, too, follow a code of honor handed on to us by our forefathers . . . Beware, you sons of rebels. When we can take no more of your impertinent meddling, we'll *secede* from you!

.   .   .

Some Northerners contend that the South has no adequate historical background for its culture. Certain Southerners, however, argue that their way of life is a direct continuation of Western European culture. I think it's provable that the Southerners are right.

In rural areas of the South, for generations, it was the custom for the wife always to walk ten paces behind the husband, even when going to a meeting of the League of Women Voters. This solemn and sensible custom was one of the South's cultural acquisitions from Western Europe.

Then quite suddenly, around 1945, the procedure was reversed. All over the South it was noted that women were now walking ten paces *ahead* of their husbands. Sociologists were baffled for a while, and then they made an illuminating discovery. During that same year, throughout Western Europe, wives had started walking ahead of husbands. Through some strange extra-sensory, telephotic transmission (controlled perhaps from Duke University) the people of the South *felt* the change in the European habit and, without discussing it, followed suit.

And why did the change occur in Europe? Simple. At the conclusion of World War II thousands of unexploded land mines remained in the ground of Western Europe. So husbands put their wives out in front.

. . .

It is sometimes said, by misguided Yankees, that Southern towns have more than the national average of feeble-minded people wandering their streets. This is not true. Several years ago I was visiting friends in a town in Unoccupied Florida, up near the Georgia border. They were building a new hospital in this town and, though construction had not started, the excavation was almost finished—an immense pit nearly a block long.

It happened that a Mr. Dabney, one of the town's leading citizens, was showing me the site. We were standing when a boy about twelve years old came along. He was by reputation the town half-wit—that is, he was

one of them. He came alongside of us and stared into the excavation and finally he said, "Mista Dabney, what they gonna do with that big ole hole when they finey git 'er dug?" Mr. Dabney smiled at the boy and then said, "Well, Hoab, I tell you. When they get 'er dug they're gonna take all the sons-of-bitches in this town and pile 'em in there." The boy reflected on this information a bit and then said, "Who they gonna git to cover 'em up?"

Thus, you see, a feeble-minded person in the South only *appears* to be feeble-minded.

. . .

I know of a Charleston family named Pinckney in which there is a three-year-old child. This child came into the house one day carrying a worm she had found in the yard. She was treating the worm with great tenderness and hospitality, and her mother, humoring her, agreed that the worm was one of the nicest worms she had ever seen. "Has the worm got a name?" she asked the child. "Oh yes," said the little girl. "What is its name?" asked the mother. "Its name," said the child, "is Worm Pinckney." Family is everything below Broad street in Charleston.

The South in the South Pacific

J. BRYAN, III

J. Bryan, III, who wrote Admiral Halsey's Story, *served in the South Pacific from 1942 to 1945.*

A PART of the Solomons campaign, waged eight years later and half a world away from the Civil War, was fought by Confederate troops. I know. I was one of them. Our "official" title was "The Confederate Forces of the Solomons," or, Navy-fashion, CONFORSOLS.

I don't remember what brought us "Confederates" together in the first place. The colonel thinks it began with that famous squawk of "Steep" Hill's: "The Navy plucks me out of my home in Atlanta and totes me eight thousand miles, and where am I? Spang in the

middle of Georgia and the South again—only this time it's *New* Georgia and the South *Pacific*. I should have stood in bed!"

The frail little fantasy might have expired right there, if I hadn't made it an item in my next letter home to Richmond. Father mentioned it to Dr. Douglas Southall Freeman, General Lee's biographer, and the Doc sent me a small Confederate flag, with a "commission" to "claim and colonize in the name of Jefferson Davis." We tacked the Flag to a dowel and stuck it in an old jelly jar.

Fighter Command's headquarters was an old tunnel in Kokengolo hill. Almost every man who saw the Flag in the jelly jar felt called on to give us some guff like: "*I know; you could have licked 'em with corn-stalks, only they wouldn't fight with corn-stalks, huh?*" or "*Pompey, you no-good rascal you, fetch me mah julep afore Ah sells you to Simon Legree!*"

The night-fighters had a lot of time to kill, so they sketched in a series of blackouts with a cast of characters that included Cap'm Cul-peper Randolph, Old Marse an' Ole Mist'is, Major Fauntleroy Taliaferro,* Miss Amanda and Miss Hydrangea, Leftenant Cyahteh Breckinridge, and assorted riverboat gamblers, slave traders and body servants. When an AA gun cut loose, one would draw an imaginary saber: "*We have fah'd on Fo't Sumteh! Hit means—wah!*" Or when a bomb fell: "*South'-ners, on yo' feet. Yankees, undeh the table. The battle's about to begin.*" Or climbing into the cockpit: "*Jes' show me the hang o' these hyah wee-pons, and p'int out who you wants kilt!*"

One of their favorite exit lines was "*A brigadier's sash ere dawn—or six feet of hon-ored clay!*" Another was "*Tonight I wateh mah hoss in the Tennessee River—or in hell!*" The pilots named their planes Dixie Belle, Traveller, Mrs. Suratt, Scarlett O'Hara and even Belle Watling.

Our "enemy," Danny O'Neill, announced that he was naming *his* plane Barbara Frietchie; otherwise he took no part in the act beyond asking, "*Who's this Robert E. Levy I hear you guys gabbing about? . . . You say it's 'Lee'? Back home in Berkeley there's a laun-dryman named Lee—Ching Lee. Guess they're any kin?*" Or, "*Wasn't it his army that that Frenchman wrote the book about, Lee's Miser-ables?*"

Such nonsense helped us forget the stink-ing tunnel, the sleepless night and the frightful food. But presently November 1 was on top of us—L-Day for the invasion of Bougainville—and we stopped playing "Dixie." The whole Confederacy rigmarole would have withered like any other fad but for Staff Sergeant James

*(Pronounced Tolliver, or Tollivah, of course.—H.T.K.)

L. Moore, USMC, of *Jackson* Street—he liked to emphasize—Starkville, Mississippi.

Lt. Comdr. John E. Lawrence, USNR, of Boston, Air Combat Intelligence, flew in on inspection. We Southerners may be mush-mouths, as Danny O'Neill claims, but every syllable Johnny spoke was a stave from "Carry Me Back to Old Back Bay." He'd had time to say scarcely more than "Hi!," but that was enough. Moore twitched a thread and a pla-card swung down, revealing in heavy red letters:

I SMELL YANKEE!

Johnny and I laughed so loud, the colonel came in. He started laughing, and pretty soon we had drawn a crowd. The story was all over Munda by evening. . . . It gathered momentum during the night. Next morning Southern ac-cents had thickened—or been adopted—in the most unlikely places. At breakfast, Kansans, State-of-Mainers, Hoosiers and Dakotans alike were noisily demanding grits-an'-gravy, pot-licker, ham hocks an' turnip tops, hush pup-pies, cornpone, hoppin' john and hoecake. Lt. Francis Bowen, USNR, of North Hollywood, was heard to declare, "Cunnel Custis, de ve'y bes' thing for sooplin' up a blacksnake whup is a b'ilin' o' possum fat." At the regular 0800 staff meeting the grave major who usually concluded his weather forecast with "Late af-ternoon and evening, heavy thundershowers over the land areas," ended instead, giggling, "Todes lightnin'-bug time, hit'll po' down rain!"

When Colonel Brice and I got back to our offices, we found a crowd waiting—Army, Navy and Marine; officers and enlisted men; friends and strangers—all clamorously insisting that the Confederacy organize its forces and that the colonel command them. They shouted down his refusal, and presently he issued his General Order Number 1:

CONFEDERATE FORCES SOLOMONS
HEADQUARTERS OF THE COMMANDER
—17 NOV., 1943
Effective at once, the following enemy priori-ties are assigned: Yankees fust, Japs second.

Even the original condition for membership in CONFORSOLS, Southern birth or residence, was waived on occasion. We accepted two New Zealanders because they came from South Island. We accepted Gus Widhelm, a Nebraskan, because he lived on the south side of his home town, Humphrey. (Danny jeered that Humphrey was so small, it didn't have but one side.) Gus' membership becoming known, Art Chamberlin, nicknamed Senator Flannelmouth, applied, as from the south side of Seattle.

At meetings the order of business was: 1. A rendition, by the colonel himself, of a stanza or two from our national anthem, "I'm a good old rebel." 2. The following "re-po't" by the "Sec'tary of Commus" in the following words (we permitted no variation): "The impo'ts an' expo'ts of the Southe'n po'ts fo' nineteen-fo'ty-fo' will be fo'teen percent mo' than the impo'ts an' expo'ts of the Southe'n po'ts fo' fo' years befo'." An account, by a different volunteer at every meeting, of a "gin-u-wine conversation between mah gran'pappy an' Ginral Lee."

An example of these accounts: "Ginral Lee ast mah gran'pappy, 'Cap'm, how many bluecoats up ahaid?' Mah gran'pappy said, 'Ginral, suh, Ah reckons they's nigh onto a thousan' o' the scoun'els.' Ginral Lee ast, 'Cap'm, how many men *you* got?' Mah gran'pappy said, 'Ginral, suh, they's me an' a wounded corp'ral and two li'l drummer boys.' Ginral Lee said, 'Cha-a-a-a-ahge!' "

On November 21, according to the CONFORSOLS war diary, Sergeant Moore introduced an ingenious security system, under which anyone seeking entrance to CONFORSOLS territory would be *shown* the password and challenged to pronounce it. Moore's list included *cigarette, hotel, dispatch, insurance, guitar, direct*—all words that only someone Southern-bred would accent on the first syllable. (Our usual passwords were lush with Jap-baffling l's: lily of the valley, lollapalooza, Vella Lavella, Lulu Belle.)

December 3 was the memorable date when Senator Flannelmouth reapplied for admission. As a character witness he offered Lieutenant Booth from the PT boats. Asked, "Are you a Southerner?", Booth cracked his knuckles and finally blurted out: "Not ex-

actly, sir, but my gre't-grandfather's cousin, John Wilkes Booth—"

We elected Senator Flannelmouth by acclamation, and Booth, too.

December 20, Secession day, was an anniversary so sacred for such passionate South Carolinians as the colonel and Caldwell Withers that we staged a special event in their honor: a raid on a "Yankee fo'tress"—actually, a dive-bombing attack on the Jap Airfield at Buka by two SBDs, each displaying a Confederate flag and carrying, in addition to its bombs, a dozen old beer bottles stuffed with notices: "Revenge for Gettysburg!," "This is for the *Merrimac!*," "Even-Stephen for Atlanta!" What do you suppose the Japs thought when they came out of their foxholes and picked up those papers and had them translated?

Then three things happened at once: Johnny Lawrence notified me that I'd be relieved any day now, and from that moment I had no heart for anything else . . . A cousin on duty in the Secretary of the Navy's office wrote me to dismember CONFORSOLS on the double and bury the fragments—the Republicans were primed to make an issue of it. . . . And a young replacement pilot, reporting to the colonel, pointed toward our Flag and asked, "What's that? Bolivia?" Plainly, it was time to shut up shop.

The Sec'tary of Commus gave his repo't on the Southe'n po'ts for the last time. And I heard for the last time a gin-u-wine account of what Ginral Lee had said to somebody's gran'pappy: " 'Cap'm,' Ginral Lee said, 'cap'm, Ah give daily thanks to the Almight that you's on ouah side, but in humanity's name, cap'm, cease yo feahful cahnage.' " CONFORSOLS disbanded.

I had been promised that I would have my orders by February 10, but the day passed with no word. On the eleventh there was still nothing. I was frantic when, early next morning, the Personnel Cfficer brought them.

He was a Vermonter, a friend of Danny O'Neill's. "Reb," he said, "I might have had 'em for you yesterday, but I wanted to make at least one Southerner thankful for Abe Lincoln's birthday."

Acknowledgments

MORE than any book which I have prepared, this one has represented happy labor. The thought of an anthology growing out of the history of the South, or of the various Souths, came to me about a decade ago. Since then I have gathered materials and notes on scores of trips about the area, on visits to England and France, including periods of work at the British Museum and the Bibliothèque Nationale; talked over aspects of the subject with friends, library authorities and specialists. But my trunkfuls of data, scattered in several rooms in New Orleans, had no particular focus or emphasis until about three years ago, when an old publishing friend, Jack Geoghegan of Coward-McCann, asked me, through my agent Mavis McIntosh, if I would be interested in treating the subject as part of the company's American Vista Series. After a few weeks' thought and my resifting of the material, we agreed on the project.

The shaping of *The Romantic South* involved far more additional time and application than I had anticipated—including the removal, during one perspiring week, of 110,000 words, to make way for more varied selections, to slim down the volume and to make it more emphatic. Throughout, I have attempted to represent all or most schools of thought and writing about the South and, not less importantly, to remain faithful to the spirit of the originals. If a writer is now and then a bit coy, or pompous, or overviolent, so be it. The primary tests which I tried to apply were ones of life and inherent interest: Was this passage more vivid than another on the subject; were its facts accurate in the main?

All choices are, to be sure, in a certain measure personal ones. The selection of necessity must appeal to the writer-editor, and have meaning for him. In most cases, however, it was advisable to take material which formed a clear, understandable unit; more diffuse, though equally well-written accounts, had to be passed over. I have sought to strike a balance between widely known, "classic" material, and less familiar selections, which sometimes represent better work.

Many individuals and groups of friends were generous during meetings in New Orleans, Atlanta, Richmond, Dallas, Houston, Forth Worth, Baltimore, Washington, Louisville, Memphis and elsewhere, in talking with me regarding Southern life, history and writings. For years, many forwarded notes—on backs of envelopes, memorandum pads, grocery-store bills in one case—whenever a book, an essay or a poem occurred to them. "Don't forget A. . . ." "I wonder if you've thought of B. . . ." "I don't see how you could leave out C. . . ." For five years one librarian sent me a message every few weeks, listing items that might be of interest. And when the manuscript finally shaped up, publisher- and author-friends proved more than helpful. In only a few cases was it impossible or difficult to obtain permissions.

In the last stages the gifted editor Tom Coffey of Coward-McCann gave dedicated service in laboring with me for many full days, over potfuls of coffee, omelets, cups of cheer (which both of us needed) and the like. Miss Jessica Diaz, New Orleans, worked conscientiously in helping process much material, as did Mrs. Eleanora Wharton, New Orleans; Vernon Spencer, who aided in sifting library material in New York, as he did with my previous *Gone Are the Days* and other books; Robert Meyer, Jr., of Festival Information Service, New York; Angela Gregory, the distinguished sculptor of New Orleans; Mrs. Marion Harris and Mrs. Zelda Soignier of the Harris Bookstore, Metairie, La., Bonnie Kate and Harold Leisure of the Plantation Bookstore, New Orleans; Lena Centanni of D. H. Holmes book department, and Kay Archer of the Maison Blanche book department, who assisted in the location of books, new and old.

I owe particular thanks, too, to Robert Talmadge, director of the Tulane University Library; Roy Kidman, assistant director; Mrs. Pat Segleau, head of the circulation department; Mrs. Dorothy Whittemore, head of the reference department; Mrs. Clayre Barr, library secretary;

Mrs. Connie Griffith of archives; Robert Greenwood of the acquisitions department. Betsy Swanson of the Newcomb School of Art helped handsomely in the processing of illustrations, and special aid came from John Hall Jacobs, former librarian of the New Orleans Public Library; George King Logan, assistant; Mrs. Ruth Robbins, acting librarian; Ruth Renaud, head of reference, and Margaret Ruckert, head of the Louisiana department.

Among others who gave counsel, help in tracking down data, locating rare items, etc., were Gerald Capers, of the Newcomb College history department and author of an important new study of John Calhoun; Mary Militano, Mr. and Mrs. Cameron Plummer of the Haunted Bookstore, Mobile; Captain Robert Estachy of the French Line, New Orleans, and Nesta Estachy; Alistair Maitland, British consul-general at New Orleans, and Betty Maitland; Robert Turner of the consulate-general staff; Lily and Albert Lieutaud of the Lieutaud Print Store, New Orleans; Mrs. Earle Rowe Glenn and Mrs. Edith Wyatt Moore, Natchez.

Mrs. Wallace Westfeldt and Mrs. Frances Bryson Moore, New Orleans; Mrs. Paula Coad, Savannah; Gordon L. Atwater, New Orleans; Captain William Lewis of the Dock Board, New Orleans, and formerly of the U. S. Engineers' Corps; Jacob Morrison, William J. Long and Edith Long, New Orleans; Mrs. Robert G. Robinson of the Louisiana Landmarks Society; Dr. Alfred Leland Crabb, Nashville, Tennessee; Admiral Whittaker Riggs, Walter Hoover, Val Mogensen, Kenneth Langguth, New Orleans; Edward Stagg and Edward Stiemel, Baton Rouge; Mrs. Margaret Dixon of the *Morning Advocate* and Essae M. Culver of the Louisiana State Library.

Lambert Davis of the University of North Carolina Press; Dr. Hugh Lefler of the University history department; William S. Powell, director, North Carolina Collection at the University library; James W. Patton, director of the library's Southern Historical Collection; Dr. Christopher Crittenden, director of the North Carolina Department of Archives and History, Raleigh, North Carolina; Mrs. Joye E. Jordan, administrator of the museum of the department; Samuel M. Boone, head of photo reproduction at the Chapel Hill Library.

Assistance in library searches came from Vergil Bedsole, archivist at Louisiana State University; John Andreassen, formerly of Baton Rouge, now of New Orleans; James Meeks, librarian of the Dallas Public library; Mrs. Margaret Pratt, head of the Texas Local History and Genealogy Department, and Marie Stanley of the staff, and Chip Chafetz of New York City.

Mrs. Mary Eleanor Clark of Chattanooga; Mr. and Mrs. Jay W. Johns, Charlottesville, Virginia; Curtis Carroll Davis, Baltimore; James Bailey, Baton Rouge, Louisiana; Mr. and Mrs. Robert Armstrong Andrews, Edisto Island and Charleston, South Carolina; S. J. ("Stonewall Jackson") Birshtein, Clarksburg, West Virginia; Dr. and Mrs. Robert Judice, New Orleans; Mrs. Helene Farris, Lyria Dickason; Judge Anna Judge Veters Levy, S. Sanford Levy and Dolly Veters, Mrs. Camilla Mays Frank and Mrs. Marion Crawford Adams, New Orleans.

Mrs. Ralph Catterall of the Valentine Museum and Miss Elizabeth J. Dance of her staff gave aid in several matters, as did John Jennings, director of the Virginia Historical Society; David J. Mays, chairman of the Virginia Library Board; Randolph Church, state librarian; Milton Russell, head of the reference department; W. Edwin Hemphill of *Cavalcade*, the library's magazine.

Jonathan Daniels of Raleigh and Virginia Dabney of Richmond both assisted in research details, as did Peter A. Brannon of the Alabama History and Archives Department, Montgomery; Bill Sharpe, publisher of *The State*, Raleigh, North Carolina; Lovick Pierce, publisher, and Leland D. Case, editor, of *Together*, Methodist Publishing House journal, who aided in material on Southern religious pioneering.

Charlotte Capers of the Mississippi Department of History and Archives; the late Jean Selby and Ella Beth Selby, Vicksburg; Mrs. Eva Davis, Vicksburg historical leader; David J. Harkness, University of Tennessee extension division at Chattanooga; Colonel Allen Julian of the Atlanta Historical Society and Beverley DuBose, Atlanta; India Thomas and Eleanor Brockenbrough of the Confederate Museum in Richmond; Joe Templeton, director of the Mobile Public Library, and Caldwell Delaney, authority on Mobile history.

Senator George Radcliffe, president of the Maryland Historical Society; James W. Foster, the society's director; Louis Azrael, Frederick Stieff and Mrs. Ferdinand Latrobe of Baltimore.

In Charleston, particular help came from Virginia Rugheimer of the Charleston Library Society; Mrs. Granville Prior of the Charleston Historical Society; Helen McCormack of the Gibbes Museum; Milby Burton, director of the Charleston Museum; Emily Sanders of the Charleston County Free Library, Elizabeth Allen and others, including Samuel Gaillard Stoney, Charleston author and historian. Robert Molloy, author of many perceptive Charleston studies, also counseled with me.

At Randolph-Macon College, Lynchburg, Dr. Robert D. Meade gave advice on the colonial period in Virginia. In Lexington, Thomas D. Clark, authority on Kentucky history; Winston ("Squire") Coleman of Winburn Farm, near Lexington; Paul Harris of the J. B. Speed Art Museum of Louisville; Mrs. Isabelle McMeekin of Louisville; Mary and Barry Bingham; Richard

Hill of the Filson Club, and Ken Meeker answered specific queries in a series of instances.

Ralph Newman and Margaret April of the Abraham Lincoln Bookstore in Chicago; Pete Long, Lincoln authority of Chicago; Clifford Dowdey, perceptive Virginia historian of Richmond, and William Lacy, Jr., Richmond; Stanley Horn, Confederate authority, Nashville; Mr. and Mrs. Roy Bird Cook, Stonewall Jackson experts; the late Boyd Stutler of Charleston, West Virginia, hunted down varied information.

Additional help came from Caroline S. Coleman, Fountain Inn, South Carolina; Ruby Parker, Pensacola, Florida; Dr. N. Philip Norman, New York; North Callahan, Bronxville, New York; Frank Daniell, Atlanta; Mrs. Edythe Capreol, Beaumont; Mrs. Kay B. McCracken, Corpus Christi, Texas; Mary Herbert, Pensacola; Mrs. E. Randolph Preston, Winston-Salem, North Carolina; Allen Maxwell of the *Southwest Review*.

Lon Tinkle, Dallas; Lile Chew, St. Petersburg, Fla., John Hundley Adams, Chicago; Mrs. R. C. Haynes, Ennis, Texas; Vernol Mayers, Houston; Bill Fountaine, Columbus, Ohio; Daisy Poole and Flo Field, New Orleans; Sallie Hill, Birmingham; James Murfin, Hagerstown, Maryland; Mrs. F. M. Robinson, McAllen, Texas; Elizabeth Jarrett, Chattanooga; Mrs. B. Morrison Sales, Lexington, Virginia.

Mrs. Merrill Parrish Hudson, Memphis; Edna H. Fowler, Los Angeles; Mrs. Walter C. White, Gates Mills, Ohio; Mrs. Edith Amsler, Houston; Mrs. Marie Jackson Arnold Pifer, Buckhannon, West Virginia; Marc and Lucille Antony, New Orleans; John K. Bettersworth, State College, Mississippi, and Mrs. Edith Amsler, Houston, Texas.

Gladys Peyronnin, Mrs. Alice V. Westfeldt, Mrs. Ellen Tilger, Ruth Scheuermann, Mrs. Bernice Zibilich, Mrs. Mary Lee, Mrs. William Spinos, Anna May McCurdy, Mrs. Marilyn Wilkins, Marion Mason, Adelaide Schmidt, Mrs. Susan Baughman, Mrs. Marion Borchers, Mrs. Elizabeth Buchanan, Mrs. Marie Sheets, Charles Daniel of the New Orleans Public Library.

Mrs. Beverly Peery, Mrs. Camille Jones, Mrs. Laura Hope, Mrs. Molly Eustis, Mrs. Alice McCausland, Mrs. Edith Ricketson, Mrs. Orahlee Handlin, Mrs. Elizabeth Thomson, Betty Maihles, Mrs. Mary Anna Blick, Mrs. Marjery Ohlsen, Mrs. Fay Swanson, Mrs. Elizabeth Beelman, Anna Wood, Mrs. Eunice Van Kirk, Mrs. Berthe Baker and the late Mrs. Aline Richter Stevens, all of the staff of the Tulane University Library.

Muriel Bultman, James Bezou, the late Roger Baudier, Joseph M. Shields, Jr., Dan S. Leyrer, Arthur Feitel, Fred Bultman, Morgan Doyle, Harry England, Paul Martin and Roy Hill, all of New Orleans.

Richard Walser, Raleigh, North Carolina; Dr. Alfred J. Hanna and Mrs. Kathryn Abbey Hanna, Winter Park, Florida; Sidney S. Field, New York; Anna Barringer, Charlottesville, Va.; Louis Engelke, San Antonio; Mary McGuire, Pensacola, and Ruby Donahey, St. Petersburg, Florida; Junius R. Fishburne, Charlottesville, Va.; John Barringer, Richmond; J. Walker Caldwell, Roanoke, North Carolina; Mr. and Mrs. Ted Swolm, Sarasota, Florida.

Betty and Carl Carmer, New York City; Bertha Worms, New Orleans; Ken Gormin, New Orleans; Stanley P. Deas, New Orleans; Howard Gwaltney, Smithfield, Virginia; Robert H. North, Washington, D. C.; Mrs. Edward Bailey and Mrs. Catherine Ellick, Jackson, Mississippi; Mrs. Powers McElveen, Sumter, South Carolina; Joseph E. Jenkins, Charleston; Mrs. Cambridge M. Trott; the Rev. S. Grayson Clary, and Mrs. St. Julien R. Childs, Charleston.

Mrs. Gertrude Carruth, Beaumont, Texas; Dr. Francis Haber, Department of Social Sciences, University of Florida, Gainesville; John G. Baker, National Audubon Society, New York; Karl Bickel, Sarasota; Marian Murray, Sarasota, Florida; Ruel McDaniel, Port La Vaca, Texas; Mrs. Grace Siewers, archivist of the Moravian Archives, Winston-Salem, North Carolina; Mrs. Kate Pyron, librarian of Salem College, Winston-Salem; and Mrs. Lloyd T. Presley of Old Salem, Inc.

Frank H. Wardlaw, Austin, director of the University of Texas Press; Congressman Charles E. Bennett of Jacksonville, Florida; Arless Nixon, librarian of the Fort Worth Public Library; James Record of the Fort Worth *Star-Telegram;* Evelyn Oppenheimer, Dallas; Kate Savage, Baltimore; A. C. Greene, Dallas; James W. Dyson, librarian of Loyola University, New Orleans; Elizabeth Litsinger of the Enoch Pratt Library, Baltimore, and Martha Ann Peters, her assistant in the Maryland Room; Mrs. Marie Eggleston Thompson, Charleston, South Carolina.

Mrs. P. G. Dearing, Alexandria, Virginia; Mrs. Mary Autry Higgins of San Antonio; Dr. Harriet H. Shoen of New York; Mr. George Person, Sr., Rembert Moon, R. H. Allen, Memphis; Allan Nevins, professor of history at Columbia University; Van Dyke MacBride; the late W. M. (Billy) Steele; John Bakeless, Seymour, Conn.; Mrs. Florence H. Barber, St. Petersburg, Fla.; Robert Selph Henry, Alexandria, Va.; Mrs. Glendy Culligan, Washington; Jerri Schmal, Chicago; Charles Claggett, Baltimore.

Mrs. Ethel Moore Mullins, Meadville, Miss.; Louise Koppel, Gulfport, Miss.; Mrs. Maud O'Bryan Ronstrom, Dorothy Blackman, New Orleans; Mrs. Charles O'Neal, Jackson, Miss.; Mrs. Rosa Oliver, librarian of Louisiana State Museum, and Charles E. Frampton, executive of the museum staff; Mrs. E. C. Harris, Mobile; Harry Shaw Newman of the Old Print Shop,

New York, and Robert L. Harley of the staff of the shop; Anthony Ragusin, Biloxi, Miss.

George B. Eager of the Colonial Williamsburg staff assisted materially in tracing items there, as did Thad Tate, Jr., Lucius Battle, Donald Gonzales, Van McNair and Rose Belt.

At the New York Public Library Elizabeth E. Roth, first assistant in the print room, located some unusual photographic items, and directed me to other collections. Virginia Daiker, reference librarian at the Library of Congress; Milton Kaplan of the maps division, and David Mearns, head of the manuscripts division, gave generously of their time and information.

Others were Charles W. Porter, III, Roy M. Stubbs, C. R. Vinten and Herbert Evison of the National Park Service. In Memphis, Lamar Wallis, Jesse Cunningham, Mary Davant and Carey Moore of the Public Library; Franklin M. Garrett, Atlanta; Pollard White, Cadiz, Texas; Ivy W. Duggan, Atlanta; McHenry Jones of Pensacola; Walter A. Anderson, Jacksonville, Fla.; David Westheimer, Houston; Mrs. Margaret Young Page, Houston; Edith Dupre and Mrs. Marie Nehrbass, Lafayette; David Replogle, Washington, D. C.; Mrs. David Terry, Little Rock, Ark.

Mrs. Fay Profilet, St. Louis; Mr. Monroe F. Cockrell, Evanston, Ill.; Hazel and Clothilde Lindsey, Pensacola, Fla.; Lydia and Ed Jervis, Greensboro, North Carolina; Edythe Thornton McLeod, New York; Mrs. Elmer Deiss, Lexington, Kentucky; Louise Guyol, New Orleans; Chalmers Davidson, of Davidson, N. C.; Mrs. Yvon du Quesnay and Yvonne du Quesnay, New Orleans; Dr. H. C. Nixon, Nashville; Mrs. H. Welge Lewis, Fredericksburg, Texas; Mrs. Shackelford Miller, Louisville, Ky.

Mrs. Esther de Vasques, San Antonio; Mrs. Jessie Smith Young, Cartersville, Georgia; Sylvester Vigilante, Ossining, New York; Mrs. Ed Vandergriff, Blacksburg, Virginia; Dr. J. Morris Hutcheson, Richmond; Mrs. W. F. McFarland, Florence, Alabama.

Mrs. Alice Hook, picture division of the Special Libraries Association, Cincinnati; Mrs. Forman Hawes, librarian of Georgia Historical Society; Walter Stilwell, Sr., president of the Savannah Historical Research Association; Dorothy Dodd, state librarian, Tallahassee, Fla.; Louise Crawford, librarian, and May G. Edwards of the City-County Memorial Library, Bay St. Louis.

Fant H. Thornley, director, Birmingham, Alabama, Public Library, and Helen Stamps, his assistant; Floyd Shoemaker, secretary, and Sarah Guitar, reference librarian, State Historical Society of Missouri, Columbia; Charles Ravenswaay, director, and Mrs. Eileen J. Cox, reference, Missouri Historical Society, St. Louis; Clarence E. Miller, librarian, and Elizabeth Tindall, reference librarian, St. Louis Mercantile Library Association.

Helen C. Frick, director of the Frick Art Reference Library, New York, and Mrs. H. W. Howell, Jr., librarian; Miss Lucia M. Tryon, librarian, Pensacola Public Library; Doris C. Wailes, administrative assistant, St. Augustine Historical Society; J. Paul Hudson, Museum specialist, National Park Service, Richmond; Virginia Ebeling, Ohio County Public Library, Wheeling, West Virginia; Eleanor Norton, librarian, Front Royal Public Library, Virginia; Mrs. Bettie Giles, Roanoke Public Library, Virginia; Mrs. Josephine Johnston, reference department, Louisville; Sarah E. Maret, librarian of the Athens Regional Library.

Mrs. Miriam G. Reeves, librarian, Louisiana State Department of Education; Gertie Espenan, Baton Rouge, Louisiana; Janice S. Brown, chief of reference and circulation departments, Smithsonian Institution; Mrs. Phyllis S. Burson, La Retama Public Library, Corpus Christi, Tex.; Annie Lou Flesher, librarian, Free Public Library of St. Augustine, Florida.

Ted R. Worley, executive secretary, Arkansas Department of Archives and History; Orville W. Taylor, staff member, Little Rock; Josephine Cobb, archivist in charge of the still picture branch, General Services Administration, Washington; Frances L. Gerard, head of the reference department, Kanawha County Public Library, Charleston, West Virginia.

Kenneth K. McCormick, historian and archivist, Arkansas Department of History, Little Rock; Geraldine LeMay, director, Savannah Public Library, and Joy Trulock, assistant in reference; Mrs. Adrian Belt, librarian, Morgantown Public Library, West Virginia; Gratia A. Meyers, librarian of Carnegie Library of Bradenton, Florida.

Mildred Stevenson, head of reference department, Rosenberg Library, Galveston, Tex.; Ella May Thornton, state librarian, Atlanta, and Vera Jameson, associate librarian; Marie Berry, head of reference, San Antonio Public Library; Betty W. Service, Saratoga Public Library, Florida; May Sherard, librarian of the Vicksburg Public Library, Mississippi.

Llerena Friend, librarian of Texas Collection, University of Texas, Austin; James H. Renz, librarian of Florida Collection, Miami Public Library; Stanley Pargellis, librarian of the Newberry Library, Chicago; Norah Albanell, chief of Public Services, Columbus Memorial Library of the Pan American Union, Washington, D. C.

Foster L. Barnes, Stephen Foster Memorial Commission, White Springs, Florida; Emerson Greenaway, director, Philadelphia Free Public Library; Maria Person, librarian of the Gulfport-Carnegie-Harrison County Library, Miss.; Erin Humphrey, librarian of El Paso Public Library,

Texas; Francis R. Berkeley, Jr., curator of manuscripts, and William H. Runge, assistant, Alderman Library, University of Virginia, Charlottesville.

Mrs. Elizabeth Edwards, librarian, and Mrs. Kathryn P. Arhold of the Chattanooga Public Library staff; Mrs. Mildred B. Turnbull, librarian, Warder Public Library, Springfield, Ohio; Margaret F. Willis and Jessie Orgain, of the reference staff, Kentucky State Library Extension, Frankfort, Ky.; Mrs. W. W. Griffith, librarian, Public Library of Fredericksburg, Va.; Cornelia Davis, librarian of the Chester, Maryland, Public Library; Mrs. Margaret Armstrong, librarian, Palmetto Public Library, Florida; Mrs. Grace Carnahan, librarian, Pulaski County Free Library, Virginia; Norma B. Cass, reference librarian, University of Kentucky, Lexington.

Lindsey O. House, Warrington, Fla.; Mr. and Mrs. Leander Marx, New Orleans; William W. Wells, assistant director, Louisiana State Parks Commission; Mrs. Gay White, Pressly Phillips of St. Petersburg, Florida; Bob Aldredge, Beaumont; Katharine Holmes, Corpus Christi; Fred W. Holder, Theodore, Alabama; Stanley Babb, Galveston; Ira Harkey, Jr., and Easton King, Pascagoula, Mississippi.

And, as on many earlier occasions, Florence Kane Reynolds, my sister, gave endless hours of assistance, as did my mother, Mrs. W. J. Kane, and my other sister, Anna Kane.

Picture Credits